W9-CLG-463

CHAPTER 8

8-1e   Total Accounts Receivable, $2,200
8-2e   Total Accounts Payable, $3,000
8-3   Sales Journal, $1,950
8-4a   Cash Received, $12,338
8-5a   Cash Received, $19,045
8-6a   Cash Payments, $3,612
8-7   Cash Payments, $7,873
8-8a   Sales Journal, $5,850
8-9a,c Ending Cash Balance, $26,918

CHAPTER 9

9-1   Cumulative Earnings, $23,080
9-2   Net Pay, $50,804
9-3a Total Taxes, $4,950
9-4a Total Taxes, $341.78
9-7a Net Pay, $1,027.94
9-8a Accumulated Earnings, $22,967.25
9-10 Net Taxes, $5,032
9-11 Net Taxes, $3,835.91
9-12 FUTA Tax, $98
9-13 FUTA Tax, $168

CHAPTER 10

10-6c   Reconciled Balance, $5,028
10-7a   Reconciled Balance, $2,730
10-8a   Reconciled Balance, $6,500
10-9a   Reconciled Balance, $1,081
10-10a Reconciled Balance, $3,521
10-11a Reconciled Balance, $2,777
10-12c Reconciled Balance, $4,245

CHAPTER 11

11-2   Book Value, 19-C, $3,300
11-3   Book Value, 19-C, $3,072
11-5c Plant Assets, $71,220
11-6c Plant Assets, $14,200
11-8a Book Value, 19-C, $2,500
11-9a Book Value, 19-B, $2,500

CHAPTER 11 APPENDIX

A11-3b Intangible Assets, $8,480

CHAPTER 12

12-1b   Gross Profit, $5,400
12-2b   Gross Profit, $4,560
12-3e   Gross Profit, $56,000
12-4c   Cost of Goods Sold, $45,400
12-5c   Cost of Goods Sold, $9,800
12-6d $6,950
12-7c   Net Income, $1,000
12-8   Ending Inventory @ Retail, $16,500
12-9   Ending Inventory @ Retail, $9,200
12-10 Cost of Goods Sold, $12,900
12-11 Cost of Goods Sold, $50,400
12-12b Cost of Goods Sold, $10,100

CHAPTER 13

13-3b Mason, $6,000
13-8   Drew, $12,706
13-9b Loss on Sale of Assets, $2,000
13-10 Gain on Sale of Assets, $1,200
13-11 Total Assets, $52,500

CHAPTER 14

14-1 Dividends Payable, $6,250
14-2 Dividends Payable, $9,750
14-3 Dividends Payable, $14,000
14-4 Dividends Payable, $6,750
14-5 Total Paid-in Capital, $200,000
14-6 Total Paid-in Capital, $530,000
14-7 Total Assets, $916,000

(continued on inside back cover)

COLLEGE ACCOUNTING
A COMPREHENSIVE APPROACH

COLLEGE ACCOUNTING
A COMPREHENSIVE APPROACH

Phebe M. Woltz
Richard T. Arlen

Schoolcraft College
Livonia, Michigan

McGRAW-HILL BOOK COMPANY
New York St. Louis
San Francisco
Auckland Bogotá
Hamburg Johannesburg
London Madrid
Mexico Montreal
New Delhi Panama
Paris São Paulo
Singapore Sydney
Tokyo Toronto

To Bob and Tom

COLLEGE ACCOUNTING: A COMPREHENSIVE APPROACH

Copyright © 1983 by McGraw-Hill, Inc. All rights reserved. This book includes Chapters 1 to 14 of *College Accounting: An Introduction,* Second Edition by Phebe M. Woltz and Richard T. Arlen, copyright © 1983 by McGraw-Hill, Inc. All rights reserved. Printed in the United States of America. Except as permitted under the United States Copyright Act of 1976, no part of this publication may be reproduced or distributed in any form or by any means, or stored in a data base or retrieval system, without the prior written permission of the publisher.

1234567890   DOCDOC   898765432

ISBN 0-07-071481-9

This book was set in Baskerville by Progressive Typographers.
The editors were Donald G. Mason and Gail Gavert;
the designer was Charles A. Carson;
the production supervisor was Charles Hess.
The cover photograph was taken by Martin Bough.
R. R. Donnelley & Sons Company was printer and binder.

Library of Congress Cataloging in Publication Data

Woltz, Phebe M.
    College accounting.

    Chapters 1–14 published separately as: College accounting : an introduction / Phebe M. Woltz, Richard T. Arlen. 2nd ed. © 1983.
    Includes index.
    1. Accounting. I. Arlen, Richard T. II. Title.
HF5635.W852 1983   657'.044   82-4683
ISBN 0-07-071481-9

CONTENTS

PREFACE   xiii

CHAPTER 1 **Introduction to the**
           Accounting System   1

Background   2
Accounting Today   2
Financial and Managerial
  Accounting   2
Accounting as a
  Profession—Areas of
  Specialization   3
Purpose of Accounting   4
Accounting versus Bookkeeping   4
The Five Basic Parts of
  Accounting   5
    Assets | Liabilities | Owner's
    Equity | Revenue | Expenses
Accounting Terms   7
    Transactions | Account |
    Fiscal Period | Double-Entry
    System | Cash versus
    Accrual Accounting
Basic Financial Statements   9
    Balance Sheet | Basic
    Accounting Equation;
    Balance Sheet Illustrated |
    Income Statement | Net
    Income Formula | Income
    Statement Illustrated |
    Owner's Equity Section of
    Balance Sheet Illustrated
Illustrative Problems   12
Accounting Principles   16
    Cost Principle | Entity
    Principle | Full Disclosure
    Principle | Going Concern
    Principle | Materiality
    Principle | Objectivity
    Principle

Summary   18
Glossary   19
Questions   21
Exercises   21
Problems   24

CHAPTER 2 **The Recording**
           Process   29
Part I   **The Account and**
         General Journal   30

Chart of Accounts   30
Accounting Manual   31
The Account   31
Parts of an Account   32
Account Forms   33
Account Balance   33
Normal Balances   35
General Journal   36
Journalizing Transactions in
  General Journal   36
Analyzing and Journalizing
  Transactions   38

Part II **Posting Transactions in**
         General Ledger   44

General Ledger   44
Posting   44
Trial Balance   48
The First Three Steps in the
  Accounting Cycle   49
Debit-Credit Rules to Remember   50
Drawing Account   50
Summary   51
Glossary   52
Questions   53
Exercises   53
Problems   55

2017

CHAPTER 3 **Adjusting Entries** 63

Adjustments 64
Adjusting for Expenses 65
*Prepaid Expenses | Alternate
Method for Recording
Prepaid Expenses | Accrued
Expenses | Depreciation*
Summary 76
Glossary 77
Questions 78
Exercises 78
Problems 80

CHAPTER 4 **Adjusting Entries**
(Continued) 87
Adjusting for Revenue 88
*Accrued Revenue | Revenue
Received in Advance |
Alternate Method for
Recording Revenue
Received in Advance*
Adjusted Trial Balance 97
Four Points to Remember
The Accounting Cycle 98
Summary 98
Glossary 98
Questions 99
Exercises 99
Problems 102

CHAPTER 5 **Accounting Cycle
and Financial
Statements** 110
Work Sheet 112
Work Sheet Preparation 112
*Summary of Work Sheet
Preparation*
Recording Adjusting Entries from
Work Sheet 126
Recording Closing Entries from
Work Sheet 128
Financial Statements 131
Account Classifications 134
Post-Closing Trial Balance 135
Four Points to Remember
The Accounting Cycle 136
Summary 136
Glossary 137
Questions 138
Exercises 139
Problems 142

CHAPTER 6 **Accounting for a
Merchandising
Business** 149

Sales and Related Accounts 150
*Sales | Sales Returns &
Allowances | Sales Discount*
Purchases and Related Accounts 154
*Purchases | Purchase
Returns & Allowances |
Purchase Discount*
Shipping Charges on
Merchandise Purchased or Sold 157
*FOB Destination |
FOB Shipping Point*
Merchandise Inventory 159
Debit and Credit Memoranda 160
Trade Discounts 161
Sales Taxes 162
Summary 163
Glossary 164
Questions 165
Exercises 165
Problems 167

CHAPTER 7 **Accounting for a
Merchandising
Business** (Continued) 173

Work Sheet for Merchandising
Concern 174
Financial Statements 176
*Income Statement | Balance
Sheet | Adjusting Entries |
Closing Entries | Post-Closing
Trial Balance*
Summary 185
Glossary 186
Questions 186
Exercises 187
Problems 189

CHAPTER 8 **Special Journals and
Ledgers for
Pegboard
Accounting** 196

Sales Journal 199
*Control Accounts and
Subsidiary Ledgers |
Summary Illustration | Proof
of Ledger Accuracy*

Purchases Journal 204
Control Accounts and Subsidiary Ledgers / Posting from Purchases Journal to Ledgers / Summary Illustration / Proof of Ledger Accuracy
Cash Receipts Journal 209
Posting from Cash Receipts Journal to Ledgers / Summary Illustration
Cash Payments Journal 211
Posting from Cash Payments Journal to Ledgers / Summary Illustration
Summary of Journalizing and Posting to Special Journals 214
General Journal Entries 214
Opposite Balances in Receivables and Payables 215
Pegboard Accounting 215
Accounts Receivable System
Summary 218
Glossary 220
Questions 221
Exercises 221
Problems 225

Chapter 8 Appendix: Bad Debts 235

Adjustment for Bad Debts 235
Methods for Estimating Bad Debts 236
Percentage of Sales or Income Statement Method / Percentage of Accounts Receivable or Balance Sheet Method
Direct Write-Off Method 238
Writing Off Accounts Receivable under Allowance Method 239
Reinstatement of Accounts Receivable 240
Summary 241
Glossary 242
Questions 242
Exercises 243
Problems 243

CHAPTER 9 Payroll Accounting 247

Government Regulations Important to Payroll 248

Rules for Employee Earnings 249
Federal Income Tax Withheld / State and City Income Tax Withheld
Social Security Act 251
Federal Insurance Contributions Tax
Other Deductions 253
Rules for the Employer 253
Federal Insurance Contributions Tax
Unemployment Compensation Tax 253
Federal Unemployment Compensation Tax / State Unemployment Compensation Tax
Fair Labor Standards Act 257
Payroll Records and Control 257
Payroll Register (How to Figure the Payroll) / Employee Earnings Record / Other Payroll Reports / Important Points to Remember
Accounting for Payroll 264
Recording the Employee's Earnings / Recording the Employer's Payroll Tax Expense
Payroll Controls 267
Pegboard Accounting for Payroll 269
Payroll System
Summary 272
Glossary 273
Questions 274
Exercises 275
Problems 277

CHAPTER 10 Accounting for Cash 283

Objectives of Cash Control 284
Petty Cash 284
Systems and Forms / Accounting for a Petty Cash Fund / Replenishing the Petty Cash Fund / Changing the Original Amount of the Petty Cash Fund / Cash Over and Short
Bank Reconciliation 290
Bank Checking Account /

Bank Reconciliation Procedure | Preparing the Bank Reconciliation Statement | Journal Entries to Correct the Cash Balance | Illustration of a Bank Reconciliation Statement

Summary 301
Glossary 302
Questions 303
Exercises 303
Problems 305

Chapter 10 Appendix: Notes and Interest 311

Promissory Note 311
Computation of Interest 312
Simple Interest | 60-Day, 6 Percent Method of Computing Interest
Maturity Date of Note 314
Maturity Value 315
Recording Promissory Notes 315
Obtaining a Bank Loan 317
Summary 319
Glossary 320
Questions 320
Exercises 321
Problems 322

CHAPTER 11 Plant Assets 325

Plant Asset Depreciation 326
Plant Asset Cost 327
Useful Life and Salvage Value
Depreciation Methods 329
Straight-Line Method | Units-of-Production Method | Sum-of-Years'-Digits Method | Double-Declining Balance Method
Depreciation for a Partial Year 333
Adjusting Entries for Recording Depreciation 335
Balance Sheet Presentation 336
Revenue versus Capital Expenditures 337

Disposing of Plant Assets 337
Discarding or Selling a Plant Asset | Trading in Plant Assets
Points to Remember 343
Effect of Trade-In Method on Yearly Depreciation 343
Natural Resources 344
Depreciation Methods Established by the Economic Recovery Act of 1981 345
Summary 346
Glossary 347
Questions 348
Exercises 348
Problems 350

Chapter 11 Appendix: Intangible Assets 354

Balance Sheet Presentation 354
Copyright 355
Franchise 355
Goodwill 355
Leasehold and Leasehold Improvements 355
Patents 356
Trademark and Trade Name 357
Summary 357
Glossary 357
Questions 358
Exercises 358
Problems 358

CHAPTER 12 Inventories 360

Inventory Valuation 362
Basic Pricing Methods 363
Specific Invoice | First-In, First-Out | Last-In, First-Out | Weighted Average
Estimated Systems 366
Retail Method | Gross Profit Method
Perpetual versus Periodic Inventory System 368
Perpetual Inventory System | Periodic Inventory System

Summary of Entries for
  Perpetual versus
  Periodic Systems   374
Consistency of Reporting—
  I.R.S. Rules   375
Effect of Errors on Inventory   375
Summary   378
Glossary   379
Questions   379
Exercises   380
Problems   382

CHAPTER 13 **Accounting for a
            Partnership**   388

Advantages and Disadvantages
  of Forming a Partnership   390
Partnership Formation   391
Accounting Differences   391
Division of Earnings   392
Dissolving a Partnership   396
Statement Presentations   401
Summary   403
Glossary   404
Questions   404
Exercises   405
Problems   407

CHAPTER 14 **The Corporate Form
            of Business
            Organization**   411

Advantages and Disadvantages   413
Organization Costs   413
Common Stock   413
Retained Earnings   417
Accounting Differences   417
Dividends   419
Balance Sheet Presentation   420
Summary   421
Glossary   422
Questions   423
Exercises   423
Problems   424

CHAPTER 15 **Corporations:
            Common, Preferred,
            and Treasury Stock** 429

Sources of Capital   430
Accounting for Common Stock   431

Preferred Stock   436
    *Preference as to Dividends /
    Preference as to Assets /
    Callable Option /
    Convertible Option*
Accounting for Preferred Stock   438
Balance Sheet Presentation of
  Common and Preferred Stock   440
Treasury Stock   441
    *Accounting for Treasury
    Stock / Donated Treasury
    Stock / Legal Restrictions on
    Treasury Stock / Balance
    Sheet Presentation of
    Treasury Stock*
Summary   446
Glossary   448
Questions   450
Exercises   450
Problems   452

CHAPTER 16 **Corporations:
            Cash and Stock
            Dividends**   459

Cash Dividends   460
    *Cash Dividend Preferences
    to Preferred Stockholders*
Stock Dividends   464
Stock Splits   468
Summary   469
Glossary   470
Questions   471
Exercises   472
Problems   474

CHAPTER 17 **Corporations:
            Income Taxes, Work
            Sheet, and Financial
            Statements**   479

Corporate Income Taxes   480
Adjusting Entry for Income Taxes 480
Work Sheet for a Corporation   484
    *Six Steps for Preparing a
    Corporate Work Sheet*
Journalizing Adjusting and
  Closing Entries from the
  Corporate Work Sheet   487
    *Adjusting Entries /
    Closing Entries*

Corporate Financial Statements
Prepared from Corporate
Work Sheet   489
Post-Closing Trial Balance   490
Summary   492
Glossary   492
Questions   492
Exercises   493
Problems   494

CHAPTER 18 **Corporations:**
            Retained Earnings   499

Appropriated Retained Earnings   500
Adjustments and Corrections to
  Retained Earnings   501
Preparing the Retained Earnings
  Statement   503
Combined Income and Retained
  Earnings Statement   504
Earnings per Share   504
Extraordinary Gains and Losses   505
Book Value per Share of Capital
  Stock   507
Summary   508
Glossary   509
Questions   509
Exercises   510
Problems   512

CHAPTER 19 **Long-term**
            Liabilities   517

Issuance of Bonds   518
Types of Bonds   519
Quotation of Bonds   520
Selling Price of Bonds   520
Accounting for Bonds   522
Year-End Adjustments for
  Accrued Interest on Bonds   524
Retirement of Bonds   526
Classification of Bonds and
  Related Accounts   527
Summary   529
Glossary   530
Questions   531
Exercises   532
Problems   534

CHAPTER 20 **Investments in**
            Stocks and Bonds   537

Long-term Investments   538
  *Long-term Investment in
  Stock | Receipt of Dividends
  on Stock Investments | Sale
  of Long-term Investment in
  Stock | Long-term
  Investment in Bonds |
  Accounting for the Purchase
  of Bonds | Sale of Long-term
  Investment in Bonds*
Temporary Investments in
  Stocks and Bonds   550
  *Temporary Investments in
  Stock | Receipt of Cash
  Dividends | Temporary
  Investment in Bonds |
  Receipt of Interest on Bond
  Investment | Sale of
  Short-term Investments
  in Securities*
Summary   553
Glossary   554
Questions   555
Exercises   556
Problems   557

Chapter 20 **Appendix: Parent and**
            Subsidiary
            Corporations and
            Consolidated Balance
            Sheets   563

Parent and Subsidiary
  Corporations   563
Investment in Subsidiary   565
Consolidated Statements   565
Summary   568

CHAPTER 21 **Budgets**   569

Advantages of a Budget   570
Preparing a Budget   571
Sales Forecast   571
Sales Budget   572
Purchases Budget   572
Expense Budget   574

Cash Budget 577
Flexible Budget 579
Summary 580
Glossary 581
Questions 582
Exercises 582
Problems 584

CHAPTER 22 **Statement of Changes in Financial Position** 591

Purpose of Preparing the Statement of Changes in Financial Position 592
 Sources of Funds | Uses or Application of Funds
Preparing the Statement of Changes in Financial Position 596
 Statement of Changes in Accounts | Working Papers for Analyzing the Changes in Noncurrent Accounts | Statement of Changes in Financial Position
Summary 609
Glossary 610
Questions 611
Exercises 611
Problems 613

Chapter 22 Appendix: Cash Flow 618

Purpose for Preparing a Cash Flow Statement 618
Conversion of Income Statement to a Cash Basis 618
 Cash Received from Customers | Cash Paid for Merchandise Sold | Cash Paid for Operating Expenses | Preparing the Conversion of Income Statement to a Cash Basis
Cash Flow Statement 623
 Preparing the Cash Flow Statement
Summary 625

CHAPTER 23 **Manufacturing Accounting** 627

Manufacturing Costs 628
Manufacturing Accounts 629
 Raw Materials | Indirect Materials | Direct Labor | Indirect Labor | Factory Overhead
Manufacturing Inventories 630
 Raw Materials Inventory | Goods in Process Inventory | Finished Goods Inventory
Cost of Goods Manufactured Statement 631
Cost of Goods Sold Section of Income Statement 632
Manufacturing Work Sheet 633
Financial Statements for a Working Capital Manufacturing Concern 637
Closing Entries Prepared from Manufacturing Work Sheet 639
Summary 642
Glossary 643
Questions 644
Exercises 645
Problems 647

CHAPTER 24 **Job Order Cost System** 651

Manufacturing Costs 652
Cost Accounting Systems 652
Job Order Cost Accounting System 653
Job Order Cost Sheet 653
 Materials Ledger Card | Material Requisition | Direct Labor Time Tickets | Factory Overhead Costs
Completing the Job Order Cost Sheet 660
Distribution of Costs on Job Order Cost Sheet 662
Summary of Job Order Cost Procedure 665
Summary 667
Glossary 668
Questions 668
Exercises 669
Problems 672

CHAPTER 25 **Process Cost Accounting System** 677

Equivalent Units of Production 679
Unit Costs 681
Cost of Ending Goods in
Process Inventory 682
Cost of Goods Transferred to
Finished Goods Inventory 682
Cost of Goods Sold and Cost of
Ending Finished Goods
Inventory 683
Production Cost Report 684
Journal Entries for Flow of Costs 684
Summary 688
Glossary 689
Questions 689
Exercises 689
Problems 691

CHAPTER 26 **Individual Income Tax** 695

Requirements for Filing an
Income Tax Return 696

Income Excluded from Taxes 697
Gross Income, Adjusted Gross
Income, and Taxable Income 698
Deductions for Exemptions 699
Form 1040A and Form 1040 703
*Interest and Dividend
Income | Other Income |
Self-Employment Income |
Allowable Business
Deductions | Allowable
Nonbusiness Personal
Deductions (Itemized
Deductions) | Completing
Form 1040 | Itemizing
Personal Deductions |
Income Averaging*
Summary 725
Glossary 726
Questions 728
Exercises 728
Problems 730

INDEX 737

PREFACE

College Accounting: A Comprehensive Approach has been designed primarily for college students who have had no previous exposure to accounting and desire a one-year course in accounting fundamentals. Accounting and other business majors as well as nonbusiness majors will find that this text's practical approach enables them to use the information in other accounting or business courses, in their jobs, or for their own personal use.

The outstanding feature of this text is its *clear, practical approach.* The written material is interspersed with a variety of easy-to-understand examples and illustrations, especially where calculations are involved. Our major objective was to treat each topic comprehensively and then to follow up with exercises and problems presented in graduated levels to enable students to master the material. Therefore, a great number of exercises and problems provide the instructor with sufficient demonstration materials for each concept without diminishing the variety and supply for student assignments.

PEDAGOGICAL FEATURES

Specific objectives or skills students should attain are presented at the beginning of each chapter, and throughout the text *marginal notes* highlight and reinforce the key concepts. End-of-chapter materials include: a chapter *summary;* a *glossary,* to help the student review definitions of new accounting terms indicated in the text by boldface; and an abundance of *questions, exercises,* and *problems.* All the exercises and problems are labeled and grouped in the same order as key concepts presented in each chapter. Each chapter also contains one or more problems that review all the concepts presented in one or more chapters.

TEXT ORGANIZATION

The topics covered in the text have been selected to meet the needs of undergraduate business students majoring in accounting or other areas of business and includes information needed to give students the necessary background in introductory accounting. Chapters 1–14 and Chapters 15–26 may be covered in two semesters of 13 to 16 weeks of instruction or the material may be easily divided to be used in three quarters instead. (For those who need only a one-term course, Chapters 1–14 are available separately as *College Accounting: An Introduction,* Second Edition.)

The first seven chapters present basic accounting procedures, account classifications, debit and credit analysis, and the complete accounting cycle for a service and a merchandising concern. Chapters 3 and 4 are devoted exclusively to the adjusting process to give students the information for preparing adjusting entries before introducing the work sheet and closing entries. Step-by-step instructions with numerous illustrations are provided to make a difficult subject more understandable and to help students approach the preparation of adjusting entries with more ease and self-confidence. An in-depth coverage of special journals and ledgers, payroll accounting, cash, and pegboard accounting for accounts receivable and payroll are covered in Chapters 8 through 10.

Chapters 11 through 14 deal with the acquisition, depreciation, and disposal of plant assets, inventory pricing methods and systems, and an introduction to partnership and corporate accounting. Bad debts, notes, and intangible assets have been included as appendixes at the end of Chapters 8, 10, and 11. Separating these discussions into appendixes allows instructors the option of including or omitting these three mini chapters without having any effect on the continuity of the course. A separate set of questions, exercises, and problems is provided at the end of each appendix.

An introduction to corporate accounting is given in Chapter 14 and the discussion continues in Chapter 15. Chapters 15–18 contain a detailed presentation of the accounting procedures required for capital stock, cash and stock dividends, the corporate work sheet and financial statements, corporate income tax, and retained earnings. The discussion of corporate income tax in Chapter 17 includes the recent changes in the tax law that affect corporate profits. Chapter 18 provides a simple, basic presentation of book value per share of capital stock, earnings per share of capital stock, and extraordinary gains and losses.

Accounting for the issuance of stocks and bonds and the purchase of short- and long-term securities using the equity method are presented in Chapters 19 and 20, which include many examples to help explain the material. The discussion of budgets in Chapter 21 is designed to give students a better understanding of both the process and the purpose of budgeting for a small or large organization. To simplify the explanation, examples of each type of budget have been prepared for a small dental laboratory to give students a realistic picture of the preparation of various types of budgets for a small organization.

The discussion of the statement of financial position presented in Chapter 22 contains detailed explanations and illustrations to make a difficult subject easier to comprehend. Included in the appendixes to Chapter 20 and 22 are simple, basic presentations of parent and subsidiary corporations, consolidated balance sheets, and cash flow. Once again, separating the discussion of these topics into appendixes gives you the option of either including or omitting these topics from the course outline without having any effect on continuity.

Chapter 23 deals with manufacturing accounting, and Chapters 24 and 25 introduce cost accounting to give students a basic explanation of its role in the business enterprise. Various forms used with job order and process cost systems are fully explained, including details of the cost procedures. These fundamental cost accounting chapters present the flow of costs through the manufacturing process with very clear diagrams.

Individual income taxes are discussed in the last chapter to help students understand the preparation of their individual income tax return. The information includes the latest revisions in the income tax law. This chapter may be introduced earlier in the text if desired.

SUPPORTING SUPPLEMENTS

Supplementary materials for both the instructor and the student are part of the *College Accounting* package. They are designed to help instructors teach more effectively and students master the material in the text more completely.

Instructor Aids

1. The *Solutions Manual* contains for each chapter a brief description, a grading level of difficulty, and the estimated time limit required to complete each problem in the text. The manual also includes a suggested course syllabus, outline for the first day of class, outline for each chapter, answers to text questions, solutions to exercises and text problems, plus answers for the two sets of achievement tests and three practice sets. The *Solutions Manual* is available in two parts: one manual for Chapters 1–14 and *Practice Sets I* and *II* for the first semester and a manual for Chapters 15–26 and *Practice Set III* for the next semester.
2. Preprinted, packaged sets of *Achievement Tests and Comprehensive Examinations* are available free to adopters. The four packages—two for each semester—consist of Set A, Chapters 1–14 and Set B, Chapters 1–14 as well as Set A, Chapters 15–26 and Set B, Chapters 15–26. Every set has four tests, covering two to three chapters in each; the comprehen-

sive exams cover Chapters 1–10, 1–14, and 15–26. Every package contains 20 copies of each test and examination.

3. Two *Additional Examination Questions* manuals (one for each semester) contain 15 true or false statements, 15 multiple-choice questions, 1 to 2 matching exercises of 5 to 15 questions, and 1 to 2 mini-problems for each of the 26 chapters plus the appendixes for Chapters 8, 10, 11, 20, and 22. These examination questions have been designed for computer scoring equipment.

4. Sets of *overhead transparencies* with solutions to selected end-of-chapter text problems can be obtained by adopters of the text. The transparencies are available for Chapters 1 to 14 and for Chapters 15 to 26.

Student Aids

1. A *Checklist of Key Figures* for the problems is provided on the inside of the front and back covers of the text to give students an instant check on the accuracy of the intermediate stages of their solutions.

2. A combined *Study Guide and Working Papers* supplement is available for text problems. This is also divided into two parts: one workbook for Chapters 1 to 14 and another for Chapters 15 to 26. The *Study Guide* contains a variety of short problems to self-test and review the material for each chapter with solutions available at the end of the book to provide instant feedback. This *Study Guide* also contains working papers for the text problems. Many of the forms are partially filled in with initial data to eliminate time spent on copying material.

3. Three practice sets are available: *Practice Set I* is for a professional dental laboratory, *Practice Set II* is for a cable TV installation service, and *Practice Set III* is for a sewing specialty company. *Practice Set I* is unique because it may be started after completing Chapter 2 and covers the material in Chapters 1 through 7. This practice set, designed for a small dental laboratory, uses a general journal and a general ledger. *Practice Set II* may be started after completing Chapter 8 and covers the material in Chapters 1 through 10. This practice set, based on a small cable TV installation service, uses five journals and three ledgers. *Practice Set III* may be started after completing Chapter 14 and covers the material in Chapters 1 through 18. This practice set concerns a sewing specialty company that operates as a corporate form of business organization. It uses five journals and three ledgers, and the student is required to issue checks and keep a running account of the amount of cash on hand. All three practice sets have been designed to run parallel with the text, enabling students to utilize the new information presented in each chapter to work the practice set as the course progresses.

ACKNOWLEDGMENTS

I would like to extend my sincere appreciation to the staff of McGraw-Hill Book Company for all their support and assistance in the completion of the first edition of the text—especially Donald G. Mason, accounting editor and Gail Gavert, editing supervisor. A special acknowledgment and deep gratitude go to Professors Candis E. Martin and Sharon A. Cotton, Schoolcraft College, for the many hours they spent in reading the manuscript, working and proofreading exercises and problems, and for their constructive suggestions and assistance in preparing the text. I also would like to express my thanks for the many useful comments and suggestions provided by colleagues who reviewed this text during the course of its development, especially to Douglas C. Gordon, Arapahoe Community College; Charles F. Grant, Skyline College; Robert J. McCarter, Macomb Community College; Raymond Machinist, Catonsville Community College, Alexander MacKenzie, Lewis & Clark Community College; Tony Merlonghi, Napa College; and William A. Serafin, Community College of Allegheny County, who reviewed the first part as *College Accounting: An Introduction*, Second Edition, and to Albert J. Arsenault, Hillsboro Community College; David Bayley, Santa Monica College; Duane Hought, Central Oregon Community College; and John D. Mallonee, Manatee Junior College, who reviewed the entire text. Duane Hought also took on the task of checking all of the exercises in the text for their accuracy, for which I am grateful. A special thanks goes to Pat Gall, an accounting student at Schoolcraft College, and to all the students in A202, A221, and A222, fall and winter term, 1980 and 1981, Schoolcraft College for their assistance in testing the exercises and problems; and to Bert L. Heckenlaible, C.P.A., Carmel Valley, CA; Charles Kaye, C.P.A., Farmington, MI; and Joseph B. Pfister, attorney at law, Redford, MI, for their support and suggestions for the manuscript.

I wish to thank the Reynolds & Reynolds Company for the use of their material on pegboard accounting and the Internal Revenue Service for the use of various tax forms and other tax information.

Finally, a special thanks to my husband, Bob, for all his patience and understanding, helpful suggestions, and assistance in preparing the manuscript plus a deep appreciation to my son, Tom, for his support and assistance in supplying technical data as well as various illustrations and forms for the text and practice sets.

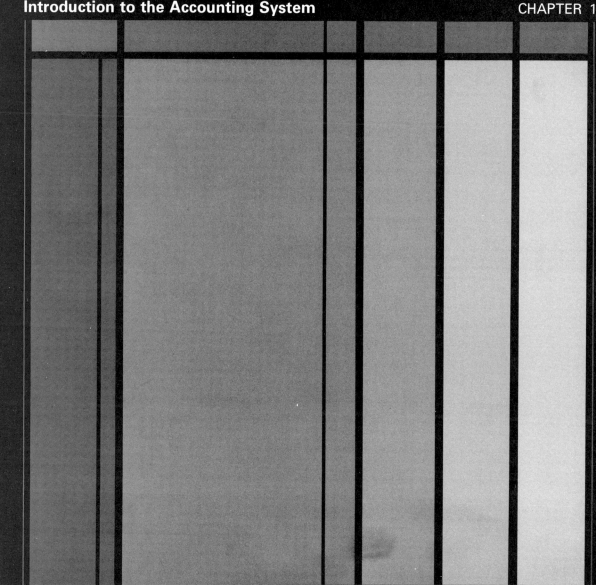

After completing this chapter, you should be able to:

1. **Define accounting**

2. **Explain the Entity, Going Concern, and Cost Principles**

3. **State the difference between bookkeeping and accounting**

4. **Describe the five basic classifications of accounts**

5. **Define transaction, account, fiscal period, double-entry system, and cash and accrual accounting**

6. **Explain the basic accounting equation and net income formula**

7. **Prepare a simple income statement and balance sheet**

BACKGROUND

Accounting is a service designed to provide historical information concerning the financial activities of a business, an organization, or an individual. Before the development of accounting, business people of the ancient world recognized the need for keeping records of their business transactions, debts, and taxes and used a very elementary recording system. Eventually these recording techniques were improved, and simple bookkeeping methods were developed. These methods steadily improved and led to the modern, more complex accounting methods used today, and accounting became known as the "language of business."

ACCOUNTING TODAY

Present accounting methods are capable of giving more detailed financial information with greater ease and flexibility. This financial information is valuable to business, government, and individuals in that it enables them to evaluate past performance and helps them plan for the future and achieve their financial goals.

FINANCIAL AND MANAGERIAL ACCOUNTING

While accounting provides financial information to business, government, and individuals, it is also needed and used by financial analysts, trade associations, stock exchanges, and educational institutions. The information required by these groups will vary according to their needs, but usually they are interested in the financial position and profits or losses of a company.

The gathering and presentation of this information for external financial reporting is known as *financial accounting,* and it is the main approach used in this text. The use of this financial information through analysis and in combination with information from other areas such as economics, government activities, business trends, and market changes for the purpose of arriving at business decisions for internal management purposes is known as *managerial accounting.*

ACCOUNTING AS A PROFESSION—AREAS OF SPECIALIZATION

The field of professional accounting is divided into three general categories:

1. *Public accounting* is an area of accounting where accountants perform their services for the general public rather than for a single organization. The basic services provided by a public accountant are auditing, preparing tax reports, assisting in various tax problems, and making recommendations for business decisions.
2. *Private accounting* is an area of accounting where accountants perform their services for a single organization. The private accountant maintains the accounting records and provides management with financial data needed for business decisions.
3. *Government accounting* is an area of accounting where accountants perform their services for local, state, and federal governmental agencies. The government accountant performs all the functions of a private or public accountant.

An *accountant* employed in any one of these areas may specialize in general accounting, cost accounting, taxation, financial analysis, budgeting and forecasting, accounting systems and design, or auditing. However, in many large as well as small business organizations, the accountant may be required to be knowledgeable in several of these specialized fields.

The most widely known area of accounting is the public sector, which primarily involves accounting firms that employ the certified public accountant, known as a CPA. The requirements for becoming a CPA are established by the American Institute of Certified Public Accountants (AICPA) and are governed by state laws. These laws set the educational requirements and actual work experience necessary for receiving the CPA designation and license. Public accounting firms are primarily engaged in auditing. *Auditing* consists of checking and testing an organization's financial records to determine if sound accounting practices have been used and if management policies have been followed. After the audit has been completed, the external or independent auditor is in a position to express an opinion on the fairness and reliability of the financial statements. The internal auditors of a company review operating and management practices and procedures to determine if they adhere to company policy and generally accepted accounting practices and procedures as well as assisting in the financial planning of the company in developing cost-saving techniques and operating efficiency policies. In the past few years, the services of certified public accounting (CPA) firms have been expanded to provide specialists in taxation, accounting system design analysis, and general management consulting services.

PURPOSE OF ACCOUNTING

Accounting is a system designed to record financial activities in a meaningful, orderly manner and to summarize and communicate their meaning. This procedure includes:

1. *Recognizing and Analyzing.* By installing a system that will collect all the data important to the business for analysis before recording the information in the accounting records.
2. *Recording and Classifying.* By setting up procedures for recording and classifying all the necessary information from the daily business activities or events on the permanent records so that they will be easily understood.
3. *Summarizing and Reporting.* By arranging recorded and classified information on financial statements that will show the income earned for a period of time and the financial position of the business as of a certain date.
4. *Interpreting.* By using the data on financial statements and comparing changes that have taken place from previous periods as well as using the data for comparison with other companies and current government indicators for the industry.

The methods and techniques presented in this text may be applied to all financial activities including those of government, nonbusiness organizations, informal groups, institutions, and individuals as well as a single proprietorship, partnership, or a corporate type of business organization.

ACCOUNTING VERSUS BOOKKEEPING

The term "bookkeeping" has been used for many years to define the process for maintaining financial records. It is often used and confused with the term "accounting." **Bookkeeping** is the process of recording and reporting routine accounting information, usually under the guidance of a supervisor. Accounting is understanding the theoretical and practical applications of accounting principles and the entire financial recording system. The accountant should be able to handle systems design, problem analysis, and present solutions to accounting problems in addition to performing and supervising routine operations.

THE FIVE BASIC PARTS OF ACCOUNTING

The accounting structure basic to all accounting systems is simple in nature. There are several concepts, definitions of terms, classifications, generally accepted accounting principles, and government regulations that explain the various parts of an accounting system and how these parts are interrelated. All these parts will be explained in detail throughout the text. Knowledge of the concepts, definitions, and rules governing one part of the accounting structure is essential to an understanding of the other parts and how they work together. Constructing an accounting system is similar to constructing a brick wall. At the beginning, it may be hard to visualize the finished design of the wall, but if the plans or instructions are followed carefully, all the parts of the design will fall into place properly. This is also true of a well-constructed accounting system.

The accounting structure has only five basic parts or classifications:

Five basic classifications

1. Assets
2. Liabilities (payables)
3. Owner's equity or capital
4. Revenue
5. Expense

Assets

An *asset* is anything of value that is owned by a business or an individual. The value of an asset is determined by the actual cost of the item. The different types of assets held by a business vary according to the nature of the enterprise. A small service-type business may only have a truck, supplies, and an office in the owner's home. A large store or manufacturing concern may have buildings, furniture, machines, and equipment. Some examples of assets are cash, supplies, land, building, machinery, equipment, and furniture.

Liabilities

Liabilities represent the debts owed to others known as creditors and are referred to as "payables." Creditors have first claim on the assets of the business, and the owners have the second claim. Accountants refer to these claims as the *equities* of a business. Should the business be dissolved, the creditors would be paid first with the cash received from the sale of the assets, and the balance of any cash would be paid to the owners. Some examples of liabilities are accounts payable, salaries or wages payable, taxes payable, and mortgage payable.

Owner's Equity

Owner's equity, often referred to as *capital,* represents the portion of the assets that belong to the owner of the business. It is the difference between the amount of the assets owned and the amount of the liabilities owed by a business. "Proprietorship" and "net worth" are other terms that are often used to designate owner's equity.

Owner's equity or capital may be *increased* in two ways:

1. Owner investing additional cash or other assets into the business
2. Revenues earned from the sale of a product or service

Owner's equity may be *decreased* in two ways:

1. Owner withdrawing cash or other assets from the business for personal use
2. Expenses incurred for the purpose of earning revenue

A single proprietorship-type business is owned by one person. The owner has the right to remove cash or other assets from the business for personal use at any time. Whenever the owner withdraws assets, these withdrawals decrease the owner's equity in the business and are called *drawings.* The drawing account is discussed in Chapter 2.

Revenue

Revenue represents assets coming into the business from the sale of a service or a product to a customer for cash or credit. When a customer does not pay cash for the service or product, this sale on credit is called a "receivable." Revenue is recognized as earned when the service is performed or the product is sold and not when cash is received. Revenue increases the owner's equity in the business. Some examples of revenue are:

1. *Revenue from Fees.* Fees earned for professional services performed by an accountant, doctor, attorney, dentist, etc., or fees earned for providing some type of service for a customer
2. *Sales.* Revenue earned from the sale of a product to a customer

Expenses

Expenses represent assets that are used, consumed, or worn out as a result of employing them in the business for the purpose of earning revenue. Expenses are often referred to as "the cost of doing business." Expenses decrease the owner's equity in the business. Some examples of expenses are rent, insurance, supplies, travel, gas and oil, maintenance and repairs, and miscellaneous expenses.

To summarize, the five basic parts or classifications that form the framework of the entire accounting system are assets, liabilities, owner's equity, revenue, and expenses.

ACCOUNTING TERMS

The language of accounting involves the use of several specialized words or terms that identify various activities. They are a part of the working vocabulary of the accountant, and their meanings are important to an understanding of the accounting system. A few of the more important terms are explained below.

Transactions

The activities of the day-to-day events of a business are known as *transactions.* Every business will usually have financial transactions as well as nonfinancial transactions. From an accounting standpoint we are only concerned with the financial transactions of the business. Those transactions involve the sale of a service or a product to a customer or the acquiring of services or materials from a creditor. Every transaction of a business affects the assets and/or equities (liabilities or owner's equity).

Each business transaction will result in one of the following:

1. Increase one asset and decrease another asset
2. Decrease one equity and increase another equity
3. Increase an asset and increase an equity
4. Decrease an asset and decrease an equity

Examples are illustrated below:

Transaction	Effect on Assets and Equities
1. Purchased $100 of supplies for cash	Increase asset: supplies for $100 Decrease asset: cash for $100
2. Paid $500 owed to creditor with a note*	Decrease liability (equity): accounts payable for $500 Increase liability (equity): notes payable for $500
3. Owner invested equipment valued at $200 in business	Increase asset: equipment for $200 Increase owner's equity: owner's capital for $200
4. Paid creditor $50 on account	Decrease asset: cash for $50 Decrease liability (equity): accounts payable for $50

* Notes will be discussed in the Chapter 10 appendix.

Account

An *account* is a place to record the increases and decreases for each item of a business transaction (see Figure 2-2). For example, all increases and decreases to cash are recorded in the Cash account. Every accounting system will have a separate account for each type of asset, liability, owner's equity, revenue, and expense.

Fiscal Period

The results of business transactions are summarized and reported to the owner at the end of a certain period of time known as a *fiscal period.* The most common accounting period is the fiscal year, consisting of a 12-month period which may or may not be the same as a calendar year. It is common to also account for a fiscal period of less than 1 year, such as 1 month (monthly) or 3 months (quarterly). Each business entity determines its own financial reporting needs, but an annual or fiscal year report of all business activities is a federal government requirement.

Double-Entry System

The *double-entry system* of recording business events simply means that both sides of a business transaction are recorded. For example, if supplies were purchased for $200 from a supplier on credit, a business would own supplies costing $200 and owe the creditor $200 for the purchase on account. Both sides of the transaction would be recorded, showing the increase to the Supplies (asset) and the increase to the Accounts Payable (liability) for the purchase. The records would show:

$$\textbf{Assets} \qquad = \qquad \textbf{Liabilities}$$
$$\text{Amount of supplies} = \text{amount owed to creditor}$$
$$\$200 = \$200$$

This equation states that

$$\text{What you own} = \text{what you owe}$$

Cash versus Accrual Accounting

The easiest way to keep a record of business transactions is to record them when there is an exchange of cash. This is the *cash* system of *accounting.* For example, when a business sells services to customers, the revenue earned would be recorded when cash is actually received. Therefore, only cash sales would be recorded as revenue earned for a period, whereas sales on account or charge sales would not be recognized until the customer paid the account.

A more meaningful method used by most businesses, and the one used throughout this text, is called the *accrual* system of *accounting.* This system recognizes revenue when earned *regardless of when the cash is received.* A sale on account is recorded as revenue earned even though the cash has not been received. Expenses for the period are recognized when they are incurred even if they have not been paid.

This principle is used in Chapters 1 and 2 and will be fully developed in Chapters 3 and 4.

BASIC FINANCIAL STATEMENTS

Balance Sheet

The **balance sheet** is a financial statement that shows the financial condition or financial position of a business on a specific date. The statement shows the assets (what the business owns), the liabilities (what the business owes), and the owner's equity (the owners' share of the assets).

Basic Accounting Equation. The first three classifications of the accounting structure—assets, liabilities, and owner's equity—form the **basic accounting** or balance sheet **equation.** The double-entry system is a direct result of the basic accounting equation. When you record both sides of a business transaction, you are keeping the books in balance. The equation is expressed as follows:

Basic accounting equation

Assets	=	**Liabilities**	+	**Owner's Equity**
Items of value owned	=	amount owed *or* creditor's claim on assets	+	capital invested by owner *or* owner's claim on assets

This equation shows the ownership of the assets as divided between the rights of the creditors, who have first claim on the assets (these claims are liabilities), and the rights of the owner, who has the second claim on the assets (these claims are capital).

Figure 1-1 illustrates the basic accounting equation using Tony's TV service.

Balance Sheet Illustrated. Although the basic accounting equation illustrated in Figure 1-1 for Tony's TV Service will give the total of the assets, liabilities, and owner's equity, a formal statement called a balance sheet should be prepared. The balance sheet shows the financial position of a company on a certain date.

Assume that the transactions for Tony's TV Service took place during the first week of business operations, ending June 30 of the current year. The financial position of the business as of June 30 is shown in the following balance sheet.

The balance sheet is a financial statement showing assets, liabilities, and owner's equity on a certain date

TONY'S TV SERVICE
BALANCE SHEET
June 30, 19___

Assets		
Cash	$2,200	
Supplies	600	
Equipment	1,200	
Total Assets		$4,000
Liabilities		
Accounts Payable	$1,200	
Owner's Equity		
Tony Taylor, Capital	2,800	
Total Liabilities and		
Owner's Equity		$4,000

FIGURE 1-1

Example: To illustrate the basic accounting equation, a few transactions for Tony's TV Service that occurred during the first week of business operations are shown below.

TONY'S TV SERVICE

Transaction	Assets + Cash	+ Supplies	+ Equipment	= Liabilities = Accounts Payable	+ Owner's Equity + Capital
a. Invested cash in business	+ $2,800			=	+ $2,800
b. Paid cash for supplies	− 600	+ $600			
Balance	+ $2,200	+ $600		=	+ $2,800
c. Equipment on account			+ $1,200	= $1,200	
Ending balance	+ $2,200	+ $600	+ $1,200	= + $1,200	+ $2,800

Total assets = $4,000   Total equities = $4,000

Invested Cash
a. Tony Taylor made a contribution or investment of cash to start his TV service business on June 24 and the assets and owner's equity both increased by $2,800.

Paid Cash for Supplies
b. Tony purchased repair supplies for cash, exchanging one asset for another. The total amount of assets did not change, but now there are two assets, Cash and Supplies. *The owner's equity was not affected and did not change.*

Equipment on Account
c. Tony purchased equipment on account. This transaction increased the assets by $1,200 without changing the owner's equity, but it did increase the liabilities for the amount owed. As a result, the creditors have a $1,200 claim on the assets.

After all the transactions are recorded, the accounting equation remains in balance and the assets equal the equities.

Notice that the heading of the balance sheet consists of three lines which show:

1. The name of the business
2. The title of the statement
3. The date

Every financial statement will usually have three lines in the heading.

Income Statement

The last two basic classifications—revenue and expense—are shown on a financial statement called the *income statement* which summarizes the results of the company operations over a period of time. The difference between the revenue and expense is presented in the owner's equity section of the balance sheet.

Net Income Formula. The difference between the last two basic classifications (revenue and expense) forms the basis of the net income formula. The *net income formula* is

Net income formula

$$\text{Revenue} - \text{expenses} = \text{net income}$$

FIGURE 1-2

Example: To illustrate the net income formula, assume that the following revenue and expense transactions for Tony's TV service occurred during the month of July.

TONY'S TV SERVICE

Transaction	Revenue Services Fees	−	(Wages	+	Expenses Telephone	+	Advertising	+	Miscellaneous)
a. Repaired TVs for customers	$1,500								
b. Paid helper's wages			$600						
c. Paid telephone bill				+	$200				
d. Paid advertising						+	$100		
e. Paid miscellaneous expenses								+	$50
Totals	$1,500	−	($600	+	$200	+	$100	+	$50)

Total revenue $1,500 − total expenses $950 = net income $550

Repaired TVs
a. Tony Taylor repaired TVs for customers and the revenue was increased in the amount of $1,500.
Paid Expenses
b. Paid wages for a helper and an expense was incurred.
c. Paid telephone bill for July and an expense was incurred.
d. Paid for advertising his TV service in the local newspaper and an expense was incurred.
e. Paid miscellaneous expenses for the business and an expense was incurred.

After all the revenue and expense transactions are recorded, the net income formula shows that the revenue exceeds the expenses and net income was earned in the amount of $550 for July.

This combination will result in either an increase or a decrease in the owner's capital account. If the revenue is greater than the expenses, the difference is called "net income"; net income will increase capital. But if the expenses are greater than the revenue, the company will incur a "net loss"; net loss will decrease capital.

Figure 1-2 illustrates the net income formula using Tony's TV Service.

Income Statement Illustrated.   After all the revenue and expense transactions are recorded for July, this information is summarized on a formal income statement as shown below. Notice that the first three lines of the statement show the *name* of the company, the title of the *statement,* and the *period of time* covered by the statement.

Income earned for a 1-month period

**TONY'S TV SERVICE
INCOME STATEMENT
For the Month Ended July 31, 19___**

Revenue		
Repair Fees Earned		$1,500
Expenses		
Wages	$600	
Telephone	200	
Advertising	100	
Miscellaneous	50	
Total Expenses		950
Net Income		$ 550

Owner's Equity Section of Balance Sheet Illustrated.   After all the transactions for July are recorded, the owner's capital would have a balance of $3,350 ($2,800 + $550). These increases and decreases to the Owner's Capital account would be shown in the Owner's Equity section of the balance sheet as illustrated below:

Owner's equity section on the balance sheet

Owner's Equity	
Tony Taylor, Capital, July 1	$2,800 (amount invested)
Add: Net income	550 (revenue − expenses)
Tony Taylor, Capital, July 31	$3,350 (ending capital)

ILLUSTRATIVE PROBLEMS

All the definitions of accounting terms and the rules and concepts for application are combined in Figure 1-3 (p. 13). This illustration analyzes 10

FIGURE 1-3

THE ACCOUNTING PROCESS

Jane Walsh started a general repair service business called Walsh Repair Service Company and engaged in several business transactions during the month of March. These transactions are financial events which increased and decreased the assets, liabilities, and owner's equity of the business. After each transaction, the assets equal the equities. The effects of the transactions on the accounting equation were analyzed and recorded on a transaction work sheet as illustrated in Figure 1-4. A transaction work sheet is a simple device used to illustrate the process of increasing (adding) or decreasing (subtracting) amounts from the asset, liability, and owner equity accounts. This process of recording information on a transaction work sheet is not used in business; however, similar recording methods are used and they are discussed in Chapters 2 to 5. The explanation of 10 transactions that occurred during March for Walsh Repair Service Company follow.

Transaction	Explanations
1.	Jane Walsh invested $5,000 in cash to start the Walsh Repair Service Company. She deposited the money in a business checking account. The asset (Cash) and the owner's equity (Jane Walsh, Capital) increased.
2.	Purchased used equipment for $500 cash. One asset (Cash) is exchanged for another asset (Equipment).
3.	Purchased repair supplies for $2,000 on account. An asset (Supplies) is gained, increasing the liability (Accounts Payable) of the company. Owner's equity is not affected.
4.	Performed a large repair job for $1,500 on account. An asset (Accounts Receivable) and revenue (Service Fees) is increased because revenue has been earned from the sale of services. *Remember:* Revenue is recognized when the service has been performed under the accrual basis, even though no cash has been collected. Revenue indirectly increases owner's equity.
5.	Paid $20 for 1 month's liability insurance. An asset (Cash) is decreased, which causes an increase in an expense (Insurance Expense). The increase in the expense account indirectly causes a decrease in owner's equity.
6.	Repair services were performed for $2,000 cash. The asset (Cash) is increased, and there is an increase in revenue (Service Fees) earned from the sale of the service.
7.	The customer in transaction 4 made a partial payment of $720 on account. An asset (Cash) is increased for the cash received. The asset (Accounts Receivable) is decreased because the customer made a payment on account.
8.	Paid $100 for the March telephone bill; $500 for the March rent; $900 for the helper's wages; and $50 for miscellaneous items. When the asset (Cash) is used to generate (earn) revenue, the accounts become expenses (Telephone Expense, Rent Expense, Wages Expense, and Miscellaneous Expense) for the period. The asset Cash decreased and the expenses increased which indirectly decreased owner's equity.
9.	Complete the net income formula: Revenue − expenses = net income which increases capital. The net result of the last two columns is transferred to the Capital column and added to the amount because profit increases capital.
10.	The owner, Jane Walsh, withdrew $800 for personal use. This reduces the asset (Cash) and reduces Owner's Equity (Jane Walsh, Drawing). The withdrawal is not an expense of the business, because the asset was not used for the production of revenue.

FIGURE 1-4

WALSH REPAIR SERVICE COMPANY
TRANSACTION WORK SHEET
For the Month Ended March 31, 19____

	Assets				=	Liabilities +	Owner's Equity			
	Cash	+ Accounts Receivable	+ Supplies	+ Equipment	=	Accounts Payable	+ Capital	+ Net Income Revenue	− Expense
1. Owner invested cash	+5,000				=		+5,000		
2. Purchased equipment for cash	−500			+500					
Balance	4,500			500			5,000		
3. Purchased repair supplies on credit			+2,000		=	+2,000			
Balance	4,500		2,000	500		2,000	5,000		
4. Service fees earned on account		+1,500			=			+1,500	
Balance	4,500	1,500	2,000	500		2,000	5,000	1,500	
5. Paid 1 month's insurance	−20				=				20
Balance	4,480	1,500	2,000	500		2,000	5,000	1,500	20
6. Cash received for service fees	+2,000				=			+2,000	
Balance	6,480	1,500	2,000	500		2,000	5,000	3,500	20
7. Cash received on account	+720	−720			=				
Balance	7,200	780	2,000	500		2,000	5,000	3,500	20
8. Paid telephone bill	−100								100
Paid March rent	−500								500
Paid helper's wages	−900								900
Paid miscellaneous expenses	−50								50
Balance	5,650	780	2,000	500	=	2,000	5,000	3,500	1,570
9. Transfer net income to capital							+1,930 ←	(3,500 − 1,570)	
Balance	5,650	780	2,000	500		2,000	6,930		
10. Owner withdrew cash for personal use	−800						−800		
Ending balance	4,850	780	2,000	500	=	2,000	6,130		

8,130 →   ← $8,130

transactions that occurred during March, the first month of business operations, for Jane Walsh, the owner of Walsh Repair Service Company.

Now that the transactions have been recorded on the transaction work sheet and each column totaled at the end of March, all the necessary information is available for the preparation of the financial statements.

The income statement is prepared first, because the amount of net income is needed to determine the amount of ending capital for the owner on the balance sheet. All the information for this statement is found in the last two columns of the transaction work sheet, Figure 1-4.

Income statement prepared from transaction work sheet

WALSH REPAIR SERVICE COMPANY
INCOME STATEMENT
For the Month Ended March 31, 19__

Revenue		
Service Fees Earned		$3,500
Expenses		
Insurance	$ 20	
Telephone	100	
Rent	500	
Wages	900	
Miscellaneous	50	
Total Expenses		1,570
Net Income		$1,930

Balance sheet showing increases and decreases to owner's equity

WALSH REPAIR SERVICE COMPANY
BALANCE SHEET
March 31, 19__

Assets		
Cash	$4,850	
Accounts Receivable	780	
Supplies	2,000	
Equipment	500	
Total Assets		$8,130
Liabilities		
Accounts Payable		$2,000
Owner's Equity		
Jane Walsh, Capital, March 1, 19__		$5,000
Net Income for March	$1,930	
Less: Drawings	800	
Net Increase in Capital	1,130	
Jane Walsh, Capital, March 31, 19__		6,130
Total Liabilities and Owner's Equity		$8,130

After the income statement is completed, the balance sheet is prepared. All the information for this statement is found under the headings of Assets, Liabilities, and Owner's Equity in Figure 1-4.

Each of the five basic parts or classifications of the accounting structure are clearly identified on the statements. The dollar amounts are arranged in an orderly manner to assist the reader in finding the desired data. Notice that the dollar signs are placed at the beginning of each column of figures and with the final number or total. Underscored single and double lines are also very important. Single lines indicate the addition or subtraction of the numbers appearing above each line, and double lines indicate a final number or total.

ACCOUNTING PRINCIPLES

When accounting was recognized as a business tool for recording and reporting financial information to business, government, individuals, and other groups, guidelines were developed by the accounting profession. These guidelines are called *accounting principles,* standards, or concepts and are referred to as "generally accepted accounting principles" (GAAP). The guidelines make it possible for owners, investors, government agencies, and the interested public to (1) analyze business performance, (2) compare one business to another, and (3) gather important financial data about any business.

Owners and professional managers are responsible for the accounting practices of their business. They must make sure that government regulations are followed and that the generally accepted accounting principles are used when recording and reporting financial information. Failure to do so produces misleading financial statements, poor management information, and inaccurate government reporting.

A good understanding of the generally accepted accounting principles is necessary if accounting methods are to be applied fairly and consistently. Several accounting principles are discussed below to provide a better understanding of the procedures used for recording and reporting accounting information in the following chapters.

Cost Principle

The *Cost Principle* states that for accounting purposes all business transactions will be recorded at cost or the actual dollars paid. These costs will be maintained in the accounting records until the assets are sold, expired, or consumed. Cost provides a reliable measurement of the asset's value at the time it is acquired, eliminating the possibility of someone's overvaluing or undervaluing the asset. If an asset were recorded at its market value, the amount would be based on an opinion or estimate which could not be verified until the asset was sold.

Entity Principle

When recording financial information, it is essential that the activities of the business unit be kept separate and distinct from the owner's personal finances. Each business or economic unit should be treated as an individual unit or entity. This is known as the ***Entity Principle.*** If a person owns more than one business, accounting for the assets, liabilities, owner's equity, revenue, and expenses should be maintained separately for each unit or business entity. Separate records must also be maintained for the owner's personal financial activities. If records for each business unit are not kept separate, it will be difficult to evaluate the results of each business operation. For example, assume that Jane Judge is an attorney engaged in the practice of law. Over the years, Jane was able to build an office building large enough to house her own offices and provide for several rental offices. In this situation there are three distinct entities for accounting purposes.

1. The personal finances of Jane Judge, such as salary, other income, and other personal expenditures
2. The law practice
3. The office building or rental property business

Although one person or company may be the controlling factor in several economic or business activities, each unit or entity should be accounted for separately.

Full Disclosure Principle

The ***Full Disclosure Principle*** requires that financial statements provide the reader with adequate information regarding the accounting methods used, the terms of long-term liabilities, and important management decisions that affect the future operation or direction of the company. The purpose is to provide enough information to the user of financial statements to present an accurate picture of the financial position of a business.

Going Concern Principle

Under the ***Going Concern Principle***, business transactions are accounted for under the assumption that the business will remain in operation for an indefinite period of time and will continue to operate in a normal manner from one year to the next. This is in contrast to accounting for a business that may be slowing down, shutting down, or going out of business completely. If a business plans to discontinue operations in the future, this information must be disclosed as a footnote on the balance sheet. Otherwise, the reader of a financial statement may assume that the business will continue to do business in the future as it has in the past.

Materiality Principle

The *Materiality Principle* allows the accountant to decide if an asset should be expensed or capitalized (charged to an asset account) and depreciated. If the cost of an item will have a great effect on the income or the assets of a business, it should be charged to an asset account and depreciated. If the cost of the item is so small that it would not materially affect the income or the assets of a business, the item could be charged to an expense account under the principle of materiality. In a large business, an item costing several thousand dollars might be charged to (recorded in) an expense account when it is purchased, because the net income would not be materially affected by the decision. However, a smaller business buying an item for a few thousand or even several hundred dollars would not be justified in charging the amount to an expense, because the purchase would make a significant change in the assets and materially distort the net income.

Accounting decisions in this area require a depth of knowledge and experience.

Objectivity Principle

The *Objectivity Principle* requires business transactions and financial statements to be based upon objective and verifiable evidence. Each accounting transaction should be supported by business documents (known as source documents) such as invoices, purchase orders, receipts, or canceled checks so the information on the accounting records and financial statements can be verified.

SUMMARY

Accounting is a system for recording financial business activities or financial transactions. The system provides financial information for owners, managers, and other interested groups in making decisions about future business operations.

The accounting system comprises five basic parts or classifications. The first three parts—assets, liabilities, and owner's equity—form the basic accounting equation:

$$\text{Assets} = \text{liabilities} + \text{owner's equity}$$

This equation is the backbone of the accounting structure. The values of these classifications are shown in a financial report called the balance sheet.

The last two classifications—revenue and expense—form the equation for net income:

$$\text{Revenue} - \text{expense} = \text{net income or loss}$$

This relationship affects the owner's equity section of the balance sheet equation, because net income will increase the owner's equity or capital and net loss will cause a decrease. The amounts of revenue and expense are presented in a financial report called the income statement.

The financial activities of a business are known as financial transactions, and the increases and decreases for each item are accumulated in an account. Every accounting system will have a separate account for each type of asset, liability, owner's equity, revenue, and expense. Recording both sides of every transaction in the accounting records is called the double-entry system.

The accrual basis of accounting recognizes revenues when they are earned and expenses when they are incurred. The cash basis of accounting recognizes revenue when cash is received and expenses when they are paid.

Financial statements are prepared at the end of a fiscal period which is usually 1 year. However, the fiscal period may be for 1, 3, 6, or 9 months. The income statement is the first statement prepared and is dated to show the period of time required to earn the net income or loss. The information on the income statement is needed to complete the balance sheet. The balance sheet is prepared next and shows the assets, liabilities, and owner's capital as of a certain date. Accounting principles developed by the accounting profession and government agencies are the guidelines used to provide a better understanding of the accounting procedures used for recording and reporting accounting information. The Cost Principle states that all transactions will be recorded at cost or actual dollars paid. Under the Entity Principle, each business or economic unit is treated as an individual unit or entity. The Full Disclosure Principle requires financial statements to include information to present an accurate picture of the financial position of the business. Under the Going Concern Principle, business transactions are accounted for under the assumption that the business is going to continue to operate in the future as it has in the past. Any foreseeable suspension of operations must be disclosed on the financial statements. The Materiality Principle allows the accountant to decide if an asset should be recorded as an expense or an asset, taking into consideration the value of its effect on the overall financial position of the business. The Objectivity Principle requires business transactions and financial statements to be based upon objective and verifiable evidence.

GLOSSARY

Account: A device used to accumulate the increases and decreases of a business transaction.

Accountant: An individual who understands the accounting principles, their theoretical and practical application, and can manage, analyze, and interpret the accounting records.

Accounting: A system for maintaining accurate financial records for business and government purposes.

Accounting Principles: Guidelines established to ensure the reliability of accounting information.

Accrual Accounting: The recognition of revenues and expenses when they are incurred regardless of when cash is received or paid.

Assets: Items of value owned by the business.

Auditing: A check on the accuracy of the accounting records and testing the procedures used in the system.

Balance Sheet: A financial statement showing the financial condition or financial position of a business on a specific date. The statement shows the assets (what the business owns), the liabilities (what the business owes), and the owner's equity (the owner's share of the assets).

Basic Accounting Equation: Assets = liabilities + owner's equity.

Bookkeeping: The process of recording and reporting routine accounting information.

Capital: A name given to the account representing the owner's equity in the business and owner's claim on the assets.

Cash Accounting: The recognition of revenue and expenses when cash is received or paid.

Cost Principle: The principle that states that all transactions will be recorded at cost or actual dollars paid.

Double-Entry System: Recording both sides of a business transaction.

Drawing (Withdrawals): The name of the account used to record the assets removed from the business by the owner for personal use. The account is not an expense.

Entity Principle: Each business unit is a separate independent unit, and the activities of the business should be kept separate from the activities of the owners.

Equity: The right to ownership. An investment or interest in the assets of a business.

Expense: The consumption or using up of assets as they are employed by the business to generate revenue.

Financial Accounting: Accounting for the financial position and profits and losses of a business.

Fiscal Period: The period of time chosen by a business to report the results of business transactions.

Full Disclosure Principle: Requires that financial statements include adequate information to present an accurate picture of the financial position of the business.

Going Concern Principle: Assumes that the business is going to continue to operate in the future as it has in the past. Any foreseeable suspension of operations must be disclosed on the financial statements.

Government Accounting: An area of accounting where accountants perform their services for local, state, and federal governmental agencies.

Income Statement: A financial report showing the amount of income earned or loss incurred over a stated period of time.

Liabilities: Debts the business owes to creditors and creditors' claims on the assets.

Managerial Accounting: Using financial information through analysis and in combination with other related information for the purpose of arriving at business decisions.

Materiality Principle: Allows the accountant to decide if an asset should be recorded as an expense or an asset, taking into consideration the value of its effect on the overall financial position of the business.

Net Income Formula: Revenue − expenses = net income or loss.

Objectivity Principle: The principle that requires business transactions and financial statements to be based upon objective and verifiable evidence.

Owner's Equity: The difference between the assets and liabilities of a business.

Private Accounting: An area of accounting where accountants perform their services for a single organization.

Public Accounting: An area of accounting where accountants perform their services for the public rather than for a single organization.

Revenue: Assets coming into the business from the sale of goods or services.

Transaction: The activities of the day-to-day events of a business.

QUESTIONS

1. Define the Entity, Cost, and Going Concern Principles.
2. Explain the difference between bookkeeping and accounting.
3. Name and briefly define the five classifications of accounts.
4. Two formal financial statements are prepared at the end of the fiscal period. Give (a) the name of the statement that shows the net income or loss for the period, and (b) the name of the statement that presents the financial position of a company on a certain date.
5. Show the basic accounting equation and the formula for determining net income.
6. What is the difference between the headings required for the income statement and those used in the balance sheet?
7. List two ways to increase owner's equity and two ways to decrease owner's equity.
8. Explain the difference between the accrual and cash bases of accounting.
9. Describe the double-entry system of accounting by using an example for your explanation.
10. What effect will the purchase of equipment on account have on the basic accounting equation?

EXERCISES

Basic Accounting Equation

1. For each of the following activities, (1) indicate the effect on assets, liabilities, and owner's equity and (2) identify the items affecting owner's equity

as either an investment, revenue, expense, or drawing as shown in the following example:

Example: Sold services to customers for cash.

Answer:

$$Assets \quad = \quad Liabilities \quad + \quad Owner's\ Equity$$
$$Increase \quad No\ Effect \quad Increase \quad (revenue)$$

(a) The owner invested cash to start the business.
(b) Paid rent for the current month.
(c) Purchased office supplies for cash.
(d) Bought used office furniture on account.
(e) Received cash from customers for services performed.
(f) Paid utility bill for the current month.
(g) Paid for used office furniture purchased in item **d**.
(h) Sent monthly statements to customers for services performed on account.

2. Using the basic accounting equation, find the missing numbers.

$$Assets \quad = \quad Liabilities \quad + \quad Owner's\ Equity$$
$$\$8,500 = (a)\ \$\_\_\_\_ + \quad \$2,500$$
$$4,000 = \quad 1,000 + (b)\ \_\_\_\_$$
$$(c)\ \_\_\_\_ = \quad 3,500 + \quad 6,000$$

Net Income Formula

3. Using the net income formula, supply the missing numbers.

$$Revenue \quad - \quad Expenses \quad = \quad Net\ Income$$
$$\$18,000 - \quad \$10,000 = (a)\ \$\_\_\_\_$$
$$12,000 - (b)\ \_\_\_\_ = \quad 4,000$$
$$(c)\ \_\_\_\_ - \quad 5,000 = \quad 3,000$$

Classification of Accounts

4. Identify each of the items below as an asset, liability, capital, revenue, or expense account.

(a) Cash   (e) Supplies
(b) Wages Expense   (f) Rent Revenue
(c) Wages Payable   (g) Equipment
(d) Land   (h) Service Fees Earned

5. Using the data given below, determine the total assets.

Accounts Payable	$ 400	Cash	$2,000
Accounts Receivable	600	Land	1,000
Building	5,000	Rent Revenue	800
Joe College, Capital	8,000	Equipment	1,500

6. Using the following data, determine the total liabilities.

Accounts Receivable	$1,000	Rent Revenue	$6,000
Notes Payable	4,000	Rent Expense	500
Land	2,000	Wages Expense	2,000
Wages Payable	600	Accounts Payable	3,000

7. Using the following data, determine the total owner's equity.

Wages Payable	$ 600	Office Furniture	$2,000
Cash	4,000	Accounts Payable	4,000
Supplies	800	Building	8,000
Accounts Receivable	300	Land	2,000

Balance Sheet

8. Using the following information, prepare a balance sheet in good form for the Good Service Company as of December 31 of the current year.

Cash	$8,000	Wages Payable	$ 500
Accounts Receivable	3,300	D. Good, Capital, 1/1	6,000
Office Supplies	300	D. Good, Drawing	8,000
Office Furniture	1,500	Service Fees Earned	65,000
Accounts Payable	600	Operating Expenses	51,000

9. On December 31 of the current year, the College Company owned assets in the amount of $10,000 and owed creditors $3,000. The owner's capital account amounted to $5,000 on December 1, net income amounted to $3,000, and the owner withdrew $1,000 for personal use during December. Prepare the Owner's Equity section of the balance sheet as of December 31.

Accounting Principles

10. List the accounting principle given in column 1 that illustrates each of the situations described in column 2.

Accounting Principle

(a) Entity
(b) Going Concern
(c) Cost
(d) Materiality
(e) Full Disclosure

Situation

_____ **1.** The personal assets of an owner are separated from the assets of the business when preparing the company's balance sheet.

_____ **2.** Land valued at $5,000 was purchased and recorded at the purchase price of $4,000.

_____ **3.** A business plans to expand their operations within 6 months. This information is noted on the balance sheet.

_____ **4.** Office furniture purchased for $10 was recorded as an expense instead of an asset.

_____ **5.** A business plans to continue operations during the following year as it has in the past.

PROBLEMS

Basic Accounting Equation

1-1. For each activity listed below, (1) indicate the effect on assets, liabilities, and owner's equity and (2) identify the items affecting the owner's equity as either an investment, revenue, expense, or drawing as shown in the following example.

Example: Paid the telephone bill.

Answer:

Assets	**= Liabilities**	**+ Owner's Equity**
Decrease	No Effect	Decrease (expense)

(a) Purchased a pickup truck for cash.
(b) Purchased an office desk and chair on account.
(c) The owner invested additional cash in the business.
(d) Paid employees' wages.
(e) Sold services to customers for cash.
(f) Paid creditor for purchase in item **b.**
(g) The owner withdrew cash for personal use.
(h) Mailed statement to customers for services performed during month.
(i) Borrowed money from the local bank.
(j) Received bill from the local gas station for products and services charged during the month.

1-2. Using the instructions given in Problem 1-1, determine the effects of the following transactions.

(a) Sold services to customers on credit.
(b) The owner invested additional cash and equipment in the business.
(c) Purchased supplies for future use on account.
(d) Paid monthly rent.
(e) Sold services to customers for cash.
(f) Paid employees' salaries.
(g) Paid for the supplies purchased in item **c.**
(h) Owner withdrew cash for personal use.
(i) Borrowed money from the local bank.
(j) Placed an order for new equipment.

Determining Income Statement and Balance Sheet Amounts

1-3. Determine the missing amounts:

A.

Assets	**= Liabilities**	**+ Owner's Equity**
$10,000 =	$4,000 +	(a) $_____
(b) _____ =	8,000 +	12,000
15,000 =	(c) _____ +	10,000

B.

	Revenue	–	Expenses	= Net Income/(Loss)
(d)	$_____	–	$ 9,000 =	$12,000
	12,000	– (e) _____ =		4,000
	18,000	–	11,000 = (f)	_____

1-4. Determine the missing amounts:

	1	2	3	4
Beginning capital	$10,000	$12,000	(c) $_____	$25,000
Investment	5,000	(b) _____	0	10,000
Net income or (loss)	8,000	15,000	25,000	(2,000)
Drawing	(a) 5000	10,000	15,000	6,000
Ending capital	18,000	20,000	30,000	(d) _____

	5	6
	$30,000	$40,000
	5,000	8,000
	(e) _____	(f) _____
	12,000	18,000
	45,000	35,000

Classification of Accounts

1-5. Classify the following items as assets, liabilities, owner's equity, revenue, or expense accounts.

(a) Cash
(b) Accounts Receivable
(c) Wages Payable
(d) Ruth Jacobs, Capital
(e) Rent Earned
(f) Equipment

(g) Utilities Expense
(h) Accounts Payable
(i) Wages Expense
(j) Land
(k) Service Fees
(l) Building

1-6. Classify the following items as assets, liabilities, owner's equity, revenue, or expense accounts.

(a) Land
(b) Service Supplies
(c) Accounts Receivable
(d) Furniture & Fixtures
(e) Wages Payable
(f) Machinery

(g) Rent Revenue
(h) Accounts Payable
(i) J. B., Capital
(j) Professional Fees
(k) Rent Expense
(l) Building

Transaction Work Sheet

1-7. During April of the current year, Brian James started a lawn care service called Love Lawns. For recording purposes, he set up the following accounts: Cash, Accounts Receivable, Equipment, Accounts Payable, and B. James, Capital. The business transactions for April were as follows:

1. Invested $5,000 cash by opening a bank account in the name of the business.

2. Purchased used lawn mowers and miscellaneous yard equipment for $1,500 cash.
3. Bought a used van for $1,800. Paid $1,000 in cash and agreed to pay the $800 balance in 90 days.
4. Bought $150 of lawn care products at the local hardware store on account (use Supplies Expense for the account).
5. Collected $1,300 cash from customers for lawn care services.
6. Paid helper $300 for the last 2 weeks of April.
7. Sent bills amounting to $500 to charge customers for services performed in April.
8. Paid the hardware store for purchase in item 4.
9. Paid $85 to a printing company for advertising fliers.
10. The owner withdrew $400 for personal use.

Required

(a) From the data in the first paragraph, prepare a transaction work sheet for Love Lawns for the month of April. Use the form illustrated in Figure 1-4.
(b) Show the effects of the transactions, and total the columns and prove the equality of the equation on April 30. Remember to identify the reason for the change in the owner's equity section as investment, revenue, expense, or drawing.
(c) Prepare an income statement for April.
(d) Prepare a balance sheet as of April 30.

1-8. Ruth Roberts operates an exclusive pet care service called the Posh Poodle. On May 1 of the current year, the assets and liabilities of the business were Cash, $2,700; Accounts Receivable, $800; Supplies, $100; Equipment, $7,500; Accounts Payable, $1,800; and Ruth Roberts, Capital, $9,300. The transactions for May were as follows:
1. Received $850 cash for work performed for customers.
2. Paid $650 rent for May.
3. Paid $500 on Accounts Payable.
4. Received $600 from customers as payment on account.
5. Purchased $300 worth of supplies on account.
6. Mailed bills totaling $1,650 to charge customers for services performed in May.
7. Purchased new equipment for $1,400, giving $1,000 in cash and charging $400 on account.
8. Ruth Roberts, owner, withdrew $500 in cash for personal use.
9. Paid $30 for monthly utility bills and paid $70 for advertising.
10. Paid $400 for monthly salaries of employees.

Required

(a) From the data in the first paragraph, prepare a transaction work sheet for the Posh Poodle. Using the form shown in Figure 1-4, place the amounts or beginning balances on the first line.

(b) Record the transactions, total the columns, and prove the equality of the equation as of May 31.

(c) Prepare an income statement for the month ended May 31.

(d) Prepare a balance sheet as of May 31.

1-9. On January 1 of the current year, Ted Taylor purchased a delivery service and changed the name to Century Carrier Company. The company had the following assets on January 1: Trucks, $5,000; Supplies, $500; and Office Equipment, $1,000. To purchase the business and provide operating cash of $2,500, Taylor invested $9,000 cash from his personal account. The following transactions occurred in January.

1. Purchased $50 of supplies on account.
2. Paid $30 for newspaper ad appearing in local paper today.
3. Billed customers $3,500 for services performed in January.
4. Paid $500 for truck driver's wages.
5. Paid $400 for truck operating expenses.
6. Received $2,000 from customers on account.
7. Ted Taylor, owner, withdrew $600 cash for personal use.
8. Paid monthly bills for utilities, $30; telephone, $55; and miscellaneous expenses, $5.

Required

(a) Prepare a transaction work sheet for the Century Carrier Company using the asset accounts Cash, Accounts Receivable, Supplies, Trucks, and Office Equipment; and a liability account Accounts Payable; and owner's equity account, Ted Taylor, Capital. Enter the beginning balance on the first line for the accounts listed in the first paragraph plus the beginning balance for Ted Taylor, Capital. Record the information for January, total all columns, and prove the equality of the equation.

(b) Prepare an income statement for the month ended January 31.

(c) Prepare a balance sheet as of January 31.

Accounting Principles

1-10. One or more accounting principles have been violated in each of the following unrelated situations. Determine the principles involved.

(a) Ruth Tate owns a small apartment building and a beauty salon. All cash received and payment for the building, beauty salon, and her personal expenses are handled from her personal checking account.

(b) Slip Shod Company purchased a building valued at $10,000 for $7,000 cash. The accountant recorded $10,000 in the building account.

(c) Nit Pick Company purchased a stapler for $2.50. The $2.50 was added to the Office Equipment account.

(d) Ding Company had a very successful year and entered into a 20-year lease for a new office building. It also was negotiating a $100,000 loan for an addition to the company plant. Neither of these events were mentioned in the annual balance sheet.

Balance Sheet

1-11. The following is an alphabetical list of the accounts of the Hey-Bob Company, a single proprietorship, as of December 31 of the current year.

Accounts Payable	$6,000	Machinery	$ 3,000
Accounts Receivable	1,500	Net Income for Year	12,000
Building	5,000	Paula Jones, Capital 1/1	7,500
Cash	2,000	Paula Jones, Drawing	6,000
Furniture & Fixtures	2,300	Trucks	5,400
Land	500	Wages Payable	200

Required

Prepare a balance sheet in good form.

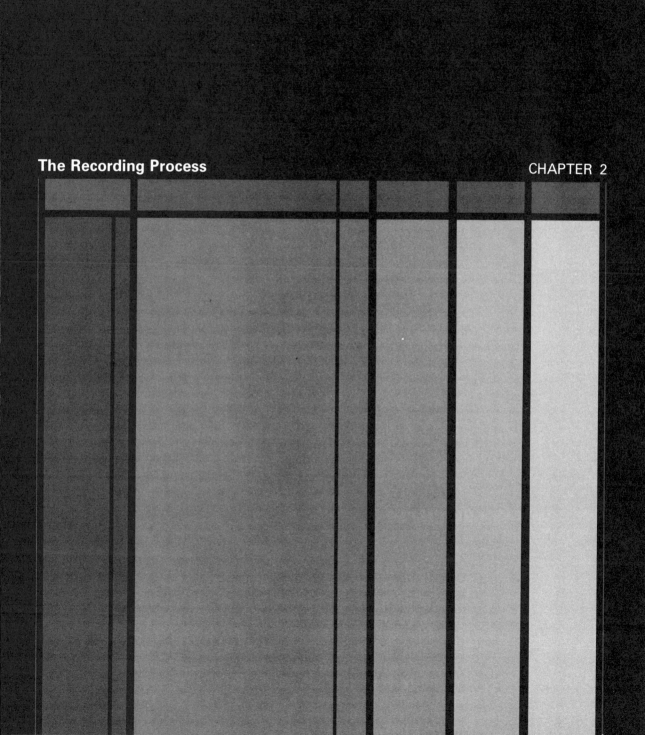

The Recording Process

After completing this chapter, you should be able to:

1. **List the six basic parts of a ledger account**
2. **State the difference between debit and credit and the normal balance for each of the five basic types of accounts**
3. **Analyze and journalize business transactions**
4. **Post the information from the general journal to the general ledger**
5. **Prepare a trial balance and state its purpose**
6. **Describe the first three steps of the accounting cycle**

Chapter 2 will explain the recording process of accounting and show how to keep books in balance. The chapter is divided into two parts. Part I will show the parts of an account and how they are used. Part II will show how business transactions or activities are recorded, summarized, and checked for accuracy.

Part I:

The Account and General Journal

As you may recall from Chapter 1, business transactions are sorted by groups of like items called "accounts." This is done in much the same manner as the postal worker sorting mail in the post office by placing the letters in the proper boxes according to the address or box number on each piece of mail.

The accountant wants to sort out the many business activities into their individual places; that is, all cash transactions in the Cash account, all office supplies transactions in the Office Supplies account, all accounts payable in the Accounts Payable account, and so on. If there is a need for more items, more accounts are added to meet the need.

CHART OF ACCOUNTS

Even the smallest accounting system should have a *chart of accounts*, which is the index to the accounting system. It should list the names or titles of the accounts, and each account should be assigned a number so they can be easily identified and located. The accounts should be arranged in the order of the five basic parts or classifications of accounts: assets, liabilities, owner's equity, revenue, and expense. Assigning a number to each basic account usually depends upon the size of the company and how many accounts will be necessary to handle their accounting information. In this text, the first digit in each number has been assigned to each of the five basic accounts. For example, the first digit 1 has been assigned to asset accounts, 2 to liability accounts, 3 to owner's equity accounts, 4 to revenue accounts, and 5 and 6 to expense accounts.

ACCOUNTING MANUAL

Usually the accountant will set up an accounting manual for the accounting system. The *accounting manual* is a separate book where you will find, in addition to the account numbers and titles, a detailed description of exactly what is to be recorded in each account. This manual serves as a reference for recording accounting information.

Using both the chart of accounts (usually found in the front of the accounting manual) and the more detailed manual information (see Figure 2-1), you can get a good look at the parts of the accounting system and see where things should go. *When in doubt as to what account to use,* check the chart of accounts and/or the manual.

THE ACCOUNT

A separate account is used for each individual asset, liability, owner's equity, revenue, and expense. The increases and decreases for different items of a business transaction are recorded in these five types of accounts. Each account has one column on the left side which is called the debit side, and each account has another column on the right side which is called the credit side. A skeleton picture or representation of an account is shown in Figure 2-2 and is known as a T account.

FIGURE 2-1

Directory to accounting system

CHART OF ACCOUNTS

Account Number	Account Title
100	Cash
120	Notes Receivable
150	Accounts Receivable

ACCOUNTING MANUAL

Account Number	
150	Accounts Receivable—This account is for the recording of monies due from customers for the sale of services on account.

FIGURE 2-2

Skeleton form of T account

Account Title	
(left side)	(right side)
or	or
Debit side	Credit side

The T account is a simple or quick method of illustrating the process of increasing and decreasing an account.

When increasing and decreasing accounts, we use the terms debit and credit. The term **debit (Dr)** means left side and the term **credit (Cr)** means right side of an account. These debit and credit terms are merely terms of direction and only have meaning within the rules of the accounting structure. When used, depending on the classification of the account under consideration, the debit (Dr) and credit (Cr) tells the accountant if the account should be increased or decreased as shown in Examples 1 and 2.

EXAMPLE 1   *To increase an asset or expense account, we use the term debit. To decrease an asset or expense account, we use the term credit as illustrated in the T account form below:*

Assets and Expense Accounts	
(left side)	(right side)
Debit side	Credit side
+	−
Normal balance and	
Increase side	Decrease side

EXAMPLE 2   *To increase a liability, owner's capital, or revenue account, we use the term credit. To decrease a liability, owner capital, or revenue account, we use the term debit as illustrated in the T account form below:*

Liabilities, Owner's Capital, and Revenue Accounts	
(left side)	(right side)
Debit side	Credit side
−	+
	Normal balance and
Decrease side	Increase side

PARTS OF AN ACCOUNT

The account form used in business has six basic parts.

1. A *title*, heading, or name

2. An account *number*

3. A *date* column
4. A *debit* side
5. A *credit* side
6. An account *balance*

ACCOUNT FORMS

There are several forms available for recording information in the accounts. The T account, Figure 2-2, is a quick, informal way for the accountant to determine the proper debits and credits for a business transaction.
It is not used for maintaining formal accounting records. Most businesses
use printed forms that are available. The forms provide places for all the
essential information very similar to the T account.

One form is arranged like the T account.

Formal T account

				CASH				Account No.: 100
Date	Explanation	Ref.	Debit	Date	Explanation	Ref.	Credit	
19__ Mar. 5			1,000	19__ Mar. 7			300	

Debit side
Credit side

A modification of the above form, which is very popular, is the one you
will use for all problems in this text. This form is called a three-column,
running balance account form, because it has debit and credit columns
along with a balance column. In this way the balance can easily be shown
after each transaction is posted.

*Three-column form of
ledger account*

Title: Cash   **Account No.: 100**

Date	Explanation	Ref.	Debit	Credit	Balance
19__ Mar. 5			1,000		1,000
7				300	700

Running balance

ACCOUNT BALANCE

The *account balance,* or the amount remaining in the account, is the difference between the debit and credit columns. When using the T account

FIGURE 2-3

*T accounts require pencil
footings and balance*

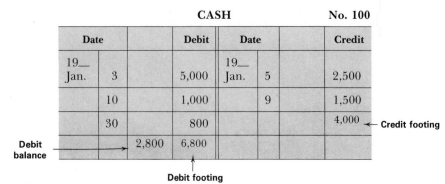

		CASH				No. 100	
Date			**Debit**	Date			**Credit**
19__ Jan.	3		5,000	19__ Jan.	5		2,500
	10		1,000		9		1,500
	30		800				4,000 ← Credit footing
Debit balance →		2,800	6,800				

↑ Debit footing

form, the account balance is determined by adding the debit and credit columns. The totals of the debit and credit columns are written in pencil under each column in small figures. These totals are called *footings*. The balance of the account is found by subtracting the total amount of the debits from the total amount of the credits. The column with the larger amount determines whether the balance is a debit or credit as illustrated in Figure 2-3.

When using the three-column account form with debit, credit, and balance columns, the account balance is determined after each debit or credit entry. The account balance shown in the balance column represents a debit or credit balance depending upon the classification of the account. Accounts classified as an asset, expense, or owner drawing account normally will have a debit balance. Accounts classified as a liability, owner capital, or revenue account normally will have a credit balance. The $2,800 shown in the balance column of the Cash account illustrated in Figure 2-4 represents a debit balance as of January 30 because Cash is classified as an asset account.

If an entry causes an account to have the opposite type of balance that it normally has, the balance is circled or recorded in parenthesis ( ). If an entry causes an account to have a zero balance, a zero is recorded in the

FIGURE 2-4

*Three-column form with
account balance shown
after each entry*

Title: Cash | | | | | | **Account No.: 100**

Date		Explanation	Ref.	Debit	Credit	Balance
19__ Jan.	3				5,000	5,000
	5				2,500	2,500
	9				1,500	1,000
	10			1,000		2,000
	30			800		2,800

↑ Debit balance

FIGURE 2-5

Three-column account form with a debit, zero, and credit balance

Title: **Accounts Payable**   Account No.: **200**

Date		Explanation	Ref.	Debit	Credit	Balance	
19__							
Jan.	5				5,000	5,000	
	8			2,000		3,000	
	10			6,000		(1,000)	← Debit balance
	14				1,000	–0–	← Zero balance
	20				7,000	7,000	

Credit balance ↑

balance column. To illustrate, an Accounts Payable account is shown in Figure 2-5 with a debit balance as of January 10, a zero balance as of January 14, and a credit balance as of January 20. The last amount of $7,000 shown in the balance column represents a credit balance as of January 20 because Accounts Payable is classified as a liability account.

NORMAL BALANCES

The *normal* or usual *balance* in an account is whatever it takes—debit or credit—to *increase* the account. Since it requires a debit to increase asset and expense accounts, the normal balance for such accounts is a debit. Since it requires a credit to increase a liability, owner capital, or revenue accounts, the normal balance for such accounts is a credit as summarized in Figure 2-6.

Before going on, take careful note of the terms and rules for increasing or decreasing an account. *They do not change.* Learn them because the

FIGURE 2-6

Financial Statement	Basic Account Classification	Normal Balance and Increase Side		Decrease Side	
		Debit	Credit	Debit	Credit
Balance sheet	(1) Assets	✔			✔
	(2) Liabilities		✔	✔	
	(3) Owner's Equity		✔	✔	
Income statement	(4) Revenue		✔	✔	
	(5) Expenses	✔			✔

rules must become automatic to record business transactions or activities with ease.

GENERAL JOURNAL

Business activities or transactions take place every day that involve investing cash or other assets in the business by the owner, selling services to customers, buying needed items from suppliers, and paying the bills. These transactions must be recorded in the accounting records in an orderly manner. The first step in the accounting process is to enter each transaction in a book called a ***general journal*** which is also known as the "book of original entry."

This first step in the accounting process provides the business with a complete history or record of financial events in chronological order and in one place. Each transaction entered must have at least one debit and one offsetting or equal credit. An entry that has more than one debit and one credit is known as a "compound" entry. (Compound entries are illustrated in the journal entries for August 4 and August 15 shown in Figure 2-7.)

At all times, the sum of the debits in each journal entry must equal the sum of the credits. This is known as double-entry accounting, and it is essential to remember this rule when thinking through transactions for the purpose of journalizing the general journal entries. The entry must balance to be correct.

JOURNALIZING TRANSACTIONS IN GENERAL JOURNAL

Recording business transactions or events in the general journal is a process known as ***journalizing.*** When journalizing a business transaction, each ***journal entry*** requires a date, debit account and amount, credit account and amount, and a brief but complete explanation as summarized below.

Six basic parts to each journal entry

1. Date
2. Debit account(s)
3. Debit amount(s)
4. Credit account(s)
5. Credit amount(s)
6. Explanation

These six basic parts are explained below.

1. Date is recorded in the Date column.
2. Debit account title/s are recorded in the Explanation column right next to the left margin.

FIGURE 2-7

A transaction for the Century Service Company on August 1: The owner, Gail Goer, invested $10,000 in cash by depositing the money in a local bank in the name of the business. The entry would look like this:

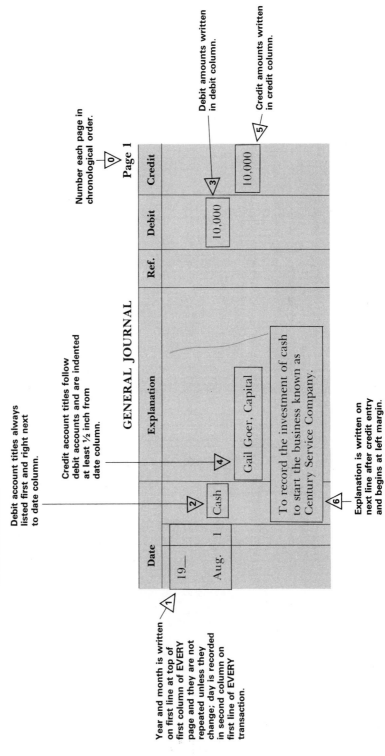

GENERAL JOURNAL Page 1

Date	Explanation	Ref.	Debit	Credit
19— Aug. 1	Cash		10,000	
	Gail Goer, Capital			10,000
	To record the investment of cash to start the business known as Century Service Company.			

Number each page in chronological order. ⓪

Debit amounts written in debit column. ③

Credit amounts written in credit column. ⑤

Debit account titles always listed first and right next to date column. ②

Credit account titles follow debit accounts and are indented at least ½ inch from date column. ④

Explanation is written on next line after credit entry and begins at left margin. ⑥

Year and month is written on first line at top of first column of EVERY page and they are not repeated unless they change; day is recorded in second column on first line of EVERY transaction. ①

37

3. Debit amount/s are recorded on the same line as the debit account title/s in the Debit Amount column.

4. Credit account title/s are recorded in the Explanation column at least one-half inch from the left margin.

5. Credit amount/s are recorded on the same line as credit account title/s in the Credit Amount column.

6. A brief but complete explanation is written on the next line after the credit entry beginning at the left margin.

To illustrate the correct format for recording transactions in the general journal, the first business transaction for the Century Service Company is shown in Figure 2-7. This illustration shows the format recognized by the entire accounting profession. All journal entries should be accurate and the explanation should be clear. Remember that you and others will have to read and understand them at some later date.

Figure 2-7 illustrates the correct form which is recognized by the entire accounting profession. *Remember* to journalize your entries clearly and accurately because you and others will have to read and understand them at some later date.

ANALYZING AND JOURNALIZING TRANSACTIONS

A narrative or description of the type of thinking or analysis that is necessary to journalize each transaction properly is listed in the three steps below. The procedure is basically the same in all cases.

Step 1. Analyze the transaction and decide what types of accounts are involved.

Step 2. Classify these accounts into one of the five basic classifications of accounts (assets, liabilities, owner's equity, revenue, or expense).

Step 3. Determine if these accounts will be increased or decreased with a debit or a credit.

Remember! Check to make sure that the sum of the debits equal the sum of the credits for each entry.

To illustrate, we will use nine transactions of the Century Service Company for the month of August, the first month of business. The analysis and journal entry for each transaction is shown below.

TRANSACTION ① On August 1, Gail Goer organized the Century Service Company as a single proprietorship-type business. She began by investing $10,000 of her own money and depositing it in a bank account for the company.

Analysis

1. Cash and Gail Goer, Capital accounts are involved in this transaction.
2. Cash is an asset account and Gail Goer, Capital is an owner's equity account.
3. Cash is an asset which is increased with a debit, and Gail Goer, Capital is an owner's equity account which is increased with a credit.

The company's Cash and Capital accounts increased because the owner, Gail Goer, is making an investment of capital (cash) in the business. The debit and credit amounts are equal, because the $10,000 debit to Cash equals the $10,000 credit to Gail Goer, Capital.

Journal entry 1

Aug. 1	Cash	10,000	
	Gail Goer, Capital		10,000
	Gail Goer invested cash to start		
	Century Service Company.		

②   On August 2, Goer located a suitable office and workroom space for the business. She agreed to a month-to-month lease and paid $450 for first month's rent.

Analysis

1. This transaction deals with the Rent Expense and Cash accounts.
2. Rent Expense is an expense account and Cash is an asset account.
3. Rent Expense is an expense account which is increased with a debit, and Cash is an asset account which is decreased with a credit.

Whenever you see the word "paid" in a transaction, immediately translate it into the word "cash." The Cash account was decreased, because Goer paid for 1 month's rent, creating an expense for the company. The expense account increased because $450 was added (debited) to the Rent Expense account. The debits and credits are equal, because $450 was debited to Rent Expense and $450 was credited to Cash.

Journal entry 2

Aug. 2	Rent Expense	450	
	Cash		450
	Paid rent for August.		

③   On August 4, Goer purchased used office furniture for $2,500. She paid $1,800 down and agreed to pay the balance in 90 days.

Analysis

1. In this transaction, there are three accounts involved: Office Furniture, Cash, and Accounts Payable.
2. Office Furniture and Cash are asset accounts, and the Accounts Payable account is a liability.
3. The asset account, Office Furniture, has increased; therefore, the account was debited. The asset account, Cash, is credited because the account was decreased. Accounts Payable is a liability account that was increased, and liabilities are increased with a credit.

The Office Furniture and Accounts Payable accounts increased because $2,500 was added to the furniture account and $700 was added to the payable account. A portion of the purchase was paid in cash causing the Cash account to decrease $1,800. The debits and credits are equal, because $2,500 was debited to Office Furniture, $1,800 was credited to Cash, and $700 was credited to Accounts Payable.

Journal entry 3

Aug. 4	Office Furniture	2,500	
	Cash		1,800
	Accounts Payable		700
	Purchased used furniture with cash of $1,800 agreeing to pay the $700 balance in 90 days.		

④ On August 7, Goer hired an assistant to be the receptionist, typist, and bookkeeper for $150 per week.

Analysis

1. No journal entry is necessary for this transaction because this is a nonfinancial transaction and no changes were made to any account.

⑤ On August 15, $200 of miscellaneous small tools and $75 of supplies were purchased from the local hardware store on account.

Analysis

1. This transaction deals with Tools, Supplies, and Accounts Payable.
2. Tools and Supplies are asset accounts and Accounts Payable is a liability account.
3. Tool and Supplies are asset accounts and assets are increased with a debit. Accounts Payable is a liability and liability accounts are increased with a credit.

Tools is an asset which was increased by $200. Supplies is an asset because they represent something of value owned by the company; they do not become an expense until they are used. These two purchases have not been paid; therefore, a liability was incurred increasing the liability account, Accounts Payable, for $275.

Journal entry 4

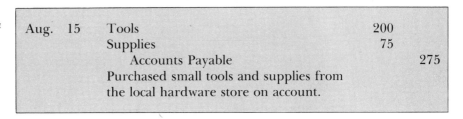

Aug.	15	Tools	200	
		Supplies	75	
		Accounts Payable		275
		Purchased small tools and supplies from the local hardware store on account.		

⑥ On August 28, Goer paid $50 for the August phone bill received today.

Analysis

1. The transaction deals with the Telephone Expense and Cash accounts.
2. The use of the telephone created an expense for the company and the expense was paid with cash which is an asset.
3. The expense account, Telephone Expense, was increased and expenses are increased with a debit. Cash is an asset which decreased, and assets are decreased with a credit.

Journal entry 5

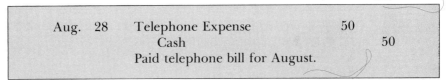

Aug.	28	Telephone Expense	50	
		Cash		50
		Paid telephone bill for August.		

⑦ On August 31, cash of $2,000 was received from customers for services performed today.

Analysis

1. The transaction deals with the Cash and Service Fees accounts.
2. Cash is an asset account and Service Fees is a revenue account.
3. Cash is an asset account and assets are increased with a debit. Service Fees is a revenue account and revenues are increased with a credit.

Whenever you see the word "received cash" in a transaction, it indicates that the Cash account was increased. If you received cash for performing services, it indicates that revenue was earned by the business. In this transaction, the asset and revenue accounts increased by $2,000. The debits and credits are equal, because $2,000 was debited to Cash and $2,000 was credited to Service Fees.

Journal entry 6

Aug. 31	Cash	2,000	
	Service Fees		2,000
	Received cash for services performed in August.		

⑧   On August 31, 2 weeks wages amounting to $300 were paid to the assistant.

Analysis

1. The Wages Expense and Cash accounts are involved in this transaction.
2. The payment of wages created an expense for the company and the expense was paid with cash which is an asset.
3. Wages Expense was increased, and expenses are increased with a debit. Cash was decreased for the payment and assets are decreased with a credit.

Journal entry 7

Aug. 31	Wages Expense	300	
	Cash		300
	Paid 2 weeks wages to the assistant.		

⑨   On August 31, statements totaling $800 were mailed to customers for services performed in August.

Analysis

1. This transaction deals with the Accounts Receivable and Service Fees accounts.
2. Statements mailed to customers for amounts owed to the company increased the asset account, Accounts Receivable. The revenue account, Service Fees, was increased for the services performed during the month.
3. Accounts Receivable is an asset that was increased, and assets are increased with a debit. Service Fees is a revenue account, and revenues are increased with a credit.

Whenever the words "sent bills" occur in a transaction, it indicates that revenue was earned but payment has not been received. The debits and credits are equal, because the asset account, Accounts Receivable, was debited and the revenue account, Service Fees, was credited for the increase amounting to $800.

Journal entry 8

Aug.	31	Accounts Receivable	800	
		Service Fees		800
		Billed charge account customers for services performed in August.		

The general journal for Century Service Company after all the entries have been journalized and posted (see Part II) for the month of August is illustrated in Figure 2-8.

FIGURE 2-8

GENERAL JOURNAL   **Page 1**

Date		Explanation	Ref.	Debit	Credit
19__					
Aug.	1	Cash	100*	10,000	
		Gail Goer, Capital			10,000
		Gail Goer invested cash to start Century Service Company.			
	2	Rent Expense	620	450	
		Cash	100		450
		Paid rent for August.			
	4	Office Furniture	130	2,500	
		Cash	100		1,800
		Accounts Payable	200		700
		Purchased used furniture with cash of $1,800 agreeing to pay the $700 balance in 90 days.			
	7	No entry required.			
	15	Small Tools	120	200	
		Supplies	112	75	
		Accounts Payable	200		275
		Purchased small tools and supplies from the local hardware store on account.			
	28	Telephone Expense	640	50	
		Cash	100		50
		Paid phone bill for August.			
	31	Cash	100	2,000	
		Service Fees	400		2,000
		Received cash for services performed in August.			
	31	Wages Expense	600	300	
		Cash	100		300
		Paid 2 weeks wages to the assistant.			
	31	Accounts Receivable	110	800	
		Service Fees	400		800
		Billed charge account customers for services performed in August.			

* The account numbers shown in the Reference column are explained in Part II of this chapter.

Part II:

Posting Transactions in General Ledger

The ledger is an individual or separate record of increases or decreases for specific items in the accounting system, such as cash, accounts receivable, and accounts payable.

GENERAL LEDGER

The *general ledger* or "book of final entry" is the name given to the entire group of individual accounts. Thus, if there were 100 individual accounts in the system, you would refer to an individual account as a *ledger account* and to all (total) of the 100 accounts as the general ledger.

POSTING

The next step in the accounting cycle is *posting* or transferring (copying) the information from the journal to the individual ledger accounts.

Figure 2-9 shows the posting of the August 1 entry for the Century Service Company. Posting is usually done on a daily basis to keep the ledger up to date. This is a very important operation, and it demands complete accuracy if good accounting records are to be maintained and accurate financial information is to be presented to management.

Posting procedure (A) Start with the debit account(s) *first.* Locate the Cash ledger account, and record the amount(s) in the debit column or debit side with the proper date. Dollar signs are *not used* in journals or ledgers.

(B-1) The symbol for the journal and its page number (J1) is recorded in the reference (Ref.) column of the ledger. This recording provides the user with a complete cross-reference between the two records.

(B-2) The ledger account number 100 for the debit entry is entered in the reference (Ref.) column of the journal.

(C) The credit entry information is then recorded in the credit column of the Gail Goer, Capital account in the same manner as the debit accounts, including the cross-references.

FIGURE 2-9

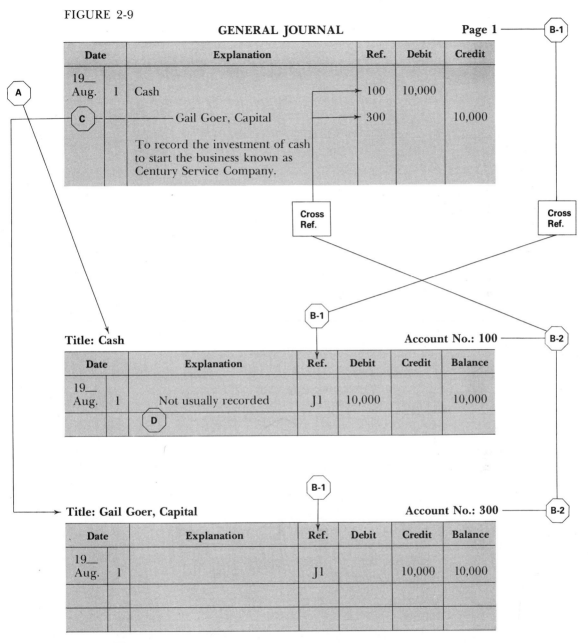

GENERAL JOURNAL

Page 1

Date			Explanation	Ref.	Debit	Credit
19__ Aug.	1		Cash	100	10,000	
			Gail Goer, Capital	300		10,000
			To record the investment of cash to start the business known as Century Service Company.			

Cross Ref.

Cross Ref.

B-1

B-2

Title: Cash

Account No.: 100

Date			Explanation	Ref.	Debit	Credit	Balance
19__ Aug.	1		Not usually recorded	J1	10,000		10,000

B-1

Title: Gail Goer, Capital

Account No.: 300

Date			Explanation	Ref.	Debit	Credit	Balance
19__ Aug.	1			J1		10,000	10,000

D Note that explanations are *not* usually transferred to the ledger accounts. Special notations may be entered.

Figure 2-9 illustrates a general journal page for the Century Service Company which is completely posted to the ledger accounts shown in Figure 2-10.

FIGURE 2-10

GENERAL LEDGER

Title: Cash   Account No.: 100

Date		Explanation	Ref.	Debit	Credit	Balance
19__ Aug.	1		J1	10,000		10,000
	2		J1		450	9,550
	4		J1		1,800	7,750
	28		J1		50	7,700
	31		J1	2,000		9,700
	31		J1		300	9,400

Title: Accounts Receivable   Account No.: 110

Date		Explanation	Ref.	Debit	Credit	Balance
19__ Aug.	31		J1	800		800

Title: Supplies   Account No.: 112

Date		Explanation	Ref.	Debit	Credit	Balance
19__ Aug.	15		J1	75		75

Title: Small Tools   Account No.: 120

Date		Explanation	Ref.	Debit	Credit	Balance
19__ Aug.	15		J1	200		200

FIGURE 2-10 (*Continued*)

Title: Office Furniture   **Account No.: 130**

Date		Explanation	Ref.	Debit	Credit	Balance
19__ Aug.	4		J1	2,500		2,500

Title: Accounts Payable   **Account No.: 200**

Date		Explanation	Ref.	Debit	Credit	Balance
19__ Aug.	4		J1		700	700
	15		J1		275	975

Title: Gail Goer, Capital   **Account No.: 300**

Date		Explanation	Ref.	Debit	Credit	Balance
19__ Aug.	1		J1		10,000	10,000

Title: Service Fees   **Account No.: 400**

Date		Explanation	Ref.	Debit	Credit	Balance
19__ Aug.	31		J1		2,000	2,000
	31		J1		800	2,800

Title: Wages Expense   **Account No.: 600**

Date		Explanation	Ref.	Debit	Credit	Balance
19__ Aug.	31		J1	300		300

FIGURE 2-10 (*Continued*)

Title: Rent Expense   Account No.: **620**

Date		Explanation	Ref.	Debit	Credit	Balance
19__ Aug.	2		J1	450		450

Title: Telephone Expense   Account No.: **640**

Date		Explanation	Ref.	Debit	Credit	Balance
19__ Aug.	28		J1	50		50

TRIAL BALANCE

After all the transactions have been posted for the accounting period, a *trial balance* is usually prepared. A trial balance is simply a check of the general ledger to determine if the debit balances and credit balances are equal. The preparation of the trial balance consists of:

1. Preparing the proper heading.
2. Listing the account titles from the ledger in the proper order (assets, liabilities, owner's capital, revenue, and expenses).
3. Recording the debit or credit balances in the debit or credit column of the trial balance for each account with a balance that is found in the general ledger. Omit accounts with a zero balance.
4. Totaling both debit and credit columns. The two columns should be equal.

The August 31, 19__, trial balance for the Century Service Company is shown in Figure 2-11. Notice that the debit and credit columns are equal. However, *this does not mean that the accounting is correct.* Why? Because although the journal entries may be journalized correctly, the posting could have been done incorrectly. The amount may have been placed in the wrong account, the account could have been debited instead of credited, or there could be compensating or offsetting errors. But, if the trial balance is in balance, you may for all practical purposes consider that it is correct and move on to the next step. Other methods for determining the accuracy of the ledger will be discussed in later chapters.

FIGURE 2-11

CENTURY SERVICE COMPANY
TRIAL BALANCE
August 31, 19__

Account Title	Debit	Credit
Cash	$ 9,400	
Accounts Receivable	800	
Supplies	75	
Small Tools	200	
Office Furniture	2,500	
Accounts Payable		$ 975
Gail Goer, Capital		10,000
Service Fees		2,800
Wages Expense	300	
Rent Expense	450	
Telephone Expense	50	
Totals	$13,775	$13,775

If the trial balance does not balance, the following steps will help in finding the error:

1. Re-add the individual figures on the trial balance.
2. Obtain the difference between the debit and credit column totals. (A single error may be causing the columns not to balance.) A lot of time can be saved by using these tests after step 2.
   (a) Errors in the amount of $0.01 to $0.10 or of even tens are usually due to incorrect addition or subtraction.
   (b) If the difference is divisible by 2, the error could be a debit entered as a credit, or vice versa.
   (c) If the difference is divisible by 9, it may be due to a transposition error ($34.25 posted as $43.25) or a misplaced decimal point ($6.50 posted as $65.00).
3. Look carefully to see if any figures were placed in the wrong column.
4. Double-check to see if you have picked up the right numbers from the ledger and placed them in the right debit or credit columns.
5. Recheck the addition after you make any changes.

THE FIRST THREE STEPS IN THE ACCOUNTING CYCLE

The sequence of accounting functions used in actual practice is referred to as the *accounting cycle.* The first three steps were illustrated with the nine transactions of the Century Service Company and are as follows:

1. Analyzing and journalizing the transactions
2. Posting the transactions (journal to ledger)
3. Preparing the trial balance

DEBIT-CREDIT RULES TO REMEMBER

The debit-credit rules for increasing and decreasing the five basic classifications of accounts are summarized below in the balance sheet equation and net income formula.

Normal balance and increase and decrease side for five basic account classifications

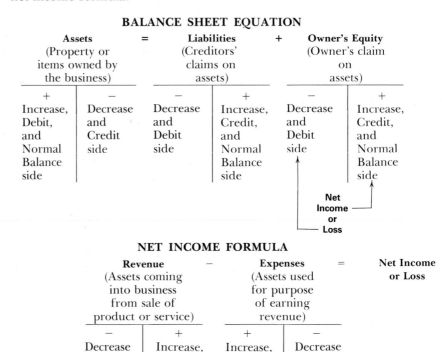

BALANCE SHEET EQUATION

Assets = (Property or items owned by the business)		Liabilities + (Creditors' claims on assets)		Owner's Equity (Owner's claim on assets)	
+	−	−	+	−	+
Increase, Debit, and Normal Balance side	Decrease and Credit side	Decrease and Debit side	Increase, Credit, and Normal Balance side	Decrease and Debit side	Increase, Credit, and Normal Balance side

Net Income or Loss

NET INCOME FORMULA

Revenue − (Assets coming into business from sale of product or service)		Expenses = (Assets used for purpose of earning revenue)		Net Income or Loss
−	+	+	−	
Decrease and Debit side	Increase, Credit, and Normal Balance side	Increase, Debit, and Normal Balance side	Decrease and Credit side	

DRAWING ACCOUNT

Whenever the owner of a single proprietorship withdraws cash or other assets from the business for personal use, the amount is debited to the owner's drawing account. The owner's drawing is a separate account established for the purpose of recording all withdrawals made by the owner as illustrated in the following T account.

Normal balance and increase and decrease side of owner's drawing account

Owner's Name, Drawing	
+	−
Debit, Increase, and Normal Balance side	Credit and Decrease side

The owner's drawing account includes the name of the owner and it is classified as a *contra*[1] owner's equity account. Therefore, the drawing account should always have a debit or zero balance.

Any withdrawals of cash or assets by the owner for personal use are not an expense of the business because they are not paid to generate revenue. These withdrawals by the owner for personal use are shown on the balance sheet as a deduction from owner's capital.

For example, assume that on August 30 Gail Goer withdrew $1,000 from the business for personal use. The entry to record the withdrawal on August 30 is:

Owner withdrew cash for personal use

19__				
Aug.	30	Gail Goer, Drawing	1,000	
		Cash		1,000
		Cash withdrawn for personal use.		

The owner's equity section of the balance sheet for Century Service Company on August 31 is illustrated below:

CENTURY SERVICE COMPANY
PARTIAL BALANCE SHEET
August 31, 19__

Partial balance sheet showing changes in owner's equity

Owner's Equity			
Gail Goer, Capital, Aug. 1, 19__	$10,000		
Add: Net Income	2,000	$12,000	
Less: Withdrawals		1,000	
Gail Goer, Capital, Aug. 31, 19__			$11,000

SUMMARY

This chapter showed how accounts are increased and decreased by employing the terms debit and credit. Each account has a debit or left side and a credit or right side. The difference between the two sides is the account balance. An individual account is called a ledger account, and the book containing all the accounts is called the general ledger or book of final entry.

Since it would be very difficult to reconstruct transactions from the ledger, each transaction is recorded, in the order in which it occurs, in a *general journal* or *book of original entry*. After being recorded in the journal, each debit and credit is then copied or posted to the proper account in the ledger. After all the monthly, quarterly, or yearly entries for the financial

[1] An account directly related to another account, it has the opposite type of balance of its related account.

period are journalized in the journal and posted to the ledger accounts, the account balances are listed on a trial balance. The trial balance is a check on whether the debit and credit balances of the general ledger are equal.

Whenever the owner of a single proprietorship withdraws assets from the business for personal use, the amount is debited to a separate owner's drawing account. The drawing account is not an expense of the business because it was not paid to generate revenue.

GLOSSARY

Account Balance: The difference between the total debit and credit amounts. If the total debits exceed the credits, the account has a debit balance; if the total credits exceed the debits, the account has a credit balance.

Accounting Cycle: Sequence of accounting functions or steps used in recording business transactions and repeated each accounting period.

Accounting Manual: A detailed description of what should be recorded in each account along with the account title and ledger account number.

Chart of Accounts: Index to the accounting system showing account titles and ledger account numbers.

Contra Account: An account directly related to another account, it has the opposite type of balance of its related account.

Credit: Right side of an account.

Debit: Left side of an account.

Footing: The temporary total of the debit and credit side of a T account that is recorded in pencil.

General Journal: The first place that a transaction is recorded. The transactions are recorded in the order in which they occur. Also referred to as a book of original entry.

General Ledger: The entire group of individual accounts; also known as the book of final entry.

Journal Entry: A business transaction or event recorded in a journal (book of original entry).

Journalizing: The process of recording transactions in the journal (book of original entry).

Ledger Account: An individual or separate record used to record the increases and decreases for a specific item in the accounting system, such as Cash, Accounts Receivable, Accounts Payable, etc.

Liability: The debts owed to creditors who have first claim on the assets.

Net Income: The difference between total revenues and total expenses for a particular period of time.

Normal Balance: The usual balance of an account. Assets, expenses, and owner's drawing accounts normally have debit balances, and liability, revenue, and owner's capital accounts normally have credit balances.

Posting: The process of transferring information from the journal to the general ledger.

Trial Balance: A check on the accuracy of the ledger to determine if the debit and credit balances are equal.

QUESTIONS

1. What is a T account?
2. List the six basic parts of an account form used in business.
3. List the classes of accounts that are increased by debits and by credits.
4. Give the normal balance for the five basic classifications of accounts.
5. Define and explain the function of the (*a*) general journal and (*b*) general ledger.
6. Explain the process of recording information in the general ledger.
7. What is meant by the account balance?
8. What is a trial balance, and what does it prove?
9. What are the three steps in the accounting cycle presented in this chapter?

EXERCISES

Debit and Credit Rules

1. For the following list of account titles, provide the necessary information under each column heading. Use the following abbreviations: A, Asset; L, Liability; OE, Owner's Equity; R, Revenue; E, Expense; Dr, Debit; Cr, Credit.

Account Title	Account Classification	Increase Dr or Cr	Decrease Dr or Cr	Normal Balance Dr or Cr
(*a*) Cash				
(*b*) Accounts Payable				
(*c*) Owner's Capital				
(*d*) Service Revenue				
(*e*) Rent Expense				

2. Prepare a form using the same column headings as in Exercise 1, and complete the data for the following account titles.
   - (*a*) Office Supplies
   - (*b*) Building
   - (*c*) Accounts Receivable
   - (*d*) Wages Expense
   - (*e*) Owner's Capital
   - (*f*) Accounts Payable
   - (*g*) Service Fees
   - (*h*) Land

3. Use the same column headings as in Exercises 1 and 2 and complete the data for the following account titles.

(a) Maintenance Supplies (f) Cash
(b) Furniture (g) Accounts Payable
(c) Owner's Capital (h) Fees Earned
(d) Accounts Receivable (i) Owner's Drawing
(e) Machinery (j) Salary Expense

Journalizing Business Transactions

4. Write general journal entries for the following business transactions of the Taylor Company. Use the account titles listed in Exercise 6.

19—

July 1 Ron Taylor started his business by depositing $25,000 cash in a bank account in the name of the company.

   2 Purchased a small building for $5,000 and land for $500. Paid $5,000 cash and signed a 90-day note payable for the $500 balance.

   4 Purchased $2,000 worth of equipment for cash.

   5 Purchased $300 of supplies on account.

   10 Cash of $35 received for services performed. (Use Service Revenue for the account title.)

   15 Paid $60 for newspaper advertising. (Use Advertising Expense for account title.)

   18 Ordered a $75 heavy-duty vise for the shop.

   20 Completed a $250 repair job for the Lock Company on account.

5. Journalize the following transactions in good general journal form. (Use the account titles listed in Exercise 7.)

19—

Apr. 2 Lois Gordon started the Gordon Lawn Service Company and deposited $5,000 of her personal money in an account with the local bank in the name of the business.

   3 Purchased a used truck for $1,750 cash.

   4 Paid $80 for a newspaper ad appearing in the local paper today.

   7 Received $90 cash for lawn service work completed today.

   9 Completed yard service work for a nursing home. The home charged the $150 on account.

   10 Paid $75 to a part-time helper for 3 days work.

   15 Received road service bills amounting to $15 for changing flat tire on pickup truck. (Use Truck Expense for account title.)

   28 Lois Gordon, owner, withdrew $100 cash for personal use.

Posting from Journal to Ledger and Preparing Trial Balance

6. Using the transactions in Exercise 4, set up T accounts for Cash; Accounts Receivable; Supplies; Equipment; Land; Building; Accounts Payable; Notes Payable; Ron Taylor, Capital; Service Revenue; and Advertising Expense. Post the journal entries and prepare a trial balance as of July 31.

7. Using the transactions in Exercise 5, set up T accounts for Cash; Accounts Receivable; Truck; Accounts Payable; Lois Gordon, Capital; Lois Gordon, Drawing; Service Revenue; Wages Expense; Truck Expense; and Advertising Expense. Post the journal entries and prepare a trial balance as of April 30.

Preparing Corrected Trial Balance

8. The following trial balance, with the correct amount for the account balances, has several errors. Prepare a corrected trial balance. Be sure to list the asset accounts first followed by the liability, owner's capital, revenue, and expense accounts.

HOT AIR COMPANY
TRIAL BALANCE
December 31, 19___

Account Title	Debit	Credit
Cash	$ 5,000 *3000*	
Hans Arnold, Capital		$20,000
Accounts Payable	6,000	
Land		2,000
Building		16,000
Accounts Receivable		9,000
Supplies	500	
Telephone Expense	500	
Notes Payable		5,000
Wages Expense	6,000	
Service Revenue		8,000
Totals	$18,000	$60,000

ARNOLD DRAWING   2000

PROBLEMS

Journalizing Business Transactions

2-1. The chart of accounts for the Lorraine Auto Wash, a single proprietorship, is listed on the next page.

Account Number	Account Title	Account Number	Account Title
110	Cash	128	Office Equipment
112	Accounts Receivable	210	Accounts Payable
115	Washing Supplies	300	Lorraine Long, Capital
120	Land	400	Car Wash Revenue
122	Building	501	Wages Expense
124	Signs	502	Advertising Expense
126	Truck	503	Telephone Expense

During the first month of operations, the following transactions took place:

19—

Mar. 1 Long Deposited $50,000 cash in a bank account under the name of the business, Lorraine Auto Wash.

2 Purchased the Sudzy Car Wash building for $18,000 and land for $2,000 giving $15,000 in cash and agreeing to pay the $5,000 balance in 6 months.

4 Purchased a used pickup truck for $1,200 cash.

5 Placed an order for chemicals for the washer and 50 pounds of toweling for drying the cars.

7 Purchased a used typewriter and adding machine for $300 cash.

10 Received the shipment and statement for $175 for chemicals and toweling ordered on March 5 on account.

11 Placed an ad in the local paper for $180 on account.

15 Paid $500 for new signs on the building.

17 Cash of $1,700 was received for washing cars on the opening day.

19 Paid $450 for wages to employees.

25 Car wash revenue amounting to $135 was charged by the local police department.

27 Paid $65 telephone bill for March.

Required

Journalize the transactions for March.

2-2. The following account numbers and titles are for the Merry Hair Salon, a single proprietorship: 100 Cash; 110 Accounts Receivable; 115 Beauty Supplies; 120 Land; 122 Building; 124 Equipment; 126 Signs; 200 Accounts Payable; 210 Notes Payable; 300 Mary Moore, Capital; 318 Mary Moore, Drawing; 400 Hair Styling Revenue; 501 Wages Expense; 502 Electric Expense; and 503 Advertising Expense.

During the first month of operations, the following transactions took place.

19__

Feb. 1 Moore deposited $25,000 cash in a bank account under the name of the business, Merry Hair Salon.

3 Purchased a building for $20,500 and land for $2,500. A cash payment of $12,000 was made and a 5-year note was signed for the balance.

10 Completed redecorating and remodeling the interior of the building and paid the contractor $5,000. (Use Building for the account title.)

12 Charged $3,500 on account for 10 new hair dryers with moisture sensors plus accessory equipment.

13 New exterior signs were installed for $1,500. Paid $500 in cash and signed a 120-day note payable for the balance.

18 Received bills amounting to $200 for newspaper advertising.

19 Purchased $150 of beauty supplies on account.

23 Received $1,000 cash for hair styling services performed during the first week.

24 Paid $400 for beauty operator's wages.

25 Billed customers $1,700 for hair styling services performed in February.

27 Received $350 cash from customers on account.

28 Paid $52 for electric bill.

28 Moore, owner, withdrew $750 cash for personal use.

Required

Journalize the transactions for February.

2-3. The following account numbers and titles are for Pat's Bookkeeping Service organized on May 1 of the current year: 100 Cash; 110 Accounts Receivable; 115 Office Supplies; 116 Prepaid Insurance; 120 Office Equipment; 200 Accounts Payable; 300 Pat Pall, Capital; 318 Pat Pall, Drawing; 400 Bookkeeping Revenue; 501 Wages Expense; 502 Electric Expense; 503 Rent Expense; 504 Maintenance Expense; and 505 Advertising Expense.

During the first month of operations, the following transactions took place.

19__

May 1 Pat Pall started a business by depositing $10,000 cash in a bank account under the name of the company, Pat's Bookkeeping Service.

3 Rented office space for $450 a month and paid the rent for May.

5 Purchased a used desk, typewriter, adding machine, and several chairs for $1,500. Paid $500 in cash and charged the $1,000 balance on account.

7   Paid $750 for minor repairs and painting of the rented office space.

8   Purchased office supplies for $275 on account.

15   Paid $300 for one week's wages to the bookkeeper.

17   Mailed statements amounting to $1,800 to clients for bookkeeping services performed.

18   Received cash amounting to $2,300 for bookkeeping services performed in May.

23   Paid $100 for newspaper advertising.

25   Purchased a 2-year liability insurance policy for $240 on account. Payment due on June 15. (Charge amount to Prepaid Insurance.)

27   Paid wages amounting to $300.

28   Paid $275 to creditors on account.

28   Paid $50 electric bill for May.

29   Pall, owner, withdrew $950 cash for personal use.

30   Received $675 cash from clients for payment on account.

Required

Journalize the transactions for May.

Posting from Journal to Ledger and Preparing Trial Balance

2-4.   Prepare a general ledger for the accounts listed in Problem 2-1, and
(a) Post information from the general journal to the general ledger.
(b) Prepare a trial balance as of March 31.

2-5.   Prepare a general ledger for the accounts listed in Problem 2-2, and
(a) Post information from the general journal to the general ledger.
(b) Prepare a trial balance as of February 28.

2-6.   Prepare a general ledger for the accounts listed in Problem 2-3, and
(a) Post information from the general journal to the general ledger.
(b) Prepare a trial balance as of May 31.

Journalizing, Posting, and Preparing Trial Balance

2-7.   Sam Short started a real estate business called Short Sales Realty. The first month's transactions are listed below.

19__

Sept.   1   Sam Short started the Short Sales Realty Company by contributing $10,000 cash and office furnishings valued at $2,500.

2   Bought office supplies for $150 on account.

5   Collected a $1,000 cash commission on the sale of a house.

8   Paid $60 for newspaper ad that appeared in the local paper today.

12 Paid printing costs of $175 for personalized stationery and pens. (Charge amount to the Office Supplies account.)

15 Paid $120 for the office secretary's salary.

17 Paid for the supplies purchased on September 2.

22 Earned a $3,000 commission, and the customer paid $2,000 cash and charged the $1,000 balance on account.

23 Sent bills amounting to $300 to clients for property appraisals.

25 Paid $60 for electric bill.

26 Sam Short, owner, withdrew $1,000 cash for personal use.

29 Paid $120 for September telephone bill.

30 Paid $400 for rental of office building for September.

Required

(a) Prepare a ledger for the following accounts: 100 Cash; 110 Accounts Receivable; 115 Office Supplies; 123 Office Furniture; 200 Accounts Payable; 300 Sam Short, Capital; 318 Sam Short, Drawing; 400 Commissions Earned; 410 Appraisal Fees Earned; 501 Salary Expense; 502 Advertising Expense; 503 Electric Expense; 504 Telephone Expense; and 505 Rent Expense.

(b) Journalize the transactions for September.

(c) Post the journal transactions to the ledger.

(d) Prepare a trial balance as of September 30.

2-8. Sally True, Attorney, started her law practice and opened an office in July of the current year. The following transactions occurred in July.

19__

July 1 True started her law practice by opening a bank account under the name of her firm, Sally True, Attorney, and depositing $2,500 cash.

5 Found a suitable suite of offices and paid $400 cash for the first month's rent.

6 Transferred her entire law library, valued at $1,000, to the business.

12 Purchased used office furniture and equipment for $2,500. Paid $500 cash and Sally signed a note agreeing to pay the balance in 6 months. (Use Notes Payable for the account title.)

15 Performed legal services for $5,500. The clients paid $3,500 in cash and promised to pay the $2,000 balance in 30 days.

19 Purchased office supplies amounting to $200 on account.

21 Paid $500 for legal secretary's semimonthly salary.

23 Sent bills amounting to $2,500 to four clients for services rendered during the month.

25 Sally True, owner, withdrew $1,500 cash for personal use.

27 Paid $175 for the July telephone bill.

28 Received $1,200 from clients to apply on account.
30 Paid $35 for July electric bill.

Required

(a) Open the following accounts: 100 Cash; 110 Accounts Receivable; 115 Office Supplies; 120 Law Library; 122 Furniture & Equipment; 200 Accounts Payable; 210 Notes Payable; 300 Sally True, Capital; 318 Sally True, Drawing; 400 Legal Fees Earned; 501 Salary Expense; 502 Rent Expense; 504 Telephone Expense; and 505 Electric Expense.
(b) Journalize the transactions for July.
(c) Post to the ledger accounts.
(d) Prepare a trial balance as of July 31.

2-9. Last month Mark Mann started the High Fence Installation Company and incurred the following business transactions.

19__
June 2 Mark Mann invested $10,000 in cash; a new pickup truck, $5,300; and equipment valued at $1,000 to start the High Fence Installation Company.
3 Rented a building with an office, workshop, and storage yard for $450 a month. Paid $1,350 for the first 3 months rent in advance. (Use Prepaid Rent for the account title.)
6 Paid a 3-year premium of $600 for liability insurance on the truck. (Use Prepaid Insurance for the account title.)
7 Completed job of installing an 8-foot fence for $1,500 cash.
9 Paid $800 for wages of two helpers.
14 Sent bills amounting to $2,800 for four jobs completed today.
15 Paid $45 for electric bill.
17 Paid $150 for newspaper ads.
20 Purchased a new posthole digger for $300 on account. (Debit Equipment.)
23 Purchased $1,200 of supplies on account.
24 Charged $125 for gas and minor repairs at corner service station.
24 Received $1,400 cash from customers on account.
27 Completed two jobs for $750 cash.
28 Paid $125 for telephone bill.
29 Paid for supplies purchased on June 23.
30 Mark Mann withdrew $850 cash for personal use.

Required

(a) Open the following accounts: 100 Cash; 110 Accounts Receivable; 115 Supplies; 116 Prepaid Rent; 117 Prepaid Insurance; 120 Trucks; 122

Equipment; 200 Accounts Payable; 300 Mark Mann, Capital; 318 Mark Mann, Drawing; 400 Installation Revenue; 501 Wages Expense; 502 Advertising Expense; 503 Truck Expense; 504 Electric Expense; and 505 Telephone Expense.

(b) Journalize the transactions for June.

(c) Post to the ledger accounts.

(d) Prepare a trial balance as of June 30.

Preparing a Trial Balance

2-10. The Sun Service Company, owned and operated by James Bryan, services and repairs swimming pools. The ledger accounts as of June 30 of the current year appear below. The accounts are not in the proper order.

Required

Determine the balance in each account, and prepare a trial balance with the accounts listed in proper order as of June 30.

Cash		Rent Expense	Trucks	Pool Supplies
10,000	3,500	450	3,500	1,000
3,000	450			
5,000	1,500			
	500			
	250			

Accounts Payable		Service Revenue	Accounts Receivable	James Bryan, Capital
	1,000	2,000	2,000	10,000
	130	5,000		
		3,000		

Truck Expense	Insurance Expense	Office Equipment	Miscellaneous Expense
130	500	1,500	250

2-11. Charles Gage started Charlie's Garage, Inc., at the beginning of August of the current year. Gage hired an inexperienced bookkeeper who prepared the following trial balance at the end of the first month of business operations.

CHARLIE'S GARAGE, INC.
TRIAL BALANCE
August 31, 19___

Account Title	Debit	Credit
Advertising Expense		$ 650
Accounts Payable	$ 8,500	
Accounts Receivable		3,000
Cash	10,000	
Prepaid Insurance		4,500
Office Supplies		2,500
Notes Payable	4,000	
Notes Receivable		3,300
Electric Expense		250
C. Gage, Capital	25,000	
Furniture		2,500
Service Revenue	23,500	
Rent Expense	1,500	
Equipment	8,000	
Tow Trucks	22,000	
Wages Expense	2,800	
Totals	$105,300	$16,700

Required

Prepare a corrected trial balance in good form. The amounts are correct, but they may not be in the proper debit or credit column.

After completing this chapter, you should be able to:

1. **State the reason for recording adjusting entries**
2. **Name the four types of accounts that require adjustments at the end of an accounting period**
3. **Journalize the adjusting entries for prepaid, accrued, and depreciation expense**

The first three steps of the accounting cycle were explained in Chapters 1 and 2 as follows:

1. Journalize the daily business transactions or events.
2. Post the entries from the journal to the general ledger.
3. Prepare a trial balance to check the accuracy of your general ledger accounts (debit balances must equal credit balances).

After the daily transactions have been journalized and posted and a trial balance prepared, the next step in the accounting cycle is to make adjustments to bring the account balances up to date. These adjustments are prepared on the last day of the accounting year or fiscal period. Adjustments are necessary because some of the assets and liabilities appearing on the trial balance have increased or decreased and some of the revenues and expenses have accrued (accumulated or increased) but have not been recorded in the accounting records. These accounts must be adjusted so they will have the correct balance before the year-end financial statements are prepared.

Asset and liability accounts needing adjustments are called *mixed accounts* because a portion of their balance affects an income statement and balance sheet account. Adjusting entries match revenues for the period with the expenses incurred in earning the revenue, a process called the *Matching Concept.*

ADJUSTMENTS

All the financial events that are taking place in the business must be recorded in the accounting system so that the journal and general ledger will have a complete record of all the business transactions for the period. If an event or transaction has not been recorded, the balances in the accounts will not show the correct amount at the end of the accounting period. For example, when office supplies are purchased for use in the business, the asset account, Office Supplies, is normally debited as shown in the following journal entry.

Purchase of office supplies
for cash

19_A				
Jan.	10	Office Supplies	100	
		Cash		100
		Purchased office supplies for cash.		

When the transaction is posted into the general ledger account, the Office Supplies account will show a debit balance of $100 as shown.

Office Supplies

19_A		
Jan.	10	100

The $100 balance in the Office Supplies account represents something of value owned by the business. These items are recorded as an asset until they are used. During the accounting period, as the office supplies are being used, the asset account is decreasing. Therefore, an adjusting entry is necessary to show the decrease in the asset account, Office Supplies, and to record the expense of the supplies used during the period. Failure to make an adjustment to record the expense of using the office supplies in the business operations and the decrease in the corresponding asset account will cause the operating expenses to be understated and the net income to be overstated on the income statement, and the asset account, Office Supplies, and Owner's Capital account to be overstated on the balance sheet.

Your accounting system is like a highly developed camera. The camera can take pictures, but it cannot show all the details without having someone make adjustments to bring the picture in focus. A good accounting system, like a good camera, will work properly if someone adjusts and records the events that are taking place in the business.

As the financial business transactions are taking place, certain types of asset, liability, revenue, and expense accounts are increasing and decreasing; and these accounts must be adjusted at the end of each accounting period. When you adjust the revenue and expense accounts, you are matching the related expense to the revenue earned during the period to determine the correct net income, and at the same time, you are adjusting the balance sheet accounts to their correct balance at the end of the period. These entries to adjust and bring the asset, liability, owner's equity, revenue, and expense accounts to their correct balance at the end of the accounting period are known as **adjusting entries.** Each adjusting entry usually affects an income statement and balance sheet account.

ADJUSTING FOR EXPENSES

All adjusting entries for accrued expenses and expenses recorded as an asset when paid require a *debit* to an *expense* account and a *credit* to an *asset or liability* account. Therefore, if you fail to make an adjusting entry to record an expense, the amount for the expense appearing on the income statement will be understated, causing the net income for the period to be overstated.

Three types of adjustments for expenses are:

1. Prepaid expenses recorded as an asset or expense when paid
2. Expenses accrued but not yet recorded or paid
3. Spreading the cost of a plant asset over its useful life through the process of depreciation

Prepaid Expenses

A *prepaid expense* is classified as a short-term or current asset,[1] and it occurs when you purchase items that will benefit one or more future accounting periods. Prepaid expenses are also known as deferred expenses because they represent the postponement or recognition of an expense that has been paid in advance. When the item is purchased before the expense has been incurred or expired, normally the asset account Prepaid Expense is debited because it represents an unexpired cost which will be used in future periods to earn revenue. As time passes, you begin to use this asset and an adjusting entry must be made to show as an expense the portion used for the period and to record the decrease in the asset account as shown in the following illustration.

Debit an Expense account
Credit a Prepaid Asset account

After the adjustment, the Prepaid Expense account will show the unused or unexpired portion; the corresponding expense account will show the correct amount of expense for the period. There are many different types of expenditures that are made by a business which will benefit future accounting periods. Some common examples of prepaid expenses are insurance and office supplies as shown in Examples 1 and 2.

EXAMPLE 1
PREPAID
INSURANCE

Mr. Irving M. Good owns a TV repair shop called the Good TV Service & Repair Shop. He realized that he needed protection against loss of the equipment and purchased a 3-year insurance policy paying the entire premium of $510 on the first day of January 19_A. At the time of payment, he made the following entry:

Entry for prepaid expense recorded as asset when paid

19_A				
Jan.	1	Prepaid insurance	510	
		Cash		510
		Paid 3-year insurance premium covering equipment.		

---

[1] *Current assets* are assets that will be consumed during the normal operating cycle and are explained further in Chapter 5.

The Prepaid Insurance account is an asset until the insurance expires, because it represents something of value owned by the company. If the insurance policy is canceled, the unexpired portion of the payment usually is returned by the insurance company.

On December 31, 19_A, one year has passed (January 1 to December 31) since the policy was purchased. An adjustment would be necessary to record the cost of the expired portion of the Prepaid Insurance account, which amounts to one-third of $510, or $170. The adjusting entry requires a debit to Insurance Expense and a credit to Prepaid Insurance for $170 as illustrated in the following entry:

Prepaid expense adjustment recognizing expired insurance

19_A			
Dec. 31	Insurance Expense	170	
	Prepaid Insurance		170
	Record insurance cost for 1 year.		

This adjusting entry would be recorded at the end of every accounting period to decrease the Prepaid Insurance account for the amount of insurance that has expired and transfer the amount to the Insurance Expense account.

Insurance Expense would be shown as an operating expense[2] on the income statement for $170.

Income statement presentation for expired insurance

Operating Expenses:
    Insurance Expense $170

Prepaid Insurance would be shown on the balance sheet as an asset for $340 ($510 − $170).

Balance sheet presentation for Prepaid Insurance

Assets
Prepaid Insurance $340

The two accounts in the general ledger would appear as follows:

Prepaid Insurance				**Insurance Expense**		
19_A		19_A		19_A		
Jan. 1	510	Dec. 31	170	Dec. 31	170	

The asset, through use, becomes an expense.

**EXAMPLE 2
OFFICE SUPPLIES**

Good needed stationery, carbon paper, paper clips, and other office supplies on hand to use in his business. On March 15, 19_A, he purchased $800 worth

[2] ***Operating expenses*** are all the expenses incurred in earning revenue from selling a service or a product. These expenses are discussed in Chapter 7.

of supplies, enough to last for a year. On March 15 he made the following entry:

19_A			
Mar.	15	Office Supplies	800
		Cash	800
		Purchased stationery, carbon paper, paper clips, and other office supplies.	

The Office Supplies account is an asset which represents a prepaid expense that usually benefits more than one accounting period. The account will be treated the same as the Prepaid Insurance account.

At the end of the year, Good would have to count the office supplies that he still has on hand to determine the amount that was used during the period. His count revealed that he had $200 of office supplies still on hand. Since he started with $800 on March 15, he used $600 of supplies.

$800 on hand Mar. 15
Less: 200 on hand Dec. 31
= $600 used

This $600 represents the Office Supplies Expense for the year, and the adjusting entry will be:

19_A			
Dec.	31	Office Supplies Expense	600
		Office Supplies	600
		Supplies used during the year.	

The Office Supplies Expense account would be shown on the income statement under Operating Expenses for $600.

Operating Expenses:	
Insurance Expense	$170
Office Supplies Expense	600

The Office Supplies account would be shown on the balance sheet as an asset for $200 ($800–$600).

Assets	
Prepaid Insurance	$340
Office Supplies	200

The two accounts in the general ledger would appear as follows:

Office Supplies				Office Supplies Expense	
19_A		19_A		19_A	
Mar. 15	800	Dec. 31	600	Dec. 31	600

The asset, through use, becomes an expense.

Alternate Method for Recording Prepaid Expenses

All prepayments of expenses are normally recorded in an asset account at the time the expenditure is made, and the adjusting process for these prepayments is handled as previously discussed and illustrated. However, occasionally an accountant may use the income statement account to record the expense when paid. When an income statement account is used to record the initial entry, an expense account may have to be adjusted to remove any unused or unexpired portion and transfer the amount to a balance sheet account. To illustrate, we will use the data given in the previous example.

Assume that when the office supplies were purchased by Mr. Good on March 15, 19_A, the following entry was made:

Prepaid expense recorded as expense when paid

19_A				
Mar. 15	Office Supplies Expense		800	
	Cash			800
	To record purchase of stationery, carbon paper, paper clips, and other office supplies.			

When the inventory taken on December 31 revealed $200 of office supplies on hand, the following adjusting entry would be made:

Adjusting entry for prepaid expense recorded as expense when paid

19_A				
Dec. 31	Office Supplies		200	
	Office Supplies Expense			200
	To correct expense account to actual amount of supplies used during period and to record amount of unused office supplies in asset account.			

After the entries were posted in the general ledger accounts, the expense account would show $600 ($800 − $200) as the amount of supplies used or expense for the period, and the asset account would show $200 of supplies on hand.

Accrued Expenses

Many businesses will incur certain expenses for an accounting period before recording the entry or making any payment. Expenses that are accumulating are called *accrued expenses* and an adjusting entry must be made to record them in the accounting records. These expenses have not been recorded in the accounting records because they will not be paid until the next accounting period; therefore, cash is not used when recording accrued expenses.

The adjustment for accrued expenses requires a debit to an expense account and a credit to a related payable (liability) account as shown in the following illustration.

> Debit an Expense account
> Credit a Liability account

Some common examples are Salaries and Wages Payable to employees and Interest Payable for money borrowed on an interest-bearing note that will be paid at some future date as shown in Examples 3 and 4.

EXAMPLE 3
ACCRUED
SALARIES AND
WAGES

Good pays salaries and wages to his two employees every Friday as follows:

> Gloria Beam $50 per day
> Robert Rite $5 per hour

On December 31, 19_A, Good wants the records to show the total amount of salaries and wages expense for 19_A and any amounts owing to the employees.

On Friday, December 26, he paid the salaries and wages for the week beginning on Monday, December 22. Good figured he owed salaries and wages for Monday, Tuesday, and Wednesday, December 29, 30, and 31, as follows:

> Gloria Beam 3 days × $50 a day   = $150
> Robert Rite 22 hours × $5 per hour = 110
> Total amount owed $260

At the end of December, these expenses would not be on the books, because they will not be paid until January 2, 19_B, the end of the next payroll period. The following adjusting entry should be made:

Adjusting entry for accrued salaries and wages

19_A			
Dec. 31	Salaries & Wages Expense	260	
	Salaries & Wages Payable		260
	Salaries and wages owed for Monday, Tuesday, and Wednesday, December 29, 30, and 31.		

After journalizing and posting the adjustment, the general ledger account in T account form will show:

Salaries & Wages Expense		Salaries & Wages Payable
19_A		19_A
Dec. 31 Bal. 18,000		Dec. 31 Adj. 260
31 Adj. 260		

The accrual increases the expense and liability accounts.

 Good will not pay for these expenses until the next payroll period, which will be on Friday, January 2, 19_B. However, these expenses were incurred in 19_A, and they must be recorded in the accounting records to show the correct amount of salaries and wages expense for that period (matching concept).

 The Salaries & Wages Payable for $260 will be shown on the balance sheet in the Liability section.

Balance sheet presentation for Salaries & Wages Payable

Liabilities

Salaries & Wages Payable $260

When the employees are paid on January 2, 19_B, they will receive salaries and wages earned for Monday, Tuesday, Wednesday, and Friday (December 29 to January 2). The shop was closed on Thursday, January 1. Salaries and wages earned for Friday are:

Gloria Beam 1 day × $50 per day = $50
Robert Rite 8 hours × $5 per hour = 40
   Total amount owed $90

 The liability for the salaries and wages for December will be paid along with the salaries and wages earned for January 2. The entry will be

Entry to record payment of salaries and wages and recognize expense for period

19_B			
Jan. 2	Salaries & Wages Payable	260	
	Salaries & Wages Expense	90	
	Cash		350
	Paid salaries and wages for the week of		
	Dec. 29 to Jan. 2.		

After posting the payment, the liability account in the ledger in T account form will appear as follows:

Salaries & Wages Payable	
19_B	19_A
Jan. 2 260	Dec. 31 260

The payment of the accrual decreases the liability.

EXAMPLE 4 ACCRUED INTEREST

Interest charged on a short-term (30-, 60-, or 90-day) loan is the expense or cost of borrowing the money. The liability for interest is accumulating as time passes, but payment of the amount borrowed plus the interest will not be paid until the due date of the loan.

For example, Good borrowed $1,200 from the Citizens Bank on December 1, 19_A, and signed a note agreeing to pay back the amount borrowed on January 30, 19_B, with interest of 12 percent or $24[3] ($1,200 × 0.12 × 60/360) for the 60-day period. Although Good has not paid any interest, an interest expense of $12 ($1,200 × 0.12 × 30/360) has accrued for the 30 days that have passed since he signed the note (December 1 to December 31). An adjusting entry will be necessary to recognize the amount of interest expense for the period and to record the amount of accrued interest that will be paid on January 30, 19_B, the due date of the loan. The adjusting entry will be:

Adjusting entry for 30 days interest accrued on note payable

19_A			
Dec. 31	Interest Expense	12	
	Interest Payable		12
	Interest accrued for 30 days on note due		
	Jan. 30.		

The ledger accounts would appear as follows:

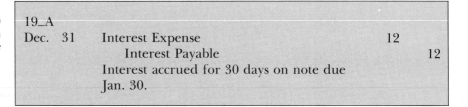

Interest Expense			**Interest Payable**	
19_A			19_A	
Dec. 31	12		Dec. 31	12

The expense and liability increase for the interest accrued.

Interest of $12 will be shown under the Other Expense[4] section of the income statement.

Income statement presentation for accrued interest

Other Expense:
  Interest Expense $12

The Interest Payable will be shown under Liabilities on the balance sheet.

Balance sheet presentation for Interest Payable

Liabilities

Interest Payable $12

---

[3] The computation of interest is discussed in the Chapter 9 appendix.

[4] **Other Expenses** are nonoperating expenses that are not incurred in selling a service or a product. These expenses are listed after the Other Revenue section on the income statement. Other expenses are discussed in Chapter 7.

The liability for the interest accrued in December will be paid on January 30, 19_B, along with the interest expense for the first 30 days in January plus the $1,200 borrowed. The entry will be:

Entry for payment of note plus interest and recognition of interest expense for period	19_B		
	Jan. 30	Interest Payable	12	
		Interest Expense	12	
		Notes Payable	1,200	
		Cash		1,224
		Recorded interest for January, payment of interest accrued in December, and $1,200 borrowed on note dated Dec. 1, 19_A.		

The liability decreases when payment is made as illustrated below:

Interest Payable

19_B		19_A	
Jan. 30	12	Dec. 31	12

Depreciation

The process of writing off or spreading the cost of a plant asset, except land,[5] over its estimated useful life is called depreciating the asset or depreciation. *Plant assets* are long-term or long-lived assets with an estimated useful life of more than 1 year purchased for the purpose of using them in the business operations to generate revenue (explained in Chapter 5). Since the business will receive benefits from these assets each year of its estimated useful life, a portion of the asset's cost should be charged to Depreciation Expense to match the expenses against the revenues for the period (based on the accounting principle called the Matching Concept).

When you spread the cost of a plant asset over its estimated useful life, you debit the *Depreciation Expense* account for the portion which applies to the current period, and you credit an account called *Accumulated Depreciation.* A special account is used for the depreciation that has accumulated instead of crediting the related asset account so the total of the accumulated depreciation and the original cost of the plant asset will be known. The depreciation expense for each year is accumulating in the Accumulated Depreciation account, which is classified as a *Contra Plant Asset*[6] and is shown on the balance sheet as a deduction to the related asset.

Depreciation is an estimate of the benefits obtained from using a plant asset and a process of charging the cost of a plant asset over its estimated

[5] Land is normally not subject to depreciation, because it has an unlimited useful life.
[6] An offset or minus account which is deducted from its related asset on the balance sheet to show the book value of the asset.

useful life, not a process for valuing the asset. Therefore, the difference between the cost of the plant asset and the accumulated depreciation is called the ***book value.*** Book value should not be mistaken for market value, as market value is the amount you would receive if the asset were sold. Some examples of depreciable plant assets are a van and a building purchased for use in the business as shown in Examples 5 and 6.

EXAMPLE 5
VAN

*On January 10, 19_A, Good purchased a van for the repair shop with an estimated useful life of 5 years for $8,000 cash. At the end of 5 years, Good estimates that the van will have a **salvage value**[7] of $800. He made the following entry after the purchase:*

Purchased asset for cash

19_A				
Jan. 10	Van		8,000	
	Cash			8,000
	Purchased a van with a useful life of 5 years and a salvage value of $800.			

  At the end of the first year, Good made an adjusting entry to record $1,440 depreciation expense. He determined the amount of depreciation as follows:

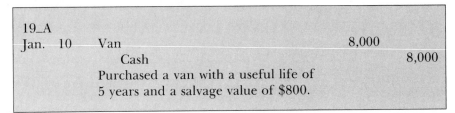

$$\$8,000 - \$800 \text{ salvage} = \$7,200 \text{ total amount to be depreciated}$$
$$\frac{\$7,200}{5\text{-year useful life}} = \$1,440 \text{ depreciation expense each year[8]}$$

The adjusting entry will be:

Adjusting entry recognizing depreciation expense for van

19_A				
Dec. 31	Depreciation Expense/Van		1,440	
	Accumulated Depreciation/Van			1,440
	Record depreciation for first year.			

The two accounts in the general ledger are shown as follows:

---

[7] Estimated value, scrap value, or residual value of an asset at the end of its useful life.
[8] This method is called the straight-line method and is one of four methods discussed in Chapter 11.

Depreciation Expense/Van		Accumulated Depreciation/Van	
19_A			19_A	
Dec. 31 1,440			Dec. 31 1,440	

The expense and contra asset increase when depreciation for the year is recorded.

The Depreciation Expense/Van account would be shown as an Operating Expense for $1,440 on the income statement.

Income statement presentation for depreciation of van

Operating Expenses:	
Insurance Expense	$ 170
Office Supplies Expense	600
Salaries & Wages Expense	18,260[9]
Depreciation Expense/Van	1,440

The Accumulated Depreciation/Van account would be shown on the balance sheet as follows:

Balance sheet presentation for plant asset

Assets		
Plant Assets:		
Van	$8,000	
Less: Accumulated Depreciation	1,440	$6,560

**EXAMPLE 6
BUILDING**

On July 1, 19_A, Good purchased a parcel of land with a small building to be used for his TV service repair shop. He paid $10,000 for the land and $40,000 for the building. The building had an estimated useful life of 40 years and no salvage value. He purchased the land and building by paying $50,000 cash and recorded the transaction as follows:

Purchased plant asset for cash

19_A			
July 1	Land	10,000	
	Building	40,000	
	Cash		50,000
	Purchased land and a building for the TV service repair shop.		

On December 31, an adjusting entry was recorded for depreciation on the building in the amount of $500 for the first 6 months. (Remember, land is not depreciated because it normally has an unlimited useful life.)

---

[9] Balance on December 31 before adjustment + adjustment ($18,000 + $260).

$$\frac{\$40,000}{40 \text{ years}} = \$1,000 \text{ depreciation expense each year}$$

$$\$1,000 \times {}^{6}/_{12} = \$500 \text{ depreciation expense for 6 months or } \frac{1}{2} \text{ year}$$
$$(\text{July 1 to December 31})$$

Adjusting entry
recognizing 6 months
depreciation on building

19_A

Dec. 31   Depreciation Expense/Building   500
               Accumulated Depreciation/Building   500
               Record first 6 months depreciation on
               building purchased July 1.

The expense and contra asset accounts below show the increase for depreciation after the adjusting entry is posted.

Depreciation Expense/Building	Accumulated Depreciation/Building
19_A	19_A
Dec. 31 500	Dec. 31 500

The cost of an asset, through use, becomes an expense.
Depreciation Expense/Building would be shown on the income statement as an Operating Expense for $500.

Income statement
presentation for
depreciation of building

Operating Expenses:	
Insurance Expense	$ 170
Office Supplies Expense	600
Salaries & Wages Expense	18,260
Depreciation Expense/Van	1,440
Depreciation Expense/Building	500

The Accumulated Depreciation/Building account would appear on the balance sheet as follows:

Balance sheet presentation
for plant assets

Assets		
Plant Assets:		
Van	$ 8,000	
Less: Accumulated Depreciation	1,440	$ 6,560
Building	$40,000	
Less: Accumulated Depreciation	500	39,500

SUMMARY

Adjusting entries are recorded on the last day of the accounting period to bring the account balances up to date. All adjusting entries for prepaid expenses recorded as an asset when paid and accrued expenses (expenses incurred but not paid) require a debit to an expense account and a credit to an asset or liability account. The cash account is not used when recording adjustments for prepaid expenses recorded as an asset when paid. Cash is not used for accrued expense adjustments because cash has not been paid. Three types of expense adjustments are prepaid expenses recorded as an asset (or expense) when paid, accrued expenses, and depreciation of plant assets.

Each adjusting entry for an expense affects a balance sheet and income statement account. Failure to make an adjustment will result in an overstatement or an understatement of the financial position of the company.

GLOSSARY

Accrued Expense: Expenses incurred that are accumulating and have not been paid or recorded in the accounting records.

Accumulated Depreciation: A contra asset account used to record all the depreciation taken on a plant asset since the date of purchase. Land is not depreciated, because it has an unlimited life.

Adjusting Entry: A journal entry that will bring the accounts up to date at the end of each accounting period. These adjustments are necessary to report the correct income and financial position of the business at the end of an accounting period.

Book Value: The difference between the cost of a plant asset and the total in its related Accumulated Depreciation account.

Contra Plant Asset: An offset or minus account that is subtracted from its related asset account on the balance sheet to show the book value of the asset.

Current Assets: Short-term assets that will be consumed during the normal operating cycle.

Deferred Expense: The postponement or recognition of an expense that has been paid in advance.

Depreciation Expense: Title of the account used to record the writing off or spreading of the cost of a plant asset over its estimated useful life.

Matching Concept: A basic accounting principle which states that revenues for a period should be matched with the expenses incurred in earning the revenue to report the correct net income.

Mixed Account: A portion of the balance of an asset or liability account that affects an income statement and a balance sheet account.

Operating Expenses: All the expenses incurred in earning revenue from the sale of a service or product.

Other Expense: Expenses incurred that are not a cost of selling a service or product. These expenses are listed after the Other Revenue section in the income statement.

Plant Assets: Long-term assets with an estimated useful life of more than 1 year purchased for the purpose of using them in the business operations to generate revenue.

Prepaid Expenses: Payment of an expense that will benefit one or more future accounting periods and recorded as an asset until expired or used.

Salvage Value: Estimated value, scrap value, or residual value of an asset at the end of its useful life.

QUESTIONS

1. Explain briefly the reason for recording an adjusting entry.
2. Name the three types of adjustments for expenses.
3. What effect would the failure to make an adjusting entry for office supplies used have on the net income for the period?
4. Define accrued expenses and give two examples.
5. If a 2-year insurance policy were purchased on June 30, 19_A, for $440, what adjustment would be required on December 31, 19_A, the end of the accounting period?
6. A business paid $400 for 2 months rent on December 1. Give the entry required on December 1, and the adjusting entry required on December 31.
7. What effect would the failure to make an adjusting entry for accrued wages in the amount of $200 have on the net income for the period?
8. A truck was purchased on July 1, 19_A, for $10,000 with a $1,000 salvage value and a 5-year life. What is the amount of depreciation expense that would be shown on the income statement for the year ended December 31, 19_A?

EXERCISES

Prepaid Expense Adjustments

1. On January 1, 19_A, the Office Supplies account had a balance of $900. An inventory taken on December 31, 19_A, showed $200 of supplies on hand.
   (a) Journalize the adjusting entry required on December 31.
   (b) Determine the dollar amount that will be shown on the (1) income statement and (2) balance sheet as of December 31, 19_A.

2. The Color Paper Products Company organized on April 1, 19_A, purchased store supplies for cash in the amount of $300 on April 2, 19_A. An inventory taken on December 31, 19_A, the end of the fiscal period, showed supplies on hand in the amount of $40.
   (a) Journalize the entries required on (1) April 2 and (2) December 31, 19_A.
   (b) Give the income statement presentation for the store supplies used during 19_A.

(*c*) Give the balance sheet presentation for the balance in the Store Supplies account on December 31, 19_A.

3. On December 15, 19_A, Saxony Company rented a machine from the Equipment Rental Company. The agreement called for a $75 rental fee per month, payable in advance. Saxony Company paid $75 on December 15 for the period December 15, 19_A, to January 15, 19_B.

    (*a*) Journalize the entry required on (1) December 15 and (2) December 31, 19_A.

    (*b*) Give the income statement presentation for the equipment rent expense for December 19_A.

    (*c*) Give the balance sheet presentation for the Prepaid Equipment Rent account as of December 31, 19_A.

4. The Color Paper Products Company in Exercise 2 purchased additional store supplies for cash in the amount of $200 on January 4, 19_B and $500 on October 2, 19_B.

    (*a*) Journalize the entries required on (1) January 4; (2) October 2; and (3) December 31, 19_B. An inventory taken on December 31, 19_B, showed $240 of store supplies on hand.

    (*b*) Determine the dollar amount to be shown on the (1) income statement and (2) balance sheet as of December 31, 19_B.

    Hint: Don't forget to consider the balance on hand on January 1, 19_B.

Accrued Expense Adjustments

5. Using the following information, journalize the entries required on December 31, 19_A, and January 2, 19_B, for the Easy-VU TV Company.

    (*a*) Four employees earn a total of $180 per day. On December 31, 19_A, 3 days salaries had accrued in the amount of $540.

    (*b*) Payment of the accrued salaries was made on January 2, 19_B.

6. Bantam Products has three employees who earn $4.50 per hour, one employee who earns $6 per hour, and one employee who earns a salary of $80 per day. All employees are paid each week. On December 31, 19_A, 2 days wages and salaries had accrued, and the company was closed on Wednesday, January 1, 19_B. All the employees worked 8 hours per day and none of the employees were paid for New Year's Day. Journalize the entries required on:

    (*a*) December 31, 19_A

    (*b*) January 3, 19_B

7. Waterford Sales had three hourly employees who earned a total of $104 per day and one employee who earned a salary of $60 per day. All employees work 8 hours per day and are paid every Friday. Journalize the entries required on (*a*) Friday, December 26, and (*b*) Wednesday, December 31, 19_A.

Depreciation Expense Adjustments

8. A company purchased office equipment for $2,400 on July 3, 19_A. The equipment had an 8-year life and no salvage value.
   (a) Journalize the entries required on (1) December 31, 19_A, and (2) December 31, 19_B.
   (b) Determine the book value of the office equipment on (1) December 31, 19_A, and (2) December 31, 19_B.

PROBLEMS

Journalizing Expense Adjustments

3-1. The following data applies to the Extra Good Bakery Company.
   (a) Employees earned a total of $220 per day. Salaries for 4 days had accrued by December 31.
   (b) On November 1 the company borrowed $2,000 from the First Savings Bank. Interest of $12 had accrued by December 31.
   (c) Depreciation on equipment is $1,200 per year. The equipment was purchased on July 1 of the current year.
   (d) A car was rented on December 20 for 30 days at a cost of $12 per day payable on January 18. Twelve days rent has accrued as of December 31. (Use Car Rental Expense and Accounts Payable for account titles.)
   (e) The Prepaid Insurance account had a balance of $240 before adjustment, representing the amount paid for a 2-year policy purchased on July 1 of the current year.
   (f) Three employees are paid $4.50 per hour, and all of the employees work 7½ hours each day. Wages have accrued for Monday to Thursday, December 28, 29, 30, and 31. (Use Wages Expense and Wages Payable for account titles.)
   (g) Furniture with a 6-year life and no salvage value was purchased on March 1 of the current year for $7,200 cash.
   (h) Prepaid rent in the amount of $96 had expired on December 31.

Required

Journalize the adjusting entries for December 31.

3-2. Selected account balances on the unadjusted trial balance for U Joint Plumbing Company as of December 31 appear below.

Prepaid Insurance	$ 320
Prepaid Rent	1,200
Shop Supplies	900
Delivery Equipment	2,000

Accumulated Depreciation/Delivery Equipment	200
Plumbing Revenue Earned	48,000
Salaries & Wages Expense	33,000
Gas & Oil Expense	1,200
Telephone Expense	980
Utilities Expense	2,400
Miscellaneous Expense	200

Required

Journalize the adjusting entries required for December 31 using the following data.

1. Prepaid insurance represents a 2-year policy purchased on October 1.
2. Prepaid rent was paid on July 1 for 8 months rent in advance.
3. An inventory of shop supplies showed $50 on hand on December 31.
4. Depreciation on the delivery equipment amounts to $500 per year.
5. Two days salaries and wages have accrued for one office employee and three shop employees. The office employee receives a salary of $80 per day, and each shop employee is paid $6 per hour (each shop employee worked 8 hours each day).
6. A telephone bill for $90 was received on December 31 and was not recorded or paid.
7. Special equipment was rented on December 20 at a cost of $10 per day. Twelve days rent had accrued but was not recorded or paid. (Use Equipment Rent Expense and Equipment Rent Payable for account titles.)

3-3. The following data applies to the Little Advertising Company who adjust their books each December 31, the end of the fiscal period.

(a) Two employees are paid wages of $5 per hour and one employee is paid a salary of $60 per day. All employees were paid on Friday, December 26. The current year ended on Wednesday, December 31, and all three employees worked on Monday, Tuesday, and Wednesday, December 29, 30, and 31. The two hourly employees worked a total of 30 hours.

(b) A 4-year insurance policy was purchased on July 1 of the current year for $1,200 cash.

(c) On September 1 of the current year, equipment with an 8-year life and no salvage value was purchased for $1,344 cash.

(d) On January 1 of the current year, the Office Supplies account had a debit balance of $150. During the year additional supplies were purchased for $600 cash. An inventory taken on December 31 revealed supplies on hand amounting to $475.

(e) Prepaid rent in the amount of $80 had expired on December 31 but had not been recorded.

(f) Depreciation on furniture amounts to $600 per year.

(g) Equipment rent amounting to $300 for December had not been recorded or paid as of December 31.

Required

Journalize the adjusting entries required on December 31.

Journalizing and Posting Expense Adjustments

3-4. The Adco Company adjusts their books on December 31, the end of the fiscal period.

Required

(a) Open general ledger accounts for 110 Cash; 112 Prepaid Insurance; 130 Office Equipment; 138 Accumulated Depreciation/Office Equipment; 210 Salaries Payable; 510 Salaries Expense; 512 Insurance Expense; and 538 Depreciation Expense/Office Equipment.

(b) Post the following balances as of December 31; 19_C: Cash, $5,000 debit; Prepaid Insurance, $1,200 debit; Office Equipment, $4,200 debit; Accumulated Depreciation/Office Equipment, $1,050 credit; and Salaries Expense, $10,000 debit. Enter the word "balance" in the Explanation column, and put a check mark (✔) in the Ref. column.

(c) Journalize and post the adjusting entries required on December 31, 19_C, using the following information.

1. The company has one employee who receives a salary of $40 per day and is paid every Friday for a 5-day week beginning on the preceding Monday. The employee was paid on Friday, December 27. Record the adjusting entry that should be made on Tuesday, December 31, to record the salary owed for Monday and Tuesday, December 30 and 31 but unpaid as of that date.

2. The Prepaid Insurance balance of $1,200 represents a 4-year policy purchased on July 1, 19_C. Record the adjusting entry required on December 31.

3. The balance in the Office Equipment account represents the cost of equipment that was purchased in 19_A. The equipment has an 8-year life and no salvage value. Depreciation has been recorded for 19_A and 19_B; record the depreciation for 19_C.

(d) Give the book value of the Office Equipment on December 31, 19_C, after all the adjustments have been journalized and posted.

3-5. Listed below is a partial trial balance (before adjustments) for the Color-Coded Paint Company as of December 31, 19_B.

COLOR-CODED PAINT COMPANY
PARTIAL TRIAL BALANCE
December 31, 19_B

Accounts Receivable	$ 4,000
Prepaid Insurance	800
Supplies	600
Equipment	12,000

Accumulated Depreciation/Equipment		$ 1,000
Accounts Payable		1,000
Jane Code, Capital		21,000
Jane Code, Drawings	9,000	
Salaries Expense	7,200	
Wages Expense	500	
Rent Expense	4,400	
Miscellaneous Expense	400	

Required

(a) Open general ledger accounts for 110 Accounts Receivable; 112 Pre-paid Insurance; 114 Supplies; 120 Equipment; 128 Accumulated Depreciation/Equipment; 210 Accounts Payable; 212 Salaries Payable; 213 Rent Payable; 214 Wages Payable; 330 Jane Code, Capital; 338 Jane Code, Drawings; 505 Salaries Expense; 510 Wages Expense; 511 Rent Expense; 512 Insurance Expense; 514 Supplies Expense; 518 Depreciation Expense/Equipment; and 520 Miscellaneous Expense. Enter the balances shown in the partial trial balance; use December 31 as the date, write the word "balance" in the Explanation column, and put a check mark (✔) in the Ref. column.

(b) Journalize and post the adjusting entries using the following data and the related information in the partial unadjusted trial balance.
1. The balance in the Prepaid Insurance account represents the amount paid for a 2-year policy that started on July 1, 19_B.
2. The supplies on hand at Dec. 31, 19_B, amounted to $120.
3. The equipment is estimated to last 6 years with no scrap value and was purchased on July 1, 19_A. The depreciation for 19_A has been recorded. Record the depreciation for 19_B.
4. Wages expense amounts to $500 for a 5-day week, and the employees are paid every Friday; Dec. 31, 19_B, falls on a Monday. Record the wages accrued for Monday, December 31.
5. Rent amounting to $400 for December had not been recorded or paid.
6. The bookkeeper receives a salary of $70 per day. Four days salaries had accrued but had not been paid or recorded by December 31.

(c) Give the book value of the equipment on December 31, 19_B, after all the adjusting entries have been journalized and posted.

3-6. The following year-end balances appeared in the records for Cleaner Homes as of December 31:

Accounts Receivable	$ 650
Prepaid Insurance	180
Office Supplies	380
Cleaning Supplies	420
Cleaning Equipment	1,800
Accumulated Depreciation/Cleaning Equipment	200
Accounts Payable	750
Jodie Casper, Capital	8,125

Jodie Casper, Drawing	6,000
Wages Expense	4,050
Gas & Oil Expense	1,260
Miscellaneous Expense	340

Required

(a) Journalize the following adjusting entries in general journal form using the related information above.
1. The Prepaid Insurance account represents a 1-year policy that started on October 1.
2. Cleaning supplies on hand, $110.
3. Depreciation for the cleaning equipment amounted to $400.
4. Accrued wages amounted to $305.
5. Gas and oil bill received on December 31 for $165 has not been recorded or paid.
6. Office supplies used during the year amounted to $280.
7. Miscellaneous expenses of $25 had accrued but were not recorded or paid.

(b) Post the adjusting entries in the ledger accounts in the workbook accompanying the text.

Journalizing and Posting Daily Transactions and Expense Adjustments

√ **3-7.** The following selected transactions apply to the Ellis Industries:

19_A

Jan.   5   Purchased a 3-year insurance policy and paid cash of $480.
       10   Purchased store equipment for $12,000, paying $2,000 cash and applying the balance on account. The equipment had a 10-year life and a $2,000 salvage value.

Feb.   2   Purchased office furniture in the amount of $600 on account from Correc-O Supplies Company. The furniture had a 10-year life and no salvage value.

Apr.   2   Paid the office rent for 1 year in advance (April 1, 19_A to April 1, 19_B), $3,600.

Required

(a) Open general ledger accounts for 115 Prepaid Insurance; 116 Prepaid Rent; 130 Office Furniture; 138 Accumulated Depreciation/Office Furniture; 141 Store Equipment; 148 Accumulated Depreciation/Store Equipment; 525 Insurance Expense; 526 Rent Expense; 538 Depreciation Expense/Office Furniture; and 548 Depreciation Expense/Store Equipment.
(b) Journalize and post the transactions required for January 5 to April 2.
(c) Journalize and post the adjusting entries required for December 31.

3-8. Office Equipment with an 8-year life and no salvage value was purchased on January 4 for $3,800; and a 4-year insurance policy was purchased for $800 cash on July 5, 19_A.

Required

(a) Journalize the entries for January 4 and July 5, 19_A.
(b) Journalize the adjusting entries required on December 31, 19_A.
(c) Journalize the adjusting entries required on December 31, 19_B.
(d) Open general ledger accounts for 108 Prepaid Insurance; 130 Office Equipment; and 138 Accumulated Depreciation/Office Equipment. Post the data recorded in a, b, and c.
(e) Give the balance sheet presentation for Prepaid Insurance and Office Equipment as of December 31, 19_B.

3-9. The following plant assets were purchased during 19_A.

July 1 Purchased a portable storage building with a 10-year life and no salvage value for $25,000 cash.
Sept. 2 Purchased furniture with an 8-year life and no salvage value for $9,000 cash.

Required

(a) Journalize the entries required on July 1 and September 2, 19_A.
(b) Journalize the adjusting entries required for December 31, 19_A.
(c) Journalize the adjusting entries required for December 31, 19_B.
(d) Open general ledger accounts for 130 Building; 138 Accumulated Depreciation/Building; 140 Furniture; and 149 Accumulated Depreciation/Furniture. Post the data recorded in a, b, and c.
(e) Give the balance sheet presentation for the building and the furniture as of December 31, 19_B.

3-10. Nonskip Pen Company purchased the following assets during 19_B.

19_B
Feb. 10 Purchased office supplies for $800 cash.
Apr. 2 Purchased office furniture for $4,000 cash.
June 6 Purchased a 2-year insurance policy for $240 cash.

Additional Data
1. On January 1, 19_B, the company had $80 of office supplies on hand, and the office supplies on hand on December 31, 19_B, amounted to $120.
2. The office furniture purchased on April 2, 19_B, had a 10-year life and no salvage value.

3. Seven months insurance had expired as of December 31, 19_B.
4. Salaries and wages accrued on December 31, 19_B, amounted to $320.

Required

(a) Open general ledger accounts for 112 Office Supplies; 115 Prepaid Insurance; 130 Office Furniture; 138 Accumulated Depreciation/Office Furniture; 210 Salaries & Wages Payable; 514 Office Supplies Expense; 525 Insurance Expense; 538 Depreciation Expense/Office Furniture; and 540 Salaries & Wages Expense. Enter debit balances of $80 in the Office Supplies account and use the date January 1, 19_B; enter $9,200 in the Salaries & Wages Expense account and use the date December 31, 19_B. Enter the word "balance" in the Explanation column for each of these two accounts, and put a check mark (✔) in the Ref. column.

(b) Journalize and post the entries for February, March, and June 19_B.

(c) Journalize and post the adjusting entries required for December 31, 19_B.

(d) Give the balance sheet presentation for the Office Furniture account as of December 31, 19_B.

Review Problem

3-11. The account balances of Loop-d-Loop Company are shown in the general ledger accounts in the workbook accompanying the text.

Required

(a) Journalize and post the adjusting entries required for December 31, 19_B.
    1. A count of office supplies revealed $40 of unused supplies.
    2. Equipment with a 5-year life and no salvage value was purchased on September 1 of the current year. Record the depreciation for 4 months.
    3. Accrued wages amount to $800.
    4. Shop supplies on hand amount to $12.
    5. Utilities accrued but not paid or recorded amount to $70.
    6. Prepaid insurance represents the cost of a 3-year policy purchased on September 1, 19_B.

(b) Give the balance sheet classification for the following accounts:
    1. Office Supplies DR.
    2. D. Loop, Capital CR.
    3. Shop Supplies DR.
    4. Prepaid Insurance DR.
    5. Equipment DR.
    6. Accumulated Depreciation/Equipment CR.
    7. Wages Payable CR.
    8. Utilities Payable CR.

After completing this chapter, you should be able to:

1. **Journalize the adjusting entries for accrued revenue and revenue received in advance from customers**

2. **Prepare an adjusted trial balance**

3. **List five steps of the accounting cycle**

Chapter 4 continues the discussion of Step 4 in the accounting cycle— the adjusting entries necessary to bring the account balances up to date before the year-end financial statements are prepared. The adjustments in Step 4 occur after the daily transactions have been journalized and posted and a trial balance is prepared to check on the accuracy of the ledger. There are five types of adjustments necessary to bring the account balances up to date.

Five types of adjusting entries

Type of Adjustment	Type of Account	
	Debited	**Credited**
1. Prepaid expense	Expense	Prepaid Asset
2. Accrued expense	Expense	Liability (Payable)
3. Depreciation expense	Depreciation Expense	Contra Asset (Accumulated Depreciation)
4. Accrued revenue	Asset (Receivable)	Revenue
5. Revenue received in advance	Liability (revenue received in advance)	Revenue

The first three types of adjustments covering the expenses were discussed in Chapter 3. Chapter 4 will complete the discussion by explaining the types of adjustments required to bring the revenue account balances up to date.

The last part of Chapter 4 will continue with the accounting cycle through Step 5 and prepare an adjusted trial balance to check on the accuracy of the general ledger after all the daily transactions and adjusting entries have been journalized and posted. Chapter 5 will complete the discussion of the accounting cycle for a service-type of business organization. In Chapter 5 we will learn that adjustments are recorded on a work sheet before they are journalized and posted into the permanent records of the business.

ADJUSTING FOR REVENUE

All adjustments for accrued revenue and revenue recorded as a liability when paid in advance require a *debit* to an *asset or liability* account and a *credit* to a *revenue* account. The adjustments for revenue are necessary to recognize all revenue earned for the period so the net income will be stated correctly on the income statement. Failure to make an adjustment for accrued revenue or revenue recorded as a liability when paid in advance will cause the revenue and the net income for the period to be understated as well as violating the Matching Concept.

Two types of adjustments for revenue are:

1. Revenue accrued but not collected in cash or recorded
2. Payment received in advance from a customer for services or merchandise to be delivered in the future and recorded in a liability or revenue account when cash is received

Accrued Revenue

Revenue may be earned before cash has been received from the customer or the transaction entered in the accounting records. These revenues that have been earned but not received or recorded are called *accrued revenues.* At the end of the accounting period, an adjusting entry must be made for accrued revenues to present the correct amount of revenue earned on the income statement and the correct amount of Accounts Receivable on the balance sheet.

The adjustment for accrued revenue requires a debit to a receivable (asset) account and a credit to a revenue account as shown in the following illustration.

Debit an asset account
Credit a revenue account

Some common examples are Accounts Receivable for repair services earned and Royalties Receivable for royalties earned on publications.

**EXAMPLE 1
REPAIR SERVICE
REVENUE**

Mr. Good signed a contract on November 30, 19_A, with the Sleepy Hollow Motel to maintain and repair the TVs in the guest rooms of the motel. The contract agreement stated that the service and repair shop was to be paid $200 per month payable the tenth day following the month the service was completed.

On December 31, 19_A, no entry had been made on the books to show the $200 earned for December, because payment will not be received until January 10, 19_B. An adjusting entry will be required to show the service revenue earned and the amount owed to the repair shop. The following adjusting entry will be made:

*Adjusting entry
recognizing revenue
earned but not received*

19_A			
Dec. 31	Accounts Receivable/Sleepy Hollow Motel	200	
	Repair Service Revenue		200
	Record revenue earned for December.		

After the adjustment is posted, the general ledger accounts affected show the increase as follows:

Accounts Receivable		Repair Service Revenue	
19_A			19_A
Dec. 31 200			Dec. 31 200

The Repair Service Revenue account would be shown under the **Operating Revenue**[1] *section on the income statement for $200.*

Income statement presentation for revenue earned but not received

> Operating Revenue:
>   Repair Service Revenue $200

The Accounts Receivable account would appear in the Asset section of the balance sheet.

Balance sheet presentation for Accounts Receivable

Assets

Accounts Receivable $200

The receivable for the revenue earned in December will be received on January 10, 19_B. The entry when payment is received will be:

Entry to record receipt of revenue earned in prior period

19_B			
Jan. 10	Cash	200	
	Accounts Receivable/Sleepy Hollow Motel		200
	Received revenue earned for December as per agreement.		

After the customer has paid for the services, the Accounts Receivable account will show the decrease as follows:

Accounts Receivable	
19_A	19_B
Dec. 31 200	Jan. 10 200

**EXAMPLE 2
ROYALTIES
EARNED**

Good wrote and designed a pamphlet for the repair shop entitled "Easy Steps for TV Maintenance." He signed a contract with the Quickee Publishing Company to print and sell the pamphlet. The agreement stated that the repair shop will receive a royalty of $0.10 on each pamphlet sold. Payment was to be made twice a year on January 15 and July 15. On December 31, 19_A, Good received notice that royalties in the amount of $600 had accrued for the period July 1 to December 31, 19_A, and a check would be mailed on

---

[1] Operating revenue is all the revenue earned from selling a service or a product. Operating revenue is discussed in Chapter 7.

January 15, 19_B. The repair shop has earned the $600 in 19_A, although payment will be received in 19_B, the next accounting period. An adjustment was made to record the receivable and the royalties earned for the period as follows:

Royalty revenue earned but not received

19_A			
Dec. 31	Royalties Receivable/Quickee Publishing Co.	600	
	Royalties Earned		600
	Record royalties earned for the last 6 months of 19_A.		

The ledger below shows the increase to the asset and revenue accounts.

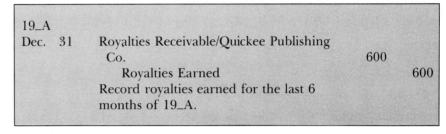

Royalties Receivable	Royalties Earned
19_A	19_A
Dec. 31 600	Dec. 31 600

The asset increases when revenue is recognized.
Royalties Receivable for $600 would be shown in the Asset section of the balance sheet.

Balance sheet presentation for Royalties Receivable

Assets	
Accounts Receivable	$200
Royalties Receivable	600

*Royalties Earned for $600 would be shown under the **Other Revenue**[2] section of the income statement.*

Income statement presentation for Royalties Earned

Other Revenue:
    Royalties Earned $600

When the $600 is received on January 15, 19_B, the following entry will be made:

Receipt of revenue earned in prior period

19_B			
Jan. 15	Cash	600	
	Royalties Receivable/Quickee Publishing Co.		600
	Received royalty payment for July 1 to Dec. 31, 19_A.		

[2] Other revenue is revenue that is not earned from selling a service or a product, and it is listed after the Operating Expense section of an income statement. Other revenue is discussed in Chapter 7.

The asset is decreased when the royalties are received as shown in the ledger account below:

Royalties Receivable

19_A		19_B	
Dec. 31	600	Jan. 15	600

Revenue Received in Advance

When a customer pays for services in advance, Cash is debited and normally a liability account called **Unearned Revenue** or Revenue Received in Advance is credited because the service has not been performed and the revenue has not been earned. Revenue received in advance from customers is also known as a **deferred revenue** because the payment represents the postponement or recognition of revenue received but not earned.

For example, when a customer pays $1,000 for services in advance, the following journal entry is recorded:

19_A			
July 1	Cash	1,000	
	Unearned Service Revenue		1,000
	Received advance payment for services		
	from customer.		

When the transaction is posted into the general ledger, the Unearned Service Revenue account will show a credit balance of $1,000.

Unearned Service Revenue

	19_A	
	July 1	1,000

The $1,000 balance in the Unearned Service Revenue account represents a liability to the company, because the service has not been performed at the time payment was received. During the accounting period, as the services are being performed, the liability account is decreasing. Therefore, at the end of the accounting period, an adjusting entry is required to show the decrease in the liability account, Unearned Service Revenue, and to record the revenue earned during the period. The Unearned Revenue account is debited for the decrease in the liability and a related revenue account is credited to record the amount earned during the period as shown in Examples 3 and 4.

Failure to make an adjustment to record the revenue earned for the period and to decrease the liability account will cause the revenue account on the income statement to be understated and the liability account, Unearned Service Revenue, on the balance sheet to be overstated. Some common examples are Repair Service Revenue and Rent Earned on property owned by the company.

EXAMPLE 3
REPAIR SERVICE
REVENUE

On October 1, 19_A, the repair shop sold repair service contracts to 10 cus-tomers covering all labor and parts for a 1-year period (October 1, 19_A, to October 1, 19_B). The contracts sold for $240 each, payable in advance. Upon receipt of the $2,400 (10 × $240), the following entry was made:

Liability account used when advance payment received from customer

19_A				
Oct. 1	Cash		2,400	
	Unearned Repair Service Revenue			2,400
	Record advance payments for ten 1-year service contracts beginning Oct. 1, 19_A, to Oct. 1, 19_B.			

One-fourth, or $600, of the contract price ($2,400 × ³/₁₂) has been earned at the end of 19_A. The liability resulting from the revenue received in advance would have to be reduced to recognize the amount earned. Good made the following adjusting entry:

Adjustment to recognize revenue earned

19_A			
Dec. 31	Unearned Repair Service Revenue	600	
	Repair Service Revenue		600
	Record revenue earned for the last 3 months of 19_A.		

The income statement would show $600 for Repair Service Revenue under the Operating Revenue section.

Income statement presentation for revenue earned

Operating Revenue:
Repair Service Revenue $600

The balance sheet would show $1,800 of Unearned Repair Service Rev-enue in the Liability section.

Balance sheet presentation for Unearned Revenue

Liabilities

Unearned Repair Service Revenue $1,800

After the adjustment is posted, the ledger accounts would appear as follows:

Unearned Repair Service Revenue			**Repair Service Revenue**	
19_A		19_A		19_A
Dec. 31 600		Oct. 1 2,400		Dec. 31 600

The liability decreases when revenue is earned.

EXAMPLE 4
RENT EARNED

Good, realizing that the repair shop could not use all the space in the building, partitioned off a portion for rental purposes. On November 1, 19_A, he
rented this space to the Easy-Vu TV Company, receiving $1,200 for 6 months
rent in advance (November 1, 19_A, to April 30, 19_B), and he recorded the
payment as follows:

*Liability increased for
advance payment of rent*

19_A			
Nov.	1	Cash	1,200	
		Unearned Rent		1,200
		Received 6 months rent (Nov. 1,		
		19_A, to Apr. 30, 19_B) for building		
		space from Easy-Vu TV Company.		

On December 31, 19_A, 2 months rent in the amount of $400
($1,200 × ²/₆) had been earned. An adjustment was made to decrease the
liability account and transfer the amount earned to the revenue account. The
following entry was made:

*Liability decreased when
rent revenue recognized
as earned*

19_A			
Dec.	31	Unearned Rent	400	
		Rent Earned		400
		Rent earned for November and		
		December for space rented to Easy-Vu		
		TV Company.		

Unearned Rent would be shown for $800 in the Liability section of the
balance sheet.

*Balance sheet presentation
for Unearned Rent*

Liabilities	
Unearned Repair Service Revenue	$1,800
Unearned Rent	800

Rent Earned would be shown on the income statement for $400 under
the Other Revenue section.

*Income statement
presentation for Rent
Earned*

Other Revenue:	
Royalties Earned	$600
Rent Earned	400

The two general ledger accounts after the adjustment was journalized and
posted would appear as follows:

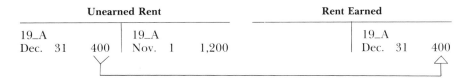

The liability decreases when revenue is earned.

Alternate Method for Recording Revenue Received in Advance

All *revenue received in advance* from customers is normally recorded in a liability account at the time payment is received, and the adjusting process for these advance payments is handled as previously discussed and illustrated. However, occasionally an accountant may use an income statement account when the advance payment was received. When an income statement account is used to record the initial entry, a revenue account may have to be adjusted to remove any unearned revenue and transfer the amount to a balance sheet account. To illustrate, we will use the data given in the previous example.

Assume that when the repair shop received 6 months rent in advance (November 1, 19_A, to April 30, 19_B) from the Easy-Vu TV Company on November 1, 19_A, the following entry was made:

Advance payment from customer recorded as revenue earned

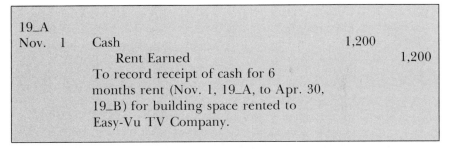

On December 31, 19_A, only two-sixths, or $400 ($1,200 × 2/6), of the $1,200 had been earned. The revenue account must be adjusted to remove the unearned portion and transfer the amount to a liability account, Unearned Rent, as shown in the following entry:

Adjustment to reduce revenue and increase liability for unearned revenue

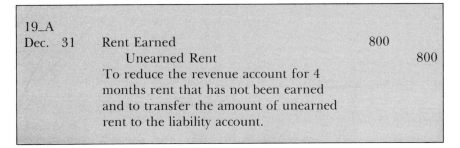

After these entries were posted, the revenue account, Rent Earned, would show $400 ($1,200 − $800) of rent earned during the period, and the liability account, Unearned Rent, would show $800 of unearned rent at the end of the period.

After the adjusting entries for expenses and revenue (discussed in Chapters 3 and 4) were posted, the general ledger accounts (in T account form) for Good TV Service & Repair Shop are shown below:

Cash		Accounts Receivable		Royalties Receivable	
Bal. 6,700		Bal. 12,000		Adj. 600	
		Adj. 200			

Prepaid Insurance		Office Supplies		Van	
Bal. 510	Adj. 170	Bal. 800	Adj. 600	Bal. 8,000	

Accumulated Depreciation/Van		Land		Building	
	Adj. 1,440	Bal. 10,000		Bal. 40,000	

Accumulated Depreciation/Building		Accounts Payable		Salaries & Wages Payable	
	Adj. 500		Bal. 10,700		Adj. 260

Interest Payable		Unearned Rent		Unearned Repair Service Revenue	
	Adj. 12	Adj. 400	Bal. 1,200	Adj. 600	Bal. 2,400

I. M. Good, Capital		I. M. Good, Drawing		Repair Service Revenue	
	Bal. 23,988	Bal. 19,028			Bal. 78,700
					Adj. 200
					Adj. 600

Salaries & Wage Expense		Insurance Expense		Depreciation Expense/Van	
Bal. 18,000		Adj. 170		Adj. 1,440	
Adj. 260					

Depreciation Expense/Building		Office Supplies Expense		Utilities Expense	
Adj. 500		Adj. 600		Bal. 1,950	

Rent Earned		Royalties Earned		Interest Expense	
	Adj. 400		Adj. 600	Adj. 12	

ADJUSTED TRIAL BALANCE

After the adjusting entries have been journalized and posted, an *adjusted trial balance* is prepared to check on the accuracy of the ledger before preparing the year-end financial statements.

The adjusted trial balance prepared from the general ledger accounts of Good TV Service & Repair Shop is shown below:

GOOD TV SERVICE & REPAIR SHOP
ADJUSTED TRIAL BALANCE
December 31, 19_A

Account Title	Debit	Credit
Cash	$ 6,700	
Accounts Receivable	12,200	
Royalties Receivable	600	
Prepaid Insurance	340	
Office Supplies	200	
Van	8,000	
Accumulated Depreciation/Van		$ 1,440
Land	10,000	
Building	40,000	
Accumulated Depreciation/Building		500
Accounts Payable		10,700
Salaries & Wages Payable		260
Interest Payable		12
Unearned Rent		800
Unearned Repair Service Revenue		1,800
I. M. Good, Capital		23,988
I. M. Good, Drawings	19,028	
Repair Service Revenue		79,500
Salaries & Wages Expense	18,260	
Insurance Expense	170	
Depreciation Expense/Van	1,440	
Depreciation Expense/Building	500	
Office Supplies Expense	600	
Utilities Expense	1,950	
Rent Earned		400
Royalties Earned		600
Interest Expense	12	
Totals	$120,000	$120,000

FOUR POINTS TO REMEMBER

1. All adjustments for accrued expenses and prepaid expenses recorded as an asset when paid require a debit to an expense account and a credit to an asset or liability account.
2. All adjustments for accrued revenue and revenue recorded as a liabil-

ity when paid in advance require a debit to an asset or liability account and a credit to a revenue account.

3. Each adjusting entry affects a balance sheet and income statement account.

4. The recording of adjusting entries for accrued or prepaid revenue and expenses never involve a debit or credit to cash.

THE ACCOUNTING CYCLE

The five steps in the accounting cycle covered in Chapters 2, 3, and 4 are as follows:

1. Analyze and journalize the daily transactions or events.
2. Post entries from the journal into the ledger.
3. Prepare a trial balance to check the accuracy of the ledger.
4. Journalize and post the adjusting entries.
5. Prepare an adjusted trial balance.

SUMMARY

Revenue adjustments are recorded on the last day of the accounting period to bring the revenue account balances up to date so that they will have the correct balance before the year-end financial statements are prepared. All adjusting entries for revenue recorded as a liability when paid and revenue accrued but not recorded require a debit to a liability or asset account and a credit to a revenue account. The cash account is not used when recording adjustments for prepaid revenue recorded as a liability when payment was received. Cash is not used for accrued revenue adjustments because cash has not been received. Two types of revenue adjustments are accrued revenue and revenue received in advance and recorded as a liability (or revenue) when payment is received.

Each revenue adjustment affects a balance sheet and income statement account. Failure to make an adjustment will result in an overstatement or an understatement of the financial position of the company.

After the daily transactions and the adjusting entries for expenses and revenues have been recorded, an adjusted trial balance is prepared to check on the accuracy of the general ledger.

GLOSSARY

Accrued Revenue: Revenue earned but payment has not been received from the customer or recorded in the accounting records.

Adjusted Trial Balance: A list of account balances taken after the daily transactions and the adjusting entries are journalized and posted to check that the debit balances equal the credit balances in the general ledger.

Deferred Revenue: Revenue received in advance from customers that has been deferred because the payment represents the postponement or recognition of revenue received but not earned.

Operating Revenue: Revenue earned from selling a service or a product.

Other Revenue: Revenue that is not earned from selling a service or a product, such as interest earned on a note receivable. Other Revenue is listed after the Operating Expense section on the income statement.

Revenue Received in Advance: Account title credited when a customer pays for a service or product in advance. The account is classified as a liability account.

Unearned Revenue: Revenue received in advance from a customer and recorded as a liability until earned.

QUESTIONS

1. Explain briefly the reason for adjusting the account entitled Revenue Received in Advance.
2. Name the two types of adjustments for revenue.
3. What effect would the failure to make an adjusting entry for revenue received in advance have on the net income for the period.
4. Define accrued revenues and give two examples.
5. If a customer paid $2,400 on September 1, 19_A, for a 6-month service contract (September 1, 19_A, to February 28, 19_B), what adjustment would be required on December 31, 19_A, the end of the accounting period?
6. A tenant paid $400 for 2 months rent on December 1, 19_A. Give the account that would be credited on December 1 and the adjusting entry required on December 31, 19_A.
7. When and why is an adjusted trial balance prepared.
8. List the five steps in the accounting cycle covered in Chapters 2 to 4.

EXERCISES

Adjustments for Accrued Revenue

1. The Rite-Light Company earned $400 for electrical repair services performed on December 28, 19_A. No entry has been made because the customer has not yet been billed. Record the necessary adjusting entry for December 31, 19_A, the end of the accounting period.

2. On December 27, 19_A, a dentist completed a root canal for a patient. The patient will not be billed for the $200 owed for the dental work until January 19_B.

(*a*) Record the adjusting entry required on December 31, 19_A, the end of the accounting period.

(*b*) Give the balance sheet presentation for the $200 owed by the patient as of December 31, 19_A.

3. An accountant bills her clients on the first of every month for work completed during the previous month. During December 19_A, the accountant completed accounting work amounting to $4,000. The clients will not be billed until January 19_B.

(*a*) Record the adjusting entry required on December 31, 19_A, the end of the accounting period.

(*b*) Give the income statement presentation for the $4,000 on December 31, 19_A.

Adjustments for Revenue Received in Advance

4. The Better Made Clothing Company received $600 in advance payments on September 1, 19_A, from customers for a special type of winter jacket. The $600 was credited to the Unearned Revenue account. All the jackets were shipped to the customers by December 31, 19_A.

Journalize the entry for (*a*) September 1 and (*b*) December 31, 19_A.

5. On December 15, 19_A, the Equipment Rental Company rented a machine to the Saxony Company for $75 per month, payable in advance. The Equipment Rental Company received $75 from the Saxony Company for the period December 15, 19_A, to January 14, 19_B.

(*a*) Journalize the entry required on (1) December 15 and (2) December 31, 19_A.

(*b*) Give the balance sheet presentation for the unearned amount of equipment rent as of December 31, 19_A.

(*c*) Give the income statement presentation for the amount of rent earned on the equipment as of December 31, 19_A.

6. The Monthly Tax Magazine sold 10, 6-month subscriptions for a total of $90. Customers are required to pay the total cost of the subscription when the agreement is signed, and the company received $90 on November 15, 19_A, from the 10 subscribers. The magazines are shipped on the first day of every month. All the December issues were shipped on December 1, 19_A.

(*a*) Journalize the entries required on (1) November 15 and (2) December 31, 19_A.

(*b*) Determine the amount to be shown on the (1) income statement for the revenue earned for the subscriptions issued in December and (2) balance sheet for the Unearned Subscription Revenue account as of December 31, 19_A.

Adjusted Trial Balance

7. The debit and credit balances for the general ledger accounts of Jackson Electrical Service are as follows:

Debit Balances

Cash	$ 2,120
Accounts Receivable	2,000
Prepaid Insurance	120
Supplies	400
Van	5,000
J. Jackson, Drawing	6,000
Wages Expense	2,100
Supplies Expense	1,800
Telephone Expense	360
Depreciation Expense/Van	1,000
Miscellaneous Expense	100

Credit Balances

Accounts Payable	$ 1,900
Unearned Electric Revenue	800
Accumulated Depreciation/Van	1,500
J. Jackson, Capital	6,200
Electric Revenue Earned	10,600

Prepare an adjusted trial balance as of December 31, 19_A. Be sure to place the accounts in correct order by listing the assets, liabilities, and owner's equity accounts before the revenue and expense accounts.

Review Exercise for Revenue Adjustments

8. Prepare the adjusting entries required on December 31, 19_A, the end of the accounting period for Brickley Industries, using the following data:
   (a) Office space rented for $150 per month covering the period December 15, 19_A, to January 14, 19_B, had not been paid by the tenant as of December 31, 19_A.
   (b) Service contracts are issued for a 4-month period. Customers paid $500 on November 30 for the 4-month period beginning on December 1, 19_A, and ending on March 31, 19_B.
   (c) Carpenter work amounting to $600 had been completed during December 19_A. Payment has not been received, because the customers will not be billed until the first week in January 19_B. (Use the account title Carpenter Revenue.)
   (d) Deposits for two jobs amounting to $200 was received on December 15, 19_A, and the Unearned Paint Revenue account was credited. As of December 31, 19_A, $150 had been earned but not recorded.

Review Exercise for Classification of Accounts

9. From the following alphabetical list of accounts, state the (1) income statement classifications and the (2) balance sheet classifications on the same line as the account title. The first account has been completed as an example.

	Account Title	Account Classification
Example: **a.**	Accounts Receivable	Asset
b.	Accumulated Depreciation/Building	_____
c.	Depreciation Expense/Building	_____
d.	Insurance Expense	_____
e.	Interest Expense	_____
f.	Interest Payable	_____
g.	Royalties Earned	_____
h.	Supplies	_____
i.	Supplies Expense	_____
j.	Unearned Rent	_____

PROBLEMS

Journalizing Revenue Adjustments

4-1. The following data applies to the U-Joint Plumbing Company.

(*a*) A customer paid for a 3-month service contract on November 1, 19_A (November 1, 19_A, to January 31, 19_B). The Unearned Revenue account was credited for $300 when payment was received on November 1.

(*b*) Payment of $900 was received from customers for work to begin on December 1, 19_A, and to be completed by January 10, 19_B. As of December 31, 70 percent of the work had been completed. Decrease the Unearned Revenue account for the amount earned as of December 31.

(*c*) A job was completed for plumbing work in a new commercial building on December 28. A portion of the cost has been paid and recorded. The $6,000 balance has not been recorded or paid because the customer will not be billed until January 19_B.

(*d*) Plumbing parts for $800 were sold to customers who have not yet been billed. Debit the Accounts Receivable account for the amount owed but not recorded.

Required

Prepare the adjusting entries required on December 31, 19_A.

4-2. The Ace Rental Company adjusts their books on December 31, the end of the accounting period. Data for the revenue adjustments appear below.

(*a*) A portion of the office space was rented for $90 per month. The first month's rent for the period December 20, 19_A, to January 19, 19_B, was paid by the tenant on December 20. The rent earned for the first 10 days has not been recorded.

(*b*) Land was rented to a farmer for planting 10 acres of corn. The agreement called for a payment of $150 for the planting season, payable on

July 1. On December 31, the accountant discovered that payment had not been received because the office clerk neglected to bill the farmer for the rental of the land.

(c) The company owned several storage lockers that are rented on a yearly basis. Payment of $720 was received from one renter for a 1-year period beginning on October 1, 19_A, and ending on September 30, 19_B. Unearned Storage Fees was credited when payment was received on October 1.

(d) Office buildings owned by the company are rented on a monthly basis. Payment of $500 has not been received from one tenant for December.

Required

Prepare the adjusting entries required on December 31, 19_A.

4-3. RA Newspaper Publishers sell papers on a daily and monthly basis, and they adjust their books on December 31, the end of the accounting period. Data for the revenue adjustments appear below.

(a) Fifty subscriptions for a 1-month period were sold on December 10. Daily delivery will begin on December 15 and continue until January 15, 19_B. Payment of $350 was received and recorded in the Unearned Subscription Revenue account on December 10, 19_A. One-half of the revenue has been earned but not recorded.

(b) The newspaper carriers for home delivery of the papers pay for their orders on the first day of each month. The carriers owed $1,200 for December which has not been recorded or received by the publishers.

(c) Mail orders are received on a weekly basis and the customers pay in advance. Weekly orders amounting to $140 for the week beginning on December 27, 19_A, and ending January 2, 19_B, were received on December 26; the Unearned Subscription Revenue account was credited for $140 on that date. The revenue earned for the period December 27 to December 31 has not been recorded.

(d) Commercial customers are billed on the fifteenth of every month for a 4-week period. As of December 31, 2 weeks service amounting to $350 has been earned but not billed or recorded.

Required

Prepare the adjusting entries required on December 31, 19_A.

Journalizing Revenue and Expense Adjustments

4-4. Rose Budd started her dental practice on October 1, 19_A. She adjusts her books on December 31, the end of her fiscal period. Adjustment data appears below.

(a) Salaries accrued amount to $800 as of December 31. The salaries owed have not been recorded or paid because the payroll period ends on January 5, 19_B.

(b) Dr. Budd paid $600 for a 6-month insurance premium which expires on March 31, 19_B. Prepaid Insurance was debited for $600 when the premium was paid on October 2. Three months insurance has expired as of December 31.

(c) Dental work completed on December 27 for $175 has not been recorded or paid as of December 31, 19_A.

(d) On October 1, 19_A, Dr. Budd purchased used dental equipment for $42,000 with a 10-year life and a $2,000 salvage value.

(e) Dr. Budd entered into an agreement to perform dental services 1 day each week for the children in a local orphanage for a fee of $50 per month. Payment of $150 was received in advance on November 30 for December 19_A, and January and February 19_B. The Unearned Dental Revenue account was credited when payment was received on November 30.

(f) A portion of the office space was rented at a cost of $80 per month. The tenant paid 3 months rent in advance on November 1, and the Unearned Rent account was credited for $240.

Required

Prepare the adjusting entries required on December 31, 19_A.

4-5. Fred Poole started the Genie Office Cleaning business on July 1, 19_B. He adjusts his books on December 31, the end of his fiscal period. Adjustment data for the business appears below.

(a) Poole purchased cleaning equipment for $1,500 on July 1 with a 10-year life and no salvage value. Depreciation has not been recorded for the 6-month period ending December 31.

(b) Accrued wages amounted to $500 as of December 31.

(c) Cleaning supplies amounting to $300 were purchased during the year. An inventory taken on December 31 showed that there were $40 of supplies on hand.

(d) Three contracts for a 6-month period (November 1, 19_A, to April 30, 19_B) were received on November 1. Payment accompanied the contracts and $600 was credited to the Unearned Revenue account.

(e) Cleaning revenue earned but not received or paid as of December 31 amounted to $200.

(f) The garage behind the business was rented for $75 per month. Rent for December has not been received or recorded as of December 31.

Required

Prepare the adjusting entries required on December 31, 19_B.

4-6. Jessie Carroll opened the Cut & Curl beauty salon on January 10, 19_C. She adjusts her books on December 31, the end of her accounting period.

Adjustment data for the beauty salon appears below.

(*a*) During 19_C, beauty supplies were purchased for $2,700 cash. As of December 31, 19_C, there were $400 of supplies on hand.

(*b*) Accrued wages amounted to $800 on December 31.

(*c*) Carroll rented space in her beauty salon to a manicurist for $100 per month. Payment for December has not been received or recorded.

(*d*) One day each week, Carroll performs beauty services for the senior citizens residing at the Sunset Retirement Village. Payment of $100 was received on December 15 for the period of December 15, 19_C, to January 15, 19_D. Unearned Revenue was credited for the $100 payment received on December 15. One-half of the payment was earned as of December 31.

(*e*) Equipment costing $10,000 with an 8-year life and a $2,000 salvage value was purchased on January 11. Depreciate the equipment for the 1-year period ending December 31.

Required

Prepare the adjusting entries required on December 31, 19_C.

Journalizing and Posting Revenue and Expense Adjustments

4-7. Selected account balances on the unadjusted trial balance for Evers Service station as of December 31, 19_C, appear below:

Accounts Receivable	$ 600
Prepaid Insurance	180
Supplies	440
Equipment	1,800
Accumulated Depreciation/Equipment	200
Accounts Payable	700
Unearned Service Revenue	800
Service Revenue	14,300
Wages Expense	4,050
Telephone Expense	600
Miscellaneous Expense	340

Required

(*a*) Journalize the following adjusting entries as of December 31, 19_C, using the related information above.

1. Services earned but not billed, $150.
2. The Prepaid Insurance account represents a 1-year policy that started on October 1, 19_C.
3. Supplies on hand, $130.
4. Depreciation for the equipment amounted to $400.
5. Accrued wages amounted to $305.

      6. One-half of unearned service revenue has been earned.

      7. Telephone bill received on December 31, 19_C, for $165 has not been recorded or paid.

   (b) Post the adjusting entries in the ledger accounts in the workbook accompanying the text.

4-8. The following year-end balances appeared in the records for Cleaner Homes as of December 31, 19_B:

Prepaid Insurance	$ 320
Prepaid Rent	1,200
Cleaning Supplies	900
Equipment	2,000
Accumulated Depreciation/Equipment	200
Unearned Cleaning Revenue	9,000
Cleaning Revenue	12,600
Salaries & Wages Expense	3,900
Gas & Oil Expense	1,100
Miscellaneous Expense	340

Required

(a) Journalize the adjusting entries required for December 31, 19_B, using the following data.

    1. Prepaid insurance represents a 2-year policy purchased on October 1, 19_B.

    2. Prepaid rent was paid on July 1, 19_B, for 8 months rent in advance.

    3. An inventory of cleaning supplies showed $50 on hand on December 31, 19_B.

    4. Depreciation on the equipment amounts to $500 per year.

    5. A customer paid for 3 months service in advance on November 1, 19_B, and the Unearned Cleaning Revenue account was credited when payment was received.

    6. Salaries and wages accrued amount to $1,200 as of December 31, 19_B.

(b) Post the adjusting entries in the ledger accounts in the workbook accompanying the text.

4-9. Listed below is an unadjusted trial balance for Maxey Paint Company as of December 31, 19_B.

MAXEY PAINT COMPANY
TRIAL BALANCE
December 31, 19_B

Cash	$ 8,300
Accounts Receivable	4,000
Prepaid Insurance	800
Supplies on Hand	600
Equipment	12,000

Accumulated Depreciation/Equipment		$ 1,000
Accounts Payable		1,000
Unearned Paint Revenue		600
Jane Maxey, Capital		21,000
Jane Maxey, Drawing	9,000	
Paint Revenue		12,000
Wages Expense	500	
Miscellaneous Expense	400	

Required

(a) Open general ledger accounts for 100 cash; 110 Accounts Receivable; 112 Prepaid Insurance; 114 Supplies on Hand; 120 Equipment; 128 Accumulated Depreciation/Equipment; 210 Accounts Payable; 212 Unearned Paint Revenue; 214 Wages Payable; 330 Jane Maxey, Capital; 338 Jane Maxey, Drawings; 440 Paint Revenue; 510 Wages Expense; 512 Insurance Expense; 514 Supplies Expense; 518 Depreciation Expense/Equipment; and 520 Miscellaneous Expense. Enter the balances shown in the trial balance; use December 31 as the date, write the word "balance" in the Explanation column, and put a check mark (✔) in the Ref. column.

(b) Journalize and post the adjusting entries using the following data and the related information in the unadjusted trial balance.
1. Paint for $800 had been sold to customers who have not yet been billed. Debit the Accounts Receivable account.
2. The balance in the Prepaid Insurance account represents the amount paid for a 2-year policy that started on July 1, 19_B.
3. The supplies on hand on December 31, 19_B, amounted to $120.
4. The equipment is estimated to last 6 years and was purchased on July 1, 19_A. The depreciation for 19_A has been recorded. Record the depreciation for 19_B.
5. Wages expense amounts to $500 for a 5-day week, and the employees are paid every Friday; December 31, 19_B, falls on a Monday. Record the wages accrued for Monday, December 31, 19_B.
6. Two-thirds of the Unearned Paint Revenue is earned by December 31, 19_B.

Preparation of an Adjusted Trial Balance

4-10. Prepare an adjusted trial balance for the Maxey Paint Company as of December 31, 19_B, using the general ledger completed in Problem 4-9.

4-11. The account balances before adjustments for Bell Snack Shop on December 31, 19_C, are shown below:

Cash	$ 2,000
Accounts Receivable	1,400
Restaurant Supplies	6,400
Prepaid Insurance	200

Restaurant Equipment	4,000
Accounts Payable	1,900
Notes Payable	2,000
Jack Bell, Capital	4,580
Jack Bell, Drawing	7,200
Restaurant Revenue	25,420
Wages Expense	8,000
Rent Expense	4,000
Utilities Expense	480
Miscellaneous Expense	220

The following adjustments are required:
1. Insurance expired, $100.
2. Restaurant supplies used, $4,400.
3. Depreciation, $480.
4. Accrued wages, $240.
5. Accrued interest on notes payable, $35.

Required

Prepare an adjusted trial balance as of December 31, 19_C. (*Hint:* Don't forget to consider adjustments.)

Review Problem Involving Revenue and Expense Adjustments Plus the Preparation of an Adjusted Trial Balance

4-12. The P & B Nursery School adjusts their books on December 31, the end of their accounting period.

Required

(*a*) Open general ledger accounts and record the December 31 balances for the following accounts: 110 Cash, $9,000; 112 Prepaid Insurance, $360; 113 Supplies, $210; 130 Playground Equipment, $4,400; 138 Accumulated Depreciation/Playground Equipment, $400; 200 Accounts Payable, $200; 210 Wages Payable; 212 Unearned Tuition Revenue, $300; 300 J. Bek, Capital, $5,300; 318 J. Bek, Drawing, $8,430; 400 Tuition Revenue, $28,000; 512 Insurance Expense; 513 Supplies Expense; 520 Wages Expense, $11,800; and 538 Depreciation Expense/Playground Equipment.

(*b*) Journalize and post the adjusting entries required for the following information on December 31, 19_D.
  1. The balance in the Prepaid Insurance account represents the amount paid on March 2 of the current year for a 3-year insurance policy.
  2. The balance in the Unearned Tuition Revenue account represents tuition paid in advance on December 15, 19_D, for a 1-month period (December 15, 19_D, to January 15, 19_E).
  3. The nursery school has two part-time employees who are paid $100

each every Friday for a 5-day, 20-hour week. The employees were paid on Friday, December 28. Wages are accrued for Monday, December 31.

4. An inventory of supplies disclosed $80 of supplies on hand.
5. Depreciation amounted to $400 per year on the playground equipment purchased 2 years ago.

(*c*) Prepare an adjusted trial balance as of December 31, 19_D.

Accounting Cycle and Financial Statements

CHAPTER 17

After completing this chapter, you should be able to:

1. **Define, prepare, and complete the six steps of a work sheet**

2. **Journalize and post the adjusting and closing entries from the work sheet**

3. **Prepare the income statement and balance sheet in good form from the information in the work sheet**

4. **Prepare a post-closing trial balance and explain why revenue, expense, and owner's drawing accounts are not shown on the statement**

5. **State the seven steps of the complete accounting cycle**

One of the main objectives of an accounting system is to provide owners and managers with current financial information for appraising the past performance of a business and for evaluating the future potential of the company. This information is presented to management in the financial statements at the end of each fiscal period. Before the statements can be prepared, the accountant must do a considerable amount of work gathering all the facts necessary to journalize and post the adjusting and closing entries. All the year-end procedures must be completed quickly if the financial information reported is to be timely and reliable. Therefore, a device is needed that will allow the accountant to summarize the activities at the end of the fiscal period, prepare the financial statements promptly, and complete the mechanics of journalizing and posting the adjusting and closing entries.

WORK SHEET

The device or method used by the accountant for summarizing the activities at the end of the fiscal period is called a *work sheet.* Completing the work sheet gives the accountant an opportunity to check the accuracy of the accounting records, make any necessary corrections, complete the adjustments, and arrange the information for the preparation of financial statements.

The work sheet is a 10-column form prepared in pencil so any error may be easily corrected. It is designed to allow for an orderly progression of events and a smooth work flow to bring together all the information needed to complete the accounting cycle.

WORK SHEET PREPARATION

The most common work sheet is the 10-column form illustrated in Figure 5-1 for the Mop-It Janitorial Service. Note that the heading includes the

FIGURE 5-1
Steps 1 and 2

MOP-IT JANITORIAL SERVICE
WORK SHEET
For the Month Ended June 30, 19___

Account Title	Trial Balance Dr	Trial Balance Cr	Adjustments Dr	Adjustments Cr	Adjusted Trial Balance Dr	Adjusted Trial Balance Cr	Income Statement Dr	Income Statement Cr	Balance Sheet Dr	Balance Sheet Cr
Cash	4,500									
Accounts Receivable	1,300									
Prepaid Insurance	700									
Supplies	450									
Truck	6,800									
Acc. Dep./Truck		500								
Equipment	3,000									
Acc. Dep./Equip.		850								
Notes Payable		1,000								
Accounts Payable		900								
Unearned Janitor Fees		2,400								
T. Mop, Capital		10,700								
T. Mop, Drawing	800									
Janitor Fees Earned		3,800								
Wages Expense	1,500									
Rent Expense	500									
Utilities Expense	200									
Vehicle Expense	400									
	20,150	20,150								

name of the business, the name of the document (work sheet), and the date. The date shows the period of time covered by the report, which is the same as the heading on the income statement. The 10 columns of the work sheet consist of five pairs of debit and credit columns. In the first pair of columns, the trial balance is entered, and changes or adjustments to these account balances are made in the Adjustment columns. The balances in the first two pairs of columns are combined, where necessary, and carried over to the Adjusted Trial Balance columns. These columns contain all the information needed for the Income Statement and Balance Sheet columns.

There are six steps for completing a work sheet.

Step 1. Enter the proper heading on the work sheet and the headings for each of the five pairs of columns: Trial Balance, Adjustments, Adjusted Trial Balance, Income Statement, and Balance Sheet. The work sheet shown in Figure 5-1, is for the month ended June 30, 19__.

Step 2. Enter the account titles and amounts in the Trial Balance columns. Dollar signs are not required on a work sheet. The information for the Trial Balance columns of the work sheet is obtained from the general ledger. Starting with the asset accounts in the general ledger, enter each account *with a balance* in the Trial Balance columns. Draw a single line under the debit and credit columns and total both columns. The debit column total should be equal to the credit column total. Double-underline these totals as shown in Figure 5-1.

Step 3. Enter the necessary changes or adjustments to the original account balances in the Adjustments columns of the 10-column work sheet to bring these balances up to date. The adjustments for Mop-It Janitorial Service are listed below:

(*a*) The $700 balance in the Prepaid Insurance account represents the amount paid on January 2 for a 1-year insurance policy. One month's insurance amounting to $100 ($1,200 × $^{1}/_{12}$) has expired for the month of June. An adjustment was made to record the insurance expense for June, which reduces the amount of unexpired insurance in the asset account. The adjustment required a debit to the Insurance Expense and a credit to the Prepaid Insurance account for $100. Since the Insurance Expense account did not appear in the beginning Trial Balance, it was added on the next free line below the Trial Balance totals. Whenever necessary, add any additional accounts and amounts on the first available line below the Trial Balance total to complete the adjustments as shown in the partial work sheet on page 115.

Each adjusting entry has been referenced by placing a letter next to the amount. This makes it possible to match the corre-

MOP-IT JANITORIAL SERVICE
WORK SHEET
For the Month Ended June 30, 19__

Account Title	Trial Balance		Adjustments	
	Dr	Cr	Dr	Cr
Cash	4,500			
Accounts Receivable	1,300			
Prepaid Insurance	700			(a) 100
Vehicle Expense	400			
Totals	20,100	20,100		
Insurance Expense			(a) 100	

sponding debit and credit for each entry. An optional brief explanation may be noted at the bottom of the work sheet for each adjustment that is entered in the Adjustments column.

(b) On June 30, Mr. Mop took an inventory of the supplies on hand and determined that $300 had been used during the month, because there were $150 of supplies on hand. The $450 balance in the Trial Balance columns was decreased to show the amount used in June. The Supplies Expense account was debited and the Supplies account was credited for $300. After the adjustment, the Adjusted Trial Balance columns will show a balance of $150 as shown in the partial work sheet shown below. This

MOP-IT JANITORIAL SERVICE
WORK SHEET
For the Month Ended June 30, 19__

Account Title	Trial Balance		Adjustments	
	Dr	Cr	Dr	Cr
Cash	4,500			
Accounts Receivable	1,300			
Prepaid Insurance	700			(a) 100
Supplies	450			(b) 300
Vehicle Expense	700			
Totals	20,100	20,100		
Insurance Expense			(a) 100	
Supplies Expense			(b) 300	

amount represents the balance in the Supplies account on June 30.

(c) The monthly depreciation is $100 for the truck and $50 for the equipment. The adjustment for depreciation on the truck required the Depreciation Expense/Truck account to be debited and the Accumulated Depreciation/Truck account to be credited for $100. The adjustment for depreciation on the equipment required the Depreciation Expense/Equipment account to be debited and the Accumulated Depreciation/Equipment account to be credited for $50. The Depreciation Expense/Truck and Depreciation Expense/Equipment accounts did not appear in the beginning Trial Balance columns because they had a zero balance, and they were written on the next free line of the work sheet as shown below:

MOP-IT JANITORIAL SERVICE
WORK SHEET
For the Month Ended June 30, 19__

Account Title	Trial Balance		Adjustments	
	Dr	Cr	Dr	Cr
Cash	4,500			
Accounts Receivable	1,300			
Prepaid Insurance	700			(a) 100
Supplies	450			(b) 300
Truck	6,800			
Accumulated Depreciation/Truck		500		(c) 100
Equipment	3,000			
Accumulated Depreciation/Equipment		850		(c) 50
Vehicle Expense	400			
Totals	20,100	20,100		
Insurance Expense			(a) 100	
Supplies Expense			(b) 300	
Depreciation Expense/Truck			(c) 100	
Depreciation Expense/Equipment			(c) 50	

(d) Last month Mr. Mop borrowed $1,000 from his bank for 2 months with interest at 6 percent. One month's interest of $5 has accrued. The adjustment for the accrued interest on the note required the Interest Expense account to be debited and the Interest Payable account to be credited for $5. Neither of these accounts appeared in the beginning Trial Balance columns, and they were written on the next free line of the work sheet as shown below:

MOP-IT JANITORIAL SERVICE
WORK SHEET
For the Month Ended June 30, 19___

Account Title	Trial Balance Dr	Trial Balance Cr	Adjustments Dr	Adjustments Cr
Cash	4,500			
Accounts Receivable	1,300			
Prepaid Insurance	700			(a) 100
Supplies	450			(b) 300
Truck	6,800			
Accumulated Depreciation/Truck		500		(c) 100
Equipment	3,000			
Accumulated Depreciation/Equipment		850		(c) 50
Vehicle Expense	400			
Totals	20,150	20,150		
Insurance Expense			(a) 100	
Supplies Expense			(b) 300	
Depreciation Expense/Truck			(c) 100	
Depreciation Expense/Equipment			(c) 50	
Interest Expense			(d) 5	
Interest Payable				(d) 5

(e) The company received $2,400 in advance from customers for janitorial services. This amount is represented as a credit in the Unearned Janitor Fees account. During June, $1,200 of the Unearned Janitor Fees was earned requiring a debit to this account and a credit to the Janitor Fees Earned account. This adjustment shows the amount of revenue that was earned in June. Since both these accounts appeared in the beginning Trial Balance, it was not necessary to add any new accounts as shown in the work sheet on page 118.

(f) Wages earned by the helper but not paid by June 30 amounted to $125. The Wages Expense and Wages Payable accounts were increased to show the additional expense and liability for June. Wages Expense was debited and Wages Payable was credited for $125. The Wages Payable account was added to the next

MOP-IT JANITORIAL SERVICE
WORK SHEET
For the Month Ended June 30, 19___

Account Title	Trial Balance		Adjustments	
	Dr	Cr	Dr	Cr
Cash	4,500			
Accounts Receivable	1,300			
Prepaid Insurance	700			(a) 100
Supplies	450			(b) 300
Truck	6,800			
Accumulated Depreciation/Truck		500		(c) 100
Equipment	3,000			
Accumulated Depreciation/Equipment		850		(c) 50
Notes Payable		1,000		
Accounts Payable		900		
Unearned Janitor Fees		2,400	(e) 1,200	
Janitor Fees Earned		3,800		(e) 1,200

free line because it did not appear in the beginning Trial Balance columns (shown on page 119). After all the adjustments are properly entered on the work sheet, draw a single line under the debit and credit columns. Total both columns to check that the debit column total equals the credit column total, and then double-underline these totals as shown in Figure 5-2.

Step 4. Combine the figure in the Adjustments columns with the figures in the Trial Balance columns and enter the result in the Adjusted Trial Balance. Start with the first account on the work sheet and continue, one line at a time, until each amount has been entered in the Adjusted Trial Balance columns. A ruler is most helpful in this work.

For example, the Trial Balance figure for the Prepaid Insurance account has a $700 debit, and a $100 credit appears in the Adjustments column. It is necessary to subtract the $100 credit from the $700 debit to obtain the Adjusted Trial Balance amount of $600 ($700 − $100), as shown in the partial work sheet (*a*) on p. 120.

A little farther down on the work sheet, the Wages Expense account has a debit of $1,500 and a $125 debit in the Adjustments column. The two debits are added to arrive at the Adjusted Trial Balance amount of $1,625 ($1,500 + $125), as shown in the partial work sheet (*b*) on p. 120.

FIGURE 5-2
Step 3

MOP-IT JANITORIAL SERVICE
WORK SHEET
For the Month Ended June 30, 19___

Account Title	Trial Balance Dr	Trial Balance Cr	Adjustments Dr	Adjustments Cr	Adjusted Trial Balance Dr	Adjusted Trial Balance Cr	Income Statement Dr	Income Statement Cr	Balance Sheet Dr	Balance Sheet Cr
Cash	4,500									
Accounts Receivable	1,300									
Prepaid Insurance	700			(a) 100						
Supplies	450			(b) 300						
Truck	6,800									
Acc. Dep./Truck		500		(c) 100						
Equipment	3,000									
Acc. Dep./Equip.		850		(c) 50						
Notes Payable		1,000								
Accounts Payable		900								
Unearned Janitor Fees		2,400	(e) 1,200							
T. Mop, Capital		10,700								
T. Mop, Drawing	800									
Janitor Fees Earned		3,800		(e) 1,200						
Wages Expense	1,500		(f) 125							
Rent Expense	500									
Utilities Expense	200									
Vehicle Expense	400									
Totals	20,150	20,150								
Insurance Expense			(a) 100							
Supplies Expense			(b) 300							
Depreciation Expense/Truck			(c) 100							
Depreciation Expense/Equip.			(c) 50							
Interest Expense			(d) 5							
Interest Payable				(d) 5						
Wages Payable				(f) 125						
Totals			1,880	1,880						

(a)

MOP-IT JANITORIAL SERVICE
WORK SHEET
For the Month Ended June 30, 19__

Account Title	Trial Balance		Adjustments		Adjusted Trial Balance	
	Dr	Cr	Dr	Cr	Dr	Cr
Cash	4,500				4,500	
Accounts Receivable	1,300				1,300	
Prepaid Insurance	700			(a) 100	600	
Insurance Expense			(a) 100		100	

(b)

MOP-IT JANITORIAL SERVICE
WORK SHEET
For the Month Ended June 30, 19__

Account Title	Trial Balance		Adjustments		Adjusted Trial Balance	
	Dr	Cr	Dr	Cr	Dr	Cr
Wages Expense	1,500		(f) 125		1,625	
Wages Payable				(f) 125		125

The accounts that have not been adjusted are transferred to the Adjusted Trial Balance columns with the amounts that appeared in the beginning Trial Balance. After completing the Adjusted Trial Balance, draw a single line under the debit and credit columns. Add the two columns to check the equality of the debit and credit column totals and double-underline both these columns as shown in Figure 5-3.

Step 5. Extend all the amounts in the Adjusted Trial Balance to either the Income Statement or Balance Sheet columns. The first accounts are assets, liabilities, and owner's equity, which are transferred to the Balance Sheet columns. The next accounts, the revenue and expenses, are transferred to the Income Statement columns. Notice that the last two accounts on the work sheet, Interest Payable and Wages Payable, are liabilities that were extended to the Balance Sheet credit column. Begin with the first account on the work sheet

FIGURE 5-3

Step 4

MOP-IT JANITORIAL SERVICE
WORK SHEET
For the Month Ended June 30, 19__

Account Title	Trial Balance Dr	Trial Balance Cr	Adjustments Dr	Adjustments Cr	Adjusted Trial Balance Dr	Adjusted Trial Balance Cr	Income Statement Dr	Income Statement Cr	Balance Sheet Dr	Balance Sheet Cr
Cash	4,500				4,500					
Accounts Receivable	1,300				1,300					
Prepaid Insurance	700			(a) 100	600					
Supplies	450			(b) 300	150					
Truck	6,800				6,800					
Acc. Dep./Truck		500		(c) 100		600				
Equipment	3,000				3,000					
Acc. Dep./Equip.		850		(c) 50		900				
Notes Payable		1,000				1,000				
Accounts Payable		900				900				
Unearned Janitor Fees		2,400	(e) 1,200			1,200				
T. Mop, Capital		10,700				10,700				
T. Mop, Drawing	800				800					
Janitor Fees Earned		3,800		(e) 1,200		5,000				
Wages Expense	1,500		(f) 125		1,625					
Rent Expense	500				500					
Utilities Expense	200				200					
Vehicle Expense	400				400					
Totals	20,150	20,150								
Insurance Expense			(a) 100		100					
Supplies Expense			(b) 300		300					
Depreciation Expense/Truck			(c) 100		100					
Depreciation Expense/Equip.			(c) 50		50					
Interest Expense			(d) 5		5					
Interest Payable				(d) 5		5				
Wages Payable				(f) 125		125				
Totals			1,880	1,880	20,430	20,430				

FIGURE 5-4

MOP-IT JANITORIAL SERVICE
WORK SHEET
For the Month Ended June 30, 19___

Account Title	Trial Balance Dr	Trial Balance Cr	Adjustments Dr	Adjustments Cr	Adjusted Trial Balance Dr	Adjusted Trial Balance Cr	Income Statement Dr	Income Statement Cr	Balance Sheet Dr	Balance Sheet Cr
Cash	4,500				4,500				4,500	
Accounts Receivable	1,300				1,300				1,300	
Prepaid Insurance	700			(a) 100	600				600	
Supplies	450			(b) 300	150				150	
Truck	6,800				6,800				6,800	
Acc. Dep./Truck		500		(c) 100		600				600
Equipment	3,000				3,000				3,000	
Acc. Dep./Equip.		850		(c) 50		900				900
Notes Payable		1,000				1,000				1,000
Accounts Payable		900				900				900
Unearned Janitor Fees		2,400	(e) 1,200			1,200				1,200
T. Mop, Capital		10,700				10,700				10,700
T. Mop, Drawing	800				800				800	
Janitor Fees Earned		3,800		(e) 1,200		5,000		5,000		
Wages Expense	1,500		(f) 125		1,625		1,625			
Rent Expense	500				500		500			
Utilities Expense	200				200		200			
Vehicle Expense	400				400		400			
Totals	20,150	20,150								
Insurance Expense			(a) 100		100		100			
Supplies Expense			(b) 300		300		300			
Depreciation Expense/Truck			(c) 100		100		100			
Depreciation Expense/Equip.			(c) 50		50		50			
Interest Expense			(d) 5		5		5			
Interest Payable				(d) 5		5				5
Wages Payable				(f) 125		125				125
Totals			1,880	1,880	20,430	20,430	3,280	5,000	17,150	15,430

and continue one line at a time. To avoid making any errors, do not skip around. Make sure that each amount in the Adjusted Trial Balance columns is carried over to its proper place in *only one of the last four columns* (Income Statement and Balance Sheet) as shown in Figure 5-4.

Step 6. Draw a single line under the debit and credit columns of the Income Statement and Balance Sheet and add both columns to obtain a subtotal. Calculate the net income or loss for the period by obtaining the "difference" between the subtotal of debit and credit columns in the Income Statement. The difference for the Mop-It Janitorial Service amounts to a debit of $1,720 ($5,000 − $3,280) and is entered in the debit column as a *balancing figure*. The $1,720 difference between the Income Statement column subtotals is transferred to the credit column of the Balance Sheet to show the increase to owner's equity for the net income earned in June. Enter any difference between the debits and credits of the Income Statement columns in the column with the smaller total.

When the difference requires an amount to be entered in the debit column, net income has been earned for the period. The words "net income" were written in the account title column on the same horizontal line as the $1,720 amount. Draw a single line across the debit and credit columns (below the net income figure) of the Income Statement and Balance Sheet. Total the last four columns. The net income was a balancing figure, so the totals of the debits and credits of these last four columns should be equal. Double-underline these totals. If the totals of the Balance Sheet columns are equal, the work sheet is in balance and complete as shown in the partial work sheet, Figure 5-5.

Note: When the difference between the debits and credits of the Income Statement columns requires an amount to be entered in the credit column, a net loss has been incurred for the period. The words "net loss" would be written in the account title column.

Summary of Work Sheet Preparation

The six steps for completing a work sheet are summarized below:

Six steps in work sheet preparation

1. Enter the proper headings on the work sheet and the heading for each of the five pairs of columns: Trial Balance, Adjustments, Adjusted Trial Balance, Income Statement, and Balance Sheet.
2. Enter the account titles and amounts in the Trial Balance columns and total the debits and credits.
3. Enter the necessary changes or adjustments to the original account balances in the Adjustments columns to bring these balances up to date (see Figure 5-2 for letter references to actual entries).
4. Combine the figure in the Adjustments columns with the figure in the

FIGURE 5-5
Step 6

MOP-IT JANITORIAL SERVICE
WORK SHEET
For the Month Ended June 30, 19___

Account Title	Income Statement Dr	Income Statement Cr	Balance Sheet Dr	Balance Sheet Cr
Cash			4,500	
Accounts Receivable			1,300	
Prepaid Insurance			600	
Supplies			150	
Truck			6,800	
Accumulated Dep./Truck				600
Equipment			3,000	
Accumulated Dep./Equip.				900
Notes Payable				1,000
Accounts Payable				900
Unearned Janitor Fees				1,200
T. Mop, Capital				10,700
T. Mop, Drawing			800	
Janitor Fees Earned		5,000		
Wages Expense	1,625			
Rent Expense	500			
Utilities Expense	200			
Vehicle Expense	400			
Totals				
Insurance Expense	100			
Supplies Expense	300			
Depreciation Expense/Truck	100			
Depreciation Expense/Equip.	50			
Interest Expense	5			
Interest Payable				5
Wages Payable				125
Totals	3,280	5,000	17,150	15,430
Net Income	1,720			1,720
Totals	5,000	5,000	17,150	17,150

- Single line under debit and credit columns.
- Subtotal debit and credit columns.
- Enter difference in columns with smaller subtotals and label net income or net loss.
- Balance debit and credit columns.
- Double lines under debit and credit columns.

Trial Balance columns and enter the result in the Adjusted Trial Balance columns.

5. Extend all the amounts in the Adjusted Trial Balance either to the Income Statement or Balance Sheet columns. Assets, Liabilities, and Owner's Equity are transferred to the Balance Sheet columns; Revenue and Expenses are transferred to the Income Statement columns.

6. Draw a single line under the debit and credit columns of the Income Statement and Balance Sheet and obtain a subtotal of the columns. Calculate the net income or net loss and enter the amount in the columns

FIGURE 5-6

MOP-IT JANITORIAL SERVICE
WORK SHEET
For the Month Ended June 30, 19___

Account Title	Trial Balance Dr	Trial Balance Cr	Adjustments Dr	Adjustments Cr	Adjusted Trial Balance Dr	Adjusted Trial Balance Cr	Income Statement Dr	Income Statement Cr	Balance Sheet Dr	Balance Sheet Cr
Cash	4,500				4,500				4,500	
Accounts Receivable	1,300				1,300				1,300	
Prepaid Insurance	700			(a) 100	600				600	
Supplies	450			(b) 300	150				150	
Truck	6,800				6,800				6,800	
Acc. Dep./Truck		500		(c) 100		600				600
Equipment	3,000				3,000				3,000	
Acc. Dep./Equip.		850		(c) 50		900				900
Notes Payable		1,000				1,000				1,000
Accounts Payable		900				900				900
Unearned Janitor Fees		2,400	(e) 1,200			1,200				1,200
T. Mop, Capital		10,700				10,700				10,700
T. Mop, Drawing	800				800				800	
Janitor Fees Earned		3,800		(e) 1,200		5,000		5,000		
Wages Expense	1,500		(f) 125		1,625		1,625			
Rent Expense	500				500		500			
Utilities Expense	200				200		200			
Vehicle Expense	400				400		400			
Totals	20,150	20,150								
Insurance Expense			(a) 100		100		100			
Supplies Expense			(b) 300		300		300			
Depreciation Expense/Truck			(c) 100		100		100			
Depreciation Expense/Equip.			(c) 50		50		50			
Interest Expense			(d) 5		5		5			
Interest Payable				(d) 5		5				5
Wages Payable				(f) 125		125				125
Totals			1,880	1,880	20,430	20,430	3,280	5,000	17,150	15,430
Net Income							1,720			1,720
Totals							5,000	5,000	17,150	17,150

Steps 1 & 2

Step 3

Step 4

Step 5

Steps 5 & 6

Step 6

with the smaller totals; write the words *net income* or *net loss* on the horizontal line in the account title column. Total the four columns and double underline.

Figure 5-6 shows a completed work sheet.

RECORDING ADJUSTING ENTRIES FROM WORK SHEET

When the work sheet is completed, the adjusting entries are journalized and posted to the general ledger accounts. The information for the adjustments is obtained from the Adjustments columns on the work sheet. Journalize each adjustment that appears on the work sheet beginning with item (a); use the data on the work sheet. The adjusting entries for the Mop-It Janitorial Service appear below:

19__				
June	30	Insurance Expense	100	
		Prepaid Insurance		100
		To record insurance expense for June		
	30	Supplies Expense	300	
		Supplies		300
		To record supplies used for June.		
	30	Depreciation Expense/Truck	100	
		Depreciation Expense/Equipment	50	
		Accumulated Depreciation/Truck		100
		Accumulated Depreciation/ Equipment		50
		To record depreciation for June.		
	30	Interest Expense	5	
		Interest Payable		5
		To record interest accrued on note payable for June.		
	30	Unearned Janitor Fees	1,200	
		Janitor Fees Earned		1,200
		To reduce the liability account for the amount of fees earned during June.		
	30	Wages Expense	125	
		Wages Payable		125
		To record wages accrued for June.		

General ledger T accounts after adjustments   The general ledger for the Mop-It Janitorial Service after the adjusting entries are posted is shown below:

Cash

19__ June	1		4,500		4,500

Accounts Receivable

19__ June	1		1,300		1,300

Prepaid Insurance

19__ June	1		700		700
	30	Adj.		100	600

Supplies

19__ June	1		450		450
	30	Adj.		300	150

Truck

19__ June	1		6,800		6,800

Accumulated Depreciation/Truck

19__ June	1			500	500
	30	Adj.		100	600

Equipment

19__ June	1		3,000		3,000

Accumulated Depreciation/Equipment

19__ June	1			850	850
	30	Adj.		50	900

Notes Payable

19__ June	30	Balance		1,000	1,000

Accounts Payable

19__ June	30	Balance		900	900

Wages Payable

19__ June	30	Adj.		125	125

Unearned Janitor Fees

19__ June	30	Balance		2,400	2,400
	30	Adj.	1,200		1,200

Interest Payable

19__ June	30	Adj.		5	5

T. Mop, Capital

19__ June	30	Balance		10,700	10,700

T. Mop, Drawing

19__ June	30	Balance	800		800

Janitor Fees Earned

19__ June	30	Balance		3,800	3,800
	30	Adj.		1,200	5,000

Wages Expense

19__					
June	30	Balance	1,500		1,500
	30	Adj.	125		1,625

Rent Expense

19__					
June	30	Balance	500		500

Utilities Expense

19__					
June	30	Balance	200		200

Vehicle Expense

19__					
June	30	Balance	400		400

Insurance Expense

19__					
June	30	Adj.	100		100

Supplies Expense

19__					
June	30	Adj.	300		300

Depreciation Expense/Truck

19__					
June	30	Adj.	100		100

Depreciation Expense/Equipment

19__					
June	30	Adj.	50		50

Interest Expense

19__					
June	30	Adj.	5		5

After the adjusting entries have been journalized and posted, the balances in the general ledger accounts should agree with the amounts shown in the Adjusted Trial Balance columns of the work sheet.

RECORDING CLOSING ENTRIES FROM WORK SHEET

After recording adjusting entries, the next step in the accounting cycle is closing the revenue, expense, and owner's drawing accounts. Closing the accounts simply means that all temporary accounts (revenue, expense, and owner's drawing) are reduced to a zero balance by transferring the amounts to the owner's capital account. Closing these accounts is necessary to accumulate the revenues, expenses, and owner's drawing for only one period and to show the year-end balance of the owner's capital account on the balance sheet.

Because the revenue, expense, and owner's drawing accounts are closed, they are called *temporary* or *nominal accounts*. The assets, liabilities, and owner's capital accounts are not closed and are called the *permanent* or *real accounts*.

Revenue and expense accounts are closed by transferring their balances to a temporary closing account called *Income Summary* which is used only at the end of the period for the purpose of recording the closing entries. The Income Summary account is used for closing revenue and expense accounts. After the revenue and expense account balances have been transferred to the Income Summary account, the balance in this account represents the net income or loss for the period. This balance is transferred to the owner's capital account, resulting in a zero balance in the Income Summary account. The owner's drawing account balance is the last account closed, and this account is closed by transferring the balance to the capital account. The owner's capital account is used for closing the Income Summary and owner's drawing accounts.

The closing process increases the owner's capital account by the amount of net income for the period. The capital account is decreased for the amount of cash or other assets taken out of the business by the owner for personal use, or if the business incurred a loss for the period.

The procedures for the four closing entries are shown below for the Mop-It Janitorial Service.

1. *Closing the Revenue Accounts.* Debit the revenue accounts and credit the amount to the Income Summary account (total of the Income Statement credit column of work sheet).

19__				
June	30	Janitor Fees Earned	5,000	
		Income Summary		5,000
		To close the revenue account.		

2. *Closing the Expense Accounts.* Debit the Income Summary account for the total of all the expenses (subtotal appearing in Income Statement debit column of work sheet), and credit all the individual expense accounts.

19__				
June	30	Income Summary	3,280	
		Wages Expense		1,625
		Rent Expense		500
		Utilities Expense		200
		Vehicle Expense		400
		Insurance Expense		100
		Supplies Expense		300
		Depreciation Expense/Truck		100
		Depreciation Expense/Equipment		50
		Interest Expense		5
		To close the expense accounts.		

3. *Closing the Income Summary Account.* Debit the Income Summary account for the amount of net income (revenue minus expenses; amount appearing after subtotal shown in Income Statement debit column of work sheet) and credit the owner's capital account. If a net loss was incurred for the period, debit the capital account and credit the Income Summary account.

19__				
June	30	Income Summary	1,720	
		T. Mop, Capital		1,720
		To close income summary and		
		record net income into capital.		

4. *Closing the Owner's Drawing Account.* Debit the capital account and credit the owner's drawing for the balance in the drawing account (amount appearing in Balance Sheet debit column of work sheet).

19__				
June	30	T. Mop, Capital	800	
		T. Mop, Drawing		800
		To close the drawing account.		

General ledger T accounts after closing entries

After the closing entries are posted, the general ledger accounts for capital, drawing, revenue, expenses, and income summary would appear as follows:

T. Mop, Capital

19__						
June	30	Balance			10,700	10,700
	30	Clos.			1,720	12,420
	30	Clos.	800			11,620

T. Mop, Drawing

19__						
June	30	Balance	800			800
	30	Clos.			800	–0–

Janitor Fees Earned

19__						
June	30	Balance			3,800	3,800
	30	Adj.			1,200	5,000
	30	Clos.	5,000			–0–

Wages Expense

19__						
June	30	Balance	1,500			1,500
	30	Adj.	125			1,625
	30	Clos.			1,625	–0–

Rent Expense

19__						
June	30	Balance	500			500
	30	Clos.			500	–0–

Utilities Expense

19__						
June	30	Balance	200			200
	30	Clos.			200	–0–

Vehicle Expense

19—					
June	30	Balance	400		400
	30	Clos.		400	–0–

Insurance Expense

19—					
June	30	Adj.	100		100
	30	Clos.		100	–0–

Supplies Expense

19—					
June	30	Adj.	300		300
	30	Clos.		300	–0–

Depreciation Expense/Truck

19—					
June	30	Adj.	100		100
	30	Clos.		100	–0–

Depreciation Expense/Equipment

19—					
June	30	Adj.	50		50
	30	Clos.		50	–0–

Interest Expense

19—					
June	30	Adj.	5		5
	30	Clos.		5	–0–

Income Summary

19—					
June	30	Rev.		5,000	5,000
	30	Exp.	3,280		1,720
	30	Net Inc.	1,720		–0–

FINANCIAL STATEMENTS

After completing the adjusting and closing entries, formal financial statements are prepared from the completed work sheet. The amounts that will appear on the income statement and the balance sheet are clearly identified in the work sheet columns. When preparing the income statement, arrange the accounts on the work sheet with their amounts by listing the revenue accounts first and the expense accounts last to arrive at the net income or loss for the period.

The format for an income statement consists of four steps:

Format for income statement

1. Statement heading
2. Revenue section
3. Expense section
4. Net income or net loss amount

Note carefully the format, arrangement of the headings, main classifications, subclassifications, placement of the figures, location of dollar signs, and single and double rulings for each statement illustrated for the Mop-It Janitorial Service.

The income statement for the Mop-It Janitorial Service for the month ended June 30 is illustrated below:

Income statement shows
revenue − expenses
= net income

MOP-IT JANITORIAL SERVICE
INCOME STATEMENT
For the Month Ended, June 30, 19__

Revenue		
Janitorial Fees Earned		$5,000
Operating Expenses		
Wages	$1,625	
Rent	500	
Utilities	200	
Gas and Oil	400	
Insurance	100	
Supplies	300	
Depreciation/Truck	100	
Depreciation/Equipment	50	
Interest	5	
Total Operating Expenses		3,280
Net Income		$1,720

When preparing a classified[1] balance sheet, arrange the accounts on the work sheet with their amounts by listing the asset accounts first, followed by the liability and owner's equity accounts. In the asset section, the current assets should be listed first followed by the plant assets; in the liability section, the current liabilities should be listed first followed by the long-term liabilities.

The format for a balance sheet usually consists of:

Format for balance sheet

1. Statement heading
2. Asset heading
3. Subclassifications of assets: current assets, long-term investments,[2] plant assets, and intangible assets[2]
4. Total assets
5. Liability heading
6. Subclassifications of liabilities: current and long-term liabilities
7. Total liabilities

[1] A classified balance sheet is a statement that lists each asset and liability account in their various groups—current assets, long-term investments, plant assets, intangible assets, current liabilities, and long-term liabilities—to present a more detailed balance sheet. These groups are discussed under the heading "Account Classifications" of this chapter.
[2] Long-term investments are investments in stocks, bonds, etc., that are expected to be held for more than 1 year and are not used in the business operations. Intangible assets have no physical substance; for example, goodwill and patents. Intangible assets is discussed in Chapter 11.

8. Owner's equity heading
9. Details of changes in owner's equity
10. Total liabilities and owner's equity

The balance sheet for Mop-It Janitorial Service as of June 30 is illustrated below.

MOP-IT JANITORIAL SERVICE
BALANCE SHEET
June 30, 19__

Assets

Current Assets:			
Cash		$ 4,500	
Accounts Receivable		1,300	
Prepaid Insurance		600	
Supplies		150	
Total Current Assets			$ 6,550
Plant Assets:			
Truck	$ 6,800		
Less: Accumulated Depreciation	600	$ 6,200	
Equipment	$ 3,000		
Less: Accumulated Depreciation	900	2,100	
Total Plant Assets			8,300
Total Assets			$14,850

Liabilities

Current Liabilities:		
Notes Payable	$ 1,000	
Accounts Payable	900	
Unearned Janitor Fees	1,200	
Wages Payable	125	
Interest Payable	5	
Total Current Liabilities		$ 3,230

Changes in owner's equity

Owner's Equity

T. Mop, Capital, June 1, 19__	$10,700		
Add: Net Income	1,720	$12,420	
Less: Drawings		800	
T. Mop, Capital, June 30, 19__			11,620
Total Liabilities and Owner's Equity			$14,850

As your study of accounting progresses, you will find that there are several variations or slightly different ways of presenting financial statement information. These different methods will be discussed in other chapters of this text.

ACCOUNT CLASSIFICATIONS

Four of the five basic classifications of accounts introduced in Chapter 1—assets, liabilities, revenue, and expenses—are divided into subclassifications. Subclassifications for assets and liabilities are explained below; revenue and expense subclassifications are explained in Chapter 6.

Assets are divided into four subclassifications:

1. *Current assets* are cash and other assets that can be easily converted into cash, or assets that are expected to be consumed or sold within 1 year or within the normal operating cycle. The order in which these assets are listed on the balance sheet is based on the ease with which they can be converted into cash. Examples include cash, *marketable securities* (temporary investments), accounts receivable, notes receivable, and prepaid expenses (supplies, insurance, and rent).

2. *Long-term investments*[3] are items of value purchased by the business for investment purposes. These assets are purchased by the company for the purpose of holding them for a period of more than 1 year and will not be used in the operations of the business. Examples include land held for future use, long-term investments in stocks or bonds, and pension funds.

3. *Plant assets* have a life span of more than 1 year. They are used in the operations of the business to help generate revenue and are not purchased for the purpose of resale. Several types of plant assets owned by a business are land, buildings, machinery and equipment, furniture and fixtures, and automobiles and trucks.

4. *Intangible assets*[4] have no physical dimension or structure and are represented by some type of document. Some examples of intangible assets are copyrights, franchises, goodwill, organization costs (costs of forming a corporation), and patents.

There are two subclassifications for liabilities.

1. *Current liabilities* represent amounts owed to creditors on a current basis which the business plans to pay within 1 year or within the normal operating cycle. These liabilities are usually paid with current assets. There is no established method for listing the liabilities on the balance sheet; however, usually Notes Payable is listed first followed by the Accounts Payable, and the other liabilities are listed in any convenient order. Examples of current liabilities are notes payable, accounts payable, taxes payable, wages payable, rent payable, and advances from customers.

[3] Long-term investments in stocks and bonds are discussed in Chapter 20 of *College Accounting: A Comprehensive Approach.*
[4] Intangible assets are discussed in Chapter 11.

2. *Long-term liabilities* represent amounts owed to creditors for debts that will be paid over a period of more than 1 year. Examples are notes payable (due in 3 years), mortgage payable (due in 15 years), and bonds payable (due in 20 years).

There are no subclassifications for owner's equity.

POST-CLOSING TRIAL BALANCE

After the closing entries have been journalized and posted, a final check is made on the accuracy of the ledger by preparing a *post-closing trial balance.* If the books have been closed properly, the post-closing trial balance should only list a balance for assets, liability, and owner's capital accounts. All the other accounts would not be shown because they should have a zero balance. Assuming everything has been closed properly, the post-closing trial balance for Mop-It Janitorial Service would appear as follows:

Only permanent accounts have a balance after closing entries

MOP-IT JANITORIAL SERVICE
POST-CLOSING TRIAL BALANCE
June 30, 19__

Account Title	Debit	Credit
Cash	4,500	
Accounts Receivable	1,300	
Prepaid Insurance	600	
Supplies	150	
Truck	6,800	
Accumulated Depreciation/Truck		600
Equipment	3,000	
Accumulated Depreciation/Equipment		900
Notes Payable		1,000
Accounts Payable		900
Wages Payable		125
Interest Payable		5
Unearned Janitor Fees		1,200
T. Mop, Capital		11,620
Totals	16,350	16,350

FOUR POINTS TO REMEMBER

1. All revenue and expense accounts are closed to the Income Summary account.
2. Income Summary and the owner's drawing account are closed to the owner's capital account.
3. Closing entries are made at the end of *each* accounting period.
4. Only balance sheet accounts (permanent accounts) have a balance after the closing entries are posted; all other accounts have a *zero* balance.

THE ACCOUNTING CYCLE

The steps in the complete *accounting cycle* are listed below:

1. Analyze and journalize the business transactions.
2. Post the information from the journal to the general ledger.
3. Prepare the work sheet beginning with the the trial balance.
4. Journalize the adjusting and closing entries.
5. Post the adjusting and closing entries.
6. Prepare the formal income statement and balance sheet.
7. Prepare a post-closing trial balance.

These seven steps are illustrated in the flowchart shown in Figure 5-7.

SUMMARY

The work sheet is an organized way for an accountant to summarize the financial information at the end of the period before preparing the financial statements and closing the books. Although the work sheet is not a formal financial statement, proper headings are important, especially the date. The work sheet has five pairs of columns: Trial Balance, Adjustments, Adjusted Trial Balance, Income Statement, and Balance Sheet. If the adjustments require the addition of accounts that do not appear on the beginning Trial Balance, these extra accounts are added on the next free line in the account title column. All items on the work sheet must be labeled, and the final total for each debit and credit column must be double-

FIGURE 5-7

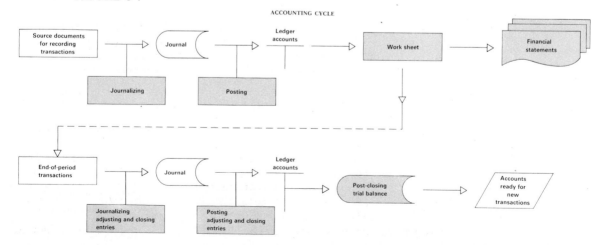

underlined. Two or more account activities are not combined; each is listed separately.

When the work sheet is completed, the next two steps of the accounting cycle require the journalizing and posting of the adjusting and closing entries.

The revenue, expense, and owner's drawing accounts are closed. When these accounts are closed, the balances are transferred to the owner's capital or Income Summary account. Income Summary is a temporary account used for the purpose of closing the revenue and expense accounts for the period. The Income Summary and owner's drawing are closed into the owner's capital account so the capital account will show the correct year-end balance.

When the closing entries have been posted, only asset, liability, and owner's capital accounts will have a balance. All the other accounts, namely, revenue, expenses, and owner's drawing, will have a zero balance.

The next step in the accounting cycle is the preparation of the income statement and balance sheet.

The last step in the accounting cycle is the preparation of a post-closing trial balance to test the accuracy of the general ledger. The debit and credit balances should be equal, and only asset, liability, and owner's capital accounts should have a balance.

Chapter 5 concludes the presentation of the complete accounting cycle.

GLOSSARY

Accounting Cycle: A term that summarizes the basic steps in the accounting process beginnning with the analyzing and journalizing of activities through the completion of the procedures at the end of the fiscal period and preparation of a post-closing trial balance.

Closing Entry: A general journal entry that will bring the account balance to a zero by transferring the balance to another account. The revenue, expense, owner's drawing, and Income Summary accounts are temporary accounts that are closed. Asset, liability, and owner's capital accounts are permanent or real accounts, and they are not closed.

Current Assets: Assets that will be converted into cash or consumed within the current fiscal year or normal operating cycle.

Current Liabilities: Liabilities or debts that are due within one fiscal period or normal operating cycle.

Financial Statements: Formal accounting reports known as the income statement and balance sheet prepared monthly or at the end of the accounting cycle or fiscal period. The income statement summarizes the operating activities for a period of time, and the balance sheet shows the financial position of a business on a certain date.

Intangible Assets: Assets that have no physical form but are presented or identified by documents, contracts, agreements, or descriptions. A few examples are copyrights, patents, and franchises.

Long-term Investments: Investments made by a company for the purpose of holding them for a period of more than 1 year. These assets are not used in the operations of the business.

Long-term Liabilities: Liabilities or debts that will be paid over a period that extends beyond 1 year.

Marketable Securities: Temporary investments which can be converted to cash quickly made by a company for the purpose of holding them for a short period of time (less than a year). They are classified as a current asset.

Nominal Accounts: Another name for temporary accounts.

Owner's Equity: The owner's claim on the assets of the business.

Permanent Accounts: Assets, liabilities, and owner's capital accounts are not closed and are called permanent or real accounts.

Plant Assets: Assets that have a life of more than 1 year and are employed in the routine operations of the business for the purpose of earning revenue. They are not purchased for the purpose of resale.

Post-Closing Trial Balance: A list of the account balances after the closing entries have been journalized and posted to check that the debit balances equal the credit balances in the ledger and to check that only the permanent accounts have a balance.

Real Accounts: Another name for permanent accounts.

Temporary Accounts: Revenue, expense, and owner's drawing accounts are closed at the end of the accounting period and are called temporary or nominal accounts.

Work Sheet: A device for summarizing the accounting activities at the end of the fiscal period and providing information for the preparation of financial statements, adjusting entries, and closing the books.

QUESTIONS

1. State the purpose for the preparation of a work sheet.
2. How is the work sheet dated?
3. List the headings for each of the five pairs of columns on a 10-column work sheet.
4. What are the headings of the three pairs of columns in which the debit and credit sides should balance?
5. If the Income Statement debit column subtotal is $12,000 and the credit column subtotal is $18,500, what does the difference represent? Where is this difference entered on the work sheet?
6. If the subtotal of the Income Statement debit column is $12,000 and the credit subtotal is $8,500, what does the difference represent? Where is this difference entered on the work sheet?
7. What is the purpose of the post-closing trial balance?
8. List the seven steps in the accounting cycle as stated in Chapter 5.
9. Name the account that would be debited to close the Insurance Expense account.

10. Give the closing entry required for a business that made a profit for the period.
11. When closing revenue accounts, what accounts are debited and credited?
12. After all closing entries have been posted, what types of accounts will have a balance?

EXERCISES

Adjusting and Closing Entries

1. On December 31 of the current year, the Prepaid Insurance account had a balance of $480 before adjustment. One-fourth of the insurance had expired and the correct adjustment was recorded.
   (a) Prepare the adjusting and closing entry required on December 31.
   (b) What dollar amount will be shown on the (1) income statement and (2) the balance sheet after the adjusting entry has been journalized and posted.

Work Sheet

2. On the work sheet for the Bobber Company, the Income Statement debit column has a subtotal of $87,500 and the credit column has a subtotal of $63,000.
   (a) What does the difference represent?
   (b) Where should the amount be entered on the work sheet?
   (c) If the subtotal of the debit column amounted to $57,500, what does the difference represent?

   A partial work sheet is shown on page 140. Indicate with a check mark (✔) where each of the accounts listed should be entered. The first account (Cash) has been completed as an example.

4. The Adjusted Trial Balance taken from the work sheet of the Zip Company for the year ending December 31 of the current year is listed below. (The amounts are in one and two digit numbers for simplicity.)

Cash	$ 4	
Accounts Receivable.............	8	
Vehicles	10	
Accumulated Depreciation/Vehicles		$ 4
Accounts Payable		2
Wages Payable..................		1
Notes Payable (due in 3 years)		3
Ron Zip, Capital		12
Ron Zip, Drawing...............	2	
Service Revenue		8
Wages Expense	3	
Utilities Expense	1	
Depreciation Expense	2	
Totals.....................	$30	$30

	Income Statement		Balance Sheet	
Account Title	**Dr**	**Cr**	**Dr**	**Cr**
Cash (Example)			✔	
Notes Payable				✔
Machinery			✔	
Copyrights			✔	
Wages Expense	✔			
Accounts Payable				✔
Accumulated Depreciation				✔
Drawing			✔	
Service Fees Earned		✔		
Rent Expense	✔			
Prepaid Insurance			✔	
Capital				✔
Accounts Receivable			✔	
Unearned Rent				✔
Net Income	✔			✔
Net Loss		✔	✔	

Required

Prepare a six-column work sheet beginning with the Adjusted Trial Balance. Enter the account titles and amounts given in the first pair of columns, and complete the work sheet.

Closing Entries

5. Using the information in Exercise 4, journalize the closing entries.

6. The adjusted trial balance as of December 31 of the current year for Spotless Cleaning Company included the following balances:

M. Dry, Capital	$16,000
M. Dry, Drawing	2,000
Service Revenue	18,000
Cleaning Supplies Expense	9,000
Utilities Expense	1,200

Gas & Oil Expense	900
Salaries & Wages Expense	12,000
Depreciation Expense/Delivery Equip.	600

Prepare the four closing entries required on December 31.

Post-Closing Trial Balance

7. Prepare a post-closing trial balance in proper order for the Flight Instruction Company as of December 31 of the current year. The accounts are arranged in alphabetical order.

Accounts Receivable	$ 4,000
Accounts Payable	6,000
Accumulated Dep./Equipment	400
B. Flight, Capital	10,100
Cash	10,000
Equipment	4,000
Notes Payable	4,000
Prepaid Insurance	2,000
Shop Supplies	500

Owner's Equity Section

8. The account balances taken from the records of the Unhappy Baking Company as of December 31 of the current year appear below:

Assets	$25,000
Liabilities	12,000
A. Ray, Capital	5,000
A. Ray, Drawing	10,000
Revenue Earned	40,000
Operating Expenses	22,000

Assuming that the correct closing entries have been journalized and posted, prepare the Owner's Equity section of the balance sheet.

Classification of Accounts

9. Classify each account title listed below as a current asset (CA), plant asset (PA), current liability (CL), or long-term liability (LTL).

(a) Cash
(b) Accounts Receivable
(c) Building
(d) Accounts Payable
(e) Notes Payable (due in 6 months)
(f) Supplies
(g) Machinery
(h) Furniture & Fixtures

(*i*) Notes Payable (due in 2 years)
(*j*) Wages Payable
(*k*) Unearned Revenue

10. Classify each account title listed below as a current asset (CA), plant asset (PA), current liability (CL), long-term liability (LTL), owner's equity (OE), revenue (R), or expense (E). For all the contra asset or owner's equity accounts, use the lowercase letter c before the classification letters.

(*a*) Notes Receivable
(*b*) Accumulated Depreciation
(*c*) Rent Payable
(*d*) Owner's Capital
(*e*) Advertising Expense
(*f*) Owner's Drawing

(*g*) Office Supplies
(*h*) Accounts Payable
(*i*) Service Fees
(*j*) Wages Expense
(*k*) Utilities Expense

PROBLEMS

Work Sheet

5-1. The general ledger of Hawk Realty Company had the following account balances as of June 30, 19_B, the end of the fiscal year.

Cash	$ 8,000
Commissions Receivable	10,000
Prepaid Insurance	300
Office Supplies	500
Cars and Trucks	15,000
Accumulated Depreciation/Cars & Trucks	7,500
Furniture and Equipment	4,000
Accumulated Depreciation/Furniture & Equipment	400
Accounts Payable	1,200
Unearned Commissions	6,300
T. Hawk, Capital	11,700
T. Hawk, Drawing	10,000
Commissions Earned	40,000
Salaries Expense	8,500
Rent Expense	7,200
Utilities Expense	1,200
Travel Expense	2,400

Additional data

(*a*) The balance in the Prepaid Insurance account represents a 3-year insurance policy purchased on January 1, 19_B.

(*b*) An inventory of office supplies showed $400 worth of supplies used during the year.

(*c*) The annual depreciation is $3,000 for the cars and trucks and $400 for the furniture and equipment.

(d) Commissions earned but the customers have not been billed amounted to $2,000.

(e) Salaries accrued but not paid amounted to $350.

(f) One-half of the commissions received in advance have been earned.

Required

Prepare a 10-column work sheet in good form.

5-2. The general ledger of the Jolt Taxi Company on December 31 of the current year, shows the following accounts and balances.

Cash	$ 2,550
Accounts Receivable	750
Supplies.......................................	300
Prepaid Insurance..............................	2,000
Taxicabs.......................................	20,000
Accumulated Depreciation/Taxicabs..............	8,000
Furniture and Equipment........................	4,500
Accumulated Depreciation/Furniture & Equipment..	800
Accounts Payable...............................	2,500
J. Jolt, Capital.................................	13,600
J. Jolt, Drawing	7,200
Fares Earned	25,000
Wages Expense	8,000
Utilities Expense	1,800
Taxi Maintenance Expense.......................	2,300
Advertising Expense............................	500

Additional data

(a) Billed flat-rate customers for December fares, $350.

(b) One-half of the Prepaid Insurance has expired.

(c) Annual depreciation is $8,000 for the cabs and $400 for the furniture and equipment

(d) Accrued wages, $700.

(e) Supplies on hand amounted to $100 on December 31.

Required

Prepare a 10-column work sheet in good form.

✓ 5-3. The Trial Balance for the No Answering Service Company on March 31 of the current year is shown below.

Cash	$ 4,200	
Accounts Receivable	2,800	
Prepaid Insurance	600	
Office Supplies	150	
Equipment	8,000	
Accumulated Depreciation/Equipment		$ 800
Accounts Payable		2,300

Unearned Service Revenue		1,000
U. No, Capital		11,900
U. No, Drawing	700	
Answering Service Revenue		5,500
Wages Expense	2,000	
Rent Expense	2,750	
Utilities Expense	200	
Miscellaneous Expense	100	
Totals	$21,500	$21,500

Additional data

(*a*) Expired insurance amounted to $300.

(*b*) Office supplies on hand on March 31 amounted to $50.

(*c*) Depreciation on equipment as of March 31 amounted to $150.

(*d*) Accrued wages as of March 31 amounted to $350.

(*e*) Forty percent of revenue received in advance had been earned as of March 31.

Required

Prepare a 10-column work sheet for March.

Adjusting and Closing Entries Plus Financial Statements

5-4. Using the work sheet prepared for Problem 5-1,

(*a*) Prepare an income statement and balance sheet.

(*b*) Journalize the adjusting and closing entries.

5-5. Using the work sheet prepared for Problem 5-2,

(*a*) Prepare an income statement and balance sheet.

(*b*) Journalize the adjusting and closing entries.

5-6. Using the work sheet prepared for Problem 5-3,

(*a*) Prepare an income statement and balance sheet.

(*b*) Journalize the adjusting and closing entries.

Work Sheet, Journalizing and Posting Closing Entries, Plus Post-Closing Trial Balance

5-7. The adjusted trial balance for the Happy Hour Tennis Club as of June 30 of the current year is listed below.

HAPPY HOUR TENNIS CLUB
ADJUSTED TRIAL BALANCE
June 30, 19___

100	Cash	$ 7,200
110	Accounts Receivable	5,400
130	Equipment	4,100

138	Accumulated Depreciation/Equipment		$ 1,625
210	Wages Payable		165
211	Unearned Service Revenue		210
310	C. Happy, Capital		3,800
318	C. Happy, Drawing	8,850	
410	Service Revenue		38,900
510	Wages Expense	13,500	
511	Rent Expense	3,600	
512	Depreciation Expense/Equipment	650	
513	Utilities Expense	1,250	
514	Miscellaneous Expense	150	
	Totals	$44,700	$44,700

Required

(a) Open a general ledger for the accounts listed above and post the balances as of June 30. Open a ledger account for 700 Income Summary.
(b) Journalize the closing entries.
(c) Post the closing entries.
(d) Prepare a post-closing trial balance.

5-8. The adjusted trial balance for John Law, CPA, as of December 31 of the current year is shown below:

JOHN LAW, CPA
ADJUSTED TRIAL BALANCE
December 31, 19__

Cash	$ 4,000	
Accounts Receivable	11,000	
Office Supplies	500	
Prepaid Insurance	600	
Law Library	30,000	
Accumulated Depreciation/Law Library		$ 6,000
Accounts Payable		7,000
Notes Payable		5,000
John Law, Capital		18,000
John Law, Drawing	23,000	
Professional Fees Earned		60,000
Salaries Expense	20,000	
Depreciation Expense/Law Library	3,000	
Utilities Expense	1,200	
Rent Expense	2,400	
Miscellaneous Expense	300	
Totals	$96,000	$96,000

Required

(a) Prepare an income statement for the year ended December 31.
(b) Journalize the closing entries for December 31.
(c) Prepare a balance sheet as of December 31.
(d) Prepare a post-closing trial balance.

Complete Accounting Cycle

5-9. The accounts in the general ledger of the Hammer Repair Service Company that had a balance on July 1 of the current year are Cash, $4,300; Accounts Receivable, $1,850; Prepaid Insurance, $3,000; Repair Supplies, $175; Truck, $7,300; Accumulated Depreciation/Truck, $1,200; Equipment, $10,000; Accumulated Depreciation/Equipment, $1,800; Accounts Payable, $700; Wages Payable, $300; Notes Payable (due in 2 years), $5,000; and Jack Hammer, Capital $17,625.

Transactions for July

19—
July 2 Purchased repair supplies on account, $350.
   6 Paid $600 for wages which includes the $300 balance in the Wages Payable account.
   10 Mr. Hammer invested an additional $5,000 in the business.
   12 Cash received from customer as payment on account, $1,500.
   15 Paid truck repair bill for July, $125.
   17 Purchased $2,500 of welding equipment for cash.
   19 Paid utility bills for July, $350.
   20 Cash received for services performed, $1,350.
   23 Paid truck gas and oil bill for July, $275.
   27 Paid wages, $300.
   29 Mr. Hammer withdrew $950 cash for personal use.
   30 Repair fees earned for services performed on account during July amounted to $3,400.

Additional data
(1) Insurance expired, $300.
(2) Accrued wages, $175.
(3) Depreciation amounts to $200 on the truck and $150 on the equipment.
(4) Repair supplies used in July, $325.
(5) Unbilled repair services performed for customers, $275.

Required

(a) Enter the account balances for July 1 in the general ledger.
(b) Journalize and post the transactions for July.
(c) Prepare and complete a 10-column work sheet.
(d) Prepare an income statement and balance sheet.
(e) Journalize and post the adjusting and closing entries.
(f) Prepare a post-closing trial balance.

5-10. Sassy Sally's Hair Salon closes its books on December 31 of the current year. The ledger balances on December 1 are as follows:

Cash	$ 2,800
Accounts Receivable	300

Prepaid Insurance	2,400
Beauty Supplies	1,850
Van	6,500
Accumulated Depreciation/Van	2,000
Equipment	9,000
Accumulated Depreciation/Equipment	3,300
Accounts Payable	450
Wages Payable	225
Taxes Payable	185
Sue Sally, Capital	16,690

Transactions for December

19—
Dec.
	3	Paid $550 for wages including the $225 balance in wages payable.
	5	Purchased beauty supplies on account, $210.
	7	Cash received from customers for services, $850.
	9	Paid taxes payable, $185.
	10	Paid $325 on accounts payable.
	13	Paid December rent, $750.
	15	Received cash from customers on account, $250.
	18	Paid gas, oil, and tune-up on van, $180.
	19	Paid wages, $225.
	21	Paid utilities, $125.
	21	Paid telephone bill, $95.
	22	Sally withdrew $500 cash for personal use.
	23	Received cash from customers for services, $1,350.
	28	Billed charge customers for service, $2,350.

Additional data
(1) Accrued wages, $250.
(2) The Prepaid Insurance represents a 1-year insurance policy purchased on November 30.
(3) Supplies on hand December 31, $1,300.
(4) Depreciation for December for the van, $200, for equipment, $150.
(5) Unbilled services performed for customers in December, $50.

Required

(*a*) Enter the account balances for December in the general ledger.
(*b*) Journalize and post the transactions for December.
(*c*) Prepare and complete a work sheet.
(*d*) Prepare an income statement and balance sheet.
(*e* Journalize and post the adjusting and closing entries.
(*f*) Prepare a post-closing trial balance.

5-11. The business activities for the month of April for Brian Service Company are as follows:

19__
Apr. 4 Purchased office supplies on account, $200.
    6 Received $900 from customers on account.
    10 Received $1,100 from cash customers for services performed.
    15 Paid wages of $1,250 which includes the wages payable amounting to $350.
    30 Paid $800 on accounts payable; rent for April, $750; utilities for April, $180; and miscellaneous expenses, $130.
    30 Ms. Brian withdrew $750 cash for personal use.

Additional data for April
(1) Expired insurance, $30.
(2) Office supplies used during April, $75.
(3) Depreciation on equipment, $150.
(4) Accrued wages, $275.
(5) Unbilled services performed for customer in April, $80.

Required

(*a*) Open ledger accounts and enter the balances for April 1 as shown for the following: 100 Cash, $4,300; 110 Accounts Receivable, $1,800; 112 Prepaid Insurance, $1,200; 114 Office Supplies, $50; 130 Equipment, $8,000; 138 Accumulated Depreciation/Equipment, $950; 210 Accounts Payable, $1,300; 212 Wages Payable, $350; 310 Georgia Brian, Capital, $12,750; 318 Georgia Brian, Drawing; 400 Service Revenue; 510 Insurance Expense; 512 Office Supplies Expense; 514 Rent Expense; 516 Utilities Expense; 517 Wages Expense; 518 Depreciation Expense/Equipment; 519 Miscellaneous Expense; 700 Income Summary.
(*b*) Journalize and post the April transactions.
(*c*) Prepare a 10-column work sheet for April.
(*d*) Prepare an income statement and balance sheet for April.
(*e*) Journalize and post the adjusting and closing entries for April.
(*f*) Prepare a post-closing trial balance.

Accounting for a Merchandising Business

After completing this chapter, you should be able to:

1. **Journalize the entries for sales and purchases of merchandise**
2. **State the purpose of the Sales Returns & Allowance and Purchase Returns accounts**
3. **Distinguish between cash discounts and trade discounts**
4. **Explain the process of clearing the beginning inventory and recording the ending inventory**
5. **State the difference between FOB destination and FOB shipping point**

The accounting procedures for a service business were introduced in Chapters 1 through 5. This chapter will introduce the accounting procedures for a *merchandising concern,* a business that buys products for the purpose of reselling the products for more than their original cost.

Accounting for a merchandising concern requires the addition of several new accounts for recording the buying and selling of a product. These additional accounts are Sales, Sales Returns & Allowances, Sales Discounts, Purchases, Purchase Returns & Allowances, Purchase Discount, Transportation In, Transportation Out, and Merchandise Inventory. All of these accounts are shown in the income statement, and the ending balance of the Merchandise Inventory account is also shown on the balance sheet.

SALES AND RELATED ACCOUNTS

Sales

Sales is the account title used to record the sale of merchandise. Accounting for the Sales account is handled in the same manner as the Service Revenue account. When merchandise is sold, an asset account (cash or a receivable if the merchandise is sold on account) is debited and the Sales account is credited. The entry for the sale is journalized when the product is shipped to a customer, as shown in the following examples for the A-1 Desk Company.

EXAMPLE 1

On March 4, 19_A, A-1 Desk Company sold and shipped 40 desks to Bea Distributing Company for $50 each, a total of $2,000.

Sale of merchandise on account

19_A			
Mar. 4	Accounts Receivable/Bea Distributing Company		
	Company	2,000	
	Sales		2,000
	Sold 40 desks for $50 each to Bea Distributing Company on account.		

EXAMPLE 2   *Sold 24 desks for $50 each to customers for cash on March 6, 19_A.*

```
19_A
Mar.  6    Cash                         1,200
              Sales                                  1,200
           Sold 24 desks for cash.
```

The Sales account is only used for the sale of merchandise. When a business sells an asset, cash or a receivable account is debited and the asset account is credited as shown in the following example.

EXAMPLE 3   *On March 7, sold office supplies at their cost price of $200 as a convenience to a customer.*

Sale of office supplies

```
19_A
Mar.  7    Cash                         200
              Office Supplies                     200
           Sold office supplies for their cost price as
           a convenience to a customer.
```

Sales Returns & Allowances

Whenever a business is involved in selling merchandise, there usually are a few customers who will return all or a portion of the goods that they purchased. The returns will be made for a variety of reasons: the merchandise may have been damaged in shipment, the customers may have changed their minds and did not want or need the goods, or the customers may have purchased more than needed.

A special account called **Sales Returns & Allowances** is used to record the returns so that the amount of goods returned is always known. If there are too many returns, necessary steps may be taken to eliminate or reduce the amount of returns before they become excessive. Returns are costly to a company because of the extra expense of recording, packaging, handling, and shipping the merchandise. The journal entry for a return from a customer is shown in the example on p. 152.

Sales Returns & Allowances is classified as a contra revenue account and would be shown on the income statement as follows:

Operating Revenue		
Gross Sales	$3,200*	
Less: Sales Returns & Allowances	50	
Net Sales		$3,150

* Credit sales, $2,000 + $1,200 cash sales.

EXAMPLE 4

On March 8, the A-1 Desk Company accepted the return of one desk from the Bea Distributing Company that was damaged in shipment. Credit of $50 was given on the Bea Distributing Company account.

Sales Returns &
Allowances account
debited for merchandise
returned from customer

19_A			
Mar. 8	Sales Returns & Allowances	50	
	Accounts Receivable/Bea Distributing Company		50
	Credit given for return of one desk that was damaged in shipment dated Mar. 4.		

Sales Discount

To encourage customers to pay their accounts promptly, a *cash discount* is frequently given if payment is received within a certain number of days from the date of the sale. Cash discounts may be offered to a customer for a partial as well as a full payment depending upon the credit terms of each company. A business that offers a cash discount will show the terms for payment on the sales invoice. Some common examples of cash discount terms when a customer pays their account in full are shown below:

2/10, n/30: 2 percent may be deducted from the amount due if the customer pays within 10 days after the date of the sales invoice. The invoice must be paid in full in order to deduct the discount. If the customer does not pay within 10 days, the net (n) or full amount must be paid within 30 days from the date of the sales invoice.

2/10, 1/15, n/60: 2 percent may be deducted from the amount due if the customer pays the account in full within 10 days, 1 percent may be deducted if paid in full within 11 to 15 days, or the net amount is due within 60 days from the date of the sales invoice if paid after 15 days.

2/10 EOM, n/60: 2 percent may be deducted from the amount due if the customer pays the account in full by the tenth of the month following the sales invoice. If the customer does not pay by the tenth of the month following the sale, the net amount must be paid within 60 days from the date of the sales invoice.

The cash discount is shown in an account called **Sales Discount.** The following example illustrates payment received from a customer within the discount period.

EXAMPLE 5

On March 14, A-1 Desk Company received full payment on account from Bea Distributing Company, less the $50 return and the 2 percent cash discount allowed for payment within 10 days. The amount received amounted to $1,911, computed as follows:

Sale on Mar. 4	$2,000
Less: Return on March 8	50
Amount Owed before Discount	$1,950
Less: 2% Discount ($1,950 × 0.02)	39
Amount Received from Customer	$1,911

The following journal entry was made for payment received from Bea Distributing Company on March 14.

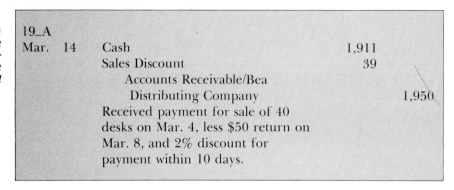

Sales Discount account debited for cash discount given customer for payment within discount period

19_A
Mar. 14   Cash   1,911
          Sales Discount   39
               Accounts Receivable/Bea
               Distributing Company   1,950
          Received payment for sale of 40
          desks on Mar. 4, less $50 return on
          Mar. 8, and 2% discount for
          payment within 10 days.

The Sales Discount account is a contra revenue account and would be shown on the income statement as a deduction to the Sales account as illustrated below:

Operating Revenue

Sales		$3,200
Less: Sales Returns &		
Allowances	$50	
Sales Discount	39	89
Net Sales		$3,111

The Sales, Sales Returns & Allowances, and Sales Discount accounts are closed at the end of the fiscal period to the Income Summary account as shown below:

Closing Sales, Sales Returns, and Sales Discount accounts

19_A
Dec. 31   Sales   3,200
               Income Summary   3,200
          To close the Sales account.

     31   Income Summary   89
               Sales Returns & Allowances   50
               Sales Discount   39
          To close the Sales Returns &
          Allowances and Sales Discount
          accounts.

After posting the entries on page 153 to the Income Summary account, the balance of the account is equal to net sales as shown in the general ledger account below:

Title: Income Summary   Account No.: 70

Date		Explanation	Ref.	Debit	Credit	Balance
19_A Dec.	31				3,200	3,200
	31			89		3,111

PURCHASES AND RELATED ACCOUNTS

Purchases

A merchandising business buys goods for the purpose of reselling the merchandise for more than its original cost. The cost of the goods purchased is recorded in an account called *Purchases.* Purchases is referred to and classified as a Cost of Goods Sold account. The Purchases account appears on the income statement and is closed at the end of the fiscal period to the Income Summary account.

The Purchases account is only used to record goods purchased for resale. When purchasing assets that will be used in the operation of a business an asset account is debited. For example, when purchasing office supplies, debit the Office Supplies account. When purchasing merchandise for the purpose of resale, debit the Purchases account and credit the Cash or Accounts Payable account, if the purchase was made on credit. The entry for purchases made by Bea Distributing Company from the A-1 Desk Company is illustrated below.

Purchase of merchandise on account

19_A			
Mar. 4	Purchases	2,000	
	Accounts Payable/A-1		
	Desk Company		2,000
	Purchased 40 desks from A-1 Desk		
	Company for $50 each, receiving		
	terms of 2/10, n/30.		

Purchase Returns & Allowances

Sometimes it will be necessary for a company to return some of the merchandise purchased because the goods were damaged in shipment, the goods were defective, or more goods may have been purchased than needed, etc. After the supplier has agreed to accept the return and give credit on account, the Accounts Payable account is debited and the account called **Purchase Returns & Allowances** is credited. If the Purchases account was used for the credit, you would not be able to know the cost of the goods returned without going through every purchase entry on your records. Maintaining a separate account for purchase returns enables a business to take steps, when necessary, to eliminate future returns which may have been caused by poor packaging, shipping, purchasing procedures, or inferior merchandise.

The Purchase Returns & Allowances account is classified as a contra purchases account and would be shown on the income statement as a subtraction to the cost of the goods purchased. The Purchase Returns & Allowances account normally has a credit balance and is closed at the end of the accounting period to the Income Summary account.

The journal entry to record merchandise returned to the A-1 Desk Company is illustrated below:

Purchase Returns & Allowances account credited for merchandise returned

19_A			
Mar. 8	Accounts Payable/A-1 Desk Company	50	
	Purchase Returns & Allowances		50
	Returned one desk to A-1 Desk Company		
	damaged in shipment and received credit of		
	$50 on account.		

Purchase Discount

Most suppliers will offer a cash discount if payment for a purchase was made before a specified date. The **Purchase Discount** account is used to record the amount that was saved by paying the account promptly. Consider the previous illustration regarding the purchase of 40 desks from the A-1 Desk Company, less the $50 return on March 8, with terms of 2/10, n/30. If payment is made on the tenth day, the amount to be paid would be $1,911.

40 desks @ $50 each	$2,000	
Less: 1 desk returned on March 8	50	
Amount owed before discount	$1,950	
Less: 2% discount ($1,950 × 0.02)	39	
Amount to be paid		$1,911

The journal entry required if payment is made on March 14 is shown on page 156.

Payment to creditor within discount period

> 19_A
> Mar. 14   Accounts Payable/A-1 Desk
>   Company   1,950
>   Purchase Discount   39
>   Cash   1,911
>   Paid balance owed on account to A-1
>   Desk Company, less $50 return on
>   Mar. 8, and 2% discount received for
>   payment within discount period.

If Bea Distributing Company did not pay the balance owed to A-1 Desk Company until March 31, the entry would be:

Payment to creditor after discount period

> 19_A
> Mar. 31   Accounts Payable/A-1 Desk
>   Company   1,950
>   Cash   1,950
>   Paid balance owed to A-1 Desk
>   Company.

The Purchases, Purchase Returns & Allowances, and Purchase Discount accounts are closed at the end of the fiscal period to the Income Summary account as illustrated below.

Closing Purchases, Purchase Returns, and Purchase Discount accounts

> **Closing Entries**
>
> 19_A
> Dec. 31   Income Summary   2,000
>   Purchases   2,000
>   To close the Purchases account.
>
>   31   Purchase Returns & Allowances   50
>   Purchase Discount   39
>   Income Summary   89
>   To close the Purchase Returns and
>   Allowances and Purchase Discount
>   accounts.

After posting the above entries to the Income Summary account, the balance of the account is equal to net purchases as shown in the general ledger account on page 157.

Title: Income Summary   Account No.: **70**

Date		Explanation	Ref.	Debit	Credit	Balance
19_A Dec.	31 31			2,000	 89	2,000 1,911

SHIPPING CHARGES ON MERCHANDISE PURCHASED OR SOLD

When goods are purchased for resale and when the goods are sold, there may be a cost for shipping the merchandise. The shipping costs will be paid by the buyer or seller depending upon the arrangements made prior to the purchase or sale of the merchandise. The shipping arrangements are listed on the invoice as freight terms or shipping terms of *FOB destination* or *FOB shipping point* as explained and illustrated in Examples 1 and 2.

EXAMPLE 1 Free on board (FOB) destination *means that the* seller *has agreed to pay all the shipping costs and the purchaser receives title to goods at point of destination.*

Shipping charges that a seller pays when selling merchandise FOB destination is debited to an account called **Transportation Out***. This account is an expense of selling the product and is classified as a selling expense that is listed in the Operating Expense section of the income statement.*

The journal entry involving transportation expenses paid by the seller is illustrated by using the A-1 Desk Company as an example.

For Destination

Assume that A-1 Desk Company gave shipping terms of FOB destination for the 40 desks sold and shipped to Bea Distributing Company on March 4. When A-1 Desk Company paid the shipping costs of $40 on March 4, the following entry would be recorded. No entry is required on the books of the purchaser.

FOB destination requires entry on seller's books

19_A		
Mar. 4	Transportation Out	40
	Cash	40
	To record payment of transportation costs for 40 desks shipped and sold to Bea Distributing Company.	

Transportation Out has a debit balance and is closed to the Income Summary account. The closing entry for the A-1 Desk Company is illustrated on page 158.

Closing entry on seller's books for transportation costs

Closing Entry		
19_A		
Dec. 31 Income Summary	40	
Transportation Out		40
To close the transportation account.		

EXAMPLE 2

Free on board (FOB) shipping point *means that the* purchaser *has agreed to pay all the shipping costs and the purchaser receives title to goods at shipping point.*

Shipping charges that a purchaser pays when buying merchandise with terms of FOB shipping point are an additional cost of the purchase. These costs are debited into an account called **Transportation In,** and the account with its amount is shown on the income statement as an addition to the cost of purchases. The income statement for a merchandising concern is discussed and illustrated in Chapter 7.

The journal entry involving transportation expenses paid by the purchaser is illustrated by using the Bea Distributing Company as an example.

For Shipping Point

Assume that Bea Distributing Company received shipping terms of FOB shipping point from A-1 Desk Company for the 40 desks purchased and received on March 4. When Bea Distributing Company paid the shipping costs of $40 on March 4, the following entry would be recorded. No entry is required on the books of the seller.

FOB shipping point requires entry on purchaser's books

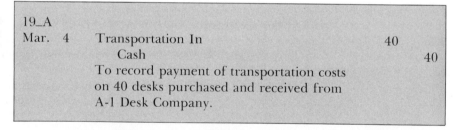

19_A		
Mar. 4 Transportation In	40	
Cash		40
To record payment of transportation costs on 40 desks purchased and received from A-1 Desk Company.		

Transportation In has a debit balance and is closed to the Income Summary account. The closing entry for Bea Distributing Company is illustrated below.

Closing entry on purchaser's books for transportation costs

Closing Entry		
19_A		
Dec. 31 Income Summary	40	
Transportation In		40
To close the transportation account.		

MERCHANDISE INVENTORY

Whenever a business is involved in buying and selling merchandise, usually some of the merchandise will remain unsold at the end of the accounting period. These goods on hand that have not been sold at the end of a fiscal period are debited to an account entitled *Merchandise Inventory.* The merchandise on hand at the end of one fiscal or accounting period would be the beginning merchandise inventory for the next fiscal period.

At the end of each fiscal period, the Merchandise Inventory account must be adjusted to show the correct amount of merchandise on hand. The inventory account is adjusted through the Income Summary account requiring two journal entries. For example, assume that the inventory for the A-1 Desk Company amounted to $5,000 on January 1, 19_A, and $8,000 on December 31, 19_A. The two entries required to record the ending inventory and to close the beginning inventory is illustrated in Entries 1 and 2.

ENTRY 1   *The (ending) inventory on hand on December 31, 19_A, amounting to $8,000 is recorded in the accounting records by debiting the Merchandise Inventory account and crediting the Income Summary account.*

Entry to record ending inventory

19_A			
Dec. 31	Merchandise Inventory	8,000	
	Income Summary		8,000
	To record the ending inventory on hand at the end of the period.		

ENTRY 2   *The (beginning) inventory for January 1, 19_A, amounting to $5,000 is closed or removed from the accounting records by debiting the Income Summary account and crediting the Merchandise Inventory account.*

Entry to close beginning inventory

19_A			
Dec. 31	Income Summary	5,000	
	Merchandise Inventory		5,000
	To transfer the beginning inventory to the Income Summary account.		

The beginning and ending balance in the Merchandise Inventory account is shown in the income statement and is discussed and illustrated in Chapter 7. The ending balance in the Merchandise Inventory account is also shown on the balance sheet as a current asset as illustrated on page 160 for the A-1 Desk Company.

Assets
Current Assets:
Merchandise Inventory $8,000

DEBIT AND CREDIT MEMORANDA

When a company accepts a return of merchandise from its customer, a *credit memorandum* is issued by the seller. To illustrate, assume that the credit memorandum in Figure 6-1 was issued by the A-1 Desk Company to the Bea Distributing Company for the return of the desk damaged in shipment.

This credit memorandum is used by the seller to record the return by the customer in the accounting records. The journal entry required by the A-1 Desk Company for the return of the desk requires a debit to the Sales Returns & Allowances account and a credit to the Accounts Receivable/Bea Distributing Company account for $50 as shown below.

Entry for return from customer

19_A			
Mar. 8	Sales Returns & Allowances	50	
	Accounts Receivable/Bea Distributing Company		50
	To record the return of one desk damaged in shipment of Mar. 4, Credit Memorandum No. 101.		

FIGURE 6-1

Credit Memorandum No. ___101___

A-1 DESK COMPANY
1002 First Avenue
Livonia, Michigan 48102

To: Bea Distributing Company   **Date:** March 8, 19_A

2001 Peru Street

Livonia, Michigan 48694

We are crediting your account with the following:

Quantity	Description	Reason	Amount
1	Walnut Desk	Damaged in shipment.	$ 50 00

When a company issues the form to a supplier for the return of merchandise, the form is called a ***debit memorandum,*** similar to the illustration in Figure 6-1. The company uses the debit or credit memorandum to record the return to the supplier. The journal entry required by the Bea Distributing Company for the return of the desk requires a debit to the Accounts Payable/A-1 Desk Company account and a credit to the Purchase Returns & Allowance account for $50 as shown below.

Entry to record return of merchandise to creditor

19_A			
Mar. 8	Accounts Payable/A-1 Desk Company	50	
	Purchase Returns & Allowances		50
	To record return of desk damaged in		
	shipment received on Mar. 8.		

TRADE DISCOUNTS

When a business firm gives customers a reduction in the list price of merchandise, it is called a ***trade discount.*** Trade discounts are given by manufacturers or merchandisers to encourage customers to purchase merchandise from their companies. The amount of trade discount given usually varies with the amount of merchandise purchased. Large orders usually receive more of a discount than small orders. Sales are credited for the list price less the trade discount; trade discount is not shown in the records of the buyer or seller, as illustrated in the following example.

The Dri-Cloth Company sold the Quickee Car Wash 1,000 pounds of rags for drying cars. The catalog list price was $0.50 per pound, with a 10 percent trade discount for orders of 250 to 500 pounds plus an additional 10 percent trade discount for orders of 500 to 1,000 pounds. Cash discount terms were 2/10, n/30. The sales price would be computed as follows:

List price (1,000 lb × $0.50)	=	$500
Less: First discount ($500 × 0.10)	=	50
Balance after first discount		$450
Less: Second discount ($450 × 0.10)	=	45
Sales price		$405

The journal entry to record the sale would be:

Trade discounts reduce the amount of the sale

Accounts Receivable/Quickee Car Wash	405	
Sales		405
Sold 1,000 pounds of rags with a list price of $0.50		
per pound, giving trade discounts of 10% on the first		
500 pounds and another 10% on second 500 pounds.		

If the Quickee Car Wash paid the account within 10 days, the amount they would pay would be $396.90; $405 − $8.10 ($405 × 0.02). The journal entry that the Dri-Cloth Company would record when payment was received is illustrated below:

Customer paid within discount period

Cash	396.90	
Sales Discount	8.10	
Accounts Receivable/Quickee Car Wash		405.00
Received payment on account less 2% discount for payment within discount period.		

SALES TAXES

Many states have enacted laws requiring a retail business to collect a sales tax from the buyer whenever certain items of merchandise are sold. The seller acts as a collection agent for the state and remits the amount collected for taxes from customers to the proper governmental agency. A sales tax report accompanied with the amount of taxes collected is filed monthly, quarterly, or annually, depending upon state regulations.

When a sale is made, an account called *Sales Tax Payable* is credited for the amount of sales tax collected from the customer. For example, if the Ace Handy Company operating in the state of Michigan sold merchandise on January 4 for $200 and collected 4 percent for sales taxes (sales tax rate for Michigan), it would receive $200 plus $8 ($200 × 0.04) from the customer for the sale. The journal entry to record the sale is shown below:

Jan. 4	Cash	208	
	Sales		200
	Sales Tax Payable		8
	Sale of merchandise for $200 plus a 4 percent sales tax amounting to $8.		

The taxes collected are paid to the state when the sales tax return is filed. The entry to record a quarterly payment to the state is illustrated in the following example:

Assume that the Ace Handy Company collected sales taxes in the amount of $70 for the first quarter of a year and paid the amount to the state on April 10. The following entry would be recorded:

Apr.	10	Sales Tax Payable	70	
		Cash		70
		To record payment of sales tax liability for the first quarter of the year.		

The Sales Tax Payable account is classified as a Current Liability and would have a credit or zero balance.

SUMMARY

A merchandising concern buys goods for the purpose of resale. The basic accounting difference between a merchandising concern and a business that sells a service to its customers is the addition of several new accounts necessary to handle the buying and selling of the merchandise. These accounts will help determine the cost of the goods sold.

When the merchandise is sold and shipped to the customer, the sale is credited in a revenue account called Sales. When goods are returned by the customer, Sales Returns and Allowances is debited for the return. Recording returns in a separate account enables management to take the necessary steps to eliminate or reduce the amount of returns before they become excessive.

When a company buys goods for the purpose of resale, a Purchases account is debited. The purchase represents the expense of the sale and is classified as a Cost of Goods Sold account. When the purchaser returns goods to the creditor, the return is credited to the Purchase Returns and Allowances account. Using a separate account enables the purchaser to take the necessary steps to eliminate future returns which may have been caused by improper packaging, shipping, or purchasing procedures.

Trade and cash discounts are given when selling or purchasing goods. Trade discounts are given to encourage trade, while sales discounts are given to encourage customers to pay their accounts promptly. Cash discounts are debited to a Sales Discount account on the books of the seller and credited to a Purchase Discount account on the books of the purchaser.

Whenever goods are purchased and sold, there will be shipping costs. Shipping costs will be paid by the buyer or seller depending upon the arrangements made prior to the sale. When the seller is required to pay the shipping costs, the terms are stated FOB destination. Shipping costs to be paid by the purchaser are stated FOB shipping point. The shipping costs on the sale of merchandise are debited to an account called Transportation Out and are classified as an operating/selling expense; shipping costs on merchandise purchased is debited to an account called Transportation In. At the end of the accounting period, merchandise remaining unsold is debited to the Merchandise Inventory account. The beginning inventory is removed by crediting the Merchandise Inventory account and the ending inventory is recorded by debiting the Merchandise Inventory account.

Many states have levied a sales tax on certain types of merchandise which must be paid by the buyer. A retail business is required to act as a collection agent for the state and remit the monies collected to the proper governmental agency. A sales tax report accompanied with the amount of taxes collected is filed according to state regulations.

GLOSSARY

Cash Discount: Discount given to encourage customers to pay their accounts within a specified number of days. These discounts are shown as Sales Discounts on the books of the seller and as Purchase Discounts on the books of the purchaser.

Credit Memorandum: A form issued by the seller to record return of merchandise by purchaser.

Debit Memorandum: A form issued to a supplier for the return of merchandise.

FOB: Free on board.

FOB Destination: Shipping costs to be paid by the seller and the purchaser has title to goods at point of distination.

FOB Shipping Point: Shipping costs to be paid by the purchaser and the purchaser has title to goods at shipping point.

Merchandise Inventory: The title of the account used to record merchandise (purchased for resale) on hand at the end of the accounting period. The Merchandise Inventory account is classified as a current asset.

Merchandising Concern: A business that buys merchandise and sells it for more than the cost paid.

Purchase Discount: Contra cost of purchases account credited to record cash discounts given by the creditor for payment received before a specified date.

Purchase Returns & Allowances: The title of the account that is credited to record the return of merchandise purchased for resale. Purchase Returns and Allowances is a contra purchases account and is shown as a deduction to the Purchases account in the Cost of Goods Sold section of the income statement.

Purchases: Account title given to record merchandise purchased for the purpose of resale and classified as Cost of Goods Sold.

Sales: Title of a revenue account that is credited to record the sale of a product.

Sales Discount: A contra revenue account debited to record a cash discount given to a customer for prompt payment. Sales Discount is shown on the income statement as a deduction to the Sales account.

Sales Returns & Allowances: The title of the account that is debited to record the return of merchandise by a customer. Sales Returns and Allowances is a contra revenue account that is deducted from the Sales account on the income statement.

Trade Discounts: A discount given on the list price of an item to encourage customers to purchase merchandise. Trade discounts are not shown on the records of the buyer or seller.

Transportation In: Account debited for shipping costs paid by purchaser for merchandise purchased for the purpose of resale. Transportation In is shown in the Cost of Goods Sold section on the income statement as an addition to purchases.

Transportation Out: An Operating/Selling Expense account that is debited for shipping costs paid by seller for sales of merchandise to customers. Shipping terms of FOB destination will be shown on the sales invoice.

QUESTIONS

1. Name the two contra revenue accounts.
2. What is the difference between a cash discount and a trade discount?
3. If a customer purchased goods with a list price of $2,000 and was given a trade discount of 10 percent, what amount will be recorded for the sale?
4. Give the journal entries for: (a) sale of merchandise on account, and (b) sale of office equipment on account.
5. Define the shipping terms FOB shipping point and FOB destination.
6. Give the general journal entry required for payment of merchandise purchased on June 14 for $1,800 with terms of 2/10 EOM, n/60, assuming payment was made on July 6.
7. Explain the difference between a merchandising and a service business.

EXERCISES

Journal Entries for Sales and Purchases of Merchandise

1. Selected transactions for Johnson Supply appear below:

Feb. 12 Sold $1,000 of merchandise on account to Salty Foods; terms: n/30.

16 Accepted return of merchandise from Salty Foods and issued a credit memorandum for $100.

28 Received payment in full from Salty Foods.

Required

Journalize the entries required for the:
(a) Johnson Supply
(b) Salty Foods

2. Borman Electrical sold electric parts for cash and on account. Selected transactions for April are shown below:

Apr. 6 Sold $600 of parts to Jay Sales on account; terms: n/30.
      8 Issued credit memorandum for $30 to Jay Sales for parts returned today.
     10 Sold office furniture no longer needed in the business to Jay Sales for $500 cash.
     28 Received payment in full from Jay Sales.

Required

Journalize the entries for the:
(a) Borman Electrical
(b) Jay Sales

Cash and Trade Discounts

3. Determine the amount to be paid for the following purchases, assuming payment was made within the discount period.

	Amount Purchased	Trade Discount	Terms	Merchandise Returned
a.	$1,400	None	2/10, n/30	$200
b.	2,800	5%	2/10 EOM, n/60	–0–
c.	3,600	10%	1/15, n/30	500

4. Using the information in Exercise 3, journalize the entries required for item **c** on the:
(a) Books of the seller
(b) Books of the purchaser

5. A company sold merchandise on February 8 with a list price of $3,000, giving a trade discount of 5 percent and terms of 2/10, n/30. Journalize the entries required on February 8 and for payment received on February 14 for the:
(a) Seller
(b) Purchaser

Cash and Sales Discounts Plus Shipping Charges

6. During the month of May a company sold merchandise with a list price of $8,000 on account and terms of 2/10, n/30, FOB destination. Merchandise was returned and a credit of $400 was given on the customer's account. Determine the following:
(a) Amount of sale
(b) Amount received from customer assuming payment was received within the discount period

(c) Amount received from customer assuming payment was received 20 days after the discount period had passed

7. Journalize the entries for Dundee Company for the following transactions that occurred during the month of June.

June 1 Purchased merchandise from Power Sales with a list price of $800 receiving terms of 1/10, n/30, FOB shipping point.

3 Paid transportation charges of $20 on merchandise received from Power Sales.

5 Sold equipment no longer needed in the business for $350 cash.

6 Sold merchandise for $1,100 cash.

8 Sold merchandise with a list price of $2,400 to Cullen Brothers with terms of 2/10, n/30, FOB destination.

8 Paid transportation charges of $60 on merchandise shipped to Cullen Brothers.

12 Issued a $150 credit memorandum to Cullen Brothers for merchandise returned today.

18 Received payment from Cullen Brothers.

30 Paid amount owed to Power Sales.

PROBLEMS

Journal Entries for Purchases, Sales, and Cash Discount

6-1. Selected transactions for Hoosier Company for the month of February of the current year are shown below:

Feb. 2 Purchased merchandise for $5,000 from the Arte Company on account; terms: 2/10, 1/15, n/30.

3 Returned $250 worth of damaged merchandise and Arte Company gave credit on our account.

6 Sales for the week were as follows: cash, $8,000; charge, $3,500.

9 Customers returned merchandise for cash, $200; credit, $150.

15 Paid Arte Company, less return of February 3 and 1 percent discount for payment within 15 days.

16 Received payment from charge customers, less returns of February 9 and 2 percent cash discount.

Required

(a) Journalize the transactions for the Hoosier Company.

(b) Journalize the entries required by the Arte Company on February 2, 3, and 15.

6-2. Selected transactions for the Jensen Company for the month of May of the current year are shown below:

May   2   Jensen sold and shipped merchandise worth $4,400 to Mason Company, terms of 1/15, n/30.

      4   Mason Company reported $200 of merchandise damaged in shipment, and credit was given on its account.

      6   Purchased office supplies for $280 cash.

      7   Sold and shipped $1,800 of merchandise to Mason Company with terms of 1/15, n/30.

     10   Sold and shipped used office equipment no longer needed in the business to Mason Company for $450 cash.

     12   Purchased merchandise for $3,200 cash.

     15   Cash sales for first 15 days of May amounted to $2,100.

     17   Jensen received full payment from Mason Company less the return and discount.

     18   Purchased $4,000 of merchandise on account from Daily Industries and received terms of 2/10, n/30.

     22   Purchased office equipment for $700 cash.

     28   Paid Daily Industries for balance owed on account less 2 percent discount.

     30   Cash sales for last 15 days of May amounted to $1,900.

     31   Received payment from Mason Company for sale of May 7.

Required

(*a*) Journalize the transactions for May on the books of the Jensen Company.

(*b*) Journalize the transactions for May 2, 4, 7, 10, 17, and 31 on the books of the Mason Company.

6-3. Selected transactions for Wax Works for the month of December of the current year are shown below:

Dec.   2   Sold $750 of merchandise to Sally's, a local gift shop, with terms of 2/10, n/30.

      4   Purchased $1,800 of wax supplies from CD Company on account; terms: 2/10, 1/15, n/30.

      6   Sold merchandise for $400 cash.

      9   Sold the company truck for $3,200 to Kelly Company receiving $2,000 cash and gave terms of n/30 for the $1,200 balance.

     10   Returned $150 of wax supplies damaged in shipment and received credit on account from CD Company.

     11   Gave $50 credit on account to Sally's for merchandise returned today.

     12   Sally's paid their account in full.

     18   Paid amount owed to CD Company.

24 Sold $2,800 of merchandise to KK Sales with terms of 2/10, 1/15, n/30.

30 Purchased $200 of office supplies from Bay Supply on account and received terms of n/30.

Required

Journalize the entries for December.

Journal Entries for Purchases, Sales, and Cash Discount

6-4. Selected transactions for Wally's Music Store for the month of November for the current year are shown below:

Nov. 2 Purchased merchandise from Music Suppliers with a list price of $3,800 and received terms of 2/10, n/30.

4 Purchased $800 of merchandise for cash.

5 Returned merchandise to Music Suppliers and received $250 credit on account.

7 Sold $5,800 of merchandise to Corbin's on account with terms of 1/15, n/60.

8 Purchased office supplies for $300 cash.

11 Paid balance owed on account to Music Suppliers.

18 Purchased $2,600 of merchandise on account from Music Suppliers with terms of 2/10, n/30.

20 Sold $4,100 of merchandise to Corbin's on account with terms of 1/15, n/60.

22 Corbin's returned goods damaged in shipment of November 20 and credit of $80 was given on their account.

22 Received payment from Corbin's for sale of November 7.

26 Paid Music Suppliers for purchase dated November 18.

30 Cash sales for November amounted to $6,300.

Required

Journalize the entries for:
(a) Wally's Music Store.
(b) Music Suppliers for November 2, 5, 11, 18, and 26.

6-5. The following sales occurred during July of the current year for Secretarial Products:

July 3 Sold merchandise with a list price of $8,000 and terms of 2/10, 1/15, n/30 to Branton Services.

8 Sold company car for its cost and received $3,100 cash.

10 Issued a $600 credit memorandum to Branton Services for merchandise returned today.

15 Cash sales for first half of July amounted to $4,400.
18 Received payment from Branton Services for balance owed on account.
30 Cash sales for last half of July amounted to $3,900.

Required

Journalize the entries required for:
(a) Secretarial Products for July.
(b) Branton Services for July 3, 10, and 18.

6-6. The transactions for the month of October of the current year for Suzy's Wallets are shown below:

Oct. 1 Purchased merchandise from Leather Works with a list price of $2,500 and received terms of 2/10, n/30.
4 Sold $1,500 of merchandise to Manley's Stores with terms of 2/15, n/30.
6 Issued a $50 credit memorandum to Manley's Stores for merchandise returned today.
15 Cash sales amounted to $850.
18 Received payment from Manley's Stores for balance owed on account.
20 Sold $3,400 of merchandise to Bates Stores with terms of 2/10, n/30.
22 Paid Leather Works for balance owed on account.
24 Purchased merchandise from Leather Works with a list price of $600 receiving terms of 2/10, n/30.
29 Cash sales amounted to $1,050.
30 Received credit of $50 for merchandise returned to Leather Works today.
31 Paid Leather Works for balance owed on account.

Required

Journalize the entries on the books of:
(a) Suzy's Wallets for October.
(b) Leather Works for October 1, 22, 24, 30, and 31.

Review Problems with Shipping Costs

√ **6-7.** On July 8 of the current year, the Clean Laundry Company purchased $6,000 of merchandise from the Fast Service Supply Company, receiving terms of 2/10 EOM, n/60, FOB shipping point. The account was paid in full on August 9. Shipping charges of $60 were paid on July 10.

Required

(a) Give the journal entries on the books of the Clean Laundry Company for July 8 and 10 and August 9.

(b) Give the journal entries on the books of the Fast Service Supply Company for July 8 and August 9.

(c) Give the journal entry for July 10 on the books of the Fast Service Supply Company, assuming shipping terms of FOB destination.

6-8. Selected transactions for January of the current year for Queens Company are presented below:

Jan. 2 Sold merchandise to L. Hopp, a customer, on account, $750, FOB shipping point.

4 Purchased merchandise from the Larie Company on account, $2,600; shipping terms, FOB shipping point; cash discount terms: 2/10, 1/15, n/30.

5 Paid shipping charges of $50 for merchandise purchased January 4.

5 Purchased office equipment for $950 from the Office Sales Company on account; terms: n/30, FOB destination.

9 Received $50 of merchandise broken in shipment from L. Hopp and credit was given on account.

11 Returned $100 of damaged merchandise to the Larie Company and the amount was deducted from our account.

12 Received payment from L. Hopp less the return and 2 percent discount.

18 Purchased merchandise from the Serts Company on account for $4,000 and received terms of 2/10, n/30, FOB shipping point.

19 Paid shipping charges of $120 on merchandise purchased from Serts Company on November 18.

22 Sold merchandise to B. Crowe for $16,760 on account; shipping terms, FOB shipping point.

23 Defective merchandise was returned by B. Crowe and a credit memorandum was issued for $200.

26 Paid Larie Company less the return of January 11.

28 The owner, Ann Queen, withdrew $800 cash for personal living expenses.

Required

(a) Journalize the transactions for January. All merchandise is sold with terms of 2/10, n/30.

(b) Journalize the closing entries for January. The inventory balance on January 1 amounted to $11,900 and $2,400 on January 31.

6-9. The May transactions for the current year for Wald Company appear below.

May 2 Purchased merchandise on account from Thomas Company, $1,365; terms: 1/10, n/30, FOB shipping point.

2 Paid $30 shipping charges for purchase from Thomas Company.

3 Sold $1,800 of merchandise on account to the Black Company; shipping terms, FOB shipping point.

5 Purchased merchandise for cash amounting to $800.

6 Returned damaged merchandise that cost $465 to the Thomas Company and received credit on account.

9 Paid the Thomas Company less the return and discount.

11 Received payment from the Black Company less the discount.

12 Purchased merchandise on account from the Exeter Company with a list price of $3,000, receiving terms of 2/10, n/30, FOB shipping point.

12 Paid $60 shipping charges for purchase from Exeter Company.

16 Cash sales amounted to $2,666.

17 Sold merchandise on account to the Blue Company for $6,000, shipping terms, FOB destination.

17 Paid $80 shipping charges for shipment of merchandise to Blue Company.

23 Blue Company complained that merchandise had arrived broken, and a credit memorandum for $180 was issued.

29 Paid balance owed to Exeter Company.

29 Charles Wald, owner, withdrew $600 cash for personal expenses.

31 Paid May expenses: selling, $800; general & administrative, $952.

31 Received payment from the Blue Company less return of May 23.

Required

(*a*) Journalize the transactions for May. All merchandise is sold with terms of 2/10, n/30.

(*b*) Journalize the closing entries for May. The merchandise inventory account had a balance of $4,500 on May 1 and $1,948 on May 31.

Accounting for a Merchandising Business (Continued)

CHAPTER 7

After completing this chapter, you should be able to:

1. **Complete a work sheet for a merchandising concern**

2. **Complete the accounting cycle for a merchandising concern beginning with the work sheet**

3. **State the formula for obtaining cost of goods sold**

Steps 1 and 2 of the accounting cycle for a merchandising concern, journalizing and posting the daily transactions, were discussed in Chapter 6. Chapter 7 will continue the discussion on accounting for a merchandising concern beginning with Step 3 of the accounting cycle—the preparation of a work sheet—and continuing through the entire accounting cycle as shown below:

Work Sheet

Financial Statements

Journalizing and Posting Adjusting and Closing Entries

Post-closing Trial Balance

WORK SHEET FOR MERCHANDISING CONCERN

The nine new accounts introduced in Chapter 6 were: Sales, Sales Returns & Allowances, Sales Discounts, Purchases, Purchase Returns & Allowances, Purchase Discount, Transportation In, Transportation Out, and Merchandise Inventory. These nine accounts appear on the work sheet for a merchandising concern, and they are handled the same as any other revenue or expense account with the exception of the adjustment of the beginning and ending inventory. The beginning inventory is listed in the debit columns of the beginning Trial Balance, Adjusted Trial Balance, and Income Statement columns. Ending inventory is recorded as a credit in the Income Statement columns and as a debit in the Balance Sheet columns.

To illustrate the work sheet for a merchandising concern, a work sheet was prepared for the Wonder Products Company for the year ended December 31 as shown in Figure 7-1. The amounts entered in the beginning Trial Balance, Adjustments, and Adjusted Trial Balance columns of the work sheet were taken from the records of Wonder Products. Six steps were necessary to complete the Income Statement and Balance Sheet columns of the work sheet. These six steps are listed below:

Step 1. Extend the beginning inventory of $8,000 shown in the debit column of the Adjusted Trial Balance column to the debit column of the Income Statement.

FIGURE 7-1

WONDER PRODUCTS COMPANY
WORK SHEET
For Year Ended December 31, 19_B

Account Title	Trial Balance Dr	Trial Balance Cr	Adjustments Dr	Adjustments Cr	Adjusted Trial Balance Dr	Adjusted Trial Balance Cr	Income Statement Dr	Income Statement Cr	Balance Sheet Dr	Balance Sheet Cr
Cash	4,650				4,650				4,650	
Accounts Receivable	2,500				2,500				2,500	
Notes Receivable	600				600				600	
Merchandise Inventory (Beg.) (new)	8,000				8,000		①8,000	②23,000	②23,000	
Prepaid Insurance	960			(a) 320	640				640	
Office Supplies	25				25				25	
Office Equipment	5,000				5,000				5,000	
Accum. Dep./Office Equip.		900		(b) 450		1,350				1,350
Accounts Payable		2,815				2,815				2,815
Notes Payable		200				200				200
Art Wonder, Capital		13,000				13,000				13,000
Art Wonder, Drawing	7,150				7,150				7,150	
Sales		29,600				29,600		29,600		
Sales Returns & Allowances	60				60		60			
Sales Discounts	900				900		900			
Purchases	5,000				5,000		5,000			
Purchase Returns & Allowances		76				76		76		
Purchase Discounts		100				100		100		
Transportation In	100				100		100			
Wages Expense/Selling	3,255		(c) 50		3,305		3,305			
Rent Expense/Selling	960				960		960			
Transportation Out	54				54		54			
Office Salaries Expense	7,000		(c) 30		7,030		7,030			
Rent Expense/Gen. & Adm.	480				480		480			
Interest Earned		9				9		9		
Interest Expense	6				6		6			
Totals	46,700	46,700								
Insurance Exp./Gen. & Adm.			(a) 320		320		320			
Depreciation Exp./Office Equip.			(b) 450		450		450			
Wages & Salaries Payable				(c) 80		80				80
Totals			850	850	47,230	47,230	26,665	32,785	23,565	17,445
Net Income							6,120			6,120
Totals							32,785	32,785	23,565	23,565

Step 1 Step 2 Step 3 Step 4 Step 5 Step 6

175

Step 2. Enter the ending inventory of $3,000 as a credit in the Income Statement column and extend the amount to the debit column of the Balance Sheet columns.

Step 3. Extend the sales and sales related accounts, cost of goods sold accounts, operating expenses, and other revenue and expense account balances in the Adjusted Trial Balance columns to the proper debit and credit columns of the Income Statement. Total the debit and credit columns.

Step 4. Extend the asset (other than merchandise inventory) and liability account balances in the Adjusted Trial Balance columns to the proper debit and credit columns of the Balance Sheet. Total the debit and credit columns.

Step 5. Calculate the difference between the debit and credit columns of the Income Statement to determine the net income or loss for the year. The credit column for the Wonder Products Company is larger than the debit column, representing net income earned in the amount of $6,120 ($32,785 − $26,665). Enter this amount in the debit column of the Income Statement and extend the amount to the credit column of the Balance Sheet columns. Enter the words "Net Income" on the same line in the Account Title column.

Step 6. Total the debit columns of the Income Statement and Balance Sheet and double-underline the totals.

Note: All final debit and credit totals should be *equal.*

FINANCIAL STATEMENTS

After the work sheet is completed, the formal financial statements are prepared from the data appearing in the Income Statement and Balance Sheet columns. The income statement is usually prepared before the balance sheet.

Income Statement

The income statement for a merchandising concern has two main classifications for revenue and expenses called:

1. *Operating Revenue* and *Operating Expenses*
2. *Other Revenue* and *Other Expenses*

A special classification for the direct costs of selling the product is shown on the income statement in a special section called Cost of Goods Sold.

The income statement begins with the Operating Revenue section.

Operating Revenue. The first item listed in the Operating Revenue section is the *gross sales* which is all the revenue earned from selling a product. Next, the total of the sales returns and allowances and sales discounts are deducted from gross sales to arrive at *net sales.*

To illustrate the various sections of the income statement for a merchandising concern, the data appearing in the income statement columns of the work sheet in Figure 7-1 for the Wonder Products Company was used for all the examples.

The Operating Revenue section is illustrated in Example 1.

EXAMPLE 1
Operating Revenue section
of income statement

Operating Revenue:			
Sales		$29,600	
Less: Sales Returns & Allowances	$ 60		
Sales Discounts	900	960	
Net Sales			$28,640

After arriving at net sales, all the direct costs of selling the product are shown in the Cost of Goods Sold section.

Cost of Goods Sold. The Cost of Goods Sold section of the income statement appears after the net sales figure. *Cost of goods sold* is determined by adding the beginning inventory to the net cost of purchases (purchases + transportation in − purchase returns and allowances − purchase discounts) and deducting the ending inventory. The *cost of goods sold formula* is:

Beginning Merchandise Inventory

+ Net Cost of Purchases

= Cost of Goods Available for Sale

− Ending Merchandise Inventory

= Cost of Goods Sold

Cost of goods sold is subtracted from net sales to obtain gross profit. *Gross profit* is the profit before deducting operating expenses to arrive at net operating income as shown in Example 2.

Operating Expenses. Operating expenses are all the expenses incurred in earning the operating revenue. The operating expenses are divided into two groups or subclassifications called:

1. Selling Expenses
2. General & Administrative Expenses

All expenses that are directly related to the sales department, such as salespeople's salaries, advertising expense, transportation out, rent, utili-

EXAMPLE 2

*Cost of Goods Sold section
of income statement*

Net Sales			$28,640
Cost of Goods Sold:			
Merchandise Inventory, Jan. 1, 19__		$ 8,000	
Purchases	$5,000		
Add: Transportation In	100	$5,100	
Less: Purchase Returns			
& Allowances	$ 76		
Purchase Discounts	100	176	
Net Cost of Purchases		4,924	
Cost of Goods Available for Sale		$12,924	
Less: Merchandise Inventory, Dec. 31, 19__		3,000	
Cost of Goods Sold			9,924
Gross Profit			$18,716

ties, depreciation, insurance, and other expenses related to the sales department, would be shown as an Operating/***Selling Expense*** on the income statement.

The expenses for the office salaries, administrative salaries, rent, utilities, depreciation, insurance, taxes, and other expenses related to the office and administrative department are classified as Operating/***General & Administrative Expenses*** on the income statement.

Total Operating Expenses (selling and general & administrative expenses) are subtracted from gross profit to arrive at *net operating income* as shown in Example 3.

EXAMPLE 3

*Operating Expense Section
of income statement*

Gross Profit			$18,716
Operating Expenses:			
Selling Expenses			
Wages	$3,305		
Rent	960		
Transportation Out	54		
Total Selling Expenses		$4,319	
General & Administrative Expenses:			
Office Salaries	$7,030		
Rent	480		
Insurance	320		
Depreciation/Office Equipment	450		
Total General & Administrative Expenses		8,280	
Total Operating Expenses			12,599
Net Operating Income			$ 6,117

After arriving at net operating income, the other revenue and other expenses are recorded to obtain the net income for the period.

Other Revenue and Other Expense. Revenue and expenses incurred during the period that are not directly related to the principal business activity of the company are classified as *Other Revenue* and *Other Expense*. These revenue and expenses are shown in the last section of the income statement. Accounts classified as other revenue would include interest earned on notes received from customers and gains received from the sale of a plant asset. Accounts classified as other expense would include interest expense resulting from a note payable or mortgage payable and losses incurred from the sale of a plant asset.[1]

Other revenue is added to net operating income and other expense is subtracted to arrive at the net income for the period as shown in Example 4.

EXAMPLE 4
Other Revenue and Other Expense section of income statement

Net Operating Income		$6,117
Other Revenue:		
Interest Earned	$9	
Other Expense:		
Interest Expense	6	3
Net Income		$6,120

Expanded Income Statement. The correct format for the preparation of a classified income statement for a merchandising concern is

Format for classified income statement

Operating revenue

− cost of goods sold

= gross profit

− operating expenses: selling, and general & administrative

= net operating income

+ other revenue

− other expense

= net income

To illustrate the complete income statement for a merchandising concern, the income statement for the Wonder Products Company shown in Example 5 was prepared from the Income Statement columns of the work sheet in Figure 7-1.

Balance Sheet

A balance sheet prepared for a merchandising concern is basically the same as a balance sheet prepared for a service-type of business. The only difference in the statements is the addition of the ending inventory which is shown after listing the cash and receivable accounts in the Current Asset section. To illustrate, the balance sheet for Wonder Products Company was prepared from the data appearing in the Balance Sheet columns of the work sheet in Figure 7-1.

[1] Gains and losses from the sale of plant assets are discussed in Chapter 11.

EXAMPLE 5

*Income statement for
merchandising concern*

WONDER PRODUCTS COMPANY
INCOME STATEMENT
For Year Ended December 31, 19_B

Operating Revenue:			
Sales		$29,600	
Less: Sales Returns & Allowances	$ 60		
Sales Discount	900	960	
Net Sales			$28,640
Cost of Goods Sold:			
Merchandise Inventory, Jan. 1, 19_B		$ 8,000	
Purchases	$5,000		
Add: Transportation In	100		
Total	$5,100		
Less: Purchase Returns & Allowances	$ 76		
Purchase Discount	100	176	
Net Cost of Purchases		4,924	
Cost of Goods Available for Sale		$12,924	
Less: Merchandise Inventory, Dec. 31, 19_B		3,000	
Cost of Goods Sold			9,924
Gross Profit			$18,716
Operating Expenses:			
Selling Expenses:			
Wages	$3,305		
Rent	960		
Transportation Out	54		
Total Selling Expenses		$ 4,319	
General & Administrative Expenses:			
Office Salaries	$7,030		
Rent	480		
Insurance	320		
Depreciation/Office Equipment	450		
Total General & Administrative Expenses		8,280	
Total Operating Expenses			12,599
Net Operating Income			$ 6,117
Other Revenue:			
Interest Earned		$ 9	
Other Expenses:			
Interest Expense		6	3
Net Income			$ 6,120

Adjusting and Closing Entries

The next step in the accounting cycle is to journalize and post the adjusting
and closing entries.[2]

[2] The adjusting and closing entries may also be prepared before the preparation of the financial statements as shown in Chapter 5.

Merchandise inventory is shown in Current Asset section of balance sheet

WONDER PRODUCTS COMPANY
BALANCE SHEET
December 31, 19_B

Assets

Current Assets:
Cash	$ 4,650	
Accounts Receivable	2,500	
Notes Receivable	600	
Merchandise Inventory	3,000	
Prepaid Insurance	640	
Office Supplies	25	
Total Current Assets		$11,415

Plant Assets:
Office Equipment	$ 5,000	
Less: Accumulated Depreciation	1,350	
Total Plant Assets		3,650
Total Assets		$15,065

Liabilities

Current Liabilities:
Accounts Payable	$ 2,815	
Notes Payable	200	
Wages & Salaries Payable	80	
Total Current Liabilities		$ 3,095

Owner's Equity

Art Wonder, Capital, Jan. 1, 19_B	$13,000	
Add: Net Income	6,120	$19,120
Less: Art Wonder, Drawing		7,150
Wonder, Capital, Dec. 31, 19_B		11,970
Total Liabilities & Owner's Equity		$15,065

Adjusting Entries. The adjusting entries are prepared from the data in the Adjustments column of the work sheet. To illustrate, the adjusting entries (shown on page 182) were prepared from the work sheet of the Wonder Products Company shown in Figure 7-1.

The posting of the adjusting entries was illustrated in Chapter 5 on page 127 and will not be shown here.

Closing Entries. The four closing entries are prepared from the data appearing in the Income Statement columns of the work sheet, and the amount for the owner's drawing account is taken from the Balance Sheet debit column. When preparing the closing entries for a merchandising concern, the accounts with their amounts appearing in the Income State-

Adjusting entries

		Adjusting Entries		
19_B				
Dec.	31	Insurance Expense/General & Administrative	320	
		Prepaid Insurance		320
	31	Depreciation Expense/Office Equipment	450	
		Accumulated Depreciation/Office		
		Equipment		450
	31	Wages Expense/Selling	50	
		Office Salaries Expense	30	
		Wages & Salaries Payable		80

ment debit column are usually closed first to bring the Merchandise Inventory account to a zero balance. The beginning inventory is shown in the Income Statement debit column and after the first closing entry is journalized and posted, the Merchandise Inventory account will have a zero balance. The ending inventory appears in the Income Statement credit column, and after the credit accounts with their amounts are closed in the second closing entry, the Merchandise Inventory account will show the ending amount of inventory. To illustrate, the four closing entries shown below were prepared from the work sheet of the Wonder Products Company. The posting of the Merchandise Inventory account is illustrated in Examples 1, 2, and 3. Posting of the other accounts in the four closing entries was illustrated in Chapter 5 and will not be shown here.

EXAMPLE 1   *On December 31, 19_A, the inventory account showed a balance of $8,000, as illustrated in the ledger account. This balance represents the amount of merchandise on hand at the beginning of the fiscal period.*

Title: Merchandise Inventory   **Account No.: 116**

Date		Explanation	Ref.	Debit	Credit	Balance
19_A						
Dec.	31		J1	8,000		8,000

Closing Entry 1

General Journal		Page 12
19_B		
Dec. 31 Income Summary		26,665
Merchandise Inventory	116	8,000
Sales Returns & Allowances		60
Sales Discount		900
Purchases		5,000
Transportation In		100
Wages Expense/Selling		3,305
Rent Expense/Selling		960
Transportation Out		54
Office Salaries Expense		7,030
Rent Expense/Gen. & Adm.		480
Interest Expense		6
Insurance Expense/Gen. & Adm.		320
Depreciation Expense/Office Equip.		450
To close the beginning inventory, Sales Returns & Allowances, Sales Discount, and expense accounts.		

EXAMPLE 2   *The posting of the first closing entry as a credit to the Merchandise Inventory account for $8,000 is shown in the ledger account below. This entry clears out the beginning inventory, bringing the balance in the account to a zero as indicated in the general ledger account.*

Title: Merchandise Inventory   **Account No.: 116**

Date		Explanation	Ref.	Debit	Credit	Balance
19_A Dec.	31		J1	8,000		8,000
19_B Dec.	31		J12		8,000	–0–

Closing Entry 2

19_B		
Dec. 31	Merchandise Inventory	116	3,000
	Sales		29,600
	Purchase Returns & Allowances		76
	Purchase Discount		100
	Interest Earned		9
	Income Summary			32,785
	To close the revenue, Purchase		
	Returns & Allowances, Purchase		
	Discount accounts, and record the		
	ending inventory.		

EXAMPLE 3   *The second closing entry is posted by debiting the Merchandise Inventory account for $3,000. The ledger account now shows the amount of inventory on hand on December 31, 19_B, the end of the fiscal period.*

Title: Merchandise Inventory   **Account No.: 116**

Date		Explanation	Ref.	Debit	Credit	Balance
19_A Dec.	31		J1	8,000		8,000
19_B Dec.	31		J12		8,000	–0–
	31		J12	3,000		3,000

Closing Entry 3

19_B		
Dec. 31	Income Summary	6,120	
	Art Wonder, Capital		6,120
	To close the Income Summary		
	account and record the net income in		
	the capital account.		

Closing Entry 4

19_B		
Dec. 31	Art Wonder, Capital	7,150	
	Art Wonder, Drawing		7,150
	To close the drawing account.		

Post-Closing Trial Balance

The post-closing trial balance is the last step in the accounting cycle, and it is prepared after the adjusting and closing entries have been journalized and posted. After the posting process is completed, the only accounts that should have a balance are the asset, liabilities, and owner's capital accounts. The post-closing trial balance shown below was prepared from the ledger of the Wonder Products Company. The capital account would have a balance of $11,970 as shown on the balance sheet on page 181.

Post-closing trial balance

WONDER PRODUCTS COMPANY
POST-CLOSING TRIAL BALANCE
December 31, 19_B

Cash	$ 4,650	
Accounts Receivable	2,500	
Notes Receivable	600	
Merchandise Inventory	3,000	
Prepaid Insurance	640	
Office Supplies	25	
Office Equipment	5,000	
Accumulated Depreciation/Office Equipment		$ 1,350
Accounts Payable		2,815
Notes Payable		200
Wages & Salaries Payable		80
Art Wonder, Capital		11,970
Totals	$16,415	$16,415

SUMMARY

The nine new accounts involved in purchasing a product and reselling the product for a profit appear on the work sheet for a merchandising concern. These nine accounts are handled the same as any other revenue or expense accounts with the exception of the adjustment for the beginning and ending inventory.

The income statement for a merchandising concern includes a special section showing the cost of the goods that are sold. These costs are subtracted from net sales to arrive at gross profit.

There are generally two types of operating expenses: selling and general & administrative expenses. The operating expenses are deducted from gross profit to arrive at net operating income.

Revenue earned and expenses incurred during the period that are not classified as an operating revenue or operating expense are listed in the Other Revenue and Other Expense section of the income statement. Net operating income plus other revenue and less other expenses equals the net income for the period.

The ending balance of the Merchandise Inventory account is listed after the cash and receivable accounts in the Current Asset section of the balance sheet.

GLOSSARY

Cost of Goods Sold: The cost of the merchandise sold to the customer and shown on the income statement as a deduction to net sales to arrive at gross profit.

Cost of Goods Sold Formula: Beginning merchandise inventory plus net cost of purchases less ending merchandise inventory equals the cost of goods sold.

General & Administrative Expenses: A subclassification of operating expenses that represents expenses directly related to the office and administrative staff.

Gross Profit: The profit obtained after deducting the cost of goods sold from net sales. Gross profit represents the profit before considering operating expenses and other expenses and other revenue.

Gross Sales: All the revenue earned from selling a product.

Net Sales: Net sales is determined by subtracting the sales returns and allowances and sales discounts from the gross sales (revenue earned from selling a product).

Operating Expenses: Expenses incurred in selling a service or a product.

Operating Revenue: Revenue earned from selling a service or a product.

Other Expense: Expenses incurred during the period that are not a cost of selling the product or an operating expense.

Other Revenue: Revenue earned during the period from sources other than selling a product or service.

Selling Expense: A subclassification of operating expenses listing the expenses directly related to the selling of the product.

QUESTIONS

1. State the correct format for the preparation of an income statement for a merchandising concern.
2. Classify the following accounts: Purchases, Sales Returns and Allowances, Transportation In, and Transportation Out.
3. In what two columns of the work sheet is the ending merchandise inventory recorded?
4. State the formula for determining cost of goods sold.
5. What is the difference between gross sales and net sales?
6. What is the difference between net operating income and net income?
7. Give the classification for interest earned and interest expense.

EXERCISES

Work Sheet

1. Arrange the following items in the appropriate order for the completion of the Income Statement and Balance Sheet columns of a work sheet for a merchandising concern.

   (a) Enter the beginning inventory in the Income Statement columns.

   (b) Enter the ending inventory in the Income Statement and Balance Sheet columns.

   (c) Extend the amounts in the Adjusted Trial Balance columns to the proper Balance Sheet columns, and total the debit and credit columns.

   (d) Determine the amount of net income or loss, and record in the proper columns of the Income Statement and Balance Sheet columns.

   (e) Record the final totals of the Income Statement and Balance Sheet columns.

   (f) Extend the amounts in the Adjusted Trial Balance columns to the proper Income Statement columns. Total the debit and credit columns.

2. For the partial work sheet below, indicate with a check (✔) mark the column/s where the amounts would appear for each of the following accounts. The first account has been completed as an example.

Account Titles	Income Statement Dr	Income Statement Cr	Balance Sheet Dr	Balance Sheet Cr
Merchandise Inventory 1/1	✔			
Merchandise Inventory 12/31				
Sales				
Sales Returns & Allowances				
Sales Discounts				
Purchases				
Purchase Returns & Allowances				
Purchase Discounts				
Transportation In				
Transportation Out				
Net Income				
Net Loss				

3. The adjusted trial balance for Walker Sales appears below. (The amounts are shown in one and two digit figures for simplicity.)

WALKER SALES
ADJUSTED TRIAL BALANCE
December 31, 19__

Merchandise Inventory	$ 2	
Other Current Assets	10	
Plant Assets	20	
Current Liabilities		$12
Long-term Liabilities		10
A. Walker, Capital		9
A. Walker, Drawing	6	
Sales		28
Sales Returns & Allowances	2	
Sales Discount	1	
Purchases	10	
Purchase Returns & Allowances		3
Purchase Discount		1
Transportation In	2	
Selling Expenses	5	
General & Administrative Expenses	6	
Interest Earned		2
Interest Expense	1	
Totals	$65	$65

Prepare a work sheet for the year ended December 31 of the current year beginning with the Adjusted Trial Balance columns. The merchandise inventory on December 31 amounts to $1.

Income Statement

4. On January 1 of the current year, the balance of the Merchandise Inventory account was $1,962. During the year, purchases totaled $80,000 and the cost of goods sold amounted to $78,400. Give the (a) two journal entries required to remove the beginning merchandise inventory and record the ending merchandise inventory on December 31, the end of the accounting period; (b) balance sheet presentation for merchandise inventory on December 31; and (c) Cost of Goods Sold section of the income statement.

5. The following data appeared in the records of DA Sales:

Net Income	$12,000	Cost of Goods Sold	$4,200
Interest Earned	240	Gross Profit	7,000
Interest Expense	130		

Determine the (a) net operating income, (b) net sales, and (c) classification for Interest Earned and Interest Expense accounts.

6. Prepare the Cost of Goods Sold section of the income statement from the following data:

Merchandise Inventory 1/1	$ 2,000
Purchases	60,000
Purchase Returns	1,100
Merchandise Inventory 12/31	1,500
Purchase Discounts	800
Transportation in	400

Closing Entries

7. Give the closing entries required for the following data:

Merchandise Inventory 1/1	$ 400
Transportation In	200
Merchandise Inventory 12/31	840
Transportation Out	90
Purchases	4,690
Selling Expense	1,210
Sales	9,960
General & Administrative Expenses	2,420
Interest Earned	80
Interest Expense	30
A. Parks, Drawing	1,000

PROBLEMS

Work Sheet

7-1. A list of selected accounts taken from the adjusted trial balance of the Stacey Company as of December 31 of the current year appears as follows:

STACEY COMPANY
ADJUSTED TRIAL BALANCE
December 31, 19__

Cash	$ 12,600	
Accounts Receivable	14,100	
Notes Receivable	2,200	
Interest Receivable	20	
Merchandise Inventory 1/1	14,105	
Prepaid Insurance	550	
Advertising Supplies	165	
Land	16,000	
Building	24,000	
Accumulated Depreciation/Building		$ 6,000
Office Equipment	4,800	
Accumulated Depreciation/Office Equipment. .		960
Accounts Payable		10,400
Interest Payable		80
Salaries & Wages Payable		750
Mortgage Payable		9,000
E. Stacey, Capital		37,000

E. Stacey, Drawings	10,800	
Sales		198,000
Sales Returns & Allowances	2,600	
Sales Discounts	2,960	
Purchases	110,400	
Purchase Returns & Allowances		2,600
Purchase Discounts		2,200
Transportation In	940	
Selling Expenses	28,460	
General & Administrative Expenses	22,300	
Interest Earned		110
Interest Expense	100	
Totals	$267,100	$267,100

The merchandise inventory on December 31 amounts to $6,050.

Required

Prepare a work sheet for the Stacey Company.

✓ **7-2.** The trial balance for Wolner Company as of December 31 of the current year appears below.

WOLNER COMPANY
TRIAL BALANCE
December 31, 19__

Cash	$ 19,700	
Accounts Receivable	9,000	
Merchandise Inventory 1/1	4,000	
Office Supplies	1,000	
Store Supplies	600	
Store Equipment	38,000	
Accumulated Depreciation/Store Equipment		$ 8,000
Accounts Payable		15,000
Notes Payable		6,000
J. Wolner, Capital		45,500
J. Wolner, Drawing	11,500	
Sales		85,700
Sales Returns & Allowances	3,000	
Sales Discount	2,400	
Purchases	48,000	
Purchase Returns & Allowances		3,500
Purchase Discount		8,200
Transportation In	2,800	
Sales Salaries Expense	10,000	
Store Rent Expense	2,400	
Insurance Expense/Selling	600	
Telephone Expense/Selling	200	
Miscellaneous Selling Expense	1,500	
Office Salaries Expense	14,000	
Office Rent Expense	1,800	

Insurance Expense/General	300	
Telephone Expense/General	800	
Miscellaneous General Expense	300	
Totals	$171,900	$171,900

Additional data

(a) Estimated depreciation for store equipment, $4,000.
(b) Store supplies remaining on hand total $100.
(c) Office supplies remaining on hand total $300.
(d) Unpaid office salaries total $600; sales salaries total $500.
(e) Merchandise inventory on December 31 amounted to $3,600.

Required

Prepare a work sheet for the Wolner Company.

Determining Income Statement Amounts and Ending Capital

7-3. Selected data taken from the records of the Diane Company on December 31 of the current year are shown below.

Merchandise Inventory 1/1	$ 4,295
Merchandise Inventory 12/31	8,035
Sales	22,000
Sales Returns & Allowances	100
Sales Discounts	605
Purchases	10,500
Purchase Returns & Allowances	50
Purchase Discounts	210
Transportation In	60
S. Diane, Capital 1/1	10,880
S. Diane, Drawings	9,200

Required

Determine the following:

(a) Net sales
(b) Cost of goods available for sale
(c) Gross profit
(d) S. Diane, Capital on December 31, assuming that operating expenses amounted to $4,550

7-4. From the following data, prepare a partial income statement through gross profit on sales in good form for the J. P. Sales Company for the year ending on December 31 of the current year.

Merchandise Inventory 1/1	$15,000
Merchandise Inventory 12/31	7,000
Purchases	25,000
Purchase Returns & Allowances	400

Purchase Discounts	450
Transportation In	110
Sales	40,000
Sales Returns & Allowances	800
Sales Discounts	650

√ 7-5. The following information was taken from the records of Feder Associates on December 31 of the current year.

Joan Feder, Capital 1/1	$ 7,600
Joan Feder, Drawing	5,800
Interest Earned	90
Merchandise Inventory 1/1	920
Merchandise Inventory 12/31	1,200
Operating Expenses	2,200
Purchases	8,100
Purchase Returns & Allowances	250
Purchase Discount	340
Sales	17,200
Sales Returns & Allowances	100
Sales Discount	210
Transportation In	150

Required

Determine the following:

(a) Net Sales

(b) Cost of Goods Sold

(c) Gross Profit

(d) Net Operating Income

(e) Net Income

(f) Joan Feder, Capital 12/31

Journalizing Adjusting and Closing Entries Plus Owner's Equity Section and Income Statement

7-6. The data appearing in the Income Statement columns of the work sheet for Brian Service Company for the year ended December 31 of the current year is shown below.

	Income Statement Debit	Income Statement Credit
Merchandise Inventory	$ 700	$ 400
Sales		18,900
Sales Returns & Allowances	500	
Sales Discount	900	
Purchases	10,700	
Purchase Returns & Allowances		50
Purchase Discount		150
Transportation In	380	
Selling Expenses	2,900	
General & Administrative Expenses	3,600	
Interest Earned		50
Interest Expense	20	
Totals	$19,700	$19,550
Net Loss		150
Totals	$19,700	$19,700

Required

(a) Journalize the closing entries.
(b) Prepare a formal classified income statement.
(c) Prepare the Owner's Equity Section of the balance sheet using the following additional information: Brian Levey, Capital 1/1, $10,600; Brian Levey, Drawings, $6,000.

7-7. A list of selected accounts taken from the Adjusted Trial Balance columns of the work sheet for Ace Company as of December 31 of the current year appears below:

ACE COMPANY
ADJUSTED TRIAL BALANCE
December 31, 19___

Cash	$ 2,600	
Accounts Receivable	4,100	
Notes Receivable	2,200	
Interest Receivable	20	
Merchandise Inventory 1/1	4,105	
Prepaid Insurance	550	
Advertising Supplies	165	
Land	6,000	
Building	24,000	
Accumulated Depreciation/Building		$ 6,000
Office Equipment	4,800	
Accumulated Depreciation/Office Equipment		960
Accounts Payable		8,400
Interest Payable		80
Salaries & Wages Payable		650
Mortgage Payable		5,000
E. Ace, Capital		7,000
E. Ace, Drawings	7,800	
Sales		98,000
Sales Returns & Allowances	1,600	
Sales Discounts	1,960	
Purchases	35,620	
Purchase Returns & Allowances		2,600
Purchase Discounts		1,200
Transportation In	380	
Selling Expenses	18,000	
General & Administrative Expenses	16,000	
Interest Earned		110
Interest Expense	100	
Totals	$130,000	$130,000

The merchandise inventory on December 31 amounted to $2,105.

Required

(a) Journalize the closing entries.
(b) Prepare an income statement.

7-8. Use the work sheet prepared for Wolner Company in Problem 7-2 and prepare the following:

(a) Journalize the adjusting and closing entries.

(b) Prepare a formal classified income statement.

Accounting Cycle Beginning with Work Sheet

7-9. The adjusted trial balance for the Hillier Company as of June 30, 19_B, the end of the fiscal year, is shown below:

HILLIER COMPANY
ADJUSTED TRIAL BALANCE
June 30, 19_B

Cash	$ 3,600	
Notes Receivable	2,000	
Accounts Receivable	7,200	
Merchandise Inventory 6/30/A	6,100	
Prepaid Insurance	460	
Office Supplies	320	
Land	2,000	
Building	26,000	
Accumulated Depreciation/Building		$ 4,200
Equipment	8,100	
Accumulated Depreciation/Equipment		1,100
Accounts Payable		6,800
Notes Payable		10,000
Salaries & Wages Payable		500
A. Hillier, Capital		11,000
A. Hillier, Drawing	10,900	
Sales		145,900
Sales Returns & Allowances	2,800	
Sales Discount	1,400	
Purchases	58,600	
Purchase Returns & Allowances		1,700
Purchase Discount		1,800
Transportation In	1,300	
Selling Expenses	22,000	
General & Administration Expenses	31,000	
Interest Earned		900
Interest Expense	120	
Totals	$183,900	$183,900

Required

(a) Complete the work sheet.

(b) Journalize the closing entries.

(c) Prepare a classified income statement.

(d) Prepare a classified balance sheet. *36,280 Ending Capital*

(e) Prepare a post-closing trial balance.

The merchandise inventory as of June 30, 19_B, amounts to $9,200.

7-10. The adjusted trial balance on December 31 of the current year for the Lasso Company appears below.

LASSO COMPANY
ADJUSTED TRIAL BALANCE
December 31, 19__

Cash	$ 3,900	
Accounts Receivable	12,300	
Notes Receivable	4,800	
Merchandise Inventory 1/1	13,100	
Prepaid Insurance	360	
Supplies	250	
Equipment	15,000	
Accumulated Depreciation/Equipment		$ 4,500
Accounts Payable		14,200
Notes Payable		1,200
Salaries & Wages Payable		400
C. Lasso, Capital		36,260
C. Lasso, Drawings	14,000	
Sales		98,900
Sales Returns & Allowances	900	
Sales Discounts	1,750	
Purchases	54,850	
Purchase Returns & Allowances		770
Purchases Discounts		1,700
Transportation In	880	
Sales Salaries Expense	10,800	
Transportation Out	400	
Supplies Expense/Selling	450	
Miscellaneous Selling Expenses	1,800	
Rent Expense/Selling	2,700	
Insurance Expense/Selling	80	
Depreciation Expense/Equipment	1,500	
Office Salaries Expense	16,000	
Miscellaneous General Expense	550	
Rent Expense/General	900	
Insurance Expense/General	40	
Supplies Expense/General	600	
Interest Earned		40
Interest Expense	60	
Totals	$157,970	$157,970

The merchandise inventory on December 31 amounted to $5,200.

Required

(*a*) Complete the work sheet.
(*b*) Journalize the closing entries.
(*c*) Prepare a classified income statement.
(*d*) Prepare a classified balance sheet.
(*e*) Prepare a post-closing trial balance.

After completing this chapter, you should be able to:

1. **Explain the need for special journals**

2. **Journalize business transactions in the sales journal, purchases journal, cash receipts journal, and cash payments journal**

3. **Explain the function of the accounts receivable and accounts payable subsidiary ledgers**

4. **Post information in the special journals to the general ledger daily and monthly**

5. **Present the receivables and payables properly on the balance sheet**

6. **Give the balance sheet presentation of overpayments by customers and overpayments to creditors**

7. **Define pegboard accounting**

8. **Explain the advantages of a pegboard system**

9. **State the advantages of using a pegboard system for accounts receivable**

Recording business transactions in the general journal is adequate for a business which has a small number of transactions. However, as the volume of activity or the size of the business increases, it soon becomes apparent that the general journal is inadequate for recording all the transactions. The posting and journalizing of each debit and credit for hundreds or perhaps thousands of entries becomes impractical. Therefore, it is necessary to develop a system that will simplify the journalizing procedures and reduce the amount of posting.

Accounting systems will vary depending on the type and size of the business. Small businesses may use simple hand-operated accounting systems. As the size of the business and volume of activity increase, accounting machines and computers combined with hand operations may be employed to handle many of the routine accounting procedures.

The first step toward improving the handling of a greater work load is to separate high-volume activities from the general work flow and group similar activities together and record them in special journals. Close examination of the day-to-day transactions show that there are four areas with a high frequency of activity. They are:

1. Sale of service and/or goods on account
2. Purchase of goods and services for business operations on account
3. Receipt of cash
4. Payment or disbursement of cash

In previous chapters, all these transactions were recorded in the general journal. Now each transaction will be separated according to categories and recorded in one of four special journals as listed below:

Four special journals
1. Sales journal
2. Purchases journal
3. Cash receipts journal
4. Cash payments journal

Each of these **special journals** is designed to handle only one type of transaction, thereby simplifying the work of the accountant and helping to make the system more efficient by reducing the time spent on journalizing and posting procedures.

SALES JOURNAL

The *sales journal* illustrated in Figure 8-2 is a one amount column special journal designed to record *all* sales of merchandise on account. Cash sales are recorded in another special journal.

FIGURE 8-1

SALES OR PURCHASE INVOICE*
Job Sales Company
10 Second Avenue
Livonia, MI   48154

Sold to: Conrad Company

6 First Street

Livonia, MI   48152

Shipped to: same

Terms: 2/10; n/30

Invoice No. 123

Invoice Date 5/3/C

Your Order No. 99

Date Shipped 5/3/C

Shipped via USP

Quantity	Description	Price	Amount
33 dozen	X32R 5-Column Journal Paper	$10	$330
7 gross	PS8N Mimeo Paper	60	420
	Total		$850

* The invoice is called a sales invoice by the seller and a purchase invoice by the purchaser.

When merchandise is sold on account, usually a multicopy, prenumbered sales slip or invoice is issued by the seller to the customer. To illustrate, an invoice was prepared by the Job Sales Company for merchandise sold to the Conrad Company as shown in Figure 8-1.

Note that the sales invoice contains the name of the customer, date of sale, credit terms, description of items sold, quantity, method of shipment, and the amount. A copy of the sales slip or invoice is used for recording the sale of merchandise on account in the sales journal.

To illustrate, assume that the Job Sales Company had the following sales of merchandise on account during May of the current year.

Sales of merchandise on account for Job Sales Company in May

19—		
May	3	Sold merchandise to Conrad Company on account, $850.
	10	Sold merchandise to Alice Company on account, $1,500.
	16	Sold merchandise to Taylor Company on account, $1,000.
	20	Sold merchandise to Bab Company on account, $500.

If these transactions were recorded in the general journal, it would require four separate journal entries consisting of four debit and four credit entries. After journalizing the four entries, it would require eight separate postings to the general ledger (four to Accounts Receivable and four to Sales). However, the work is considerably reduced when using the special sales journal because each entry only takes one line as shown in Figure 8-2.

Note that the sales journal in Figure 8-2 contains a column for each item of information. If more information is needed, such as credit terms, another column could be added.

In a general journal each sale would require one line for the debit entry, one line for the credit entry, and one to three lines for the explanation. In the sales journal, each of the four sales requires only one line for recording all the information about the transaction. This is possible because the one-column sales journal is designed to record only one type of transaction that requires a debit to the Accounts Receivable account and a credit to the Sales account. This journal also eliminates the need for an ex-

FIGURE 8-2

SALES JOURNAL   **Page 2**

Date		Account Debited	Invoice No.	Ref.	Amount
19—					
May	3	Conrad Company	123	✓	850
	10	Alice Company	124	✓	1,500
	16	Taylor Company	125	✓	1,000
	20	Bab Company	126	✓	500
	31	Accounts Receivable Dr/Sales Cr			3,850
					(110)(400)

planation. If additional information is needed regarding a particular sale, it may easily be found on the file copy of the prenumbered sales invoice which is referenced in the Invoice Number column of the sales journal.

Control Accounts and Subsidiary Ledgers

In previous chapters every transaction involving a sale of merchandise or services to a customer on account was recorded in the Accounts Receivable account. The balance in the Accounts Receivable account represented the total amount owed to the firm by all customers; it did not show the amount due from each individual customer. This information could be obtained by going through each individual journal entry or sales invoice. To provide this information, a separate record is maintained for each customer. These records of customers' *subsidiary accounts* are arranged in alphabetical order in a ledger called the *accounts receivable subsidiary ledger* or "customers' subsidiary ledger."

Posting from sales journal to ledgers

The *Accounts Receivable* account in the general ledger is known as the control account. This *control account* contains the total or balance of all the individual customer accounts shown in the subsidiary ledger. The balance for each individual customer is shown in the subsidiary ledger. Control accounts serve as a check on the accuracy of the subsidiary ledgers. For example, the balance in the Accounts Receivable account in the general ledger should equal the sum of the balances as shown in each customer's account in the subsidiary ledger if all the posting has been done properly. It is important to keep each customer's account up-to-date. Daily posting of these charges to the customer's account in the subsidiary ledger makes it possible to know how much each customer owes on a daily basis. As each sale is posted to the subsidiary ledger, a check mark (✔) is placed in the Reference column of the sales journal. A check mark is used because the customers' accounts in the subsidiary ledger do not have account numbers; they are arranged alphabetically.

At the end of the month the sales journal is totaled and the amount is double-underlined. In Figure 8-3, the amount ($3,850) is posted as a debit to the Accounts Receivable control account and as a credit to the Sales account in the general ledger. The account numbers are written below the column total to indicate that the posting of this total has been completed. Posting from the special sales journal required only six postings (two to the general ledger and four to the subsidiary ledger) as compared to 12 postings that would have been necessary had we used the general journal to record the transactions. This simplifies the journalizing and posting procedure, resulting in a significant saving of time especially for a company with many charge sales each month.

Summary Illustration

The procedures for posting from the sales journal to the general ledger accounts and individual customers' accounts in the accounts receivable subsidiary ledger are listed below.

① The individual sales are posted daily to the accounts receivable subsidiary ledger. The subsidiary ledger has a separate account for each customer arranged in alphabetical order.

② A check mark (✔) is placed in the Reference column of the sales journal to indicate that the posting to the subsidiary ledger is complete.

③ At the end of the accounting period, usually monthly, the sales column is totaled and posted as a debit to the Accounts Receivable control account and as a credit to the Sales account in the general ledger.

④ The Accounts Receivable and Sales account numbers are entered below the total of the sales column in the sales journal to show that the posting to the general ledger is complete.

⑤ In the Reference column of the general ledger and of the accounts receivable subsidiary ledger, "S2" is entered, indicating that the source of the data was obtained from page 2 of the sales journal.

To illustrate the complete flow of posting, the sales journal, general ledger, and accounts receivable subsidiary ledger were prepared for the Job Sales Company for the month of May as shown in Figure 8-3.

Proof of Ledger Accuracy

The total of all the debit balances of customer accounts in the subsidiary ledger should be the same as the debit balance of the Accounts Receivable control account in the general ledger, if all the journalizing and posting has been completed correctly.

Periodically, usually monthly, a trial balance or a *schedule of accounts receivable* should be prepared as a check on the accuracy of the accounts receivable subsidiary ledger. This total should agree with the balance in the Accounts Receivable control account. This gives the accountant another check on the accuracy of the accounting records which is important for internal control.

The schedule of accounts receivable prepared from the Job Sales Company's accounts receivable subsidiary ledger is shown in Figure 8-3. Note that the total of the customer accounts amounts to $3,850, the same amount as the balance of the Accounts Receivable account in the general ledger.

Schedule of accounts receivable provides a verification of the accuracy of the Accounts Receivable control account

JOB SALES COMPANY
SCHEDULE OF ACCOUNTS RECEIVABLE
May 31, 19—

Alice Company	$1,500	
Bab Company	500	
Conrad Company	850	
Taylor Company	1,000	
Total Accounts Receivable		$3,850

FIGURE 8-3

SALES JOURNAL

②   Page 2

Date		Account Debited	Invoice No.	Ref.	Amount
19__ May	3	Conrad Company	123	✔	$ 850 ←
	10	Alice Company	124	✔	1,500 ←
	16	Taylor Company	125	✔	1,000 ←
	20	Bab Company	126	✔	500 ←
	31	Accounts Receivable Dr/Sales Cr			$3,850 ←
					(110)(400)

①

④

GENERAL LEDGER

Accounts Receivable   ⑤   → No. 110

19__ May	31		S2	3,850		3,850 ←

③

Sales   → No. 400

19__ May	31		S2		3,850	3,850 ←

ACCOUNTS RECEIVABLE SUBSIDIARY LEDGER

Alice Company

19__ May	10		S2	1,500		1,500 ←

Bab Company

19__ May	20		S2	500		500 ←

Conrad Company

19__ May	3		S2	850		850 ←

Taylor Company

19__ May	16		S2	1,000		1,000 ←

The general design and work-flow patterns developed for the explanation of the sales journal will be applied to all four special journals. Special journals have columns for recording single items, posting of column totals to general ledger accounts, posting of individual accounts to subsidiary ledger accounts, and cross-references between the journal and ledgers clearly shown. The diagrams of the special journals show the flow of work and should be studied carefully.

PURCHASES JOURNAL

The *purchases journal* is a special journal designed to record all items purchased on credit (charged on account). Cash purchases are entered in another special journal.

Usually a *purchase order* is issued by the buyer to the seller as authorization for the purchase. When the supplier ships the merchandise, an invoice is mailed to the purchaser. This invoice is called a *purchase invoice* by the purchaser and a *sales invoice* by the seller. It is used by the buyer and

FIGURE 8-4

PURCHASE ORDER   Order No. ___99___
Conrad Company
6 First Avenue
Livonia, MI 48152

To: ___Job Sales Company___   **Date:** ___May 3, 19___

___10 Second Avenue___   **Ship via:** ___USP___

___Livonia, MI 48154___   **Terms:** ___2/10, n/30___

Please enter our order for the following:

Quantity	Description	Price	Total
33 dozen	X32R 5-Column Journal Paper	$10	$330
7 gross	PS8N Mimeo Paper	60	420
	Total		$850

Company

By: ___R. L. Conrad___

seller to record the entry in the accounting records. There are different purchase order forms available, but each one usually contains the same information as the purchase order illustrated in Figure 8-4 prepared by the Conrad Company to the Job Sales Company on May 3.

After the purchase order is issued, the goods are shipped and a purchase invoice is issued to the buyer. Some companies will prepare a receiving report when the merchandise is received. This report will show the type of merchandise received, amount, and if the material was received in good condition. Before payment is made, the purchase invoice is checked with the purchase order and with the receiving report, Figure 8-5, to verify the proper receipt of goods and to check terms and prices. The purchase invoice or receiving report is used to obtain the information for recording the purchase in the purchases journal.

Every entry recorded in the purchases journal requires a credit to the Accounts Payable account. This journal will have the necessary number of columns to show the various items frequently purchased on account—mer-

FIGURE 8-5

RECEIVING REPORT — No. 10

Received from:

Job Sales Company

10 Second Avenue

Livonia, MI   48154

Date 5/3/C

Purchase Order No. 99

Supplier's Invoice No. 123

Received via USP

Quantity	Description	Condition
33 dozen	X32R 5-Column Journal Paper	Excellent
1 gross	PS8N Mimeo Paper	Excellent

Counted and inspected by: _R. Wolfe_

chandise (Purchases), supplies, and other items. The number of columns in the purchases journal may vary depending on how many are necessary to decrease the amount of posting and simplify the recording of all purchases on account. The purchases of the Job Sales Company for May are listed below. All purchases of merchandise were made on account with cash discount terms of 2/10, n/30.

Purchase of merchandise on account for Job Sales Company in May

19__
May   2   Purchased merchandise from Socko Company, $2,700.
         4   Purchased merchandise from Adhoc Supply Company, $1,500.
        18   Purchased merchandise from Rip Tide Company, $750.
        24   Purchased office supplies from Write Office Supplies Company, $350.
        30   Purchased a new desk from Office Furniture Company, $275.

These transactions are recorded in a multicolumn purchases journal and posted to the proper accounts in the general ledger as shown in Figure 8-6. Each transaction is entered on one line with debit and credit amounts recorded in the proper column. If a particular item is purchased often, e.g., office supplies, a special column could be added to accommodate these purchases. Other special columns may be added as needed. Items purchased infrequently are recorded in the Other Accounts column.

Control Accounts and Subsidiary Ledgers

In previous chapters every transaction involving a purchase of materials or merchandise on credit was recorded in the Accounts Payable account. The balance in the Accounts Payable account represented the total amount or balance owed to all creditors. The amount owed to each individual creditor could only be obtained by going through each individual journal entry or purchase invoice. To provide this information, a separate record is maintained for each creditor. These records of creditors' *subsidiary accounts* are arranged in alphabetical order in a ledger called the *accounts payable subsidiary ledger* or "creditors' subsidiary ledger."

The *Accounts Payable* account in the general ledger is known as the control account. This *control account* contains the total or balance of all the individual creditor accounts shown in the subsidiary ledger. The balance for each individual creditor is shown in the subsidiary ledger. Control accounts serve as a check on the accuracy of the subsidiary ledgers. For example, the balance in the Accounts Payable account in the general ledger should equal the sum of the balances as shown in each creditor's account in the subsidiary ledger if all the posting has been done properly.

Posting from Purchases Journal to Ledgers

Transactions appearing in the Other Accounts and the Accounts Payable columns are posted daily to the respective accounts in the general ledger and the respective creditors accounts in the accounts payable subsidiary ledger with proper dates and cross-references. Credit information for cash discounts may be taken directly from the invoice or a column for "terms" may be added to the purchases journal.

At the end of the month, each column is totaled and double-underlined. The sum of all the debit columns should equal the sum of all the credit columns to ensure the equality of debits and credits. The column totals are posted to the proper general ledger accounts, and the numbers of the general ledger accounts are placed below each column total to indicate that the posting for each of these totals is complete. The total of the Other Accounts column is not posted; therefore, a check mark (✔) is placed below the column total to indicate that each individual item in the column has been posted separately to the general ledger.

Summary Illustration

The procedures for posting from the purchases journal to the general ledger accounts and individual creditors' accounts in the accounts payable subsidiary ledger are listed below.

① Post daily the amounts appearing in the Other Accounts column to the respective accounts in the general ledger. Post daily the amounts appearing in the Accounts Payable column to the creditors' accounts in the accounts payable subsidiary ledger. The subsidiary ledger has a separate account for each creditor arranged in alphabetical order.

② Record a check mark (✔) in the Reference column of the purchases journal to indicate that the posting to the subsidiary ledger is complete.

③ Record the account number of the general ledger accounts in the Reference column to indicate that the posting to the accounts appearing in the Other Accounts column is complete.

④ At the end of the period, usually monthly, total the amount columns and check that the sum of the debit columns equals the sum of the credit columns and double-underline the totals.

⑤ Post the totals of the special columns to the proper accounts in the general ledger and enter the account number below the column totals to show that the posting is complete. Do not post the total of the Other Accounts column (each amount has been posted individually) but place a check mark (✔) below the total to indicate that the total has not been posted.

⑥ In the Reference column of the general ledger and the accounts payable subsidiary ledger, "P2" is entered; indicating that the source of the data was obtained from page 2 of the purchases journal.

To illustrate the complete flow of posting, the purchases journal, general ledger, and accounts payable subsidiary ledger were prepared for the Job Sales Company for the month of May as shown in Figure 8-6.

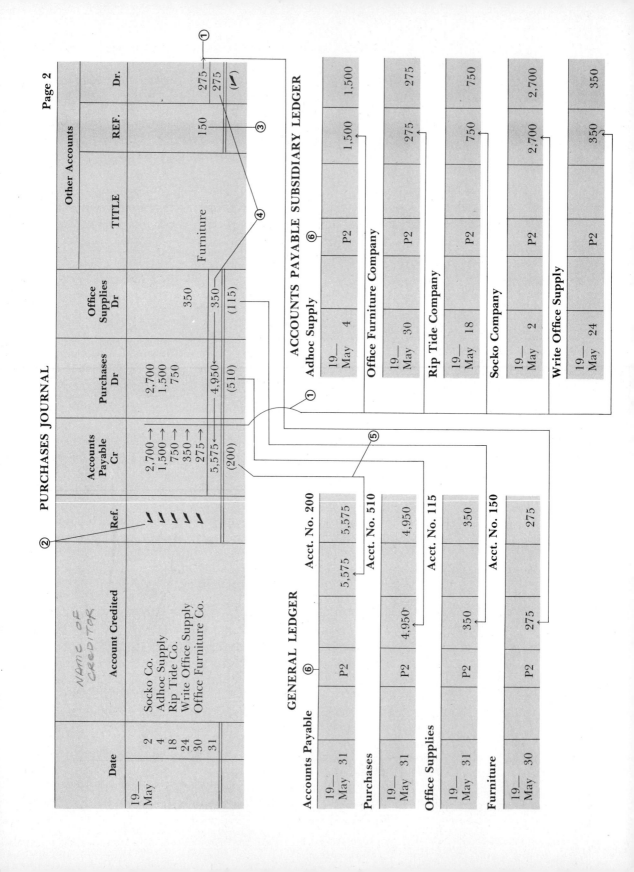

Proof of Ledger Accuracy

The total of all the balances of individual creditor accounts in the subsidiary ledger should be the same as the credit balance of the Accounts Payable control account in the general ledger.

Periodically, usually monthly, a *schedule of accounts payable* should be prepared as a check on the accuracy of the accounts payable subsidiary ledger. This total should agree with the balance of the Accounts Payable control account. This gives the accountant another check on the accuracy of the accounting records.

The schedule of accounts payable prepared from the Job Sales Company's accounts payable subsidiary ledger is shown in Figure 8-6. Note that the total of the creditors accounts amounts to $5,575, the same amount as the balance of the Accounts Payable control account in the general ledger.

Schedule of accounts payable provides a check on the Accounts Payable control account

JOB SALES COMPANY
SCHEDULE OF ACCOUNTS PAYABLE
May 31, 19—

Adhoc Supply	$1,500
Office Furniture Company	275
Rip Tide Company	750
Socko Company	2,700
Write Office Supply	350
Total Accounts Payable	$5,575

CASH RECEIPTS JOURNAL

The *cash receipts journal* is a special journal designed to record all transactions in which any cash is received. Every entry recorded requires a debit to the Cash account. This journal usually has several columns to show the various sources of cash—cash sales of merchandise (Sales), payments received from credit customers (Accounts Receivable), sale of assets, and other sources. The number of columns in a cash receipts journal depends on how many are necessary to decrease the amount of posting and simplify the recording of cash receipts for a business.

As an example, let us use the Job Sales Company that sells all merchandise with terms of 2/10, n/30. The transactions involving cash receipts for May of the current year are shown on page 210.

The May cash receipts journal for the Job Sales Company is illustrated in Figure 8-7. This journal has three credit columns: Other Accounts, Sales, and Accounts Receivable, and two debit columns: Sales Discounts and Cash. Note that each transaction is recorded on one line with the amounts entered in the proper column.

At the end of the month, each column in the journal should be totaled

19__
May 2 Sold equipment for $3,000 cash.
     4 Received full payment on account from Ajax Company for $500
        balance less 2 percent discount.
    10 Cash sales for the first 10 days of May totaled $1,300.
    13 Received full payment on account from Conrad Company, $850
        balance less 2 percent discount.
    18 H. Job, owner, invested an additional $2,000 in the business.
    25 Cash sales from May 10 to May 25 totaled $2,100.
    27 Rocket Sales Company made a partial payment of $700. No cash
        discounts are given on partial or late payments.

and double-underlined. The sum of the debit column totals and the sum of the credit column totals should be equal to check on the equality of the debits and credits.

Posting from Cash Receipts Journal to Ledgers

The Accounts Receivable subsidiary accounts are posted individually and a check mark (✔) is placed in the Reference column. After posting, each subsidiary account should have either a zero or a debit balance. If a customer account has been overpaid, the account will have a credit balance and this amount will be shown on the balance sheet as a current liability as illustrated on page 215.

The total of the debit columns for Cash ($10,423) and Sales Discounts ($27) and the total of the credit columns for Sales ($3,400) and Accounts Receivable ($2,050) are posted to the proper general ledger accounts. The general ledger account number is entered below the column total to indicate that the posting for that column is complete.

Any amounts in the Other Accounts column are posted individually each day as a credit to the proper general ledger account. The account number of each item is entered in the Reference column, and the posting to the general ledger is dated as of the date of the entry. The total of this column is needed to determine if the sum of the debits equals the sum of the credits, but the total is not posted to any account. A check mark (✔) is placed under the double lines to indicate that the amount is not posted.

Summary Illustration

The procedures for posting from the cash receipts journal to the general ledger accounts and individual customers' accounts in the accounts receivable subsidiary ledger are the same as the procedures for posting from the purchases journal. But in the reference column of the general ledger and accounts receivable subsidiary ledger, "CR2" is entered, indicating that the source of the data was obtained from page 2 of the cash receipts journal.

To illustrate the complete flow of posting, the cash receipts journal, general ledger, and accounts receivable subsidiary ledger were prepared for the Job Sales Company for the month of May as shown in Figure 8-7.

FIGURE 8-7

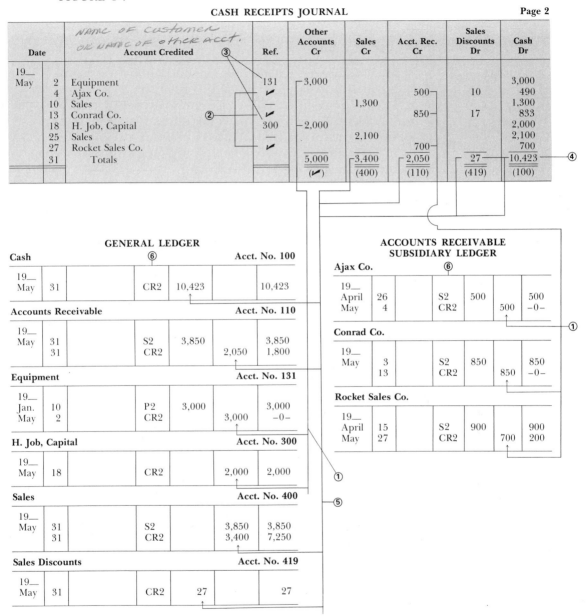

CASH RECEIPTS JOURNAL — Page 2

Date	Account Credited ③	Ref.	Other Accounts Cr	Sales Cr	Acct. Rec. Cr	Sales Discounts Dr	Cash Dr
19__ May 2	Equipment	131	3,000				3,000
4	Ajax Co.	✔			500	10	490
10	Sales	—		1,300			1,300
13	Conrad Co. ②	✔			850	17	833
18	H. Job, Capital	300	2,000				2,000
25	Sales	—		2,100			2,100
27	Rocket Sales Co.	✔			700		700
31	Totals		5,000	3,400	2,050	27	10,423 ④
			(✔)	(400)	(110)	(419)	(100)

NAME OF customer or NAME of other acct.

GENERAL LEDGER ⑥

Cash — Acct. No. 100

19__ May	31		CR2	10,423		10,423

Accounts Receivable — Acct. No. 110

| 19__ May | 31 | | S2 | 3,850 | | 3,850 |
| | 31 | | CR2 | | 2,050 | 1,800 |

Equipment — Acct. No. 131

| 19__ Jan. | 10 | | P2 | 3,000 | | 3,000 |
| May | 2 | | CR2 | | 3,000 | –0– |

H. Job, Capital — Acct. No. 300

| 19__ May | 18 | | CR2 | | 2,000 | 2,000 |

Sales — Acct. No. 400

| 19__ May | 31 | | S2 | | 3,850 | 3,850 |
| | 31 | | CR2 | | 3,400 | 7,250 |

Sales Discounts — Acct. No. 419

| 19__ May | 31 | | CR2 | 27 | | 27 |

ACCOUNTS RECEIVABLE SUBSIDIARY LEDGER

Ajax Co. ⑥

| 19__ April | 26 | | S2 | 500 | | 500 |
| May | 4 | | CR2 | | 500 | –0– ① |

Conrad Co.

| 19__ May | 3 | | S2 | 850 | | 850 |
| | 13 | | CR2 | | 850 | –0– |

Rocket Sales Co.

| 19__ April | 15 | | S2 | 900 | | 900 |
| May | 27 | | CR2 | | 700 | 200 |

① ⑤

CASH PAYMENTS JOURNAL

The *cash payments journal* is a special journal designed to record all cash payments. Every entry recorded in the cash payments journal requires a credit to the Cash account. This journal usually has several columns to show the various payments of cash—cash purchases of merchandise (Purchases), payments to creditors (Accounts Payable), purchase of assets, and other purchases for cash. The number of columns in the cash payments journal depends on how many are necessary to decrease the amount of posting and simplify the recording of cash payments.

The cash payments journal illustrated in Figure 8-8 has four columns consisting of Other Accounts, Accounts Payable, Purchase Discounts, and Cash. These four columns are used to record payments to creditors and to record transactions requiring a credit to Cash and Purchase Discounts and a debit to a creditor in payment on account or for a cash purchase.

The Job Sales Company had the following transactions involving cash payments during May of the current year.

Cash payments made in May by Job Sales Company

19__
May   3   Paid rent expense for May, $625.
       5   Purchased merchandise and paid $300 cash.
      10   Paid Socko Company in full, $2,700 balance less a 2 percent discount.
      15   Paid Adhoc Supply in full, $1,500 balance less a 2 percent discount.
      25   H. Job, owner, withdrew $550 cash for personal use.
      27   Paid Rip Tide Company $500 on account.
      29   Paid advertising expenses, $75.

These transactions are recorded in a cash payments journal and posted to the proper accounts in the general ledger as shown in Figure 8-8. This journal has two debit columns, Accounts Payable and Other Accounts, and two credit columns, Purchase Discounts and Cash. Each transaction is recorded on a separate line, and the sum of the debits must equal the sum of the credits for each entry.

After all the entries have been journalized in the cash payments journal, the columns are totaled and cross-balanced to test the equality of the debits and credits.

Posting from Cash Payments Journal to Ledgers

The entries appearing in the Accounts Payable column are posted individually each day to the accounts payable subsidiary ledger, and a check mark (✔) is placed in the Reference column. After posting to each creditor's account, the account should have a zero or a credit balance. If a creditor was overpaid, the account will have a debit balance and this amount will be shown on the balance sheet as a current asset. The sum of the individual postings in the accounts payable subsidiary ledger should equal the debit of $4,700 shown in the Accounts Payable control account in the general ledger. Any transactions appearing in the Other Accounts column are posted individually each day to the proper general ledger account, and the

FIGURE 8-8

CASH PAYMENTS JOURNAL

Page 2

Date	Account Debited *(Name of creditor or name of other acct.)*	Check No.	Ref.	Other Accounts Dr	Accounts Payable Dr	Purchase Discounts Cr	Cash Cr
19__ May 3	Rent Expense	425	625	625			625
5	Purchases	426	510	300			300
10	Socko Company	427	✔		2,700	54	2,646
15	Adhoc Supply	428	✔		1,500	30	1,470
25	H. Job, Drawing	429	319	550			550
27	Rip Tide Company	430	✔		500		500
29	Advertising Expense	431	640	75			75
31	Totals			1,550	4,700	84	6,166
				(✔)	(200)	(519)	(100)

GENERAL LEDGER

Cash ⑥   Acct. No. 100

19__ May	31		CR2	10,423		10,423
	31		CP2		6,166	4,257

Accounts Payable   Acct. No. 200

19__ May	31		P2		5,575	5,575
	31		CP2	4,700		875

Hal Job, Drawing   Acct. No. 319

19__ May	25		CP2	550		550

Purchases   Acct. No. 510

19__ May	5		CP2	300		300
	31		P2	4,950		5,250

Purchase Discounts   Acct. No. 519

19__ May	31		CP2		84	84

Rent Expense   Acct. No. 625

19__ May	3		CP2	625		625

Advertising Expense   Acct. No. 640

19__ May	29		CP2	75		75

ACCOUNTS PAYABLE SUBSIDIARY LEDGER*

Adhoc Supply ⑥

19__ May	4		P2		1,500	1,500
	15		CP2	1,500		–0–

Rip Tide Company

19__ May	18		P2		750	750
	27		CP2	500		250

Socko Company

19__ May	2		P2		2,700	2,700
	10		CP2	2,700		–0–

* The Office Furniture Company and Write Office Supply accounts were not shown, because there were no payments made to these creditors during May. Refer to Figure 8-6. page 208.

account number is placed in the Reference column. Each column should be posted to the general ledger, except the total of the Other Accounts column, and the account number placed below the total to indicate that the posting is complete. A check mark (✔) is placed under the Other Accounts column to indicate that the amount was not posted.

Summary Illustration

The procedures for posting from the cash payments journal to the general ledger accounts and the individual creditors' accounts in accounts payable subsidiary ledger are the same as the procedures for posting from the purchases journal. However, in the reference column of the general ledger and accounts payable subsidiary ledger, "CP2" is entered, indicating that the source of the data was obtained from page 2 of the cash receipts journal.

To illustrate the complete flow of posting, the Cash Payments Journal, General Ledger, and Accounts Payable Subsidiary Ledger were prepared for the Job Sales Company for the month of May as shown in Figure 8-8.

SUMMARY OF JOURNALIZING AND POSTING TO SPECIAL JOURNALS

When special journals are used in an accounting system, very few transactions will be recorded in the general journal. Most of the transactions will be recorded in four special journals as summarized below.

Types of transactions recorded in special journals

1. All sales of merchandise on account in the sales journal
2. All purchases on account in the purchases journal
3. All cash received by the business in the cash receipts journal
4. All disbursements paid with a check in the cash payments journal

Before posting the totals of the columns to the general ledger accounts, a check must be made to ensure that the sum of the debit columns equals the sum of the credit columns. The amounts appearing in the Other Accounts, Accounts Receivable, and Accounts Payable columns are posted individually to the general ledger accounts and to the customers' and creditors' accounts in the subsidiary ledger.

GENERAL JOURNAL ENTRIES

Special journals reduce the number of transactions recorded in the general journal. When special journals are used, the general journal is used for recording the following types of transactions:

1. Merchandise returned from a customer and credit given on account. The return of cash sales would be recorded in the cash payments journal.
2. Purchases returned to a creditor and credit given on account. The return of cash purchases would be recorded in the cash receipts journal.

3. Adjusting entries.
4. Closing entries.

Other special transactions that do not involve cash, sales and purchases on account, sales and purchase returns for credit on account, adjusting, or closing entries are discussed in other accounting courses and will not be covered in this text. Keep in mind that if the transaction is not a purchase on account, or sale of merchandise on account, or the receipt or payment of cash, the entry is recorded in the general journal.

OPPOSITE BALANCES IN RECEIVABLES AND PAYABLES

An overpayment made by a customer or to a creditor will result in a credit balance in a customer's account and a debit balance in a creditor's account in the subsidiary ledgers. When these subsidiary accounts have a balance opposite from the normal balance, these amounts should be listed separately on the balance sheet instead of deducting the amount from the control accounts.

The procedure for handling these overpayments is illustrated in the following examples:

EXAMPLE 1

Accounts receivable subsidiary ledger with 50 accounts.
48 accounts have debit balances of $10,000.
2 accounts have credit balances of $200.

BALANCE SHEET PRESENTATION

Balance sheet presentation for overpayments by customers and overpayments to creditors

Current Assets:	
Accounts Receivable	$10,000
Current Liabilities:	
Credit Balances in Customer Accounts	$ 200

EXAMPLE 2

Accounts payable subsidiary ledger with 30 accounts.
29 accounts have a credit balance of $5,000.
1 account has a debit balance of $100.

BALANCE SHEET PRESENTATION

Current Assets:	
Debit Balances in Creditor Accounts	$ 100
Current Liabilities:	
Accounts Payable	$5,000

PEGBOARD ACCOUNTING — omit

Computer systems and highly sophisticated accounting machines are available for maintaining the accounting records of a business, but these systems are expensive and usually too elaborate for a small- or medium-sized business. Pegboard accounting is a multi-records system designed by many companies to meet the accounting needs of a small- or medium-sized business or professional practice with a minimum amount of cost.

Pegboard systems handle different accounting operations, such as payroll, accounts receivable, accounts payable, cash receipts, cash payments, and purchases. The system uses standardized accounting forms and procedures providing convenience and accuracy for the bookkeeper while reducing the clerical time involved in recording the necessary information. Low costs are attained because the pegboard reduces the amount of writing and eliminates the posting procedure. The system can be operated by employees who have a minimum amount of accounting training, such as secretaries or medical assistants in doctors' or dentists' offices.

The basic foundation of a pegboard system is the device that gives it its name—the pegboard (Figure 8-9). The pegboard is also known as the "accounting board," or "writing board." The size of the pegboard varies depending on the company producing it and the purpose of the board. Pegboards are constructed of formica or metal with a row of pegs down one side, both sides, or across the top. The forms used in the system have a series of holes which enable the bookkeeper to place the forms on the writing board in proper position. When the information is written on the top form, it will be reproduced on all the forms beneath it because of the special carbonized forms used on the pegboard.

A "one-write" *pegboard system for accounts receivable* records the same

FIGURE 8-9

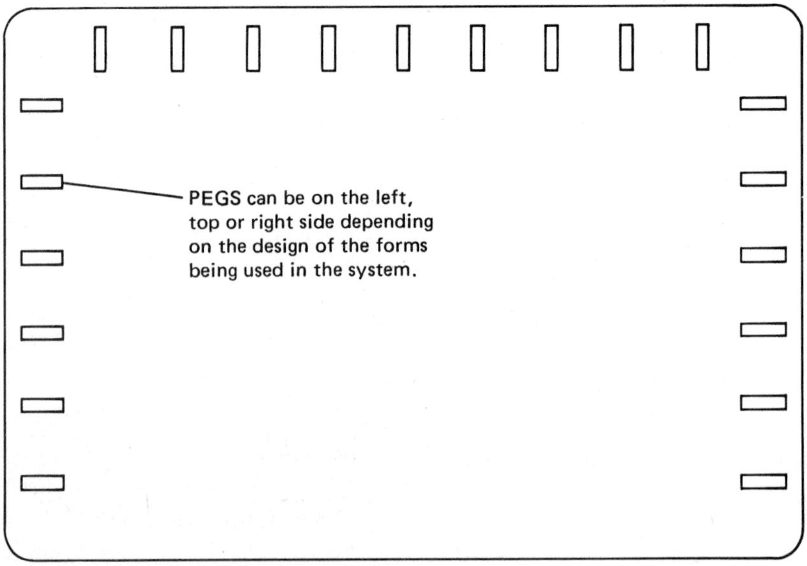

PEGS can be on the left, top or right side depending on the design of the forms being used in the system.

FIGURE 8-10

FIGURE 8-11

A 'ONE WRITE' ACCOUNTS RECEIVABLE SYSTEM

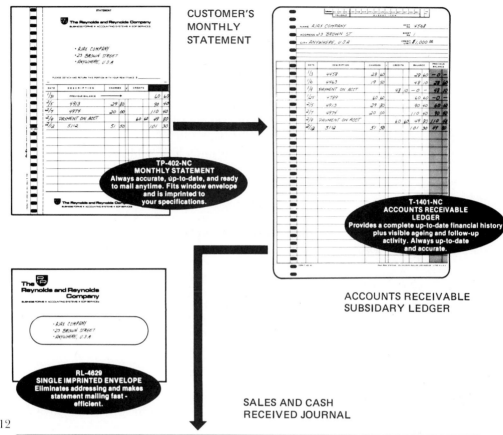

CUSTOMER'S MONTHLY STATEMENT

TP-402-NC MONTHLY STATEMENT
Always accurate, up-to-date, and ready to mail anytime. Fits window envelope and is imprinted to your specifications.

T-1401-NC ACCOUNTS RECEIVABLE LEDGER
Provides a complete up-to-date financial history plus visible ageing and follow-up activity. Always up-to-date and accurate.

ACCOUNTS RECEIVABLE SUBSIDARY LEDGER

RL-4629 SINGLE IMPRINTED ENVELOPE
Eliminates addressing and makes statement mailing fast - efficient.

SALES AND CASH RECEIVED JOURNAL

FIGURE 8-12

T-747-NC RECORD OF SALES AND CASH RECEIVED JOURNAL
A daily listing and control of all charges and cash receipts, daily proof of posting and balances proving this journal simultaneously proves ledger and statement postings. Has 14 distribution columns and 1 miscellaneous of face, plus 10 more distribution columns on the recerse side. Column headings blank for flexibility.

information on several types of forms with one writing through the use of carbonized forms. An example of a one-write system for accounts receivable is described below.

Accounts Receivable System

The pegboard system for accounts receivable offers an inexpensive method of recording accounts receivable and improving accuracy by reducing the number of time-consuming procedures.

Three different forms required for the accounts receivable pegboard system are completed with one writing, reducing the copying time considerably. These three forms are listed below, and they are illustrated in Figures 8-10, 8-11, and 8-12.

Forms used in a pegboard accounts receivable system

1. Record of sales and cash received journal (Figure 8-12)
2. Customer's accounts receivable subsidiary ledger card (Figure 8-11)
3. Monthly statement (Figure 8-10)

The procedures require arranging the forms in proper order. The accounts receivable journal is placed on the pegboard first, the customer's accounts receivable subsidiary ledger card placed on top of the journal, and the monthly statement is placed on top of these two forms. All three forms must be properly aligned so that the information will be recorded on the proper line on all three forms at the same time.

When the transaction is recorded on the customer's monthly statement, the information will be recorded on all three forms with one writing. The distribution is recorded on the right side of the journal to complete the transaction, and the monthly statement and ledger card are filed.

At the end of the month, the completed monthly statements are removed from the ledger file and mailed to the customers. New statements are addressed for the next month and filed with the customer's accounts receivable subsidiary ledger card. The accounts receivable journal is totaled and balanced.

SUMMARY

As a business expands and the number of transactions increase, it becomes necessary to install efficient, time-saving accounting methods. Special journals have been developed that allow the business to process accounting data more efficiently. Four special journals used frequently are the sales journal, purchases journal, cash receipts journal, and the cash payments journal.

The sales journal is a one-column journal used to record charge or credit sales on account. The total of the Amount column is posted at the end of a month as a debit to the Accounts Receivable and as a credit to the Sales account in the general ledger. The individual items in the sales journal are posted to the customers' accounts in the accounts receivable subsidiary ledger. The sum of the individual postings to the accounts receivable subsidiary ledger should equal the balance shown in the Accounts Receivable control account in the general ledger.

All items purchased on account are recorded in a multicolumned journal called the purchases journal. This journal has a column for the purchase of merchandise for resale, columns for any other frequently used debit accounts, an Other Accounts column for occasionally used items, and an Accounts Payable credit column. The column totals of the Accounts Payable, Purchases, Office Supplies, etc., are posted to their respective general ledger accounts. The amounts appearing in the Accounts Payable column are posted to each individual creditor's account in the accounts payable subsidiary ledger, and the items appearing in the Other Accounts column are also posted individually to their respective general ledger accounts. The balance shown in the Accounts Payable control account in the general ledger should equal the sum of the individual accounts in the accounts payable subsidiary ledger.

All cash receipts are recorded in the cash receipts journal. The totals of the Cash and Sales Discounts column are posted as a debit, and the totals of the Accounts Receivable and Sales columns are posted as a credit in the proper general ledger account. Each item in the Other Accounts column is posted individually to the general ledger. The cash payments received from customers (Accounts Receivable column) is posted individually to the customer's account in the accounts receivable subsidiary ledger.

All cash payments are recorded in the cash payments journal. The totals of the Accounts Payable column is debited, and the totals of the Cash and Purchase Discounts columns are credited to their respective general ledger accounts. Each item in the Other Accounts column is posted as a debit to the appropriate account in the general ledger. The cash paid to a supplier or creditor (Accounts Payable column) is posted individually to the creditor's account in the accounts payable subsidiary ledger.

Most transactions are recorded in one of the four special journals. Only transactions that involve the return of merchandise from customers for credit, the return of purchases by the business for credit, and the adjusting and closing entries are recorded in the general journal.

The accounts receivable system is only one of the many accounting functions that can be performed by pegboard accounting methods. All the pegboard systems for different accounting functions are based on the one-write procedure. This procedure as explained for accounts receivable allows accounting information to be recorded on several different forms at one time through the use of carbonized forms.

The pegboard system offers an inexpensive method of recording accounting information and improving accuracy by reducing the number of time-consuming procedures. These systems are used frequently by small-

and medium-sized business operations and professional practices that are not large enough to require sophisticated computerized systems and machines.

GLOSSARY

Accounts Payable Control: A liability account in the general ledger representing the total amount owed to short-term creditors which should agree with the total of the creditors' accounts in the accounts payable subsidiary ledger.

Accounts Payable Subsidiary Ledger: Group of individual creditors' accounts arranged in alphabetical order showing details of charge purchases. The total amount owed to creditors should agree with the accounts payable control account in the general ledger.

Accounts Receivable Control: An asset account in the general ledger representing the total amount owed by customers. The total of the control account should agree with the total of the individual customers' accounts in the accounts receivable subsidiary ledger.

Accounts Receivable Subsidiary Ledger: Group of individual customers' accounts arranged in alphabetical order showing the details of charge sales. The total amount owed by customers should agree with the accounts receivable control account in the general ledger.

Cash Payments Journal: A special journal for recording all cash payments of a business.

Cash Receipts Journal: A special journal for recording all cash received by a business.

Control Account: A general ledger account that summarizes the total of individual accounts in a subsidiary ledger. The balance in the control accounts should equal the sum of the individual account balances in the subsidiary ledger.

Pegboard System for Accounts Receivable: A one-write system that records the same information on several types of forms for accounts receivable with one writing.

Purchase Invoice: A form completed by the seller and sent to the purchaser that gives all the information about the terms of a business transaction.

Purchases Journal: A special journal for recording all purchases on credit.

Purchase Order: A document issued by the buyer authorizing a seller to deliver goods or services.

Sales Invoice: A form completed by the seller that gives all the information about the terms of a business transaction.

Sales Journal: A special journal for recording credit sales of merchandise.

Schedule of Accounts Payable: Listing of the balances owed to creditors which is prepared as a check on the accuracy of the accounts payable subsidiary ledger.

Schedule of Accounts Receivable: Listing of the balances owed by customers which is prepared as a check on the accuracy of the accounts receivable subsidiary ledger.

Special Journal: A journal designed to record a large amount of transactions quickly and efficiently.

Subsidiary Ledger: A book containing individual accounts that are represented by a controlling account in the general ledger. The total of the balances in the subsidiary ledger should equal the balance of the general ledger control account.

QUESTIONS

1. Define the meaning of a special journal.
2. What is a control account?
3. What is a subsidiary ledger?
4. Explain the relationship between the control account and the subsidiary ledger.
5. Zoom Toy Company made 1,000 credit sales in August.
   (a) If each of these transactions was recorded in a general journal, how many times would the account title "Sales" be written, and how many postings would be needed?
   (b) If a sales journal had been used, how many postings to the Sales account would be needed?
6. Name the two control accounts in the general ledger that show the balance owed by customers and the balance owed to creditors.
7. Is the balance of the controlling account always equal to the total of its subsidiary accounts? Explain.
8. What method is used to arrange the accounts in the subsidiary ledgers?
9. How would you prove that a subsidiary ledger agrees with the control account?
10. Give the balance sheet presentation for an overpayment on account by a customer and an overpayment to a creditor.

EXERCISES

Journalizing in Special Journals

1. Zoom Sales Company uses the four special journals as shown in this chapter plus a general journal. Indicate in which journal each of the following transactions should be recorded:

   Sales, S   Cash Receipts, CR
   Purchases, P   Cash Payments, CP
   General, J

   ___S___ (a) Sold merchandise on account (example).
   _____ (b) Owner withdraws cash for personal use.
   _____ (c) Purchased merchandise for cash.
   _____ (d) Sold merchandise for cash.

_____ (e) Returned merchandise sold on account.
_____ (f) Purchase equipment for cash.
_____ (g) Closed revenue account.
_____ (h) Returned goods purchased on account.
_____ (i) Owner invests additional cash in the business.
_____ (j) Recorded depreciation for the year.
_____ (k) Merchandise purchased on account.
_____ (l) Purchased supplies on account.
_____ (m) Paid monthly rent.

2. The Colin Company uses the four special journals as shown in the chapter plus a general journal. Indicate in which journal each of the following transactions should be recorded:

Sales, S   General, J   Cash Payments, CP
Purchases, P   Cash Receipts, CR

_____ (a) Purchased $50 of merchandise on account from Ace Sales.
_____ (b) Sold $500 of merchandise on account to Townley's.
_____ (c) Sold $500 of equipment to the Medlin Company on account.
_____ (d) Purchased $60 of merchandise for cash.
_____ (e) The owner invested additional cash of $1,000 in the business.
_____ (f) Sold merchandise for $500 cash.
_____ (g) Credit of $40 was received from creditor for merchandise broken in shipment.
_____ (h) Paid account owed to creditor within discount period and received a 2 percent discount.

Posting from Special Journals

3. Open T accounts for Cash, Accounts Receivable, Sales, Sales Discount, Johnson Distributors, and Allrite Company. Post the following data recorded in a sales and cash receipts journal to the general ledger and accounts receivable subsidiary ledger.

Sales Journal
(a) Johnson Distributors, $1,500.
(b) Allrite Company, $2,000.

Cash Receipts Journal
(c) Received payment on account from Johnson Distributors less a 2 percent discount.
(d) Received partial payment of $1,000 from Allrite Company (no discounts given on partial payments).

4. Open T accounts for Cash, Office Supplies, Accounts Payable, Purchases, Purchase Discounts, Purchase Returns, Dalsey Company, and Preston Supply Company. Post the following data recorded in a purchases, general, and cash payments journal to the general ledger and accounts payable subsidiary ledger.

Purchases Journal

(*a*) Purchased merchandise on account from Dalsey Company, $4,000.

(*b*) Purchased office supplies on account from Preston Supply, $400.

General Journal

(*c*) Returned merchandise to Dalsey Company and received a $200 credit on account.

Cash Payments Journal

(*d*) Paid account in full to Dalsey Company less return and 2 percent discount for payment within discount period.

(*e*) Paid Preston Supply for balance owed on account (no discount given).

5. From the list below, select the answer/s that best describes how each of the following column totals of the purchases, cash receipts, and cash payments journal should be posted.

Answers

(*a*) Posted as a debit to the general ledger.

(*b*) Posted as a credit to the general ledger.

Purchases Journal

(1) Accounts Payable, $40,000 (example)	*b*
(2) Purchases, $36,000	_____
(3) Office Equipment, $3,000	_____
(4) Store Supplies, $1,000	_____

Cash Receipts

(5) Cash, $50,000	_____
(6) Sales Discount, $1,100	_____
(7) Accounts Receivable, $32,000	_____
(8) Sales, $19,000	_____

Cash Payments

(9) Cash, $32,000	_____
(10) Purchase Discount, $6,200	_____
(11) Accounts Payable, $37,400	_____
(12) Automobile Expense, $800	_____

6. Open T accounts for Cash, Accounts Receivable, Store Supplies, Office Equipment, Accounts Payable, Sales, Sales Discount, Purchases, Purchase Discount, and Automobile Expense. Post the information from Exercise 5 into the proper T account. Identify the amounts in the T accounts with the item number.

7. Indicate whether the following columns in a purchases, cash receipts, cash payments, and sales journal are posted as a debit (Dr) or credit (Cr), are posted individually each day, or whether the total is posted at the end of the month. Use a D for daily and E for end of month. Some items may require two answers.

Item	Column	Journal	Dr or Cr	Daily or End of Month
a	Other Accounts	Purchases (example)	_Dr_	_D_
b	Accounts Payable	Cash Payments	___	___
c	Purchases Discount	Cash Payments	___	___
d	Cash	Cash Receipts	___	___
e	Sales	Cash Receipts	___	___
f	Accounts Payable	Purchases	___	___
g	Individual amounts	Sales	___	___
h	Total	Sales	___	___

Schedule of Accounts Receivable and Accounts Payable

8. On December 31 of the current year, the Accounts Receivable control account for the College Company had a debit balance of $950. The accounts receivable subsidiary ledger had three accounts with debit balances of $600 for A, $300 for B, and $100 for C. The D Company account ended with a credit balance of $50. Prepare a schedule of accounts receivable as of December 31.

9. The accounts payable subsidiary ledger for the College Company has the following credit balances as of January 31: Dick Company, $400; C. Jones, $600; and U. R. Rite, $400. Prepare a schedule of accounts payable for January 31 of the current year.

10. Prepare a schedule of accounts receivable from the accounts receivable subsidiary ledger below for Lasko Products as of May 31 of the current year.

Acro Binder Company

19__					
May	2		6,000		6,000
	18			3,000	3,000

Bertan Distributors

19__					
May	20		2,000		2,000
	25			500	1,500
	30			750	750

Wilcox Sales Company

19__					
May	20		500		500
	30			500	–0–

11. Prepare a schedule of accounts payable from the accounts payable subsidiary ledger (shown at the top of the next page) for the Comrad Company as of June 30 of the current year.

Compton Products

19—					
June	2			4,000	4,000
	12		2,500		1,500

Norton Company

19—					
June	4			1,000	1,000
	10		100		900
	14		900		–0–

Wabash Company

19—					
June	16			2,000	2,000
	27			1,000	3,000

PROBLEMS

Sales and Purchases Journal

8-1. The Tango Company's charge sales for the month of July of the current year are shown below:

July	5	Jean Taylor	$150
	7	Robert David	450
	12	Sara Short	300
	15	Jean Taylor	250
	18	Carl Robe	400
	21	Robert David	200
	26	Sara Short	350
	29	Carl Robe	100

Required

(a) Record the transactions in a sales journal. Use the form illustrated in the chapter. (Begin with invoice No. 40.)

(b) Open customers' accounts in the accounts receivable subsidiary ledger for Robert David, Carl Robe, Sara Short, and Jean Taylor.

(c) Open general ledger accounts for 110 Accounts Receivable; and 400 Sales.

(d) Post into the accounts receivable subsidiary ledger and the general ledger the data from the sales journal.

(e) Prepare a schedule of accounts receivable using the information in the subsidiary ledger.

8-2. The Giddy Novelty Company's purchases on account during May are as follows:

May 3 Merchandise purchased from Skip Company, $400.

5 Office supplies purchased from ABC Supply Company, $100.

9 Merchandise purchased from Acme Company, $200.

10 Merchandise purchased from Hardy Company, $750.
15 Merchandise purchased from Skip Company, $900.
27 New desk chair purchased from ABC Supply Company, $150.
29 Merchandise purchased from Acme Company, $500.

Required

(a) Record the transactions in a purchases journal. Use the form shown in this chapter.
(b) Open general ledger accounts for 115 Office Supplies; 130 Furniture & Fixtures; 200 Accounts Payable; and 510 Purchases.
(c) Open accounts payable subsidiary ledger accounts for ABC Supply Company, Acme Company, Hardy Company, and Skip Company.
(d) Post into the accounts payable subsidiary ledger and the general ledger the information from the purchases journal.
(e) Prepare a schedule of accounts payable using the information in the subsidiary ledger.

8-3. The All Right Shop's sales and purchases on account for the month of May of the current year are as follows:

May 3 Sold merchandise to Jane Barker on account, $150.
4 Purchased merchandise from ABC Company on account, $500.
5 Sold merchandise to Ken Cole on account, $250.
6 Sold merchandise to Karen Dawn on account, $450.
7 Purchased merchandise from Pine Company on account, $750.
10 Purchased merchandise from Top Ten Company on account, $900.
11 Sold merchandise to Joyce Eaton on account, $600.
12 Purchased merchandise from ABC Company on account, $1,000.
13 Purchased secretarial desk chair from Supply House on account, $65. (Record in Furniture account.)
15 Purchased merchandise from Barton Company on account, $800.
20 Sold merchandise to Ken Cole on account, $300.
24 Purchased merchandise from Pine Company on account, $1,200.
30 Sold merchandise to Jane Barker on account, $200.
30 Purchased office supplies from Supply House on account, $75.

Open general ledger accounts for 110 Accounts Receivable; 115 Office Supplies; 130 Furniture; 200 Accounts Payable; 400 Sales; and 510 Purchases. Open accounts receivable subsidiary ledger accounts for Jane Barker, Ken Cole, Karen Dawn, and Joyce Eaton. Open accounts payable subsidiary ledger accounts for ABC Company, Barton Company, Pine Company, Supply House, and Top Ten Company.

Required

(*a*) Record the above transactions in the sales or purchases journal. Start with invoice No. 101 for all sales of merchandise.

(*b*) Post from the journals to the general ledger and subsidiary ledger accounts.

Sales and Cash Receipts Journal

8-4. The Taylor Company's transactions for cash receipts during April of the current year are as follows:

Apr. 4 George Taylor invested an additional $3,000 cash in the business.

7 Received payment from Acme Company on account, $500 balance less 2 percent discount.

12 Received payment from Todd Company on account, $100 balance less 2 percent discount.

15 Cash sales for first half of April, $1,500.

19 Received $250 from Ajax Company on account, no discount.

21 Borrowed $5,000 from the bank and signed a note payable in 6 months.

26 Cash sales for second half of April amounted to $2,000.

Required

(*a*) Record the transactions in a cash receipts journal. Use the form shown in the chapter.

(*b*) Open accounts for 100 Cash; 110 Accounts Receivable; 210 Notes Payable; 300 G. Taylor, Capital; 400 Sales; and 419 Sales Discount. The Accounts Receivable account had a debit balance of $1,350 as of April 1 of the current year.

(*c*) Open subsidiary accounts receivable for the following customers and record the debit balances as of April 1, for Acme Company, $500; Ajax Company, $750; and Todd Company, $100.

(*d*) Post from the cash receipts journal to the accounts receivable subsidiary ledger and the general ledger.

8-5. The sales on account and cash received during the month of April of the current year for Konstructo Supply Company are shown below:

Apr. 4 Sold merchandise on account to Tucker Builders, $3,200.

5 Sold merchandise on account to Bill Long, $1,000.

7 Sam Kon, owner, invested an additional $2,500 in the business.

8 Sold merchandise on account to Rick Monroe, $550.

11 Sold merchandise on account to Tucker Builders, $700.

12 Received a check from Bill Long for invoice No. 216, less 2 percent discount.

14 Cash sales to date, $5,350.

15 Sold merchandise on account to Sid Strong, $350.

18 Received a $300 check from Rick Monroe for partial payment on invoice No. 217.

20 Borrowed $1,000 from the bank on a 6 percent, 30-day note.

21 Received a check from Sid Strong for the amount due on invoice No. 219, less 2 percent discount.

22 Sold merchandise on account to Mary Pick, $600.

25 Received a check from Tucker Builders for invoice Nos. 215 and 218, less the discount.

26 Sold merchandise on account to Rick Monroe, $250.

29 Cash sales for the balance of the month, $4,750.

Required

(*a*) Record the above transactions in a sales and cash receipts journal. Terms of all sales on account are 2/10 EOM, n/30. No discounts are allowed on partial payments. Start with sales invoice No. 215 for transactions entered in the sales journal.

(*b*) Open the following general ledger accounts: 100 Cash; 110 Accounts Receivable; 205 Notes Payable; 300 Sam Kon, Capital; 400 Sales; and 409 Sales Discounts.

(*c*) Open the following customers' accounts in the accounts receivable subsidiary ledger: Bill Long, Rick Monroe, Mary Pick, Sid Strong, and Tucker Builders.

(*d*) Post from the journals to the ledgers; post to the subsidiary ledgers after each transaction involving a customer's account; and post the data in the Other Accounts column daily.

(*e*) Prepare a schedule of accounts receivable as of April 30.

Purchases, Cash Payments, and General Journal

8-6. The cash payment transactions during March for the Badger Company appear below:

Mar. 3 Paid March rent, $650.

7 Paid the Sims Company on account, $500 balance less a 2 percent discount.

10 Cash purchase of merchandise, $400.

12 Purchased a used filing cabinet for cash, $65. (Record in the Furniture account.)

17 Paid the Pen Company on account, $900 balance less a 2 percent discount.

25 Paid the telephone bill, $125.

28 Paid Rollo Company $1,000 for merchandise purchased on account (no discount on partial payment).

Required

(a) Record the transactions in a cash payments journal. Use the form shown in the chapter. (Start with check No. 840.)

(b) Open general ledger accounts for 100 Cash; 150 Furniture; 200 Accounts Payable; 510 Purchases; 519 Purchase Discounts; 602 Rent Expense; and 603 Telephone Expense. Enter a balance of $5,000 in the Cash account and $2,900 in the Accounts Payable account as of March 1 of the current year.

(c) Open subsidiary accounts payable ledgers with credit balances as of March 1 of the current year for Pen Company, $900; Rollo Company, $1,500; and Sims Company, $500.

(d) Post from the cash payments journal to the ledgers.

8-7. The purchases on account and the cash payments for the month of July of the current year for Hanson Housewares appear below:

July 1 Paid $1,200 for a 1-year liability insurance policy. (Start with check No. 101.)

5 Purchased merchandise on account from Baily Products amounting to $2,500.

6 Paid $550 cash for merchandise.

7 Received a credit for $100 for merchandise returned to Baily Products.

8 Paid Baily Products the amount due on account less the return and discount.

11 Purchased merchandise on account from Dorsey Company, $1,000.

13 Purchased merchandise on account from Endor Company, $800.

15 Received a credit of $200 from Dorsey Company for the return of damaged merchandise.

18 Purchased merchandise on account from Baily Products, $200.

19 Received credit on account from Endor Company for merchandise returned, $50.

20 Paid Dorsey Company the amount due less the return and discount.

21 Paid $180 for advertising.

22 John Hanson, owner, withdrew $500 for personal use.

23 Paid $392 ($400 less a 2% discount of $8) to Endor Company to apply on account. Endor allows discounts on partial payments.

25 Purchased merchandise on account from Hess Company, $1,200.

26 Purchased store supplies on account from Peters Supply Company, $350.

27 Paid telephone bill for July, $115.

29 Paid monthly salaries, $1,800.

Required

(a) Record the transactions in the purchases, cash payments (start with check No. 101), or general journal. Credit terms for all purchases of merchandise are 2/10, n/30.

(b) Open the following general ledger accounts and record the balances as of July 1: 100 Cash, $9,740; 114 Prepaid Insurance; 116 Store Supplies; 200 Accounts Payable; 319 J. Hanson, Drawing; 510 Purchases; 518 Purchase Returns & Allowances; 519 Purchases Discounts; 600 Salaries Expense; 601 Advertising Expense; 602 Telephone Expense.

(c) Open the following creditors' accounts in the accounts payable subsidiary ledger: Baily Products, Dorsey Company, Endor Company, Hess Company, and Peters Supply Company.

(d) Post from the journals to the ledgers. Post daily from Other Accounts columns and general journal to the subsidiary ledgers.

(e) Prepare a schedule of accounts payable as of July 31.

Review Problems Covering All Five Journals

8-8. The Debbie Darlin Shops general ledger has account balances on August 1 of the current year as follows:

No.	Title	Balance August 1, 19__
100	Cash	$15,000
110	Accounts Receivable	2,000
114	Prepaid Insurance	
115	Office Supplies	
200	Accounts Payable	2,050
300	Debra Mayor, Capital	14,950
400	Sales	
408	Sales Returns and Allowances	
409	Sales Discounts	
500	Purchases	
518	Purchases Returns and Allowances	
519	Purchase Discounts	
600	Salary Expense	
601	Telephone Expense	
602	Utilities Expense	
603	Rent Expense	

The August 1 balances in the subsidiary ledger are as follows:

ACCOUNTS RECEIVABLE

Customer	Date of Sale	Terms	Balance
Allison Company	July 25	2/10, n/30	$500
Hilo Company	July 27	2/10, n/30	900
Macoy Company			−0−
Yargo Company	July 29	2/10, n/30	600

ACCOUNTS PAYABLE

Creditor	Date of Purchase	Terms	Balance
Audit Supply Company			
Castro Company	July 15	2/10 EOM, n/30	$750
Ken's Supply Company	July 8	n/30	900
Lindy Company	July 21	1/15, n/30	400

Transactions for August are:

Aug. 1 Purchased merchandise from Ken's Supply Company on account, $700, n/30.

2 Paid $1,000 for a 1-year insurance policy. (Start with check No. 400.)

3 Issued Yargo Company a credit memo for $100 for merchandise damaged in shipment.

3 Received full payment from the Allison Company for the July 25 transaction less 2 percent discount.

4 Paid Lindy Company for purchase on July 21 less 1 percent discount.

4 Purchased merchandise on account from Castro Company, $450, 2/10 EOM, n/30.

5 Cash sales for the week, $4,300.

5 Paid Ken's Supply for the purchase of July 8.

5 Paid the August rent, $500.

8 Paid Castro Company for the purchase on July 15 less 2 percent discount.

9 Sold merchandise on account to Macoy Company, $1,200.

10 Debra Mayor, owner, invested an additional $3,000 in the business.

11 Received full payment from the Hilo Company for the sale of July 27.

12 Sold merchandise on account to Allison Company, $1,500.

12 Cash sales for the week, $3,900.

15 Purchased merchandise on account from Lindy Company, $1,300, 1/15, n/30.

15 Paid semimonthly salaries, $720.

16 Sold merchandise on account to the Macoy Company, $1,600.

16 Purchased office supplies on account from Audit Supply Company, $65.

17 Issued a debit memo to Castro Company for merchandise returned, $250.

18 Received a partial payment of $882 from Allison Company on account. This amount represents a payment of $900 less a 2% discount. Discounts allowed on partial payments received within 10 days from date of sale.

19   Cash sales for the week, $4,850.
22   Sold merchandise on account to Hilo Company, $750.
22   Purchased merchandise for cash, $625.
24   Received full payment from the Macoy Company for the August 16 sale less 2 percent discount.
26   Cash sales for the week, $4,275.
29   Paid Lindy Company for the purchase of August 15 less 1 percent discount.
30   Paid utility bill, $165.
31   Paid semimonthly salaries, $720.
31   Paid telephone bill, $95.
31   Purchased merchandise on account from Lindy Company, $1,500, 1/15, n/30.
31   Sold merchandise on account to Yargo Company, $800.

Required

(*a*) Record the transactions in a sales, purchases, cash receipts, cash payments (start with check No. 400), or general journal. Terms of all sales on account are 2/10, n/30. (Use invoice Nos. 300 to 304.)

(*b*) Open the general ledger and subsidiary ledger accounts and record the account balances as of August 1 from the data given in the problem.

(*c*) Post from the journals to the ledgers. Post daily from Other Accounts columns and general journal to the subsidiary ledgers.

(*d*) Prepare a schedule of accounts receivable and a schedule of accounts payable as of August 31.

8-9.   The general ledger of Karl's Auto Parts Company had the following account balances as of May 1:

No.	Account Title	Balance, May 1, 19__
100	Cash	$12,000
110	Accounts Receivable	3,500
114	Prepaid Insurance	
117	Store Supplies	
200	Accounts Payable	2,800
300	Karl Kope, Capital	12,700
400	Sales	
408	Sales Returns & Allowances	
409	Sales Discounts	
500	Purchases	
518	Purchase Returns & Allowances	
519	Purchase Discounts	
600	Salaries Expense	
601	Telephone Expense	
602	Utilities Expense	
603	Rent Expense	

The May 1 balances in the subsidiary ledgers are shown below:

ACCOUNTS RECEIVABLE

Customer	Sale Date	Terms	Balance
Alice's Auto Repair	April 24	2/10, n/30	$1,350
Downtown Service	April 25	2/10, n/30	700
George's Garage	April 27	n/30	1,000
Max's Repair Company	April 28	2/10, n/30	450

ACCOUNTS PAYABLE

Creditor	Purchase Date	Terms	Balance
ABC Supply Company			–0–
Bart Parts	April 20	2/10 EOM, n/30	$ 800
Clint Auto Suppliers			–0–
Eden Products	April 25	2/10 EOM, n/30	1,400
Jax Company	April 28	n/30	600

Transactions for May are: *Select the Journal*

May 1 Purchased $1,000 of merchandise on account from Jax Company; terms: n/30.

2 Paid $1,200 for a 1-year insurance policy. (Start with check No. 300.)

3 George's Garage returned $200 of parts it had purchased on April 27. A credit memorandum was issued.

4 Received full payment from Alice's Auto Repair for sale of April 24 less a 2 percent discount.

5 Paid Eden Products for April 25 purchase less a 2 percent discount.

5 Cash sales for week, $3,800.

5 Received full payment from Downtown Service for sale of April 25 less a 2 percent discount.

5 Paid May rent, $850.

8 Purchased $1,500 of merchandise from Bart Parts; terms: 2/10 EOM, n/30.

8 Received full payment from Max's Repair Company for sale of April 28 less a 2 percent discount.

9 Sold $300 of parts to Alice's Auto Repair; terms: 2/10, n/30.

10 Paid Bart Parts for purchase of April 20 less a 2 percent discount.

11 Cash sales for week, $4,200.

12 Purchased $2,000 of parts from Eden Products; terms: 2/10, n/30.

15 Paid semimonthly salaries, $800.

16 Sold $500 of merchandise to Max's Repair Company; terms: 2/10, n/30.

17 Purchased $175 of store supplies from ABC Supply Company; terms: n/30.

18 Received payment for sale of May 9 from Alice's Auto Repair less a 2 percent discount.

19 Cash sales for week, $3,500.

22 Sold $600 of merchandise to Downtown Service; terms: 2/10, n/30.

23 Purchased merchandise for cash, $250.

24 The owner, Karl Kope, invested an additional $2,500 in the business.

25 Received payment for sale of May 16 from Max's Repair Company less a 2 percent discount.

26 Received full payment from George's Garage for sale of April 27, less return of May 3.

26 Paid Jax Company for April 28 purchase.

26 Cash sales for week, $3,900.

29 Sold $700 of merchandise to Max's Repair Company; terms: 2/10, n/30.

30 Issued a debit memorandum for $300 to Eden Products for damaged merchandise.

30 Paid utility bill for May, $225.

30 Paid May telephone bill, $135.

31 Paid semimonthly salaries, $800.

31 Sold $250 of merchandise to George's Garage; terms: n/30.

31 Purchased $750 of merchandise from Clint Auto Suppliers; terms: 2/10, n/30.

Required

(*a*) Open a general ledger and accounts receivable and accounts payable subsidiary ledger for the accounts listed, and record the account balances as of May 1.

(*b*) Record the transactions for May in a sales, purchases, cash receipts, cash payments, or general journal. Post daily from Other Accounts columns and general journal to the subsidiary ledgers.

(*c*) Total and balance the four special journals at the end of the month and post to the general ledger.

(*d*) Prepare a schedule of accounts receivable and a schedule of accounts payable as of May 31.

Chapter 8 Appendix:

Bad Debts

Normally, a business that sells merchandise and services on credit will have a few customers who do not pay their accounts. These uncollectible accounts are known as bad debts, and they are classified as a ***Bad Debts Expense*** account under Operating/General & Administrative Expense on the income statement. The amount of Bad Debts Expense resulting from uncollectible accounts will vary according to the general credit policies of the company.

At the end of each accounting period, the amount of uncollectible accounts is estimated to obtain a reasonable amount for the Bad Debts Expense shown on the income statement. When some customers' accounts become doubtful or uncollectible, the Accounts Receivable account should be decreased to show the estimated amount of collectible accounts. Otherwise, the net realizable amount of Accounts Receivable shown on the balance sheet will not be accurately stated, and the financial position of the business may be misleading to management, creditors, and other interested groups.

ADJUSTMENT FOR BAD DEBTS

It is usually difficult to determine the specific customers who will not pay their account. Therefore, it becomes necessary to obtain an estimate for the amount of accounts receivable that will eventually become uncollectible if the Accounts Receivable is to be stated correctly on the balance sheet.

An estimated amount for uncollectible accounts is used when recording the adjusting entry recognizing the Bad Debts Expense for the period. This adjusting entry requires a debit to Bad Debts Expense and a credit to a contra asset account called ***Allowance for Doubtful Accounts.*** The Accounts Receivable would not be directly credited for this estimated amount, because this figure is merely an estimate of customer accounts that may prove to be uncollectible and does not represent any specific customer.

In general journal form, the entry is:

19__		
Dec. 31	Bad Debts Expense	
	Allowance for Doubtful Accounts	
	Estimated bad debts expense for period.	

The Allowance for Doubtful Accounts normally has a credit balance.

METHODS FOR ESTIMATING BAD DEBTS

There are two basic methods of estimating losses for bad debts, and both these methods are acceptable by the Internal Revenue Service as long as they are applied consistently.

Method 1. The *percentage of sales or income statement method* estimates Bad Debts Expense by using a percentage of net credit sales to arrive at a reasonable amount. To arrive at the estimated rate, it is necessary to examine and analyze the percentage of losses experienced for the *total net credit sales* of prior periods.

The estimated percentage is then applied to the total net charge sales for the period less the amount of sales returns and allowances. Any balance remaining in the Allowance for Doubtful Accounts from any prior periods would not be added or subtracted to arrive at a dollar amount for the adjustment of bad debts.

To illustrate the adjustment for Bad Debts Expense under the income statement method, assume that the College Company made sales on account of $100,000 and had sales returns amounting to $10,000. After a careful review, the accountant estimated that 2 percent of the net charge sales recorded may not be collectible. The adjustment for Bad Debts Expense would amount to 2 percent of $90,000 ($100,000 − $10,000), or $1,800.

The Allowance for Doubtful Accounts had a credit balance of $50 before the year-end adjustment. This $50 balance *would not* be added to or subtracted from the $1,800.

The adjusting entry necessary would be:

Adjusting entry for estimated uncollectible accounts using income statement method

19__			
Dec. 31	Bad Debts Expense	1,800	
	Allowance for Doubtful Accounts		1,800
	Estimated bad debts expense using		
	2% of net charge sales amounting to		
	$90,000.		

General ledger accounts after the adjusting entry is posted:

BALANCE SHEET ACCOUNT

Allowance for Doubtful Accounts					
Date		Explanation	Debit	Credit	Balance
19__					
Dec.	31	Bal.		50	50
	31	Adj.		1,800	1,850

INCOME STATEMENT ACCOUNT

Bad Debts Expense					
Date		Explanation	Debit	Credit	Balance
19— Dec.	31	Adj.	1,800		1,800

BALANCE SHEET PRESENTATION

Current Assets:
  Accounts Receivable/Trade $200,000
    Less: Allowance for Doubtful Accounts   1,850 $198,150

Over a period of time, the small balances that remain in the year-end allowance account could eventually add up to a significant amount. Therefore, this method may not disclose the estimated net realizable amount of Accounts Receivable. This may be corrected with an adjusting entry whenever the amount becomes excessive; the Allowance for Doubtful Accounts would be debited and the Bad Debts Expense or Correction of Prior Period Income account would be credited.

Method 2. The *percentage of accounts receivable or balance sheet method* estimates the amount of Bad Debts Expense by taking a percentage of the balance remaining in the Accounts Receivable account.

To arrive at a reasonable percentage, an analysis should be made of the Accounts Receivable collections over a considerable length of time plus an analysis of the age of the current accounts receivable. The rate or percentage determined would be applied to the balance of the Accounts Receivable to obtain the estimated dollar amount for the adjustment to Bad Debts Expense and the Allowance for Doubtful Accounts.

Keep in mind that the percentage or rate you use is merely an estimate. Therefore, this estimate will probably never equal the exact amount of uncollectible accounts for the year, and the allowance account may have a debit or credit balance at the end of the accounting period before adjustments. This year-end debit or credit balance in the allowance account must be considered when making the adjusting entry using the balance sheet method.

Any debit balance[1] should be added to the amount estimated for Bad Debts Expense and any credit balance[2] should be subtracted.

The following examples illustrate this method.

EXAMPLE 1   *The balance of the Accounts Receivable at the end of the year amounted to $100,000, and it was estimated that 1 percent would be uncollectible*

---

[1] A debit balance indicates an underestimate of uncollectible accounts.
[2] A credit balance indicates an overestimate of uncollectible accounts.

($100,000 × 0.01 = $1,000). The Allowance for Doubtful Accounts had a credit balance of $50. ($1,000 − $50 = $950.) The necessary adjusting entry would be:

19__			
Dec. 31	Bad Debts Expense	950	
	Allowance for Doubtful Accounts		950
	Estimated expense for bad debts using		
	the balance sheet method.		

EXAMPLE 2   *The balance of the Accounts Receivable at the end of the year amounted to $100,000, and it was estimated that 1 percent would be uncollectible ($100,000 × 0.01 = $1,000). The Allowance for Doubtful Accounts had a debit balance of $50. ($1,000 + $50 = $1,050.) The necessary adjusting entry would be:*

19__			
Dec. 31	Bad Debts Expense	1,050	
	Allowance for Doubtful Accounts		1,050
	Estimated expense for bad debts		
	using the balance sheet method.		

Some companies may arrive at an estimated amount of uncollectible accounts receivable by using a process of "aging" each balance in the customers accounts according to the date in which the transaction occurred. This method is accomplished by grouping the balances into those accounts that are 30 days past due, 31 to 60 days past due, 61 to 90 days past due, and over 90 days past due and taking a percentage of these amounts based on their age. The total of these groups determine the amount that should appear as the balance in the Allowance for Doubtful Accounts at the end of the accounting period.

DIRECT WRITE-OFF METHOD

Some companies may wait until they are unable to collect a specific customer's account before making any adjustment for bad debts expense.

When it becomes clear that an account is uncollectible, they use the *direct write-off method.* Thus, the Bad Debts Expense account would be debited and the Accounts Receivable account in the general ledger and the appropriate customer's account in the accounts receivable subsidiary ledger would be credited for the uncollectible amount owed by the customer.

Under this method the Allowance for Doubtful Accounts would not be used, as the Bad Debts Expense would be recorded as an expense in the period in which the account was written off and not when the sale was made. As a result, assets may be overstated on the balance sheet and the revenue may be overstated on the income statement when no provision has been made to adjust the Accounts Receivable for any estimated losses for uncollectible accounts. This method violates the matching principle, because the expenses are not matched with the revenue to determine the net income for the period.

WRITING OFF ACCOUNTS RECEIVABLE UNDER ALLOWANCE METHOD

When a customer's account becomes uncollectible, the account should be removed from the accounting records. To record the write-off, the journal entry requires a debit to the Allowance for Doubtful Accounts and a credit to the Accounts Receivable Account, with the customer's name.

To illustrate, assume that on February 15, 19_B, the College Company received notice that the Student Company had declared bankruptcy. The accounts receivable ledger for the College Company shows a debit balance of $1,000 for the Student Company as of January 1, 19_A.

The journal entry to record the write-off is:

Customer's account written off as uncollectible

19_B			
Feb. 15	Allowance for Doubtful Accounts	1,000	
	Accounts Receivable/Student Co.		1,000
	Account written off as uncollectible		
	due to bankruptcy.		

General ledger and subsidiary ledger accounts after the write-off are:

ACCOUNTS RECEIVABLE SUBSIDIARY LEDGER

Student Company

Date	Explanation	Debit	Credit	Balance
19_A Jan. 1	Bal.	1,000		1,000
19_B Feb. 15	Write off		1,000	–0–

GENERAL LEDGER

Accounts Receivable

Date	Explanation	Debit	Credit	Balance
19_B Jan. 1	Bal.	100,000		100,000
Feb. 15			1,000	99,000

Allowance for Doubtful Accounts

Date	Explanation	Debit	Credit	Balance
19_A Dec. 31	Bal.		4,000	4,000
19_B Feb. 15	Write off	1,000		3,000

Generally, a customer's account would not be written off as uncollectible until all reasonable efforts to collect the account have been unsuccessful. Notice that an expense account is not involved at the time an account is written off, because the expense was taken when the adjusting entry for bad debts expense was recorded in a previous period. Writing off a customer's account has no effect on the net realizable amount of accounts receivable for the period. For example, before writing off the $1,000 owed by the Student Company in our example, the net realizable amount of Accounts Receivable on December 31, 19_A amounted to $96,000:

Accounts Receivable balance	$100,000	
Less: Allowance for Doubtful Accounts	4,000	$96,000

After writing off the account of the Student Company on February 15, 19_B, the net realizable amount of Accounts Receivable still amounts to $96,000:

Accounts Receivable balance	$99,000	
Less: Allowance for Doubtful Accounts	3,000	$96,000

REINSTATEMENT OF ACCOUNTS RECEIVABLE

Occasionally an account that has been written off as uncollectible may be collected in full or in part at a later date. The write-off entry would be reversed when payment is received, placing the account back on the records and permitting a posting to the customer's account. After recording the reversing entry and the collection received on account, the records will show that the account was written off and recovered at a later date. In the event that the customer makes a charge purchase in the future, all the necessary data with which to approve or reject the customer's order will be shown on the records.

To illustrate, assume that the account of Joe College for $500 was written off as uncollectible on March 1.

19__			
Mar. 1	Allowance for Doubtful Accounts	500	
	Accounts Receivable/Joe College		500
	Write off account of Joe College as uncollectible.		

On November 1, a $400 check was received from Joe College as a partial payment on his past-due account. The entry to record this information would be recorded by the following two entries:

Entries for reinstatement of Accounts Receivable and receipt of payment from customer

19__			
Nov. 1	Accounts Receivable/Joe College	400	
	Allowance for Doubtful Accounts		400
	To reinstate $400 of the account of Joe College written off March 1 for $500.		
1	Cash	400	
	Accounts Receivable/Joe College		400
	Cash received on account.		

Any additional payments received from the customer would require the same two entries.

SUMMARY

Overpayments by customers or overpayments to creditors should be designated as overpayments on the balance sheet instead of deductions from the totals of the Accounts Receivable and Accounts Payable accounts.

There are two methods for estimating and recording credit losses for charge sales to customers. A percentage of net sales is one method, whereas the other method takes a percentage of the ending balance in the Accounts Receivable to bring the allowance account to a desired balance.

A business with a limited amount of charge sales or sales on account may use a direct write-off method for recording credit losses. Under this method, a debit to Bad Debts Expense and a credit to Accounts Receivable is made when a specific account becomes uncollectible.

Writing off an Accounts Receivable as uncollectible by using the allowance method results in a debit to Allowance for Doubtful Accounts and a credit to the Accounts Receivable control account and related customer's subsidiary account.

Comparison of methods reveals that the balance sheet and income statement methods match the expenses of a period with the related revenues, and the direct write-off method records the Bad Debt Expense in the period when the account becomes uncollectible and not when the sale was made.

GLOSSARY

Allowance for Doubtful Accounts: A contra account to Accounts Receivable established to show the estimated amount of uncollectible accounts receivable. The Allowance for Doubtful Accounts is subtracted from the Accounts Receivable on the balance sheet to show the estimated realizable amount of accounts receivable.

Bad Debts Expense: The account used at the end of the accounting period to show the estimated amount of accounts receivable that will be uncollectible and/or the amount actually written off using the direct write-off method. The account is classified as an Operating/General & Administrative Expense on the income statement.

Direct Write-Off Method: A procedure which does not recognize any Bad Debts Expense until a specific customer's account proves to be uncollectible.

Percentage of Accounts Receivable or Balance Sheet Method: Taking a percentage of open accounts receivable at the end of a period to estimate the Bad Debts Expense.

Percentage of Sales or Income Statement Method: Taking a percentage of net sales for the fiscal period to estimate the amount of Bad Debts Expense.

QUESTIONS

A1. Describe briefly two basic methods of estimating Bad Debts Expense when the allowance method is used.

A2. How do the direct write-off and allowance methods of handling losses differ with respect to the recognition of the Bad Debt Expense?

A3. What account titles are used in the adjusting entry when estimating the amount of uncollectible accounts?

A4. Under what circumstances would you reinstate a customer's account that was previously written off as a bad debt?

A5. What two entries are required for a payment received from a customer on an account that was previously written off the company records?

EXERCISES

Estimating Bad Debts Expense

A1. On December 31 of the current year, selected accounts in the ledger of the Book Company showed the following balances:

Credit Sales	$60,000	Accounts Receivable	$80,000
Sales Discounts	500	Allowance for Doubtful Accounts	100*
Sales Returns	1,000		

* Credit balance.

Determine the amount needed to record the Bad Debts Expense under each of the following methods:
(*a*) Income statement method using a 4 percent rate.
(*b*) Balance sheet method using a 2 percent rate.

Journalizing Adjusting Entry for Bad Debts

A2. From the information in Exercise A1, prepare the adjusting entry in general journal form for items *a* and *b*.

Writing Off Accounts Receivable

A3. Prepare the general journal entry required on March 2 to write off the $240 uncollectible account of A. Storm and Company, and give the general journal entry to record the receipt of $140 on December 10 from A. Storm and Company.

Posting to Accounts Receivable

A4. Set up general ledger accounts for Accounts Receivable and the Allowance for Doubtful Accounts and record the beginning balances of $1,000 (debit) and $500 (credit), respectively. Post from the general journal in Exercise A3 and post the information that affects these two accounts.

PROBLEMS

Journalizing Adjusting Entry for Bad Debts

A8-1. The Lite Company adjusts and closes its books each December 31. The accounts for all prior years have been properly adjusted and closed. Given below are a number of the company's account balances prior to the adjustments on December 31.

	Debit	Credit
Accounts Receivable	$60,000	
Allowance for Doubtful Accounts		$ 120
Sales		90,000
Sales Discounts	2,000	
Sales Returns & Allowances	1,000	

Required

(a) Prepare the adjusting entry required for Bad Debts Expense on December 31, assuming that for the past few years the company had experienced losses on Accounts Receivable equal to 2 percent of net sales.
(b) Prepare an alternate adjusting entry under the assumption that the Bad Debts Expense is estimated to be 3 percent of the Accounts Receivable.

Estimating Bad Debts Expense

A8-2. At the end of the fiscal year, selected accounts in the general ledger of the Welco Corporation show the following balances:

Accounts Receivable	$60,000
Sales	70,000
Sales Discounts	4,000
Sales Returns & Allowances	5,000

Required

Determine the amount needed to record the Bad Debts Expense under each of the following assumptions:
(a) The Bad Debts Expense is estimated to be 2 percent of net sales.
(b) The Bad Debts expense is estimated to be 2 percent of the Accounts Receivable. The Allowance for Doubtful Accounts before the adjusting entry has a credit balance of $300.
(c) The Bad Debts Expense is estimated to be 2 percent of the Accounts Receivable. The Allowance for Doubtful Accounts before the adjusting entry has a debit balance of $100.

A8-3. The Cole Company makes all sales on account and does not offer cash discounts. The collections from customers and write-offs of uncollectible accounts for a 2-year period are summarized below.

Year	Sales	Accounts Receivable Collections	Accounts Receivable Written Off
1	$400,000	$280,000	$1,500
2	500,000	450,000	1,200

The Cole Company uses the direct write-off method of recognizing losses for uncollectible accounts.

Required

(a) What amount of Bad Debts Expense would be recognized each year?
(b) What would the total amount of Accounts Receivable be on the balance sheet at the end of each year?

Review Problems for Bad Debts

A8-4. On January 1, the beginning of the current period, the Buckley Industries had the following balances for the accounts listed below:

Accounts Receivable	$100,000	(debit)
Allowance for Doubtful Accounts	2,000	(credit)

During this year, sales on account amounted to $160,000 and collections of Accounts Receivable amounted to $140,000. Selected transactions during the year appear below:

Mar.   8   Wrote off the account of Carbon Company, $400.
May   14   Wrote off the account of Stover, Inc., $1,800.
Oct.   10   Carbon Company paid $200 of the $400 written off on March 8. This $200 is not included in the $140,000 of collections.
Dec.   12   Wrote off the account of Suns Specialities, $50.
       31   Recorded the total sales on account for the year.
       31   Recorded the total collections on Accounts Receivable for the year.
       31   Recorded the adjusting entry for Bad Debts Expense using 1 percent of net sales.

Required

(a) Open general ledger accounts for 112 Accounts Receivable; 118 Allowance for Doubtful Accounts; and 618 Bad Debts Expense. Post the beginning balances as of January 1.
(b) Journalize the transactions above and post to the general ledger.
(c) Give the balance sheet presentation on December 31 for Accounts Receivable and Allowance for Doubtful Accounts.

A8-5. The Supreme Corporation uses the direct write-off method for recognizing uncollectible accounts. At the beginning of the calendar year, Accounts

Receivable had a balance of $160,000. During the year, the following selected transactions were recorded:

Mar. 12 Wrote off the account of Haskins & Jones, $520.
June 8 Wrote off the account of Crest & Crest, $720.
Nov. 6 Wrote off the account of Jacks, Inc., $220.

Required

(*a*) Open general ledger accounts for 112 Accounts Receivable and 618 Bad Debts Expense, and enter the beginning balance for Accounts Receivable as of January 1.
(*b*) Journalize the transactions above, and post to the general ledger.
(*c*) What amount will be recorded on the income statement for Bad Debts Expense?

√**A8-6.** Selected transactions during the current fiscal period for D & E Company appear below. The normal balance in the Accounts Receivable and the Allowance for Doubtful Accounts on January 1 amounted to $180,000 and $3,600, respectively.

May 18 Wrote off the account of Swift Corporation, $1,400.
July 19 Wrote off the account of Leeds Specialities, $600.
Oct. 3 Received $700 from Swift Corporation as partial payment of the $1,400 previously written off the records.
Nov. 6 Received 40 percent of $5,000, owed by Sunlit Company. The company is bankrupt, and the remaining balance was written off as uncollectible.
Dec. 31 Recorded the total credit sales for the year, $200,000.
     31 Recorded collections of 60 percent of the Accounts Receivable balance on December 31.
     31 Recorded the adjusting entry for Bad Debts Expense by an amount equal to 2 percent of the Accounts Receivable balance on December 31.

Required

(*a*) Open general ledger accounts for 112 Accounts Receivable; 118 Allowance for Doubtful Accounts; and 618 Bad Debts Expense. Post the beginning balances as of January 1.
(*b*) Journalize and post the transactions above.
(*c*) Give the balance sheet presentation on December 31 for Accounts Receivable and Allowance for Doubtful Accounts.

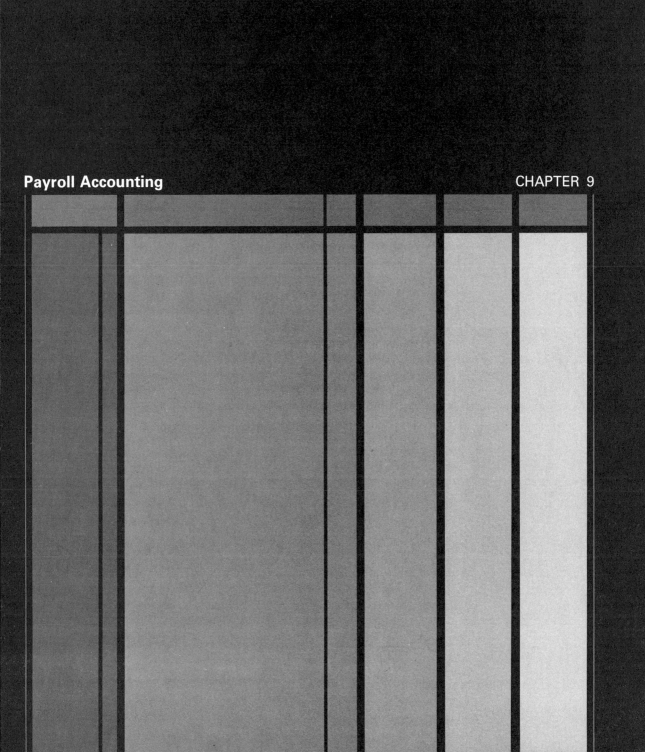

After completing this chapter, you should be able to:

1. **State the purpose of an Employee's Withholding Allowance Certificate (W-4) and the Wage and Tax Statement (W-2)**

2. **List the payroll taxes paid by employees and employers**

3. **Define merit rating as it applies to state unemployment**

4. **Describe the Fair Labor Standards Act**

5. **List the payroll records each employer is required to maintain**

6. **Compute the wages earned and taxes paid by employees and journalize the payroll entries**

7. **Compute the employer's taxes for a payroll and record the entry for payroll tax expense**

8. **Prepare a payroll register and an employee earnings record**

9. **State the advantage of using a one-write pegboard system for payroll**

Most people who work for someone else depend upon the payroll department to figure the amount of their earnings correctly and make all the proper deductions. Therefore, it is very important for those working in the payroll department to be familiar with the rules and regulations affecting the earnings of the employees and the taxes levied on the employers for having people work for them.

This chapter will discuss three things:

1. The federal, state, and local laws that place certain restrictions on the method for recording and reporting payroll information
2. How payroll accounting and control works for the wages earned and paid to the employees and for the taxes the employer must pay on the earnings of the employee
3. How payroll information may be recorded by using a one-write pegboard accounting method

GOVERNMENT REGULATIONS IMPORTANT TO PAYROLL

Several laws require employees to pay taxes on wages earned. These laws require employers to deduct or withhold these taxes from earnings and pay them to the proper government agencies. Also, there are laws that require employers to pay payroll taxes to the government because they have people working for them. All these laws have important rules which govern the computing of the payroll.

RULES FOR EMPLOYEE EARNINGS

Federal Income Tax Withheld

The Internal Revenue Code requires an employer to withhold federal income tax on an employee's gross wages. The purpose is to have the employer withhold this tax and send to the *Internal Revenue Service* (*I.R.S.*) a sufficient amount each pay period that will approximately equal what the employee will owe the government in federal income tax for the year. This is known as the "pay-as-you-go method." This means that the government receives your tax payments each pay period, saving you from making one federal income tax payment at the end of the year. The amount that the employer is required to withhold (there are some exceptions) depends on your marital status, number of exemptions claimed, total wages earned, and how often you get paid.

When hired, each employee must fill out a Form W-4, *Employee's Withholding Allowance Certificate* (Figure 9-1), indicating the marital status and the number of exemptions claimed. After the date of hire, it becomes the employee's responsibility to fill out a new Form W-4 if there is any change in the number of exemptions.

When figuring the amount of taxes to be withheld from an employee's wages, the employer may use *Circular E,* an I.R.S. publication that furnishes tables showing how much tax should be withheld for each employee, thereby eliminating any calculations. A section from Circular E is shown in Figure 9-2.

Assume that a male employee is married, has four exemptions including himself, and is paid weekly. The earnings for the week total $205. Look

FIGURE 9-1

Form **W-4**
(Rev. October 1979)

Department of the Treasury—Internal Revenue Service
Employee's Withholding Allowance Certificate

Print your full name ▶ | Your social security number ▶

Address (including ZIP code) ▶

Marital status: ☐ Single ☐ Married ☐ Married, but withhold at higher Single rate
Note: *If married, but legally separated, or spouse is a nonresident alien, check the single block.*

1 Total number of allowances you are claiming (from line F of the worksheet on page 2) . . . .

2 Additional amount, if any, you want deducted from each pay (if your employer agrees) . . . . $

3 I claim exemption from withholding because (see instructions and check boxes below that apply):
  a ☐ Last year I did not owe any Federal income tax and had a right to a full refund of **ALL** income tax withheld, **AND**
  b ☐ This year I do not expect to owe any Federal income tax and expect to have a right to a full refund of **ALL** income tax withheld. If both

  a and **b** apply, enter "EXEMPT" here . . . . ▶
  c If you entered "EXEMPT" on line 3b, are you a full-time student? . . . . ☐ Yes ☐ No

Under the penalties of perjury, I certify that I am entitled to the number of withholding allowances claimed on this certificate, or if claiming exemption from withholding, that I am entitled to claim the exempt status.

Employee's signature ▶ | Date ▶ | , 19

Employer's name and address (including ZIP code) **(FOR EMPLOYER'S USE ONLY)** | Employer identification number

FIGURE 9-2

Table from Circular E

MARRIED Persons — WEEKLY Payroll Period

And the wages are—		And the number of withholding allowances claimed is—										
At least	But less than	0	1	2	3	4	5	6	7	8	9	10 or more
		The amount of income tax to be withheld shall be—										
$0	$60	$0	$0	$0	$0	$0	$0	$0	$0	$0	$0	$0
60	62	.10	0	0	0	0	0	0	0	0	0	0
62	64	.40	0	0	0	0	0	0	0	0	0	0
64	66	.70	0	0	0	0	0	0	0	0	0	0
66	68	1.00	0	0	0	0	0	0	0	0	0	0
68	70	1.30	0	0	0	0	0	0	0	0	0	0
70	72	1.60	0	0	0	0	0	0	0	0	0	0
72	74	1.90	0	0	0	0	0	0	0	0	0	0
74	76	2.20	0	0	0	0	0	0	0	0	0	0
76	78	2.50	.30	0	0	0	0	0	0	0	0	0
78	80	2.80	.60	0	0	0	0	0	0	0	0	0
80	82	3.10	.90	0	0	0	0	0	0	0	0	0
82	84	3.40	1.20	0	0	0	0	0	0	0	0	0
84	86	3.70	1.50	0	0	0	0	0	0	0	0	0
86	88	4.00	1.80	0	0	0	0	0	0	0	0	0
88	90	4.30	2.10	0	0	0	0	0	0	0	0	0
90	92	4.60	2.40	.20	0	0	0	0	0	0	0	0
92	94	4.90	2.70	.50	0	0	0	0	0	0	0	0
94	96	5.20	3.00	.80	0	0	0	0	0	0	0	0
96	98	5.50	3.30	1.10	0	0	0	0	0	0	0	0
98	100	5.80	3.60	1.40	0	0	0	0	0	0	0	0
100	105	6.30	4.10	2.00	0	0	0	0	0	0	0	0
105	110	7.10	4.90	2.70	.50	0	0	0	0	0	0	0
110	115	8.00	5.60	3.50	1.30	0	0	0	0	0	0	0
115	120	8.90	6.40	4.20	2.00	0	0	0	0	0	0	0
120	125	9.80	7.20	5.00	2.80	.60	0	0	0	0	0	0
125	130	10.70	8.10	5.70	3.50	1.40	0	0	0	0	0	0
130	135	11.60	9.00	6.50	4.30	2.10	0	0	0	0	0	0
135	140	12.50	9.90	7.30	5.00	2.90	.70	0	0	0	0	0
140	145	13.40	10.80	8.20	5.80	3.60	1.50	0	0	0	0	0
145	150	14.30	11.70	9.10	6.50	4.40	2.20	.10	0	0	0	0
150	160	15.70	13.10	10.50	7.90	5.50	3.30	1.20	0	0	0	0
160	170	17.50	14.90	12.30	9.70	7.10	4.80	2.70	.50	0	0	0
170	180	19.30	16.70	14.10	11.50	8.90	6.30	4.20	2.00	0	0	0
180	190	21.10	18.50	15.90	13.30	10.70	8.10	5.70	3.50	1.40	0	0
190	200	22.90	20.30	17.70	15.10	12.50	9.90	7.30	5.00	2.90	.70	0
200	210	24.70	22.10	19.50	16.90	14.30	11.70	9.10	6.50	4.40	2.20	0
210	220	26.50	23.90	21.30	18.70	16.10	13.50	10.90	8.30	5.90	3.70	1.50
220	230	28.40	25.70	23.10	20.50	17.90	15.30	12.70	10.10	7.50	5.20	3.00
230	240	30.60	27.50	24.90	22.30	19.70	17.10	14.50	11.90	9.30	6.70	4.50
240	250	32.80	29.60	26.70	24.10	21.50	18.90	16.30	13.70	11.10	8.50	6.00
250	260	35.00	31.80	28.60	25.90	23.30	20.70	18.10	15.50	12.90	10.30	7.70
260	270	37.20	34.00	30.80	27.70	25.10	22.50	19.90	17.30	14.70	12.10	9.50
270	280	39.40	36.20	33.00	29.80	26.90	24.30	21.70	19.10	16.50	13.90	11.30
280	290	41.80	38.40	35.20	32.00	28.90	26.10	23.50	20.90	18.30	15.70	13.10
290	300	44.30	40.70	37.40	34.20	31.10	27.90	25.30	22.70	20.10	17.50	14.90
300	310	46.80	43.20	39.60	36.40	33.30	30.10	27.10	24.50	21.90	19.30	16.70
310	320	49.30	45.70	42.10	38.60	35.50	32.30	29.10	26.30	23.70	21.10	18.50
320	330	51.80	48.20	44.60	41.00	37.70	34.50	31.30	28.20	25.50	22.90	20.30
330	340	54.30	50.70	47.10	43.50	39.90	36.70	33.50	30.40	27.30	24.70	22.10
340	350	56.80	53.20	49.60	46.00	42.40	38.90	35.70	32.60	29.40	26.50	23.90
350	360	59.30	55.70	52.10	48.50	44.90	41.30	37.90	34.80	31.60	28.40	25.70
360	370	62.10	58.20	54.60	51.00	47.40	43.80	40.10	37.00	33.80	30.60	27.50
370	380	64.90	60.80	57.10	53.50	49.90	46.30	42.60	39.20	36.00	32.80	29.60
380	390	67.70	63.60	59.60	56.00	52.40	48.80	45.10	41.50	38.20	35.00	31.80
390	400	70.50	66.40	62.40	58.50	54.90	51.30	47.60	44.00	40.40	37.20	34.00
400	410	73.30	69.20	65.20	61.20	57.40	53.80	50.10	46.50	42.90	39.40	36.20
410	420	76.10	72.00	68.00	64.00	59.90	56.30	52.60	49.00	45.40	41.80	38.40
420	430	78.90	74.80	70.80	66.80	62.70	58.80	55.10	51.50	47.90	44.30	40.70
430	440	81.80	77.60	73.60	69.60	65.50	61.50	57.60	54.00	50.40	46.80	43.20

250

down the left-hand column under "Wages" until you arrive at "$200 to $210." Then follow the chart across to the column for four exemptions and locate "$14.30," which is the amount to be deducted from the wages earned by the employee for federal income taxes.

State and City Income Tax Withheld

Most states and a few cities have levied an income tax on the total earnings of employees which must be withheld each pay period by the employer. The payroll procedures for withholding, remitting, and reporting these state and local income taxes are similar to the pattern established for federal income taxes, with a variety of tax rates and forms. Therefore, it is important that anyone working on payroll carefully check all requirements and follow the rules established by each individual state and city government.

SOCIAL SECURITY ACT

The Social Security Act approved in August 1935 is a complex law that provides for many benefits, and since its enactment, the rates and maximum amount of wages subject to the tax has been constantly increased by various amendments. A person working on the payroll for a business does not need to know all the details of the legislation to complete the payroll properly. Therefore, this text will present only the necessary information involving the two major parts of the Act: the Federal Insurance Contributions Act (FICA) for both the employee and employer and the Federal Unemployment Tax Act (FUTA) for employer—with a few exceptions.

Federal Insurance Contributions Tax

Under the *Federal Insurance Contributions Act* (*FICA*) the employee is required to pay a percentage of his or her earnings for social security. The 1981 rate is 6.65 percent on the first $29,700 of taxable earnings, or $1,975.05 ($29,700 × 0.0665). Once the employee has earned $29,700 in any calendar year, no more FICA tax has to be paid. Current tables for withholding FICA from employees may be found in Circular E, Employer's Tax Guide, published by the Internal Revenue Service. A section from Circular E is shown in Figure 9-3.

For example, if employee A earns $32,000 during 1981, only $29,700 would be subject to FICA tax. The employer must withhold $1,975.05 ($29,700 × 0.0665) from the wages of employee A, and the employer must pay another $1,975.05 on behalf of the employee, for a total of $3,950.10 to be paid to the federal government. When this text went into press, there was considerable discussion in Congress covering drastic changes to the Act regarding the increasing of the age limits before a worker becomes eligible for social security, decreasing the amount of benefits and the tax rate, etc.

FIGURE 9-3

Social Security Employee Tax Table for 1981—Continued
(6.65%)

Wages At least	But less than	Tax to be withheld
$61.28	$61.43	$4.08
61.43	61.58	4.09
61.58	61.73	4.10
61.73	61.88	4.11
61.88	62.04	4.12
62.04	62.19	4.13
62.19	62.34	4.14
62.34	62.49	4.15
62.49	62.64	4.16
62.64	62.79	4.17
62.79	62.94	4.18
62.94	63.09	4.19
63.09	63.24	4.20
63.24	63.39	4.21
63.39	63.54	4.22
63.54	63.69	4.23
63.69	63.84	4.24
63.84	63.99	4.25
63.99	64.14	4.26
64.14	64.29	4.27
64.29	64.44	4.28
64.44	64.59	4.29
64.59	64.74	4.30
64.74	64.89	4.31
64.89	65.04	4.32
65.04	65.19	4.33
65.19	65.34	4.34
65.34	65.49	4.35
65.49	65.64	4.36
65.64	65.79	4.37
65.79	65.94	4.38
65.94	66.10	4.39
66.10	66.25	4.40
66.25	66.40	4.41
66.40	66.55	4.42
66.55	66.70	4.43
66.70	66.85	4.44
66.85	67.00	4.45
67.00	67.15	4.46
67.15	67.30	4.47
67.30	67.45	4.48
67.45	67.60	4.49
67.60	67.75	4.50
67.75	67.90	4.51
67.90	68.05	4.52
68.05	68.20	4.53
68.20	68.35	4.54
68.35	68.50	4.55
68.50	68.65	4.56
68.65	68.80	4.57
68.80	68.95	4.58
68.95	69.10	4.59
69.10	69.25	4.60
69.25	69.40	4.61
69.40	69.55	4.62
69.55	69.70	4.63
69.70	69.85	4.64
69.85	70.00	4.65
70.00	70.16	4.66
70.16	70.31	4.67
70.31	70.46	4.68
70.46	70.61	4.69
70.61	70.76	4.70
70.76	70.91	4.71
70.91	71.06	4.72
71.06	71.21	4.73
71.21	71.36	4.74
71.36	71.51	4.75
71.51	71.66	4.76
71.66	71.81	4.77
71.81	71.96	4.78
71.96	72.11	4.79

Wages At least	But less than	Tax to be withheld
$72.11	$72.26	$4.80
72.26	72.41	4.81
72.41	72.56	4.82
72.56	72.71	4.83
72.71	72.86	4.84
72.86	73.01	4.85
73.01	73.16	4.86
73.16	73.31	4.87
73.31	73.46	4.88
73.46	73.61	4.89
73.61	73.76	4.90
73.76	73.91	4.91
73.91	74.07	4.92
74.07	74.22	4.93
74.22	74.37	4.94
74.37	74.52	4.95
74.52	74.67	4.96
74.67	74.82	4.97
74.82	74.97	4.98
74.97	75.12	4.99
75.12	75.27	5.00
75.27	75.42	5.01
75.42	75.57	5.02
75.57	75.72	5.03
75.72	75.87	5.04
75.87	76.02	5.05
76.02	76.17	5.06
76.17	76.32	5.07
76.32	76.47	5.08
76.47	76.62	5.09
76.62	76.77	5.10
76.77	76.92	5.11
76.92	77.07	5.12
77.07	77.22	5.13
77.22	77.37	5.14
77.37	77.52	5.15
77.52	77.67	5.16
77.67	77.82	5.17
77.82	77.97	5.18
77.97	78.13	5.19
78.13	78.28	5.20
78.28	78.43	5.21
78.43	78.58	5.22
78.58	78.73	5.23
78.73	78.88	5.24
78.88	79.03	5.25
79.03	79.18	5.26
79.18	79.33	5.27
79.33	79.48	5.28
79.48	79.63	5.29
79.63	79.78	5.30
79.78	79.93	5.31
79.93	80.08	5.32
80.08	80.23	5.33
80.23	80.38	5.34
80.38	80.53	5.35
80.53	80.68	5.36
80.68	80.83	5.37
80.83	80.98	5.38
80.98	81.13	5.39
81.13	81.28	5.40
81.28	81.43	5.41
81.43	81.58	5.42
81.58	81.73	5.43
81.73	81.88	5.44
81.88	82.04	5.45
82.04	82.19	5.46
82.19	82.34	5.47
82.34	82.49	5.48
82.49	82.64	5.49
82.64	82.79	5.50
82.79	82.94	5.51

Wages At least	But less than	Tax to be withheld
$82.94	$83.09	$5.52
83.09	83.24	5.53
83.24	83.39	5.54
83.39	83.54	5.55
83.54	83.69	5.56
83.69	83.84	5.57
83.84	83.99	5.58
83.99	84.14	5.59
84.14	84.29	5.60
84.29	84.44	5.61
84.44	84.59	5.62
84.59	84.74	5.63
84.74	84.89	5.64
84.89	85.04	5.65
85.04	85.19	5.66
85.19	85.34	5.67
85.34	85.49	5.68
85.49	85.64	5.69
85.64	85.79	5.70
85.79	85.94	5.71
85.94	86.10	5.72
86.10	86.25	5.73
86.25	86.40	5.74
86.40	86.55	5.75
86.55	86.70	5.76
86.70	86.85	5.77
86.85	87.00	5.78
87.00	87.15	5.79
87.15	87.30	5.80
87.30	87.45	5.81
87.45	87.60	5.82
87.60	87.75	5.83
87.75	87.90	5.84
87.90	88.05	5.85
88.05	88.20	5.86
88.20	88.35	5.87
88.35	88.50	5.88
88.50	88.65	5.89
88.65	88.80	5.90
88.80	88.95	5.91
88.95	89.10	5.92
89.10	89.25	5.93
89.25	89.40	5.94
89.40	89.55	5.95
89.55	89.70	5.96
89.70	89.85	5.97
89.85	90.00	5.98
90.00	90.16	5.99
90.16	90.31	6.00
90.31	90.46	6.01
90.46	90.61	6.02
90.61	90.76	6.03
90.76	90.91	6.04
90.91	91.06	6.05
91.06	91.21	6.06
91.21	91.36	6.07
91.36	91.51	6.08
91.51	91.66	6.09
91.66	91.81	6.10
91.81	91.96	6.11
91.96	92.11	6.12
92.11	92.26	6.13
92.26	92.41	6.14
92.41	92.56	6.15
92.56	92.71	6.16
92.71	92.86	6.17
92.86	93.01	6.18
93.01	93.16	6.19
93.16	93.31	6.20
93.31	93.46	6.21
93.46	93.61	6.22
93.61	93.76	6.23

Wages At least	But less than	Tax to be withheld
$93.76	$93.91	$6.24
93.91	94.07	6.25
94.07	94.22	6.26
94.22	94.37	6.27
94.37	94.52	6.28
94.52	94.67	6.29
94.67	94.82	6.30
94.82	94.97	6.31
94.97	95.12	6.32
95.12	95.27	6.33
95.27	95.42	6.34
95.42	95.57	6.35
95.57	95.72	6.36
95.72	95.87	6.37
95.87	96.02	6.38
96.02	96.17	6.39
96.17	96.32	6.40
96.32	96.47	6.41
96.47	96.62	6.42
96.62	96.77	6.43
96.77	96.92	6.44
96.92	97.07	6.45
97.07	97.22	6.46
97.22	97.37	6.47
97.37	97.52	6.48
97.52	97.67	6.49
97.67	97.82	6.50
97.82	97.97	6.51
97.97	98.13	6.52
98.13	98.28	6.53
98.28	98.43	6.54
98.43	98.58	6.55
98.58	98.73	6.56
98.73	98.88	6.57
98.88	99.03	6.58
99.03	99.18	6.59
99.18	99.33	6.60
99.33	99.48	6.61
99.48	99.63	6.62
99.63	99.78	6.63
99.78	99.93	6.64
99.93	100.00	6.65

The multiples of the withholding for **FICA** on $100 are

Wage	Tax to be withheld
$100	$6.65
200	13.30
300	19.95
400	26.60
500	33.25
600	39.90
700	46.55
800	53.20
900	59.85
1,000	66.50

OTHER DEDUCTIONS

In the states of Alabama, Alaska, New Jersey, and Rhode Island, the employee is required to pay a portion of the state unemployment insurance tax. And, in a few cases, the employee must pay a tax to provide funds for disability benefits.

At the request of or authorization by the employee, the employer may make other deductions and payments, such as union dues, credit union deposits, life and hospitalization insurance, retirement programs, and contributions to charities (United Fund, etc.).

RULES FOR THE EMPLOYER

Various government regulations require employers to pay certain taxes because they have people working for them. Such taxes are not deducted from the employee's earnings, but they are an additional operating expense for the employer.

Federal Insurance Contributions Tax (Social Security)

The FICA law requires the employer to pay a tax equal to that of the employee. For every dollar that the employee pays for social security taxes, the employer must add or match it dollar for dollar. All FICA tax rates and the amount of earnings subject to FICA taxes are the same as for the employee.

UNEMPLOYMENT COMPENSATION TAX

Unemployment compensation programs are set up under federal laws authorizing the states to set the standards and rules for paying unemployment benefits. As a result, there are two separate taxes known as Federal Unemployment Compensation Tax (FUTA) and State Unemployment Compensation Tax (SUTA) that must be paid by the employer for unemployment benefits.

Federal Unemployment Compensation Tax (FUTA)

The *Federal Unemployment Tax Act* known as FUTA requires every employer to:

1. Pay an excise tax of 0.7 percent (0.007) on the first $6,000 of earnings paid to the employee
2. File a Form 940, *Employer's Annual Federal Unemployment Tax Return* (Figure 9-4)

FIGURE 9-4

Form 940

Form **940** Department of the Treasury Internal Revenue Service	**Employer's Annual Federal Unemployment Tax Return** ▶ For Paperwork Reduction Act Notice, see page 2.	OMB No. 1545–0028 **1981**

			T	
If incorrect, make any necessary change. ▶	Name (as distinguished from trade name)	Calendar Year **1981**	FF	
	Trade name, if any	Employer identification number	FD	
			FP	
	Address and ZIP code		I	
			T	

A Did you pay all required contributions to your State unemployment fund by the due date of Form 940? . . . . . . ☐ Yes ☐ No

If you check the "Yes" box, enter amount of contributions timely paid to your State unemployment fund . . . ▶ $_____

B Are you required to pay contributions to only one State? . . . . ☐ Yes ☐ No

If you checked the "Yes" box, (1) Enter the name of the State where you are required to pay contributions . . . ▶ _____

(2) Enter your State reporting number(s) as shown on State unemployment tax return . . . . ▶ _____

Part I	**Computation of Taxable Wages and Credit Reduction (To Be Completed by All Taxpayers)**

1 Total payments (including exempt payments) during the calendar year for services of employees . . . . .

2 Exempt payments. (Explain each exemption shown, attaching additional sheets if necessary) ▶ _____ | Amount paid

3 Payments for services in excess of $6,000. Enter only the excess over the first $6,000 paid to individual employees exclusive of exempt amounts entered on line 2. Do not use State wage limitation . . .

4 Total exempt payments (add lines 2 and 3) . . . .

5 **Total taxable wages** (subtract line 4 from line 1). (If any portion is exempt from State contributions, see instructions) . ▶

6 Credit reduction because of unrepaid advances to the States listed. Enter in lines (a)–(k) the wages included on line 5 above for each State and multiply by the rate shown.

(a) CT _____ × .007 _____	(e) ME _____ × .006 _____	(i) RI _____ × .006 _____
(b) DE _____ × .006 _____	(f) NJ _____ × .006 _____	(j) VT _____ × .006 _____
(c) DC _____ × .006 _____	(g) PA _____ × .006 _____	(k) VI _____ × .006 _____
(d) IL _____ × .006 _____	(h) PR _____ × .006 _____	

7 Total credit reduction (add lines 6(a) through 6(k) and enter on line 2, Part II or line 4, Part III) . . . . ▶

Part II	**Tax Due or Refund (Complete if You Checked the "Yes" boxes in Both Items A and B Above)**

1 FUTA tax. Multiply the wages on line 5, Part I, by .007 and enter here . . . .

2 Enter amount from line 7, Part I . . . .

3 Total FUTA tax (add lines 1 and 2) . . . .

4 Less: Total FUTA tax deposited from column d, line 5, Part IV . . . .

5 **Balance due** (subtract line 4 from line 3—If over $100, see Part IV Instructions). Pay to IRS . . . . . ▶

6 Overpayment (subtract line 3 from line 4) . . . . ▶

Part III	**Tax Due or Refund (Complete if You Checked the "No" Box in Either Item A or Item B Above)**

1 Gross FUTA tax. Multiply the wages on line 5, Part I, by .034 . . . .

2 Maximum credit. Multiply the wages on line 5, Part I, by .027 . . . .

3 Enter the smaller of the amount on line 11, Part V, or line 2, Part III . . . .

4 Enter amount from line 7, Part I . . . .

5 Credit allowable (subtract line 4 from line 3) . . . .

6 Total FUTA tax (subtract line 5 from line 1) . . . .

7 Less: Total FUTA tax deposited from column d, line 5, Part IV . . . .

8 **Balance due** (subtract line 7 from line 6—if over $100, see Part IV Instructions). Pay to IRS . . . . . ▶

9 Overpayment (subtract line 6 from line 7) . . . . ▶

Part IV	**Record of Federal Tax Deposits for Unemployment Tax (Form 508) (Do not include contributions paid to State)**

	a. Quarter	b. Liability for quarter	c. Date of deposit	d. Amount of deposit
1	First			
2	Second			
3	Third			
4	Fourth			
5	Total for year			

If you will not have to file returns in the future, write "Final" here (see general instruction "Who Must File") . . ▶

Under penalties of perjury, I declare that I have examined this return, including accompanying schedules and statements, and to the best of my knowledge and belief, it is true, correct, and complete, and that no part of any payment made to a State unemployment fund claimed as a credit was or is to be deducted from the payments to employees.

Date ▶ _____ Signature ▶ _____ Title (Owner, etc.) ▶ _____

State Unemployment Compensation Tax (SUTA)

States have various unemployment compensation programs. These State Unemployment Tax programs known as SUTA are supported by taxing employers (except where exempt by law) and requiring them to:

1. Pay a maximum tax of 2.7 percent (0.027) on an employee's wages. The amount of an employee's wages subject to the tax varies from $6,000 to $10,000. Twenty-seven states pay 2.7 percent on the first $6,000 earned by each employee. Alaska is the only state requiring employers to pay 2.7 percent on the first $10,000 earned by each employee. Each employer receives an annual rate from the state.
2. File the necessary state tax reports.

The employer subject to a FUTA or SUTA payroll tax would be any business or organization employing one or more persons at any time in each of 20 different calendar weeks or paying wages of $1,500 or more in any one calendar quarter. The temporary benefits received from the unemployment insurance fund are payable to unemployed workers for limited periods in accordance with programs created by each state and approved by the federal government.

During periods of high unemployment, the federal government may provide states with additional funds so that unemployment benefits can be extended.

At the present time, the average joint (state and federal) tax rate is 3.4 percent of the first $6,000 of wages paid to each employee during a calendar year. However, the federal government gives an employer credit against this tax for payments made to the state up to a maximum of 2.7 percent. Consequently, states have set their rates at the maximum allowed; therefore, the federal unemployment tax generally amounts to 0.7 percent (3.4 percent − 2.7 percent). As a result, an employer pays the larger portion of unemployment tax to the state.

State laws provide employers a reward, called a *merit rating* or an *experience rating,* to encourage employers to establish a record of stable employment. This rating reduces the basic rate of state unemployment tax but does not increase the federal rate.

Computation of federal and state unemployment taxes is illustrated in the following examples:

EXAMPLE 1

Employer A has a payroll of $10,000 subject to unemployment taxes. The tax rate is 3.4 percent: 2.7 percent to the state and 0.7 percent for the federal government.

State tax ($10,000 × 0.027) $270
Federal tax ($10,000 × 0.007)   70

FIGURE 9-5

Payroll register

PAYROLL REGISTER

| NAME | PERIOD ENDING | HOURS WORKED | EARNINGS | | | | ★ | DEDUCTIONS | | | | | NET PAY | ACCUMU-LATED EARNINGS | CHECK NUMBER | LINE NO. |
			REGULAR	OVERTIME	OTHER	TOTAL		FEDERAL INC. TAX	FICA	STATE INC. TAX	OTHER	TOTAL				
TOTALS BROUGHT FORWARD ➡																
Salesman A	1/29		700			700		100	46.55	35		181.55	518.45	1400	1403	1
Employee B	1/29	80	400			400		53	26.60	20		99.60	300.40	800	1404	2
Office #1	1/29		300			300		30	19.95	15		64.95	235.05	600	1405	3
Office #2	1/29		300			300		30	19.95	15		64.95	235.05	600	1406	4
Office #3	1/29		300			300		30	19.95	15		64.95	235.05	600	1407	5
																6
																7
																8
																9
																10
																11
																12
																13
																14
																15
																16
																17
																18
																19
																20
																21
																22
																23
																24
																25
																26
																27
																28
																29
																30
TOTALS FORWARD ➡			2000			2000		243	133.00	100		476.00	1524	4000		
			1	2	3	4						5	6			

FORM B-935-2 NC

PROOF OF POSTINGS
The totals of Column 1 (Regular Earnings) + Column 2 (Overtime Earnings) + Column 3 (Other Earnings) = Column 4 (Total Earnings) − Column 5 (Total All Deductions) = Column 6 (Net Pay).

THE REYNOLDS & REYNOLDS CO. DAYTON OHIO   LITHO IN U.S.A.

PAYROLL PERIOD ENDING __1/29/82__

EXAMPLE 2   *Employer B has a payroll of $10,000 subject to unemployment taxes. The tax rate is 3.4 percent: 2.7 percent to the state and 0.7 percent to the federal government. Employer B has had an excellent record of stable employment for the employees and received a merit rating reducing the state unemployment tax rate from 2.7 to 2.1 percent.*

State Tax ($10,000 × 0.021) $210
Federal tax ($10,000 × 0.007)   70

FAIR LABOR STANDARDS ACT

The *Fair Labor Standards Act,* commonly known as the *Federal Wage and Hour Law,* involves businesses directly engaged in the production of goods for interstate commerce. The Act requires an employer to pay each employee a minimum hourly rate established by the government plus an overtime rate of *time and one-half* (hourly rate plus half the hourly rate) for all hours worked beyond 40 hours per week. This act does not limit total working hours, but it does establish the 40-hour workweek as the basis for overtime pay. Many companies have extended the overtime premium pay to hours worked beyond 8 hours per day as well as those in excess of 40 hours per week. Some state laws require employers to pay employees overtime premium for any hours worked in excess of 8 hours per day.

PAYROLL RECORDS AND CONTROL

All states require an employer to keep certain payroll records in addition to the tax records and reports. Although the specific requirements vary from state to state, the following requirements are standard.

Payroll records required by state

1. A record of each pay period called a payroll register (Figure 9-5) showing the date, hours, earnings, and deductions of each employee
2. A record of each employee's earnings called an employee or individual earnings record (Figure 9-6) showing:
   (*a*) Date of employment, layoff, rehire, or discharge
   (*b*) Social security number
   (*c*) Rate or method of pay
   (*d*) Summary of wages and deductions by quarter and calendar year

Payroll Register (How to Figure the Payroll)

Each pay period a detailed record for all the employees is summarized in a payroll register similar to the illustration in Figure 9-5. This *payroll register* contains columns showing the amount of cumulative earnings for the cal-

FIGURE 9-6

EMPLOYEE EARNINGS RECORD

NAME __Employee B__

ADDRESS __27468 W. Taylor Street, Livonia, MI   48151__

RATE __$5.00 Hour__

SOCIAL SECURITY NO. __362-30-1312__

DATE HIRED: __1/2/82__

NO. OF EXEMPTIONS __2__

MARITAL STATUS __M__

NAME	PERIOD ENDING	HOURS WORKED	EARNINGS				*	DEDUCTIONS					NET PAY	ACCUMULATED EARNINGS	CHECK NUMBER	PERIOD
			REGULAR	OVERTIME	OTHER	TOTAL		FEDERAL INC. TAX	FICA	CITY INC. TAX	STATE INC. TAX	TOTAL				
TOTALS BROUGHT FORWARD →																
Employee B	1/15	80	400			400		53	26.60		20	99.60	300.40	400	1399	1
Employee B	1/29	80	400			400		53	26.60		20	99.60	300.40	800	1404	2
																3
																4
																5
																6
																7
																8
																9
																10
																11
																12
																13
																14
TOTAL																
YEAR TO DATE																

FIGURE 9-7

WEEKLY TIME CARD

EMPLOYEE'S NUMBER _22_

EXEMPTIONS _2_

WEEK ENDING _1/15/82_

NAME _Jack Baker_

DAY	JOB
10	11
11	11
12	11
13	11
14	11
15	11

						TOTALS		TOTAL	
					UNION	OTHER		9320	40000
					-0-	-0-			
F.I.C.A.	FED. W.T.	STATE W.T.					TOTAL	306 80	
24.20	53.00	16.00							
BALANCE DUE									

DAILY TIME SHEET

TICKET NO.:

Employee Name: _Jack Baker_

Employee No.: _22_   Date: _1/15/82_

Job Description: _Fasteners_

Job Order No.: _11_   Department No.: _8_

T I M E			Hourly Rate	Amount
Start	Stop	Total Hours		
8 a.m.	5 p.m.	8	$ 5.00	$40.00

Jack Baker
Employee

Basil Writers
Foreman

endar year, gross earnings for the payroll period, the various deductions to be subtracted from gross earnings, and the net amount of earnings (amount to be paid) for each employee.

Gross earnings is the total amount earned by the employee before any deductions are made. At the end of each payroll period, time cards and time sheets (Figure 9-7) or other similar documents prepared by the employees showing the total hours worked are sent to the payroll department. This department determines the total regular and overtime hours worked for the period. Gross earnings are calculated by applying the hourly rate to the total regular hours. If the employer is subject to the Fair Labor Standards Act, the overtime hours would be computed at $1\frac{1}{2}$ times the regular hourly rate. Assume, for example, that employee A worked a total of 48 hours for the week and earned an hourly rate of $5 per hour. Employee A's regular earnings would amount to $200 (40 hours × $5) and overtime earnings would amount to $60 (8 hours × $7.50 or $5 + $2.50), for total earnings of $260 for the week.

Employee Earnings Record

An individual earnings record must be maintained for each employee (Figure 9-6). At the top of the record, all the personal data about the employee is shown, including the social security number, employee number, date of hire, number of withholding allowances, and marital status. The body of the record should contain the regular and overtime wages earned, hourly rate of pay, an itemized list of all the deductions, total cumulative gross earnings, and the check number and net amount paid for each pay period.

This detailed information is necessary for the employer to determine the amount of tax to be withheld for FICA. It is also important for the employer to know when the individual earnings have exceeded the maximum amounts for applying unemployment and FICA taxes.

This record provides all the data needed for issuing an individual's paycheck and for preparing Form W-2 (Wage and Tax Statement) and Form 941 (Employer's Quarterly Federal Tax Return).

The information for the individual record of each employee is obtained from the payroll register.

Other Payroll Reports

In addition to the employee payroll records, the employer is required by law to file the following reports:

Payroll forms filed by employer to state and federal government

1. *Form 941: **Employer's Quarterly Federal Tax Return.*** This report illustrated in Figure 9-8 shows the amounts withheld from employees' wages for federal income tax and FICA tax, plus the employer's share of FICA taxes. Along with the report, the employer must remit any moneys withheld not previously paid to the I.R.S. or deposited in a Federal Reserve bank or federally approved financial institution. Only the very smallest business is not subject to the deposit requirements.

FIGURE 9-8

Form **941**
(Rev. March 1981)
Department of the Treasury
Internal Revenue Service

Employer's Quarterly Federal Tax Return

			T	
			FF	
			FD	
			FP	
			I	
			T	

Your name, address, employer identification number, and calendar quarter of return. (If not correct, please change.)

Name (as distinguished from trade name)
Thomas R. Evans

Date quarter ended
March 1981

Trade name, if any
Tom's Drive-in Restaurant

Employer identification number
52-8986027

Address and ZIP code
559 S. Main Street, Moosic, Va. 19827

If address is different from prior return, check here ▶

1 Number of employees (except household) employed in the pay period that includes March 12th (complete first quarter only)	1	
2 Total wages and tips subject to withholding, plus other compensation . . . . ⟶	5898	00
3 Total income tax withheld from wages, tips, annuities, sick pay, gambling, etc.	602	10
4 Adjustment of withheld income tax for preceding quarters of calendar year		
5 Adjusted total of income tax withheld . . . . ⟶	602	10
6 Taxable FICA wages paid . . . . $ 5425 00 times 13.3% =TAX	721	53
7 a Taxable tips reported . . . . $ 473 00 times 6.65% =TAX	31	45
b Tips deemed to be wages (see instructions) . . $ _____ times 6.65% =TAX		
8 Total FICA taxes (add lines 6, 7a, and 7b) . . . . ⟶	752	98
9 Adjustment of FICA taxes (see instructions)		
10 Adjusted total of FICA taxes . . . . ⟶	752	98
11 Total taxes (add lines 5 and 10)	1355	08
12 Advance earned income credit (EIC) payments, if any (see instructions)		
13 Net taxes (subtract line 12 from line 11)	1355	08

▶ ☐ Check if you are a first-time 3-banking-day depositor (see Specific Instructions on page 6).

Record of Federal Tax Deposits

Deposit period ending:		a. Tax liability for period	b. Date of deposit	c. Amount deposited
Overpayment from previous quarter . . .				
First month of quarter	1st through 3rd day . . . . . A			
	4th through 7th day . . . . . B			
	8th through 11th day . . . C			
	12th through 15th day . . . D			
	16th through 19th day . . . E			
	20th through 22nd day . . . F			
	23rd through 25th day . . . G			
	26th through last day . . . . H			
I First month total	**I**	420.05		
Second month of quarter	1st through 3rd day I			
	4th through 7th day . . . . . J			
	8th through 11th day . . . K			
	12th through 15th day . . . L			
	16th through 19th day . . . M			
	20th through 22nd day . . . N			
	23rd through 25th day . . . O			
	26th through last day . . . P			
II Second month total	**II**	484.90	2/28/81	904.95
Third month of quarter	1st through 3rd day . . . . . Q			
	4th through 7th day . . . . . R			
	8th through 11th day . . . S			
	12th through 15th day . . . T			
	16th through 19th day . . . U			
	20th through 22nd day . . . V			
	23rd through 25th day . . . W			
	26th through last day . . . X			
III Third month total	**III**	373.20		
IV Total for quarter (add items I, II, and III) .		1,278.15		904.95
V Final deposit made for quarter. (Enter 0 if included in item IV.) .				–0–
VI Total deposits for quarter. Add items IV and V. Enter here and on line 14 on next page .				904.95

Lines 13a-18 continued on back of this page.

261

FIGURE 9-8 *Continued*

13 a Net taxes. Enter amount from line 13 on front · . . . .   1355 | 08 ← ⑩

14 Total deposits for quarter. Enter amount from item VI on front · . . . .   904 | 95 ← ⑪

15 Undeposited taxes due (subtract line 14 from line 13a). Pay to Internal Revenue Service and enter here . . . ▶   450 | 13 ← ⑫

16 If line 14 is more than line 13a, enter overpayment here ▶ $ and check if to be: ☐ Applied to next return, or ☐ Refunded.

17 Number of Forms W–4 enclosed. Do not send originals. (See General and Specific Instructions.) . . . .

18 If you are not liable for returns in the future, write "FINAL" (see instructions) ▶   Date final wages paid ▶

Under penalties of perjury, I declare that I have examined this return, including accompanying schedules and statements, and to the best of my knowledge and belief it is true, correct, and complete.

Date ▶ April 30, 1981   Signature ▶ *Thomas R. Evans*   Title ▶ Owner

Please file this form with your Internal Revenue Service Center (see instructions on "Where to File").

⑬

Instructions for Form 941

① `This space is for your name, address, employer identification number, and the last month in the quarter covered by the return. These entries are ordinarily made before the Form 941 is mailed to you. Be sure to write this information on your copy of the return. If it is incorrect, or if your address changes, draw a line through the error and type or print the correction.

② Be sure to answer Item 1 (first quarter return only).

③ Show the total of: all wages paid, tips reported, and other compensation paid to your employees, even if you do not have to withhold income or FICA tax on it. Do not include annuities, supplemental unemployment compensation benefits, or gambling winnings, even if you withheld income tax on them.

④ Show the total income tax withheld on wages, tips, annuities, supplemental unemployment compensation benefits, and gambling winnings.

⑤ Enter the total wages taxable under FICA that you paid your employees during quarter. Show amount before deductions. Do not include tips on this line.

⑥ Enter on Line 7a all tips employees reported during quarter. If you pay any employees (that report $20 or more in tips a month) less than the Federal minimum wage, you must pay employer FICA tax on the difference as the amount is considered to be wages and this amount is entered on Line 7b. There are no tips to be reported on Line 7b in this case.

⑦ Multiply the FICA wages by the rates applicable, 13.3%; that is, 6.65% employer tax and 6.65% employee tax. The total in this case is $721.53.

⑧ Multiply the tips reported on Line 7a by 6.65%. The total is $31.45.

⑨ Subtract amount on Line 12 from Line 11 to obtain net taxes.

⑩ Enter amount from Line 13 on Page 1 to Line 13 on Page 2.

⑪ Enter the total amount deposited for quarter; amount on Line VI.

⑫ Enter the undeposited taxes and amount of taxes due with return. The amount due for this return is $450.13 ($1,355.08 − $904.95).

⑬ Sign return, date it, show your title, and include a check for amount shown on Line 15; amount in this case is $450.13.

⑭ Record of Federal tax deposits: If you deposit taxes, please complete all three columns. In column 1, show tax due for each quarter-monthly period in which you had a pay day. If your total taxes for any month are less than $3,000, show your tax on the "total" line for that month. The totals in this case are $420.05, $484.90, and $373.20 for a total for the quarter of $1,278.15. In column 2, show the date of deposit; and in column 3, show the amount deposited. The amount deposited on February 28, 1981, was $904.95 which is also the total deposited for the quarter.

FIGURE 9-9

FORM 1099

For Official Use Only

Type or print PAYER'S name, address, ZIP code, and Federal identifying number.

Statement for Recipients of 19

Miscellaneous Income

Copy A

For Internal Revenue Service Center

95 ☐

Recipient's identifying number	1 Rents	2 Royalties	3 Commissions and fees to nonemployees (No Form W-2 items)	4 Prizes and awards to nonemployees (No Form W-2 items)

Name ▶ Type or print RECIPIENT'S name, address, and ZIP code below (Name must aline with arrow).

5 Other fixed or determinable income
a. Amount
b. Source

For instructions on completing this form, see "Instructions for Form 1096."

Form 1099–MISC ☆ GPO : 1976—O-218-096 EI NO. 22-1832268 Department of the Treasury—Internal Revenue Service

2. *Form 1099:* ***Information Return.*** If an employer makes payments to others for dividends, interest, or miscellaneous income (commissions or tips), this information must be applied on Form 1099, shown in Figure 9-9. A copy must be given to the individual and the Internal Revenue Service within 1 month after the end of the calendar year.
3. *Form 940:* ***Employer's Annual Federal Unemployment Tax Return.*** An annual return for federal unemployment taxes must be filed on Form 940 (Figure 9-4) on or before January 31 following the end of the calendar year. Any tax due must be paid with the return.

FIGURE 9-10

1 Control number	222	2 Employer's State number		For Official Use Only	
3 Employer's name, address, and ZIP code			4 Sub-total ☐ Cor-rection ☐ Void ☐	5 Yes ☐ Jan–Mar No ☐	6 Yes ☐ Apr–Jun No ☐
			7 Employer's identification number	8 Yes ☐ Jul–Sep No ☐	9 Yes ☐ Oct–Dec No ☐
10 Employee's social security number	11 Federal income tax withheld		12 Wages tips, other compensation	13 FICA tax withheld	14 Total FICA wages
15 Employee's name (first, middle, last)			16 Pension plan coverage? Yes/No	17*	18 FICA tips
			20 State income tax withheld	21 State wages, tips, etc.	22 Name of State
19 Employee's address and ZIP code			23 Local income tax withheld	24 Local wages, tips, etc.	25 Name of locality
Wage and Tax Statement 19				COPY A For Social Security Administration *See Instructions for Forms W-2 and W-2P and back of Copy D	

Form W–2 Department of the Treasury—Internal Revenue Service

4. State and local quarterly and annual income and unemployment tax forms would be required for employers subject to these taxes under state and local regulations.

5. *Form W-2: **Wage and Tax Statement**.* At least two copies of Form W-2 (Figure 9-10) must be given to each employee on or before January 31 following the end of the calendar year or 30 days after termination of employment showing the total yearly earnings (gross pay) and total deductions for taxes and health insurance.

IMPORTANT POINTS TO REMEMBER

The government is continually changing the regulations governing payroll taxes. Therefore, it is very important to check carefully at the beginning of every year to verify the:

1. Tax rates
2. Tax base or cutoff points for FICA and FUTA
3. Any other changes in rules and regulations, especially the dates for filing government reports

It is **your responsibility** to keep up with current rules and legislation concerning payroll.

ACCOUNTING FOR PAYROLL

Now that the basic rules governing payroll activities have been covered, it can be seen that the accounting or recording of the payroll has two basic parts or expenses: the employee's earnings and the employer's taxes.

Recording the Employee's Earnings

An expense is created or incurred because a business employs people. In exchange for their labor or services, the business agrees to give them some type of compensation for their efforts. This compensation may take the form of hourly wages, piecework, wages for various incentive programs, salaries, commissions, fees, or the acceptance of goods and services.

For example, biweekly payroll information of the Robert Company for the period ending January 29 is as follows:

Salesperson A earns a salary of $350 per week.

Employee B in the sales office works 40 hours per week at a rate of $5 per hour.

Three office employees earn a salary of $150 each per week, a total of $450.

FICA tax rate 6.65 percent

State income tax rate, 5 percent

FUTA tax rate, 0.7 percent

SUTA tax rate, 2.7 percent

Federal income taxes withheld, $280

All the employees are paid biweekly, and *all* the salaries and wages earned are subject to all taxes.

Computation of employees'
earnings and taxes

	Gross Earnings	
A: $350 × 2 =	$700	
B: $200 (40 × $5) × 2 =	400	$1,100
3 × $150 = $450 × 2 =		900
Total payroll		$2,000
FICA tax: $2,000 × 0.0665 = $133		
State income tax: $2,000 × 0.05 = $100		

The first step in recording the salaries and wages expense for the payroll period is to determine the total amount earned by the employee, which is known as **gross earnings** or **taxable earnings.** This is the amount that is debited to the proper salary or wages expense account.

Next, the amounts to be deducted from the employee's gross earnings to pay for federal, state, and local income taxes, social security taxes, and other items must be determined. These amounts are credited to various liability accounts. Be sure to keep in mind that the business or employer is only a collector of these deductions and is not permitted to keep this money. Payments must be made to the various government agencies as the law requires.

When the sum of all the deductions is subtracted from the gross earnings, the difference is the amount that is actually paid to the employee. This amount (gross earnings − deductions) is known as **net earnings** or **take-home pay.**

The general journal entries to record the biweekly payroll for the Robert Company is shown at the top of the following page.

<table>
<tr><td>Entry to record salaries and wages earned by employees and taxes withheld</td><td>

19__
Jan. 29

</td></tr>
</table>

Entry to record salaries and wages earned by employees and taxes withheld	19__ Jan. 29	Sales Salaries & Wages Expense	1,100
		Office Salaries Expense	900
		Federal Income Taxes Payable		280
		FICA Taxes Payable		133
		State Income Taxes Payable		100
		Salaries and Wages Payable		1,487
		Record payroll for the period ending January 29.		
Payment of salaries and wages to employees	29	Salaries and Wages Payable	1,487	
		Cash		1,487
		Issued payroll checks to employees for payroll period ending January 29.		

Note that these are summary entries and that the amounts in the first entry are supported by a separate set of calculations for each employee on the individual earnings records.

Recording the Employer's Payroll Tax Expense

The employer's payroll tax expense is caused or incurred because federal, state, and local governments have laws that require a business to pay taxes when employees are hired. Remember, there are three taxes that the employer is required to pay:

Employer's taxes on payroll	**1.** Federal Insurance Contributions Act (FICA)
	2. Federal Unemployment Tax Act (FUTA)
	3. State Unemployment Tax Act (SUTA)

Assuming that the Robert Company records its payroll tax expense at the same time that it does its payroll, and that its state tax rate for unemployment has been set at 2.7 percent (0.027), the payroll tax liability for the employer for the week ending January 29 is as follows:

Entry to record payroll tax expense	19__ Jan. 29	Payroll Tax Expense	201
		FICA Taxes Payable (0.0665 × 2,000)		133
		Federal Unemployment Taxes Payable (0.007 × 2,000)		14
		State Unemployment Taxes Payable (0.027 × 2,000)		54
		Record employer's taxes on payroll ending January 29.		

Payroll taxes levied on the employer are classified as an operating expense of the business, and they are shown on the income statement. Salaries and wages for the employees of the sales department would be classified as Operating/Selling Expenses; other salaries and wages would be classified as Operating/General or Administrative Expenses.

Any payroll taxes that have not been paid at the time the books are closed, the payable or liability for paying these taxes, would be shown on the balance sheet as a current liability.

Payroll information presented on income statement and balance sheet

INCOME STATEMENT

Operating Expenses:	
Selling Expenses:	
Sales Salaries & Wages Expense	$1,100
General or Administrative Expenses:	
Office Salaries Expense	$ 900

BALANCE SHEET

Current Liabilities:	
FICA Taxes Payable	$ 266
Federal Income Taxes Payable	280
State Income Taxes Payable	100
Federal Unemployment Taxes Payable	14
State Unemployment Taxes Payable	54

PAYROLL CONTROLS

The writing of a paycheck involves the disbursement of cash and should be handled in the same careful way as all other cash payments.

Employees should be paid with prenumbered checks issued from a special payroll checking account. Payroll checks should be provided with an attached stub (Figure 9-11) showing the employee's gross earnings, regular hours and premium hours worked, deductions, and net or take-home pay. Many payroll accounting systems in larger businesses have pay stubs that show deductions for the current pay period and year-to-date totals.

The payroll register may be used as a special journal, and all necessary information would be posted directly to the general ledger. Usually, this register is used as the basis for determining the amount of the employer's payroll taxes and for journalizing and posting payroll information in the accounting records. Therefore, one payroll register is prepared for each pay period.

Referring to the payroll register in Figure 9-5, notice that the net pay plus the deductions equals the gross pay for each employee.

FIGURE 9-11

COLLEGE COMPANY   116 Park   Livonia, MI 48152

NO. 16700

Total Hours	Earnings			Deductions			Net Pay	Period Ending	Number
	Regular	Overtime	Gross Pay	FICA	Fed. With.	State With.			
80	80	-0-	$400	$26.60	$53	$20	$300.40	1/29/82	140

Pay Statement — Detach and Retain

PAYROLL
CHECK

COLLEGE COMPANY
116 Park
Livonia, MI. 48152

NO. 16700

$$\frac{62\text{-}9}{311}$$

DATE *January 29* 19 *82*

PAY
TO THE ORDER OF *Barry Barton* $ *300.40*

Three Hundred and 40/100 ———————————— DOLLARS

LIVONIA TRUST COMPANY
Livonia, Michigan

COLLEGE COMPANY

Robert Maxwell
President

PEGBOARD ACCOUNTING FOR PAYROLL

Recording payroll information is one of the many accounting functions that can be performed by pegboard accounting methods discussed in Chapter 8. All the pegboard systems for different accounting functions are based on the one-write procedure. This procedure allows payroll information to be recorded on several different forms at one time through the use of carbonized forms.

The pegboard system for payroll offers an inexpensive method of recording payroll information and improving accuracy by reducing the number of time-consuming procedures. These systems are used frequently by small- and medium-sized business operations and professional practices that are not large enough to require sophisticated computerized systems and machines.

A *"one-write" pegboard system for payroll* records the same payroll information on several types of payroll forms with one writing through the use of carbonized forms. An example of a one-write principle for payroll is described below.

Payroll System

There are three payroll forms required to complete the payroll:

Forms used in a one-write payroll system

1. Payroll register (Figure 9-14)
2. Employee's individual earnings record (Figure 9-13)
3. Payroll checks with an attached record stub for the employee (Figure 9-12)

In an ordinary manually operated accounting system, preparing these three forms requires that the information be written three times with three opportunities for errors, taking three times as long to record.

With a payroll pegboard system, all three forms are completed with *one* writing, reducing the copying time considerably.

The procedures for a one-write payroll system are (Figure 9-15):

Procedures for a one-write payroll system

1. Arrange the forms by placing the payroll register on the pegboard. Next place the checks arranged in numerical order so that they overlap. We refer to this group of checks as "shingled checks" in the pegboard system. Align the first pay stub with the proper line for recording the first employee's earnings information on the register. Insert the employee's earnings record between the payroll register and the checks, making sure that the first blank line is directly underneath the top line of the checkstub of the first check.
2. Complete the checkstub information. As this is being written, the information will be recorded on all three forms with one writing. Flip the

FIGURE 9-12

A COMPLETE 'ONE-WRITE' PAYROLL SYSTEM

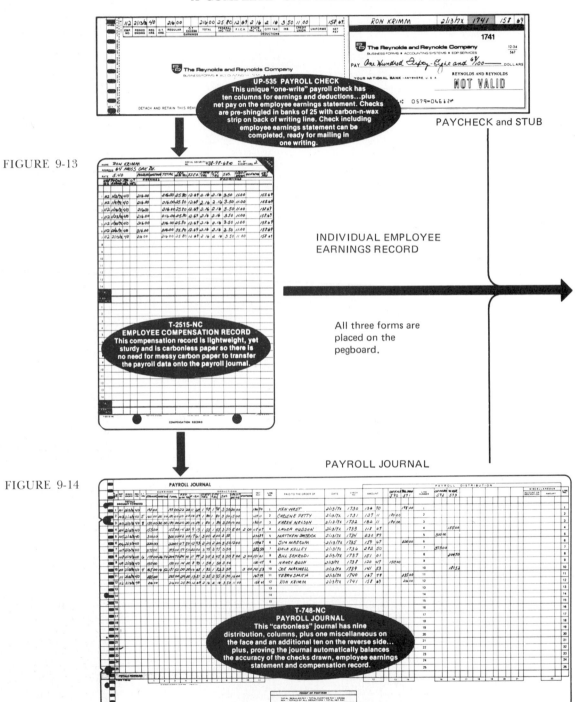

FIGURE 9-13

FIGURE 9-14

PAYCHECK and STUB

INDIVIDUAL EMPLOYEE EARNINGS RECORD

All three forms are placed on the pegboard.

PAYROLL JOURNAL

FIGURE 9-15

1. The pegboard
2. The Payroll Journal
3. The Employee Individual Earnings Record
4. The paycheck

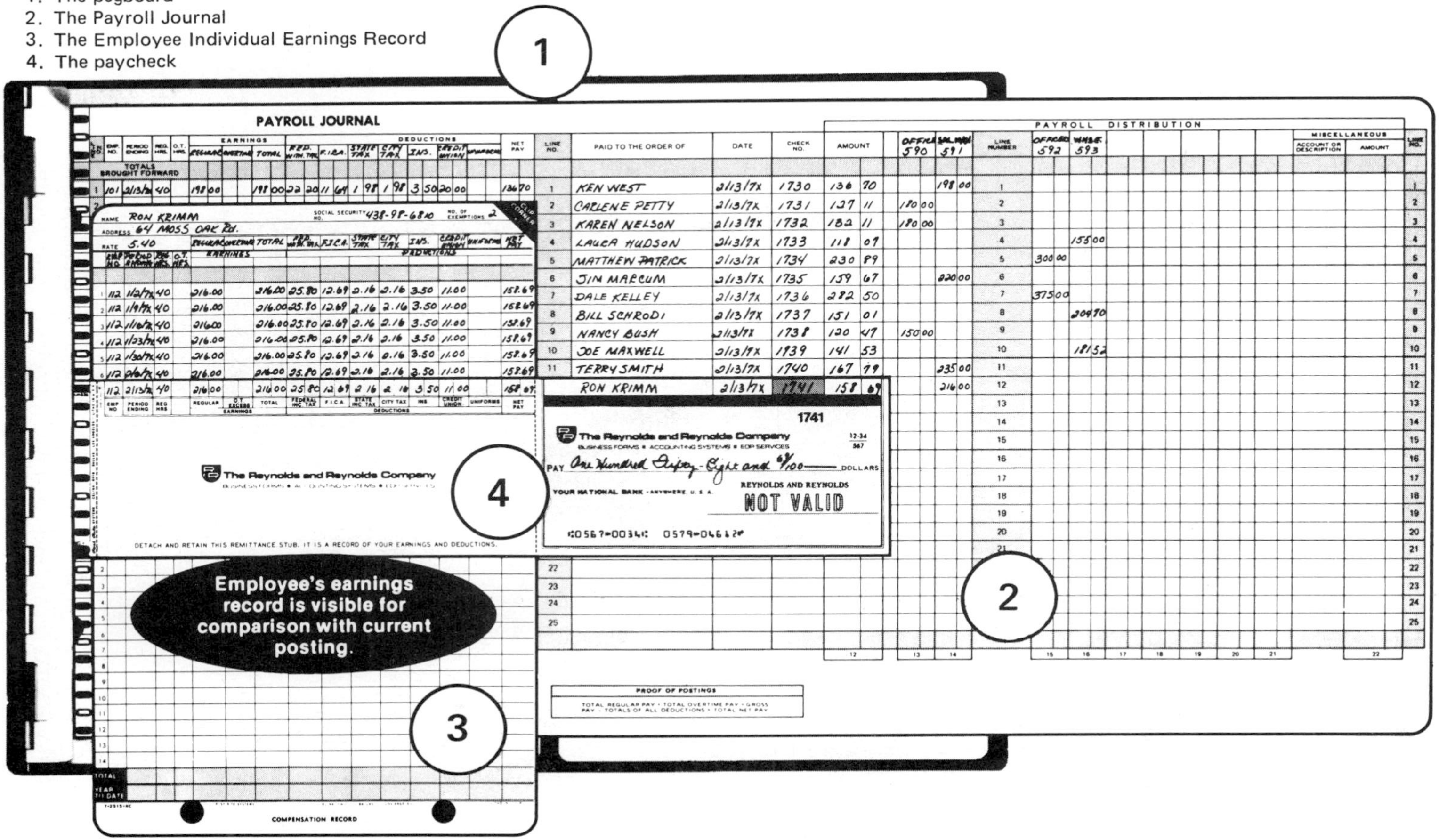

check with the completed stub over to the left and return the employee's earning record to the file. Note that the actual check is not written until the accuracy of the payroll register is proved. Insert the next employee's earning record and repeat the process until all the paycheck stubs are completed.

3. Complete the payroll register by totaling all columns and proving the balance of the journal and payroll distribution.

4. Remove those checks from the pegboard which have a completed checkstub and write or type the information on the check.

The system is now ready for the next payroll period.

SUMMARY

Payroll accounting requires employers to maintain accurate, up-to-date, and proper employee earning records for the purpose of issuing payroll checks and remitting and reporting the required payroll information to the proper government agency. Persons working in the payroll department must have some knowledge of federal, state, and local laws that have imposed taxes on the employer and employee.

The Internal Revenue Code requires employers to withhold federal income tax and social security (FICA) tax from employee earnings. A Form 941 report must be filed quarterly with a remittance for any amount withheld not previously deposited in a federally approved bank or financial institution. Circular E, an Internal Revenue publication, furnishes the employer with the necessary information for withholding, remitting, and reporting taxes to the federal government.

Most states and some cities have levied an income tax on employee earnings which must also be withheld each pay period. Employers are required by law to follow the rules and regulations established by these government agencies.

Employers are subject to three payroll taxes because they have people working for them. Such taxes are not paid by the employee but are operating expenses of the business. Social Security (FICA) taxes represent the largest amount of tax expense imposed on the payroll. Unemployment taxes are a joint federal and state tax levied for the purpose of providing temporary benefits to unemployed workers.

The Fair Labor Standards Act requires a business engaged in the production of goods for interstate commerce to pay employees an overtime rate of $1\frac{1}{2}$ times the hourly rate for all hours worked over 40 hours per week.

At the end of the calendar year, employers are required to file Forms W-2, 940, 941, 1099, and several state and local tax forms.

The laws are constantly changing, and the employer is responsible for keeping current with the various rules and regulations.

Recording payroll information is one of the many accounting functions that can be performed by pegboard accounting methods. This procedure as explained for payroll allows accounting information to be recorded on several different forms at one time through the use of carbonized forms. For example, the pegboard system for payroll is designed so that the employee's individual earnings information is recorded on the payroll register, employee's earnings record, and check stub in one writing.

GLOSSARY

Circular E: Employer's Tax Guide publication of the Internal Revenue Service providing information about the responsibilities of an employer for employment taxes and withholding tables.

Employee's Withholding Allowance Certificate: Form W-4 required for every new employee designating the number of exemptions claimed for income tax purposes.

Employer's Annual Federal Unemployment Tax Return: Form 940, which must be filed by January 31, for the reporting of taxes under the Federal Unemployment Tax Act (FUTA).

Employer's Quarterly Federal Tax Return: Form 941 required to be filed by the employer reporting the federal income and FICA taxes withheld from the wages of employees and the employers's share of FICA taxes.

Experience Rating: Another name for a merit rating described below.

Fair Labor Standards Act: Law imposed on businesses engaged in interstate commerce requiring the employer to pay an overtime rate of 1½ times the regular rate of hours worked over 40 hours per week.

Federal Insurance Contributions Act (FICA): A tax imposed on the employer and the employee for social security.

Federal Unemployment Tax Act (FUTA): A tax imposed on wages and salaries and paid by an employer to build a fund which helps finance a joint federal and state unemployment tax program.

Federal Wage and Hour Law: Another name for Fair Labor Standards Act described above.

Gross Earnings: Total amount of taxable wages earned before any deductions.

Information Return: Form 1099 required by the federal government for reporting any compensation paid other than wages and salaries.

Internal Revenue Service: A department of the Treasury known as the I.R.S. responsible for the collection of federal income and social security taxes.

Merit Rating: A reduction in the state unemployment tax rate given to an employer for a record of stable employment. Also known or referred to as an experience rating.

Net Earnings: Take-home pay or amount to be paid an employee for earnings after all deductions have been made from the total gross earnings.

One-Write Pegboard System for Payroll: A system that records the same payroll information on several types of forms with one writing.

Payroll Register: A detailed record prepared each payroll period, stating the amount of cumulative earnings, gross earnings for the period, the various deductions to be made, and the net amount of earnings to be paid each employee.

Taxable Earnings: Total money earned (gross earnings) on which taxes must be paid.

Wage and Tax Statement: Form W-2 required by law to be given each employee by January 31, showing total earnings and deductions for taxes and health insurance, during the previous year.

QUESTIONS

1. Explain the difference between the individual employee's earnings record and the payroll register.
2. List three common payroll taxes imposed on the employer and give the rate for each tax (assuming no experience rating).
3. Name two taxes that the employer is required to withhold from an employee's earnings.
4. State the advantage of using a one-write pegboard system for payroll.
5. Explain the use of the following forms:
   (a) W-2   (c) 940
   (b) W-4   (d) 941
6. Discuss fully the term merit rating.
7. Journalize in general journal form, without amounts, for recording the following payroll data: Salaries and wages earned by employees plus deductions for FICA and federal and state income taxes.
8. Classify the following accounts:
   (a) Payroll tax expense for the sales staff
   (b) Federal income taxes withheld
   (c) State unemployment tax liability
   (d) Salaries earned by office workers
9. Explain briefly three possible uses of the payroll register.
10. Describe the benefits to the employer for obtaining a copy of Circular E.
11. Classify the following operating expenses as to selling or general:
    (a) Sales Commissions
    (b) Office Salaries
    (c) Delivery Wages
12. Which deductions listed below would not be withheld by the employer from an employee's wages?
    (a) Union dues
    (b) Federal income tax
    (c) FUTA
    (d) FICA
    (e) State income tax

EXERCISES[1]

Computation of Employee Earnings

1. A company has two office employees who earn a salary of $200 per week each for a 40-hour week and one office manager who earns a salary of $400 per week. One office employee worked 40 hours and the other office employee worked 45 hours during the current payroll period. The two office employees are paid 1½ times the regular hourly rate for all hours worked over 40 hours per week. Compute the gross wages earned by each employee and the total gross wages for the payroll period ending April 7.

2. An employer had four employees and was subject to the Fair Labor Standards Act. Payroll data for the three employees is shown below.

Employee	Hours Worked	Hourly Rate
1	46	$4.00
2	40	6.00
3	48	5.00
4	42	4.50

Determine the gross earnings for each employee.

FICA Taxes

3. Compute the amount of FICA taxes to be withheld from the earnings of each of the following employees for the current year.
    (a) Employee 1 earned $400 a week for 22 weeks and $450 a week for 30 weeks.
    (b) Employee 2 received a salary of $200 a week for 52 weeks.
    (c) Employee 3 was paid an annual salary of $32,000.

4. The Wixom Company had five employees who earned wages for the week ending December 15 as follows:

Employee	Weekly Earnings	Cumulative Earnings	Federal Income Tax
1	$200	$ 9,800	$20
2	400	19,700	48
3	700	34,600	84
4	650	31,900	69
5	450	22,500	52

[1] *Note:* For simplicity and ease of calculation, all the exercises and problems in this chapter will use a FICA rate of 6 percent (0.06) on the first $30,000 of earnings and a SUTA rate of 2.7 percent (0.027) on the first $6,000 of earnings.

Compute the FICA taxes and net pay for each employee for the week ending December 15.

SUTA and FUTA Taxes

5. Compute the employer's SUTA and FUTA tax liability for each of the following unrelated assumptions.
   (a) Total payroll for January amounted to $10,000.
   (b) An employer had one employee with earnings of $300 per week and four employees with earnings of $250 per week each for 52 weeks during the current year. Determine the unemployment tax liability for the current year.
   (c) A company with a total payroll of $20,000 subject to unemployment taxes received a merit rating reducing the SUTA tax to 2.2 percent.
   (d) An employee earns $150 per week. In how many weeks would the employees wages become tax exempt for SUTA and FUTA taxes.

Journalizing Payroll Entries

6. Payroll data for the period ending May 4 is shown below:

   Office Salaries Expense, $800
   Delivery Wages Expense, $650
   Federal Income Taxes Withheld, $230
   FICA taxes, $87

   All earnings are subject to FUTA and SUTA taxes. Prepare the payroll entries for:
   (a) Salaries and wages earned by the employees
   (b) Salaries and wages paid to the employees
   (c) Payroll tax expense for the employer

7. Payroll data for the period ending November 10 appears below:

   Salaries & Wages Expense, $2,600
   Federal Income Taxes Withheld, $650
   FICA Taxes Withheld, $120

   Only $700 of the payroll is subject to FUTA and SUTA taxes. Prepare the journal entries for:
   (a) Salaries and wages earned by the employees
   (b) Salaries and wages paid to the employees
   (c) Payroll tax expense for the employer

Classification of Accounts

8. Complete the last two columns for the following list of accounts. The first item has been completed as an example.

Account	Classification	Financial Statement
a. State Income Taxes Payable	Current Liability	Balance Sheet
b. Salesperson's Commissions		
c. FICA Taxes Payable		
d. Delivery Wages Expense		
e. Administrative Salaries Expense		
f. Salaries & Wages Payable		
g. Payroll Tax Expense		

9. Complete the last two columns for the following list of accounts:

Account	Classification	Financial Statement
a. City Income Tax Payable		
b. Sales Salaries Expense		
c. FUTA Tax Payable		
d. Office Salaries Expense		
e. Office Salaries Payable		
f. SUTA Tax Payable		
g. FUTA Tax Payable		

PROBLEMS

Determining Employee Taxes and Net Pay

9-1. Jack Coin pays his four employees on a biweekly basis. Cumulative earnings for the payroll period ending January 1 to April 15 are: Employee A, $4,800; B, $4,000; C, $8,000; and D, $3,680. Complete the schedule below for the payroll period April 16 to April 30 assuming a state income tax rate of 5 percent.

Employee	Earnings	Federal Income Taxes	State Income Taxes	FICA Tax	Total Taxes	Net Pay	Cumulative Earnings
A	$ 600	$ 50					
B	500	70					
C	1,100	200					
D	400	40					
Totals	$2,600	$360					

9-2. Assuming that each employee in Problem 9-1 earns the same wages every biweekly pay period for the year, complete the schedule on page 278.

TOTAL YEARLY TAXES WITHHELD

Employee	Yearly Earnings	FICA Taxes	State Income Taxes	Federal Income Taxes	Total Taxes	Net Pay
A						
B						
C						
D						

Computation of Payroll Tax Expense and Journal Entry

9-3. Ralph Help has five employees who are paid semimonthly. Employees 1, 2, 4, and 5 earned the same salary (listed below) throughout the year; employee 3 earned the same salary (listed below) for only the last five months of the year. The company earned a merit rating from the state reducing its state unemployment tax rate from 2.7 percent to 1.5 percent. The semimonthly salaries earned by each employee are listed below:

Employee	Semimonthly Salary
1	$ 500
2	400
3	300
4	800
5	1,200

Required

(Use form provided in your *Study Guide* Workbook for Requirement *a*.)

(*a*) Compute the total amount of taxes to be paid by the employer during the year for FICA, SUTA, and FUTA.

(*b*) Journalize the entry to record the information in requirement *a* assuming this entry is recorded at the end of each year.

9-4. John Backus has two employees who are paid a biweekly salary of $750, one office manager who is paid a biweekly salary of $1,250, and three employees who earn an hourly rate of $5, $4, and $6 respectively. Each of the hourly employees are paid 1½ times their regular hourly rate for all hours worked over 40 hours per week. All the employees are paid every two weeks, and for the payroll period ending March 31 the hourly workers worked 80, 88, and 90 hours respectively.

Required

(*a*) Complete the following schedule. All earnings are subject to unemployment taxes except the office manager.

EMPLOYER'S PAYROLL TAXES
FOR PAYROLL PERIOD ENDING MARCH 31, 19___

Employee	Employee Earnings	FICA Taxes	SUTA Taxes	FUTA Taxes	Total Taxes
1	$ 750				
2	750				
3	1,250				
4	?				
5	?				
6	?				

(b) Journalize the entry for the payroll tax expense for the period ending March 31 using the data in part a.

Journalizing Payroll Entries

9-5. For its March payroll, the employees of the Thar Company had gross earnings of $9,000 from which $800 of federal income tax was withheld. The state income tax rate is 5 percent, and all the earnings are subject to all taxes.

Required

(a) Record the payroll.
(b) Record payment to employees.
(c) Record employer's taxes on payroll.

9-6. The following wages and salaries were earned during the month of December:

Salaries, $10,000
Wages, $5,000

The federal income tax withheld amounted to $3,000; all wages and salaries were subject to FICA and state income taxes with a rate of 5 percent; and $5,000 of the wages and salaries subject to unemployment taxes. The company received a merit rating from the state reducing the SUTA tax rate to 2.2 percent.

Required

Prepare the journal entries for the following:
(a) Payroll for the month of December
(b) Wages and salaries paid to the employees
(c) Employer's payroll tax expense

Payroll Register and Payroll Entries

9-7. Data pertaining to the payroll for the Mark Company for the week ending November 30 of the current year appears on page 280.

Employee	Gross Earnings to Date	Hours Worked	Hourly Rate	Federal Income Tax Withheld	State Income Tax Withheld	Check No.
A	$10,000	40	$ 4	$21.90	$ 8.00	912
B	5,000	44	4	17.30	9.20	913
C	14,000	36	6	19.50	10.80	914
D	8,000	48	8	59.90	20.80	915
E	29,700	40	10	84.10	20.00	916

Required

(a) Prepare a payroll register for the week ending November 30. Use the form in the *Study Guide* Workbook or prepare one using Figure 9-5 in the text. The state income tax rate is 5 percent on all earnings, and the SUTA tax rate is 2.2 percent.

(b) Prepare the journal entries to record the payroll and the payment to the employees.

(c) Prepare the journal entries to record the employer's taxes on the payroll.

9-8. Data pertaining to the payroll for the College Company for the week ending April 30 of the current year appears below:

Employee	Hours Worked	Hourly Rate	Gross Earnings to Date	Federal Income Taxes Withheld
1	32	$4.00	$2,400	$20
2	40	4.50	4,000	22
3	49	3.50	6,000	30
4	42	4.00	6,500	15
5	40	5.00	3,200	25

Required

(a) Prepare a payroll register using the form in your *Study Guide* Workbook or prepare one using Figure 9-5 in the text. Employees were paid with check numbers beginning with No. 438.

(b) Prepare the journal entries to record the payroll and the payment to the employees.

(c) Prepare the journal entries to record the employer's taxes on the payroll.

Additional Data

State income tax rate is 5 percent.

Employee Earnings Record

9-9. Prepare an Employee's Earnings Record for (*a*) employee 3 and (*b*) employee 5 for the College Company in Problem 9-8. Use the form in your *Study Guide* Workbook or construct one like Figure 9-6 in the text.

Preparation of Form 941

9-10. Complete Form 941 (Employer's Quarterly Federal Tax Return) in your *Study Guide* Workbook for the Coin Factory, 105 Sixth Street, Novi, MI 48164, for the quarter ending June 30 of the current year. The identification number for Coin Factory is 58-3500307. Jack Coin, the president, had four employees working for his company since January 1. The total income taxes withheld from the employees wages during the second quarter amounted to $2,505, and the total wages subject to withholding amounted to $19,000. All employees are paid on a biweekly basis. Data relative to the period April 1 to June 30 (last payroll period for second quarter) is given below. Jack Coin paid the balance due as of June 30 on July 2.

Tax Liability		Federal Tax Deposits for Federal Income and FICA Taxes	
Period	Amount	Date Deposited	Amount
April	$1,376	4/23	$1,376
May	1,334	5/21	1,334
June	2,209	6/30	2,209

9-11. Complete Form 941 (Employer's Quarterly Federal Tax Return) in the *Study Guide* Workbook for Joe College, owner of the College Company, 1848 Lowell Avenue, Livonia, MI 48190, for the quarter ending March 31 of the current year. The employer's identification number for the College Company is 62-4611408. The company has five employees, the total income taxes withheld amounted to $1,247, and the total wages subject to withholding amounted to $19,465.52. Joe College paid the balance due as of March 31 on April 2.

Additional Data

Tax Liability		Federal Tax Deposits for Federal Income and FICA Taxes	
Period	Amount	Date Deposited	Amount
January	$1,083.47	1/31	$1,083.47
February	1,091.22	2/28	1,091.22
March	1,627.64	4/2	1,627.64

Preparation of Form 940

9-12. Complete Form 940 (Employer's Annual Federal Unemployment Tax Return) in your *Study Guide* Workbook for John Byron, owner of the Plastics Company for the year ended December 31 of the current year. The wages earned by the three employees of the company amounted to $20,000, $10,000, and $2,000 respectively. Total wages subject to unemployment taxes amounted to $14,000 at a SUTA rate of 2.7 percent and a FUTA rate of 0.7 percent. The SUTA taxes of $378 were paid on time to the state, and the identification number of the company is 59-3861943. Plastics Company is located at 1796 Howe Street, Livonia, Michigan, 48260. Mr. Byron paid the FUTA taxes on January 6.

9-13. Complete Form 940 (Employer's Annual Federal Unemployment Tax Return) in your *Study Guide* Workbook for the Coin Factory (Problem 9-10) for the year ended December 31 of the current year. The wages earned by the four employees of the Coin Factory amounted to $15,600, $13,000, $28,000 and $11,700 respectively. Total wages subject to unemployment taxes amounted to $24,000 at a SUTA rate of 2.7 percent and a FUTA rate of 0.7 percent. Jack Coin, President, made a state tax deposit of $648 on time and he made a federal tax deposit of $112.03 on April 2 and of $37.97 on July 3 and the balance of $18 was paid on January 5.

After completing this chapter, you should be able to:

1. **Describe the function of the petty cash fund**

2. **Journalize the entries for establishing and replenishing a petty cash fund**

3. **Explain the purpose of the Cash Over and Short account**

4. **Describe the procedures for opening a checking account for a business**

5. **List the steps for reconciling the bank account and journalize the entries necessary to correct the cash account**

Cash is the most liquid asset of a business, and an adequate system of control is needed to prevent theft and to prevent employees from using cash belonging to the company for their personal use.

Most individuals tend to think of cash as the amount of money they have on hand at any given time. However, in business and accounting, *cash* consists of coins, paper money, bank drafts, checks, money orders, certified checks, cashier's checks, and any balance in checking and other types of bank accounts.

Most business transactions begin or end with cash, and special care must be taken when handling cash to ensure the financial success and growth of the business.

OBJECTIVES OF CASH CONTROL

Some objectives for the internal control of cash are to take all the necessary precautions to prevent theft and to establish an accurate method of reporting for cash in the accounting records. A good accounting system separates the handling of cash from the recording function by providing for the division of duties among several employees. Individuals who receive cash should not be responsible for recording, disbursing, or depositing cash receipts in the bank. All cash receipts should be recorded and deposited daily, and all cash payments should be made by check.

PETTY CASH

A good system for the control of cash requires that all payments be made by check to protect against the loss or theft of cash. However, it is costly to write a check for a small amount in payment of delivery charges and the purchase of postage, newspapers, and other miscellaneous items. Therefore, most companies have a cash fund available for these small payments, and this fund is called a *petty cash* or imprest fund.

Systems and Forms

A petty cash system is usually handled by one person referred to as the *petty cashier* who is responsible for making payments from the fund. When the accountant determines the amount of petty cash needed, a check is issued payable to the petty cashier. The check is usually written for an even amount ($25, $50, $100, etc.) that is sufficient to handle small payments for a reasonable length of time—at least 1 month. After the check has been cashed by the petty cashier, the money is usually placed in a strongbox or other suitable place for safekeeping. Whenever the need arises, the petty cashier will make payments and issue a *petty cash receipt* or *petty cash voucher* (Figure 10-1) to verify the payment made from the petty cash fund.

The petty cash receipt is filed in the strongbox containing the petty cash fund. Some companies require a signed receipt from the person receiving the money as verification that payment was made. At all times, the petty cashier should have the total amount of the fund on hand in the form of money and/or petty cash receipts.

Accounting for a Petty Cash Fund

When the petty cash fund is established and a check issued, the petty cashier will cash the check in exchange for small amounts of currency and coin to make payments from the fund. An entry debiting Petty Cash and crediting Cash is recorded in the journal when the fund is established.

FIGURE 10-1

Petty cash receipt for purchase of office supplies

PETTY CASH RECEIPT

No.   1   **Date**   June 10, 198_

Paid to   Office Supply Company $ 18.00

For   typing paper and carbon paper

Account   Office Supplies

Approved by: **Payment Received by:**

Carey Brooks   *John Adelson*

To illustrate the petty cash procedure, assume that Nu-Fabric Company established a petty cash fund of $100 on June 1 of the current year. A check was issued payable to Carey Brooks, petty cashier. The following journal entry was recorded on June 1.

Journal entry to establish petty cash fund

19__			
June 1	Petty Cash	100	
	Cash		100
	Establish petty cash fund and issue check payable to Carey Brooks, petty cashier.		

Petty Cash

Petty cash account after fund is established

Date		Explanation	Ref.	Dr	Cr	Balance
19__						
June	1			100		100

The Petty Cash account is classified as a current asset and would be shown on the balance sheet with other cash accounts as illustrated in the entry below:

Balance sheet presentation of cash and petty cash accounts

Assets
Current Assets:
  Cash $2,000
  Petty Cash   100

After the fund has been established, the Petty Cash account would not be debited or credited unless the fund is increased, decreased, or eliminated.

Replenishing the Petty Cash Fund

Whenever the cash balance in the petty cash fund is low, the petty cashier informs the proper individual, generally the immediate supervisor. A report is prepared by the petty cashier for the accountant to show the reasons and amounts paid from the fund and the amount of cash on hand. When the report is approved, a check is issued to replenish the fund for the total of the petty cash receipts or the amounts paid from the fund.

Using the Nu-Fabric Company example, assume that the summary received from Carey Brooks revealed that the following payments were made in June: postage, $22; delivery expense, $30; newspaper, $10; office supplies, $18; and $12 for personal expenses of the owner, A. Tomas. Cash on hand amounted to $8. The entry on June 30 to replenish the petty cash fund is illustrated below:

19___				
June	30	Postage Expense	22	
		Freight In	30	
		Miscellaneous Expense	10	
		Office Supplies	18	
		A. Tomas, Drawing	12	
		Cash		92
		Replenish petty cash fund for June payments.		

Notice that the credit was made to Cash instead of the Petty Cash account. Remember that the Petty Cash account would not be *credited* unless the fund is decreased or the fund is eliminated.

After the check to replenish the fund is issued and cashed, Carey Brooks will have $100 in the fund ($92 + $8 balance).

Changing the Original Amount of the Petty Cash Fund

When a petty cash fund is established, the accountant estimates for a 1-month period the amount necessary to handle payments for small expenditures. If this original amount proves to be insufficient to cover all these small payments for a reasonable length of time, the accountant may decide to increase the amount of the fund. If the increase is approved, a check is issued. The journal entry to record the increase would require a debit to Petty Cash and a credit to the Cash account.

Using the replenishment entry for the Nu-Fabric Company on June 30, let us assume that the fund was increased for $10 at the time the fund was replenished. The journal entry would be:

19___				
June	30	Postage Expense	22	
		Freight In	30	
		Miscellaneous Expense	10	
		Office Supplies	18	
		A. Tomas, Drawing	12	
		Petty Cash	10	
		Cash		102
		Replenish the petty cash fund for June payments and increase the fund from $100 to $110.		

Petty Cash

Date		Explanation	Ref.	Dr	Cr	Balance
19__ June	1			100		100
	30				10	110

If the amount in the petty cash fund proves to be more than is needed for a reasonable length of time, the fund may be decreased. Usually the fund is adjusted for any decreases when the fund is replenished. The journal entry required to record the decrease of the fund would require a credit to the Petty Cash account for the amount of the decrease.

Let us assume that the Nu-Fabric Company on June 30 of the current year decreased the petty cash fund in the amount of $10 at the time the fund was replenished. The journal entry would be:

Replenished petty cash and decreased fund

19__ June	30	Postage Expense	22	
		Freight In	30	
		Miscellaneous Expense	10	
		Office Supplies	18	
		A. Tomas, Drawing	12	
		Petty Cash		10
		Cash		82
		Replenish the petty cash fund for June payments and decrease the fund from $100 to $90.		

Petty Cash

Date		Explanation	Ref.	Dr	Cr	Balance
19__ June	1			100		100
	30				10	90

Cash Over and Short

Whenever an error occurs in making payments from the petty cash fund, an account called *Cash Over and Short* is used to record the amount of shortage or overage. If the error results in an overage of cash, the Cash

Over and Short account is credited. When the error results in a cash shortage, the Cash Over and Short account is debited.

The following examples for the Nu-Fabric Company show the entries required for the Cash Over and Short account.

EXAMPLE 1   *On July 31, the petty cashier of the Nu-Fabric Company submitted the following summary of payments made from the petty cash fund during July: postage, $32; delivery expense on merchandise purchased, $48; and newspapers, $10. Cash on hand on July 31 amounted to $6. After the summary was analyzed, a shortage of $4 was discovered.*

Computation to determine any cash shortage or overage in petty cash fund

Petty Cash on hand		$100
Petty Cash Payments:		
Postage	$32	
Freight In	48	
Newspaper	10	
Total Payments		90
Cash on hand *should amount to*		$ 10
Actual cash on hand		6
Cash Shortage		$ 4

The journal entry to replenish the fund for payments made in July and to record the $4 shortage is shown below:

Entry to record shortage of cash and replenishment of petty cash fund

19__			
July	31	Postage Expense	32
		Freight In	48
		Miscellaneous Expense	10
		Cash Over and Short	4
		Cash		94
		Replenish the petty cash fund for July payments and record a shortage of $4.	

At the end of the period, if the balance of the Cash Over and Short account has a debit balance, it represents an expense and is shown on the income statement under Operating Expenses/General & Administrative.

INCOME STATEMENT

Income statement presentation of cash shortage

Operating Expenses:
General & Administrative:
Cash Over & Short $4

EXAMPLE 2   *Carey Brooks, petty cashier for the Nu-Fabric Company, submitted the following summary of payments made from the petty cash fund as of August 31: postage, $41; freight on merchandise purchased, $36; newspapers, $10; and $12 personal expenses for the owner, A. Tomas. Cash on hand on August 31 amounted to $3. After the summary was analyzed, a $2 overage was discovered. Cash on hand should have been $1 instead of $3 as reported;*

$100 − $99 ($41 + $36 + $10 + $12) = $1. The journal entry for replenishing the fund for payments made in August and to record the $2 overage is shown below:*

Cash overage recorded at time fund is replenished

19__				
Aug.	31	Postage Expense	41	
		Freight In	36	
		Miscellaneous Expense	10	
		A. Tomas, Drawing	12	
		Cash Over & Short		2
		Cash		97
		Replenish petty cash fund for August and record a cash overage of $2.		

The Cash Over and Short account with a credit balance is shown on the income statement under Other Income.

INCOME STATEMENT

Income statement presentation of cash overage

Other Income:
Cash Over & Short $2

BANK RECONCILIATION

Bank Checking Account

When a business opens a checking account, the bank requires a *signature card* to be completed by each person authorized to sign or issue company checks. This card is kept on file with the bank so that if there is any doubt about the signature on a check, a bank teller can compare the signature on the card with the signature on the check to make sure that the check is signed by a person authorized to sign company checks.

Once a checking account is opened, the bank will issue printed deposit slips and prenumbered checks with the business name, address, and account number. Every month the company will receive a statement from the bank along with canceled checks. Canceled checks are checks written by the company and paid by the bank from the company account. The *bank statement* (Figure 10-3) will show the beginning and ending cash balance, deposits, collections made by the bank for the company, checks paid, deductions for service fees and other charges, and checks deposited from customers which proved to be uncollectible by the bank. All additions and/or deductions on the bank statement that were not the result of deposits made or checks paid during the month will be identified by a code letter. An explanation of these code letters will appear on the bank statement.

Bank signature card

ACCOUNT NUMBER _____

ADDRESS _____ ZIP CODE _____ SIG'S. REQUIRED [ ]

TYPE OF BUSINESS _____ TAXPAYER NUMBER _____

NEW [ ]   REPLACEMENT [ ]

DATE

ORIGINAL OPENING

TEL. _____ DATE _____

APPROVED

OFFICE: In account with   Lowell National Bank,   Livonia, Michigan
Harding & Five Mile

The undersigned (sole proprietor) (all of the partners) doing business under the name of

hereby agree(s) that, until further notice in writing (in the form of either a properly executed replacement signature card or other acceptable instrument) the Bank shall honor checks, drafts, notes, orders and receipts drawn upon funds now or hereafter on deposit

in this account in the name of said firm signed by any _____ of the following persons.

SIGNATURE: _____

SIGNATURE: _____

SIGNATURE: _____

THE DEPOSITOR AGREES TO THE RULES, REGULATIONS, TERMS AND CONDITIONS CONTAINED ON THE REVERSE HEREOF.

In witness whereof, I/we have subscribed my/our name(s) this _____ day of _____, 19 ____

Cert. No.
(Affix signatures of all co-partners or sole proprietor here, as ☞ shown on certificate.)

F110007 (9-71)

PARTNERSHIP OR ASSUMED NAME   (OVER)

Debit memorandum issued by bank for deductions other than checks presented for payment

LOWELL NATIONAL BANK
LIVONIA, MICHIGAN

We charge your account and return the following items unpaid; REASON IS NOTED ON EACH ITEM:

OFFICE _____   DATE _____

DRAWN BY _____   DRAWN ON _____   AMOUNT _____

RETURNED ITEM

DEBIT

SAVINGS ACCOUNT NUMBER

AUTHORIZED SIGNATURE

CHECKING ACCOUNT NUMBER

43

TOTAL CHARGE

291

An illustration of a deposit slip is shown in Figure 10-2. **Deposit slips** are prepared in duplicate; the original copy is given to the bank and the carbon copy maintained in the company records providing the business with a detailed record of each item deposited. It also serves as a valuable reference in case the bank misplaces the original deposit slip. Information regarding the deposit may also be needed for auditing purposes.

A debit memorandum for all deductions other than checks (one is shown on page 291) and a credit memorandum for all additions other than deposits are included with the bank statement.

Bank Reconciliation Procedure

The cash balance shown on the bank statement (Figure 10-3) usually does not agree with the balance of the Cash account shown in the accounting records. There are several reasons for the difference between the bank balance and the book balance.

Three basic reasons why the bank cash balance may not agree with the cash balance shown on the books of a company are:

1. *Deposits in Transit.* Deposits made by the company that were too late to be included on the bank statement are referred to as **deposits in transit.** These deposits would be included in the Cash account of the company, but they would not be shown on the current bank statement.
2. *Outstanding Checks.* During the month, checks are written to creditors, to employees for wages and salaries, and to government agencies for tax payments, etc. All the checks written are not always presented to the bank for payment during the period covered by the statement. Checks that have not been presented for payment are referred to as **outstanding checks.** The cash balance of the company will include these checks as deductions, but inasmuch as some checks have not been presented to the bank for payment, the deductions will not be shown on the current bank statement.
3. *Bank Errors.* Occasionally the bank will make an error. The most common error is charging or crediting an account with the check of another company.

Five basic reasons why the cash balance shown on the books may not agree with the cash balance shown on the bank statement are:

1. *Bank Service Charges.* The bank deducts a fee called a **service charge** for handling an account. The amount of the service charge deducted by the bank will not be known until the bank statement is received.
2. *NSF Checks.* The bank may return a check received from a customer because the customer's bank account did not have sufficient funds to cover the check. These checks that are uncollectible by the bank are

FIGURE 10-2
*Deposit slip for Nu-Fabric
Company*

CHECKING ACCOUNT DEPOSIT TICKET

Nu-Fabric Products Company

Presentation of this deposit slip at any LOWELL NATIONAL SUBSIDIARY
BANK other than the bank of record authorizes Bank to open an Accommo-
dation Account for me to effect a transfer of the funds representing the deposit
to the bank named on this deposit ticket.

LOWELL NATIONAL BANK—LIVONIA, MICHIGAN

	DOLLARS	CENTS
DATE 3/4/—		
CURRENCY	25	—
COIN		
CHECKS LIST EACH SEPARATELY		
1 *Fashion Company*	50	—
2		
3		
4		
5		
6		
7		
8		
9		
10		
11		
12		
13		
14		
15		
16		
17		
18		
19		
20		
21		
22		
23		
24		
25		
26		
27		
TOTAL FROM OTHER SIDE OR ATTACHED LIST		
PLEASE RE-ENTER TOTAL HERE **TOTAL**	75	—

⑈:O7 24⣿ 1 2 38⣿: O1O1⣿OO8 1⣿6⣿

DELUXE CHECK PRINTERS 80-80

Checks and other items are received for
deposit subject to the terms and conditions of this bank's collection agreement.

FIGURE 10-3

Bank statement received by
Nu-Fabric Company for
March

LOWELL NATIONAL BANK

NU-FABRIC PRODUCTS COMPANY
1800 Silvery Park
Livonia, MI 48152

ACCOUNT NUMBER
0101 0081 6

THIS STATEMENT COVERS THE PERIOD
FROM 02/28/8_ TO 03/31/8_

DATE	CHECKS	TRANS CODE
03 01 8_	85 96	
03 03 8_	92 50	
03 08 8_	18 19	
03 10 8_	50 00	
03 16 8_	10 00	
03 17 8_	27 00	
03 22 8_	12 50	
03 23 8_	18 75	60
03 28 8_	10 85	
03 30 8_	12 79	
03 31 8_	7 32	SC

DATE	CHECKS	TRANS. CODE
03 01 8_	88 55	
03 10 8_	48 86	
03 11 8_	50 00	
03 16 8_	84 28	
03 18 8_	30 00	
03 22 8_	31 50	
03 23 8_	30 00	
03 28 8_	37 06	
03 31 8_	22 00	

DATE	DEPOSITS	TRANS CODE
03 04 8_	25 00	
03 04 8_	50 00	
03 08 8_	54 82	
03 11 8_	255 00	
03 16 8_	30 00	
03 29 8_	28 00	

INCLUDED IN STATEMENT	
NO. OF DEPOSITS 6	NO. OF CHECKS 19

TOTAL ADDED FOR DEPOSITS $ 442.82

TOTAL DEDUCTED FOR CHECKS AND CHARGES $ 768.11

FIRST LOW BALANCE
DATE | AMOUNT $

BEGINNING BALANCE $ 334.18

CURRENT BALANCE $ 8.89

TRANSACTION CODES

BLANK - CHECK
BLANK - DEPOSIT
SC - SERVICE CHARGE

3 - CREDIT MEMO
5 - DEPOSIT CORRECTION

7 - LIST CORRECTION
8 - LIST

10 - CHECK CORRECTION
12 - CHARGE CORRECTION
29 - CERTIFIED CHECK MEMO

40 - MISC. BANK CHARGE
60 - DEBIT MEMO
OD - OVERDRAWN BALANCE
61 - SAVINGS DEDUCTION

PLEASE RECONCILE YOUR STATEMENT PROMPTLY
(SEE REVERSE SIDE)

referred to as **NSF** (nonsufficient funds) **checks.** When a company deposits a check received from a customer, the bank adds the amount to the company account, but when the check proves to be uncollectible, the bank deducts the amount from the company account. The bank will mail a debit memorandum and the NSF check to the depositor (company) when the check is uncollectible. Usually the amount is not deducted from the company records until the end of the month when the bank statement is received.

3. *Collection of Notes.*[1] The bank may act as a collection agent for a company and collect the payment of a note that the company received from a customer. The bank charges a small fee for this service. When a note is collected, the bank adds the amount of the note plus any interest earned on the note and deducts the collection fee from the company bank account. The depositor (company) usually does not know if the note was collected until the bank statement is received, although some banks may send a notification (credit memorandum) when the note is collected.

4. *Note Payments.* A company may give the bank a note that is owed to a creditor, authorizing the bank to pay the note on the due date plus any interest and to deduct the amount from the company bank account. When the note is paid by the bank, a debit memorandum is usually sent to the company as notification that payment was made. Most companies will not make an entry until the bank statement is received.

5. *Book Errors.* The company may make an error in recording a cash payment or cash receipt. Usually the error is not discovered until the bank statement is received and reconciled with the cash balance as shown on the company books.

Preparing the Bank Reconciliation Statement

A **bank reconciliation** is a statement that is prepared as soon as the cancelled checks and the statement are received from the bank. The bank reconciliation statement is prepared to determine the reasons for any difference in the cash balance as shown in the books and the cash balance as shown on the bank statement.

There are two parts to the preparation of a bank reconciliation statement. In order to arrive at the correct cash balance at the end of the month, you must:

1. Account for the differences in the bank statement
2. Account for the differences in the book balance

Procedures for Reconciling the Bank Account. There are four steps or procedures for reconciling the cash balance shown on the bank statement.

---

[1] Notes are discussed in the Chapter 10 appendix.

1. Record the ending cash balance as shown on the bank statement.

Balance per bank statement	$XXXXX

2. Check for any additions to the bank balance by beginning with the stubs in your checkbook to see if the deposits made by the company agree with the deposits as shown on the bank statement. Any deposit not recorded on the bank statement is called a deposit in transit. Write the words "deposit in transit" and record the amount in the Amount column. Check for any errors made by the bank resulting in an addition to the beginning bank balance. List the type of error and the amount under the deposit in transit. Add the additions to the beginning bank balance to obtain a subtotal.

Balance per bank statement		$XXXX
Add: Deposit in transit	$XXX	
Error by bank in deducting		
check of another company	XX	XXX
Subtotal		$XXXX

3. Arrange the checks returned with the bank statement in numerical order. Next, turn to the checkstubs and check off each check that has been canceled (paid). All checks written and not returned by the bank are called "outstanding checks." Each outstanding check is listed with its check number and amount, and the outstanding checks are totaled.

Balance per bank statement			$XXXX
Add: Deposit in transit		$XX	
Error by bank in deducting			
check of another company		X	XX
Subtotal			$XXXX
Less: Outstanding Checks:			
Check Nos.: xxx	$XX		
xxx	X	$XX	

4. Check for any errors made by bank resulting in a deduction to bank balance. List the type of error and record the amount under the total of outstanding checks. Add the deductions, record the amount under the previous subtotal, and subtract the deductions from subtotal to obtain a final total. This total is called the "reconciled bank balance." Double-underline the reconciled bank balance.

```
Balance per bank statement                              $XXXX
Add: Deposit in transit                    $XX
      Error by bank in deducting
         check of another company            X          XX
   Subtotal                                             $XXXX
Less: Outstanding Checks:
   Check Nos.: xxx               $XX
              xxx                  X        $XX
      Error by bank in adding check
         of another company                  X          XX
   Reconciled Bank Balance                              $XXXX
```

Procedures for Reconciling the Book Balance. There are four steps or procedures for reconciling the cash balance as shown in the books of the company.

1. Record the ending cash balance as shown in the ledger of the company.

```
Balance per books                                       $XXXX
```

2. Check for any additions to the book balance by adding any note and interest collections made by the bank, and by looking for any errors made by the company resulting in an addition to the beginning book balance. List the type of error and the amount, and obtain a total of the additions and add to the beginning book balance to obtain a subtotal.

```
Balance per books                                       $XXXX
Add: Note and interest collected
        by bank                            $XXX
     Error in recording check
        No. xx for Office Supplies           XX         XXX
   Subtotal                                             $XXXX
```

3. Check deductions made for:
(*a*) Bank service charges
(*b*) Note collection charges
(*c*) Note and interest payment by bank
(*d*) NSF checks received from customers
(*e*) Errors made by company in recording cash receipts and cash payments

List each deduction and type of error with its amount, total the deductions, and subtract from the previous subtotal.

Balance per books		$XXXX
Add: Note and interest collected by bank	$XXX	
Error in recording check No. xx for Office Supplies	XX	XXX
Subtotal		$XXXX
Less: Bank service charge	$ X	
Note collection charge	X	
Note and interest paid by bank	XX	
NSF check received from customer	XXX	
Error in recording check No. xx for payment on account	XX	XXX

4. Obtain a final total of the additions and subtractions to the cash balance as shown on the books. This total is called the "reconciled book balance," and it should be the same as the reconciled bank balance. Double-underline the reconciled book balance.

Balance per books		$XXXX
Add: Note and interest collected by bank	$XXX	
Error in recording check No. xx for Office Supplies	XX	XXX
Subtotal		$XXXX
Less: Bank service charge	$ X	
Note collection charge	X	
Note and interest paid by bank	XX	
NSF check received from customer	XXX	
Error in recording check No. xx for payment on account	XX	XXX
Reconciled Book Balance		$XXXX

All additions should be listed first and all subtractions should be listed last on the portion of the statement reconciling the bank balance and on the portion of the statement reconciling the book balance. Therefore, check through all the items and group the additions and subtractions to the bank balance and the additions and subtractions to the book balance before preparing the bank reconciliation statement.

After the bank reconciliation statement has been completed, the reconciled bank balance and reconciled book balance should be equal if all the steps have been followed properly.

Journal Entries to Correct the Cash Balance

If any additions or subtractions were made to the book balance for cash on the bank reconciliation statement, an adjustment must be made to record them on the books. After the adjustment has been journalized and posted, the Cash account will show the reconciled balance which is the correct balance.

The total amount of *additions* on the portion of the statement reconciling the book balance should be *debited* to the Cash account. The total amount of *subtractions* on the portion of the statement reconciling the book balance should be *credited* to the Cash account.

Illustration of a Bank Reconciliation Statement

The bank reconciliation is not a formal financial statement, but it is a statement prepared monthly and kept in the permanent records of the company. The heading should have the name of the company, the name of the statement (Bank Reconciliation Statement), and the date of reconciliation.

As an illustration of a bank reconciliation statement, assume that the following data applies to the Nu-Fabric Company for the month ending September 30 of the current year.

The Cash account in the general ledger showed a debit balance of $7,552. The statement received from the bank for the month of September shows a cash balance of $6,840. After analyzing the statement received from the bank and the cash balance in the records of the company, the accountant determined that the following factors caused the difference in the bank balance and the book balance.

1. A deposit of $1,200 made by the company at four o'clock on September 30 was too late to be entered on the bank statement.
2. The bank statement showed a deduction of $200 for a check written by the Nu-Fashion Company. The accountant for the Nu-Fabric Company notified the bank of the error, and the bank informed the accountant that the company account would be corrected.
3. The bank statement included 20 canceled checks written in September and paid by the bank. However, three checks written by the company and recorded on the books were not returned. These three checks were No. 810, $60; No. 840, $305; and No. 892, $120.
4. A credit memorandum was enclosed with the bank statement for $306 representing a $300 note collected by the bank, plus interest amounting to $6.
5. The accountant discovered that check No. 834 in the amount of $78 written to the J. Bean Company in payment for office equipment purchased on September 10 was entered in the accounting records as $87. The bank deducted the correct amount of $78 from the company account.

6. Two debit memorandums issued by the bank were enclosed with the statement. One was for bank service charges amounting to $6 and the other was for a note collection fee amounting to $4.

7. An NSF check for $102 was returned with the statement. The check was received from a customer, L. Home, for payment on account. A debit memorandum issued by the bank was enclosed stating that $102 was deducted from the account of the company.

Note that items 1 and 2 are additions and item 3 is a subtraction to the cash balance as shown on the bank statement. Items 4 and 5 are additions and items 6 and 7 are subtractions to the cash balance as shown on the company books.

A bank reconciliation prepared for the Nu-Fabric Company as of September 30 of the current year is shown below.

NU-FABRIC COMPANY
BANK RECONCILIATION STATEMENT
September 30, 19—

Reconciling cash balance on bank statement with cash balance shown on company books

Balance per Bank Statement		$6,840
Add: Deposit in Transit	$1,200	
Nu-Fashion Company check deducted in error . .	200	1,400
Total		$8,240
Less: Outstanding Checks:		
No. 810	$ 60	
No. 840	305	
No. 892	120	485
Reconciled Bank Balance		$7,755
Balance per Books		$7,552
Add: Note Collection by bank	$ 300	
Interest Collected on Note	6	
Error in recording check No. 834 for office equipment purchased from J. Bean Company	9	315
Total		$7,867
Less: Bank Service Charges	$ 6	
Note Collection Fee	4	
NSF check from L. Home	102	112
Reconciled Book Balance		$7,755

After the reconciliation was prepared for the Nu-Fabric Company, the following entries were journalized and posted to correct the Cash account. Remember that only additions and subtractions to the cash balance as shown on the company books require an entry. Any changes affecting the cash balance as shown on the bank statement must be corrected by the bank.

Entries to correct cash balance

19__			
Sept. 30	Cash	315	
	Notes Receivable		300
	Interest Earned		6
	Office Equipment		9
	To record note and interest collected by bank, and correct error in recording check No. 834 on Sept. 10 for purchase of office equipment.		
30	Miscellaneous Expenses	10	
	Accounts Receivable/L. Home	102	
	Cash		112
	To record bank service charges of $6, note collection fee of $4, and NSF check for $120 received from L. Home.		

SUMMARY

Adequate control must be maintained for handling cash to prevent theft and the misappropriation of funds. A good system of control divides the receiving, recording, disbursing, and depositing of cash among several individuals.

Normally all payments of material amounts are made by check. Small payments that are impractical to make with a check are paid out of a special fund termed the petty cash fund.

A petty cash fund is usually established for an amount sufficient to handle the payment of small expenditures for a period of a month or a reasonable length of time. At the end of the period, or when the fund is exhausted, the petty cash fund is replenished and the payments made from the fund are recorded in the accounting records. Whenever the fund is replenished, any shortage or overage of cash in the petty cash fund is recorded in the Cash Over and Short account.

When a checking account is opened in the name of the business, the bank requires all persons authorized to sign company checks to sign a signature card which is kept on file with the bank. The bank will print checks and deposit slips with the name, address, and account number of the company. At the end of every month, the company receives a statement from the bank. This statement shows the beginning cash balance, deposits, amounts paid out of the account, and the ending cash balance. Upon receipt of the bank statement, the company prepares a bank reconciliation statement to determine the reasons for any differences in the amount of cash as shown on the bank statement and the amount of cash as shown on the books of the company. A journal entry is made for any additions or subtractions listed on the bank reconciliation statement affecting the cash balance as shown on the books of the company. After these entries are posted, the Cash account will show the reconciled account balance.

GLOSSARY

Bank Reconciliation: A statement prepared to determine the reasons for any differences in the cash balance as shown on the books and the cash balance as shown on the bank statement.

Bank Service Charge: A monthly fee charged by the bank for handling a checking account.

Bank Statement: A statement received by the depositor from the bank, usually monthly, showing the beginning cash balance, plus any deposits, less any deductions, and the ending cash balance.

Cash: In business, coins, paper money, bank drafts, checks, money orders, certified checks, cashier's checks, and the deposits on hand in a checking or savings account are considered as cash.

Cash Over and Short: An account that is used when the petty cash fund is replenished to record any cash shortages or cash overages. The account is shown on the income statement. A cash shortage is classified as an Operating/General & Administrative Expense. A cash overage is classified as Other Income.

Deposit Slip: Form required by a bank whenever a deposit is made in an account. All checks are listed separately along with the amount of cash deposited.

Deposits in Transit: Deposits made by a company that were too late to appear on the current bank statement. The deposit normally will appear on the statement for the following month.

NSF Checks: Checks written by a customer that proved to be uncollectible because of insufficient funds in the customer's account. The check is returned by the bank to the company that received the checks with notice that the amount was deducted from its account.

Outstanding Checks: Checks written by a company during the month that have not been presented to the bank for payment; therefore, the amounts have not been deducted from the company's account by the bank.

Petty Cash: A special fund established for the payment of small expenditures that would be impractical to pay with a check.

Petty Cash Receipt: A form issued (receipt) for cash expenditures made from a petty cash fund.

Petty Cashier: The person designated to handle the petty cash fund.

Petty Cash Voucher: Another name for petty cash receipt.

Signature Card: Card required by the bank to be signed by all persons authorized to sign checks.

QUESTIONS

1. What is the difference between the terms cash and petty cash as used in business?
2. List two objectives for the control of cash.
3. Why would a company establish a petty cash fund?
4. What account would be credited to reimburse the petty cash fund?
5. What account would be debited for a shortage of cash in a petty cash fund?
6. Give two reasons why the cash balance on the bank statement would not agree with the cash balance on the books of the company.
7. Give the journal entry required to correct the cash account for an NSF check received from O. Bert, a customer, in the amount of $45.
8. A bank collects a note receivable for a company amounting to $5,010, which includes interest of $10, and the bank deducts a collection fee of $3. Give the journal entry required by the company showing the collection of the note and interest and the deduction for the collection fee.
9. Why would a bank include a debit memorandum with the bank statement?
10. Define the following terms: signature card, deposit slip, and bank service charges.
11. List the two parts of a bank reconciliation statement.
12. State whether the following items would be an addition to or subtraction from the book portion of the bank reconciliation statement.
   (*a*) Notes Payable
   (*b*) Interest on Note Payable
   (*c*) Bank service charge
   (*d*) NSF check
   (*e*) Note Receivable
   (*f*) Interest on Note Receivable

EXERCISES

Establishing and Replenishing a Petty Cash Fund

1. On June 1 a petty cash fund was established for $25. On June 30 the petty cashier reported a balance of $3 in the fund. The following payments were made during June: postage, $10; office supplies, $5; and freight on purchase of merchandise, $7. Give the journal entries required for establishing the petty cash fund on June 1 and for replenishing the fund on June 30.

2. On July 1, a petty cash fund was established for $25. During July the following expenditures were made by the petty cashier: postage, $5; freight on merchandise purchased, $8; office supplies, $6; and $5 paid to the

owner, James Wall, for his personal use. Cash on hand on July 31 amounted to $2. Give the journal entries required for establishing the fund on July 1 and for replenishing the fund on July 31.

Determining Additions and Subtractions on a Bank Reconciliation Statement

3. Indicate whether the following items would be an addition or subtraction to the book portion of a bank reconciliation statement for the current month.
   (a) NSF check.
   (b) Note collection fee.
   (c) Note collected plus interest.
   (d) Note paid by bank plus interest.
   (e) Bank service charge for month.
   (f) Error by bookkeeper in recording payment by check for office supplies. The correct amount was $125, but the check was recorded for $152.

4. Indicate whether the following items would be an addition or subtraction to the bank portion of a bank reconciliation statement for the current month.
   (a) Outstanding checks.
   (b) Deposits in transit.
   (c) Error by bank in deducting $100 for a check issued by another company.
   (d) Error by bank in adding $200 for a deposit made by another company.

Journal Entries to Correct Cash Balance

5. The following data appeared on a bank reconciliation statement. Give journal entries required to correct the cash account.
   (a) NSF check for $200 received from B. Coombs, customer.
   (b) Note for $200 collected by the bank plus $6 interest.
   (c) Error by company in recording payment for an account payable to Janes Company. Check was written for $126 and recorded as $216; the correct amount was $126.
   (d) Bank service charges of $6.

Preparing a Bank Reconciliation Statement

6. The following data appeared in the records of the Custerd Products Company as of August 31 of the current year.
   (a) Balance per bank statement, $2,024
   (b) Balance per books, $1,280
   (c) Outstanding checks, $804
   (d) Deposit in transit, $220
   (e) Note collected by bank, $800; interest, $16

(*f*) NSF check from T. Richard, $650

(*g*) Bank service charges, $2

(*h*) Note collection fee, $4

Prepare a bank reconciliation statement and the journal entries required to correct the cash account of the Custerd Products Company.

PROBLEMS

Establishing and Replenishing Petty Cash Fund

10-1. The Bell Company established a petty cash fund on November 1 for $50. A check was made out to Roslyn Berrick, petty cashier. During the month of November, Roslyn paid the following expenses from the fund: freight on merchandise purchased for resale, $12; gas for company truck, $14; postage, $7; office supplies, $8; newspapers, $6. Cash on hand, $3.

Required

(*a*) Journal entry for establishing petty cash fund on November 1.

(*b*) Journal entry for replenishing the fund on November 30.

10-2. The Trailer Company established a petty cash fund on January 2 for $25, naming James Watters petty cashier. On January 31, Watters submitted petty cash receipts to the accountant for the following: postage, $5; freight on merchandise shipped to customer, $6; newspapers, $6.50; office supplies, $4; and $2.50 for COD package for merchandise purchased by I. Trailer, owner, for personal use. Cash on hand January 31, $2.

Required

(*a*) Journal entry for establishing petty cash fund on January 2.

(*b*) Journal entry for replenishing petty cash fund on January 31.

10-3. Trailer of Problem 10-2 increased the petty cash fund $50 on February 1. The company accepted a special contract that would require two of the office employees to work overtime for the month of February, and he agreed to pay the cost of dinner for these two employees during this period. On February 28, James Watters, petty cashier, submitted the following summary for expenses to the accountant: postage, $6; freight on purchase of merchandise, $8; office supplies, $4; newspapers, $6.50; and dinners, $46.50 (charge to Miscellaneous Expense). Cash on hand February 28, $4.

Required

(*a*) Journal entry for increasing petty cash fund on February 1.

(*b*) Journal entry to replenish the fund on February 28 and to return the fund to $25. The special contract is completed, so the fund is decreased.

10-4. The Sudzy Car Wash established a petty cash fund for $50 on June 1 and named John Hoosier petty cashier. On June 30, Hoosier submitted the following summary of expenditures for the month of June: washing solvent, $15; freight on rags purchased to dry the cars, $9; and coffee for employees, $16 (charge to Miscellaneous Expense). Cash on hand June 30, $8.

Required

(a) Journal entry for June 1.
(b) Journal entry required on June 30 to replenish and decrease the fund in the amount of $10.

Journal Entries to Correct Cash Account

10-5. The Curl-E Hair Salon prepared a bank reconciliation statement as of December 31 of the current year. The additions to correct the cash balance as shown on the books amounted to $960 for a note collected for $932 and interest of $28. The subtractions to correct the cash balance as shown on the books amounted to $434 for a $380 NSF check from customer C. Laskin; bank service charges, $7; and an error in recording check No. 742 for materials and supplies in the amount of $47.

Required

Journalize the necessary entries to correct the Cash account of the company.

Determining Additions and Deductions on Bank Reconciliation Plus Journal Entries to Correct Cash Account

10-6. The records for the Basil Seed Company showed a cash balance of $5,240 on January 31 of the current year. The bank balance showed a cash balance of $6,910. The accountant discovered the following while analyzing the records.
1. Late deposit made on January 31 for $102 was not recorded by the bank.
2. Outstanding checks: No. 110, $80; No. 124, $362; No. 146, $720; and No. 184, $822.
3. A credit memorandum for a note collected by the bank for $1,020, plus interest of $62.
4. NSF check from a customer, J. Ris, in the amount of $1,228 was returned by the bank.
5. The bookkeeper recorded check No. 112 in the amount of $206 for store supplies. The correct amount was $260.
6. Bank service charge, $8, plus note collection fee of $4.

Required

(*a*) Determine the total additions to the book balance and bank balance.
(*b*) Determine the total deductions to the book balance and bank balance.
(*c*) Determine the reconciled balance.
(*d*) Journalize the entries to correct the cash balance of the company.

Preparation of Bank Reconciliation Statement

10-7. The STE Clothing Company received the bank statement from the Eureka National Bank which showed a cash balance on January 31 of the current year of $2,700. The cash account of the company showed a balance of $1,630. After analyzing the statement, the following facts were discovered:
1. NSF check from a customer, B. Struthers, in the amount of $120 was returned by the bank.
2. A late deposit on January 31 in the amount of $520 was not recorded.
3. Checks written by the company but not presented for payment were No. 702, $400; No. 780, $100; and No. 792, $52.
4. A check for $62 written by the SFE Company was deducted in error by the bank from the company account. The bank was notified and the account was corrected. Check was returned to the bank.
5. A credit memorandum for a note collected by the bank for $930, plus interest of $31, was included with the statement.
6. The bank deducted $8.50 for service charges and $2.50 note collection fee.
7. Check No. 682 in the amount of $145 for office equipment was returned by the bank. The bank deducted the proper amount ($145), but the accountant discovered that the bookkeeper deducted $415 in error.

Required

(*a*) Prepare a bank reconciliation as of January 31.
(*b*) Journalize the necessary entries to correct the Cash account of the company.

10-8. The Drapery Company showed a cash balance of $6,804 on July 31 of the current year. The bank statement received from the Laker National Bank disclosed the following facts:
1. Balance on the bank statement as of July 31, $5,010.
2. Late deposit of $1,608 was not recorded on the bank statement.
3. A debit memorandum for $1,006 covering a note paid by the bank in the amount of $1,000, plus interest of $6.
4. Outstanding checks: No. 810, $40; No. 861, $21; No. 889, $27; and No. 906, $30.
5. The bookkeeper recorded check No. 811 in the amount of $622 for store equipment. The correct amount of the check was $226, and this amount was deducted by the bank.

6. A credit memorandum for a note collected by the bank in the amount of $310, plus interest of $8, was included with the statement.
7. Bank service charges amounted to $9 plus a $3 note collection fee.

Required

(a) Prepare a bank reconciliation as of July 31.
(b) Journalize the necessary entries to correct the Cash account of the company.

10-9. The records for Drapery Company in Problem 10-8 showed a cash balance on August 31 of $1,114. The bank statement showed a cash balance of $1,200. The accountant discovered the following while analyzing the records.
1. Late deposit made on August 31 for $660 was not recorded by the bank.
2. NSF check from customer J. Joles for $46 was returned by the bank.
3. The bookkeeper recorded check No. 927 for office supplies in the amount of $64. The correct amount of the check was $46, and this amount was deducted by the bank.
4. A check for $206 written by the Dimmer Company was deducted by the bank in error. The accountant notified the bank and returned the check. The bank corrected the account.
5. Outstanding checks: No. 926, $860; No. 981, $85. Also check No. 810, $40, for July was still outstanding.
6. Bank Service charges, $5.

Required

(a) Prepare a bank reconciliation statement as of August 31.
(b) Prepare the necessary journal entries to correct the Cash account of the company.

10-10. The Curl-E Hair Salon showed a cash balance of $3,132 on November 30, of the current year. The bank statement received from the Burlington State Bank showed a balance of $3,159. After the accountant analyzed the records, the following facts were discovered as the cause for the difference.
1. Outstanding checks: No. 1010, $100; No. 1069, $32; No. 1098, $26; and No. 1103, $69.
2. A late deposit on November 30 in the amount of $384 was not recorded by the bank.
3. A debit memorandum for a note paid by the bank in the amount of $300, plus $18 interest.
4. A credit memorandum for a note collected by the bank in the amount of $700, plus interest of $16.80.
5. The bank deducted a check written by the EZ-Curl Hair Salon in the amount of $205 in error. The bank was notified and corrected the company account.

6. The bookkeeper made an error recording check No. 1002 for beauty supplies. The amount recorded was $276, and the correct amount of $267 was deducted by the bank.
7. Bank service charges for November, $8.80, and a $10 fee for notes paid and collected by the bank.

Required

(a) Prepare a bank reconciliation statement as of November 30.
(b) Prepare the necessary journal entries to correct the cash account of the company.

10-11. The SEP Associates showed a cash balance of $3,902 on September 30 of the current year. The bank statement from Lowel National Bank showed a balance of $3,640. The accountant discovered the following facts as the cause for the difference.

1. Late deposit on September 30 for $310 did not appear on bank statement.
2. NSF check from Ward Products (customer) for $402 was returned by the bank.
3. A debit memorandum for a note paid by the bank for $700 plus $21 interest.
4. The bank deducted a $108 check written by ESP Associates in error. The bank was notified and they corrected the company account.
5. Bookkeeper for the company deducted $165 (check No. 602) for supplies purchased during September. The Bank deducted the correct amount of $156.
6. Outstanding checks: No. 584, $545; No. 600, $340; No. 628, $306; and No. 632, $90.
7. Bank charges for September: service, $7 and note payment fee, $4.

Required

(a) Prepare a bank reconciliation for September.
(b) Prepare journal entries to correct the cash account of the company.

10-12. The SEP Associates in Problem 10-11 showed a cash balance of $1,923 on October 31 of the current year, and the bank statement showed a balance of $1,998. After analyzing the records, the accountant discovered the following facts as the cause for the difference.

1. A late deposit of $1,050 on October 31 did not appear on the bank statement.
2. Outstanding checks: No. 684, $62 and No. 691, $58. Check No. 632 for $90 written in September was still outstanding.
3. Bookkeeper recorded check No. 686 as $228 for equipment purchased in October. The bank deducted the correct amount of $282.

4. NSF check for $128 from Wally's Shop (customer) was returned by the bank.
5. A credit memorandum for a $800 note collected by the bank plus interest of $20.
6. Bank added $290 to the company account for a deposit made by SEP Sales. Bank was notified of error, and they corrected the company account.
7. Bank charges for October: service, $8 and note collection fee, $5.

Required

(a) Prepare a bank reconciliation for October.
(b) Prepare journal entries to correct the cash account of the company.
(c) Prepare a bank reconciliation for November using the following data.
   1. Book balance on November 30, $4,420; bank statement balance on November 30, $3,553.
   2. Bank deducted a $620 check written by SPE Products in error. Accountant notified the bank, and they corrected company account.
   3. Bank collected a $200 note plus interest of $6 from customer John Wells.
   4. Bookkeeper deducted check No. 720 for $518 in payment of amount owed to Jackson Company. The bank deducted the correct amount of $815.
   5. NSF check for $75 from Paul Jenkins in payment on account was returned by the bank.
   6. Late deposit of $510 on November 30 did not appear on bank statement.
   7. Outstanding checks for November: No. 740, $180 and No. 748, $200. Check No. 691 for $58 written in October was still outstanding.
   8. Bank charges for November: service, $6 and note collection fee, $3.
(d) Prepare journal entries to correct the cash account for November.

Chapter 10 Appendix:

Notes and Interest

After completing this appendix, you should be able to:

1. **Give the definition of a promissory note, and account for the basic transactions of notes received from customers**

2. **Compute the interest for a note using the basic formula and 60-day, 6 percent method**

3. **Determine the maturity date and maturity value of a promissory note**

4. **Account for the basic transactions when borrowing from a bank using a promissory note**

Obtaining a loan from a financial institution or a private party usually requires that the borrower pay a fee, called interest, for the use of the money. When the loan is obtained, the borrower signs a written promise to pay, at a future date, the amount of money borrowed plus interest to the lender. This written promise signed by the borrower is called a promissory note.

Notes may be accepted by a company from a customer in payment of an account (Accounts Receivable), or notes may be given to a creditor in payment of an account (Accounts Payable). Usually, notes received from customers or notes given to creditors are in the form of a promissory note. Interest received from a customer when the note is paid is credited to Interest Earned; interest paid on a note given to a creditor is debited to Interest Expense.

This appendix will define an interest-bearing promissory note and the calculation of interest and will explain the accounting for a note received from a customer and a note given to a creditor.

PROMISSORY NOTE

A *promissory note* is a written promise made by one person to another to pay a certain sum of money on a particular date. It is a popular, economical method of obtaining or borrowing money for a short period of time. Promissory notes are signed by the maker, and they are made payable to a specific person or to bearer of note. Other basic information is shown on the note illustrated in Figure A10-1.

The note must be signed by the borrower, who is known as the *maker* of the note, and it must contain the amount, city, state, date note is written,

FIGURE A10-1
*Illustration of a
promissory note*

$1,000.00   Plymouth, Mich., July 15, 19 83

_____60 days_____ after date _I_ promise to pay to

the order of _____Rick Taylor_____

One Thousand and _____00/100_____ DOLLARS

with interest at ___9___ per cent per annum at _Plymouth Bank_____

Value received

Jean Scott

No. _47_ Due _Sept. 13, 1983_

the time payment is due, and interest rate. For the note to be negotiable (legally transferable from one person to another), it must be made out to the *order* of the person lending the money, who is known as the **payee,** or to the **bearer,** who is anyone in possession of the note.

COMPUTATION OF INTEREST

The cost or expense of borrowing money is called **interest,** which is expressed as a percentage on the note. The Truth in Lending laws of the federal government require that the lender state the **interest rate** in terms of simple annual interest. The key factor in determining the true cost of interest is the rate, not the amount of money paid for interest. The lower the interest rate, the lower is the actual cost or expense of borrowing money.

The formula used to compute the amount of interest due on a note is

*Formula for computing
interest*

$$\textbf{Principal} \times \textbf{rate} \times \textbf{time} = \textbf{interest}$$
$$P \times R \times T = I$$

Principal (P) is the amount of money borrowed on the face amount of the loan. The person or party borrowing the money is known as the "lendee" or "debtor." The person or party lending the money is known as the "lender" or "creditor."

Rate (R) is the interest to be charged stated in terms of a percentage that is applied to the amount of money borrowed or principal.

Time (*T*) is the number of days or months before the loan is due. It is important in determining the amount of interest due.

When an interest rate is quoted, it is assumed that the rate applies to a 1-year or annual period. For convenience, a 1-year or annual period is considered to have 360 days, or 12 months of 30 days each. For example, a 9 percent, $1,000 note without any specified time period is 9 percent for 1 year, or $90 ($1,000 × 0.09). If the interest rate quoted is for a period of less than 1 year, it will be indicated by stating the interest as 1½ percent per month, 2½ percent quarterly, or 3½ percent semiannually, etc.

Simple Interest

Simple interest is the cost or expense of borrowing money at a given rate for a specific period of time. The formula principal × rate × time is used to determine the interest in the following examples.

EXAMPLE 1   *$1,000 loan at 9 percent.*

$$\$1,000 \times 0.09 = \$90 \text{ interest}$$

Since no time was stated, it is assumed that the interest rate is for 1 year.

EXAMPLE 2   *$1,000 loan at 9 percent for 6 months:*

$$\$1,000 \times 0.09 \times \frac{180 \text{ days } (30 \text{ days} \times 6 \text{ months})}{360 \text{ days } (30 \text{ days} \times 12 \text{ months})} = \$45 \text{ interest}$$

or

$$\$1,000 \times 0.09 \times \frac{6 \text{ months}}{12 \text{ months } (1 \text{ year})} = \$45 \text{ interest}$$

EXAMPLE 3   *$1,000 loan at 9 percent for 1 month:*

$$\$1,000 \times 0.09 \times \frac{30 \text{ days}}{360 \text{ days}} = \$7.50 \text{ interest}$$

EXAMPLE 4   *$2,500 loan at 9 percent for 3 years:*

$$\$2,500 \times 0.09 = \$225 \text{ interest for 1 year} \times 3 \text{ years} = \$675 \text{ interest}$$

60-Day, 6 Percent Method of Computing Interest

The *60-day, 6 percent method* of computing interest offers a shortcut for determining interest. To find the interest for 60 days at 6 percent for any amount, simply move the decimal point two places to the left of the principal or amount borrowed.

EXAMPLE 1   *$2,500 loan at 6 percent for 60 days:*

60-day, 6% method: $2,500.00   = $25

Formula method: $2,500 × 0.06 × $\dfrac{60 \text{ days}}{360 \text{ days}}$ = $25

EXAMPLE 2   *$9,250 loan at 6 percent for 60 days:*

60-day, 6% method: $9,250.00   = $92.50

Formula method: $9,250 × 0.06 × $\dfrac{60 \text{ days}}{360 \text{ days}}$ = $92.50

The 60-day, 6 percent method may also be used if the interest rate is more or less than 6 percent and/or the time is more or less than 60 days. This is illustrated in the three examples shown below:

EXAMPLE 3   *$7,200 loan at 5 percent for 30 days:*

6% for 60 days: $7,200.00	=	$72
6% for 30 days = ¹/₂ of $72 or	=	$36
Less: 1% for 30 days (1%/6% or ¹/₆ of $36)	=	6
Interest @ 5% for 30 days	=	$30

EXAMPLE 4   *$5,000 loan at 6 percent for 90 days:*

6% for 60 days: $5,000.00	=	$50
Add: 6% for 30 days (¹/₂ of $50)	=	25
Interest @ 6% for 90 days	=	$75

EXAMPLE 5   *$12,000 loan at 8 percent for 120 days:*

6% for 60 days: $12,000.00	=	$120
Add: 6% for 60 days: $12,000.00	=	120
Interest @ 6% for 120 days	=	$240
Add: 2% for 120 days (2%/6% or ¹/₃ of $240)	=	80
Interest @ 8% for 120 days	=	$320

The 60-day, 6 percent method is a convenient shortcut which requires fewer calculations and can be used in many different situations.

MATURITY DATE OF NOTE

The *maturity date* is the last day of the time period on the note when the principal and interest is due. When the note is stated for a specified number of days, the maturity date is determined by using the exact number of days in the month. Using the data from Figure A10-1 the maturity date is determined as follows:

Steps to determine maturity date of note.

1. Begin with the number of days in the month of July, the month note is dated.	31
2. Subtract the day the note is dated (July 15).	15
3. This difference equals the number of days remaining in July, the first month of note.	16
4. Add the number of days in August, the second month.	31
Total number of days from July 15 to August 31	47
5. Add the number of days needed in September to obtain the number of days of loan. This number gives the maturity date or due date of note (September 13).	13
Total number of days specified on note	60

If the note is written for a specified number of months, the maturity date is determined by counting the number of months stated on note. The maturity date would be the same day as specified on the note, only several months later. For example, a 2-month note dated July 15 would be due 2 months later on September 15, exactly 2 months from July 15.

A note dated the thirty-first or last day of a month would be due on the last day of the month even if there are only 28, 29, or 30 days in that month. For example, a 3-month note dated January 31 would be due on April 30, the last day of April, which is 3 months later.

MATURITY VALUE

Maturity value is the principal or the amount borrowed plus the interest owed on the maturity date of a note. The maturity value for the Jean Scott note (Figure A10-1) is illustrated below:

Computation of maturity value

$$\$1,000 \times 0.09 \times \frac{60 \text{ days}}{360 \text{ days}} = \$15 \text{ interest}$$

$$\$1,000 \text{ principal} + \$15 \text{ interest} = \$1,015 \text{ maturity value}$$

RECORDING PROMISSORY NOTES

Occasionally a customer will be unable to make payment on an account and will ask for an extension of time by offering a note in payment of the account receivable to the seller. Accounting for the acceptance of a note in payment of an account is illustrated in the following example.

On March 25 of the current year the Sails Company sold $2,400 of merchandise to the Beyer Company with terms of $^2/_{10}$, n/30. On April 22, the Beyer Company notified Sails Company that payment could not be made within 30 days. Beyer Company offered a 60-day, 8 percent promissory note dated April 25, of the current year in payment of the account. Sails Company accepted the note, which was paid on the maturity date. The journal entries recorded on the books of the seller and the buyer are shown below:

Entries involving notes receivable and notes payable with payment on maturity date

Sails Company (Seller)			Beyer Company (Customer)		
19__					
Mar. 25 Accounts Receivable/			Purchases	2,400	
Beyer Company	2,400		Accounts Payable/		
Sales		2,400	Sails Company		2,400
Sold merchandise with			Purchased merchandise		
terms of 2/10, n/30.			with terms of 2/10, n/30.		
Apr. 25 Notes Receivable	2,400		Accounts Payable/Sails		
Accounts Receivable/			Company	2,400	
Beyer Company		2,400	Notes Payable		2,400
Accepted 60-day, 8%			Issued 60-day, 8% note		
note dated April 25 in			dated April 25 in		
payment of account.			payment of account.		
June 24 Cash	2,432		Notes Payable	2,400	
Notes Receivable		2,400	Interest Expense	32	
Interest Earned*		32	Cash		2,432
Beyer Company			Paid note due today to		
honored note due			Sails Company.		
today.					

* $\$2{,}400 \times 0.08 \times \dfrac{60 \text{ days}}{360 \text{ days}} = \$32$ interest.

Note that on the Sails Company books, or the payee, the note is recorded as Notes Receivable, which is classified as a Current Asset on the balance sheet. On the books of the Beyer Company, or the maker of the note, the note is recorded as Notes Payable, which is classified as a Current Liability on the balance sheet.

Assume that on June 24 (maturity date) the Beyer Company was unable to pay the note. When the maker does not pay the note on the maturity date, it is then a *dishonored* or *defaulted note,* and must be removed from the records. If a note is not paid on the maturity date, it is no longer negotiable. However, the Beyer Company (customer) is not released from its obligation because it dishonored its note. Therefore, the amount of the note plus the interest is entered on the records in the Accounts Receivable account. The entry on the Sails Company books (seller) recognizing this obligation for the maturity value of the note is shown below.

Customer-dishonored note

Sails Company (Seller)			Beyer Company (Customer)
19__			
June 24 Accounts Receivable/			No entry required.
Beyer Company	2,432		
Notes Receivable		2,400	
Interest Earned		32	
To record dishonored			
Beyer Company note			
and record interest			
earned.			

Assume that the Beyer Company paid the dishonored note on July 20. The entry for the payment would be:

Sails Company (Seller)			Beyer Company (Customer)		
19__					
July 20 Cash	2,432		Note Payable	2,400	
Accounts Receivable/			Interest Expense	32	
Beyer Company		2,432	Cash		2,432
Received payment on			Paid 60-day, 6 percent		
note dishonored on			note due June 24 to		
June 24.			Beyer Company.		

OBTAINING A BANK LOAN

A business may borrow money from a bank by issuing or signing a note promising to pay the principal plus a stated amount of interest on a certain date. The bank has two methods for charging interest when granting a loan:

Two methods used by bank in granting loan

1. Interest may be paid on the maturity date of the note. The borrower receives the principal amount of the note to use over the entire period of the loan. This is known as an ***interest-bearing note.***

2. Interest may be deducted from the principal amount of the loan at the time the loan is granted, and the borrower receives the ***proceeds*** or difference between the principal and interest. The borrower receives less than the principal amount to use over the period of the loan. This is known as a ***discounted*** or ***non-interest-bearing note.***

Although the same amount of interest is paid in both cases, the borrower pays a higher rate of interest in the second method. To illustrate, assume that on September 1 of the current year, the Glad Florist Shop borrowed $3,000 from the Second National Bank, signing a 90-day, 8 percent note. The note was paid on November 30, the maturity date.

METHOD 1   *The bank accepts a $3,000 interest-bearing note.*

Entries for interest-bearing note and payment on maturity date

19__				
Sept.	1	Cash	3,000	
		Notes Payable		3,000
		To record a 90-day, 8% note issued to Second National Bank.		
Nov.	30	Notes Payable	3,000	
		Interest Expense	60*	
		Cash		3,060
		Paid 90-day note due today to Second National Bank.		

$$* \ \$3{,}000 \times 0.08 \times \frac{90 \text{ days}}{360 \text{ days}} = \$60 \text{ interest.}$$

METHOD 2   *The bank discounts a $3,000 note.*

Entries for discounted note and payment on maturity date

19__				
Sept.	1	Cash	2,940	
		Interest Expense	60	
		Notes Payable		3,000
		To record 90-day, 8% discounted note issued by Second National Bank.		
Nov.	30	Notes Payable	3,000	
		Cash		3,000
		To record payment of 90-day note due today to Second National Bank.		

Notice that in Method 1, Glad Florist had use of the $3,000 for the entire 90 days at an actual interest rate of 8 percent. In Method 2, Glad Florist only had the use of $2,940 for an actual interest rate of 8.17 percent ($2,940/360 days).

SUMMARY

When a business or individual borrows money, there is a cost or charge for the use of the money known as interest. Interest is expressed in terms of a percentage and is normally stated for a 1-year or annual period.

The amount of money borrowed is known as the principal or face amount of the loan.

For convenience, a 1-year or annual period is considered to have 360 days, or 12 months of 30 days each.

There are two basic interest methods described in this appendix: simple interest and the 60-day, 6 percent shortcut method. The formula for simple interest is principal × rate × time = interest. To determine the amount of interest for 60 days at 6 percent using the shortcut method, the decimal is moved two places to the left of the principal or face amount of the loan. This method applies to any amount and can be used to find interest with terms other than 60 days at 6 percent.

A negotiable promissory note is a common method of borrowing money for a short-term period. It is used by most financial institutions for loans granted to a business or an individual. A promissory note is a written, unconditional agreement to pay to the order of a designated person, a specific amount of money, at a specified interest rate, on a particular date. It must be signed by the borrower or maker of the note. The lender is known as the payee.

Notes may be issued to pay open charge accounts. On the books of the maker of the note, it is a note payable and incurs interest expense. On the books of the payee, it is a note receivable and earns interest revenue.

When the time period on the note is expressed in days, the actual number of calendar days must be counted to arrive at the maturity date or the day the note must be paid. If the time period is expressed as a number of months, then the maturity date will occur on the same date as the note only several months later.

A business or individual may borrow money from a bank or other financial institutions. When borrowing money, there are two basic types of notes: interest-bearing and non-interest-bearing. With an interest-bearing note, the borrower receives the principal amount and the interest is paid with the principal on the maturity date. On a non-interest-bearing note, the lender withholds the interest at the time of the loan, which is called discounting a note. The borrower does not receive the full principal of the note at the time of the loan and must pay only the principal amount on the maturity date. A discounted or non-interest-bearing note produces a higher rate of interest and is therefore more costly and less desirable.

GLOSSARY

Bearer: Anyone in possession of a note.

Defaulted Note: A note that is not paid on the maturity date.

Discounted Note: Interest paid at time loan is granted, and borrower receives the difference between the principal and interest.

Dishonored Note: A note that is not paid on the maturity date; also known as a defaulted note.

Interest: The cost, price, or charge of using or borrowing money.

Interest-Bearing Note: Interest is paid on maturity date of note.

Interest Rate: An annual percentage on the amount of money being borrowed which is used to determine the interest.

Maker: The party or person borrowing money on a note.

Maturity Date: The day a loan must be paid.

Maturity Value: The total of the principal plus interest on a note.

Non-Interest-Bearing Note: Interest paid at time loan is granted.

Payee: The party or person loaning money.

Principal: The amount of money being borrowed, also known as the face amount.

Proceeds: The amount of money received by the borrower or maker of a discounted note.

Promissory Note: A written document made by one person to another stating the terms of a short-term loan.

Rate: Interest to be charged on a loan stated in terms of a percentage.

Simple Interest: Cost for using or borrowing money calculated on the principal or face amount of loan.

60-day, 6 Percent Method: Shortcut method of determining interest. Decimal is moved two places to the left of principal amount to obtain the interest on a 60-day, 6 percent loan. This method may also be used if the interest rate is more or less than 6 percent and/or the time is more or less than 60 days.

Time: Number of days or months before a loan is due.

QUESTIONS

A1. Give a brief definition of interest.

A2. State the basic interest formula.

A3. Explain the shortcut interest method.

A4. Give the definition of a promissory note.

A5. Define each of the following terms:

    (a) Principal   (d) Maturity date

    (b) Payee   (e) Maturity value

    (c) Maker

A6. What are the two methods used by a bank for charging interest when granting a loan.

A7. What does dishonor or default mean in regard to a promissory note?

A8. What entry is required when payment is received from a note receivable on the maturity date, plus interest?

EXERCISES

Maturity Date

A1. Determine the maturity date for each of the following:

(*a*) May 9, 30 days

(*b*) June 15, 90 days

(*c*) August 1, 40 days

(*d*) September 15, 2 months

Determining Interest

A2. What is the annual interest for the following notes?

(*a*) $1,000 at 9 percent   90   (*c*) $2,300 at 12 percent   276

(*b*) $1,500 at 10 percent   150   (*d*) $600 at 14 percent   84

A3. Using the basic interest formula, determine the amount of interest for each of the following situations:

(*a*) $5,000 at 6 percent, 90 days

(*b*) $3,500 at 9 percent, 180 days

(*c*) $1,800 at 8 percent, 90 days

(*d*) $750 at 10 percent, 60 days

A4. Using the 6 percent, 60-day method, determine the interest for each of the following situations:

(*a*) $3,500 at 9 percent, 60 days

(*b*) $1,800 at 8 percent, 90 days

(*c*) $2,000 at 9 percent, 60 days

(*d*) $750 at 12 percent, 90 days

Journalizing Entries for Notes Receivable

A5. Century Supply is holding a 10 percent, 60-day note received from Tardy Construction Company (in payment on account) for $3,000. Give the journal entries required to record the transactions for:

(*a*) Receipt of note

(*b*) Note honored on maturity date

(*c*) Note is dishonored

Journalizing Entries for Notes Payable

A6. Edray Fashions borrowed $3,000 from the bank on a 90-day loan at 12 percent. Give the journal entries required to record the receipt of the money and the payment of the note assuming:
(*a*) The interest was paid on the maturity date.
(*b*) The interest was deducted from the amount borrowed.

Review on Notes

A7. Little Company issued a 90-day promissory note to Big Company in payment of its $4,500 account. The note is dated March 25 and the interest rate is 12 percent. Determine the following:
(*a*) Principal   (*d*) Maturity date
(*b*) Maker   (*e*) Amount of interest
(*c*) Payee   (*f*) Maturity value

PROBLEMS

Determining Maturity Date

A10-1. Determine maturity dates for the following:
(*a*) October 10, 90 days   (*d*) June 25, 50 days
(*b*) March 15, 60 days   (*e*) April 18, 80 days
(*c*) September 5, 75 days   (*f*) July 7, 40 days

Determining Interest

A10-2. Determine the annual interest for the following:
(*a*) $800 at 8 percent   (*d*) $500 at 12 percent
(*b*) $1,500 at 9 percent   (*e*) $1,250 at 10 percent
(*c*) $2,750 at 10 percent   (*f*) $4,200 at 9 percent

A10-3. Using the basic interest formula, determine the interest for the following:
(*a*) $900 at 8 percent, 90 days
(*b*) $1,200 at 9 percent, 60 days
(*c*) $3,500 at 10 percent, 1 year
(*d*) $1,800 at 9 percent, 4 months
(*e*) $4,300 at 12 percent, 90 days
(*f*) $2,500 at 9 percent, 120 days

A10-4. Using the 6 percent, 60-day method, determine the interest for the following:
(*a*) $1,800 at 6 percent, 80 days
(*b*) $1,800 at 9 percent, 90 days
(*c*) $1,800 at 9 percent, 30 days

(d) $900 at 9 percent, 60 days
(e) $2,400 at 8 percent, 60 days
(f) $3,000 at 8 percent, 90 days

Journalizing Notes Receivable

A10-5 ✔ On August 15, Sunset Sales Company accepted a $6,000, 120-day, 12 percent note from John Raymer in payment on account. Write the journal entries to record the transactions for receiving the note and payment of the note on the maturity date. Give the correct dates for each entry.

A10-6. ✔ On March 10, XYZ Company received a $8,000, 60-day, 12 percent note from DEF Company as payment on account. Write the journal entry with the correct dates to record the transactions for:
(a) Receipt of note
(b) Note honored on maturity date
(c) Note is dishonored on maturity date

Journalizing Notes Payable

A10-7. ✔ On July 25, Toco Toys borrowed $8,000 from its bank giving a 90-day, 9 percent note. The bank discounted the note. Write the journal entries to record the transactions for receiving cash and payment of the note at maturity with the correct dates.

Review on Notes

A10-8. On March 10, Sam Flock borrowed $2,500 from his bank giving a 180-day, 9 percent note. Determine the following:
(a) Principal   (c) Maturity date
(b) Interest   (d) Maturity value

A10-9. ✔ On May 10 the ABC Bank loaned Beth Driver $4,000 for 90 days at 12 percent, and the note was discounted. Determine the following:
(a) Principal   (d) Maturity date
(b) Proceeds   (e) Maturity value
(c) Interest expense

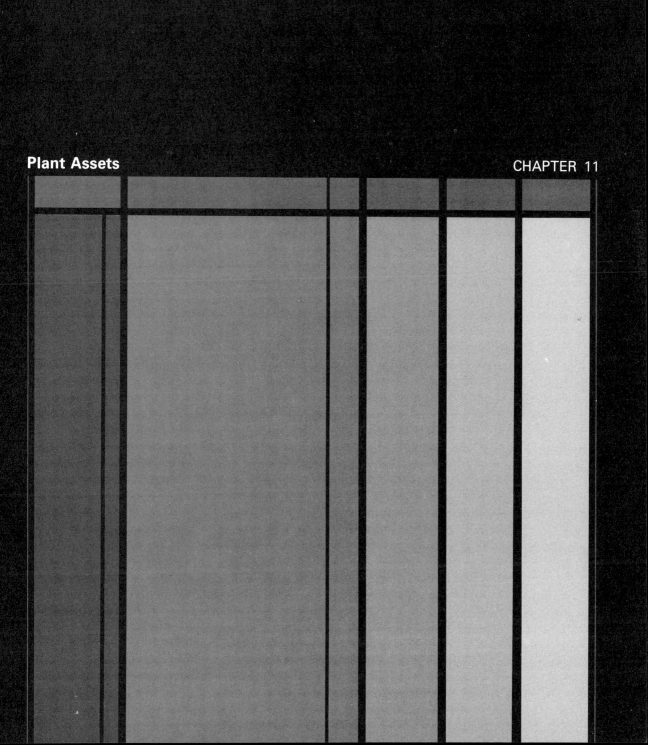

After completing this chapter, you should be able to:

1. **Give the definition of a plant asset**

2. **Explain how the cost principle applies to plant assets**

3. **Calculate the annual amount of depreciation expense using straight-line, units-of-production, sum-of-years'-digits, and double-declining balance methods**

4. **Account for a partial years depreciation using the four methods**

5. **Journalize the adjusting entries for depreciation**

6. **Give the balance sheet presentation for plant assets**

7. **Distinguish between revenue and capital expenditures**

8. **Account for the disposal and trade-in of plant assets**

9. **Define wasting assets and depletion**

Assets with a useful life of more than 1 year acquired for use in business operations for the purpose of earning revenue are called *plant assets.* These assets are referred to as the fixed, tangible or intangible assets of a business. Buildings, equipment, furniture and fixtures, machinery, automobiles, and trucks are all examples of fixed, tangible assets that are depreciated over their useful life. *Natural resources* or *wasting assets* are a form of tangible, fixed assets whose cost is allocated to future periods and charged to an expense known as depletion. Mineral deposits, oil and gas deposits, and forests are all examples of natural resources or assets that are depleted when extracted or removed from the ground. Copyrights, franchises, goodwill, leaseholds, patents, and trademarks are all examples of intangible assets and are discussed in the appendix to this chapter.

Land is a tangible asset with an unlimited life and not subject to depreciation. The Internal Revenue Service assumes that over a period of time land will probably appreciate or increase in value and any increase or possible decrease in its value will be accounted for when the land is sold.

PLANT ASSET DEPRECIATION

Although plant assets may last for several years, they will eventually wear out or become obsolete. As these assets deteriorate or wear out through use and time, the decrease in the asset value is charged to an expense known as *depreciation.* Depreciation during each fiscal period measures the amount of the asset cost or expense charged to that period. By assigning a portion of the asset cost to each fiscal period, the total cost of the asset is spread over its useful life.

PLANT ASSET COST

Under the Cost Principle, plant assets are recorded at the purchase price plus sales tax, charges for shipping, and any other costs incurred in getting the asset to the business location. Any additional costs for repairing, installing, or remodeling the asset to get it ready for use must also be charged to the asset account.

For example, assume that on January 5 of the current year a used truck was purchased at a cost of $7,500. Before the truck could be used, the engine and transmission were overhauled at a cost of $800, and four new tires were purchased for a total cost of $600. These expenditures were paid for on January 6. The journal entries and the ledger account to record the data are shown below:

Entries to record the purchase of a plant asset and the cost of getting the asset ready to use in the business

19__				
Jan.	5	Truck	7,500	
		Cash		7,500
		Purchased used truck for cash.		
	6	Truck	800	
		Cash		800
		Overhauled engine and transmission on used truck purchased January 5.		
	6	Truck	600	
		Cash		600
		Purchased four new tires for used truck purchased January 5.		

Ledger illustration of plant asset after acquisition and costs have been recorded

Truck   **No. 130**

Date			**Debit**	**Credit**	**Balance**
19__					
Jan.	1		7,500		7,500
	6		800		8,300
	6		600		8,900

The total cost of $8,900 will be used when depreciating the truck.

When a parcel of land and a building are purchased as a total package, a value must be placed on the land. The value (cost) of the land is recorded in an account separate from the Building account, because land is not subject to depreciation. All the costs involved in remodeling or getting the building ready for use would be debited to the Building account. If the building is torn down and will not be used in the business, the entire purchase price plus the cost of removing the building would be recorded in the land account.

For example, assume that on July 1 of the current year, land and a building were purchased at a total cost of $40,000. Cash of $10,000 was paid, and a 20-year mortgage was obtained on the building. The land was valued at $8,000. During July the building was remodeled at a total cost of $5,000. The work was completed on July 31, and the contractor was paid in cash. Journal entries and ledger accounts to record the original purchase and remodeling costs on the building are shown below:

Entry for allocating costs between land and building

19__				
July	1	Building	32,000	
		Land	8,000	
		Cash		10,000
		Mortgage Payable		30,000
		Purchased land and building with		
		$30,000 cash and obtained a		
		20-year mortgage on the building.		
	31	Building	5,000	
		Cash		5,000
		Paid contractor for remodeling		
		building.		

Remodeling costs are charged to building account

Building   **No. 131**

Date		Explanation	Ref.	Debit	Credit	Balance
19__ July	1			32,000		32,000
	31			5,000		37,000

The total cost of $37,000 will be used when depreciating the building.

Land   **No. 132**

Date		Explanation	Ref.	Debit	Credit	Balance
19__ July	1			8,000		8,000

Assume that on July 1 of the current year, land and a building were purchased for a total cost of $30,000. The building was not suitable for the business, but the company had to purchase the building to obtain the parcel of land. The building was torn down at a cost of $500, and the material was scrapped. The journal entries and ledger account to record the purchase and the cost of removing the building are shown below:

Purchase of land and removal of old building

19__				
July	1	Land	30,000	
		Cash		30,000
		To record the purchase of a parcel of land with a building which was dismantled and the material scrapped.		
	1	Land	500	
		Cash		500
		Cost of tearing down building and getting land ready to use.		

Land   **No. 132**

Date		Explanation	Ref.	Debit	Credit	Balance
19__ July	1			30,000		30,000
	1			500		30,500

Useful Life and Salvage Value

The *useful life* of a plant asset is the estimated number of years that a plant asset will last through use and time. Useful life of a plant asset and the salvage or scrap value is often difficult to estimate, but they must be determined before you can compute the depreciation expense for a period. Normally a company will estimate the useful life according to similar types of assets previously owned by the business. Guidelines for arriving at acceptable estimates are provided by the I.R.S. or by various trade associations.

    Salvage or *scrap value,* an estimate of what a plant asset will be worth at the end of its useful life, is also the amount that could be realized when the asset is sold or when the asset is discarded or retired from service. Estimating salvage value depends upon how much the asset is used and the maintenance and repair practice of the company. The asset cannot be depreciated below the salvage value.

DEPRECIATION METHODS

Several methods have been developed for estimating the depreciation expense of tangible plant assets. The four depreciation methods discussed in this chapter are straight-line, units-of-production, sum-of-years'-digits, and double-declining balance. These four methods are accepted by the American Institute of Certified Public Accountants for financial reporting purposes. At the time of publication of this text, the Internal Revenue Service established the Accelerated Cost Recovery System (ACRS)[1] for depreciating plant assets for income tax purposes. These depreciation methods established under ACRS are a departure from generally accepted accounting standards and are not accepted by the AICPA for financial reporting purposes.

The depreciation expense per fiscal period will vary depending upon the method selected, but the total depreciation over the asset's useful life cannot go beyond salvage value. Some depreciation methods will result in a higher expense in the early years of the asset's life, causing a significant effect on the net income for the period. Therefore, the accountant must carefully evaluate all the factors involved before selecting a method for depreciating plant assets.

Straight-Line Method

The straight-line method of depreciation allocates equal amounts of the cost of an asset to each accounting period during its estimated life. This method is used frequently because it is easy and simple to calculate. The *straight-line method* is based on the number of years of asset life as expressed in the formula

Straight-line depreciation formula

$$\frac{\text{Cost} - \text{salvage value}}{\text{years of useful life}} = \begin{array}{l}\text{amount of depreciation} \\ \text{for each year of asset} \\ \text{life } or \text{ annual} \\ \text{depreciation expense}\end{array}$$

The annual depreciation using the straight-line method for a truck costing $8,900 with an estimated useful life of 4 years and a salvage value of $500 is

$$\frac{\$8,400\ (\$8,900 - \$500)}{4\ \text{years}} = \$2,100 \text{ depreciation expense for each year}$$

or

$$\frac{100\%}{4\ \text{years}} = 25\% \times \$8,400\ (\$8,900 - \$500) = \$2,100$$

Units-of-Production Method

The *units-of-production method* allocates the cost of an asset to usage rather than years. For example, depreciation may be based on the units the asset is capable of producing, or the number of hours the asset will be operated, or

---

[1] A brief explanation of ACRS depreciation methods is on page 345 of this chapter.

the number of miles the asset will travel as expressed in the formula

* *Formula for obtaining unit cost*

$$\frac{\text{Cost} - \text{salvage value}}{\text{Units of use, hours, or miles}} = \begin{array}{c}\text{depreciation}\\\text{cost of one}\\\text{unit, hour,}\\\text{or mile}\end{array} \times \begin{array}{c}\text{no. of units,}\\\text{hours, or miles}\\\text{actually used}\\\text{during period}\end{array} = \text{depreciation expense for period}$$

For example, assume that the truck used in the previous example will be driven a total of 40,000 miles. The depreciation cost per mile is

$$\frac{\$8,400\ (\$8,900 - \$500)}{40,000\ \text{miles}} = \$0.21 \text{ depreciation cost per mile}$$

To determine the annual depreciation expense, the cost per mile ($0.21) is multiplied by the number of miles driven in that period. The calculation of the annual depreciation expense based on the number of miles the truck was driven during 4 years is shown in the following table.

Year	Cost per Mile ×	Miles	= Annual Depreciation
1	$0.21	9,000	$1,890
2	0.21	12,000	2,520
3	0.21	11,000	2,310
4	0.21	8,000	1,680
		40,000	$8,400

The straight-line and units-of-production methods allocate depreciation expense in a fairly even manner. With the straight-line method of depreciation, the amount of depreciation expense is the same for each fiscal period. With the units-of-production method, the depreciation cost is the same for each unit produced, hour used, or mile traveled, but the total depreciation expense for each period depends on how many units are produced, hours used, or miles traveled during the fiscal period.

The last two methods sum-of-year's-digits and double-declining balance are called accelerated methods of determining the annual depreciation expense. It is important to remember that you never depreciate below the estimated salvage value.

Sum-of-Years'-Digits Method

The *sum-of-years'-digits method* of depreciation (like the straight-line method) subtracts the scrap value from the cost of the asset. However, the result is multiplied by a fraction that consists of a numerator representing the number of years of asset's life remaining and a denominator representing the total of the digits for the number of years of the asset's life. Using the truck as an example, the depreciation using the sum-of-years'-

digits method is computed as follows:

$$\text{Year } 1 + \text{year } 2 + \text{year } 3 + \text{year } 4 = 10 \text{ (denominator)}$$

An easy formula may be used to obtain the denominator.

Easy formula for sum-of-years'-digits method

$$\frac{\text{Year} + (\text{year} \times \text{year})}{2} = \text{denominator}$$

$$\frac{4 + (4 \times 4)}{2} = \frac{20}{2} = 10 \text{ (denominator)}$$

The depreciation expense for year 1 can be calculated using the following figures:

Cost	−	Scrap Value	=	Amount to Be Depreciated
$8,900	−	$500	=	$8,400

$$\text{Amount to Be Depreciated} \times \frac{\text{Years of Life Remaining}}{\text{Sum of Years}} = \text{Depreciation Expense Year 1}$$

$$\$8,400 \times {}^4/_{10} = \$3,360$$

The following chart shows the calculation of the annual depreciation expense under the sum-of-years'-digits method of depreciation for the 4-year useful life of the truck that was used in the previous examples.

Sum-of-years'-digits formula illustrated

Year	Fraction ×	Amount to Be Depreciated =	Annual Depreciation
1	${}^4/_{10}$	$8,400	$3,360
2	${}^3/_{10}$	8,400	2,520
3	${}^2/_{10}$	8,400	1,680
4	${}^1/_{10}$	8,400	840
	${}^{10}/_{10}$		$8,400

The sum-of-years'-digits method provides for a larger amount of depreciation expense in the first year and a decreasing amount in the remaining years of the asset's life. This method is based on the theory that an asset depreciates more in the earlier years of its life.

Double-Declining Balance Method

A longer and more descriptive title for the double-declining balance method is double-declining balance at twice the straight-line rate. The **double-declining balance method** *does not* subtract the scrap or salvage value from the cost of the asset to obtain the amount to be depreciated. In the first year, the total cost of the asset is multiplied by a percentage that is twice the percentage of annual depreciation based on the straight-line method. In the second and remaining years, the percentage is applied to the book value of the asset. ***Book value*** represents the cost of the asset minus the accumulated depreciation.

The depreciation for the truck based on the double-declining balance method is calculated as follows:

Method of obtaining depreciation rate for double-declining balance method

$$\frac{100\%}{4\text{-year life}} = 25\% \times 2 = 50\% \text{ rate per year}$$

50% × book value (cost − accumulated depreciation)

= yearly depreciation

A chart illustrating the annual depreciation expense for the 4-year life of the truck using the double-declining balance method is shown below. (Amounts are rounded to nearest dollar.)

Illustration showing depreciation for 4 years using double-declining balance method

Year	Rate ×	Book Value (Amount to Be Depreciated)	=	Annual Depreciation	Accumulated Depreciation
1	50% ×	$8,900	=	$4,450	$4,450
		− 4,450			
2	50% ×	$4,450	=	2,225	6,675
		− 2,225			
3	50% ×	$2,225	=	1,113	7,788
		− 1,113			
4	50% ×	$1,112	=	612	8,400
		− 612			
		$ 500			

Notice that in the last year 50 percent × $1,112 = $556 instead of $612 as shown in the chart. The salvage of $500 was retained, because the asset could not be depreciated below its salvage value. Therefore, in the last year of the asset's useful life, the annual depreciation expense had to be adjusted so the total amount of accumulated depreciation expense would be equal to $8,400 ($8,900 − $500). The adjustment in the last year brought the accumulated depreciation account to $8,400 or the cost to be depreciated over the 4-year period.

DEPRECIATION FOR A PARTIAL YEAR

All the depreciation methods presented show the depreciation expense for a full year of the asset's life. Frequently a year in the life of an asset will not coincide with or be the same as the fiscal year of a business. Therefore, depreciation expense will have to be calculated for a partial year to record the correct amount of expense for the fiscal period.

Using the truck from the previous examples, assume that the truck was purchased on October 10, 19_A. If we use the straight-line method of depreciation, the depreciation expense for year 19_A would be calculated as

$$\frac{\$8,400\ (\$8,900 - \$500)}{4\ \text{years}} = \$2,100\ \text{annual depreciation}$$

$$\frac{\$2,100}{12\ \text{months}} = \$175\ \text{monthly depreciation}$$

$175 monthly depreciation
$\times$ 3 months (October, November, and December)
$= \$525$ depreciation expenses for 19_A

A chart showing the depreciation expense for the 4-year life of the truck is shown below:

Four-year depreciation chart for plant asset using straight-line method

Fiscal Year	Number of Months	$\times$	Monthly Depreciation	=	Yearly Depreciation
19_A	3*	$\times$	$175	=	$ 525
19_B	12	$\times$	175	=	2,100
19_C	12	$\times$	175	=	2,100
19_D	12	$\times$	175	=	2,100
19_E	9†	$\times$	175	=	1,575
Total amount to be depreciated over 4 years:					$8,400

* October to December.
† January through September.

Notice in the above chart that the first year of the asset's life extends beyond the company's fiscal period. With the straight-line method, each calendar month has an equal amount of depreciation. Therefore, the only difference to be accounted for in calculating the depreciation for a fiscal year is in the first year and year of disposal, or last year. However, an equal amount of depreciation expense is not present when using sum-of-years'-digits or double-declining balance methods.

If the truck was purchased on October 10, 19_A, and the sum-of-years'-digits method was used, the depreciation expense for the first year would be calculated as

$^4/_{10} \times \$8,400\ (\$8,900 - \$500)$
$= \$3,360$ depreciation expense for year 19_A

The $3,360 depreciation expense must be allocated for 3 months (October, November, and December) that the asset was used in year 19_A.

$^3/_{12} \times \$3,360 = \$840$ depreciation expense for year 19_A

The balance of $^9/_{12} \times \$3,360$, or $2,520, would be allocated to the depreciation expense for the first 9 months (January to September) of year

19_B. The depreciation for the last 3 months (October, November, and December) of year 19_B would be calculated as

$$^3/_{10} \times \$8,400 = \$2,520 \times {}^3/_{12} = \$630$$

The total depreciation expense for year 19_B would amount to

$2,520 (last 9 months of year 1) + $630 (first 3 months of year 2) = $3,150

A chart showing the depreciation expense for the 4-year useful life of the truck using the sum-of-years'-digits method is shown below:

Four-year depreciation chart for plant asset using sum-of-years'-digits method

DEPRECIATION SCHEDULE

	Asset Year			Fiscal Year		
Year	**Calculation**	**Amount**		**Calculation**	**Amount**	**Year**
1	$^4/_{10} \times \$8,400 =$	$3,360	▷ $^3/_{12} =$	$ 840	$ 840	19_A
2	$^3/_{10} \times \$8,400 =$	2,520	▷ $^9/_{12} =$	2,520	3,150	19_B
			▷ $^3/_{12} =$	630		
3	$^2/_{10} \times \$8,400 =$	1,680	▷ $^9/_{12} =$	1,890	2,310	19_C
			▷ $^3/_{12} =$	420		
4	$^1/_{10} \times \$8,400 =$	840	▷ $^9/_{12} =$	1,260	1,470	19_D
			▷ $^3/_{12} =$	210		
			▷ $^9/_{12} =$	630	630	19_E
	Amount to be depreciated:	$8,400			$8,400	

In most cases assets are acquired at times other than the beginning of the fiscal year. It is important to remember that depreciation expense must be matched to the company's fiscal year and not to the physical life of the asset. It is often helpful to construct a chart showing the date the asset was acquired and the calculation for each fiscal year's depreciation before recording the adjusting entries for depreciation expense.

ADJUSTING ENTRIES FOR RECORDING DEPRECIATION

There are two situations when depreciation should be recorded:

1. At the end of the fiscal period—month or year
2. At the time of sale or disposal of the asset

In both situations, the Depreciation Expense account is debited and the Accumulated Depreciation account is credited. Two parts of the adjusting entry may vary with the type of asset being depreciated: the *amount* and *name* of the plant asset being depreciated. For example, to record depreciation expense for the truck (purchased on January 5, 19__) at the end of 19__, using the straight-line method, the entry is as follows:

Adjusting entry for depreciation

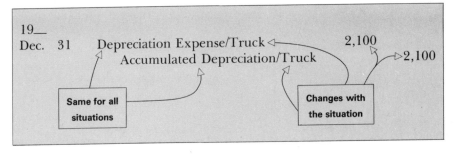

A Depreciation Expense account may be established for each individual plant asset, each group of plant assets, or one account which includes all plant assets. A small business with few plant assets may use only one Depreciation Expense account for all plant assets. However, larger companies with a wider range of plant assets may have separate Depreciation Expense accounts such as one for buildings, one for machinery, and one for trucks.

The Accumulated Depreciation account is a contra asset account which reduces or offsets the Plant Asset account. This account is not closed at the end of the accounting period but continues to increase until the asset has been fully depreciated, sold, or discarded.

BALANCE SHEET PRESENTATION

The Accumulated Depreciation account is shown on the balance sheet in the Plant Asset section as illustrated below:

Book value of each plant asset is shown on balance sheet

BOULDER SAND AND GRAVEL COMPANY
PARTIAL BALANCE SHEET
December 31, 19__

Assets			
Total Current Assets			$18,000
Plant Assets:			
Land		$ 8,000	
Building	$32,500		
Less: Accumulated Depreciation	1,600	30,900	
Machinery	$15,000		
Less: Accumulated Depreciation	1,400	13,600	
Trucks	$ 8,900		
Less: Accumulated Depreciation	2,100	6,800	
Total Plant Assets			59,300
Total Assets			$77,300

This method of presentation shows the original cost of the plant asset and the total amount of depreciation to date. The difference between the cost of the plant asset and its accumulated depreciation represents the *book value* of the asset, and *not* the market or trade-in value.

REVENUE VERSUS CAPITAL EXPENDITURES

The normal maintenance, repairs, and other expenses involved in using plant assets are classified as operating expenses and are called *revenue expenditures.* They are classified as an expense, because the benefits derived from these expenditures will be used up during the current period, and they should be matched with the revenue earned for the period in arriving at net income. Normal maintenance means keeping an asset in its standard or normal operating condition without extending its original useful life. To oil a machine at regular intervals, replace a seal, or clean the filters is considered routine maintenance. These expenditures are usually debited to a Maintenance & Repair Expense account.

Major repairs, improvements, or additions to a plant asset that either increase its useful life and/or increase its output or capacity are called *capital expenditures.* Capital expenditures are normally debited to the asset account. For example, replacing old wiring and plumbing in a building, replacing a worn-out motor with one of higher speed and capacity in a piece of equipment to achieve greater production, or replacing an old roof on a building that will last longer than the original roof are called capital expenditures. Capital expenditures are added to the cost of the plant asset and depreciated over the remaining or increased useful life of the asset.

DISPOSING OF PLANT ASSETS

Assets may be disposed of by discarding, selling, or trading them in for a new asset. When accounting for the disposal of a plant asset, the asset and Accumulated Depreciation account must be removed from the accounting records.

Regardless of how an asset is disposed of, there are only three situations that exist:

1. A gain will be realized.
2. A loss will be realized.
3. No gain or loss will be realized.

The formulas to determine the gain or loss on the disposal of a plant asset are as follows:

*Formula for obtaining
gain or loss when
disposing of plant asset*

Cost − accumulated depreciation = book value

Cash received − book value = gain realized

Book value − cash received = loss realized

Discarding or Selling a Plant Asset

A plant asset discarded or sold during an accounting year requires an entry to record the depreciation expense for the period and to bring the balance of the Accumulated Depreciation account up-to-date.

One procedure frequently used is to charge depreciation from date asset was acquired to date of disposal by allocating amounts to the nearest full month. For example, if the asset was acquired or discarded before the fifteenth day of a month, the entire month would not be considered for depreciation purposes. If the asset was acquired or discarded after the fifteenth day of a month, the month would be considered for depreciation purposes. This procedure is used for all the illustrations and problems in this text.

For example, assume that Bart Cart Company, which closes its books on December 31, purchased a machine on July 7, 19_A, at a cost of $12,000. The machine had no scrap value, a 10-year useful life, and was depreciated by the straight-line method. The machine was discarded on March 25, 19_H. Before illustrating the disposal of the machine, the following information must be determined:

1. Cost: $12,000
2. Accumulated depreciation:

$$\frac{\$12,000}{10 \text{ years}} = \$1,200 \text{ annual depreciation}$$

$$\frac{\$1,200}{12 \text{ months}} = \$100 \text{ monthly depreciation}$$

Year A: 6 months × $100   = $ 600
Years B through G: 72 months × $100 =   7,200
Accumulated depreciation balance, Dec. 31, 19_G $7,800

Normally another adjusting entry for depreciation expense would not be recorded until December 31, 19_H, but since the machine was disposed of before that date, the Accumulated Depreciation account must be brought up to date. An adjusting entry for depreciation must be made before recording the disposal of the asset to ensure that the Accumulated Depreciation account has the correct balance. This is very important in determining the book value of the asset and arriving at the current net income for the period. The entry for this example is shown below:

<table>
<tr><td rowspan="2">Entry to record
depreciation on date
of disposal</td><td colspan="2">19_H
Mar. 25   Depreciation Expense/Machine   300
                  Accumulated Depreciation/Machine   300
                  To record depreciation for the first 3
                  months, January to March, of 19_H.</td></tr>
</table>

The new balance in the Accumulated Depreciation account is now $8,100 ($7,800 + $300).

Accumulated Depreciation/Machine

Date		Explanation	Ref.	Dr	Cr	Balance
19_A Dec.	31				600	600
19_B Dec.	31				1,200	1,800
19_C Dec.	31				1,200	3,000
19_D Dec.	31				1,200	4,200
19_E Dec.	31				1,200	5,400
19_F Dec.	31				1,200	6,600
19_G Dec.	31				1,200	7,800
19_H Mar.	25				300	8,100

Cost	− Accumulated Depreciation	= Book Value
$12,000 −	$8,100	= $3,900

Remember that book value represents the value of the asset on the company's accounting records and does not represent market value.

Three different examples illustrating the disposal of the machine are shown on pages 340 and 341.

**ILLUSTRATION 1
THE MACHINE
WAS SOLD FOR
$4,500 CASH**

First, compare the cash received with the book value of the machine to determine if there is a gain or loss on the disposal:

$$\begin{array}{ccc} \textbf{Cash} & - & \textbf{Book Value} = & \textbf{Gain Realized} \\ \$4,500 & - & \$3,900 = & \$600 \end{array}$$

Second, journalize the entry to (*a*) record the cash received, (*b*) remove the accumulated depreciation, (*c*) remove the old machine, and (*d*) record the gain or loss as shown below:

*Entry to record sale
of plant asset and
recognize gain*

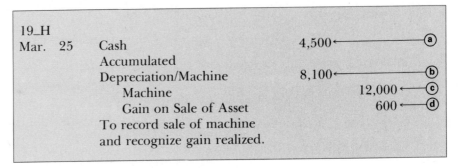

19_H
Mar. 25   Cash   4,500 — (a)
          Accumulated
          Depreciation/Machine   8,100 — (b)
            Machine   12,000 — (c)
            Gain on Sale of Asset   600 — (d)
          To record sale of machine
          and recognize gain realized.

Gain on Sale of Asset is classified as Other Revenue and appears at the bottom of the income statement under Net Operating Income.

**ILLUSTRATION 2
THE MACHINE
WAS SOLD FOR
$3,500 CASH**

$$\begin{array}{ccc} \textbf{Book Value} & - & \textbf{Cash} = & \textbf{Loss Realized} \\ \$3,900 & - & \$3,500 = & \$400 \end{array}$$

The journal entry to record the above information is shown below:

*Entry to record sale
of plant asset and
recognize loss*

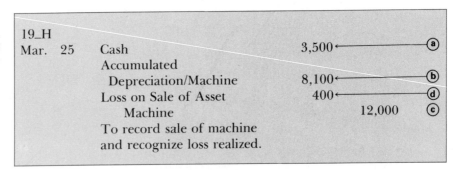

19_H
Mar. 25   Cash   3,500 — (a)
          Accumulated
            Depreciation/Machine   8,100 — (b)
          Loss on Sale of Asset   400 — (d)
            Machine   12,000 — (c)
          To record sale of machine
          and recognize loss realized.

Loss on Sale of Asset is classified as Other Expense and appears at the bottom of the income statement under Other Revenue.

**ILLUSTRATION 3
THE MACHINE
WAS SOLD FOR
$3,900 CASH**

$$\begin{array}{ccc} \textbf{Book Value} & - & \textbf{Cash} = & \textbf{Gain or Loss} \\ \$3,900 & - & \$3,900 = & 0 \end{array}$$

The journal entry to record this information is:

<table>
<tr><td>*Sale of plant asset at book value*</td><td>

19_H
Mar. 25 Cash 3,900
        Accumulated Depreciation/Machine 8,100
          Machine 12,000
        To record sale of machine for its
        book value.

</td></tr>
</table>

To illustrate the income statement presentation for Other Revenue and Other Expense using Illustrations 1 and 2, assume that the net operating income for the Bart Cart Company amounted to $21,000. A partial income statement is shown below:

Any gain or loss on sale of asset is shown on income statement

BART CART COMPANY
PARTIAL INCOME STATEMENT
For Year Ended December 31, 19_H

Net Operating Income		$21,000
Other Revenue:		
Gain on Sale of Assets	$600	
Other Expense:		
Loss on Sale of Assets	400	200
Net Income		$21,200

Trading in Plant Assets

When acquiring a new plant asset, usually the old asset is traded in and credit is received as part of the cost of the new asset. In accounting for trade-ins, there are two methods:

1. Recognition of loss called the **list-price method.** (Loss is realized when trade-in allowance is less than book value and the loss is material in amount.)
2. Nonrecognition of gain or loss called the **income tax method.**

For example, assume that a van was purchased at a cost of $4,500, and when it had been depreciated in the amount of $4,000, it was traded in for a new van. The book value of the old van at the time of the trade-in amounted to $500 ($4,500 – $4,000). Three examples to illustrate the recognition of a loss, the nonrecognition of a loss, and the nonrecognition of a gain realized at the time the old van was traded for a new van are shown below:

EXAMPLE 1: RECOGNITION OF LOSS Assume that the old van was traded in on a new van with a list price of $6,500, and the company paid cash of $6,400, receiving a trade-in allowance of $100 for the old van. A loss of $400 was realized as follows:

$$\text{Book Value} - \text{Trade-in Allowance} = \text{Loss Realized}$$
$$\$500 \quad - \quad \$100 \quad = \quad \$400$$

The entry to record the trade-in recognizing the loss is

Loss recognized on trade-in of plant asset

Van (New)	6,500	
Accumulated Depreciation/Van (Old)	4,000	
Loss on Trade-in of Asset	400	
Van (Old)		4,500
Cash		6,400
To record trade-in of van and the recognition of a realized loss amounting to $400.		

EXAMPLE 2: NONRECOGNITION OF LOSS

Using the data from Example 1, assume that the loss was not recognized (income tax method). The cost of the new van is recorded at its list price less the trade in allowance and plus the book value of the old asset as shown below.

$$\text{List Price} - \text{Trade-in Allowance} + \text{Book Value} = \text{Cost of New}$$
$$\$6,500 \quad - \quad \$100 \quad + \quad \$500 \quad = \quad \$6,900$$

or

$$\text{List Price} + \text{Loss on Trade} = \text{Cost of New}$$
$$\$6,500 \quad + \quad \$400 \quad = \quad \$6,900$$

The entry to record the trade-in with no recognition of the loss is

No recognition of loss realized on trade-in of plant asset

Van (New)	6,900	
Accumulated Depreciation/Van (Old)	4,000	
Van (Old)		4,500
Cash		6,400
To record trade-in of van with no recognition of $400 realized loss.		

EXAMPLE 3: NONRECOGNITION OF GAIN

Assume that the old van was traded in on a new van with a list price of $6,500, and the company paid cash of $5,600, receiving a trade-in allowance of $900 for the old van. A gain of $400 was realized as shown:

$$\text{List Price} - \text{Trade-in Allowance} + \text{Book Value} = \text{Cost of New Asset}$$
$$\$6,500 \quad - \quad \$900 \quad + \quad \$500 \quad = \quad \$6,100$$

or

$$\text{List Price} - \text{Gain on Trade} = \text{Cost of New}$$
$$\$6,500 \quad - \quad \$400 \quad = \quad \$6,100$$

The entry to record the trade-in with no recognition of gain is

Van (New)	6,100	
Accumulated Depreciation/Van (Old)	4,000	
Van (Old)		4,500
Cash		5,600
To record trade-in of old van with no recognition of $400 gain realized on trade.		

The Accounting Principles Board (APB) has ruled that any gain realized on the trade-in of a plant asset should not be recorded in the accounting records. Therefore, the gain decreases cost of the new asset, resulting in a decrease in the amount of depreciation expense recorded in the accounting records during its useful life.

POINTS TO REMEMBER

Remember:

1. When a realized loss is material in amount (Example 1), loss is recognized, and the new asset is recorded at its list price
2. When loss is not material in amount, the income tax method is used (Example 2), and loss is not recognized
3. When a trade-in results in a gain (Example 3), the income tax method is used because gains are not recognized by the APB and gains or losses are not recognized by the IRS

The IRS requires everyone to use the income tax method of recording the trade-in of a plant asset for tax purposes. This tax rule applies only to the trade-in of a plant asset and does not apply to the discarding or sale of a plant asset.

EFFECT OF TRADE-IN METHOD ON YEARLY DEPRECIATION

The method of recording the cost of a new asset has an effect on the amount of depreciation expense to be recorded each year during the useful life of the asset. For example, assume that the trade-in of the van illustrated in Examples 1, 2, and 3 had a useful life of 4 years, salvage value of $500, and the straight-line method of depreciation was used in determining the amount of depreciation expense for each year. The yearly depre-

Computation of yearly depreciation for plant asset acquired through trade-in of old asset

ciation expense (cost − salvage ÷ life) for each example is as follows:

EXAMPLE 1 $\dfrac{\$6,500 \text{ cost} - \$500 \text{ salvage}}{4\text{-year life}} = \$1,500$ yearly depreciation

EXAMPLE 2 $\dfrac{\$6,900 \text{ cost} - \$500 \text{ salvage}}{4\text{-year life}} = \$1,600$ yearly depreciation

EXAMPLE 3 $\dfrac{\$6,100 \text{ cost} - \$500 \text{ salvage}}{4\text{-year life}} = \$1,400$ yearly depreciation

NATURAL RESOURCES

Natural resources are recorded at cost and are classified as Plant Assets. These resources are referred to as "wasting assets," because as they are removed from their natural state, the natural resource decreases in value. Some examples of natural resources are forests, gas and oil deposits, and mineral deposits (coal, copper, iron ore, etc.). Removal of the natural resource for use is known as *depletion* and the amount removed is debited to the Depletion Expense account and credited to the Accumulated Depletion account. Natural resources appear in the Plant Asset section of the balance sheet with other depreciable assets and the Accumulated Depletion account is shown as a deduction to the natural resource (asset) account.

For example, assume that the mineral rights to an oil well estimated to have a capacity of producing 1,000,000 barrels of oil was purchased for $500,000. To determine the amount of depletion expense, the unit cost (barrel, ton, etc.) is determined and the unit cost is multiplied by the number of units produced during the accounting period. Using the oil well purchased for $500,000 as an example, the unit cost would amount to $0.50 per barrel ($500,000 cost/1,000,000 estimated barrels). The depletion expense for the first year based on a production of 100,000 barrels would amount to $50,000 (100,000 barrels × $0.50 per barrel). The adjusting entry to record depletion would require a debit to the Depletion Expense account and a credit to the Accumulated Depletion account for $50,000 as shown in the following entry:

Adjusting entry for recording depletion of a natural resource

Dec. 31	Depletion Expense/Oil Well	50,000	
	Accumulated Depletion/Oil Well		50,000
	To record depletion expense for the production of 100,000 barrels of oil for the period at $0.50 per barrel.		

The Accumulated Depletion account is classified as a contra plant asset account and would be shown on the balance sheet as a deduction to the corresponding plant asset account as shown below:

Plant Assets:		
Oil Well	$500,000	
Less: Accumulated Depletion	50,000	$450,000

DEPRECIATION METHODS ESTABLISHED BY THE ECONOMIC RECOVERY ACT OF 1981

The Economic Recovery Act of 1981 is one of the biggest tax cut bills to be passed by Congress. This act provided for a reduction in taxes that were effective in 1981 and 1982 for business and for individuals. Some of the provisions of the act provided for tax reductions to be phased in over a period of several years.

One part of this act provided for a new method of depreciating plant assets called the *Accelerated Cost Recovery System* and referred to as ACRS. This system allows a business to depreciate all its machinery, equipment, furniture, and fixtures that were purchased in 1981 or later over a shorter period of time for income tax purposes (than under the old system) using a straight-line or accelerated method of depreciation.

Prior to 1981, a business had the option of using the straight-line, sum-of-years'-digits, double-declining balance, or units of production method for depreciating plant assets for income tax purposes. However, these four methods were not completely eliminated with the passage of ACRS. Depreciable plant assets purchased prior to January 1, 1981, must continue to be depreciated for income tax purposes according to the provisions established under the old system.

Under the ACRS accelerated method, percentage tables were established by the IRS. These percentage tables cover depreciable assets purchased between January 1, 1981, and December 31, 1984, between January 1, 1985, and December 31, 1985, and for depreciable assets purchased on January 1, 1986, and thereafter.

When using the ACRS straight-line method for depreciable assets (except real property), only a half-year of depreciation is allowed in the first year the asset is acquired.

Real property purchased in 1981 or thereafter is subject to different depreciation rules for income tax purposes than the depreciation rules applying to other types of depreciable assets.

All the ACRS depreciation methods established by the IRS in 1981 for income tax purposes are discussed fully in a Federal Income Tax Accounting course.

SUMMARY

The term plant assets includes land, buildings, furniture and fixtures, machinery, trucks, and natural resources known as wasting assets. Plant assets are relatively permanent, have a useful life of more than 1 year, and have been acquired for use in the regular operation of the business. Intangible assets include patents, copyrights, franchises, leaseholds, and goodwill and are discussed in the appendix to this chapter.

Plant assets are recorded at cost, which includes the purchase price plus any other expenditures necessary to bring the asset to the proper location and get it ready to use in the business operations. All plant assets, except land, are depreciated over their estimated useful life. Depreciation expense is the term applied to tangible plant assets, and depletion expense is the term applied to natural resources.

Four depreciation methods are presented in this chapter: straight-line, units-of-production, sum-of-years'-digits, and double-declining balance. Each method has a different basis for computation resulting in a different depreciation expense for the period. The straight-line method spreads the depreciation in equal amounts over each accounting period. The units-of-production method is based on usage and allocates the depreciation expense on a unit basis depending on the asset's use during the fiscal period. Two accelerated methods, sum-of-years'-digits and double-declining balance, are applied in a manner that assigns more expense in the early years of the asset's life and less expense in the later years.

Additional expenditures for plant assets during their life are classified as revenue or capital expenditures. Revenue expenditures are assumed to benefit only the current accounting period. These revenue expenditures maintain plant assets in their normal operating condition and are classified as an operating expense for the period. Capital expenditures are major improvements that increase the value or life of the asset and are added to the original cost of the asset and depreciated over the remaining or extended useful life of the asset.

Assets may be sold, discarded, or traded in for new assets. When discarding or selling a plant asset, the gain or loss realized is measured by the difference between the cash received and the book value of the old asset. The gain or loss is always recognized when discarding or selling an asset. If an asset is traded in, the new asset may be recorded by its list price if a realized loss is material in amount, or by the income tax method which does not recognize any gain or loss realized.

Natural resources or "wasting" assets consist of material obtained from the ground such as mineral deposits and forests. When the natural resource is removed from the ground, it is recorded in the accounting records as Depletion Expense.

During 1981, Congress passed the Economic Recovery Act. One part of this act provided for a new method of depreciating plant assets called the

Accelerated Cost Recovery System. Under ACRS depreciation methods, depreciable assets purchased after December 31, 1980, were eligible for a faster write-off for income tax purposes.

GLOSSARY

Accelerated Cost Recovery System: A method of depreciating plant assets purchased after December 31, 1980, for income tax purposes. Depreciation under ACRS was established by the passage of the Economic Recovery Act of 1981 and allows for a faster write-off of depreciable assets using an accelerated or straight-line method.

Book Value: The difference between the cost of a plant asset and the accumulated depreciation.

Capital Expenditure: Major repairs, improvements, or additions to an existing plant asset that either increase its useful life and/or increase its output or capacity. These expenditures are recorded in the asset account.

Depletion: When a natural resource is extracted from the ground, the asset account is decreasing in value. Writing off this portion of the cost to an expense is called depletion.

Depreciation: The term used to record a portion of the cost of a plant asset (other than natural resources) over its useful life to an expense.

Double-Declining Balance Method: A depreciation method that uses the book value of an asset multiplied by a percentage that is twice the percentage of annual depreciation based on the straight-line basis to arrive at the depreciation expense for the period.

Estimated Salvage Value: Same as salvage value.

Estimated Useful Life: Same as useful life.

Income Tax Method: A method that does not recognize any gain or loss on the trade-in of an old asset for a new asset. The new asset is recorded at a cost equal to the book value of the old asset plus the amount of cash paid or the list price of the new asset minus a gain or plus a loss realized on the trade.

List-Price Method: A method that recognizes a loss realized on the trade-in of an old asset for a new asset if it is material in amount. The new asset is recorded at its list price when the loss is recognized.

Loss on Sale of Asset: The difference between the book value of a plant asset and the cash received. The account is classified as Other Expense on the income statement.

Natural Resources: Referred to as "wasting assets," for example, mineral deposits, oil and gas deposits, and forests.

Plant Asset: A tangible or intangible asset that has a life of more than 1 year and is used in the routine operation of the business for the purpose of earning revenue.

Revenue Expenditures: An expenditure incurred for maintaining and repairing plant assets that benefit the current fiscal period. These expenditures are recorded as an expense.

Salvage Value: An estimate of the worth of a plant asset at the end of its useful life.

Scrap Value: Another term for salvage value.

Straight-Line Method: A depreciation method based on the number of years of asset life calculated by subtracting salvage value from the cost price and dividing by the useful life of asset to arrive at the depreciation expense for the period.

Sum-of-Years'-Digits Method: An accelerated depreciation method for arriving at depreciation expense for a period that subtracts salvage value from cost price. This difference is multiplied by a fraction that consists of a numerator representing the number of years of the asset's life remaining and a denominator representing the total of the digits for the number of years of the asset's life.

Units-of-Production Method: A depreciation method based on the total number of units to be used or produced or the number of hours operated or traveled to arrive at depreciation expense for a period.

Useful Life: The estimated length of time that a plant asset will last. This estimate is needed to determine the depreciation expense for the period.

Wasting Assets: Assets consisting of natural resources such as mineral deposits, gas and oil deposits, and forests.

QUESTIONS

1. Define the term plant assets and give three examples.
2. List and define the four basic methods of depreciation.
3. Explain the difference between depreciation and depletion.
4. List four items that should be charged to the cost of a plant asset.
5. Depreciation is recorded at the end of each year. When may depreciation be recorded during the year?
6. State the difference between a capital and revenue expenditure.
7. List three situations that could result from the disposal of a plant asset.
8. List two ways of recording the trade-in of plant assets and explain the difference between the two methods.

EXERCISES

Costing and Journalizing Purchase of Plant Assets

1. A company purchased a new machine for $18,000 plus sales taxes of $900, freight charges of $750, insurance costs of $200 when the machine was in transit, and installation charges amounting to $675. What is the total cost of the machinery to be recorded on the records and used for depreciation purposes?

2. Journalize the entries necessary to record the purchase of the following assets:
   (a) Purchased a used warehouse on 10 acres of land for $50,000 paying

cash of $15,000 and signing a 5-year note for the balance. The land was valued at $2,000 per acre.

(b) Acquired a parcel of land with a small building for cash of $20,000. The building was torn down (at a cost of $1,000), because the company planned to build a new warehouse on the land.

(c) Purchased machinery for $6,800, plus sales taxes of $340, shipping charges of $90, installation material costing $200, and cost of labor for installing the machine amounted to $300.

Determining Depreciation

3. On October 3, 19_A, a company acquired a machine for $25,000. The machine has a scrap value of $2,500 and a useful life of 15 years. Using straight-line depreciation, determine:

(a) Depreciation for the year 19_A.

(b) Depreciation for the year 19_B.

(c) Assume that the machine will produce 450,000 units during its useful life. During 19_A, 21,900 units were produced; during 19_B, 30,000 units were produced. Determine the depreciation expense for years 19_A and 19_B.

4. On January 12, 19_A, a company purchased a new car for one of its executives for $8,700. At the end of its useful life of 3 years, it is estimated that the car will have a trade-in value of $1,500. Determine the amount of depreciation for:

(a) Years 19_A, 19_B, and 19_C using the sum-of-years'-digits method.

(b) Assume that the car was purchased on April 5, 19_A, and the straight-line method of depreciation was used to determine depreciation. Determine the depreciation expense for years 19_A, 19_B, 19_C, and 19_D.

5. On January 10, 19_A, a company purchased a special machine for $50,000 with a useful life of 4 years and no salvage value. Using the double-declining balance method, determine the following:

(a) Depreciation expense for each of the 4 years of its life.

(b) Assuming that the machine will have a scrap value of $5,500, determine the depreciation expense for 19_D.

Journalizing Depreciation Expense

6. Journalize the entries required for:

(a) Exercise 3, Year 19_A

(b) Exercise 4, Year 19_A of part *a*

(c) Exercise 5, Year 19_D of part *b*

Journalizing Entries for Sale of Plant Asset

7. On January 5, 19_A, a company purchased a truck for $7,700 with a useful life of 6 years and a salvage value of $500. The truck was depreciated by the straight-line method for years 19_A, 19_B, and 19_C. On December 31, 19_C, the truck was sold.

(a) Journalize the entry required to record the depreciation expense for January 1 to December 31, 19_A.

(b) Journalize the entry required to record the sale of the truck on December 31, 19_C, for $4,400.

Journalizing Entries for Trade-in of Plant Assets

8. Assume that on December 31, 19_C, the truck in Exercise 7 was traded in on a new truck with a list price of $10,750.

(a) Using the income tax method, journalize the entries required on December 31, 19_C, assuming a trade-in allowance of $3,400 was received for the old truck.

(b) Journalize the entries required for the trade-in assuming the loss realized was recognized.

Revenue versus Capital Expenditures

9. Journalize the following transactions involving revenue and capital expenditures:

(a) Replaced several sections of the sidewalk in front of the office building and paid $600 cash.

(b) Installed new lights in the office building and paid $12,000 cash.

(c) Purchased four new desk calculators with a 10-year useful life for the accounting department. The calculators cost $1,200 each, a total of $4,800 which was paid for in cash.

(d) Cleaned and painted all the offices in the office building for $1,500 cash.

(e) Replaced the switch on a machine which was damaged during installation at a cost of $350 in cash.

PROBLEMS[1]

Determining Depreciation and Book Value

11-1. On January 12, 19_A, Hip Man Record Shops purchased a new van for $10,500 with a useful life of 4 years and a scrap value of $1,000.

Required

Determine the amount of depreciation expense for 19_A and 19_B using the following methods:

(a) Straight-line

(b) Sum-of-years'-digits

(c) Double-declining balance

[1] Round all amounts to the nearest dollar.

11-2. On January 5, 19_A, the Raylite Equipment Company acquired special equipment for $6,000 with a useful life of 10 years and a salvage value of $500.

Required

Using the sum-of-years'-digits method, determine for 19_A, 19_B, and 19_C:
(*a*) The annual depreciation expense
(*b*) The accumulated depreciation on December 31
(*c*) The book value of the equipment on December 31

11-3. Assume that the equipment in Problem 11-2 is depreciated by the double-declining balance method.

Required

Determine for 19_A, 19_B, and 19_C:
(*a*) The annual depreciation expense
(*b*) The accumulated depreciation on December 31
(*c*) The book value of the equipment on December 31

11-4. On June 22, 19_A, Puncture Tire Company purchased a new retreading machine for $40,000 plus $600 freight charges and $1,400 for installation. It was estimated that the new machine would have a useful life of 5 years and a salvage value of $3,000.

Required

Prepare a schedule showing the depreciation expense for 19_A and 19_B under each of the following methods:
(*a*) Straight-line.
(*b*) Units-of-production, assuming a total operating life of 30,000 hours. Actual hours used were 3,500 in 19_A and 5,500 in 19_B.
(*c*) Sum-of-years'-digits.
(*d*) Double-declining balance.

Journalizing Purchases and Depreciation of Plant Assets

11-5. On March 28, 19_A, Fantasy Sales purchased a store on 2 acres of land for $75,000 cash. The land was valued at $15,000. The store had a useful life of 25 years and a salvage value of $6,000.

Required

(*a*) Journalize the entry required on March 28, 19_A.
(*b*) Journalize the adjusting entry to record the depreciation expense for December 31, 19_A and 19_B using the straight-line method.
(*c*) Give the balance sheet presentation on December 31, 19_B.

11-6. On January 1, 19_A, Sport-Lite Company purchased lights for the parking lot with a special automatic switch for $25,000. The lights had an estimated life of 100,000 hours and a salvage value of $1,000. During the first year, the lights were used for 20,000 hours; during the second year, the lights were used for 25,000 hours.

Required

(a) Journalize the depreciation expense for year 19_A.
(b) Journalize the depreciation expense for year 19_B.
(c) Give the balance sheet presentation on December 31, 19_B.

Sale and Trade-in of Plant Assets

11-7. On April 12, 19_A, Lance Drilling Company purchased a new truck for $9,800 with a useful life of 6 years and a salvage value of $800. The truck was depreciated under the straight-line method.

Required

Journalize the entries required to record the sale or trade-in of the truck based on each of the following transactions:

(a) Sold the truck at the end of 19_E for $3,200.
(b) Sold the truck at the end of its useful life for $500 cash.
(c) On April 12, 19_C, the truck was traded in for a new truck with a list price of $15,700, receiving a trade-in allowance of $6,000. (The loss is recognized.)
(d) Assume the same facts as in item c and record the transaction using the income tax method.

11-8. On January 10, 19_A, Crunch Manufacturing Company purchased a new punch press for $20,000 with a useful life of 4 years and a salvage value of $2,000. The press will be depreciated by the double-declining balance method.

Required

(a) Prepare a schedule showing the depreciation expense, accumulated depreciation, and book value for each of the 4 years.
(b) Journalize the entry required to record the trade-in of the machine on January 2, 19_D, on a new machine with a list price of $37,000. The company received $2,200 trade-in allowance on the old machine. (Loss is recognized.)
(c) Assume the same facts given in item b, and record the transaction using the income tax method.

Review Problem for Depreciation, Sale, and Trade-in of Plant Assets

11-9. On January 14, 19_A, Zany Products Company acquired a copying machine for $3,500. The machine had a useful life of 6 years and a trade-in value of $500.

Required

(*a*) Prepare a schedule showing the depreciation expense, accumulated depreciation, and the book value for 19_A, 19_B, and 19_C using the straight-line method.

(*b*) Journalize the entries required for each of the following unrelated assumptions:

1. The machine was sold on October 5, 19_D, for $1,500.
2. The machine was traded in at the end of 19_D for a new model with a list price of $4,700. A trade-in allowance of $1,200 was received. (Loss is recognized.)
3. Using the information given in item 2, journalize the entry assuming the income tax method was used.

Revenue versus Capital Expenditures

11-10. Journalize the following cash transactions involving revenue and capital expenditures. (Use June 30 of the current year for the date.)

(*a*) Installed a new motor on a machine for $2,500. The new motor will increase the production of the machine.

(*b*) Replaced several shingles on the roof that had blown away during a windstorm, $80.

(*c*) Removed and replaced the platform and lift on the truck for a total cost of $3,750.

(*d*) Purchased a new pocket calculator for the purchasing department for $85. The calculator has a useful life of 3 years.

(*e*) Purchased a new electronic cash register with a useful life of 10 years, $4,200.

(*f*) Replaced damaged wiring and a switch box located in the store room of the office building for $150.

Chapter 11 Appendix:

Intangible Assets

After completing this appendix, you should be able to:

1. **Give the definition of intangible assets**

2. **Present intangible assets properly on the balance sheet**

3. **List the intangible assets that have a limited life and state how their costs may be amortized**

4. **List the intangible assets that have an unlimited life**

Intangible assets are noncurrent items of value that are owned by a business but have few, if any, physical properties. They are recorded at cost and are represented by documents that describe the particular asset. Examples of intangible assets are copyrights, franchises, goodwill, leaseholds, patents, trade names, and trademarks. Most intangible assets have a limited life, and their cost is allocated to the fiscal period by a process known as *amortization*, which is similar to depreciation. Goodwill, trademarks, and trade names are examples of intangible assets not subject to amortization for tax purposes because they have an unlimited life.

Amortizing the cost of an intangible asset requires a debit to Amortization Expense and a credit to the Intangible Asset account. A contra account is not maintained for intangible assets. Therefore, the balance shown in the Intangible Asset account represents the unamortized cost.

BALANCE SHEET PRESENTATION

Intangible assets are listed on the balance sheet as the last group of assets and are shown in the condensed partial balance sheet below:

Intangible assets are the last group of assets shown on the balance sheet

COOL POP BEVERAGE COMPANY
PARTIAL BALANCE SHEET
December 31, 19__

Assets		
Total Current Assets		$ 13,000
Total Long-term Investments		25,000
Total Plant Assets		230,000
Intangible Assets:		
Copyrights	$30,000	
Patents	5,000	
Trademarks	50,000	
Total Intangible Assets		85,000
Total Assets		$353,000

COPYRIGHT

A *copyright* is issued by the U.S. government and gives the owner the sole right to publish or have published a literary or artistic piece of work. A copyright runs for the life of the author and 50 years thereafter.

Obtaining a copyright is usually not very costly; therefore the cost may be expensed in the year in which it was acquired. However, purchasing a copyright may be costly and would require the cost to be amortized.

FRANCHISE

A *franchise* is an exclusive right to make and/or sell a product under the terms of a franchise agreement. A franchise may be issued by the federal government, a state government, or a private company. When a franchise is purchased and the right is given for a specific period of time, the cost is amortized over the life of the agreement. If the franchise has an unlimited life, the cost would not be amortized; the cost of the franchise would remain on the accounting records indefinitely.

GOODWILL

Goodwill is created only when a business is purchased for more than the book value of its assets. The term *goodwill* represents the amount paid in excess of the book value of the assets. The purchaser recognizes the ability of the company to earn income greater than the normal income earned by other businesses in the industry and therefore is willing to pay more for the business. Many factors are taken into consideration when determining the amount to be paid for goodwill, such as outstanding service and customer relations, management techniques and competent employees, excellent credit rating and reputation, or any other factor that make the company unique. The amount that is paid by the buyer for goodwill is negotiated at the time of purchase. Goodwill can never be recorded in the accounting records as a result of a company's own efforts.

Goodwill has a limited life and may be amortized over a period not to exceed 40 years. However, amortization of goodwill is not allowed for federal income tax purposes.

LEASEHOLD AND LEASEHOLD IMPROVEMENTS

A document called a lease contract giving the exclusive right to a lessee (one who obtains the use of property from another under a lease) to use land, buildings, or other property for a specific period of time and under specific conditions is known as a *leasehold*. When substantial advance payments have been made to obtain these rights, the amount should be debited to an asset account titled Leasehold. These advance payments are amortized over the life of the lease by debiting Rent Expense and crediting the Leasehold account. If the contract calls for monthly payments, these payments are considered to be rent and are debited to the Rent Expense account when payment is made.

Usually some type of improvement is made to leased property by a tenant to get it ready to use in the business. Buildings may be remodeled, the land resurfaced for parking or storage, or the grounds landscaped. All these costs for improving the property are debited to an asset account called *Leasehold Improvements*. These costs are amortized over the life of the improvement or term of the lease, whichever is shorter, by debiting Rent Expense or Amortization Expense and crediting the asset account Leasehold Improvements. Accounting for leases is discussed in intermediate accounting texts.

PATENTS

Patents are exclusive rights granted by the U.S. Patent Office to an owner for a period of 17 years to prevent others from producing, using, or selling an idea or invention throughout the United States. All costs of obtaining a patent including legal fees and developmental expenses are debited to the Patent account. The cost of a patent is spread over its 17-year life. If the useful life of a patent is less than 17 years, the cost may be spread over the shorter period. Spreading the cost over its useful life or 17 years is called amortizing the patent and the amount is debited to an account called Amortization Expense and credited to the Patent account.

For example, assume that a patent with a remaining life of 15 years was purchased for $2,000. It was determined that the useful life of the asset was 10 years. The adjusting entry for amortizing the patent for a 1-year period ending on December 31, 19__, is shown below:

Amortizing cost of patent

19__				
Dec.	31	Amortization Expense/Patent	200*	
		Patent		200
		To record one-tenth the purchase cost of a patent.		

* $2,000/10 years = $200.

Patents would be shown on the balance sheet at its unamortized cost, $1,800 ($2,000 − $200), because no contra accounts are maintained for intangible assets. The Amortization Expense/Patent account would be classified as an Operating/Selling Expense on the income statement.

TRADEMARK AND TRADE NAME

A *trademark* or *trade name* is a term used to identify a particular product or service. These marks or names may be registered with the U.S. Patent Office to protect their use and ownership. The cost of a trademark or trade name is usually small, but its value may increase with its use and acceptance over a period of time. However, the cost could be high if the trademark or trade name is purchased. It is difficult to determine the life of a trademark or trade name, and for that reason, it normally is not amortized.

Certain costs associated with protecting or registering the trademark or trade name are debited to the asset account. The I.R.S. allows these costs to be amortized over a period of not less than 5 years.

SUMMARY

Intangible assets are noncurrent items owned by a business, such as a copyright, franchise, goodwill, leasehold, patents, trade names, and trademarks. For federal income tax purposes, the cost of a franchise, patent, leasehold, and leasehold improvements may be amortized over their useful life or length of agreement; costs of a trademark or trade names may be amortized over a period of not less than 5 years. Spreading the costs of these assets is referred to as amortization, and they are debited to an account called Amortization Expense and credited to the Intangible Asset account.

GLOSSARY

Amortization: Spreading the cost of an intangible asset over its useful life.
Copyright: Exclusive right issued by the U.S. government giving the owner the right to publish or have published a literary or artistic piece of work.
Franchise: An agreement giving an exclusive right to make and/or sell a product.
Goodwill: Amount paid in excess of the value of assets when purchasing a business.
Leasehold: An exclusive right to use land, buildings, or other property.
Leasehold Improvements: Improvements made by a tenant to leased property.
Patent: Exclusive right granted by U.S. Patent Office to the owner of the patent to use, produce, or sell an idea or invention.
Trademark/Trade Name: Term used to identify a particular product or service.

QUESTIONS

A1. List two types of intangible assets that may be amortized over a 5-year period for federal income tax purposes.

A2. Name one intangible asset that cannot be amortized for federal income tax purposes.

A3. What account is debited for improvements made by a tenant on leased property?

A4. What account is debited for the amortization of an advance payment on leased property?

EXERCISES

Balance Sheet Presentation

A1. Give the balance sheet presentation for the following assets:
(a) Patents: Cost, $5,000; $1,200 amortized to date
(b) Leasehold Improvements: Cost, $8,000; $2,000 amortized to date

Journalizing Adjusting Entries

A2. Journalize the adjusting entry required for the following:
(a) Leasehold Improvements: Cost, $12,000; 20-year useful life; life of lease, 10 years
(b) Patent: Cost, $8,000; 8-year useful life

PROBLEMS

Lease and Leasehold Improvements

A11-1. On January 2, of the current year, Ginger Spice Company obtained a 10-year lease on a building and parking lot for its business. The lease called for a $5,000 advance payment and $400 rent per month, payable the first day of each month. Improvements were made to the building by the Ginger Spice Company before it occupied the premises. The company paid $6,000 cash on January 10 to cover the cost of the improvements which had a useful life of 15 years.

Required

Prepare the journal entries for:
(a) January 2, of the current year
(b) January 10, of the current year
(c) Adjusting entries on December 31, of the current year

Patents

A11-2. On July 1, 19_A, the Crater Space Corporation purchased a patent for $7,500 with an estimated useful life of 5 years.

Required

Journalize the entries for:
(*a*) July 1, 19_A.
(*b*) Adjusting entry, December 31, 19_A.
(*c*) Adjusting entry, December 31, 19_B.
(*d*) What amount will appear on the balance sheet as the book value of the patent on December 31, 19_B?

A11-3. On November 1, 19_A, CosWell Manufacturing Company obtained a 17-year patent for a special golf glove from the U.S. Patent Office. The costs incurred in developing the patent amounted to $9,600. It was estimated that the patent had a useful life of 10 years.

Required

(*a*) Journalize adjusting entry required on December 31, 19_A, and 19_B.
(*b*) Give the balance sheet presentation for the patent on December 31, 19_B.

Inventories

After completing this chapter, you should be able to:

1. **Discuss the four basic methods of valuing the ending inventory, and compute the cost of the ending inventory by using each method**

2. **Explain the reasons for estimating ending inventory and the two methods available for determining the inventory cost without taking a physical count of the merchandise on hand**

3. **Distinguish between the perpetual and periodic systems for maintaining inventory records**

4. **Journalize the entries for clearing beginning inventory and recording the ending inventory under the periodic system**

5. **State the entries required for recording merchandise purchased for resale under the perpetual and periodic systems**

6. **Discuss the effect of errors on inventory in the income statement and balance sheet**

Merchandise inventory was discussed in Chapters 6 and 7 and defined as the merchandise on hand at the end of the accounting period representing goods that will eventually be sold to customers. The cost of the merchandise on hand and the cost of the goods that are sold must be obtained to match the appropriate cost against revenue to determine the proper net income for the period. This chapter will discuss the various methods available for valuing ending inventory by using either the perpetual or periodic system of maintaining inventory records.

INVENTORY VALUATION

When merchandise is purchased for resale, the purchase is recorded at the cost price less any cash discount given for prompt payment. The cost price of the merchandise includes any shipping costs paid by the purchaser, insurance expense incurred in shipping or storing the goods, plus any taxes.

Although the initial purchase of merchandise is recorded at its cost price, there are several methods available to the accountant for valuing the merchandise that has not been sold at the end of the accounting period. The method selected is important because the cost of the ending inventory will affect the cost of goods sold and net income shown on the income statement and the ending inventory shown as a current asset on the balance sheet.

BASIC PRICING METHODS

When merchandise is purchased during an accounting period, the prices usually vary with each purchase. Therefore, it is difficult for the accountant to determine the cost of the merchandise sold and the cost of merchandise on hand at the end of the period. Several methods are available to help the accountant determine the cost of the ending inventory. A method of pricing the ending inventory should be selected that will provide the business with the best measurement of net income for the period and the best method for tax purposes.

Four methods used frequently for valuing the ending inventory are the specific invoice; first-in, first-out (FIFO); last-in, first-out (LIFO); and weighted average, as discussed in the following paragraphs.

Specific Invoice

The *specific invoice method* for valuing inventory requires the recording of detailed information for each purchase transaction so that merchandise on hand at the end of an accounting period can be identified with a specific order. Each purchase may be assigned a special number, or a special tag may be placed on each specific order so that each sale can be identified to the related invoice. In this way, the merchandise on hand may be identified to a specific order and the actual cost may be obtained from the purchase invoice. The specific invoice method is best for a company that purchases goods which are easily identified by a special serial or model number or for a company that handles a limited amount of merchandise.

This method may not be practical for a large organization that purchases a considerable amount of merchandise throughout the accounting period because of the work involved in identifying and maintaining the cost records. Although the specific invoice method provides an accurate measurement of the cost of the goods on hand and the cost of the goods sold during an accounting period, it is seldom used because of the difficulty of identifying goods and the cost involved in keeping detailed records.

As an example, assume that the E-Z Lawn Products Company uses the specific invoice method for valuing the ending inventory. During its first year in business, the following purchases of merchandise were made:

Purchase Date	Quantity	Unit Price	Total Cost
Jan. 10	50 bags	$6.00	$ 300
Apr. 20	200 bags	6.50	1,300
July 15	200 bags	6.25	1,250
Sept. 5	50 bags	6.60	330
	500 bags		$3,180

During the year, 440 bags of merchandise were sold and 60 bags were on hand at the end of the year. The 60 bags in the ending inventory could be specifically identified as 30 bags acquired on September 5 and 30 bags acquired on July 15.

The cost of the ending inventory using the specific invoice method is computed as follows:

Computation of ending inventory using specific invoice method

30 bags @ $6.60 each = $198.00
30 bags @ 6.25 each =   187.50
60 bags   = $385.50 (cost of ending inventory by specific invoice method)

First-In, First-Out

The *first-in, first-out method* or FIFO method of inventory valuation assumes that the first goods purchased are the first goods sold. Therefore, the merchandise on hand at the end of the period would consist of the last or most recent purchase valued at the current or last purchase price.

Using the data given for the E-Z Lawn Products Company, the ending inventory under the FIFO method would be computed as follows:

Purchase Date	Quantity	Unit Price	Total Cost		
Jan. 10	50 bags	$6.00	$ 300	Sold 50	
Apr. 20	200 bags	6.50	1,300	Sold 200 } 440	
July 15	200 bags	6.25	1,250	Sold 190	
				On Hand 10 } 60	
Sept. 5	50 bags	6.60	330	On Hand 50	
	500 bags		$3,180		

The 500 bags of merchandise available for sale, less the 440 bags sold, left 60 bags of merchandise on hand at the end of the fiscal period. These 60 bags would be priced as follows using the FIFO method:

Computation of ending inventory using FIFO method

50 bags @ $6.60 = $330.00
10 bags @ 6.25 =   62.50
60 bags   = $392.50 (cost of ending inventory by FIFO method)

Last-In, First-Out

The *last-in, first-out method* or LIFO method of inventory valuation assumes that the last goods purchased are the first ones sold. The goods that remain unsold at the end of the period would consist of goods in the beginning inventory and/or the first goods purchased. When using the LIFO inventory pricing method, the first items purchased are assumed to be the last items sold; therefore, the ending inventory would be valued at the earliest or first purchase price.

Using the data given for the E-Z Lawn Products Company, the ending inventory under the LIFO method would be computed as follows:

Purchase Date	Quantity	Unit Price	Total Cost		
Jan. 10	50 bags	$6.00	$ 300	On Hand 50	60
Apr. 20	200 bags	6.50	1,300	On Hand 10	
				Sold 190	
July 15	200 bags	6.25	1,250	Sold 200	440
Sept. 5	50 bags	6.60	330	Sold 50	
	500 bags		$3,180		

The 60 bags of merchandise in the ending inventory would be priced under the LIFO method as follows:

Computation of ending inventory using LIFO method

50 bags @ $6.00 = $300
10 bags @ 6.50 = 65
60 bags = $365 (cost of ending inventory by LIFO method)

Weighted Average

The *weighted average method* of valuing inventory recognizes that prices will vary as merchandise is purchased during the fiscal period. Therefore, under this method the units in the ending inventory are priced at the *average unit cost* of the merchandise on hand during the *entire fiscal period*. Before computing the value of the ending inventory using the weighted average method, the average cost for one unit must be obtained and then applied to the number of units in the ending inventory.

Using the data given for the E-Z Lawn Products Company, the ending inventory under the weighted average method is computed as follows:

Purchase Date	Quantity	Unit Price	Total Cost
Jan. 10	50 bags	$6.00	$ 300
Apr. 20	200 bags	6.50	1,300
July 15	200 bags	6.25	1,250
Sept. 5	50 bags	6.60	330
	500 bags		$3,180

The average unit cost for the 500 bags of merchandise purchased during the year is shown below.

Computation of ending inventory using weighted average method

$$\frac{\$3,180 \text{ total cost}}{500 \text{ bags purchased}} = \$6.36 \text{ average unit cost}$$

When the average unit cost is obtained, the cost of the ending inventory for the weighted average method is computed as follows:

60 bags × $6.36 = $381.60 (cost of ending inventory by weighted average method)

ESTIMATED SYSTEMS

Sometimes the accountant must estimate the cost of the inventory without taking a physical count of the quantity of goods on hand. For example, when inventory is destroyed or lost due to fire, flood, wind, and theft, or when the cost of the inventory is needed for preparing interim financial statements and a physical count would be time-consuming and costly, an estimate is necessary.

There are two methods available for estimating the inventory cost.

1. The *retail method* is used primarily by chain and department stores, as well as by wholesale establishments. To estimate the cost of inventory under the retail method, a business must have records available for the cost and selling price of merchandise purchased and returned as well as the sales price of all merchandise sold during the accounting period.
2. The *gross profit method* is frequently used for estimating the cost of inventory when merchandise has been lost or destroyed. Under the gross profit method, the current accounting records and the records for the past few years are used to estimate the ending inventory.

Retail Method

Under the **retail method,** the cost price and retail price of goods available for sale must be used to obtain a ratio of cost to selling price. The ratio is then applied to the ending inventory at retail price (retail price of goods available for sale less the net sales) to obtain the ending inventory at cost price. To estimate the cost of the ending inventory under the retail method, set up a Cost Price column and a Retail Price column and record the following information in both columns unless instructed otherwise.

1. Beginning inventory
2. Add purchases for the year
3. Add transportation charges only to the Cost Price column and then subtotal both columns
4. Subtract purchase returns from the subtotal to arrive at the estimated goods available for sale
5. Subtract the net sales for the period from the estimated goods available

for sale at retail price to obtain the estimated ending inventory at retail price

6. Divide the cost price of goods available for sale by the retail price to obtain the cost to retail ratio
7. Multiply the estimated ending inventory at retail price by the cost-to-retail ratio (Step 6) to obtain the estimated ending inventory at cost price

Estimating ending inventory using retail method

The data below shows the estimated ending inventory on December 31, 19__, for the Last-Stop Company using the retail method.

	Cost Price	Retail Price
① Inventory, Jan. 1, 19__	$ 42,000	$ 50,400
② Add: Purchases	68,400	136,600
③ Transportation In	2,220	
Total	$112,620	$187,000
④ Less: Purchase Returns	1,500	1,800
Estimated Goods Available For Sale	$111,120	$185,200
⑤ Less: Net Sales		160,200
Estimated Inventory at Retail, Dec. 31, 19__		$ 25,000
⑥ Cost-to-Retail Ratio ($111,120/$185,200) = 60%		
⑦ Estimated Inventory at Cost ($25,000 × 0.60) = $ 15,000		

Gross Profit Method

To obtain a reasonable estimate of the cost of the ending inventory under the **gross profit method,** the gross profit percentage of sales must be fairly stable for the past few years. This method is described in the following six steps:

1. Add the cost of the beginning inventory to the cost of purchases plus the transportation charges and obtain a subtotal.
2. Subtract the purchase returns from the subtotal (Step 1) to obtain the cost of goods available for sale.
3. Obtain the net sales by subtracting sales returns from gross sales.
4. Multiply net sales by the gross profit percentage given to obtain the estimated gross profit.
5. Subtract the estimated gross profit from net sales to obtain the cost of goods sold.
6. Subtract the cost of goods sold (Step 5) from the goods available for sale (Step 2) to obtain the estimated ending inventory at cost price.

The illustration on page 368 for the Rolls Aero Company shows the estimated ending inventory using the gross profit method and assuming a 30 percent average gross profit rate.

Estimating ending inventory using gross profit method

Inventory, Jan. 1, 19___		$ 18,000	
Add: Purchases		62,200	
Transportation In		2,000	
① Total		$ 82,200	
Less: Purchase Returns		2,200	
② Cost of Goods Available for Sale.			$80,000
Gross Sales		$112,000	
Less: Sales Returns		12,000	
③ Net Sales		$100,000	
④ Less: Estimated Gross Profit ($100,000 × 0.30) . . .		30,000	
⑤ Cost of Goods Sold			70,000
⑥ Estimated Inventory at Cost Price, Dec. 31, 19___ . .			$10,000

The gross profit method is often used by the accountant as a check on the physical count of the ending inventory.

PERPETUAL VERSUS PERIODIC INVENTORY SYSTEM

There are two systems available for maintaining the inventory records and the Cost of Goods Sold account. These two systems are known as *perpetual* and *periodic*.

Perpetual Inventory System

The *perpetual inventory system* maintains a running balance of the amount of merchandise on hand and the cost of the goods that are sold. When merchandise is purchased, the inventory account is increased; when merchandise is sold, the inventory account is decreased and the cost of the sale is recorded. At all times, the amount of merchandise on hand and the total cost of sales for the period is available. Under the perpetual system, there usually are no Purchases, Transportation In, Purchase Returns & Allowances, or Purchase Discount accounts. Any transactions requiring debits or credits to these accounts will be recorded in the Merchandise Inventory account.

Whenever merchandise is purchased and transportation charges incurred for shipping the merchandise, the Merchandise Inventory account is debited for the purchase and transportation charges and the Accounts Payable and Cash accounts are credited. To illustrate the purchase of merchandise, assume that the Plastics Company had $400 of merchandise on hand March 1, 19___. On March 5, $1,000 of merchandise was purchased from Quick Suppliers with terms of 2/10, n/30, FOB shipping point. Under the perpetual system, the following entry would be recorded when the merchandise was received and a $50 shipping cost was paid.

Inventory is debited when purchasing merchandise under perpetual system

19__			
Mar. 5	Merchandise Inventory	1,050	
	Accounts Payable/Quick Suppliers		1,000
	Cash		50
	Merchandise purchased on account and $50 paid for shipping charges.		

When merchandise is returned, the Accounts Payable account is debited and the Merchandise Inventory account is credited. If on March 10, 19__, the Plastics Company returned $100 of merchandise that was broken in shipment, and credit was given on its account, the following entry would be recorded.

Inventory is credited for returns of merchandise under perpetual system

19__			
Mar. 10	Accounts Payable/Quick Suppliers	100	
	Merchandise Inventory		100
	Returned merchandise broken in shipment and credit received on account.		

When a creditor is paid within the discount period and a cash discount given for prompt payment, the Accounts Payable account is debited and the Merchandise Inventory and Cash accounts are credited. The Plastics Company paid Quick Suppliers on March 15.

Inventory is credited for discount received for prompt payment

19__			
Mar. 15	Accounts Payable/Quick Suppliers	900	
	Merchandise Inventory		18
	Cash		882
	Record payment on account less a 2% discount received for prompt payment.		

When merchandise is sold under the perpetual inventory system, a compound entry is necessary to record the sale plus the cost of goods sold. Using the information in the above entries, assume that on March 20 the Plastics Company sold merchandise to Serv-U Sales for $1,200 on account. The merchandise was purchased at a cost of $900. The entry requires a debit to the Cost of Goods Sold and the Accounts Receivable accounts and a credit to the Sales and Merchandise Inventory accounts.

*Compound entry for sale of
merchandise under
perpetual system*

19__					
Mar.	20	Cost of Goods Sold		900	
		Accounts Receivable/Serv-U Sales		1,200	
		Merchandise Inventory			900
		Sales			1,200
		Record the sale of merchandise and the cost of the sale, plus removing the goods sold from the Inventory account.			

The effects of these transactions on the Merchandise Inventory, Sales, and Cost of Goods Sold accounts in the general ledger are shown below:

Merchandise Inventory

19__					
Mar.	1	Balance	400		400
	5		1,050		1,450
	10			100	1,350
	15			18	1,332
	20			900	432

Sales

19__					
Mar.	20			1,200	1,200

Cost of Goods Sold

19__					
Mar.	20		900		900

Under the perpetual inventory system, the Merchandise Inventory and Cost of Goods Sold accounts will always show the balance of merchandise on hand and the total cost of goods sold for the period. The general ledger accounts for the Plastics Company show $432 of merchandise on hand on March 31 and $900 as the Cost of Goods Sold for March.

At the end of the accounting period, the Cost of Goods Sold account is closed to the Income Summary account along with the other expense accounts. To illustrate the closing entries for the preceding data, assume that the other expense and revenue accounts have already been closed.

*Closing sales and cost of
goods sold*

CLOSING ENTRIES

19__					
Mar.	31	Sales		1,200	
		Income Summary			1,200
		To close the Sales account.			
	31	Income Summary		900	
		Cost of Goods Sold			900
		To close the Cost of Goods Sold account.			

This system eliminates the need for taking a physical count of the merchandise on hand at the end of the period (although a physical count is usually taken as a check on the accuracy of the Inventory account), for recording the ending inventory, and for closing the beginning inventory, Purchases, and purchase-related accounts. It also simplifies the preparation of the Cost of Goods Sold section on the income statement inasmuch as the cost of each sale is recorded at the time the sale is made. However, this system requires the maintenance of a detailed accounting system for determining the value of the inventory on hand and for determining the cost of the inventory that has been sold. A partial income statement follows:

Partial income statement using perpetual inventory system

PLASTICS COMPANY
PARTIAL INCOME STATEMENT
For Month Ended March 31, 19__

Operating Revenue:		
Sales	$1,200	
Less: Cost of Goods Sold	900	
Gross Profit		$300

Periodic Inventory System

The *periodic inventory system* does not maintain a running balance of the merchandise on hand. The Purchases account is debited whenever merchandise is purchased for resale, and the Purchase Returns & Allowances, Purchase Discount, and Transportation In accounts are used for returns, cash discounts received for prompt payment, and transportation charges incurred for shipping the merchandise. Therefore, a physical count must be taken to determine the amount of merchandise on hand at the end of the period. The cost of goods sold is not recorded each time a sale is made under the periodic system but can be computed by using the formula given in Chapter 5:

Cost of goods sold formula

Beginning inventory

+ purchases

+ transportation in

− purchase returns & allowances

− purchase discounts

= cost of goods available

− ending inventory

= cost of goods sold

Assume that the Plastics Company used a periodic system for maintaining a record of merchandise purchased for resale. The entries for March would appear as follows:

19—				
Mar.	5	Purchases	1,000	
		Transportation In	50	
		Accounts Payable/Quick Suppliers		1,000
		Cash		50
		Merchandise purchased on account and shipping costs paid in cash.		
	10	Accounts Payable/Quick Suppliers	100	
		Purchase Returns & Allowances		100
		Merchandise returned that was broken in shipment and credit received on account.		
	15	Accounts Payable/Quick Suppliers	900	
		Purchase Discounts		18
		Cash		882
		Paid account receiving 2% discount for prompt payment.		
	20	Accounts Receivable/Serv-U Sales	1,200	
		Sales		1,200
		Sold merchandise on account.		

These transactions would not affect the Merchandise Inventory or Cost of Goods Sold accounts, and the ledger accounts would not provide any information about the amount of merchandise on hand or the cost of the sales for March. A physical count would have to be taken to determine the amount of merchandise on hand on March 31.

At the end of the period, the beginning inventory, Purchases, and purchase-related accounts would have to be closed to the Income Summary account. The amount of merchandise on hand would have to be counted and an entry made to record the ending inventory.

Using the data given, the following closing entries would be journalized if the books were closed on March 31. (This information was discussed in detail in Chapter 7.)

Closing Sales, Purchases, and purchase-related accounts under periodic system

CLOSING ENTRIES

19__				
Mar.	31	Sales	1,200	
		Purchase Returns & Allowances	100	
		Purchase Discount	18	
		Merchandise Inventory (Ending)	432	
		Income Summary		1,750
		To close the Sales, Purchase Returns & Allowances, and Purchase Discount accounts and record the ending inventory.		
	31	Income Summary	1,450	
		Purchases		1,000
		Transportation In		50
		Merchandise Inventory (Beginning)		400
		To close the Purchases, Transportation In, and the beginning inventory.		

The cost of goods sold for March would be shown on the income statement as illustrated on the following partial income statement for the Plastics Company.

Partial income statement using periodic inventory system

PLASTICS COMPANY
PARTIAL INCOME STATEMENT
For Month Ended March 31, 19__

Operating Revenue:			
Sales			$1,200
Cost of Goods Sold:			
Merchandise Inventory Mar. 1, 19__		$ 400	
Purchases	$1,000		
Add: Transportation In	50		
Total	$1,050		
Less: Purchase Returns & Allowances $100			
Purchase Discount 18	118		
Cost of Purchases		932	
Cost of Goods Available		$1,332	
Less: Merchandise Inventory, Mar. 31, 19__		432	
Cost of Goods Sold			900
Gross Profit			$ 300

SUMMARY OF ENTRIES FOR PERPETUAL VERSUS PERIODIC SYSTEMS

	PERPETUAL		PERIODIC

Comparison of perpetual and periodic systems

1. Purchased merchandise on account and paid transportation costs.

	PERPETUAL			PERIODIC		
19__ Mar. 5	Merchandise Inventory	1,050		Purchases	1,000	
	Accounts Payable		1,000	Transportation In	50	
	Cash		50	Accounts Payable		1,000
				Cash		50

2. Merchandise returned and credit received on account.

10	Accounts Payable	100		Accounts Payable	100	
	Merchandise Inventory		100	Purchase Returns & Allowances		100

3. Paid account within discount period.

15	Accounts Payable	900		Accounts Payable	900	
	Merchandise Inventory		18	Purchase Discount		18
	Cash		882	Cash		882

4. Sold merchandise on account.

20	Accounts Receivable	1,200		Accounts Receivable	1,200	
	Cost of Goods Sold	900		Sales		1,200
	Sales		1,200			
	Merchandise Inventory		900			

PERPETUAL   **PERIODIC**

5. Closing entries.

19__					
Mar. 31	Sales	1,200		Sales	1,200
	Income Summary		1,200	Purchase Returns &	
				Allowances	100
				Purchase Discount	18
				Merchandise Inventory	
				(Ending)	432
				Income Summary	1,750
31	Income Summary	900		Income Summary	1,450
	Cost of Goods Sold		900	Purchases	1,000
				Transportation In	50
				Merchandise Inventory	
				(Beginning)	400

CONSISTENCY OF REPORTING—I.R.S. RULES

There are different methods available for maintaining and valuing inventory, and every company has the option of selecting the method most suitable for its business. The method selected has a direct effect on income and could result in a substantial difference in the reporting of taxable income. Therefore, once a method for valuing the inventory is selected, it may not be changed without receiving approval from the Internal Revenue Service.

The information contained in the financial statements is used by management, creditors, government agencies, and investors. These groups evaluate the past and future performance of a company for management decisions, for granting of loans or contracts, for statistical or tax reports, and for investments. Therefore, the accountant must disclose and consistently apply the method used for valuing the inventory and other items on the statements if these groups are to arrive at reliable and meaningful comparisons. If it becomes necessary for an accountant to change methods used in prior years, and approval is obtained from the I.R.S., full disclosure regarding the effect of the change on the amounts shown on the statement must be noted.

EFFECT OF ERRORS ON INVENTORY

An error in the ending inventory will affect the net income reported on the income statement and the inventory reported in the Current Asset section of the balance sheet for the current period. When the ending inventory shows more than the actual amount on hand, this will cause the cost of the goods sold to be *lower,* resulting in a *higher* net income. When the ending inventory shows less than the actual amount on hand, this will cause the cost of goods sold to be *higher,* resulting in a *lower* net income. To illustrate the overstatement or understatement of ending inventory on net income, let us use an overstated ending inventory of $632, an understated ending inventory of $232, and a correct ending inventory of $432 for the Plastics Company. A condensed income statement showing the effect of the above inventories on net income is illustrated below:

Effect of overstatement or understatement of ending inventory on net income

PLASTICS COMPANY
INCOME STATEMENT
For Month Ended March 31, 19__

	Correct Ending Inventory	Overstated Ending Inventory	Understated Ending Inventory
Operating Revenue:			
Net Sales	$1,200	$1,200	$1,200
Cost of Goods Sold:			
Cost of Goods Available for Sale	$1,332	$1,332	$1,332
Less: Merchandise Inventory, Mar. 31, 19__	432	632	232
Cost of Goods Sold	900	700	1,100
Gross Profit	$ 300	$ 500	$ 100
Operating Expenses	100	100	100
Net Income	$ 200	$ 400	$ -0-

Assume the current assets of the Plastics Company amounted to Cash, $600; Accounts Receivable, $1,200; and Prepaid Expenses, $200. A partial balance sheet showing the correct ending inventory and the effect of the overstatement and understatement of the ending inventory is illustrated below:

Effect of overstatement or understatement of ending inventory on current assets

PLASTICS COMPANY
BALANCE SHEET
March 31, 19__

	Correct Ending Inventory	Overstated Ending Inventory	Understated Ending Inventory
Current Assets:			
Cash	$ 600	$ 600	$ 600
Accounts Receivable	1,200	1,200	1,200
Merchandise Inventory	432	632	232
Prepaid Expenses	200	200	200
Total Current Assets	$2,432	$2,632	$2,232

Remember that the ending inventory of one period is the beginning inventory of the following period. Therefore, an error will affect the current financial statements and the financial statements for the next accounting period.

The effect of an error in the current period is summarized as follows:

Ending Inventory	Current Net Income
Overstated	Overstated
Understated	Understated

The effect of an error in the current period will affect the following period as follows:

Beginning Inventory	Net Income
Overstated	Understated
Understated	Overstated

Using the Plastics Company as an example, assume that in the following month sales amounted to $1,800; net purchases, $1,100; ending inventory, $200; and operating expenses, $150. The illustration below shows the effect on the income statement for the correct beginning inventory and the effect of the overstatement and understatement of the beginning inventory.

Effect of overstatement or understatement of beginning inventory on net income

PLASTICS COMPANY
INCOME STATEMENT
For Month Ended April 30, 19__

	Correct Beginning Inventory	Beginning Inventory Overstated	Beginning Inventory Understated
Operating Revenue:			
Net Sales	$1,800	$1,800	$1,800
Cost of Goods Sold:			
Mdse. Inv., Mar. 31, 19__	$ 432	$ 632	$ 232
Add: Net Purchases	1,100	1,100	1,100
Cost of Goods Avail.	$1,532	$1,732	$1,332
Less: Mdse. Inv., Mar. 31, 19__	200	200	200
Cost of Goods Sold	1,332	1,532	1,132
Gross Profit	$ 468	$ 268	$ 668
Operating Expenses	150	150	150
Net Income	$ 318	$ 118	$ 518

SUMMARY

Inventory consists of merchandise on hand at the end of the accounting period representing goods that will eventually be sold. The valuation of the inventory is important because it affects the net income on the income statement for the current and following period, and the Current Asset section of the balance sheet for the current period.

There are four different methods available for valuing the ending inventory: specific invoice; first-in, first-out (FIFO); last-in, first-out (LIFO); and weighted average. The specific invoice method requires that detailed records be kept for the inventory so that each sale can be identified as pertaining to a specific purchase. The FIFO method assumes that the first goods purchased are the first goods sold so that the ending inventory is priced at the latest purchase price. The LIFO method assumes that the last goods purchased are the first goods sold so that the ending inventory is priced at the earliest or first purchase price. The weighted average method prices the quantity of goods in the ending inventory by multiplying the quantity by the average unit price for all goods available during the period.

There are times when it is necessary for the accountant to estimate the cost of the ending inventory without taking a physical count of the quantity of goods on hand. Two methods for estimating the ending inventory are the retail method and the gross profit method. The retail method is used primarily by retail and wholesale establishments. Under this method the accountant must have records available for the cost and selling price of the Purchases and purchase-related accounts as well as the selling price of the merchandise sold.

The gross profit method is usually used for estimating the amount of inventory lost through fire, theft, or other types of casualties, and it is often used to check on the accuracy of the physical count of the goods on hand at the end of an accounting period.

Maintaining the inventory records may be handled by the perpetual or periodic system. The perpetual system maintains a running balance of the amount of merchandise on hand and the cost of the good sold. The periodic system requires that a physical count of the merchandise on hand be taken to determine the amount of goods in the ending inventory. The perpetual system simplifies the recording process and the preparation of the income statement, but it does require maintaining detailed records of the inventory.

Whatever system is selected by the accountant for maintaining the inventory records and valuing the cost of the inventory, it must be followed consistently so reliable comparisons may be made by management, creditors, government agencies, and investors.

An error in the ending inventory will affect the income statement and balance sheet for the current period. When the ending inventory is understated or overstated, net income and current assets will be understated or overstated. The ending inventory of one period is the beginning inventory for the following period, and an error will cause the income for these periods to be misstated. Therefore, an understatement or overstatement in the beginning inventory will have an opposite effect and result in an overstatement or understatement of net income for that period.

GLOSSARY

First-In, First-Out (FIFO) Method: A method of pricing the items in the ending inventory by beginning with the prices paid for the last items purchased. This method assumes that the first items purchased are the first ones sold.

Gross Profit Method: A method used to estimate the cost of inventory by multiplying net sales by the average gross profit percentage realized on prior period sales.

Inventory: Merchandise on hand representing goods to be sold to customers.

Last-In, First-Out (LIFO) Method: A method that assumes that the last items purchased are the first ones sold; therefore, the cost of the ending inventory is priced at the earliest or first purchase price.

Periodic Inventory System: A system that records all merchandise purchased for resale in the Purchases account. This system requires a physical count of the quantity of merchandise on hand at the end of an accounting period to determine the cost of the ending inventory.

Perpetual Inventory System: A system that maintains a running balance of the Merchandise Inventory account and the cost of the goods sold. All merchandise purchased for resale is debited to the Merchandise Inventory account.

Retail Method: A method used to estimate the cost price of ending inventory. This method obtains a ratio of cost to selling price and applies the ratio to the retail price of ending inventory (goods available for sale less net sales) to obtain the cost price.

Specific Invoice Method: A method of valuing ending inventory by identifying the merchandise on hand to a specific invoice or purchase.

Weighted Average Method: A method of valuing the ending inventory by obtaining an average unit price of goods available during the period and multiplying the quantity of goods on hand by the average unit cost.

QUESTIONS

1. Name four basic methods for pricing or valuing ending inventory.
2. Briefly describe the retail method for estimating the cost of the ending inventory.
3. How is the ratio of cost to selling price obtained when using the retail method of estimating ending inventory?
4. Give two reasons for using the gross profit method of estimating ending inventory.

5. Describe two ways in which the perpetual and periodic systems differ in maintaining inventory records.

6. What is the difference between the Cost of Goods Sold section of the income statement under the periodic and perpetual inventory system?

7. If a company had a beginning inventory of 5 items that cost $5 each and purchased 10 items at $5.10 each and 20 items at $5.20 each, what is the dollar amount of goods available for sale? If the company sold 25 items, what is the cost of goods sold using the FIFO method of inventory pricing?

8. What effect will an understatement of ending inventory have on the current financial statements?

9. The inventory at the end of a period is overstated. What effect will this error have on the following period?

10. Identify the method of valuing the ending inventory that provides an accurate measurement of the cost of goods on hand and the cost of goods sold.

EXERCISES

Four Methods of Valuing Ending Inventory

1. The Serv-U Sales had a beginning inventory of 20 items purchased at $4 each. Purchases during the period: 5 items at $4.20 each, 4 items at $4.30 each, and 11 items at $4.40 each.
   (a) Compute the cost of goods available for sale.
   (b) Compute the cost of the ending inventory using the FIFO method. Sales amounted to 27 items for the period.

2. Referring to the data in Exercise 1, compute:
   (a) Cost of 15 items in the ending inventory using LIFO and weighted average
   (b) Cost of goods sold using LIFO and weighted average

3. The Renoir Company uses the specific method of inventory valuation. At the beginning of the year it had 500 units that cost $5 each. During the year it purchased 600 units at $5.50 each and 400 units at $5.45 each. At the end of the year, the inventory consisted of 200 units which could be specifically identified as 150 units in the beginning inventory and 50 units purchased at $5.45 each.
   (a) What is the cost of the goods available for sale?
   (b) What is the cost of the ending inventory?
   (c) What is the cost of the goods that were sold?

4. The inventory data for a company is listed below:

Beginning inventory	30 units @ $4.50
Purchases: January	60 units @ 4.60
April	80 units @ 4.80

July	80 units @	5.00
October	200 units @	4.80
December	50 units @	4.90

90 units remain unsold on December 31. Determine the cost of the ending inventory using:
(a) FIFO   (b) LIFO   (c) Weighted average

Perpetual versus Periodic Inventory System

5. Transactions involving purchases during May for Crestwood Company are given below:

19_A
May   7 Purchased merchandise on account from Add-It Compounds, $800; terms: 2/10, n/30; FOB shipping point.
      8 Paid transportation costs of $50.
     10 Returned $150 of merchandise and received credit on account.
     17 Paid Add-It Compounds in full.

Journalize the entries for May using the (a) perpetual, and (b) periodic inventory system.

6. Using the data in Exercise 5, prepare the *sales* entries for (a) perpetual, and (b) periodic inventory system assuming the merchandise was sold on May 20 for $870 to the Superior Company with terms of 2/10, n/30, FOB destination. The Superior Company paid the account on May 30.

Income Statement

7. Prepare an income statement for the month ended January 31 of the current year for John Storey, owner of Storey Insulation Company, from the following data: Sales, $2,800; Cost of Goods Sold, $2,010; and Operating Expenses, $490. The Storey Company uses the perpetual system for maintaining inventory records.

Closing Entries

8. Prepare the closing entries for Exercise 7 assuming the books are closed each month.

Effect of Errors on Net Income

9. The Lang Company discovered the following errors in January 19_C:

December 31, 19_A, inventory understated $4,000
December 31, 19_B, inventory overstated $2,000

Show the dollar amount by which the net income will be misstated for 19_A, 19_B, and 19_C using the following format:

Net Income

Year	Overstated	Understated
19_A		
19_B		
19_C		

10. Using the data in Exercise 9, determine the correct amount of the cost of goods sold for 19_A, assuming that the cost of goods sold reported was $28,000.

Retail versus Gross Profit Method

11. Estimate the ending inventory on December 31 of the current year for the retail method using the following data:

	Cost Price	Retail Price
Inventory, Jan. 1	$19,518	$24,400
Purchases	25,000	31,250
Purchase Returns	750	940
Sales		40,000

12. Estimate the ending inventory on December 31, 19__, for the gross profit method using the following data:

Inventory, Jan. 1, 19__	$15,000
Sales	60,000
Purchases	38,000
Purchase Returns	1,000

In the past, the gross profit percentage averaged 30 percent of net sales.

PROBLEMS

Four Methods of Estimating Ending Inventory, Plus Determining Gross Profit

12-1. The Futura Company sells a single product. The following data relates to the purchases and sales for the year ended December 31 of the current year:

	Units	Unit Price	Total Cost
Balance, Jan. 1	200	$10	$ 2,000
Purchases: January	300	12	3,600
April	100	15	1,500
September	300	13	3,900
December	100	16	1,600
Totals	1,000		$12,600

The Futura Company sold 800 units at $20 each during the year.

Required

(a) Calculate the ending inventory by each of the following methods:
   1. Weighted average
   2. FIFO
(b) Calculate the gross profit on sales from the data above, assuming the Futura Company used the LIFO method of valuing the ending inventory.

12-2. The Sunlite Company sells a single product. The following data applies to the merchandise on hand during the year.

	Units	Unit Price
Balance, Jan. 1	300	$5.00
Purchases: February	400	6.00
May	200	7.50
October	400	6.80
November	200	8.00
Total	1,500	

The Sunlite Company sold 1,200 units during the year for $10 each.

Required

(a) Calculate the cost of the ending inventory by each of the following methods:
   1. Weighted average
   2. LIFO
(b) Calculate the gross profit on sales from the data above assuming the Sunlite Company used the FIFO method of valuing the ending inventory.

Four Methods of Estimating Ending Inventory Plus Determining Cost of Goods Sold and Gross Profit

12-3. The Rosebud Company's inventory records contained the following data:

	Units	Unit Price
Balance, Jan. 1	1,000	$10
Purchases: January	4,000	11
June	2,000	12
October	3,000	14

The Rosebud Company sold 7,000 units during the year for $20 each.

Required

Compute the following:
(a) The number of units in the ending inventory.
(b) The cost of the ending inventory using LIFO and FIFO valuing methods.

(c) The cost of the ending inventory assuming that 1,000 units could be identified as goods purchased in January and 2,000 units as goods purchased in October.

(d) Determine the cost of the goods sold using the weighted average method of inventory valuation.

(e) The amount of gross profit on sales for the weighted average method of inventory valuation.

12-4. The inventory on January 1 of the current year of product A held by the White Industries consisted of 100 units at a unit cost of $53 each, for a total cost of $5,300. Purchases during the year were as follows:

Date	Units	Unit Price
Feb. 8	100	$54
Apr. 2	200	55
July 23	300	56
Sept. 18	300	58
Dec. 9	100	57

At the end of the year, 300 units were on hand as determined by a physical count.

Required

(a) Determine the cost of the ending inventory assuming a FIFO method of inventory valuation.

(b) Determine the cost of goods sold assuming a weighted average method of inventory valuation.

(c) If sales amounted to $75,000, what is the amount of gross profit on sales assuming a LIFO method of inventory valuation?

12-5. The Plastic Products Company's inventory records contained the following data:

	Units	Unit Price
Balance, Jan. 1	100	$10
Purchases: July	300	11
October	400	12
December	200	14

The Plastic Products Company sold 800 units at $20 each during the year, for a total cost of $16,000.

Required

Compute the following:

(a) Number of units in ending inventory

(b) Cost of goods sold using the FIFO method

(c) The amount of gross profit on sales assuming the LIFO method of inventory valuation

(d) The cost of the ending inventory assuming a weighted average method of inventory valuation

12-6. The ADE Company had 200 units of a product in the beginning inventory on January 1 of the current year. The per unit cost was $25, for a total cost of $5,000. Purchases during the year were as follows:

Date	Units	Unit Price
February	100	$24
April	200	26
July	300	28
September	200	29
December	500	28

On December 31 of the current year, 250 units were on hand as determined by a physical count.

Required

Determine the dollar amount of ending inventory assuming:
(a) FIFO method of inventory valuation.
(b) LIFO method of inventory valuation.
(c) Weighted average method of inventory valuation.
(d) One hundred and fifty units could be specifically identified to the purchase in September and 100 units to the purchase in April.

Determining Cost of Goods Sold, Gross Profit, and Net Income

12-7. Referring to the data in Problem 12-6, determine the following:
(a) Cost of goods sold using a LIFO method of inventory valuation
(b) The dollar amount of gross profit on sales assuming sales of $40,000 and a FIFO method of inventory valuation
(c) The net income assuming sales of $40,000 and operating expenses of $5,000 and a weighted average method of inventory valuation

Retail versus Gross Profit Method

12-8. Using the retail method, estimate the cost of the inventory as of March 31 of the current year for the Whyte Company using the information given below:

	Cost Price	Selling Price
Balance, Jan. 1	$ 7,275	$15,950
Purchases	20,718	36,030
Sales		35,250
Transportation In	102	
Purchase Returns	150	230

12-9. Compute the cost of the estimated inventory on June 30 of the current year for the Whyte Company using the retail method and the following data:

	Cost Price	Selling Price
Balance, Jan. 1	$8,910	$16,500
Sales		15,600
Purchases	6,248	8,580
Transportation In	170	
Purchase Returns	200	280

12-10. On September 1 of the current year, the management of Whyte Company had a fire that destroyed the entire inventory. Estimate the inventory loss using the following information recorded in the accounting records:

Balance in Inventory, June 30	$ 8,100
Purchases	7,800
Purchase Returns	80
Transportation In	146
Sales	17,400
Sales Returns	200

The gross profit for the prior periods amounted to 25 percent.

12-11. Estimate the ending inventory for the Label Distributors using the gross profit method. Label Distributors had an inventory of $15,420 on October 1 of the current year. The following data was taken from the accounting records on October 31:

Sales	$84,000
Purchases	56,000
Purchase Returns	1,200
Transportation In	800

Label Distributors has an average gross profit of 40 percent of net sales.

Required

Determine the estimated inventory on October 31.

Correction of Errors in Inventory

12-12. The data shown on page 387 appeared on the partial income statement prepared on December 31 of the current year for the Oasis Company. After analyzing the statement, the accountant discovered that the bookkeeper understated the ending inventory by $400.

Required

Determine the following:
(*a*) The correct cost of goods sold
(*b*) The correct gross profit for the period

OASIS COMPANY
INCOME STATEMENT
For Year Ended December 31, 19__

Operating Revenue:			
Sales			$22,000
Cost of Goods Sold:			
Merchandise Inventory, Jan. 1, 19__		$ 6,000	
Add: Purchases	$8,000		
Transportation In	500		
Total	$8,500		
Less: Purchase Returns	800		
Net Cost of Purchases		7,700	
Cost of Goods Available		$13,700	
Less: Merchandise Inventory,			
Mar. 31, 19__		3,200	
Cost of Goods Sold			10,500
Gross Profit			$11,500

Accounting for a Partnership

After completing this chapter, you should be able to:

1. **List the advantages and disadvantages of a partnership-type business**

2. **State the basic differences in the accounting records of a single proprietorship and a partnership-type business**

3. **Compute the division of profits and losses for each partner of a partnership according to the partnership agreement**

4. **Journalize the entries required in dissolving a partnership**

5. **Prepare a statement of partners' capital and the Partners' Equity section of a balance sheet**

Accounting for single proprietorships, a type of business that is owned by one person, was discussed in Chapters 1 to 12. Chapter 13 will discuss accounting for *partnerships*, a type of business that is owned by two or more persons who form a partnership as co-owners for the purpose of earning a profit from the sale of a service or product. This type of business is very simple to organize because most cities and states do not require any license or prior government approval to operate the business. All the partners have to do is open an office, store, or factory and begin operating their business. Partnerships are more common in the professional practices, such as law or accounting.

ADVANTAGES AND DISADVANTAGES OF FORMING A PARTNERSHIP

There are several advantages and disadvantages of forming a partnership. Four advantages are:

Advantages of forming a partnership

1. A partnership is relatively easy to organize.
2. A partnership is subject to very few government regulations.
3. A partnership provides for the combination of capital and special talents, expertise, and skills of several persons.
4. A partnership does not pay income taxes on any profits earned. However, the partners report their share of the partnership profits on their personal tax return.

Three disadvantages are:

Disadvantages of forming a partnership

1. *Unlimited liability:* Each partner is individually liable for *all* debts of the partnership.
2. *Mutual agency:* Each partner is an agent for the business and may enter into contracts or purchase agreements that are binding to all other

partners. If the partnership agreement limits the authority of the partners in these matters, the other partners are still liable unless the other party was informed about the limitation.

3. *Limited Life:* The life of a partnership is limited, because if one partner is unable to perform the duties of the partnership owing to illness or death, or a new partner is admitted or an existing partner retires, the partnership must be dissolved and a new partnership formed.

PARTNERSHIP FORMATION

When a partnership is formed, it is advisable for the partners to have a written contract stating the terms of the agreement. This written contract is called the *Articles of Co-Partnership.* However, a written contract is not required by law, and a partnership may be formed with an oral agreement.

When a written contract is prepared, it should contain all the information necessary to operate a successful business. Some important items to be included in a partnership agreement are:

Items to be included in partnership agreement

1. Name of each partner, name of the partnership, and the business location
2. Effective date of written contract and partnership duration
3. Amount of assets to be contributed by each partner
4. Method of maintaining the accounting records
5. Duties of each partner, salaries to be paid each partner, and the procedure for handling profits and losses
6. Amount of cash or other assets allowed to be withdrawn by each partner
7. Responsibilities for signing checks, contracts, or making large purchases or sales
8. Provision for the withdrawal of a partner or admission of a new partner and procedure for dissolution of the business

It is not required or necessary that all partners invest cash or other assets in the business. Many partners are given an interest in a business because of their knowledge, skills and abilities, or specialized talent.

ACCOUNTING DIFFERENCES

The accounting records for a single proprietorship and a partnership are basically the same. A single proprietorship will have only one capital and one drawing account. A partnership will have a separate capital account for each individual partner to record each partner's investment in the business.

There will also be a separate drawing account for each individual partner to show the amount of cash or other assets withdrawn from the business by a partner for their personal use.

When a partnership is formed, the cash and other assets contributed by each partner are debited to the respective asset accounts and credited to each partner's capital account. The assets other than cash invested in the business by a partner are recorded at their fair market value at the time of the investment or at the value agreed upon by all the partners.

For example, assume that on March 1 a partnership known as the B & F Company was formed between Arthur Buddy and Clara Friend. Mr. Buddy invested cash of $8,000 in the partnership, and Ms. Friend invested cash of $5,220 and office equipment valued at $780, for a total investment of $6,000 ($5,220 + $780). The opening journal entry for the B & F partnership required a debit to Cash for $13,220 ($8,000 + $5,220), a debit to Office Equipment for $780, and a credit to Arthur Buddy, Capital for $8,000 and a credit to Clara Friend, Capital for $6,000 as shown below:

Mar.	1	Cash	110	13,220	
		Office Equipment	120	780	
		Arthur Buddy, Capital	301		8,000
		Clara Friend, Capital	302		6,000
		To record the investment of the partners in the B & F Company.			

After the opening entry for the partnership is journalized, it is posted to the general ledger accounts as illustrated below:

Illustration of the ledger after posting opening entry of partnership

Cash   No. 110

Mar.	1		13,220		13,220

Office Equipment   No. 120

Mar.	1		780		780

Arthur Buddy, Capital   No. 301

Mar.	1			8,000	8,000

Clara Friend, Capital   No. 302

Mar.	1			6,000	6,000

DIVISION OF EARNINGS

The profits or losses of a partnership are divided among the partners according to the terms of their oral or written agreement. When the profits of an accounting period are divided, each partner's capital account is increased. If the business incurs a loss for the accounting period, the capital account of each partner is decreased. The partners must report their individual shares of the partnership profits to the Internal Revenue Service (I.R.S.) on their personal tax returns. All profits are taxable income to the partners even if they were not withdrawn from the business for personal use.

Various methods of dividing the profits or losses are shown below. Many partnerships will use one or a mixture of two or three of the five methods listed:

Methods of dividing profits and losses

1. Equally
2. In the ratio of the beginning or year-end capital balance
3. Average capital balance
4. Interest on the beginning or ending capital balance
5. Salaries paid according to the partnership agreement

When a partnership contract does not specify how the profits or losses will be divided, the law requires the profits and losses to be divided equally among the partners. If the agreement specifies how the profits are to be divided but does not mention anything about the division of losses, the losses are to be divided in the same manner as the profits.

To illustrate the division of profits and losses, four examples are given below.

EXAMPLE 1

Using the B & F Company as an example, assume that the partnership earned net income of $15,000 at the end of the first accounting period. The partnership agreement specified that profits or losses were to be divided equally, and each capital account was credited for $7,500 (50% of $15,000) to distribute the net income equally to the partners as shown below:

Each partner's capital account is credited for his or her share of the net income

Dec.	31	Income Summary	15,000	
		A. Buddy, Capital		7,500
		C. Friend, Capital		7,500
		To close the Income Summary account and to credit the partners' capital accounts for 50 percent of the $15,000 net income.		

EXAMPLE 2

Assume that the partnership agreement of the B & F Company specified that each partner would be allowed 6 percent interest on his or her beginning capital balance. The 6 percent interest was to be subtracted from net income or added to net loss and any remainder was to be divided equally. The calculation for the division of the $15,000 net income would be:

Computation for division of net income among partners

	A. Buddy	C. Friend	Total
Net Income			$15,000
6% of $8,000 and $6,000	$ 480	$ 360	(840)
Balance to be divided			$14,160
50% of $14,160	7,080	7,080	
Division of $15,000 net income	$7,560	$7,440	$15,000

The following journal entry would be recorded to increase each partner's capital account for his or her share of the net income.

Each partner's capital account is credited for his or her share of the net income

Dec.	31	Income Summary	15,000	
		A. Buddy, Capital		7,560
		C. Friend, Capital		7,440
		To close the Income Summary account and credit each partner's capital account for their share of the $15,000 net income.		

EXAMPLE 3

Assume that the B & F Company incurred a net loss of $4,000 for the first accounting period. The partnership agreement specified that Buddy was to receive a salary of $4,000 and Friend a salary of $6,000. The salaries of $10,000 ($6,000 + $4,000) were to be subtracted from net income or added to net loss and the balance was to be divided in the ratio of each partner's beginning capital balance. Calculation for division of the $4,000 loss would be computed as follows:

Computation for division of net loss among partners

	A. Buddy	C. Friend	Total
Net Loss			($ 4,000)
Salary	$4,000	$6,000	(10,000)
Total loss to be divided (Ratio: $8,000 + $6,000 = $14,000)			($14,000)
8,000/14,000 of $14,000	(8,000)		
6,000/14,000 of $14,000		(6,000)	
Division of $4,000 net loss	($4,000)	–0–	($ 4,000)

The journal entry to record the decrease to Arthur Buddy, Capital for the net loss would be:

Partner's capital account is debited for the net loss

Dec.	31	A. Buddy, Capital	4,000	
		Income Summary		4,000

To close the Income Summary account and record a net loss of $4,000 according to partnership agreement.

EXAMPLE 4

Assume that the B & F Company earned net income of $14,000, and the partnership agreement called for salaries of $4,000 to Buddy and $6,000 to Friend. The salaries of $10,000 ($6,000 + $4,000) were to be subtracted from net income or added to net loss and the balance was to be divided in the ratio of each partner's ending capital balance. During the year, Buddy invested an additional $1,000 in the business. The calculation for the division of the net income of $14,000 is as follows:

	A. Buddy	C. Friend	Total
Net Income			$14,000
Salary	$4,000	$6,000	10,000
Balance to be divided (Ratio: $8,000 + $1,000 = $9,000 + $6,000 = $15,000)			$ 4,000
$9,000/$15,000 of $4,000	2,400		
$6,000/$15,000 of $4,000		1,600	
Division of $14,000 net income	$6,400	$7,600	$14,000

The following journal entry would be recorded to increase each partner's capital account for his or her share of the net income:

Dec.	31	Income Summary	14,000	
		A. Buddy, Capital		6,400
		C. Friend, Capital		7,600

To close the Income Summary account and credit each partner's capital account for their share of the $14,000 net income.

Remember that the definition of an expense is an expenditure made to generate revenue. Therefore, any salaries, interest, or profits paid or credited to the partners' capital account are not an expense of the partnership as they represent the division of profits and losses according to the partnership agreement. Whenever the partners' capital accounts are credited or debited for the division of any profits or losses, they will not appear as an expense on the income statement of the partnership.

DISSOLVING A PARTNERSHIP

A partnership may be dissolved when one partner dies, retires or is physically unable to perform the duties of the partnership, or when the partners agree to sell the partnership to another company or discontinue doing business. When a partnership is dissolved, there are four steps required to close the books and bring the balance of every account to zero. The four steps for dissolving a partnership are:

Four steps for dissolving a partnership

1. The *noncash* assets must be sold and converted into cash.
2. Any gain or loss realized on the sale of *noncash* assets must be divided among the partners according to the terms of the partnership agreement.
3. The creditors must be paid.
4. The remaining cash must be paid to each partner in the amount of each partner's capital account balance.

For example, assume that the B & F Company dissolved their partnership on December 31, the end of their fifth year of doing business. The following balance sheet was prepared on December 31, 19_E, prior to dissolving the partnership.

Balance sheet before the dissolution of partnership

B & F COMPANY
BALANCE SHEET
December 31, 19_E

Assets		
Cash	$20,000	
Other Assets	12,000	
Total Assets		$32,000
Equities		
Accounts Payable	$18,000	
A. Buddy, Capital	9,000	
C. Friend, Capital	5,000	
Total Equities		$32,000

The partnership agreement stated that all profits and losses are to be divided equally.

Three examples are shown below illustrating the four entries required for dissolving a partnership.

1. Noncash Assets Sold at a Gain. The other assets are sold for $16,000 cash resulting in a $4,000 gain ($16,000 − $12,000).

ENTRY 1   *To record the sale of the noncash assets.*

Sale of noncash assets for more than book value

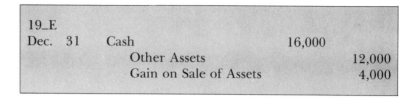

19_E			
Dec. 31	Cash	16,000	
	Other Assets		12,000
	Gain on Sale of Assets		4,000

After the entry has been posted, the ledger accounts with a balance are Cash, $36,000; Accounts Payable, $18,000; A. Buddy, Capital, $9,000; C. Friend, Capital, $5,000; and Gain on Sale of Assets, $4,000.

ENTRY 2   *To divide the gain among the partners.*

Gain divided among partners according to partnership agreement

19_E			
Dec. 31	Gain on Sale of Assets	4,000	
	A. Buddy, Capital		2,000
	C. Friend, Capital		2,000

After the entry has been posted the ledger accounts with a balance are Cash, $36,000; Accounts Payable, $18,000; A. Buddy, Capital, $11,000; C. Friend, Capital, $7,000.

ENTRY 3   *To record payment of accounts payable.*

Creditors paid before partners

19_E			
Dec. 31	Accounts Payable	18,000	
	Cash		18,000

After the entry has been posted, the ledger accounts with a balance are Cash, $18,000; A. Buddy, Capital, $11,000; and C. Friend, Capital, $7,000.

ENTRY 4   *To distribute the remaining cash to the partners.*

Remaining cash paid to partners for balance in capital account

19_E			
Dec. 31	A. Buddy, Capital	11,000	
	C. Friend, Capital	7,000	
	Cash		18,000

After the four journal entries have been posted, every account in the ledger will have a zero balance, as illustrated in the following:

Ledger accounts have a zero balance after partnership is dissolved

Cash

19_E					
Dec.	31	Balance			20,000
	31	Entry 1	16,000		36,000
	31	Entry 3		4,000	32,000
	31	Entry 4		32,000	–0–

Other Assets

19_E					
Dec.	31	Balance			12,000
	31	Entry 1		12,000	–0–

Accounts Payable

19_E					
Dec.	31	Balance			18,000
	31	Entry 3	18,000		–0–

A. Buddy, Capital

19_E					
Dec.	31	Balance			9,000
	31	Entry 2		2,000	11,000
	31	Entry 4	11,000		–0–

C. Friend, Capital

19_E					
Dec.	31	Balance			5,000
	31	Entry 2		2,000	7,000
	31	Entry 4	7,000		–0–

Gain on Sale of Assets

19_E					
Dec.	31	Entry 1		4,000	4,000
	31	Entry 2	4,000		–0–

2. Noncash Assets Sold at a Loss. The other assets are sold for $7,000 cash resulting in a $5,000 loss ($12,000 − $7,000).

ENTRY 1   *To record the sale of the noncash assets.*

Noncash assets sold for less than book value

19_E				
Dec.	31	Cash	7,000	
		Loss on Sale of Assets	5,000	
		Other Assets		12,000

After the entries have been posted, the ledger accounts with a balance are Cash, $27,000; Accounts Payable, $18,000; A. Buddy, Capital, $9,000; C. Friend, Capital, $5,000; and Loss on Sale of Assets, $5,000.

ENTRY 2   *To divide the loss among the partners.*

Partners' capital accounts are decreased for loss

19_E				
Dec.	31	A. Buddy, Capital	2,500	
		C. Friend, Capital	2,500	
		Loss on Sale of Assets		5,000

After the entry has been posted, the ledger accounts with a balance are Cash, $27,000; Accounts Payable, $18,000; A. Buddy, Capital, $6,500; and C. Friend, Capital, $2,500.

ENTRY 3   *To record the payment of the accounts payable.*

Creditors paid before partners

19_E			
Dec. 31	Accounts Payable	18,000	
	Cash		18,000

After the entry has been posted, the ledger accounts with a balance are Cash, $9,000; A. Buddy, Capital, $6,500; and C. Friend, Capital, $2,500.

ENTRY 4   *To distribute the remaining cash to the partners.*

Remaining cash distributed to partners for balance in capital account

19_E			
Dec. 31	A. Buddy, Capital	6,500	
	C. Friend, Capital	2,500	
	Cash		9,000

After the four journal entries have been posted, all the ledger accounts will have a zero balance.

3. Noncash Assets Sold at a Loss and Loss Exceeds Partners' Capital. The other assets are sold for $1,000 resulting in a $11,000 loss ($12,000 − $1,000) and a debit balance in one partner's account.

ENTRY 1   *To record the sale of the noncash assets.*

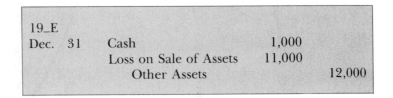

19_E			
Dec. 31	Cash	1,000	
	Loss on Sale of Assets	11,000	
	Other Assets		12,000

After the entry has been posted, the accounts with a balance are Cash, $21,000; Accounts Payable, $18,000; A. Buddy, Capital, $9,000; C. Friend, Capital, $5,000; and a $11,000 Loss on Sale of Assets.

ENTRY 2   *To divide the loss among the partners.*

19_E			
Dec. 31	A. Buddy, Capital	5,500	
	C. Friend, Capital	5,500	
	Loss on Sale of Assets		11,000

After the entry has been posted, the accounts with a balance are Cash, $21,000; Accounts Payable, $18,000; A. Buddy, Capital, $3,500; and C. Friend, Capital, has a debit balance of $500.

ENTRY 3   *To record payment of accounts payable.*

19_E			
Dec. 31	Accounts Payable	18,000	
	Cash		18,000

After the entry has been posted, the accounts with a balance are Cash, $3,000; A. Buddy, Capital, $3,500; and C. Friend, Capital with a debit balance of $500.

ENTRY 4   *To distribute the remaining cash to the partner with the credit balance and eliminate the debit balance in the other partner's account.*

Ms. Friend did not contribute $500 to the partnership to cover the loss.

Partner must absorb any deficit

19_E			
Dec. 31	A. Buddy, Capital	3,500	
	Cash		3,000
	C. Friend, Capital		500

Whenever one of the capital accounts has a debit balance, the partner is expected to pay the amount of the debit balance to the partnership or agree to pay the other partners at a later date. Remember that each partner is individually liable for all the debts of a partnership, and if a partner does not have any personal assets to cover his or her share of any losses incurred, the other partners must assume the responsibility.

If Ms. Friend paid $500 cash to offset the debit balance in her capital account, Entry 4 would have been recorded as follows:

Payment of deficit to partnership and remaining cash paid to partner with credit balance	19_E Dec.	31	Cash	500
			C. Friend, Capital		500
		31	A. Buddy, Capital	3,500
			Cash		3,500

STATEMENT PRESENTATIONS

There is very little difference in the preparation of an income statement for a partnership or a single proprietorship-type of business. However, some accountants may show the division of net income or loss among the partners as an additional section at the bottom of the income statement. To illustrate, assume that the following facts were obtained from the records of the ABC Partnership as of December 31, 19_B: Total Assets, $37,000; Accounts Payable, $7,000; Net Income for the Year, $18,000; Capital balances on January 1, 19_B: Colleen Allen, $8,000; Dan Birch, $9,000; and Mary Casey, $6,400. During the year Mr. Birch invested an additional $600 in the business; and Ms. Allen withdrew $4,000, Mr. Birch, $6,000, and Ms. Casey, $2,000 for personal use. The partnership agreement provided for all profits and losses to be divided equally.

A partial income statement showing the division of net income among the partners on the bottom portion of the statement is shown below.

Division of net income shown at the bottom of income statement

ABC PARTNERSHIP
PARTIAL INCOME STATEMENT
For Year Ended December 31, 19_B

Net Income		$18,000
Division of Net Income:		
Colleen Allen	$6,000	
Dan Birch	6,000	
Mary Casey	6,000	
Net Income		$18,000

When recording the closing entries, each capital account would be credited for $6,000 and debited for the amount withdrawn during the year. The closing entries are shown as follows:

Closing Entries

19_B				
Dec.	31	Income Summary	18,000	
		C. Allen, Capital		6,000
		D. Birch, Capital		6,000
		M. Casey, Capital		6,000
		To close the Income Summary account and record each partner's share of the net income in his or her capital account.		
	31	C. Allen, Capital	4,000	
		D. Birch, Capital	6,000	
		M. Casey, Capital	2,000	
		C. Allen, Drawing		4,000
		D. Birch, Drawing		6,000
		M. Casey, Drawing		2,000
		To close drawing accounts of each partner.		

The Equity section of a balance sheet will show the ending capital balance for each individual partner. The changes that have occurred in the capital accounts during the accounting period will be shown in a separate statement called the "statement of partners' capital" as shown below for the ABC Partnership.

ABC PARTNERSHIP
STATEMENT OF PARTNERS' CAPITAL
For Year Ended December 31, 19_B

	C. Allen	D. Birch	M. Casey	Total
Capital balance, Jan. 1, 19_B	$ 8,000	$ 9,000	$ 6,400	$23,400
Add: Additional Investments		600		600
Net Income	6,000	6,000	6,000	18,000
Total	$14,000	$15,600	$12,400	$42,000
Less: Drawings	4,000	6,000	2,000	12,000
Capital balance, Dec. 31, 19_B	$10,000	$ 9,600	$10,400	$30,000

The Equity section of the balance sheet for the ABC Partnership is as follows:

Ending capital balance of each partner shown on balance sheet

ABC PARTNERSHIP
PARTIAL BALANCE SHEET
December 31, 19__

Liabilities

Current Liabilities:	
Accounts Payable	$ 7,000

Partners' Equity

Capital Balance, Dec. 31, 19__		
Colleen Allen	$10,000	
Dan Birch	9,600	
Mary Casey	10,400	
Total Partners' Equity		30,000
Total Liabilities & Partners' Equity		$37,000

Some accountants may present the changes in each partners' capital account in the Equity section of the balance sheet instead of preparing a separate statement of partners' capital. A partial balance sheet for the ABC Partnership showing the details of changes in partners' capital during the year is illustrated below:

Balance sheet showing changes in partners' capital accounts

ABC PARTNERSHIP
PARTIAL BALANCE SHEET
December 31, 19__

Liabilities

Current Liabilities:	
Accounts Payable	$ 7,000

Partners' Equity

	C. Allen	D. Birch	M. Casey	
Capital Balance, Jan. 1, 19__	$ 8,000	$ 9,000	$ 6,400	
Add: Additional Investments		600		
Net Income	6,000	6,000	6,000	
Total	$14,000	$15,600	$12,400	
Less: Drawings	4,000	6,000	2,000	
Capital Balance, Dec. 31, 19__	$10,000	$ 9,600	$10,400	30,000
Total Liabilities & Partners' Equity				$37,000

SUMMARY

A partnership type of business organization occurs when two or more persons agree to become co-owners in a business for the purpose of earning a profit from the sale of a service or a product. The only difference in the accounting records of a partnership and a single proprietorship type of business organization is in the capital or equity section. A partnership will have an individual capital and drawing account for each partner. When a partnership is formed, the cash or other assets (valued at the current market price) contributed to the business by each partner are credited to the partner's individual capital account.

All profits and losses are divided among the partners according to the terms of the partnership contract or oral agreement. When no agreement has been made, profits and losses are divided equally. If an agreement was made for profits but not losses, losses are divided the same way as profits.

The financial statements for a partnership and single proprietorship are basically the same, although the division of net income or loss is sometimes shown in a section at the bottom of the income statement. Some accountants will prepare a separate statement of partners' capital showing all the details of changes to the partners' capital accounts during an accounting period; others may present this information in the Equity section of the balance sheet.

The net income for the period (divided according to the partnership agreement) and the drawing accounts are closed to each partner's capital account.

Dissolving a partnership requires the sale of noncash assets, payment to creditors, and payment to the partners for their capital account balance.

GLOSSARY

Articles of Co-Partnership: A written contract stating the terms of the partnership agreement.

Limited Life: If one partner is unable to perform the duties of the partnership because of illness or death, the partnership is terminated.

Mutual Agency: Each partner is bound by the actions of the other partners and all partners are liable even though they may not have agreed to the conditions of a contract or purchase agreement.

Partnership: When two or more persons agree to conduct a business as co-owners for the purpose of earning a profit from the sale of a service or a product.

Unlimited Liability: Each partner is personally liable for all the debts of a partnership.

QUESTIONS

1. List and explain briefly two advantages and disadvantages of forming a partnership.

2. List four items that should be included in a written partnership agreement.

3. The beginning capital balance of Partners A and B were $8,000 and $10,000, and net income for the period amounted to $18,000. How much would each partner receive if the partnership contract stated that all profits will be divided in the ratio of the beginning capital?

4. A partnership was dissolved, and after all noncash assets were sold and liabilities paid, the cash amounted to $28,000. Partner C has a capital balance of $20,000 and Partner D has a balance of $8,000. The partnership agreement called for all profits and losses to be divided equally. How much cash will each partner receive?

5. Prepare the journal entry required for Question 4.

6. What is the basic difference between accounting for a single proprietorship and a partnership-type business.

7. What is the name of the written contract that gives the terms of the partnership agreement.

8. Briefly list the steps required to close the books for a partnership that is dissolving their business operations.

EXERCISES

Journal Entries and Division of Profits and Losses

1. Andrew Wilcox and Basil Corrigan formed a partnership on January 1 of the current year known as the A & B Company. They each contributed cash of $20,000 to form the partnership. Journalize the following entries:
   (*a*) Entry required for the formation of the partnership.
   (*b*) Closing entry required on December 31, the end of their first year of business assuming a net income of $18,000. The partnership agreement stated that profits and losses were to be divided equally.
   (*c*) Closing entries required on December 31 assuming the partnership agreement allowed each partner to withdraw a salary of $800 per month and 25 percent of any balance was to go to Wilcox and 75 percent to Corrigan.

2. The partnership agreement for the division of profits and losses for JB Associates is shown below:

   Yearly salaries of $9,000 to John Blum and $12,000 to Betty Wilcox.

   8 percent interest on each partner's capital balance on January 1 which amounted to $18,000 to John Blum and $24,000 to Betty Wilcox.

   Any balance was to be divided equally.

Determine each partner's share of a net income of $32,100.

3. Using the data in Exercise 2, determine each partner's share of a net loss of $1,800.

Statement of Partners' Capital

4. Using the information in Exercise 2, prepare a statement of partners' capital as of December 31. Betty and John both withdrew their salary during the year.

5. The Three B Partnership earned net income of $21,000 during the year ended December 31, 19_C. The partnership agreement allowed each partner a 6 percent interest on their beginning capital balance and the balance was to be divided equally. On January 1, 19_C, the balance in the capital accounts were: James Bart, $10,000; Joan Bachek, $20,000; and Jack Breston, $12,000. Prepare a statement of partners' capital for the year ended December, 19_C. (Each partner withdrew $7,200 during the year.)

Journal Entries for Dissolving a Partnership

6. A partnership was dissolved on April 30, 19_F, and after all the noncash assets were sold and the creditors paid, the Cash account had a balance of $21,000. The balance in the partners' capital accounts were: C. Grepps, $10,000; P. Nasley, $9,000; and R. Tixley, $2,000. Prepare the entry to close the partnership.

7. On June 4, 19_B, a partnership had cash of $3,000, noncash assets of $27,000, and they owed $15,000 on account to their creditors. The partners' capital balances amounted to: E. Rice, $3,000; M. Morley, $8,000; and R. Oricole, $4,000. The partnership dissolved their business operations and sold the noncash assets for $21,000. All profits and losses are divided equally among the partners. Journalize the entries required to close the books of the partnership.

Equity Section of Balance Sheet

8. Prepare the equity section of the balance sheet for the Easy-Wax Partnership as of December 31, 19_G, using the following data:

Accounts Payable	$ 8,000
Notes Payable, Due June 1, 19_H	2,000
Arnold Buckley, Capital	12,000
Samuel Yardley, Capital	10,000
Ellis Wales, Capital	9,000

9. The accountant for the Aspen Company presents the changes in each partner's capital account in the Partners' Equity section of the balance sheet. Prepare the Partners' Equity section of a balance sheet as of December 31, 19_E, using the following data:

Cory Davis, Capital, Jan. 1	$14,000
Cory Davis, Drawings	9,600
Peter Childs, Capital, Jan. 1	8,000
Peter Childs, Drawings	9,600
Net Income for 19_E	28,200

Note: The partnership agreement allows a yearly salary of $9,600 to each partner and two-thirds of any balance to Davis and one-third to Childs.

PROBLEMS

Division of Profits and Losses

13-1. A & B Partnership was organized on June 30 of the current year with Steve Allrite investing $12,000 cash and Dorothy Bates investing $8,000 cash. The partnership agreement called for salaries to be paid each partner at the rate of $800 per month to Steve and $800 per month to Dorothy with the balance to be divided in the ratio of their beginning capital balance. During the first 6 months, the partnership earned net income of $2,400 and in the following year they earned net income of $27,000.

Required

Determine each partner's share of the net income for:
(*a*) The first year (June 30 to December 31)
(*b*) The second year of business operations

13-2. A partnership called Eric Water Products was formed by Mary Wilson and Jack Barry on January 4 of the current year. Each partner invested $9,000 in cash and other assets. Their partnership agreement called for the payment of monthly salaries of $900 to Mary and $1,000 to Jack, 8 percent interest on their beginning capital balance, and 60 percent of the balance to Mary and 40 percent to Jack.

Required

Determine each partner's share of the net income or loss for each of the following unrelated assumptions:
(*a*) Net income of $28,000
(*b*) Net income of $19,000
(*c*) Net loss of $1,800

13-3. Mike Xeod, Dennis Lawly, and Stanley Mason formed the XLM Partnership on January 1 of the current year. Each partner contributed capital in the amount of $12,000, $18,000, and $15,000 respectively. The partnership agreement stated that profits and losses would be divided as follows:

Salaries to be paid each partner in the amount of $800 per month, 6 percent interest on beginning capital, and any balance to be divided equally.

Required

Determine each partner's share of the income or loss based on the following data:
(a) Net income of $33,000
(b) Net income of $18,000
(c) Net loss of $4,500

Journalizing Entries for a Partnership

13-4. David Compton and Melissa Pratt formed the C & P Partnership on June 25 of the current year. David contributed $14,000 cash and office equipment valued at $500; Melissa contributed $8,000 cash, a van valued at $6,000, and office furniture valued at $1,200. The partnership agreement called for salaries to be paid each partner at the rate of $800 per month to David and $900 per month to Melissa and the balance of any profit or loss to be divided equally. During the first 6 months, the partnership earned net income of $12,000.

Required

Journalize the entries for:
(a) June 25
(b) Closing entries required on December 31

13-5. On January 1 of the current year, a partnership known as Jaloid Company was formed by Jacob Gale, Lois Colin, and Ida Drew. Each partner contributed $6,000 cash plus an automobile valued at $4,900 by Jacob, office furniture valued at $5,000 by Lois, and office equipment valued at $5,100 by Ida. The partnership agreement stated that Lois was to be paid a salary of $600 per month, each partner was to be paid 6 percent interest on the beginning capital balance, and the balance of any income or loss was to be divided equally. At the end of the first year of business, net income of $12,000 was earned.

Required

Journalize the entries for:
(a) January 1
(b) Closing entries required on December 31

13-6. Journalize the closing entries required on December 31 for Problem 13-3c.

Statement of Partners' Capital

13-7. Prepare a statement of partners' capital for the 6-month period ending December 31 of the current year using the data given in Problem 13-4.

13-8. Prepare a statement of partners' capital for the year ended December 31 of the current year using the data given in Problem 13-5.

Journal Entries for Dissolving a Partnership

13-9. The J, O, & B Partnership, organized 6 years ago, decided to dissolve operations as of March 15, 19___. The following account balances appeared in the accounting records:

Cash	$6,000
Accounts Receivable	4,000
Merchandise Inventory	1,000
Equipment	9,000
Accumulated Depreciation/Equipment	3,000
Accounts Payable	5,500
Notes Payable	1,500
J. Beels, Capital	3,000
O. Dike, Capital	4,000
B. Waters, Capital	3,000

Profits and losses are divided in the ratio of the partners' ending capital balance.

Required

Prepare the necessary journal entries to close the books of the partnership assuming:
(*a*) Noncash assets were sold for $13,000.
(*b*) Noncash assets were sold for $9,000.

13-10. Partners Carol Jesop, John Crowley, and William Yates decided to dissolve their partnership, known as the Curly Q Hair Salon, on June 10, 19___. As of June 10, the following account balances appeared on the accounting records:

Cash	$ 1,200
Supplies	2,800
Equipment	18,000
Accumulated Depreciation/Equipment	6,000
Accounts Payable	4,000
Notes Payable	2,000
Carol Jesop, Capital	5,000
John Crowley, Capital	3,000
William Yates, Capital	2,000

The noncash assets were sold for $16,000, and the partnership agreement stated that all profits and losses were to be divided in the ratio of the ending capital balance.

Required

Prepare the journal entries required to close the books of the partnership.

Balance Sheet for Partnership

13-11. Prepare balance sheet in good form for the E & A Partnership on December 31 of the current year.

Accounts Payable	$ 4,750
Accounts Receivable	9,000
Cash	8,300
E. Williams, Capital	20,000
A. Johnson, Capital	14,500
E. Williams, Drawing	8,000
A. Johnson, Drawing	9,500
Buildings	32,500
Accumulated Depreciation/Building	8,000
Machinery	6,000
Accumulated Depreciation/Machinery	1,000
Land	2,000
Mortgage Payable	10,000
Merchandise Inventory	1,200
Prepaid Insurance	600
Taxes Payable	400
Wages Payable	350
Patents	1,900

Net income of $20,000 was earned during the year, and the partnership agreement allowed yearly salaries of $8,000 to Williams and $9,500 to Johnson with the balance distributed equally to each partner.

The Corporate Form of Business Organization

After completing this chapter, you should be able to:

1. **Define the corporate form of business organization and state three major advantages and disadvantages**

2. **Account for common stock transactions**

3. **Define retained earnings and state how profits, losses, and dividends are handled through the Retained Earnings account**

4. **State the basic difference between accounting for a single proprietorship and for the corporate form of business structure**

5. **Define and account for cash dividends**

6. **Prepare the Stockholders' Equity section for a corporate balance sheet**

A *corporation* is a separate legal entity or invisible being which exists only by law. A corporation may enter into contracts, own property under the corporate name, and conduct business in the same manner as a person.

Corporations account for a vast majority of the dollar volume of business conducted in the United States and in the world because government regulations and taxation make the corporate form of business very attractive. The number of small businesses turning to the corporate form of business organization is increasing every day because of its many advantages over sole proprietorships and partnerships.

Each state has its own laws governing the establishment and operation of corporations. Permission to organize a corporation may be obtained when one or more individuals, called the *incorporators,* file a form with the state requesting authorization to operate a corporate form of business organization. Upon approval, the state will issue a corporate charter to the incorporators. The *charter* will list the official corporate name, the types of business activities to be conducted, and the types and amount of stock authorized. Owners of a corporation are known as "stockholders" or "shareholders."

After the corporate charter has been issued, the first act of the incorporators is to hold an organizational meeting to approve a set of bylaws, elect a board of directors, arrange for the printing and sale of stock, and decide on the major operating procedures for the business. The *board of directors* governs and assumes the primary responsibilities for the affairs of the corporation and elects the *corporate officers* who will actually be responsible for managing the business. The chief corporate officer is the president, whose authority is second only to the board of directors. There may be one or more vice-presidents depending on the size and need of the management structure. The secretary is responsible for recording and maintaining the minutes of the board of directors, stockholders' meetings, and stockholders' records. The treasurer is the chief financial officer who has custody of the corporate funds and is responsible for financial planning and reporting.

ADVANTAGES AND DISADVANTAGES

The corporate form of business organization offers several advantages that are not available to a single proprietorship or partnership. Three major advantages are:

1. The corporation is established by law as a separate legal entity or artificial being, and the owners or stockholders are separate from the corporation. This limits the claim of creditors only to the assets of the corporation, because the stockholders cannot be held responsible for the corporate debts.
2. It is easier for a corporation to raise operating capital through the sale of its stock.
3. The corporation's existence is not affected by changes in ownership through the sale of its stock or by illness or death of its managers or stockholders. The corporation can only be terminated by the state or upon the decision of the stockholders.

There are some disadvantages to the corporate form of organization. Three of the more important ones are:

1. Corporations are more closely regulated by state and federal governments. They are required by law to comply with many regulations and file numerous reports.
2. Corporations that sell their stock to the general public are required to make full disclosure of their business affairs.
3. Corporate profits are taxed twice. The corporation pays taxes on its profits, and any profits paid to the stockholders in the form of dividends are taxed again as a part of the stockholders' personal income.

ORGANIZATION COSTS

Legal fees, state incorporation fees, and any other expenses incurred in establishing a corporation are known as *organization costs*. Organization costs are classified as an Intangible Asset on the balance sheet. It is assumed that these costs will benefit the corporation's entire life, but usually they are amortized over a period of from 5 to 40 years. Since the Internal Revenue Service (I.R.S.) allows a corporation to amortize organization costs over a 5-year period, most corporations use the shorter period.

COMMON STOCK

The corporate charter allows the corporation to sell its ownership rights by issuing shares of *stock.* When the stock is sold and paid for, a *stock certifi-*

cate is issued to the buyer who becomes a part owner of the company. Each share of stock represents one unit of ownership in a corporation.

The corporate charter specifies the types of stock that the corporation may issue. If only one type has been authorized, it is known as **common stock.** Common stockholders are entitled to attend stockholders' meetings, vote for the board of directors, and vote on other business matters. One vote is granted for each share of stock owned. Common stockholders also have what is known as a **preemptive right,** a right to purchase a portion of any new stock issues so that each stockholder's original proportionate share of ownership can be maintained. The other major type of stock is known as "preferred stock" and will not be discussed in this chapter.

The corporate charter also authorizes the number of shares of stock a corporation may issue. The authorized number of shares is usually much larger than what is required for the immediate needs of the business. This provision allows the corporation to issue additional shares as the business grows without having to go back to the state for permission to increase its initial amount of authorized stock. Authorized shares of stocks that are issued and held by the stockholders are known as **outstanding stock.**

PAR OR STATED VALUE

Common stock is one of the main sources of capital for a corporation and is recorded as contributed or permanent capital when it is issued to the stockholders. Stock may be issued with a par value or with no-par value. **Par value** is an amount per share established by the board of directors which is stated in the corporate charter and printed on the stock certificate. Some directors will assign a **stated value** to no-par stock, which is an arbitrary value used for recording purposes. A few states require that no-par value stock be assigned a stated value.

Whenever shares of stock are sold and issued, the amount charged to the Capital Stock account is always computed by multiplying the number of shares issued by the *par* or *stated value*. If stock is sold for an amount above the par or stated value, the excess amount is credited to the Premium on Common Stock account. In most states, stock cannot be issued for less than the par or stated value. As a result, most stocks carry low par values. However, par or stated value *does not* indicate the true worth of the stock. Only careful analysis of the company's financial records and the *market price* of the stock can determine its value.

ACCOUNTING FOR STOCK TRANSACTIONS

When common stock is issued, the Common Stock account is credited for the par value of the stock. If the stock is sold for more than par value, the excess amount over par is credited to the **Premium on Common Stock** account. Two different situations are illustrated below.

Assume that on March 1, 19__, the Davis Corporation obtained authorization to issue 200,000 shares of common stock with a $5 par value.

SITUATION 1   *On March 10, 19__, 50,000 shares are issued for $5 per share, the par value of the stock.*

$$50,000 \text{ shares} \times \$5 = \$250,000$$

The journal entry is:

Sale of common stock at par

19__				
Mar.	10	Cash	250,000	
		Common Stock (equity acct).		250,000
		Issued 50,000 shares of $5 par value common stock.		

SITUATION 2   *On June 16, 19__, 50,000 shares are issued for $8 per share, the market price of the stock.*

$$50,000 \text{ shares} \times \$8 = \$400,000$$
$$50,000 \text{ shares} \times \$5 \text{ par value} = \$250,000$$
$$50,000 \text{ shares} \times \$3 \text{ premium} = \$150,000$$

The journal entry is:

Sale of common stock above par

19__				
June	16	Cash	400,000	
		Common Stock		250,000
		Premium on Common Stock (equity acct)		150,000
		Issued 50,000 shares of $5 par value common stock for $8 per share.		

The Common Stock account will always be recorded in terms of par or stated value in the accounting records. Premium on Common Stock will be shown as an addition to the Common Stock account on the balance sheet, representing the total paid in capital by the stockholders.

Occasionally, a corporation will accept an order for stock with a cash down payment and the balance due at a specified time. When a corporation accepts an order from a subscriber (purchaser) to purchase stock on a time or installment basis, it is referred to as a **stock subscription.** The **subscribed stock** is not issued until full payment is received on the subscription. The amount due for the subscription is debited to Subscriptions Receivable and credited to Common Stock Subscribed, which are classified as a Current Asset and a Stockholders' Equity account, respectively, on the balance sheet. To illustrate, let us use the Davis Corporation as an example.

Assume that on July 1, 19__, 50,000 shares of common stock are subscribed for at $8 per share with 50 percent of the subscription paid in cash and the balance due within 30 days. The journal entry is shown below:

Receipt of subscriptions to common stock above par

19__				
July	1	Cash	200,000*	
		Subscriptions Receivable/		
		Common Stock	200,000	
		Common Stock Subscribed		250,000†
		Premium on Common Stock		150,000
		Received subscriptions for 50,000 shares of $5 par common stock at $8 per share. One-half of subscriptions paid and balance due in 30 days.		

* 50,000 shares × $8 = $400,000 × .50 = $200,000.
† 50,000 shares × $5 par value = $250,000.

Notice that the amount in excess of par value ($3 × 50,000 shares) is credited directly to the Premium on Common Stock account.

On August 1, 19__, the subscribers paid the balance of the subscriptions and stock was issued. The journal entry is shown below:

Payment received on subscriptions and stock issued

19__				
Aug.	1	Cash	200,000	
		Subscriptions Receivable/		
		Common Stock		200,000
		Received full payment for the balance due on 50,000 shares of common stock.		
	1	Common Stock Subscribed	250,000	
		Common Stock		250,000
		Issued certificates for 50,000 shares of common stock.		

Notice that when payment is received for the subscriptions the stock certificates are issued and the amount is transferred from the subscribed account to the Common Stock account.

RETAINED EARNINGS

Retained earnings are the accumulated profits less dividends retained by a corporation. Normally the Retained Earnings account has a credit balance, but if the losses exceed the accumulated profits, the Retained Earnings account would have a debit balance. A debit balance in Retained Earnings would be termed a "deficit" on the balance sheet. Most states do not permit the distribution of dividends for more than the balance in the Retained Earnings account, preventing the distribution of unlimited amounts of corporate funds to stockholders.

In a corporation, the balance in the Income Summary account is closed into Retained Earnings. If the Income Summary account for the Davis Corporation had a *credit* balance of $50,000, a profit was earned for the period. The closing entry is:

Income Summary closed to Retained Earnings

19__				
Dec.	31	Income Summary	50,000	
		Retained Earnings *(equity acct)*		50,000
		To close the Income Summary account and transfer the net income into Retained Earnings.		

If the Income Summary account for the Davis Corporation had a *debit* balance of $50,000, a loss was incurred for the period. The closing entry is:

Retained Earnings decreased for loss

19__				
Dec.	31	Retained Earnings	50,000	
		Income Summary		50,000
		To close Income Summary and transfer the net loss to Retained Earnings.		

ACCOUNTING DIFFERENCES

Accounting for a single proprietorship, partnership, and a corporation are the same except for the recording of owner's equity transactions. A single proprietorship has one capital and drawing account, a partnership has a capital and drawing account for each partner, and a corporation has a stock account for each class of stock plus a Retained Earnings account.

The differences are illustrated by using a single proprietorship and a corporation as an example. A partnership would be the same as a single proprietorship except there would be more than one capital and more than one drawing account.

Assume that Tom Pott invested $30,000 to start a single proprietorship business. Compare this to his forming a corporation with six stockholders each purchasing 1,000 shares of common stock at $5 par value (6,000 shares × $5) for a total of $30,000. The business earned a $10,000 net income during the year. In the single proprietorship, Tom Pott withdrew $6,000 for personal expenses—as compared to the corporation declaring and paying a cash dividend of $1 per share for a total of $6,000 (6,000 shares × $1) to the stockholders. The entries for the single proprietorship and corporation are shown below:

Comparison entries for single proprietorship and corporation

SINGLE PROPRIETORSHIP			CORPORATION		
Cash	30,000		Cash	30,000	
T. Pott, Capital		30,000	Common Stock		30,000
Tom Pott invested cash in business.			Issued 6,000 shares of common at $5 par value.		
Income Summary	10,000		Income Summary	10,000	
T. Pott, Capital		10,000	Retained Earnings		10,000
To close Income Summary and record net income into capital.			To close Income Summary and record net income into Retained Earnings.		
T. Pott, Drawing	6,000		Retained Earnings	6,000	
Cash		6,000	Dividends Payable		6,000
Tom Pott withdrew cash for personal use.			Declared a dividend of $1 per share.		
			Dividends Payable	6,000	
			Cash		6,000
			Paid dividends to stockholders.		

The Equity section of the balance sheet for the single proprietorship and the corporation is illustrated as follows:

Owner's Equity section for single proprietorship and corporation

SINGLE PROPRIETORSHIP

Owner's Equity

Tom Pott, Capital, Jan. 1, 19__	$30,000		
Add: Net Income	10,000	$40,000	
Less: Drawings		6,000	
Tom Pott, Capital, Dec. 31, 19__			$34,000

CORPORATION

Stockholders' Equity

Common Stock, $5 Par Value, 6,000 shares authorized, issued, and outstanding	$30,000	
Retained Earnings	4,000*	
Total Stockholders' Equity		$34,000

* $10,000 Net Income − $6,000 Dividends = $4,000.

Notice that the total amount of equity on December 31, 19__, is the same for both types of business organizations. The only difference is in the accounting and reporting of the ownership accounts.

DIVIDENDS

Dividends are profits paid to the stockholders as a return on their investment. The payment of cash to stockholders as a return on their investment is known as a "cash dividend." Dividends can only be declared by the board of directors, which has the authority to authorize the payment of a dividend. If the directors decide to pay a dividend, they must arrange to pay the dividend to the stockholders on a certain date. Three dates are important to the dividend process.

1. *Date of declaration:* Date a dividend is declared by the board of directors. Enter on books.
2. *Date of record:* Stockholders who own the stock as of a certain date are entitled to receive the dividend. No entry on books
3. *Date of payment:* Date dividend checks will be mailed to stockholders of record.

To illustrate the accounting for dividend transactions, assume that on November 1, 19_A, the Davis Corporation's Board of Directors declared a $0.50 per share dividend on common stock to be paid to stockholders of record on December 15, 19_A, payable on January 15, 19_B. There are

25,000 shares outstanding on December 15, 19_A. This declaration would be recorded as follows:

Declaration and payment of a cash dividend

Date of Declaration

19_A					
Nov.	1	Retained Earnings		12,500	
		Dividends Payable			12,500

To establish the liability for a $0.50 per share dividend on 25,000 shares of common stock.

Date of Record

19_A		
Dec.	15	No entry required.

Date of Payment

19_B					
Jan.	15	Dividends Payable		12,500	
		Cash			12,500

To issue dividend checks to stockholders of record Dec. 15, 19_A.

BALANCE SHEET PRESENTATION

The Ownership or Equity section of the corporation balance sheet is known as the *Stockholders' Equity* section. A partial balance sheet for the Briar

Stockholders' Equity section on balance sheet

BRIAR CORPORATION
PARTIAL BALANCE SHEET
December 31, 19_

Stockholders' Equity

Common Stock, $5 Par Value, 100,000 shares authorized, 25,000 shares issued and outstanding	$125,000	
Unissued Common Stock Subscribed, 25,000 shares	125,000	
Total Common Stock Issued and Subscribed	$250,000	
Premium on Common Stock	150,000	
Total Paid-in Capital		$400,000
Retained Earnings		37,500
Total Stockholders' Equity		$437,500

Corporation (shown on page 420) is based on the following information:

1. Stock authorized: 100,000 shares of common, $5 par value
2. Stock sold: 25,000 shares at $8 per share
3. Shares outstanding: 25,000
4. Shares subscribed and not issued: 25,000 shares at $8 per share
5. Retained Earnings: $50,000 less dividends of $0.50 per share on 25,000 outstanding shares

SUMMARY

A corporation is a legal entity created under state law. Permission to start a corporation may be obtained when one or more individuals, called incorporators, request authorization from the state to operate a corporate type of business. Upon approval, the state will issue a corporate charter authorizing the corporation to issue a given number of shares of stock and operate a business as defined in the corporate charter.

Ownership in a corporation is represented by a document called a stock certificate which states the number of shares issued. There are two classes of stock, common and preferred. If only one class of stock is issued, it is called common. Par or stated value represents an arbitrary value established by the board of directors for each share of stock but does not represent the market value. When stock is sold, the Common Stock account is credited for the par or stated value, and any excess received from the sale is credited to the Premium on Common Stock account.

The board of directors govern and assume the primary responsibilities of the corporate affairs and are elected by the common stockholders. The common stockholders receive one vote for each share of stock owned and have the right to vote on corporate matters and to purchase new stock issues to maintain their proportionate share of ownership. This right is known as their preemptive right.

Profits earned by a corporation are transferred from the Income Summary account to Retained Earnings, whereas profits earned by a single proprietorship are transferred from Income Summary to the owner's capital account.

A return on investment paid to stockholders is known as a dividend. When the board of directors officially declares a cash dividend, the Retained Earnings account is debited and Dividends Payable is credited. On the date of payment, the entry requires a debit to Dividends Payable and a credit to Cash. In a single proprietorship, the owner's drawing account is debited whenever profits are taken out of the business by the owner.

The Equity section of a corporate balance sheet is titled the Stockholders' Equity section. In this section, the Common Stock and related accounts are listed first and the data for the Retained Earnings account is listed last. The only difference in the accounting records for a single proprietorship and a corporation is in the account titles and the presentation of the Equity section of the balance sheet.

GLOSSARY

Board of Directors: The group that governs the affairs of a corporation and assumes the primary responsibility of the corporate affairs.

Charter: A document issued by the state giving authorization to operate a corporate type of business. The charter includes the corporate name, type of business activity to be conducted, and types and amount of authorized stock.

Common Stock: The basic type of stock issued by a corporation.

Corporate Officers: The group responsible for managing the corporate business.

Corporation: A form of business organization that operates as a legal entity separate from its owners and exists only by law.

Date of Declaration: Date a dividend is declared by the board of directors to the stockholders of a corporation.

Date of Payment: Date dividend checks will be mailed to stockholders of record.

Date of Record: All stockholders on record as of a certain date that are entitled to receive a dividend declared by the board of directors of a corporation.

Dividends: Profits paid to stockholders as a return on their investment.

Incorporators: One or more individuals who are responsible for forming a corporation.

Organization Costs: All expenses incurred in establishing a corporation.

Outstanding Stock: Authorized shares of stocks that are issued and held by the stockholders of a corporation.

Par Value: Arbitrary value established by the board of directors for one share of stock which is printed on the stock certificate.

Preemptive Right: A right to purchase a portion of any new stock issues so that each stockholder's original proportionate share of ownership can be maintained.

Premium on Common Stock: When common stock is issued, the Common Stock account is always credited for the par or stated value and any excess contributed is credited to a Premium on Common Stock account.

Retained Earnings: The title of an account used to record the accumulated profits less dividends retained by a corporation.

Stated Value: Arbitrary value established by the board of directors for one share of no-par stock.

Stock: Represents ownership in a corporation.

Stock Certificate: A document issued by a corporation representing ownership and the number of shares owned by a stockholder.

Stockholders' Equity: The section of the balance sheet that shows the amount of assets owned by the stockholders.

Stock Subscriptions: Stock sold on a time or installment basis.

Subscribed Stock: The amount of stock sold on a subscription basis which will not be issued until full payment is received.

QUESTIONS

1. Give the definition of a corporation, and explain how a corporation is formed.
2. List two advantages and two disadvantages of a corporate type of business organization.
3. Define the term organization costs, and state how it is classified on the balance sheet.
4. What is the purpose of the Retained Earnings account?
5. What is a cash dividend and when is it paid?

EXERCISES

Journal Entries for Common Stock

1. The Candis Corporation received authorization for 50,000 shares of $3 par common stock. Journalize the entries required for:
   (a) The cash sale of 10,000 shares at $3 per share
   (b) The cash sale of 15,000 shares at $4 per share

2. Assume that on February 1, 19—, the Candis Corporation received a subscription for 25,000 shares at $5 per share. One-third of the subscription was received in cash, and the balance is to be paid in two equal monthly installments. Record:
   (a) The receipt of the subscription and cash payment
   (b) The receipt of the two installment payments
   (c) The issuance of the stock

Journal Entries for Cash Dividends

3. Assume that the Candis Corporation has 50,000 shares of common stock outstanding at the end of 19—. On December 10, the board of directors declared a $0.50 cash dividend to be paid on February 15 of the next year. On December 31, the Income Summary account has a credit balance of $50,000 after the declaration of the dividend. Prepare journal entries for:
   (a) Declaration of the dividend.
   (b) Closing entry for Income Summary.
   (c) Payment of the dividend.
   (d) Determine the balance in the Retained Earnings account on December 31.

4. The MacGuffy Corporation received authorization to issue 15,000 shares of $5 par common stock. As of December 15 of the current year, 12,000 shares have been issued. On December 20, the board of directors declared a $0.30 per share cash dividend to be paid to stockholders of record De-

cember 30, payable January 15 of the following year. Net income for the year amounted to $16,000. Prepare journal entries for:
(*a*) Declaration of the cash dividend on December 20
(*b*) Closing entry for Income Summary
(*c*) Payment of the cash dividend on January 15 of the following year

Stockholders' Equity Section of the Balance Sheet

5. The Jackson Corporation received authorization to issue 20,000 shares of $10 par common stock, and 18,000 shares had been issued at an average of $12 per share. On January 1 of the current year, there was a $8,000 credit balance in the Retained Earnings account, and net income for the current year amounted to $11,000. Cash dividends amounting to $12,000 had been declared and paid during the year. Prepare the Stockholders' Equity section of the balance sheet as of December 31 of the current year.

6. Use the following information to prepare the Stockholders' Equity section of the balance sheet in good form for Kotton Corporation on December 31 of the current year.

Retained Earnings	$105,000 (credit balance)
Premium on Common	300,000
Common Stock Subscribed, 10,000 shares	?
Common Stock, $10 par, 100,000 shares authorized, 50,000 shares issued	500,000

PROBLEMS

Journal Entries for Common Stock and Cash Dividends

✓ **14-1.** Mo-By Corporation received a charter authorizing the sale of 50,000 shares of $8 par value common stock. Journalize the following transactions.

19_A
Jan. 10 Sold for cash 10,000 shares at $10 per share.
Feb. 15 Received a subscription for 10,000 shares at $11 per share with a 50 percent cash down payment and the balance due in 60 days.
Apr. 15 Received the balance due on the subscription of February 15 and stock was issued.
Oct. 20 Sold for cash 5,000 shares at $12 per share.
Dec.   1 The board of directors declared a $0.25 cash dividend on all outstanding shares payable on February 10, 19_B.
      31 The Income Summary account has a $20,000 credit balance.
19_B
Feb. 10 Paid the dividend declared on December 1, 19_A.

14-2. Backlash Company received authorization for 100,000 shares of $5 par value common stock; 50,000 shares are outstanding. Journalize the following selected transactions.

19_A

Jan. 15 Received a subscription for 15,000 shares at $10 per share, receiving one-third down and the balance due in 3 months.

Apr. 15 Received the balance due on the subscription of January 15 and stock was issued.

Dec. 10 Declared a $0.15 cash dividend on outstanding shares to be paid on January 25, 19_B.

31 Closed the Income Summary account. The account has a $35,000 credit balance.

19_B

Jan. 25 Paid the dividend declared on December 10, 19_A.

14-3. The charter of Sanchez Corporation authorized the sale of 200,000 shares of no-par common stock. The board of directors set a stated value of $3 per share. Journalize the following transactions:

19_A

Jan. 20 Received a subscription for 20,000 shares at $4 per share. The subscribers paid 25 percent of the subscription price in cash, agreed to pay the balance in three equal installments on February 20, March 20, and April 20.

Feb. 10 Sold for cash 25,000 shares at $5 per share and stock issued.

20 Received the first payment from the subscribers for the subscription dated January 20.

Mar. 10 Sold for cash, 10,000 shares at $6 per share and stock issued.

20 Subscribers paid the second payment on the subscription received January 20.

Apr. 1 Sold for cash 15,000 shares at $7 per share and stock issued.

20 Received the final payment from the subscribers of January 20 subscriptions and stock certificates issued.

Dec. 10 The board of directors declared a $0.20 cash dividend on all outstanding shares payable January 15, 19_B, to stockholders of record on December 31, 19_A.

14-4. Tell Tail Corporation is authorized to sell 100,000 shares of $10 par value common stock. Journalize the following transactions:

19_A

Apr. 10 Sold for cash 15,000 shares at $11 a share and stock issued.

June 18 Received subscriptions for 20,000 shares at $15 a share. Subscribers paid two-thirds of the subscription as a cash down payment. They agreed to pay the balance by July 18.

July 18 Received the balance due on the June 18 subscription and issued the stock certificates.

Aug. 20 Sold for cash 10,000 shares at $12 a share and stock issued.

Dec. 5 The board of directors declared a $0.15 cash dividend per share payable January 20, 19_B, to stockholders on record January 1, 19_B.

31 Closed the Income Summary account, which has a $35,000 credit balance.

19_B

Jan. 20 Paid the dividend declared on December 5.

Stockholders' Equity Section of Balance Sheet

14-5. The accounting records of the Up Down Corporation on December 31, 19_A, contained the following information:

Common Stock, $5 par value, 50,000 shares authorized, 20,000 shares issued and outstanding	$100,000
Common Stock Subscribed, 10,000 shares	50,000
Premium on Common Stock	50,000
Retained Earnings before cash dividend	20,000

Cash dividend of $0.50 a share declared on December 31 to be paid on January 25 to stockholders of record January 10, 19_B.

Required

Prepare the Stockholders' Equity section of the balance sheet as of December 31, 19_A.

14-6. The ledger of Kort Ho Corporation provided the following information on December 31 of the current year.

Total Assets	$750,000
Total Liabilities	80,000
Common Stock, $2 par value, 200,000 shares authorized, 110,000 shares issued and outstanding	220,000
Common Stock subscribed, 5,000 shares	10,000
Premium on Common Stock	300,000
Retained Earnings	?

Required

Prepare the Stockholders' Equity section of the balance sheet in good form as of December 31.

Corporate Balance Sheet

14-7. Prepare a balance sheet in good form for the End All Corporation on December 31 of the current year.

Accounts Payable	$ 10,000
Accounts Receivable	15,000
Cash	20,000
Buildings	400,000
Common Stock, 100,000 authorized, $3 par value,	
50,000 shares issued	150,000
Common Stock Subscribed, 5,000 shares	15,000
Premium on Common	410,000
Accumulated Depreciation/Building	125,000
Machinery	350,000
Accumulated Depreciation/Machinery	50,000
Land	85,000
Land for Future Expansion	35,000
Mortage Payable, 7½%, due 19_U	200,000
Merchandise Inventory	150,000
Prepaid Insurance	6,000
Taxes Payable	4,000
Wages Payable	3,000
Common Subscriptions Receivable	25,000
Retained Earnings	?
Organization Costs	3,000
Patents	2,000

After completing this chapter, you should be able to:

1. **List the sources of corporate capital and give their balance sheet presentation**

2. **Record the sale of common stock for cash and on subscription**

3. **Explain briefly the features of callable and convertible preferred stock**

4. **Account for the issuance of preferred stock at par value and above and below par value**

5. **Prepare the Stockholders' Equity section of the balance sheet**

6. **Record the entries for the purchase and sale of treasury stock**

7. **Account for the receipt and sale of donated treasury stock**

Chapter 14 discussed the difference between accounting for a corporate form of business and a single proprietorship. The only difference is in recording transactions for the owner's equity accounts—known as stockholders' equity for a corporation. The stockholders or shareholders are the owners of a corporation which is a legal entity of its own, separate from its owners. Stockholders are not liable for corporate debts, and they may sell their ownership (represented by shares of stock) without consent from other stockholders. This chapter will continue the discussion of accounting for common stock along with the accounting for preferred stock and treasury stock.

SOURCES OF CAPITAL

All three types of business organizations obtain capital from two major sources—profits received from business operations and assets received from the owner/s, the public, or the government. A single proprietorship or partnership receives additional capital from assets contributed to the business by the owner/s. These contributed assets and realized profits are called owner's capital and are shown in the Owner's Equity section of a balance sheet. However, a corporation may receive assets from three different sources:

Sources of corporate capital

1. Sale of authorized stock
2. Gifts in the form of assets
3. Profits realized from business operations

The sale of stock and assets received as a gift are referred to as ***paid-in capital*** and ***contributed capital.*** Profits realized from operations that have not been declared as dividends by the corporate board of directors are known as ***retained earnings,*** because these earnings are being retained for operations by the corporation. Paid-in capital (contributed capital) and retained earnings represent the owner's equity in a corporation, and they are shown in the last section of a balance sheet under the classification of stockholders' equity.

ACCOUNTING FOR COMMON STOCK

Common stock is usually sold for cash; however, some companies may issue stock in payment of organization costs or the receipt of assets, or they may sell their stock on a subscription contract. When stock is issued in payment of organization costs or in payment for the purchase of assets, the related asset account is debited and the Common Stock account is credited. When stock is sold on a subscription contract, the purchaser signs a contract to buy a specified number of shares of a corporation's stock at a specified price and agrees to pay for the stock at some future date. A person who buys stock on subscription is called a subscriber. Recording entries for the sale and issuance of common stock is discussed next.

Common Stock Sold for Cash. Recording the sale of common stock for cash requires a debit to the Cash account for its selling price and a credit to the Common Stock account for its par or stated value. If common stock has no-par or stated value, the entire amount of the sale is credited to the Common Stock account. When common stock is sold for more than its par or stated value, the excess amount is credited to an account entitled *Premium on Common* for par value stock and *Paid-in Capital in Excess of Stated Value/Common* for stated value stock. When stock is sold for less than its par or stated value, the difference between par or stated value and the issuance price is debited to an account entitled *Discount on Common* for par value stock and Paid-in Capital in Excess of Stated Value/Common for stated value stock. Since some states do not allow corporate stock to be sold at a discount, stock is seldom issued for an amount less than its par or stated value.

To illustrate the sale of common stock for cash, three examples are given for the Clapp Corporation who received authorization to issue 25,000 shares of $25 par value common stock.

EXAMPLE 1   Sale of Common Stock for Par Value: *On February 10 of the current year, 1,000 shares of common stock were issued for cash at its par value of $25 per share.*

Sale of par value common stock at par

Feb.	10	Cash (1,000 shares × $25)	25,000	
		Common Stock (1,000 shares × $25 par value)		25,000
		Issued 1,000 shares of common stock at its par value.		

EXAMPLE 2   Sale of Common Stock above Par Value: *On March 5, 500 shares of common stock were issued for $27 per share, $2 per share above its par value.*

Sale of par value common above par value

Mar. 5	Cash (500 shares × $27)	13,500	
	Common Stock (500 shares × $25 par value)		12,500
	Premium on Common (500 shares × $2 above par)		1,000
	Issued 500 shares of common stock at $27 per share, $2 above par value.		

EXAMPLE 3   Sale of Common Stock below Par Value: *On March 10, 800 shares of common stock were issued for $24 per share, $1 per share below par.*

Sale of par value common below par value

Mar. 10	Cash (800 shares × $24)	19,200	
	Discount on Common (800 shares × $1 below par)	800	
	Common Stock (800 shares × $25 par value)		20,000
	Issued 800 shares of common stock at $24 per share, $1 below par value.		

After the entries for Examples 1, 2, and 3 are posted, the stockholders' equity accounts (in T account form) would show the following balances:

Common Stock		Premium on Common	
	Feb. 10 25,000		Mar. 5 1,000
	Mar. 5 12,500		
	10 20,000		

Discount on Common	
Mar. 10 800	

Common Stock Sold on Subscription Contract.   When subscribers sign the subscription contract, a journal entry is required debiting a current asset account entitled *Subscription Receivable* for the contract price and crediting a temporary stockholder equity account entitled *Common Stock Subscribed* for the par or stated value of the stock. If the common stock has no-par or stated value, the entire amount of the contract price is credited to the Common Stock Subscribed account. When subscribed stock is sold for more than its par or stated value, the excess amount is credited to an account entitled Premium on Common for par value stock or Paid-in Capital in Excess of Stated Value/Common for stated value stock. When subscribed stock is sold for less than its par or stated value, the difference between its par or stated value and the subscription contract price is debited to a Discount of Common Stock account for par value stock or Paid-in Capital in Excess of Stated Value/Common for stated value stock.

To illustrate the receipt of a common stock subscription, assume that the Clapp Corporation in Examples 1, 2, and 3 received the following subscriptions for its $25 par value common stock.

EXAMPLE 4   Receipt of Common Stock Subscription above Par Value: *On March 31, a subscription was received for 1,000 shares of common stock at $27 per share, and the subscribers paid 50 percent of the subscription price in cash.*

Receipt of common stock subscription above par value

Mar. 31	Cash (1,000 shares × $27 = $27,000 × 50%)	13,500	
	Subscriptions Receivable/Common ($27,000 − $13,500)	13,500	
	Common Stock Subscribed (1,000 shares × $25 par value)		25,000
	Premium on Common (1,000 shares × $2 above par)		2,000
	Received subscription for 1,000 shares of common stock at $27 per share, $2,000 above par value. Subscribers paid 50% of subscription price in cash.		

On April 30, the balance due on the subscription dated March 31 was received and 1,000 shares were issued to common subscribers.

Issuance of common stock subscribed above par value

Apr. 30	Cash (1,000 shares × $27 = $27,000 × 50%)	13,500	
	Common Stock Subscribed	25,000	
	Subscriptions Receivable/Common		13,500
	Common Stock (1,000 shares × $25 par value)		25,000
	Received balance due on subscription dated March 31 and 1,000 shares of common stock was issued to the subscribers.		

After the entries for Examples 1, 2, 3, and 4 are posted, the stockholders' equity accounts (in T account form) would show the following balances:

Common Stock		
	Feb. 10	25,000
	Mar. 5	12,500
	10	20,000
	Apr. 30	25,000

Common Stock Subscribed		
Apr. 30 25,000	Mar. 31	25,000

Premium on Common		
	Mar. 5	1,000
	31	2,000

Discount on Common	
Mar. 10 800	

The Common Stock, Common Stock Subscribed, and Premium on Common accounts are all classified as stockholders' equity, paid-in capital accounts. All these accounts should always have a credit balance. The Common Stock Subscribed account is actually a temporary stockholders' equity account, because when the subscription is paid in full and the stock is issued to the subscribers, the account is closed with a debit and the amount is credited to the Common Stock account. Discount on Common is classified as a contra stockholders' equity, paid-in capital account and should always have a debit or zero balance.

The Stockholders' Equity, Paid-in Capital section of the balance sheet as of April 30 follows.

Stockholders' Equity, Paid-in Capital section of balance sheet

Stockholders' Equity		
Paid-in Capital:		
Common Stock, $25 par value, 25,000 shares authorized, 3,300 shares issued and outstanding		$82,500
Premium on Common	$3,000	
Less: Discount on Common	800	2,200
Total Paid-in Capital		$84,700

Receipt of Common Stock Subscription above Stated Value. To illustrate the receipt of a common stock subscription for no-par common stock with a stated value, assume that the Carlson Shoe Corporation received authorization to issue 10,000 shares of no-par common stock with a stated value of $10 per share. On May 15, a subscription was received for 1,000 shares of no-par common stock at $12 per share. The subscribers paid 40 percent of the subscription price in cash.

Receipt of no-par common stock subscription above stated value

May	15	Cash (1,000 shares × $12 = $12,000 × 40%)	4,800	
		Subscriptions Receivable/Common ($12,000 − $4,800)	7,200	
		Common Stock Subscribed (1,000 shares × $10 stated value)		10,000
		Paid-in Capital in Excess of Stated Value/Common (1,000 shares × $2 above stated value)		2,000
		Received subscription for 1,000 shares of no-par common with a $10 stated value at $12 per share, $2 above stated value. Subscribers paid 40% of subscription price in cash.		

On June 15, the 60 percent balance due on the subscription dated May 15 was received and 1,000 shares were issued to the common subscribers.

Issuance of no-par common stock to subscribers

June	15	Cash (1,000 shares × $12 = $12,000 × 60%)	7,200	
		Common Stock Subscribed	10,000	
		Subscriptions Receivable/Common		7,200
		Common Stock		10,000
		Received balance due on subscription dated May 15 and 1,000 shares of no-par common stock was issued to the subscribers.		

Common Stock Issued in Payment for Organization Costs or a Purchase of Assets. When common stock is issued in payment for organization costs or for the purchase of assets, the asset account is debited for its cost and the stock account is credited for its par or stated value. Any difference between the amount of the organization costs and the par or stated value of the stock is credited to the account Premium on Common.

To illustrate, assume that legal costs for the organization of the Johnson Corporation amounted to $515. On April 12 of the current year, the attorney agreed to accept 25 shares of the corporation's $20 par value common stock in payment for his fees. The following journal entry would be recorded:

Common stock issued in payment for organization costs

Apr.	12	Organization Costs	515	
		Common Stock (25 shares × $20 par value)		500
		Premium on Common ($515 − $500 par value of stock)		15
		To record issuance of 25 shares of common stock in payment for legal fees incurred in organizing the corporation.		

The costs of organizing a corporation are not classified as an expense, because if these costs were not incurred, the corporation would not exist. Therefore, organization costs are classified as an intangible asset since they will benefit the corporation over its entire life. Organization costs are shown in the Intangible Asset section of a balance sheet.

The Financial Accounting Standards Board (FASB) requires that the costs of organization be written off (expensed) over a period of 40 years or less. According to current income tax regulations, organization costs may be written off over a 5-year period or more. Consequently, most corporations write off the costs of organization over a 5-year period.

PREFERRED STOCK

There are several distinctive features that separate **preferred stock** from common stock. These features give preferred stockholders certain advantages called preferences that are not given to common stockholders, such as **preference as to dividends, preference as to assets,** a convertible option, and a callable option.

Preference as to Dividends

Preferred stockholders are entitled to receive a dividend for a stipulated rate before any dividends are paid to common stockholders. However, preferred or common stockholders cannot receive any dividends unless they are declared by the board of directors. When dividends are declared, preferred stockholders receive their share of the dividends according to the preferred stock contract. The four variations of distributing dividends to preferred stockholders are discussed in Chapter 16.

Preference as to Assets

If a corporation discontinues operations and dissolves the business, preferred stockholders have first claim on the assets after all the creditors have been paid and before any assets are paid to common stockholders. Preferred stockholders are entitled to receive an amount equal to the par value of their stock. Depending upon the stock contract, they may also receive any dividends in arrears.

For example, a corporation with $25,000 of outstanding preferred stock preferred as to assets and $40,000 of common stock outstanding decides to liquidate its business. After paying off all creditors, assets amounted to $30,000. There are no dividends in arrears for preferred. Preferred stockholders would receive $25,000, and the $5,000 balance would go to the common stockholders.

If preferred stock did not have the asset preference feature, the $30,000 in the above illustration would be divided between the preferred and common stockholders according to their capital balance ratio. The preferred stockholders would receive $11,538 and common stockholders $18,462 of the $30,000 computed as follows:

	Capital Stock Outstanding
Preferred	$25,000/$65,000 × $30,000 = $11,538
Common	40,000/$65,000 × $30,000 = 18,462
Total	$65,000 _____ $30,000

Callable Option

Some preferred stock may be issued with a callable clause giving a corporation the option of calling in preferred stock on a specified date to cancel the stock and pay off the stockholders. Because the callable price of *callable preferred* stock is usually higher than the par value of the stock, the stock will be attractive to investors.

If callable preferred stock is called in at an amount above its par value, and there are paid-in capital accounts related to the issue, the journal entry requires a debit to Callable Preferred Stock, a debit to Premium on Preferred, and a credit to Cash. Any difference resulting between the call price and the issued price is debited to the Retained Earnings account.

To illustrate, assume that a corporation had 300 shares outstanding of $50 par value callable preferred stock for a total of $15,000 plus an account balance of $4,000 in Premium on Preferred related to the issue. The stock was called in on January 8 for a price of $65 per share. The journal entry to record this transaction appears below.

Journal entry to record cancelation of callable preferred stock

Jan.	8	Callable Preferred Stock	15,000	
		Premium on Preferred	4,000	
		Retained Earnings	500	
		Cash		19,500
		To record the cancelation of 300 shares of callable preferred stock at $65 per share.		

Convertible Option

Some preferred stock may be issued with a *convertible* option giving stock-holders an opportunity to convert their *preferred stock* into common stock or long-term bonds at a specified time for a specified amount. The option of converting preferred to common stock may be a distinct advantage to the stockholders, because they are usually given an opportunity to acquire common stock for a price below its market value per share and at the same time acquire voting rights in the corporation.

The convertible option on preferred stock may be combined with the callable option. For example, preferred stock may be callable at a specified time and stockholders are given the option of converting preferred stock to common stock or exchanging preferred stock for cash.

When preferred stock is converted into common, the journal entry requires a debit to the preferred stock account and a credit to the common stock account for the par value amount. The difference between the preferred and common stock amounts is debited or credited to a paid-in capital account.

To illustrate, assume that a corporation had 1,000 shares outstanding of $100 par value preferred stock with a convertible option entitling stock-holders to exchange one share of preferred stock for two shares of $25 par value common stock at $50 per share. On March 6, 500 shares of preferred stock were exchanged for 1,000 shares of common stock by preferred stockholders, and the 500 shares of preferred stock were canceled. The entry is shown below.

Journal entry for conversion of preferred stock to common stock

Mar. 6	Preferred Stock	50,000	
	Premium on Common		25,000
	Common Stock		25,000
	To record the conversion of 500 shares of preferred to 1,000 shares of $25 par value common at $50 per share. The 500 shares of preferred were canceled.		

ACCOUNTING FOR PREFERRED STOCK

Accounting for the issuance of preferred stock is handled in the same manner as recording the issuance of common stock. However, a different account title is used for each type of preferred stock issued. Preferred stock may have a par value, stated value, or no-par value, although most preferred stock is assigned a par value. Par or stated value stock is recorded at its par or stated value, and no-par stock is recorded at its selling price. When stock is sold above par value, the excess is credited to the ***Premium on Preferred*** account. The excess amount of stock sold above stated value is credited to the ***Paid-in Capital in Excess of Stated Value/Preferred*** account. If stock is sold below par or stated value, the preferred stock account is credited for the par or stated value. The difference between the par value and the selling price of preferred stock is debited to an account entitled ***Discount on Preferred.*** The difference between the stated value and selling price is debited to an account entitled Paid-in Capital in Excess of Stated Value/Preferred. If preferred stock has no-par or stated value, preferred will be credited for the selling price, and there will be no premium, discount, or paid-in capital accounts.

Preferred stock may be sold at par value or above or below its par value. To illustrate, assume that a company received authorization to issue 10,000 shares of 6 percent, $100 par value preferred. Three examples for the sale of the preferred stock are illustrated below.

EXAMPLE 1   *On February 6, 2,000 shares of 6 percent preferred stock were sold for its $100 par value. The entry required is shown below.*

Preferred stock issued at par value

Feb. 6	Cash	200,000	
	6% Preferred Stock		200,000
	To record the sale of 2,000 shares of 6% preferred stock at its $100 par value.		

EXAMPLE 2   *On February 28, 5,000 shares of 6 percent preferred stock were sold for $110 per share, $10 per share above par value. The entry required is shown below.*

Preferred stock issued above its par value

Feb. 28	Cash	550,000	
	6% Preferred Stock		500,000
	Premium on Preferred		50,000
	Issued 5,000 shares of 6% preferred stock at $110 per share, $10 per share above its $100 par value.		

EXAMPLE 3   *On March 10, 1,000 shares of 6 percent preferred stock were sold for $98 per share, $2 lower than its $100 par value. The entry required is as follows:*

Preferred stock issued below its par value

Mar. 10	Cash	98,000	
	Discount on Preferred	2,000	
	6% Preferred Stock		100,000
	Issued 1,000 shares of 6% preferred stock at $98 per share; $2 per share below its $100 par value.		

After the entries for Examples 1, 2, and 3 are posted, the stockholders' equity accounts (in T account form) would show the following balances:

Preferred Stock		Premium on Preferred
	Feb. 6 200,000	Feb. 28 50,000
	28 500,000	
	Mar. 10 100,000	

Discount on Preferred
Mar. 10 2,000

The Stockholders' Equity, Paid-in Capital section of the balance sheet for Examples 1, 2, and 3 for the 6 percent, $100 par value preferred stock as of March 10 is illustrated below.

Stockholders' Equity

Paid-in Capital:		
6% Preferred Stock, $100 par value, 10,000 shares authorized, 8,000 shares issued and outstanding		$800,000
Premium on Preferred	$50,000	
Less: Discount on Preferred	2,000	48,000
Total Paid-in Capital for Preferred		$848,000

BALANCE SHEET PRESENTATION OF COMMON AND PREFERRED STOCK

All stock issued is shown in the Stockholders' Equity, Paid-in Capital section of the balance sheet as illustrated in the previous examples. When authorization has been received for more than one type of stock, preferred stock is listed first followed by the common stock and other paid-in capital accounts. Preferred stock is listed first because they have preferences over the assets before common stockholders. To illustrate, the Stockholders' Equity, Paid-in Capital section of the balance sheet has been prepared with the data given in Examples 1 to 4 for common stock and Examples 1 to 3 for preferred stock.

Stockholders' Equity, Paid-in Capital section of balance sheet

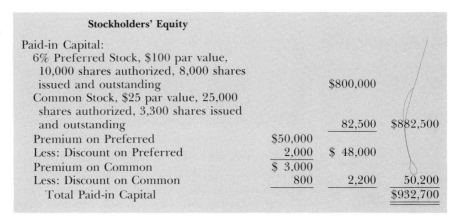

Stockholders' Equity			
Paid-in Capital:			
6% Preferred Stock, $100 par value, 10,000 shares authorized, 8,000 shares issued and outstanding		$800,000	
Common Stock, $25 par value, 25,000 shares authorized, 3,300 shares issued and outstanding		82,500	$882,500
Premium on Preferred	$50,000		
Less: Discount on Preferred	2,000	$ 48,000	
Premium on Common	$ 3,000		
Less: Discount on Common	800	2,200	50,200
Total Paid-in Capital			$932,700

TREASURY STOCK

When a corporation acquires some of its own issued and outstanding capital stock for the purpose of reissuing the stock at some future date, the stock acquired by the company is called *treasury stock.* Treasury stock may be acquired through purchase on the open market or as a gift. A stockholder may also donate shares for the treasury to raise additional funds for operations. Usually treasury stock is acquired by a corporation for the purpose of having stock available for employee stock investment plans and employee bonuses, or for issuing stock dividends to stockholders.

A corporation receives something of value when treasury shares are acquired, but the shares cannot be classified as an asset. These shares represent a partial return of capital invested by the stockholders resulting in a decrease to stockholders' equity. Therefore, a return of a stockholder's investment cannot be classified as an asset because a corporation cannot own part of itself. Treasury stock is stock that has been issued but the shares are no longer outstanding; therefore, they have no voting or dividend rights.

Since treasury stock causes a decrease to stockholders' equity, it is classified as a contra stockholders' equity account on the balance sheet. The Treasury Stock account will always have a debit or zero balance.

Accounting for Treasury Stock

The most common method of recording treasury stock transactions is referred to as the cost method. Under this method, the Treasury Stock account is debited for the purchase price following the cost principle[1] of accounting. For example, assume that on February 1 a corporation purchased 2,000 shares of its own $10 par value common stock for $15 per share, a total of $30,000 (2,000 × $15). The entry would be recorded as follows:

Purchase of treasury stock

Feb. 1	Treasury Stock/Common	30,000	
	Cash		30,000
	Purchased 2,000 shares of $10 par value common stock for $15 per share.		

If a corporation has more than one class of stock, the type of stock must be indicated after the account title as shown in the previous journal entry. It is not necessary to use the type of stock in the account title if a corporation has only one class of stock.

The ledger account for Treasury Stock/Common is shown next.

Ledger account for treasury stock

Title: Treasury Stock/Common   **Account No.: 380**

Date		Explanation	Ref.	Debit	Credit	Balance
Feb.	18			30,000		30,000

When treasury stock is sold, the Cash account is debited for the increase and the Treasury Stock account is credited for the decrease. If treasury stock is sold for more or less than its purchase price, the account *Paid-in Capital/Treasury Stock* would be used to record the difference between the selling price and purchase price. If the treasury stock is sold for more than its purchase price, the account is credited for the difference; if the treasury stock is sold for less than its purchase price, the account is debited for the difference as shown in the following examples.

EXAMPLE 1

On February 18, 500 shares of treasury stock were sold for $18 per share, a total of $9,000 (500 × $18). The stock was sold for an excess of $3 per share ($18 − $15) over the purchase price of $15 for a total of $1,500 (500 × 3). The sale is journalized below.

Sale of treasury stock above cost price

Feb. 18	Cash	9,000	
	Treasury Stock/Common		7,500
	Paid-in Capital/Treasury Stock		1,500
	Reissued 500 shares of treasury stock for $18 per share, $3 over the purchase price of $15 per share.		

---

[1] The cost principle states that for accounting purposes all business transactions will be recorded at cost or the actual dollars paid.

Note that the Treasury Stock account is credited for $7,500, the purchase price of 500 shares at $15 per share. The excess amount of $1,500 ($9,000 − $7,500) received over the purchase price is credited to the Paid-in Capital/Treasury Stock account which is classified as a stockholders' equity account.

The two stockholders' equity accounts after posting the above entry are shown below.

Ledger accounts for treasury stock

Title: Treasury Stock/Common   **Account No.: 380**

Date		Explanation	Ref.	Debit	Credit	Balance
Feb.	1			30,000		30,000
	18				7,500	22,500

Title: Paid-in Capital/Treasury Stock   **Account No.: 381**

Date		Explanation	Ref.	Debit	Credit	Balance
Feb.	18				1,500	1,500

EXAMPLE 2

On March 28, 1,000 shares of treasury stock were sold for $15 per share, a total of $15,000 (1,000 × $15). The sale is journalized below.

Sale of treasury stock at cost price

Mar.	28	Cash	15,000	
		Treasury Stock/Common		15,000
		Reissued 1,000 shares of common		
		at its purchase price of $15 per share.		

The ledger account for Treasury Stock/Common after posting the above entry is shown below.

Title: Treasury Stock/Common   **Account No.: 380**

Date		Explanation	Ref.	Debit	Credit	Balance
Feb.	1			30,000		30,000
	18				7,500	22,500
Mar.	28				15,000	7,500

EXAMPLE 3

On May 2, the last 500 shares of treasury stock were sold for $13 per share, a total of $6,500 (500 × $13). The stock was sold for $2 per share ($15 − $13) less than the purchase price of $15 for a total of $1,000 (500 × $2). The Paid-in Capital/Treasury Stock account is debited for the decrease as follows:

Sale of treasury stock below cost price

May 2	Cash	6,500	
	Paid-in Capital/Treasury Stock	1,000	
	Treasury Stock/Common		7,500
	Reissued 500 shares of common stock at $13 per share, $2 below the purchase price of $15 per share.		

The stockholders' equity accounts after the May 2 entry is posted are shown below:

Title: Treasury Stock/Common   **Account No.: 380**

Date		Explanation	Ref.	Debit	Credit	Balance
Feb.	1			30,000		30,000
	18				7,500	22,500
Mar.	28				15,000	7,500
May	2				7,500	–0–

Title: Paid-in Capital/Treasury Stock   **Account No.: 381**

Date		Explanation	Ref.	Debit	Credit	Balance
Feb.	18				1,500	1,500
May	2			1,000		500

If the last 500 shares of treasury stock were sold for $11 per share, a total of $5,500 (500 × $11), the sale would result in a decrease of $4 per share ($15 − $11) below the purchase price of $15 for a total decrease of $2,000 (500 × $4). On May 2, the Paid-in Capital/Treasury Stock account only had a $1,500 credit balance; therefore, the $500 loss ($2,000 − $1,500) from the sale of treasury stock is debited to the Retained Earnings account as shown below.

May 2	Cash	5,500	
	Paid-in Capital/Treasury Stock	1,500	
	Retained Earnings	500	
	Treasury Stock/Common		7,500
	Reissued 500 shares of treasury stock at $11 per share, $2,000 under the purchase price. Decreased the Paid-in Capital/Treasury Stock account for $1,500 balance and decreased Retained Earnings for the remaining $500.		

The Paid-in Capital/Treasury Stock account could not be debited for the entire loss of $2,000, because the account only had a $1,500 credit balance; therefore, the $500 ($2,000 − $1,500) difference was debited to the Retained Earnings account. The $500 difference may also be debited to any other Paid-in Capital account.

Donated Treasury Stock

When a corporation receives its own capital stock as a donation, a journal entry is not required because no assets are involved in the transaction. However, a notation may be entered in the journal. For example, assume that on June 3 a company received 500 shares of common treasury stock as a donation from a stockholder. The notation in the journal is shown below.

Journal notation for receipt of donated stock

June	3	Received a donation of 500 shares of common stock.

If the donated treasury stock is sold on July 6 for $18 per share, the following journal entry would be recorded:

Sale of donated stock

July	6	Cash	9,000	
		Paid-in Capital/Donated Treasury Stock		9,000
		Reissued 500 shares of donated common stock received on June 3.		

Note that the Treasury Stock account was not credited for the sale; no entry was recorded in the ledger account when the donation was received. The ***Paid-in Capital/Donated Treasury Stock*** account is credited for the entire amount received from the sale of donated common stock.

Legal Restrictions on Treasury Stock

Some state laws limit the amount of treasury stock that a corporation may acquire to the excess amount over its legal capital. ***Legal capital*** usually represents the total amount of outstanding capital stock at its par or stated value. If a corporation has no par or stated value stock, some states may designate legal capital as the amount of outstanding no-par value stock. For example, assume a corporation has 10,000 shares of $10 par value capital stock authorized, issued, and outstanding in the amount of $100,000, Premium on Common for $30,000, and Retained Earnings of $40,000. The amount of legal capital is $100,000; therefore, the corporation would be limited to treasury stock in the amount of $70,000 ($30,000 + $40,000).

States may also restrict the amount of retained earnings available for dividends to the cost of any unissued treasury stock. For example, assume the corporation with $40,000 of retained earnings had 1,000 shares of un-issued treasury stock that cost $12,000. The retained earnings would be re-stricted for the $12,000 cost of unissued treasury stock, and only $28,000 ($40,000 − $12,000) would be available for the declaration of dividends.

Balance Sheet Presentation of Treasury Stock

Once capital stock has been sold, it would be listed as issued in the Stock-holders' Equity section of a balance sheet until the stock is called in and canceled. If some issued stock is in the treasury, the cost would be shown as the last item on a balance sheet and deducted from the Total Paid-in Capi-tal and Retained Earnings section to arrive at total stockholders' equity.

The number of shares in the treasury, the restriction placed on re-tained earnings, and the cost of treasury stock would be disclosed in the Stockholders' Equity section of a balance sheet. The balance sheet presen-tation for a corporation with treasury stock is illustrated below.

Balance sheet presentation of treasury stock

Stockholders' Equity		
Paid-in Capital:		
Common Stock, $10 par value, 10,000 shares authorized and issued of which 1,000 shares are in the treasury	$100,000	
Premium on Common	30,000	
Total Paid-in Capital	$130,000	
Retained Earnings of which $15,000 is restricted for the cost of treasury stock	40,000	$170,000
Less: Cost of treasury stock		15,000
Total Stockholders' Equity		$155,000

SUMMARY

Single proprietorships and partnerships obtain operating capital from real-ized profits and assets contributed to the business from owners. Corpora-tions obtain operating capital from realized profits, the sale of capital stock, and assets received as a gift. Capital realized from the sale of authorized stock and assets received as a gift are called contributed capital or paid-in capital; profits realized from business operations are called retained earnings.

Common stock may be issued as no-par, or it may be assigned a par or stated value. No-par common stock is credited for the issuance price. Par or stated value common stock is credited for the par or stated value; any ex-cess over par or stated value is credited to the Premium on Common or Paid-in Capital in Excess of Stated Value account. When common stock is sold for less than par or stated value, the Discount on Common or Paid-in

Capital in Excess of Stated Value account is debited for the difference between the issuance price and its par or stated value. Stock sold on subscription is credited to the Common Stock Subscribed account for the par or stated value when the subscription is received. When subscribed stock is issued, the subscribed account is debited and the Common Stock account is credited.

Preferred stock derives its name from the preferences stockholders receive that are not offered to common stockholders. Preferences as to dividends and assets plus a conversion and callable option are advantages that may be given to different issues of preferred stock. If a corporation dissolves its business operations, the preferred stockholders have first claim on the assets after all the creditors have been paid and before any assets are paid to common stockholders assuring preferred stockholders a return on their investment for the amount of its par value per share. Depending upon the provisions of the contract, preferred stockholders may also receive any dividends in arrears after all creditors are paid and before any assets are paid to common stockholders.

Convertible preferred stock may be advantageous to the corporation as well as the stockholder. Convertible options give a corporation the opportunity of eliminating preferred dividends, and the preferred stockholders are given the option of converting their shares of preferred stock to common stock at a price below the market value per share or exchanging their preferred stock for cash. The conversion of preferred stock to common stock gives stockholders an opportunity to acquire common stock at a reasonable price and at the same time gives them voting rights in the corporation.

Callable preferred stock allows a corporation to call in the preferred stock at some future date, cancel the stock, and pay the preferred stockholders an amount that is usually more than the cost of their original investment.

Accounting for preferred stock requires that a different account title be used for each type of preferred stock issued. Preferred stock usually is issued with a par value, but some companies may issue no-par value stock with a stated value or it may issue preferred stock with no-par or stated value. Stock with a designated value is credited for its par or stated value when it is sold. Any excess amount above its par or stated value is credited to a Premium on Preferred or Paid-in Capital in Excess of Stated Value account. If stock is issued below par or stated value, the difference is debited to a Discount on Preferred for par value stock and a Paid-in Capital in Excess of Stated Value account for stated value stock. No-par value stock is credited for its issuance price, and there are no premium, discount, or paid-in capital accounts. When a corporation has more than one class of stock, the preferred stock is listed first in the Stockholders' Equity, Paid-in Capital section of a balance sheet.

When a company acquires some of its own stock for the purpose of reissuing the shares at some future date, the stock acquired is called treasury stock. Treasury stock is not an asset account; it represents a partial return of capital invested by the stockholders resulting in a decrease to stockholders' equity. When treasury stock is acquired, the Treasury Stock account is debited for its acquisition price following the cost principle of accounting. The Treasury Stock account is credited when the stock is sold, and any difference in the amount received and its purchase price is debited or credited to a Paid-in Capital/Treasury Stock account.

Occasionally treasury stock is donated by a stockholder to enable the corporation to reissue the stock and obtain additional funds for operations. A journal entry is not required for the receipt of donated stock because assets are not decreased when the stock is received. When the donated stock is sold, the Paid-in Capital/Donated Treasury Stock account is credited for its selling price.

Some states may place legal restrictions on the amount of treasury stock that a corporation may acquire for an amount above its legal capital. These restrictions must be shown in the Stockholders' Equity section of a balance sheet to comply with the full disclosure principle of accounting.

GLOSSARY

Callable Preferred: A type of preferred stock that gives a corporation the option of calling in the stock on a specified date to cancel the stock and pay off the stockholders an amount that is usually higher than its issuance price so the stock will be attractive to investors.

Common Stock Subscribed: A stockholders' equity account that is credited for the par or stated value of the stock when subscribers sign the subscription contract.

Contributed Capital: The amount received from the sale of stock plus the value of assets donated to a corporation.

Convertible Preferred: A type of preferred stock that gives preferred stockholders an option to convert their preferred stock into cash, common stock, or long-term bonds at a specified time and for a specified amount.

Discount on Common: The title of a contra stockholders' equity account that is used whenever common stock is sold at less than its par value. The account is debited for the difference between its par value and its issuance price.

Discount on Preferred: A contra stockholders' equity account that is debited when preferred stock is sold for less than its par value. The difference between par value and selling price is debited to a Discount on Preferred account.

Legal Capital: Legal capital represents the total amount of outstanding par or stated value capital stock. If there is no-par or stated value stock, some states may designate legal capital as the total amount of outstanding no-par value stock.

Paid-in Capital: Assets received from the sale of authorized and issued stock which represents the total stockholders' equity less the balance in the Retained Earnings account is known as paid-in capital.

Paid-in Capital/Donated Treasury Stock: Paid-in Capital/Donated Treasury Stock is a stockholders' equity account that is credited for the entire amount received from the sale of donated common stock. No entry is made into any account when a corporation receives its own common stock as a donation; only a notation is entered in the records indicating the number of shares received by the company.

Paid-in Capital in Excess of Stated Value: The title of a stockholders' equity account that is used whenever common or preferred stock is sold for more or less than its stated value. The account is credited for the difference between its stated value and issuance price whenever common or preferred stock is sold for more than its stated value. When common or preferred stock is sold for less than its stated value, the account is debited for the difference between its issuance price and stated value.

Paid-in Capital/Treasury Stock: Paid-in Capital/Treasury Stock is a stockholders' equity account that is credited or debited when treasury stock is sold for more or less than the purchase price of the stock. The Paid-in Capital/Treasury Stock account is credited for the difference between the selling price and purchase price when the treasury shares are sold for more than their cost. The Paid-in Capital account is debited for the difference when the treasury shares are sold for less than their cost.

Preference as to Assets: A preference given to preferred stockholders. The preference entitles preferred stockholders to the first claim on assets after all the creditors have been paid and before any assets are paid to common stockholders when the business operations are discontinued and liquidated.

Preference as to Dividends: A preference given to preferred stockholders. The preference entitles preferred stockholders to receive a dividend for a stipulated rate before any dividends are paid to common stockholders. However, dividends cannot be paid to any stockholder unless they are declared by the board of directors.

Preferred Stock: An issue of capital stock that gives preferred stockholders preferences as to dividends and assets plus a convertible and callable option that is not given to common stockholders.

Premium on Common: The title of a stockholders' equity account that is used whenever common stock is sold for more than its par value. The account is credited for the difference between its par value and issuance price.

Premium on Preferred: Premium on Preferred is a stockholders' equity account that is credited for the excess amount of the issuance price above the par value of preferred stock.

Retained Earnings: Profits realized from business operations that have not been paid to the stockholder in the form of a dividend; earnings retained in the business.

Subscription Receivable: A current asset account that is debited for the amount of the subscription when the subscribers sign the subscription contract.

Treasury Stock: When a company acquires some of its own issued and outstanding stock for the purpose of reissuing the shares at some future date, the stock acquired by the company is called treasury stock. The Treasury Stock account is debited when the shares are purchased and credited when the shares are sold for their cost price. The account is classified as a contra stockholders' equity account and would have a debit or zero balance.

QUESTIONS

1. A corporation obtains capital for the business from several different sources. Name the three main sources of capital for a corporation.

2. Name the two subclassifications of the Stockholders' Equity section of a balance sheet.

3. Give the two journal entries required, without amounts, for (*a*) the issuance of a common stock subscription received above par value, and (*b*) the issuance of the stock when the subscription is paid in full.

4. What accounts are debited when common stock is issued for less than its par or stated value?

5. Give the amounts credited to the common stock account for each of the following: (*a*) 1,000 shares of $10 par value common issued for $12 per share; (*b*) 500 shares of no-par common issued for $14 per share; and (*c*) 2,000 shares of no-par common with a stated value of $20 per share issued at $18 per share.

6. Give the definition of legal capital.

7. List the stockholders' equity accounts that are credited for the sale of: (*a*) preferred stock above par value; (*b*) preferred stock below par value; (*c*) common stock above stated value; and (*d*) treasury stock for more than the purchase price.

8. State two options that may be given to convertible preferred stockholders.

9. Give the balance sheet presentation for common stock, with the corresponding amounts, for a corporation that received authorization for 10,000 shares of $25 par value common stock, 8,000 shares issued at $32 per share, of which 500 shares are in the treasury.

10. Journalize the entry for the purchase of 1,000 shares of $10 par value common treasury stock with a market value of $18 per share.

EXERCISES

Common Stock Transactions for Cash and on Subscription

1. Ever-Sharp Knife Company received authorization to issue 15,000 shares of no-par value common stock; 7,500 shares were issued in the first year of operations at an average of $12 per share. Journalize the following selected transactions for the current year.

Apr.	2	Issued 2,500 shares of common stock at $11 per share.
	24	Received a subscription for 5,000 shares of common stock at $12 per share.
May	25	Subscribers paid the full amount of the subscription dated April 24 and 5,000 shares were issued.

2. Busy-Bee Products received authorization to issue 20,000 shares of $10 par value common stock and 50 percent of the shares were issued at an average price of $14 per share. On December 28, 19_A, 5,000 shares were subscribed for $15 per share. The Retained Earnings account had a credit balance of $7,930 on December 31, 19_A. Journalize the following selected transactions for 19_B.

19_B
Jan. 6 Received a payment amounting to 50 percent of the common subscriptions received on December 28, 19_A.
     29 Issued 4,000 shares of common stock at $13 per share.
Feb. 15 Common subscribers paid the balance due on the subscription of December 28, 19_A, and the 5,000 shares of common stock were issued.

Organization Costs and Preferred Stock Transactions

3. On January 1, 19__, Krawley Products was organized and received authorization to issue 5,000 shares of $50 par value preferred and 10,000 shares of $20 par value common stock.

Required

Journalize the following selected transactions for preferred stock.

19__
Jan. 10 Legal costs of organizing the corporation amounted to $2,500. The attorney agreed to accept 50 shares of preferred stock as payment for his fees and the shares were issued.
Feb. 2 Issued 1,550 shares of preferred stock for $60 per share.

Stockholders' Equity Section of Balance Sheet

4. Assume that Krawley Products of Exercise 3 sold 8,000 shares of common stock for an average price of $26 per share.

Required

Prepare the Stockholders' Equity, Paid-in Capital section of the balance sheet as of June 30, 19__; include all the information from Exercises 3 and 4.

Preferred Stock Transactions and Stockholders' Equity Section of Balance Sheet

5. Marlin Industries received authorization for 10,000 shares of $100 par value preferred and 20,000 shares of no-par value common stock with a stated value of $25 per share. On January 1, 19__, 5,000 shares of preferred stock and all the common shares had been issued. The Premium on Preferred Stock account had a credit balance of $75,000 and the Paid-in Capital in Excess of Stated Value/Common Stock account had a credit balance of $300,000.

Required

Journalize the following selected transactions for preferred stock.

19__
Feb. 10 Issued 2,000 shares of preferred stock for $120 per share.
Apr.   6 Issued 500 shares of preferred stock at par value.
July   1 Issued 1,000 shares of preferred stock for $119 per share.

6. Using the information in Exercise 5, prepare the Stockholders' Equity, Paid-in Capital section of the balance sheet as of July 31, 19__.

Treasury Stock Transactions

7. The Young Company had 40,000 shares of authorized, issued, and outstanding $10 par value common stock as of January 1, 19__. On November 8, 19__, the Young Company purchased 800 shares of treasury stock/common for $21 per share, and on November 28 they sold 400 shares for $26 per share.

Required

Journalize the entries required.

8. Ditmar Corporation had 20,000 shares of authorized, issued, and outstanding $10 par value common stock as of January 1, 19_A. On December 1, 19_A, Ditmar purchased 1,000 shares of treasury stock/common for $19 per share. Ditmar sold 500 shares for $22 per share on December 20, 19_A; and on January 8, 19_B, they sold the last 500 shares of treasury stock/common for $18 per share.

Required

Journalize the entries required.

PROBLEMS

Journalizing and Posting Common Stock Transactions and Stockholders' Equity Section of Balance Sheet

√15-1. On June 2, 19_A, Shingle Roof Products received authorization to issue 40,000 shares of no-par value common stock. The board of directors declared a stated value of $25 per share for the no-par common stock. During 19_A and 19_B the following stock transactions occurred.

19_A

June   2   Organization costs amounted to $6,200; $4,200 was paid in cash and the organizers agreed to accept 80 shares of common stock for the balance.

        4   Issued 6,000 shares of common stock for $27 per share.

July 12   Received subscriptions for 10,000 shares of common stock at $28 per share with 20 percent of the subscription price received in cash.

Aug. 10   Received a payment of 50 percent of the balance due on the subscriptions dated July 12.

Sep.   4   Received the balance due on the subscriptions dated July 12 and 10,000 shares of common stock were issued to the subscribers.

Dec.   2   Issued 2,000 shares of common stock at $25 per share.

19_B

June 14   Received a subscription for 10,000 shares of common stock at $26 per share receiving 50 percent of the subscription price in cash.

July 13   Received $65,000 as a partial payment on subscriptions dated June 14.

Aug. 14   Received balance due on subscriptions dated June 14 and 10,000 shares of common stock were issued to subscribers.

Required

(*a*) Journalize the transactions for 19_A and 19_B.

(*b*) Open general ledger accounts for: 118 Subscriptions Receivable/Common; 130 Organization Costs; 310 Common Stock; 311 Common Stock Subscribed; 312 Paid-in Capital in Excess of Stated Value/Common. Post the entries from the journal to the selected ledger accounts.

(*c*) Prepare the Stockholders' Equity, Paid-in Capital section of the balance sheet as of August 14, 19_B.

15-2.   As of January 1, 19_C, the Shingle Roof Products (Problem 15-1) had 30,000 shares of common stock outstanding; Paid-in Capital in Excess of Stated Value/Common, $60,000; Subscriptions Receivable/Common, $25,000; and 5,000 shares of Common Stock Subscribed. During 19_C the following selected transactions occurred.

19_C

Feb.   5   Received the balance due on subscriptions and issued 5,000 shares of common stock to the subscribers.

Aug.   5   Issued 4,900 shares of common stock at $28 per share.

10 A small building to be used as a storage shed was erected on company property at a cost of $2,800, and the construction company agreed to accept 100 shares of the company's common stock as full payment for the building. The stock was selling for $28 per share on the day the stock was issued.

Required

(*a*) Journalize the transactions for 19_C.
(*b*) Open general ledger accounts for: 118 Subscriptions Receivable/Common; 135 Storage Building; 310 Common Stock; 311 Common Stock Subscribed; and 312 Paid-in Capital in Excess of Stated Value/Common. Record the balances in the accounts dated as of January 1, 19_C, and post the transactions from the journal to the selected ledger accounts.
(*c*) Prepare the Stockholders' Equity, Paid-in Capital section of the balance sheet as of December 31, 19_C.

15-3. On February 2, 19_A, Loc-It Bolt Company received authorization to issue 25,000 shares of no-par value common stock. The following transactions occurred during 19_A, its first year of operations.

19_A
Feb. 20 Organization costs for legal fees amounted to $3,000 and the attorney agreed to accept 300 shares of common stock as full payment of his fees.
Mar. 2 Issued 6,000 shares of common stock at $12 per share.
Aug. 15 Issued 5,000 shares of common stock at $14 per share.
Sep. 3 Issued 700 shares of common stock at $15 per share.
Dec. 20 Received a subscription for 2,000 shares of common stock at $14 per share.

Required

(*a*) Journalize the transactions for 19_A.
(*b*) Open general ledger accounts for: 118 Subscriptions Receivable/Common; 130 Organization Costs; 310 Common Stock; and 311 Common Stock Subscribed. Post the entries from the journal to the selected ledger accounts.
(*c*) Prepare the Stockholders' Equity, Paid-in Capital section of the balance sheet as of December 31, 19_A.

15-4. On January 1, 19_C, the Loc-It Bolt Company (Problem 15-3) had 19,000 shares of no-par value common stock outstanding with an average price of $14 per share. During 19_C the following transactions occurred.

19_C
Jan. 20 Issued 3,000 shares of common stock at $16 per share.

Oct. 2 Issued 1,000 shares of common stock at $16 per share.

Dec. 10 Received a subscription for 2,000 shares of common stock at $18 per share and 50 percent of the subscription price was received in cash.

Required

(a) Journalize the transactions.
(b) Open general ledger accounts for: 310 Common Stock and 311 Common Stock Subscribed. Record the balances in the accounts as of January 1, 19_C, and post the transactions from the journal to the selected ledger accounts.
(c) Prepare the Stockholders' Equity, Paid-in Capital section of the balance sheet as of December 31, 19_C.

Organization Costs, Common and Preferred Stock Transactions, and Determining Paid-in Capital *4/12000*

15-5. Bar B-Q Products received authorization for 4,000 shares of $100 par value preferred stock and 12,000 shares of $25 par value common stock. The following selected transactions occurred during the current year.

Jan. 26 Legal fees for organization costs amounted to $3,500. The attorney agreed to accept 20 shares of preferred stock and 60 shares of common stock in payment and the stock was issued.

Feb. 28 Sold 4,000 shares of common stock for $28 per share and 500 shares of preferred stock for $103 per share.

June 26 Issued 1,000 shares of preferred stock for $100 per share.

Oct. 9 Sold 5,000 shares of common stock for $29 per share.

Required

(a) Prepare journal entries for the above selected transactions.
(b) Open the following ledger accounts: 310 Preferred Stock; 312 Premium on Preferred; 320 Common Stock; and 322 Premium on Common. Post from the journal to the selected ledger accounts.
(c) Determine the amount of total paid-in capital as of October 9.

Stockholders' Equity Section of Balance Sheet

15-6. Weaver Company organized on February 3, 19_A, received authorization for 2,000 shares of $50 par value preferred stock and 8,000 shares of $20 par value common stock. On December 31, 19_E, the following stockholders' equity accounts with amounts appeared in the ledger: Preferred Stock, $100,000; Common Stock, $140,000; Premium on Preferred, $8,000; Premium on Common, $42,000; Paid-in Capital/Donated Treasury Stock, $1,200; Paid-in Capital/Treasury Stock, $1,800; Treasury Stock/Common, $4,200. There were 200 shares of common stock in the treasury.

Required

Prepare the Stockholders' Equity, Paid-in Capital section of the balance sheet as of December 31, 19_E.

15-7. The stockholders' equity accounts and balances for Ace Company as of December 31, 19__, are as follows: Preferred Stock, $25 par value, 5,000 shares authorized, $125,000; No-Par Common Stock, $10 stated value, 10,000 shares authorized, $80,000; Premium on Preferred, $30,000; and Paid-in Capital in Excess of Stated Value/Common, $32,000.

Required

(a) Determine the number of shares outstanding for preferred and common stock as of December 31, 19__.
(b) Prepare the Stockholders' Equity, Paid-in Capital section of the balance sheet as of December 31, 19__.

Organization Costs and Capital Stock Transactions

15-8. The Easy-Vu Photo Company received authorization for 7,000 shares of $50 par value preferred stock and 10,000 shares of $20 par value common stock. Selected transactions for 19__ appear below:

19__

Jan. 12 Issued 500 shares of preferred stock and 500 shares of common stock to the organizers for their services at the par value of the stock.

Feb. 11 Sold 3,000 shares of common stock for $20 per share and 100 shares of preferred stock for $50 per share.

Mar. 8 Sold 500 shares of preferred stock for $101 per share.

18 Received a subscription for 2,000 shares of common stock at $22 per share, and the subscribers paid 50 percent of the subscription price in cash.

Apr. 20 Received the balance due from the subscription dated March 18 and the stock was issued.

Oct. 19 Received a subscription for 1,000 shares of preferred stock at $102 per share, and the subscribers paid 25 percent of the subscription price in cash.

Nov. 20 Received 25 percent of the subscription dated October 19 from the subscribers.

Dec. 20 Received the balance of the subscription dated October 19 and the stock was issued.

30 Received a subscription for 1,000 shares of common stock at $23 per share, and the subscribers paid 50 percent of the subscription price in cash.

Required

Prepare the journal entries for 19__.

Journalizing and Posting Capital Stock Transactions and Stockholders' Equity Section of Balance Sheet

15-9. Pectin Sales organized in 19_A received authorization for 5,000 shares of $100 par value preferred stock and 30,000 shares of $50 par value common stock. During 19_E the following selected transactions occurred:

19_E

Jan.	16	Issued 1,000 shares of preferred stock for $124 per share.
Apr.	2	Purchased 1,000 shares of treasury stock/common for $52 per share.
	15	Received a subscription for 5,000 shares of common stock at $53 per share with a cash payment of $26,500 of the subscription price.
May	14	Reissued 500 shares of treasury stock/common at $54 per share.
	15	Received $138,500 from the subscribers for the subscription dated April 15.
June	5	Reissued 200 shares of treasury stock/common at $51 per share.
	15	Received the balance due from the subscribers for the subscription dated April 15 and the stock was issued.
July	4	Reissued 300 shares of treasury stock/common at $51 per share.
Dec.	1	Received 1,000 shares of treasury stock/common as a gift from a stockholder.
	10	Reissued 1,000 shares of donated common stock received on December 1 for $50 per share.
	20	Purchased 500 shares of treasury stock/common for $50 per share.

Required

(*a*) Journalize the selected transactions for 19_E.

(*b*) Open the following selected ledger accounts and record the balances as of January 1, 19_E: 118 Subscriptions Receivable/Common; 310 Preferred Stock, $400,000; 312 Premium on Preferred, $72,000; 320 Common Stock, $1,250,000; 322 Premium on Common, $300,000; 323 Common Stock Subscribed; 330 Paid-in Capital/Treasury Stock; 332 Paid-in Capital/Donated Treasury Stock; 334 Treasury Stock/Common. Post the journal entries for 19_E to the selected ledger accounts.

(*c*) Prepare the Stockholders' Equity, Paid-in Capital section of the balance sheet as of December 31, 19_E.

Corporations: Cash and Stock Dividends

After completing this chapter, you should be able to:

1. **Compute the amount of cash dividends for preferred and common stockholders**

2. **Journalize the declaration and payment of cash dividends to preferred and common stockholders**

3. **Record the entries for the declaration and payment of a stock dividend**

4. **Account for the declaration of a stock split to the common stockholders**

5. **Prepare the Stockholders' Equity, Paid-in Capital section of a balance sheet which includes the Common Stock Dividend Distributable account**

When a corporation has a sufficient amount of profits realized from operations, it may distribute these profits to the stockholders in the form of a cash or stock dividend. This chapter will discuss the declaration and payment of cash dividends, stock dividends, and stock splits to the common and preferred stockholders.

CASH DIVIDENDS

When the profits of a corporation are paid in cash on a pro rata share to the stockholders, these payments are called *cash dividends.* Dividends declared by a board of directors for the profits realized by a corporation are usually paid in the form of a cash dividend to the stockholders. Occasionally the profits realized are paid in the form of a *stock dividend* and additional shares of the company's stock are issued to stockholders. All cash or stock dividends must be declared by the board of directors of a corporation before any dividends can be paid or distributed to the stockholders. Most states have restrictions on the amount of dividends that may be declared by the board of directors; these restrictions are discussed in Chapter 18.

When a cash dividend is declared by the board of directors of a corporation, they arrange to pay the dividend at a later date. Dividends are paid to stockholders who own the stock on a certain date called the *record date* which occurs between the declaration and payment dates. The declaration date, record date, and payment date are important in the dividend process, and accounting for these three dates are shown below.

Three important dates in the dividend process

Declaration Date. A journal entry is required on the *declaration date* (the day a dividend is declared by the board of directors) to decrease retained earnings and increase liabilities for the dividends owed to stockholders. The Retained Earnings account is debited and a current liability account, **Dividends Payable,** is credited because cash will be used when the dividend is paid to the stockholders.

Record Date. A journal entry is *not* required on the record date because no accounts are affected. On the record date, the corporation prepares a list of the stockholders entitled to receive the dividend on the payment date.

Payment Date. A journal entry is required on the **payment date** (the date dividend checks will be mailed to stockholders of record) to decrease the liability and cash accounts for the dividend payment. The Dividends Payable account is debited and the Cash accounts is credited on the payment date.

For example, assume that on March 1 of the current year the board of directors of a corporation declared a cash dividend of $1.50 per share to 5,000 preferred stockholders and $0.50 per share to 9,000 common stockholders of record on March 15, payable April 2. The entries to record the declaration and payment of the cash dividend are shown below.

Journal entry for the declaration of a cash dividend	Mar. 1	Retained Earnings	12,000	
		Dividends Payable/Preferred		7,500
		Dividends Payable/Common		4,500
		Cash dividends of $1.50 per share were declared to 5,000 preferred stockholders and $0.50 per share were declared to 9,000 common stockholders of record on March 15, payable April 2.		

Journal entry for the payment of a cash dividend	Apr. 2	Dividends Payable/Preferred	7,500	
		Dividends Payable/Common	4,500	
		Cash		12,000
		Payment of cash dividends declared March 1 to 5,000 peferred and 9,000 common stockholders.		

Cash Dividend Preferences to Preferred Stockholders

One of the distinctive features that separate preferred stock from common stock is a preference as to cash dividends. This feature allows preferred stockholders to receive their share of the dividends according to the preferred stock contract whenever dividends are declared. The preferred stock contract will contain one or more of four variations of distributing dividends to preferred stockholders which are discussed and illustrated below.

Dividend preferences for preferred stock

1. Cumulative. When *preferred stock* is *cumulative,* the stockholders are entitled to dividends at the rate stipulated in the preferred contract. If dividends are not declared by the board of directors in any year, the amount of preferred dividends accumulates and carries over to the following year. These accumulated dividends are known as *"dividends in arrears."* When dividends are declared, the dividends in arrears must be paid along with the dividends for the current year on preferred stock before any dividends are paid to common stockholders.

For example, assume that cumulative preferred stockholders are entitled to a $10 per share dividend each year and the dividends are 2 years in arrears. If the board of directors declare dividends to be paid in the current year, preferred stockholders would receive dividends of $30 ($10 × 2 years = $20 + $10 for the current year = $30) for each share of stock they own before any dividends are paid to common stockholders.

Dividends in arrears do not represent a liability to the corporation until they have been declared by the board of directors; therefore, they should not be shown in the Liability section of the balance sheet until they have been declared. To comply with the full disclosure principle,[1] they should be shown as a footnote on the balance sheet similar to the illustration below.

Note: Cumulative dividends of $20 per share for 1,000 shares of preferred stock outstanding for a total of $20,000 (1,000 shares × $20 per share) is in arrears for preferred stock as of the date of the balance sheet.

Most corporations issue cumulative preferred stock to make it more attractive to investors.

2. Noncumulative. *Noncumulative preferred stock* entitles stockholders to dividends at the rate stipulated in the stock contract only if the board of directors declares them in any given year. Any dividends in arrears for preferred stockholders do not carry over from one year to the next; therefore, noncumulative preferred is rarely issued because the stock is not very attractive to investors.

To illustrate, assume the same facts given in item 1. If preferred stock were noncumulative, the stockholders would receive only the current year dividend of $10 per share because the $20 in dividends for each share of

[1] The full disclosure principle was discussed in Chapter 1.

outstanding preferred stock in the previous 2 years were not cumulative and would not carry over to the current year.

3. Participating. When preferred stock entitles the stockholders to share in any excess earnings (declared by the board of directors) above the stipulated rate with the common stockholders, it is called *participating preferred stock*. However, preferred stockholders do not participate in any excess earnings declared as dividends by the board of directors until dividends at the rate stipulated in the preferred stock contract are paid to preferred and common stockholders. Preferred stockholders may share in any excess earnings by participating fully with common stockholders or participating partially with common stockholders to a designated percentage over the established rate.

For example, assume that a corporation has capital stock outstanding consisting of 10,000 shares of 6 percent, $100 par value preferred stock and 20,000 shares of $25 par value common stock.

EXAMPLE 1

The board of directors declares that a dividend of $150,000 be paid to preferred and common stockholders. Preferred stock is fully participating and there are no dividends in arrears for any prior year. The amounts to be paid each class of stock would be computed as follows:

Computation of dividends for preferred and common stockholders

	Preferred	Common	Total
Shares outstanding	10,000	20,000	30,000
Par value	× $100	× $25	
Dollar amount outstanding	$1,000,000	$500,000	$1,500,000
Specified percentage	× .06	× .06	
Regular dividend	$ 60,000	$ 30,000	$ 90,000
$60,000* excess ($150,000 − $90,000)			
divided ⅔ and ⅓	40,000	20,000	60,000
Total dividends	$ 100,000	$ 50,000	$ 150,000

* $1,000,000 outstanding for preferred/$1,500,000 = ⅔
   500,000 outstanding for common/$1,500,000 = ⅓
$1,500,000 total outstanding

Dividends received:
  Preferred stockholders $10.00 per share ($100,000 ÷ 10,000 shares)
  Common stockholders $ 2.50 per share ($50,000 ÷ 20,000 shares)

EXAMPLE 2

Using the same facts given in Example 1, assume that the preferred stock was partially participating for an additional percentage of 2 percent over the established rate of 6 percent. The dividends would be computed as follows:

	Preferred	Common	Total
Shares outstanding	10,000	20,000	30,000
Par value	× $100	× $25	
Dollar amount outstanding	$1,000,000	$500,000	$1,500,000
Specified percentage	× .06	× .06	
Regular dividend	$ 60,000	$ 30,000	$ 90,000
2% of $1,000,000 to preferred	20,000		20,000
$40,000 balance to common			
($150,000 − $90,000 − $20,000)		40,000	40,000
Total dividends	$ 80,000	$ 70,000	$ 150,000

Dividends received:
  Preferred stockholders $8.00 per share ($80,000 ÷ 10,000 shares)
  Common stockholders $3.50 per share ($70,000 ÷ 20,000 shares)

4. Nonparticipating. When *preferred stock* is *nonparticipating,* the preferred stockholders are only entitled to dividends at the rate stipulated in the preferred stock contract. They do not share in any excess earnings declared by the board of directors with the common stockholders. For example, using the data in item 3, the dividends would be computed as follows:

	Preferred	Common	Total
Shares outstanding	10,000	20,000	30,000
Par value	× $100	× $25	
Dollar amount outstanding	$1,000,000	$500,000	$1,500,000
Specified percentage	× .06	× .06	
Regular dividend	$ 60,000	$ 30,000	$ 90,000
$60,000 balance to common			
($150,000 − $90,000 = $60,000)		60,000	60,000
Total dividends	$ 60,000	$ 90,000	$ 150,000

Dividends received:
  Preferred stockholders $6.00 per share ($60,000 ÷ 10,000 shares)
  Common stockholders $4.50 per share ($90,000 ÷ 20,000 shares)

The dividends on preferred stock may be just one of the four variations of distributing dividends, or they may consist of a combination of two of the variations. For example, preferred stock may be cumulative and participating or cumulative and nonparticipating; or it may be noncumulative and participating or noncumulative and nonparticipating.

STOCK DIVIDENDS

Dividends are usually paid in cash to the stockholders of a corporation. However, occasionally the board of directors will declare a *stock dividend* to its common stockholders and additional shares of stock (for the amount of the declaration) are issued to the shareholders. Stock dividends allow a corporation to pay dividends without using any of the cash available for operations. At the same time, the stock dividend gives a stockholder the advantage of receiving a temporary tax-free dividend, because the I.R.S. does not consider a stock dividend to be taxable income until the stock is sold by the stockholder.

Stock dividends have no effect on the assets of a corporation, because only stockholder equity accounts are involved. For example, when a stock dividend is declared, the Retained Earnings account is debited for the market value of the stock. A *Stock Dividend Distributable* account is credited for the par or stated value of the stock and the difference between the par or stated value and the market value is credited to a *Paid-in Capital/Stock Dividend* account as shown below.

> Retained Earnings
> Stock Dividend Distributable
> Paid-in Capital/Stock Dividends

The Stock Dividend Distributable account is classified as a stockholders' equity, paid-in capital account and is shown in the Stockholders' Equity section of the balance sheet. A liability account is not used at the time a stock dividend is declared, because when the stock dividend is distributed, stock is issued to the stockholders instead of cash or other assets. If a liability account were used, it would indicate that cash or other assets would be used to pay off the debt to the stockholders.

To illustrate, assume that on June 5 a corporation declared a 10 percent stock dividend to its common stockholders of record on June 20, payable July 5. On June 5, there were 15,000 shares of $10 par value common stock authorized, of which 10,000 shares were outstanding with a market value of $16 per share, a Premium on Common Stock account with a balance of $8,000, and a Retained Earnings account with a credit balance of $24,000 as shown in the following ledger accounts (in T account form).

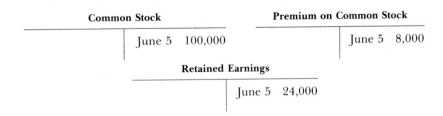

Common Stock	Premium on Common Stock
June 5 100,000	June 5 8,000

Retained Earnings
June 5   24,000

Explanation of entry for declaration and payment of stock dividend

The entry for the declaration of the dividend on June 5 is explained below.

The Retained Earnings account is debited for $16,000, the market value of the stock.

$$10,000 \text{ outstanding shares} \times 0.10 = 1,000 \text{ shares}$$

$$1,000 \text{ shares} \times \$16 \text{ market value} = \$16,000$$

The stockholders' equity account Common Stock Dividend Distributable is credited for $10,000, the par value of the stock.

$$1,000 \text{ shares} \times \$10 \text{ par value} = \$10,000$$

The difference between the market value and par value of the common stock is credited for $6,000 to the stockholders' equity account Paid-in Capital/Stock Dividends.

$$\$16,000 - \$10,000 = \$6,000$$

The following journal entry is required on June 5, the declaration date.

Declaration of stock dividend

June 5	Retained Earnings	16,000	
	Common Stock Dividend Distributable		10,000
	Paid-in Capital/Stock Dividends		6,000
	Declared a 10% stock dividend to 10,000 common stockholders of record on June 20, payable July 5; 1,000 shares at $16 per share		

The ledger accounts (in T account form) after posting the journal entry are shown below.

Common Stock	
	June 5 100,000

Common Stock Dividend Distributable	
	June 5 10,000

Premium on Common Stock	
	June 5 8,000

Paid-in Capital/Stock Dividends	
	June 5 6,000

Retained Earnings	
June 5 16,000	June 5 24,000

The Stockholders' Equity section of the balance sheet prepared on June 5 from the T accounts follows:

Balance sheet presentation
of Stockholders'
Equity section

Stockholders' Equity

Paid-in Capital:
  Common Stock, $10 par value, 15,000
    shares authorized, 10,000 shares issued
    and outstanding $100,000
  Common Stock Dividend Distributable,
    1,000 shares   10,000 $110,000
  Premium on Common $ 8,000
  Paid-in Capital/Stock Dividends   6,000   14,000
    Total Paid-in Capital $124,000
  Retained Earnings   8,000*
    Total Stockholders' Equity $132,000

* Beginning balance of $24,000 − $16,000 stock dividend = $8,000 ending balance.

When the stock is issued on July 5, the following journal entry would be recorded:

Distribution of stock
dividend

July 5	Common Stock Dividend Distributable	10,000	
	Common Stock		10,000
	Issued 1,000 shares to common stockholders of record on June 20 for stock dividend declared June 5.		

The ledger accounts (in T account form) after posting the journal entry are shown below.

Common Stock

	June 5 100,000
	July 5 10,000

Common Stock Dividend Distributable

July 5 10,000	June 5 10,000

Premium on Common Stock

	June 5 8,000

Paid-in Capital/Stock Dividends

	June 5 6,000

Retained Earnings

June 5 16,000	June 5 24,000

The Stockholders' Equity section of the balance sheet prepared on July 5 from the T accounts is as follows:

Stockholder Equity section of balance sheet after distribution of stock dividend

Stockholders' Equity		
Paid-in Capital:		
Common Stock, $10 par value, 15,000 shares authorized, 11,000 shares issued and outstanding		$110,000
Premium on Common	$8,000	
Paid-in Capital/Stock Dividends	6,000	14,000
Total Paid-in Capital		$124,000
Retained Earnings		8,000
Total Stockholders' Equity		$132,000

Note that there is no change in the total amount of stockholders' equity on the balance sheet, because a stock dividend has no effect on total assets, liabilities, or stockholders' equity.

STOCK SPLITS

A *stock split* represents additional shares of common stock that are issued by a corporation to its stockholders. A corporation may declare a stock split when they want to increase the number of its common shares and thereby decrease its market value in hopes of increasing stock sales. When additional shares are distributed after the declaration of a stock split, there is an immediate increase in the number of outstanding shares and a decrease in their book value. If a substantial number of shares are distributed, the increased number of outstanding shares will normally cause a decrease in the market price per share of stock and an increase in the sale of its stock. It takes a considerable number of shares to effect a decrease in the market price per share of stock; therefore, the number of shares distributed as a result of a stock split must be greater than the number of shares distributed in a stock dividend.

Stock splits may be declared by the board of directors in the ratio of 1 for 1, 2 for 1, 4 for 1, or any ratio that they believe will increase the marketability of the corporation's stock. The par value of stock is reduced in proportion to the number of shares that are distributed in a stock split. For example, a 2 for 1 split of $10 par value common would reduce the par value to $5 per share. A 4 for 1 split of $10 par value common would reduce the par value to $2.50 per share.

A stock split has no effect on retained earnings or the assets of a company; therefore, no journal entry is required. Occasionally, however, an accountant may journalize a stock split for the amount of outstanding shares by debiting the common stock account with the old par value and crediting the common stock account with the new par value as follows:

Journal entry for stock split

Dec.	1	Common Stock, $10 Par Value	10,000	
		Common Stock, $5 Par Value		10,000
		To record a 2 for 1 stock split		
		declared by the board of directors		
		for 1,000 shares of $10 par value		
		common to 2,000 shares of common		
		with a par value of $5 per share.		

The increase in the number of outstanding shares and the decrease in its par value are recorded in the ledger account as shown below.

Notation in ledger for stock split

Title: Common Stock   **Account No.: 338**

Date		Explanation	Ref.	Debit	Credit	Balance
Dec.	1	Balance				10,000
	1	Called in and canceled				
		1,000 shares of $10 par				
		value common.		10,000		–0–
		Issued 2,000 shares of $5 par			10,000	10,000
		value common.				

A stock split requires stockholders to return each share of stock they own as the old shares will be canceled and new shares issued. For example, if we use the data in the above example, stockholders would receive two shares of $5 par value common for each share of $10 par value stock they returned for a total of 2,000 shares (1,000 × 2). However, the $10,000 value of the 2,000 shares (2,000 × $5 par value) would be the same as the value of the 1,000 shares (1,000 × $10 par value), because the par value was reduced to $5 per share.

SUMMARY

Profits realized from the business operations of a corporation are usually paid to stockholders in the form of cash dividends. However, dividends must be declared by the board of directors of a corporation before they can be paid to stockholders. The Retained Earnings account is debited and the Dividends Payable account is credited when a dividend is declared, and the Dividends Payable account is debited and the Cash account is credited when dividends are paid.

Preferred stock derives its name from the preferences stockholders receive that are not offered to common stockholders. One preference is to cash dividends and there are four variations of dividend preferences giving preferred stockholders the right to receive a dividend each year at the rate stipulated in the preferred stock contract. Dividend preferences may be cumulative, noncumulative, participating, or nonparticipating. If the contract is participating, the preferred stockholders will receive dividends in excess of the rate stipulated in the stock contract.

Dividends may be paid in the form of cash or stock to the stockholders. Stock dividends allow a corporation to pay dividends without using any of the cash that is available for operations. At the same time, stock dividends give the stockholder a temporary tax-free dividend. The I.R.S. does not consider stock dividends to be taxable income until the stock received as a dividend is sold by the stockholder.

A corporation may declare a stock split when it wants to decrease the market value per share of its common stock. The stock split increases the number of shares of outstanding stock, but it does not increase its total value. Increasing the number of shares of common stock outstanding usually results in a decrease in the market value per share. Normally a company reduces the par value of common in proportion to the number of shares distributed in a stock split.

GLOSSARY

Cash Dividends: Profits of a corporation paid in cash on a pro rata share to the stockholders.

Cumulative Preferred: A dividend preference entitling preferred stockholders to a dividend each year at the rate stipulated in the cumulative preferred stock contract. If dividends are not declared or paid in any given year, dividends accumulate and must be paid along with the dividend for the current year before any dividends are paid to common stockholders.

Declaration Date: Date a dividend is declared by the board of directors to the stockholders of a corporation.

Dividends in Arrears: If dividends are not declared by the board of directors in any year, the amount of dividends that the cumulative preferred stockholders are entitled to (at rate stipulated in preferred contract) will accumulate and carry over to the following year. These accumulated dividends are known as "dividends in arrears."

Dividends Payable: A current liability account credited when cash dividends are declared by the board of directors. The balance in the Dividends Payable account represents the amount of cash dividends declared and owed to the stockholders.

Noncumulative Preferred: When dividends are declared by the board of directors, noncumulative preferred stockholders receive dividends for the stipulated rate. They are not entitled to any dividends that were not paid in any prior year because dividends for noncumulative preferred stock do not accumulate and carry over from one year to the next.

Nonparticipating Preferred: Nonparticipating preferred stockholders are only entitled to dividends at the rate stipulated in the preferred stock contract. They do not share in any excess earnings (declared as dividends by the board of directors) with the common stockholders.

Participating Preferred: Participating preferred stock entitles preferred stockholders to share in any excess earnings (declared as dividends by the board of directors) with common stockholders after dividends for the rate stipulated in the preferred stock contract is paid to common stockholders.

Payment Date: Date dividend checks will be mailed to stockholders of record.

Record Date: All stockholders of record as of a certain date who are entitled to receive a dividend declared by the board of directors of a corporation.

Stock Dividend Distributable: A stockholders' equity account credited when a stock dividend is declared to common stockholders. The Stock Dividend Distributable account is credited for the par or stated value amount of the dividend; if no-par or stated value has been assigned to common stock, the account is credited for its market price.

Stock Dividends: Profits realized by a corporation paid in the form of a stock dividend and additional shares of the company's stock are issued to the stockholders.

Stock Split: A stock split represents additional shares of stock that are issued by a corporation to its common stockholders for the purpose of increasing the number of outstanding shares of common stock and thereby decreasing the market value per share.

QUESTIONS

1. List the four variations of distributing dividends to preferred stockholders.
2. State the basic difference between cumulative and noncumulative and participating and nonparticipating preferred stock.
3. What term is applied to accumulated dividends on cumulative preferred stock?
4. How are accumulated dividends of $30,000 for 6 percent cumulative, fully participating preferred stock shown on the balance sheet?
5. How much would the dividends amount to for each share of 7 percent, $100 par value cumulative preferred stock that is participating to 3 percent above the established rate?
6. A 10 percent stock dividend was declared on 10,000 shares of $25 par value common with a market value of $42 per share. Give the name of the two accounts, with the corresponding amounts, that would be credited for the declaration of the dividend.
7. Why would a company declare a 2 for 1 stock split on 10,000 outstanding shares of $10 par value common stock with a market value of $48 per share? How many shares would be outstanding after the stock split had been distributed?
8. John Ames purchased 50 shares of $20 par value common stock of the Elite Corporation at $24 per share for a total cost of $1,200. The Elite

Corporation declared a 2 for 1 stock split and decreased the par value to $10 per share. What is the value of John Ames' investment after the stock split?

EXERCISES

Determining Amount of Cash Dividends to Stockholders

1. The Young Company had 10,000 shares of authorized, issued, and outstanding $50 par value, 6 percent preferred stock and 40,000 shares of authorized, issued, and outstanding $10 par value common stock. Dividends were declared by the board of directors for $80,000.

   Required

   Determine the amount of dividends to be paid to each class of stock for each of the following methods of dividend distribution:
   (a) Preferred stock was noncumulative and nonparticipating
   (b) Preferred stock was noncumulative and participating to 2 percent above the established rate
   (c) Preferred stock was cumulative and nonparticipating and preferred dividends were in arrears for the previous year

2. Ditmar Corporation issued 5,000 shares of authorized $50 par value, 6 percent cumulative and fully participating preferred stock and 20,000 shares of authorized and issued $10 par value common stock. Dividends were declared in 19_A for $5,000, 19_B for $25,000, and 19_C for $29,700.

   Required

   Determine the amount of dividends to be paid each class of stockholder for each year.

Journal Entries for Cash Dividends

3. Journalize the entry for (a) the declaration and (b) the payment of the dividend for Exercise 1, part c.

4. Journalize the entry for (a) the declaration and (b) the payment of the dividend for Exercise 2, Year 19_C.

Stockholders' Equity Section of Balance Sheet

5. The Young Company received authorization to issue 10,000 shares of $50 par value, 6 percent preferred stock and 40,000 shares of $10 par value common stock. As of December 31 of the current year, all the preferred stock was issued at an average of $80 per share, and all the common stock was issued at an average of $22 per share. Retained earnings had a credit

balance of $21,000. Prepare the Stockholders' Equity section of the balance sheet.

6. Ditmar Corporation received authorization to issue 5,000 shares of $50 par value, 6 percent cumulative and fully participating preferred stock and 20,000 shares of $10 par value common stock. As of December 31 of the current year, all the preferred stock was issued at $60 per share and all the common stock was issued for $18 per share. Retained earnings had a credit balance of $2,000 after dividends were paid for the year. Prepare the Stockholders' Equity section of the balance sheet.

Journal Entries for Stock Dividends and Stockholders' Equity Section of Balance Sheet

7. The balances in selected accounts for Zippy Tree Removal Service as of December 1, 19_B, follow.

    Common Stock, $10 par value, 10,000 shares authorized, 5,000 shares issued, $50,000; Premium on Common, $5,500; and Retained Earnings, $35,000 (credit).

    The board of directors declared a 5 percent stock dividend on December 2, 19_B, to the common stockholders of record on December 20, to be distributed January 10, 19_C. The common stock was selling at $12 per share on the open market.

    Required

    (a) Prepare the journal entries for the declaration and distribution of the stock dividend.
    (b) Prepare the Stockholders' Equity section of the balance sheet as of December 31, 19_B, and January 10, 19_C.

8. Marlin Industries received authorization for 10,000 shares of $100 par value, 6 percent cumulative preferred stock and 20,000 shares of no-par value common stock with a stated value of $20 per share. On March 10 of the current year, 7,500 shares of preferred stock and 12,000 shares of the common stock had been issued. Premium on Preferred stock had a credit balance of $115,000, Paid-in Capital in Excess of Stated Value/Common had a credit balance of $16,000, and Retained Earnings had a credit balance of $52,500. On July 1 the board of directors declared the semiannual dividend for preferred stockholders payable August 1. On the same day, the board of directors declared a 10 percent stock dividend to the common stockholders of record on July 15, to be distributed on August 1. Common stock was selling for $22 per share on the date of declaration.

    Required

    (a) Prepare the journal entries for the declaration and payment of the cash and stock dividend.

(b) Prepare the Stockholders' Equity section of the balance sheet as of July 1 and August 1.

Journal Entries for Stock Split

9. On November 20 of the current year, Marlin Industries had 20,000 shares of no-par value common stock with a $20 stated value authorized, issued, and outstanding. On this date, the board of directors declared a 2 for 1 stock split for common stockholders of record on December 1, payable December 15.

Required

(a) Journalize the entries required for November 20, December 1, and December 15.
(b) Give the balance of the Common Stock account as of December 15.

PROBLEMS

Determining Amount of Cash Dividends for Preferred and Common Stockholders

16-1. The 1,000 shares of 5 percent, $50 par value preferred stock and the 5,000 shares of $10 par value common stock authorized for Tast-e Sip Cola were issued and outstanding as of June 30 of the current year. The Retained Earnings account had a credit balance of $30,000 and dividends of $13,700 were declared on June 30, the end of the fiscal period.

Required

Determine the amount of dividends preferred and common stockholders would receive if:
(a) Preferred stockholders did not receive a dividend last year and preferred stock was cumulative and fully participating
(b) Preferred stock was noncumulative and fully participating

16-2. The Hatchery Company had 5,000 shares of $100 par value, 7 percent preferred stock and 10,000 shares of $25 par value common stock authorized, issued, and outstanding; and a credit balance in retained earnings of $80,000. On December 31 of the current year, the board of directors declared dividends of $77,000 to preferred and common stockholders. No dividends were paid the previous year.

Required

Determine the amount of dividends to be paid preferred and common stockholders for each of the following unrelated assumptions for dividend

distributions:
(*a*) Noncumulative and nonparticipating preferred
(*b*) Noncumulative and fully participating preferred
(*c*) Cumulative and nonparticipating preferred
(*d*) Noncumulative preferred with a participation of 2 percent over the established rate

16-3. The board of directors for Drake Products with capital stock of 2,000 shares of $50 par value, 6 percent preferred stock and 5,000 shares of $10 par value common stock authorized, issued, and outstanding declared dividends of $9,000 in 19_A, $5,100 in 19_B, and $12,600 in 19_C.

Required

Determine the dividends to be received by preferred and common stockholders for each year using the following unrelated assumptions for dividend distributions:
(*a*) Noncumulative and nonparticipating preferred
(*b*) Noncumulative and fully participating preferred
(*c*) Cumulative and nonparticipating preferred
(*d*) Cumulative and fully participating preferred

Journal Entries for Cash and Stock Dividends Plus Stock Splits

16-4. Pectin Sales, organized in 19_A, received authorization for 5,000 shares of $100 par value, 6 percent preferred stock and 30,000 shares of $50 par value common stock. The following selected transactions occurred during 19_F and 19_G.

19_F
Dec. 15 Declared a cash dividend of $0.35 per share to common stockholders of record on December 30, payable January 14, 19_G.
    31 Declared semiannual dividends to preferred stockholders.

19_G
Jan. 14 Dividends of $7,000 declared on December 15, 19_F, were paid to common stockholders.
    31 Semiannual dividends declared on December 31, 19_F, were paid to preferred stockholders.
June 30 The board of directors declared the regular semiannual dividends to preferred stockholders.
July 30 Dividends declared on June 30 were paid to preferred stockholders.
Aug. 1 A dividend of $0.40 per share was declared to common stockholders of record on August 15, payable September 1.
Sep. 1 Dividends declared on August 1 were paid to common stockholders.

Nov. 15 A 10 percent stock dividend was declared to common stock-holders of record on November 30, payable December 30. The market value of common stock was $52 per share.

Dec. 30 The stock dividend declared on November 15 was distributed to the common stockholders.

31 Declared semiannual dividends to preferred stockholders.

Additional Data

There is $400,000 (4,000 shares) of preferred stock outstanding and $1,000,000 (20,000 shares) of common stock outstanding.

Required

Journalize the transactions for 19_F and 19_G.

16-5. Proctor Shoe Company, organized in 19_A, received authorization for 10,000 shares of $50 par value, 6 percent cumulative, fully participating preferred stock and 20,000 shares of $20 par value common stock. All authorized stock was issued and outstanding. The following events occurred during 19_E and 19_F:

1. Annual dividends in the amount of $54,000 were declared to the preferred and common stockholders on June 30, payable July 30, 19_E. (No dividends were in arrears.)
2. A 2 for 1 stock split was declared on October 1 to common stockholders of record on October 15, payable October 30, 19_E, and the par value of common stock was reduced to $10 per share.
3. Annual dividends in the amount of $81,000 were declared to the preferred and common stockholders on June 30, payable July 30, 19_F.

All dividends were paid on the payment date.

Required

Journalize the transactions for 19_E and 19_F.

Stockholders' Equity Section of Balance Sheet

16-6. The stockholders' equity accounts and balances for Ace Company as of January 1 of the current year appear below:

6 percent Preferred Stock, $25 par value, 5,000 shares authorized, $125,000; no-par Common Stock, $10 stated value, 10,000 shares authorized, $80,000; Common Stock Dividend Distributable, $10,000; Premium on Preferred, $30,000; Paid-in Capital in Excess of Stated Value/Common, $38,000; Paid-in Capital/Stock Dividends, $5,000; and Retained Earnings, $8,000.

The following events occurred during the year:

1. The stock dividend was issued to common stockholders on January 10,

and the balance of the authorized common stock was issued on January 20 for $16 per share.

2. A 2 for 1 stock split was declared on May 4 to common stockholders of record on May 20 to be issued June 4. The stated value was decreased from $10 to $5.

Required

Prepare the Stockholders' Equity section of the balance sheet as of June 4.

16-7. Weaver Company organized on February 3, 19_A, received authorization for 2,000 shares of $50 par value, 6 percent cumulative preferred stock and 8,000 shares of $20 par value common stock. On December 31, 19_G, the following stockholders' equity accounts and amounts appeared in the general ledger:

6 percent Cumulative Preferred Stock, $100,000; Common Stock, $140,000; Common Stock Dividend Distributable, $20,000; Premium on Preferred, $8,000; Premium on Common, $42,000; Paid-in Capital/Stock Dividends, $3,500; and Retained Earnings, $9,800.

The 1,000 shares of common stock was to be distributed on January 10, 19_H.

Required

Prepare the Stockholders' Equity section of the balance sheet as of December 31, 19_G and January 10, 19_H.

Journalizing and Posting Transactions for Cash Dividends and Stock Split, and Preparing Stockholders' Equity Section of Balance Sheet

16-8. Selected transactions for Photo Company with 7,000 shares of $50 par value, 5 percent cumulative preferred stock and 10,000 shares of $20 par value common stock authorized, issued, and outstanding are shown below:

19_G no entry

Jan. 12 A 4 for 1 stock split was declared plus a reduction in the par value to $5 per share to common stockholders of record on January 22 to be issued February 10.

Feb. 10 The 10,000 shares of $20 par value common stock were received from the common stockholders and in exchange 40,000 shares of $5 par value common stock were issued.

May 6 A cash dividend of $0.20 per share was declared to common stockholders of record on May 20, payable June 6.

June 6 Cash dividends declared on May 6 were paid to common stockholders.

30 Semiannual dividends declared to preferred stockholders.

July 20 Dividends declared on June 30 were paid to preferred stockholders.

Nov. 6 Declared a cash dividend of $0.20 per share to common stockholders of record on November 20, payable December 10.

Dec. 10 Dividends declared on November 6 were paid to common stockholders.

31 Net income earned for 19_G amounted to $22,000.

31 Declared the semiannual dividend to preferred stockholders.

Required

(*a*) Journalize the transactions for 19_G.

(*b*) Open the following selected ledger accounts and record the balances as of January 1, 19_G: 310, 5 percent Cumulative Preferred Stock, $350,000; 312 Premium on Preferred, $24,000; 320 Common Stock, $200,000; 322 Premium on Common, $120,000; 340 Retained Earnings, $51,000 (credit). Post from the journal to the selected ledger accounts.

(*c*) Prepare the Stockholders' Equity section of balance sheet as of December 31, 19_G.

Corporations: Income Taxes, Work Sheet, and Financial Statements

After completing this chapter, you should be able to:

1. **Compute and record corporate income tax on earnings**

2. **Prepare a 12-column corporate work sheet**

3. **Journalize adjusting and closing entries from corporate work sheet**

4. **Prepare the year-end corporate income statement, retained earnings statement, and balance sheet**

This chapter will continue the discussion of accounting for the business activities of a corporation beginning with the liability for income tax on earnings and continuing through the entire accounting cycle.

CORPORATE INCOME TAXES

A corporation is a separate legal entity and it must pay federal income tax on earnings the same as an individual. Payment for taxes on earnings are subject to the pay-as-you-go system that requires corporations and individuals to make periodic payments for income taxes owed to the federal government. At the beginning of each year, corporations are required to estimate the amount of income tax expense for the year. A work sheet, *Form 1120W* (Figure 17-1) Corporation Estimated Tax, is provided by the Internal Revenue Service (I.R.S.) to assist a corporation in estimating its income tax liability. This work sheet is retained in the corporate records; it is *not* mailed to the I.R.S. A corporation must make quarterly payments if it expects its estimated taxes to be $40 or more. Quarterly estimated tax payments must be deposited at an authorized financial institution or Federal Reserve Bank or branch with a *Federal Tax Deposit Form* (Figure 17-2) provided by the I.R.S. by April 15, June 15, September 15, and December 15.

The tax rates on the profits realized from operations and the earnings of individuals are established by the federal government and are subject to changes by Congress. Over the past few years, there have been several changes in the corporate tax rates. However, at the time this text was printed, corporate profits were to be taxed at 15 percent on the first $25,000, 18 percent on the next $25,000, 30 percent on the third $25,000, 40 percent on the fourth $25,000, and 46 percent on any profits over $100,000. Gains realized from the sale of assets and other types of corporate income receive special treatment and are taxed at different rates.

ADJUSTING ENTRY FOR INCOME TAXES

At the end of the year, an adjusting entry debiting the Income Tax Expense account and crediting the Income Tax Payable account is required

FIGURE 17-1

*Instructions for preparing
Form 1120W (Work sheet)*

Instructions

(References are to the Internal Revenue Code.)

Effective for tax years beginning after 1981, the Economic Recovery Tax Act of 1981 reduced the corporate tax rates for the two lowest taxable income brackets. For the taxable income bracket of $25,000 or less, the tax rate has decreased for 1982, from 17% to 16%, and for 1983, to 15%. For the taxable income bracket over $25,000 but not over $50,000, the tax rate has decreased for 1982, from 20% to 19%, and for 1983, to 18%. The remaining tax rates of 30%, 40%, and 46% did not change.

Because of changes in these tax rates, fiscal year 1982–83 corporations must prorate their tax under Internal Revenue Code section 21. Use this form to compute the estimated tax.

Employee stock ownership credit.—This Act provides a credit that applies to aggregate compensation (within the meaning of section 415 (c)(3)), paid or accrued after December 31, 1982, in tax years ending after such date. See section 44G.

Calendar year corporations, use lines 1 through 32 (but are to omit lines 19 through 25(a)) to compute their estimated tax. Fiscal year corporations, use lines 1 through 32 (but are to omit line 25(b)) to compute their estimated tax.

A. Who Must Make Estimated Tax Payments.—A corporation must make estimated tax payments if it can expect its estimated tax (income tax less credits) to be $40 or more.

B. Underpayment of Estimated Tax.—A corporation that does not pay estimated tax when due may be charged an underpayment penalty for the period of underpayment (section 6655), at a rate determined under section 6621.

C. Members of a Controlled Group.—On lines 4, 6, 8, and 10, members of a controlled group (defined in section 1563) enter either the amount from the preceding line or their share of the $25,000 whichever is less.

If no apportionment plan is adopted, the members of the controlled group must share the $25,000 in each taxable income bracket equally. For example, controlled group AB consists of corporation A and corporation B. They do not elect an unequal apportionment plan. Therefore, corporation A is entitled to $12,500 (half of $25,000) in each taxable income bracket and corporation B is entitled to $12,500 in each taxable income bracket.

Members of a controlled group may elect an unequal apportionment plan and divide the $25,000 in each taxable income bracket in any way they want. They need not divide each taxable income bracket in the same way. Any member of the controlled group may be entitled to all, some, or none of the $25,000 in a taxable income bracket, as long as the total for all members of the controlled group is not more than $25,000 in any taxable income bracket.

D. Depositary Method of Tax Payment.—Deposit corporation income tax payments and estimated tax payments with a preinscribed Federal Tax Deposit (FTD) Form 503. Make these tax deposits with either a financial institution qualified as a Depositary for Federal taxes or the Federal Reserve Bank or Branch (FRB), for the area where the taxpayer is located. Records of deposits will be sent to the Internal Revenue Service for crediting to the corporation's account. See the instructions on the back of Form 503 for more information and exceptions.

Preinscribed FTD Forms 503 will be mailed to corporations on a regular basis depending on the tax year of the corporation. Corporations needing deposit forms may apply for them to the Internal Revenue Service Center where they will file their returns. The application should include the corporation's name, employer identification number, address, and the tax year for which the deposits are made.

Penalty for Overstated Tax Deposits.—If you overstate your deposits, you may be subject to a penalty. See section 6656(b).

E. Overpayment of Estimated Tax.—A corporation that has overpaid its estimated tax may apply for a "quick refund" if the overpayment is (1) at least 10% of its expected income tax liability **AND** (2) at least $500.

To apply, the corporation must file Form 4466, Corporation Application for Quick Refund of Overpayment of Estimated Tax, within 2½ months after the end of its tax year and before it files its tax return.

F. Alternative Tax.—If there is a net capital gain (which means the net long-term capital gain is more than the net short-term capital loss), use the alternative method (section 1201) to see if the resulting tax is less than the tax figured using the regular method.

Alternative tax is the total of (1) a partial tax figured at graduated tax rates on the taxable income decreased by the net capital gain, plus (2) 28% of the net capital gain.

G. Minimum Tax on Tax Preference Items.—Do not consider the minimum tax under section 56 when figuring estimated tax.

H. Late Payments.—If you miss a payment of estimated tax or if you made a mistake which caused an underpayment in earlier installments, you should make an immediate "catch-up" payment.

I. Time and Amount of Deposits.—Use the following table to determine the due date of deposits and the amount of each installment. *If any date falls on a Saturday, Sunday, or legal holiday, substitute the next regular workday.*

If a corporation's estimated tax is $40 or more, it meets the requirement for making deposits. If this requirement is first met—	The number of installments to deposit is—	And you should deposit the following percentages of the estimated tax by the 15th day of the—			
		4th month	6th month	9th month	12th month
before the 1st day of the 4th month of the tax year	4	25	25	25	25
after the last day of the 3rd month and before the 1st day of the 6th month of the tax year	3		33⅓	33⅓	33⅓
after the last day of the 5th month and before the 1st day of the 9th month of the tax year	2			50	50
after the last day of the 8th month and before the 1st day of the 12th month of the tax year	1				100

FIGURE 17-1 (*Continued*)

Form **1120–W**
(WORKSHEET)
Department of the Treasury
Internal Revenue Service

Corporation Estimated Tax
(Do Not File—Keep for Your Records)

19

1 Taxable income expected in the tax year . . . .

2 Net capital gain. (If the alternative tax does not apply, enter zero. See Instruction F for alternative tax.) . .

3 Subtract line 2 from line 1 . . . .

4 Enter the smaller of line 3 or $25,000 (members of a controlled group, see Instruction C) . . . . . .

5 Subtract line 4 from line 3 . . . .

6 Enter the smaller of line 5 or $25,000 (members of a controlled group, see Instruction C) . . . . . .

7 Subtract line 6 from line 5 . . . .

8 Enter the smaller of line 7 or $25,000 (members of a controlled group, see Instruction C) . . . . . .

9 Subtract line 8 from line 7 . . . .

10 Enter the smaller of line 9 or $25,000 (members of a controlled group, see Instruction C) . . . . . .

11 Subtract line 10 from line 9 . . . .

12 16% of line 4 . . . .

13 19% of line 6 . . . .

14 30% of line 8 . . . .

15 40% of line 10 . . . .

16 46% of line 11 . . . .

17 Alternative tax on capital gain—28% of line 2 (see Instruction F) . . . .

18 Add lines 12 through 17. Calendar year filers omit lines 19 through 25(a). Enter on line 25(b) the amount from line 18 and complete the balance of the form . . . .

19 15% of line 4 . . . .

20 18% of line 6 . . . .

21 Add amounts on lines 14, 15, 16 and 17 . . . .

22 Add amounts on lines 19, 20, and 21 . . . .

23 Line 18 × $\dfrac{\text{number of days in tax year before 1/1/83}}{\text{number of days in tax year}}$

24 Line 22 × $\dfrac{\text{number of days in tax year after 12/31/82}}{\text{number of days in tax year}}$ . . . .

25 (a) Add lines 23 and 24 . . . .

(b) Calendar year corporations only—enter the amount from line 18 . . . .

26 Estimated tax credits: Foreign tax credit, possessions tax credit, investment credit, jobs credit, nonconventional source fuel credit, alcohol fuel credit, research credit, and employee stock ownership credit . .

27 Subtract line 26 from line 25(a) or line 25(b), whichever is applicable . . . .

28 Tax from refiguring a prior year investment credit . . . .

29 Total—Add lines 27 and 28 . . . .

30 Credit for Federal tax on special fuels and oils . . . .

31 Estimated tax—Subtract line 30 from line 29 . . . .

32 Divide line 31 by the number of installments to be paid for the tax year (see instruction I).This is the amount due for each installment. *Generally, you may apply your 1981 overpayment, elected as a credit against your 1982 estimated tax, to any installment due.* For exceptions, see Rev. Rul. 77–475, 1977–2 C.B. 476 . . .

Amended Estimated Tax

If, after you figure and deposit estimated tax, you find that your estimated tax is much more or less than originally estimated because your economic condition has changed, you should refigure your estimated tax before the next installment. You may use the following lines to figure the remaining installment payments. (See instruction H for exceptions.)

33 Refigured estimated tax for 1982 . . . .

34 Amount of 1981 overpayment elected as a credit against 1982 estimated tax . . . .

35 Earlier estimated tax payments made for 1982 (include only net amounts deposited—do not include the credit taken in line 34) . . . .

36 Total amount already paid (add lines 34 and 35) . . . .

37 Unpaid balance—Subtract line 36 from line 33 . . . .

38 Divide the amount on line 37 by the number of remaining installments. This is the amount due for each remaining installment . . . .

FIGURE 17-2

*Federal Tax
Deposit Form*

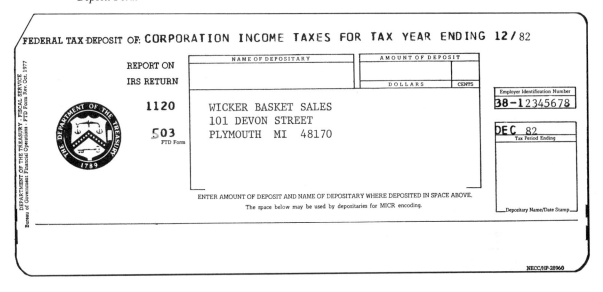

for any corporate income tax due as of December 31. To determine the amount of income tax due, the accountant must:

*Computation of corporate
income tax*

1. Determine the actual ***taxable earnings*** for the year.

$$\text{Revenue} - \text{expenses} = \text{net income}$$

2. Determine the actual income tax expense on taxable earnings using the rates established by the federal government. The current rates are:

First $25,000 × 15%
+ Second $25,000 × 18%
+ Third $25,000 × 30%
+ Fourth $25,000 × 40%
+ Balance of taxable earnings × 46%
= Total income tax expense for year

3. Determine amount of income tax due at the end of the year.
Actual income tax expense
Less: Quarterly payments for estimated taxes
= Tax owed at end of year

To illustrate, the work sheet for Wicker Basket Sales in Figure 17-3 was used to compute the income tax due as of December 31, 19__. The computation of the income tax expense for Wicker Basket Sales is shown in the following three steps.

Step 1. Taxable Earnings: Revenue − cost of goods sold +
expenses

Revenue: (sales, $69,300 + interest earned, $180)		$69,480
Less: Cost of goods sold (beginning inventory, $1,800 + purchases, $25,000 − ending inventory, $2,200)	$24,600	
Expenses (operating expenses, $9,080 + interest expense, $4,800)	13,880	38,480
= Taxable earnings		$31,000

Step 2. Income Tax Expense: Taxable earnings × tax rates

First $25,000 × 15%	= $ 3,750
Balance of earnings ($31,000 − $25,000) $6,000 × 18%	= 1,080
Actual income tax expense for the year	= $ 4,830

Step 3. Income Tax Due: Actual tax due − quarterly
payments

Less: Quarterly payments for estimated taxes	= 4,500
Tax owed as of December 31, 19__	= $ 330

The adjusting entry for the income tax due on December 31, 19__, is
shown below.

Adjusting entry for corporate income tax due

19__				
Dec.	31	Income Tax Expense	330	
		Income Tax Payable		330
		Balance of income taxes due as of December 31.		

WORK SHEET FOR A CORPORATION

At the end of an accounting year (after all the financial transactions have
been journalized and posted), the accountant prepares a work sheet. The
work sheet (Chapters 5 and 7) is a device for summarizing the accounting
activities at the end of the fiscal period and provides information for the
preparation of financial statements, including the Retained Earnings Statement, and closing the books. The work sheet for a corporation usually has
12 columns consisting of the beginning trial balance, adjustments, adjusted
trial balance, income statement, retained earnings, and balance sheet. Note
that the work sheet for a corporation has 12 columns instead of the 10-col-
umn work sheet used for a single proprietorship (Chapters 5 and 7). The
two extra columns are used to determine the amount of ending retained
earnings and to provide the information for preparing the statement of retained earnings.

To illustrate, the account balances for the year ended December 31,
19__, were used to prepare a work sheet for Wicker Basket Sales. For sim-

plicity, the balances for various asset and expense accounts are shown in the Plant Assets, Intangible Assets, and Operating Expense Control accounts instead of showing the balances for each type of asset and expense in a separate account.

Six Steps for Preparing a Corporate Work Sheet

Six steps for preparing the *corporate work sheet* are shown below.

Step 1. The account balances in the general ledger were recorded in the beginning (unadjusted) Trial Balance columns.

Step 2. The adjusting entries were recorded in the Adjustments column, the second pair of columns in the work sheet, to bring the account balances up to date. The following additional data was used:
   (*a*) Interest accrued on notes receivable, $30.
   (*b*) Insurance expired as of December 31, $120.
   (*c*) Office supplies used, $340.
   (*d*) Accrued interest on mortgage, $400.
   (*e*) Depreciation for year, $2,000.
   (*f*) Income taxes due December 31, $330.

Step 3. The amounts in the first four columns of the work sheet were combined and carried over to the Adjusted Trial Balance columns.

Step 4. All the revenue and expense accounts and beginning inventory appearing in the Adjusted Trial Balance columns were carried over to their respective debit and credit columns of the income statement. The ending inventory of $2,200 was entered in the income statement credit column and balance sheet debit column, and the income statement columns were subtotaled. Inasmuch as the credit column amounting to $71,680 was greater than the debit column of $45,510, net income of $26,170 was earned for the year. The net income was entered in the debit column for balancing purposes and the debit and credit columns were totaled and double-underlined.

Step 5. The net income appearing in the debit column of the income statement columns was carried over to the Retained Earnings credit column. The beginning retained earnings amount of $3,994 was carried over from the credit column of the Adjusted Trial Balance column to the credit column of the Retained Earnings. Subtotal the debit and credit columns. Inasmuch as the debit column is a zero, the $30,164 total of the credit column represents the retained earnings balance as of December 31. Record the $30,164 in the debit column and total the debit and credit columns. Double-underline the totals.

Step 6. The ending retained earnings appearing in the Retained Earnings debit column is carried over to the Balance Sheet credit column. All the asset, liability, and paid-in capital accounts appearing in the Adjusted Trial Balance columns are carried over to their respective

FIGURE 17-3

Corporate work sheet

WICKER BASKET SALES
WORK SHEET
For Year Ended December 31, 19__

	Trial Balance Debit	Trial Balance Credit	Adjustments Debit	Adjustments Credit	Adjusted Trial Balance Debit	Adjusted Trial Balance Credit	Income Statement Debit	Income Statement Credit	Retained Earnings Debit	Retained Earnings Credit	Balance Sheet Debit	Balance Sheet Credit
Cash	8,800				8,800						8,800	
Accounts Receivable	13,050				13,050						13,050	
Notes Receivable	2,000				2,000						2,000	
Merchandise Inventory	1,800				1,800		1,800	2,200			2,200	
Prepaid Insurance	480			(b) 120	360						360	
Office Supplies	400			(c) 340	60						60	
Plant Asset Control	48,600				48,600						48,600	
Accumulated Depreciation/Plant Asset Control		4,000		(e) 2,000		6,000						6,000
Intangible Asset Control	28,200				28,200						28,200	
Accounts Payable		9,806				9,806						9,806
Mortgage Payable		12,000				12,000						12,000
Preferred Stock		25,000				25,000						25,000
Common Stock		18,000				18,000						18,000
Premium on Common		1,600				1,600						1,600
Retained Earnings 1/1/__		3,994				3,994				3,994		
Sales		69,300				69,300		69,300				
Purchases	25,000				25,000		25,000					
Operating Expense Control	6,620		(b) 120 (c) 340 (e) 2,000		9,080		9,080					
Income Tax Expense	4,500		(f) 330		4,830		4,830					
Interest Earned		150		(a) 30		180		180				
Interest Expense	4,400		(d) 400		4,800		4,800					
Totals	143,850	143,850										
Interest Receivable			(a) 30		30						30	
Interest Payable				(d) 400		400						400
Income Tax Payable				(f) 330		330						330
Totals			3,220	3,220	146,610	146,610	45,510	71,680				
Net Income							26,170			26,170		
Totals							71,680	71,680	-0-	30,164		
Retained Earnings 12/31/__									30,164			30,164
Totals									30,164	30,164	103,300	103,300

Step 1 · Step 2 · Step 3 · Step 4 · Step 5 · Step 6

debit and credit columns of the Balance Sheet columns. The debit and credit columns were totaled and double-underlined.

The completed work sheet for Wicker Basket Sales for the year ended December 31, 19__, is shown in Figure 17-3. This 12-column work sheet provides all the information necessary to journalize the year-end adjusting and closing entries and to prepare an income statement, retained earnings statement, and balance sheet.

JOURNALIZING ADJUSTING AND CLOSING ENTRIES FROM THE CORPORATE WORK SHEET

Adjusting Entries

All the information necessary for journalizing adjusting entries appears in the Adjustments column of the corporate work sheet. For example, the following adjusting entries were prepared from the Adjustments column of the work sheet in Figure 17-3 for Wicker Basket Sales.

Adjusting entries prepared from corporate work sheet

		Adjusting Entries		
19__				
Dec.	31	Interest Receivable	30	
		Interest Earned		30
		Interest accrued on notes receivable.		
	31	Operating Expenses	120	
		Prepaid Insurance		120
		To record insurance expired as of December 31.		
	31	Operating Expenses	340	
		Office Supplies		340
		To record office supplies used during year.		
	31	Interest Expense	400	
		Interest Payable		400
		Interest accrued on mortgage.		
	31	Operating Expenses	2,000	
		Accumulated Depreciation/Plant Assets		2,000
		To record depreciation for the year.		
	31	Income Tax Expense	330	
		Income Tax Payable		330
		To record income tax due as of December 31.		

Closing Entries

There are three closing entries prepared from the information appearing in the Income Statement columns of a corporation work sheet. The information for the first closing entry is obtained from the accounts listed in the credit column (Ending Merchandise Inventory, Revenues Earned, and any Purchase Returns or Purchase Discount accounts). All these items appearing in the credit column are *debited* with their respective amounts, and the total of these debits are *credited* to the Income Summary account. To illustrate, the first closing entry prepared from the work sheet of the Wicker Basket Sales (Figure 17-3) is shown below.

First closing entry prepared from corporate work sheet

19__				
Dec.	31	Merchandise Inventory	2,200	
		Sales	69,300	
		Interest Earned	180	
		Income Summary		71,680
		To record the ending inventory and close the revenue accounts.		

In the second closing entry, all the items appearing in the debit column (Beginning Merchandise Inventory, Purchases, Transportation In, Sales Returns, Sales Discounts, all operating expenses, other expenses, and Income Tax Expense accounts) are *credited* for their respective amounts and the total of these items are *debited* to the Income Summary account. To illustrate, the second closing entry prepared from the work sheet of the Wicker Basket Sales (Figure 17-3) is shown below.

Second closing entry prepared from corporate work sheet

19__				
Dec.	31	Income Summary	45,510	
		Merchandise Inventory		1,800
		Purchases		25,000
		Operating Expenses		9,080
		Income Tax Expense		4,830
		Interest Expense		4,800
		To remove beginning inventory from the records and close Purchases and expense accounts.		

The third and last closing entry requires a *debit* to the Income Summary account for the income earned in the period (amount appears in the Income Statement debit column under the subtotal) and a *credit* to the Retained Earnings account. If the corporation has incurred a loss for the period, the amount would appear in the Income Statement credit column under the subtotal, and the entry would be reversed. Remember that the Retained Earnings account is used to record the profits earned and the losses incurred for a corporation. To illustrate, the third and last closing entry prepared from the work sheet of the Wicker Basket Sales (Figure 17-3) is shown below.

Third and last closing entry prepared from corporate work sheet

19__			
Dec. 31	Income Summary	26,170	
	Retained Earnings		26,170
	To close the Income Summary account and transfer net income for period to the Retained Earnings account.		

CORPORATE FINANCIAL STATEMENTS PREPARED FROM CORPORATE WORK SHEET

Information for the preparation of financial statements for a corporation may be obtained after a 12-column corporate work sheet has been pre-

FIGURE 17-4

Year-end corporate income statement

WICKER BASKET SALES
INCOME STATEMENT
For Year Ended December 31, 19__

Operating Revenue:			
Sales			$69,300
Cost of Goods Sold:			
Merchandise Inventory, January 1, 19__	$ 1,800		
Add: Purchases	25,000		
Cost of Goods Available		$26,800	
Less: Merchandise Inventory, December			
31, 19__		2,200	
Cost of Goods Sold			24,600
Gross Profit			$44,700
Operating Expenses			9,080
Net Income Before Other Income and			
Expense			$35,620
Other Income:			
Interest Earned		$ 180	
Other Expense:			
Interest Expense		4,800	4,620
Net Income Before Taxes			$31,000
Income Tax Expense			4,830
Net Income After Taxes			$26,170

FIGURE 17-5

Year-end retained earnings statement

WICKER BASKET SALES
RETAINED EARNINGS STATEMENT
For Year Ended December 31, 19__

Retained Earnings, January 1, 19__	$ 3,994	
Add: Net Income for 19__	26,170	
Retained Earnings, December 31, 19__		$30,164

pared. The income statement is the first statement prepared from the information appearing in the Income Statement columns of the work sheet. To illustrate, the income statement prepared from the work sheet of Wicker Basket Sales is shown in Figure 17-4.

The *retained earnings statement* is the second statement prepared from the information appearing in the Retained Earnings columns of a corporate work sheet. A retained earnings statement begins with the balance as of January 1, plus the addition of the income earned during the period, less dividends declared,[1] and ends with the balance as of December 31. The Retained Earnings account and retained earnings statement is discussed fully in Chapter 18. To illustrate, the retained earnings statement prepared from the work sheet of Wicker Basket Sales is shown in Figure 17-5.

Note: There were no dividends declared by the board of directors during 19__. However, if dividends were declared they would appear after the addition of the net income and deducted from the subtotal of the beginning balance and net income to arrive at the ending retained earnings balance.

The balance sheet is the third and last statement prepared from the information appearing in the Balance Sheet columns of the work sheet. To illustrate, the balance sheet prepared from the work sheet of Wicker Basket Sales is shown in Figure 17-6. (Wicker Basket Sales had 2,000 shares of $25 par value preferred stock authorized, and 5,000 shares of $10 par value common stock authorized. As of December 31, 19__, there were 1,000 shares of preferred stock and 1,800 shares of common stock issued and outstanding.)

POST-CLOSING TRIAL BALANCE

After the adjusting and closing entries are journalized and posted and the financial statements are prepared, a post-closing trial balance is prepared. A post-closing trial balance (Chapter 5) is prepared as a final check on the accuracy of the general ledger. If the books have been closed properly, the post-closing trial balance should only list a balance for assets, liability, and stockholders' equity accounts. All the other accounts would not be shown

---

[1] The amount of dividends declared is obtained from corporate records.

FIGURE 17-6

*Year-end corporate
balance sheet*

WICKER BASKET SALES
BALANCE SHEET
December 31, 19___

Assets

Current Assets:			
Cash	$ 8,800		
Accounts Receivable	13,050		
Notes Receivable	2,000		
Interest Receivable	30		
Merchandise Inventory	2,200		
Prepaid Insurance	360		
Office Supplies	60		
Total Current Assets		$26,500	
Plant Assets:			
Plant Assets Control	$48,600		
Less: Accumulated Depreciation	6,000		
Total Plant Assets		42,600	
Intangible Assets:			
Intangible Assets Control		28,200	
Total Assets			$97,300

Liabilities

Current Liabilities:			
Accounts Payable	$ 9,806		
Interest Payable	400		
Income Tax Payable	330		
Total Current Liabilities		$10,536	
Long-term Liabilities:			
Mortgage Payable		12,000	
Total Liabilities			$22,536

Stockholders' Equity

Paid-in Capital:			
Preferred Stock, $25 par value, 2,000 shares authorized, 1,000 shares issued and outstanding	$25,000		
Common Stock, $10 par value, 5,000 shares authorized, 1,800 shares issued and outstanding	18,000	$43,000	
Premium on Common		1,600	
Total Paid-in Capital		$44,600	
Retained Earnings		30,164	
Total Stockholders' Equity			74,764
Total Liabilities & Stockholders' Equity			$97,300

because they should have a zero balance. The accounts with a balance in the general ledger should be the same as the accounts and amounts appearing in the Balance Sheet columns of the corporation work sheet. Inasmuch as the general ledger is not shown for Wicker Basket Sales, a post-closing trial balance is not illustrated.

SUMMARY

The earnings of a corporation are subject to income tax the same as an individual. Corporations are required to make quarterly payments to the federal government for their estimated taxes. At the end of the year, the actual income tax of the corporation is compared to the estimated quarterly tax payments, and any difference represents the amount of corporate income tax due or to be refunded.

A work sheet for a corporation contains 12 columns, two extra columns for retained earnings.

GLOSSARY

Corporate Work Sheet: A device for summarizing the accounting activities at the end of a fiscal period to provide information for the journalizing of the adjusting and closing entries and the preparation of financial statements. The work sheet for a corporation usually has 12 columns consisting of a beginning (unadjusted) trial balance, adjustments, adjusted trial balance, income statement, retained earnings, and balance sheet.

Federal Tax Deposit Form: Form provided by the Internal Revenue Service (I.R.S.) that is used by a corporation when they deposit their quarterly estimated income tax payments to the federal government. These forms along with the quarterly payments are deposited at an authorized financial institution or a federal reserve bank or branch.

Form 1120W: An estimated tax work sheet provided by the Internal Revenue Service (I.R.S.) to assist a corporation in estimating their income tax liability. The work sheet is not sent to the I.R.S.; it is maintained in the company records.

Retained Earnings Statement: A report prepared after the income statement that shows the beginning balance of retained earnings, net income or loss for the period, dividends declared, and ending balance of retained earnings.

Taxable Earnings: The difference between the total amount of revenues earned and total amount of expenses incurred.

QUESTIONS

1. Are all taxable profits of a corporation taxed at one basic rate? Explain.
2. Individuals are subject to the pay-as-you-go system for paying federal income taxes. How does the federal government collect income taxes due from corporations?
3. In what way does the work sheet for a corporation differ from a work sheet prepared for a single proprietorship?
4. The subtotals of the Income Statement debit and credit columns on the

work sheet prepared for John Corporation amounted to $84,000 and $76,000 respectively. What amount is carried over to the Retained Earnings columns? Is this amount transferred as a debit or credit to the Retained Earnings columns? What does this amount represent?

5. In which of the last six columns of a corporate work sheet are the amounts for the following entered? (If the amount is entered in more than one column, name both columns.) (*a*) net income; (*b*) income tax expense; (*c*) income tax payable; (*d*) preferred stock; (*e*) premium on common; and (*f*) ending retained earnings.

6. Name the three formal financial statements prepared for a corporation in their proper order.

EXERCISES

Determining Corporate Income Tax Expense

1. Determine the amount of corporate income tax expense for the year for taxable earnings of: (*a*) $18,000; (*b*) $26,000; and (*c*) $79,000.

2. A corporation with taxable earnings of $24,900 for 19__ made quarterly payments on estimated earnings of $23,000. Determine the total amount of (*a*) income tax expense for 19__, and (*b*) amount of income tax due for 19__.

3. Aspen Sales estimated taxable earnings of $62,000 for 19__, and they made quarterly payments based on this estimate during the year. Actual taxable earnings amounted to $64,000. Determine (*a*) amount of quarterly payments paid for income tax during the year, (*b*) actual income tax expense for 19__, and (*c*) income tax due for 19__.

Journal Entry for Income Tax Due at End of Period

4. Give the journal entry required on December 31 for each of the following unrelated assumptions. Assume that all quarterly payment have been made during the year.

Corporation	Estimated Earnings	Actual Earnings
A	$23,000	$25,900
B	74,000	79,000
C	29,000	31,000

Partial Corporate Work Sheet

5. For the partial work sheet given on the following page, place a check mark (✔) in the column used to record each item.

	Income Statement		Retained Earnings		Balance Sheet	
	Dr	Cr	Dr	Cr	Dr	Cr
(a) Dividends Payable						✓
(b) Common Stock Subscribed						✓
(c) Discount on Common					✓	
(d) Retained Earnings 1/1 (Cr.)				✓		
(e) Net Income	✓			✓		
(f) Retained Earnings 12/31			✓			✓

6. For the partial work sheet shown below, place a check mark (✔) in the column used to record the following:

	Adjust- ments		Income Statement		Retained Earnings		Balance Sheet	
	Dr	Cr	Dr	Cr	Dr	Cr	Dr	Cr
(a) Merchandise Inventory 1/1			✓					
(b) Income Tax Expense	✓		✓					
(c) Income Tax Payable		✓						✓
(d) Merchandise Inventory 12/31				✓			✓	
(e) Net Loss				✓	✓		✓	

PROBLEMS

Determining Corporation Income Tax Expense

✓ **17-1.** Determine the following:

1. Income tax expense for taxable corporate earnings of:
   (a) $21,400   (b) $48,600
2. Net income after taxes for a corporation with taxable earnings of:
   (c) $60,600   (d) $110,000

Journal Entries for Corporate Income Tax

✓ **17-2.** As of January 1, 19_B, the Shingle Roof Products had a credit balance in Retained Earnings of $22,114. During 19_B the following selected transactions occurred.

19_B

Jan. 10 Paid income tax liability amounting to $520 for 19_A.

Apr. 15 Estimated taxable earnings for 19_B of $8,180, and paid the first quarterly installment for estimated income taxes. (Round amounts to nearest dollar.)

June 15 Paid the second quarterly installment for estimated income taxes.

Sept. 15 Paid the third quarterly installment for estimated income taxes.

Dec. 15 Paid the fourth quarterly installment for estimated income taxes.

31 Actual net income before taxes amounted to $9,100. Record the adjusting entry necessary for the balance due for income tax.

31 Close the Income Tax Expense account.

31 Net income after taxes amounted to $7,735. Close the Income Summary account and record net income in the Retained Earnings account. (Assume that all other closing entries have been recorded.)

Required

Journalize the selected transactions for 19_B.

17-3. On January 1, 19_B, the Loc-it Bolt Company had a credit balance in the Income Tax Payable account of $100 and a credit balance in the Retained Earnings account of $18,000. During 19_B, the following selected transactions occurred.

19_B

Jan. 10 Paid income tax liability for 19_A.

Apr. 15 Estimated taxable earnings of $2,720 for 19_B, and paid the first quarterly installment for estimated income taxes.

June 15 Paid the second quarterly installment for estimated income taxes.

Sept. 15 Paid the third quarterly installment for estimated income taxes.

Dec. 15 Paid the fourth quarterly installment for estimated income taxes.

31 Actual net income before taxes amounted to $2,900. Record the adjusting entry for income taxes due as of December 31.

31 Close the Income Tax Expense account.

31 Net income after taxes amounted to $2,465. Close the Income Summary account and record net income in the Retained Earnings account. (Assume all other closing entries have been recorded.)

Required

Journalize the selected transactions for 19_B.

17-4. Esson Shoe Company had a credit balance in the Income Tax Payable account of $350 and a credit balance in the Retained Earnings account of $5,800 as of December 31, 19_A. During the second year of operations, the following selected transactions occurred.

19_B

Jan.   10   Paid the income tax liability for 19_A.

Apr.   15   Estimated taxable earnings of $6,900 for 19_B, and paid the first quarterly installment for estimated income taxes. (Round amounts to nearest dollar.)

June   15   Paid the second quarterly installment for estimated income taxes.

Sept. 15   Paid the third quarterly installment for estimated income taxes.

Dec.   15   Paid the fourth quarterly installment for estimated income taxes.

       31   Actual net income before taxes amounted to $7,400. Record the adjusting entry for income taxes due as of December 31.

       31   Close the Income Tax Expense account.

       31   Net income after taxes amounted to $6,290. Close the Income Summary account and record the net income in the Retained Earnings account. (Assume all other closing entries have been recorded.)

Required

Journalize the selected transactions for 19_B.

Corporate Work Sheet, Year-End Entries, and Financial Statements

17-5. The adjusted trial balance as of December 31, 19_B, for Sweetheart Candy Corporation is shown below.

SWEETHEART CANDY CORPORATION
ADJUSTED TRIAL BALANCE
December 31, 19_B

Cash	$ 12,800	
Accounts Receivable	15,800	
Subscriptions Receivable/Common	4,000	
Merchandise Inventory, 1/1/_B	4,540	
Prepaid Insurance	480	
Supplies	140	
Equipment	140,000	
Accumulated Depreciation/Equipment		$ 6,000
Patents	1,600	
Leasehold Improvements	12,840	
Accounts Payable		16,400
Income Tax Payable		220

Interest Payable		60
Notes Payable due 19_F		9,000
Common Stock, $10 Par Value		80,000
Common Stock Subscribed, 800 shares		8,000
Premium on Common		16,000
Retained Earnings, 1/1/_B		18,820
Sales (Net)		140,000
Purchases (Net)	62,000	
Operating Expense Control	33,900	
Interest Expense	100	
Income Tax Expense	6,300	
Totals	$294,500	$294,500

Required

(a) Prepare a corporate work sheet for the year ended December 31, 19_B, beginning with the Adjusted Trial Balance columns. The inventory on December 31, 19_B, amounted to $2,540, and the corporation received authorization to issue 9,000 shares of $10 par value common stock.

(b) Prepare a formal income statement, retained earnings statement, and balance sheet from the data in the work sheet. Use the illustrations on pages 489–491 as a guide for the correct format.

17-6. The account balances, before adjustments, for the Can-O-Pop Corporation as of December 31, 19_A, appear below.

Cash	$ 3,400	
Accounts Receivable	2,900	
Notes Receivable	900	
Merchandise Inventory 12/31/_A	1,450	
Prepaid Insurance	240	
Furniture & Equipment	34,000	
Accumulated Depreciation/Furniture & Equipment		$ 2,400
Leasehold Improvements	8,510	
Accounts Payable		2,880
Notes Payable due 19_B		450
Notes Payable due 19_G		6,000
Common Stock, No Par Value, $10 Stated Value		20,000
Paid-in Capital in Excess of Stated Value/Common		4,000
Retained Earnings, 1/1/_A		2,090
Sales (Net)		90,400
Cost of Goods Sold	44,900	
Operating Expense Control	30,000	
Income Tax Expense	1,920	
Totals	$128,220	$128,220

Additional Data

(a) Interest of $10 has accrued on notes received from customer.

(b) Insurance expired amounts to $80.

(c) Depreciation for furniture and equipment amounts to $1,200.

(*d*) Interest of $100 has accrued on notes payable.

(*e*) Income taxes due amount to $200.

(*f*) Common stock authorized amounted to 3,000 shares of which 2,000 shares have been issued.

(*g*) A perpetual inventory system is used. *dont make an adjustment for*

Required

(*a*) Prepare a 12-column corporate work sheet for the year ended December 31, 19_A.

(*b*) Journalize the adjusting and closing entries.

(*c*) Prepare an income statement, retained earnings statement, and balance sheet using the data in the work sheet.

After completing this chapter, you should be able to:

1. **Record the entries to correct errors in reporting revenue and expenses of a prior period**

2. **Prepare a year-end retained earnings statement for a corporation**

3. **Prepare a year-end combined income statement and retained earnings statement**

4. **Compute earnings per share for common stock**

5. **Classify gains and losses realized from an unusual event as Other Revenue, Other Expense, or Extraordinary Items on an income statement**

6. **Give the income statement presentation for earnings per share of common stock**

Retained earnings are the accumulated profits of a corporation that have not been distributed as dividends to the stockholders. These earnings may not be available or distributed as dividends because (1) the board of directors declared earnings to be reserved for plant expansion, sales promotion campaigns, litigation, or other contingencies, or (2) the laws of some states may prohibit the declaration of dividends for the cost of any unissued treasury stock acquired by the corporation. Earnings reserved by the board or earnings restricted by the laws of a state are referred to as *appropriated retained earnings;* earnings available for dividends or operations are referred to as *unappropriated retained earnings.* To comply with standards established by the AICPA,[1] appropriated and unappropriated retained earnings should be shown separately on the retained earnings statement and balance sheet or as a footnote on the balance sheet.

APPROPRIATED RETAINED EARNINGS

A credit balance in the Retained Earnings account is not an indication that a corporation has an equal amount of cash on hand for the payment of dividends to stockholders. Cash on hand may not be available for the distribution of dividends as the cash may be needed for operations. Many students confuse cash on hand with the balance shown in the Retained Earnings account. However, if students will refer to the basic accounting equation (assets = liabilities + stockholders' equity), they will realize that retained earnings consist of all the assets on hand and not one particular asset; namely, cash.

Before a board declares a cash dividend to stockholders, they must re-

[1] Accounting Research Study No. 7 and SEC Accounting Series Release No. 35.

view the needs of the business. The growth or future profits of the company should not be jeopardized by using assets for the payment of dividends. At the same time, they must recognize that dividends are also important to stockholders. A consistent distribution of dividends helps make the sale of stock more attractive to investors, and the sale of stock is an important source of cash to the company. One method that may be used by the board of directors to inform stockholders that retained earnings are needed for plant expansion, sales promotion, etc., is to appropriate or reserve a portion of retained earnings for these special needs. The board may establish a special account for earnings that are reserved or appropriated for specific purposes or they may include the information as a footnote on the balance sheet. When a special account is established by the board of directors, Unappropriated Retained Earnings is debited and Appropriated Retained Earnings, with the name of the appropriation, is credited. This entry has no effect on the assets or liabilities of the company. Keep in mind that when earnings are appropriated there is no special fund being established. This procedure is simply a method of informing stockholders that assets for the amount of appropriated retained earnings are not available for dividends. Setting up a special appropriation account is not used very often today; usually a corporation will simply include this information as a footnote on the balance sheet.

ADJUSTMENTS AND CORRECTIONS TO RETAINED EARNINGS

After the books are closed, any material adjustments that affect net income or correction of errors to revenue or expense and assets or liabilities of a prior period are usually corrected by debiting or crediting the Retained Earnings account. These adjustments and corrections are called *prior period adjustments* and are shown on the retained earnings statement as an adjustment to the beginning balance of retained earnings. They are not shown on the current income statement, because they are corrections that apply to a prior period. However, when making a correction for a prior period, keep in mind the materiality principle. The materiality principle allows an adjustment or correction of a prior period to be ignored if the amount will not materially affect or distort the financial statements of the current period. A material amount for one business may be so small and insignificant for another business that it would not materially affect the usefulness or reliability of the current financial statements. Therefore, an insignificant amount for a particular business may be included when reporting the income of the current period.

Examples of an adjustment to net income and a correction to revenue or expense of a prior period that will have a material affect on the financial statements begin on the next page.

EXAMPLE 1

Several pieces of equipment purchased for $10,000 on December 30, 19_A, were deducted as an expense on the income statement. After an I.R.S. audit in 19_B, the expense deduction was disallowed and the equipment was classified as a 5-year depreciable asset. The company was assessed additional income taxes of $4,600 ($10,000 × .46). The company paid income taxes on earnings of $100,000 in 19_A; therefore, the assessment was computed at a rate of .46 percent. Reclassifying the equipment as an asset decreased expenses and increased income after taxes by $5,400 ($10,000 − $4,600 taxes). The entry to correct the records on May 4, 19_B, required a debit to the Equipment account and a credit to the Income Taxes Payable and Retained Earnings accounts as shown below.

Adjusting entry to correct error in reporting prior period net income

19_B			
May 4	Equipment	10,000	
	Income Taxes Payable		4,600
	Retained Earnings		5,400
	To record additional tax assessment for 19_A and to increase amount of equipment and retained earnings.		

EXAMPLE 2

During 19_B, the accountant discovered an error in recording supplies for the previous period. This error caused the supplies expense to be overstated by $3,000, increased the liability for income taxes by $1,380 ($3,000 × .46), and increased net income by $1,620 ($3,000 − $1,380). To correct the records on May 4, 19_B, the Supplies on Hand account was debited for $3,000, the Income Tax Payable account was credited for $1,380, and the Retained Earnings account was credited for $1,620 as shown below.

Correcting entry for overstatement of supplies used in prior period

19_B			
May 4	Supplies on Hand	3,000	
	Income Tax Payable		1,380
	Retained Earnings		1,620
	To correct the amount of supplies on hand, record additional liability for taxes, and increase the Retained Earnings account for the error in recording supplies expense in 19_A.		

Inasmuch as the books for 19_A were closed when the error was discovered, the Retained Earnings account was credited for the decrease in expense and increase in income. When the books have been closed, any correction to a prior period expense or revenue is corrected through the Retained Earnings account. Correcting an error through an expense or revenue account after the books are closed would violate the Matching Concept of accounting (revenue earned for a period must match the expenses incurred to earn the revenue).

PREPARING THE RETAINED EARNINGS STATEMENT

A separate *retained earnings statement* may be prepared at the end of an accounting period giving a detailed summary of the changes to retained earnings. The beginning balance of retained earnings is listed first on the statement; any adjustments or corrections to the income of prior periods are added or subtracted to arrive at the corrected beginning balance of retained earnings. Next, the net income is added (a loss is subtracted) and dividends are subtracted from the corrected beginning balance to arrive at ending retained earnings. The formula for the preparation of a retained earnings statement with no special appropriation accounts is shown below.

Formula for preparation of retained earnings statement

Retained Earnings, 1/1

+ or − any adjustment or correction to income of a prior period

= Corrected Retained Earnings, 1/1

+ Net Income or − Net Loss

− Cash Dividends

− Stock Dividends

= Retained Earnings, 12/31

To illustrate, a retained earnings statement has been prepared for Safety Tool Corporation for the year ended December 31, 19_B, and is shown in Figure 18-1.

FIGURE 18-1

Corporate retained earnings statement

SAFETY TOOL CORPORATION
RETAINED EARNINGS STATEMENT
For Year Ended December 31, 19_B

Retained Earnings, 1/1/_B	$100,000	
Less: Additional assessment for income taxes		
for Year 19_A	8,000	
Corrected Retained Earnings, 1/1/_B		$ 92,000
Add: Net Income after Taxes		111,272 $203,272
Less: Cash Dividends		$ 40,000
Stock Dividends		30,000 70,000
Retained Earnings, 12/31/_B		$133,272

COMBINED INCOME AND RETAINED EARNINGS STATEMENT

Many corporations prepare a *combined income and retained earnings statement* to show the revenue, expenses, net income, and changes to retained earnings during a period on one statement. Accountants have different opinions about combined statements. Some accountants believe that a combined statement of income and retained earnings emphasizes the ending balance of retained earnings because it is the last amount shown on the statement and that net income may be overlooked because it appears in the middle of the statement. Other accountants prefer the combined statement because they believe the amount of income earned from operations and changes to retained earnings can be quickly noted when they both appear on one statement.

To illustrate, a combined income and retained earnings statement has been prepared for Safety Tool Corporation for the year ended December 31, 19_B, and is shown in Figure 18-2. (For simplicity, only the final figures for Sales, Cost of Goods Sold, and Operating Expenses were recorded in the income statement section.)

EARNINGS PER SHARE

Earnings per share is the amount of current period earnings available for dividends for one share of outstanding common stock. The earnings per share of common stock is one measure used by common stockholders and investors to evaluate the company's future growth, earning capacity, and dividend potential of a corporation.

FIGURE 18-2

Combined income statement and retained earnings

SAFETY TOOL CORPORATION
COMBINED INCOME AND RETAINED EARNINGS STATEMENT
For Year Ended December 31, 19_B

Sales	$400,000	
Less: Cost of Goods Sold	140,000	
Gross Profit	$260,000	
Operating Expenses	91,440	
Net Income before Taxes		$168,560
Income Taxes		57,288
Net Income after Taxes		$111,272
Retained Earnings, 1/1/_B	$100,000	
Less: Additional assessment for income taxes in 19_A	8,000	
Corrected Retained Earnings, 1/1/_B		92,000
Total Net Income and Retained Earnings		$203,272
Less: Cash Dividends	$ 40,000	
Stock Dividends	30,000	70,000
Retained Earnings, 12/31/_B		$133,272

Earnings per share is usually shown at the bottom of an income statement to comply with Opinion No. 15 of the AICPA, Accounting Principles Board which specifies that earnings per share should be shown on the face of an income statement.

To compute earnings per share for a corporation with only one class of stock, the net income after taxes is divided by the number of common shares of stock outstanding.

Formula for computation of earnings per share

$$\frac{\text{Net income after taxes}}{\text{Number of common shares outstanding}} = \text{earnings per share}$$

If a corporation has two classes of stock, preferred and common, the net income minus any dividends owed to preferred stockholders is divided by the number of common shares of stock outstanding.

$$\frac{\text{Net income after taxes} - \text{dividends due preferred}}{\text{Number of common shares outstanding}} = \text{earnings per share}$$

For example, assume that Safety Tool Corporation had 40,000 shares of common stock outstanding on December 31, 19_B, and all the dividends were paid to the preferred stockholders.

$$\frac{\$111,272}{40,000} = \$2.78 \text{ earnings per share of common stock}$$

To illustrate, an income statement showing earnings per share of common stock has been prepared for Safety Tool Corporation for the year ended December 31, 19_B, and is shown in Figure 18-3.

EXTRAORDINARY GAINS AND LOSSES

Business transactions that result in a realized gain or loss from an unusual event or an event that occurs very infrequently[2] are classified as *extraordinary items* on an income statement. Examples of unusual events are floods, earthquakes, fires, etc. These gains or losses realized from unusual events are shown after the Other Revenue or Expense section of an income statement under the heading of Extraordinary Items. In the last section of an income statement, earnings per share is shown separately for income before extraordinary items, for extraordinary items, and for income after extraordinary items.

The AICPA, Accounting Principles Board, does not specify the types

[2] APB No. 30 states that an unusual or infrequent event is one that is not expected to reoccur in the foreseeable future.

FIGURE 18-3

*Income statement with
presentation of earnings
per share*

**SAFETY TOOL CORPORATION
INCOME STATEMENT
For Year Ended December 31, 19_B**

Sales	$400,000	
Less: Cost of Goods Sold	140,000	
Gross Profit		$260,000
Operating Expenses		91,440
Net Income before Taxes		$168,560
Income Taxes		57,288
Net Income after Taxes		$111,272
Earnings per Share of Common Stock		$ 2.78

of events that may be classified as extraordinary, but they list the following items as normal business events to be shown in the Other Revenue and Expense section of an income statement.

1. The write-down or write-off of receivables, inventories, and intangible assets
2. The exchange or translation of foreign currencies
3. The sale or abandonment of property, plant, or equipment used in the business
4. The effects of a strike
5. The adjustment of long-term contract accruals

For example, assume Safety Tool Corporation realized a gain of $4,000 from the sale of equipment and incurred an uninsured loss of $10,000 from a fire that destroyed a small warehouse. These events would be shown in the income statement as illustrated in Figure 18-4.

Notice that the net income before extraordinary items represents the income realized from operations less the taxes before considering any ex-

FIGURE 18-4

*Partial income statement
with Other Revenue,
Extraordinary Items, and
earnings per share*

**SAFETY TOOL CORPORATION
PARTIAL INCOME STATEMENT
For Year Ended December 31, 19_B**

Net Operating Income before Other Revenue		$168,560
Other Revenue:		
Gain on Sale of Equipment	4,000	$172,560
Less: Income Taxes		59,128
Net Income before Extraordinary Items		$113,432
Extraordinary Items:		
Loss due to Fire	$ 10,000	
Add: Reduction in Taxes due to Loss	4,600	5,400
Net Income after Extraordinary Items		$108,032
Earnings per Share of Common Stock:		
Net Income before Extraordinary Items		$ 2.84
Extraordinary Loss		(0.14)
Earnings on Net Income after Extraordinary Items		$ 2.70

traordinary gains or losses. The increase or decrease in taxes that result from an extraordinary gain or loss are separated from the results of operations so that these items plus or minus the tax effect will not distort the amount of income reported from operations.

BOOK VALUE PER SHARE OF CAPITAL STOCK

Book value per share of capital stock represents the amount of a stockholder's claim on the assets if a corporation discontinues operations and dissolves the business. The book value concept assumes that assets will be sold for the amounts shown in the general ledger accounts. The formula for computing book value per share for a corporation with only one class of stock is:

$$\frac{\text{Total stockholders' equity}}{\text{Number of shares outstanding}}$$

If a corporation has two classes of stock (preferred and common) the formula for book value per share of preferred is:

Formula for book value per share for preferred and common stockholders

$$\frac{\text{Total preferred stock outstanding} + \text{any dividends in arrears}}{\text{Number of shares of preferred stock outstanding}}$$

The formula for book value per share of common stock is:

$$\frac{\text{Total stockholders' equity} - \text{total preferred stock outstanding} + \text{dividends in arrears}}{\text{Number of shares of common stock outstanding}}$$

To illustrate, assume that a corporation had total stockholders' equity of $71,544 consisting of 1,000 shares of $25 preferred stock and 1,800 shares of $10 common stock issued and outstanding, premium on common of $1,600, and a credit balance in Retained Earnings amounting to $26,944. The book value per share of preferred and common stock is:

Book value per share of preferred stock

$$\frac{\text{Total preferred stock outstanding}}{\text{Number of preferred shares outstanding}} = \text{book value per share}$$

$$\frac{\$25,000}{1,000} = \$25$$

Book value per share of common stock

$$\frac{\text{Total stockholders' equity} - \text{total preferred stock outstanding}}{\text{Number of shares of common stock outstanding}} = \text{book value per share}$$

$$\frac{\$71,544 - \$25,000 = 46,544}{1,800} = \$25.86$$

SUMMARY

Retained earnings are the accumulated profits of a corporation that have not been distributed as dividends to the stockholders. All the retained earnings may not be available for dividends because some earnings may be reserved by the board of directors for any special needs of a corporation; retained earnings may also be restricted from dividends by the laws of a state. Any appropriations by a board of directors or restrictions to comply with state laws must be shown on the balance sheet as a footnote or recorded in a special appropriation account and shown in the Retained Earnings section of a balance sheet.

Cash on hand usually does not equal the balance shown in the Retained Earnings account because earnings are represented by assets and not any particular asset; namely, cash. The board of directors may establish a special account for appropriations; this procedure requires a debit to the Unappropriated Retained Earnings account and a credit to the Appropriated Retained Earnings account resulting in no change in the assets or liabilities.

After the books are closed, any adjustments and corrections to net income, revenue, or expense for a prior period are usually corrected through the Retained Earnings account. These adjustments and corrections are shown as an addition or subtraction to the beginning balance of Retained Earnings on the retained earnings statement. They are not shown on the income statement, because they apply to the earnings of a prior period.

Some corporations prepare a separate statement to show the changes in retained earnings during a period. A retained earnings statement lists beginning retained earnings first, followed by any corrections to income of prior periods, net income, and dividends declared during period to arrive at the ending balance of retained earnings. The ending balance for total retained earnings is shown on the balance sheet. Instead of preparing a separate retained earnings statement, some corporations may prepare a combined income and retained earnings statement.

Earnings per share is the amount of current period earnings available for dividends for one share of outstanding common stock. The earnings per share of common stock is one measure used by stockholders and investors to evaluate the future growth, earning capacity, and dividend potential of a corporation. To comply with AICPA standards, earnings per share is shown on the income statement.

Extraordinary items are gains or losses realized from an unusual event or an event that occurs very infrequently. These unusual events are shown after the Other Revenue and Expense section of the income statement under the heading of Extraordinary Items.

Book value per share of capital stock represents a stockholder's claim on the assets of a corporation that is dissolving business operations. The book value concept assumes that amounts realized from the sale of assets will equal the amounts shown in the general ledger accounts.

GLOSSARY

Appropriated Retained Earnings: Amount of retained earnings reserved by a board of directors for a special need of the corporation or earnings restricted by the laws of a state.

Book Value per Share: The amount of a stockholder's claim on the assets if a corporation discontinues business operations.

Combined Income and Retained Earnings Statement: A financial statement prepared at the end of an accounting period that shows the revenue, expense, net income, and changes to retained earnings during the period on one statement.

Earnings per Share: Earnings per share is the amount of current period net income available for dividends for one share of outstanding common stock.

Extraordinary Items: Business transactions that result in a realized gain or loss from an unusual event or an event that occurs very infrequently are classified as extraordinary items on an income statement.

Prior Period Adjustments: After the books are closed, any material changes to net income from a previous period are called prior period adjustments. These adjustments are corrected by debiting or crediting the Retained Earnings account. They are shown as an adjustment to the beginning balance of Retained Earnings on the retained earnings statement.

Retained Earnings: Retained earnings are the accumulated profits of a corporation that have not been distributed as dividends to the stockholders.

Retained Earnings Statement: A financial statement prepared at the end of an accounting period giving a detailed summary of the changes to retained earnings during the period.

Unappropriated Retained Earnings: Unappropriated retained earnings is the amount of accumulated profits available for the distribution of dividends to stockholders. Before any dividend can be distributed to stockholders, they must be declared or authorized by the board of directors of the corporation.

QUESTIONS

1. Give two reasons why earnings may not be distributed to stockholders in the form of dividends.
2. Explain the difference between unappropriated and appropriated retained earnings.
3. There are two methods of informing stockholders that a portion of retained earnings are not available for dividends. Give a brief explanation of each method.
4. A corporation with a $42,000 credit balance in the Retained Earnings account was assessed additional income taxes of $7,800 for the previous period after the books were closed. How would this information be disclosed on a retained earnings statement?
5. After the books were closed for 19___, the accountant discovered that depreciation on equipment was understated by $4,000. Journalize the

necessary adjusting entry assuming the corporation is subject to a tax rate of 40 percent.

6. A corporation issued 20,000 shares of $10 par value common stock for an average of $16 per share, and the Retained Earnings account had a credit balance of $7,500. Determine the book value per share of common stock.

7. A corporation with 10,000 shares of outstanding common stock reported net income after taxes of $38,000. Compute the earnings per share for common stock.

8. A corporation with beginning retained earnings of $69,000 declared dividends of $30,000 and reported net income after taxes of $51,000. What amount would be shown on the combined income and retained earnings statement for (a) the ending balance of retained earnings, and (b) what is the earnings per share for common stock if 10,000 shares of common stock are outstanding?

EXERCISES

Correcting Entries and Determining Corrected Balance of Retained Earnings

1. The Retained Earnings account for Photo Corporation had a credit balance of $75,000 on December 31, 19_A. On February 8, 19_B, the accountant for the corporation discovered that the ending inventory for 19_A was understated by $28,000.

Required

(a) Journalize the entry necessary to correct the records (disregard income tax liability for error).
(b) Determine the corrected balance for retained earnings on January 1, 19_B.

2. During 19_B, Machine Company was assessed additional income taxes of $3,200 for 19_A.

Required

(a) Journalize the adjusting entry required.
(b) Determine the corrected balance for retained earnings on January 1, 19_B, assuming the balance on December 31, 19_A, amounted to $200,000.

Retained Earnings Statement

3. Selected information for Johnson Distributors as of December 31, 19_B, appears on the next page.

Retained Earnings, 1/1/_B $81,000 (credit)
Net income after taxes   42,000
Cash dividends declared and paid   53,000

Required

(a) Prepare a retained earnings statement.

(b) Prepare the retained earnings section of the balance sheet as of December 31, 19_B, assuming there is $29,000 of unissued treasury stock. The laws of the state restrict dividends for the cost of unissued treasury stock (Chapter 15).

4. Selected information for W & P Iron Works for the year ending December 31, 19_B, appears below:

Retained Earnings, 1/1/_B $142,000 (credit)
Additional tax assessment for 19_A   12,000
Net income after taxes   112,000
Cash dividends declared and paid   144,000

Required

Prepare a retained earnings statement.

Earnings per Share of Capital Stock

5. A corporation with 12,000 shares of common stock outstanding earned net income after extraordinary items and income taxes of $46,440 in 19_A and $60,000 in 19_B. Extraordinary losses of $2,040 were incurred in 19_A and dividends amounting to $7,500 were owed to preferred stockholders at the end of 19_B. Determine the earnings per share of common stock for 19_A and 19_B.

6. Determine the earnings per share for the following three corporations:

Corporation	Net Income after Extraordinary Items & Taxes	Extraordinary Items (Net of Tax)	Dividends Owed Preferred	Outstanding Shares of Common	Unissued Treasury Stock
A	$168,000	-0-	$36,000	30,000	-0-
B	74,000	($4,800)*	-0-	43,000	3,000
C	93,000	-0-	6,000	30,000	1,000

* $4,800 loss

Book Value per Share of Capital Stock

7. Busy Bee Products has 19,000 shares of $10 par value common stock outstanding at an average price of $14 per share and a credit balance in the Retained Earnings account of $7,790. Determine the book value per share of common stock.

8. Zippy Tree Service had the following selected balances as of December 31, 19_A: Paid-in Capital, $135,000 and Retained Earnings, $4,920 credit. Common stock of Zippy had a $10 par value and an average selling price of $11.25 per share. Determine the book value per share of common stock.

9. A corporation with a total paid-in capital of $640,000 and a credit balance in Retained Earnings of $20,000 has 5,000 shares of $50 par value preferred stock and 10,000 shares of $25 par value common stock outstanding. The preferred stock sold at par value. Determine the book value per share for (a) preferred stock and (b) common stock.

10. Axle Cycle Shop has 3,000 shares of $25 par value preferred stock and 8,000 shares of $10 par value common stock outstanding. The preferred stock sold for an average of $26 per share. Total paid-in capital amounted to $334,200 and retained earnings amounted to $6,200. Determine the book value per share of (a) preferred stock and (b) common stock.

PROBLEMS

Journal Entries, Retained Earnings Statement, and Earnings per Share

18-1. On January 1, 19_B, M & N Electric had a credit balance of $26,000 in the Retained Earnings account. During 19_B, the following two selected transactions occurred:

19_B
July 22 After an I.R.S. audit of 19_A, the company was assessed additional income taxes of $1,840. On January 4, 19_A, the company purchased tools for $4,000, and they recorded the tools as an expense which was disallowed by the I.R.S. The tools had a 5-year life and no salvage value.

Dec. 31 Net income after taxes amounted to $46,550. Close the Income Summary account assuming all other closing entries have been recorded.

Required

(a) Journalize the selected entries for 19_B.
(b) Prepare a retained earnings statement for the year ended on December 31, 19_B. Cash dividends of $22,000 were declared to the common stockholders during the year.
(c) Determine earnings per share for common stock assuming the corporation has 20,000 shares issued and outstanding.

18-2. The following account balances appearing in the records of P & J Tool

Company as of January 1, 19_C:

Common Stock, $10 par value $200,000
Retained Earnings 63,400 (credit)
Treasury Stock (1,000 shares) 18,000

Selected transactions for 19_C are shown below.

19_C

May 6 The accountant discovered that ending inventory was understated $800 in 19_B. (Disregard income tax liability.)

Dec. 31 Net income after taxes amounted to $29,700. Close the Income Summary account assuming all other closing entries have been recorded.

Required

(*a*) Journalize the selected entries for 19_C.

(*b*) Prepare a retained earnings statement for the year ended on December 31, 19_C. Cash dividends of $40,000 were declared to the common stockholders during the year.

(*c*) Determine earnings per share of common stock.

Posting Selected Entries and Retained Earnings Statement

18-3. Open a general ledger account for Retained Earnings No. 320, and enter the beginning credit balance of $53,900 as of January 1, 19_C.

Required

(*a*) Post the following data for 19_C: The company was assessed additional income taxes for 19_A on May 6, 19_C, amounting to $4,800 because the depreciation of equipment was overstated. Net income for 19_C amounted to $24,000 and dividends were declared on December 30 amounting to $46,000.

(*b*) Prepare a retained earnings statement for Mays Tool Company for the year ended December 31, 19_C.

18-4. On January 1, 19_C, Major Maintenance had a credit balance of $56,400 in the Retained Earnings account. During 19_C, the following selected transactions occurred.

1. An understatement of $2,000 for depreciation of the building in 19_A was discovered on March 1, 19_C, by the accountant and the error was corrected. Additional income taxes of $920 resulted from the error, and the liability was entered in the records.

2. Dividends of $48,000 were declared to the common stockholders on December 30, 19_C.

3. Net income after taxes, $19,000.

Required

(a) Open a general ledger account for Retained Earnings No. 320, and enter the beginning balance; post the information in items 1 to 3 in the Retained Earnings account.

(b) Prepare a retained earnings statement for the year ended December 31, 19_C.

Combined Income Statement and Retained Earnings Statement

18-5. Prepare a combined income and retained earnings statement (use Figure 18-2 for an example) for Wilcox Service for the year ended December 31, 19_C, using the following information:

Common Stock, no par value, $10 stated value	$ 90,000
Retained Earnings, 1/1/_C	67,000 (credit)
Sales	370,557
Cost of Goods Sold	110,750
Operating Expenses (Control)	184,807
Uninsured loss from theft of inventory (net of taxes amounting to $1,820)	4,340
Dividends declared and paid	16,000
Income taxes	16,750

Note: Be sure to include earnings per share of common stock.

Income Statement, Retained Earnings Statement, and Partial Combined Statement

18-6. The following data was obtained from the records of Spot Treat Company as of December 31, 19_C:

Common Stock, $25 par value	$525,000
Retained Earnings, 1/1/_C	133,000 (credit)
Treasury Stock (1,000 shares)	14,000
Cash Dividends Declared	36,000
Sales	186,000
Cost of Goods Sold	46,500
Operating Expenses (Control)	91,600
Interest Earned	1,162
Income Taxes	9,062

Required

Prepare the following statements:

(a) Income statement

(b) Retained earnings statement

(c) Partial combined income statement and retained earnings statement beginning with net income after taxes

Review Problem for Chapters 15 to 18

18-7. Balances in the stockholders' equity accounts for Ace Products as of January 1, 19_B, are shown below:

Common Stock, $10 par value	$180,000
Premium on Common	90,000
Retained Earnings	47,000 (credit)

Transactions affecting stockholders' equity accounts for the years 19_B and 19_C are shown below:

19_B

Jan.   15   A cash dividend of $0.40 per share was declared to common stockholders of record January 30, payable February 18.

Feb.   18   Paid dividend to common stockholders.

Mar.   30   After the 19_A audit, the I.R.S. assessed additional income taxes of $3,000. Several small pieces of equipment, purchased on December 28, 19_A, were recorded as an expense for $10,000; entry was disallowed by I.R.S. and reclassified as a depreciable asset with no salvage value. Additional assessment is due on April 15, 19_B.

Apr.   15   Paid additional tax liability of $3,000 for 19_A.

May   4   Issued 2,000 shares of common stock for $15 per share.

July   15   A dividend of $0.40 per share was declared to common stockholders of record July 31, payable August 14.

Aug.   14   Paid dividend to common stockholders.

Dec.   31   Net income after taxes, $59,000. Close the Income Summary account assuming all other closing entries have been recorded.

19_C

Jan.   15   Dividend of $0.40 per share was declared to common stockholders of record January 30, payable February 18.

Feb.   18   Paid dividend to common stockholders.

Apr.   10   The accountant discovered an overstatement of depreciation amounting to $5,000 in 19_B. Error was corrected and the additional tax liability of $1,500 was recorded.

May   1   Paid additional tax liability of $1,500.

July   15   Dividend of $0.40 per share was declared to common stockholders of record July 31, payable August 14.

Aug.   14   Paid dividend to common stockholders.

Dec.   31   Close the following accounts: Sales, $284,000; Cost of Goods Sold, $71,000; Operating Expenses (Control), $184,800; Income Tax Expense, $5,250; Interest Revenue, $1,800; and Income Summary for the appropriate amount.

Required

(a) Open a general ledger account for: 330 Retained Earnings and enter a credit balance of $47,000 as of January 1, 19_B.

(b) Journalize transactions for the years 19_B and 19_C, and post the selected entries to the Retained Earnings account.

(c) Prepare a retained earnings statement for 19_B.

(d) Prepare a combined income statement and retained earnings statement for 19_C. (Be sure to include earnings per share of common stock.)

Long-term Liabilities

After completing this chapter, you should be able to:

1. **State the difference between a secured and a debenture bond**

2. **Give a brief description of registered serial, convertible, callable, and coupon bonds**

3. **Account for the issuance of bonds at face value and above or below face value**

4. **Amortize bond discount and bond premium**

5. **Record the retirement of bonds on their maturity date and prior to their maturity date**

6. **Give the balance sheet presentation for Bond Interest Payable, Bonds Payable, Premium on Bonds, and Discount on Bonds**

7. **Give the income statement presentation for Bond Interest Expense, Loss on Retirement of Bonds, and Gain on Retirement of Bonds**

Long-term liabilities are debts of a business that will not be paid within the current operating cycle. Most long-term debts consist of notes, mortgages, or bonds that extend over a period of several years and involve the payment of interest on the obligation.

When a business needs a large amount of money for operations or for the purchase or construction of plant assets, it may obtain the funds by borrowing on a note or by issuing stocks or bonds. It is advantageous for a corporation to obtain funds by issuing long-term notes or bonds, because these funds normally require the payment of interest, and interest is a deductible expense of a business. Issuing stocks to obtain funds normally requires the payment of dividends to stockholders, and dividends are not a deductible expense. Also, common stockholders receive one vote for each share of stock they own entitling them to vote on corporate affairs.

ISSUANCE OF BONDS

Certain legal procedures must be followed before bonds may be issued, and most corporations must also receive authorization from the stockholders. When authorization is received, the bonds are printed and presented for sale. Bonds may be sold by the issuing corporation, but usually they are sold on the open market in the same way as stocks.

Bonds, like notes, are a written promise to pay the *face value* (amount designated on bond certificate) on its *maturity date* (day bonds come due) plus a promise to pay a stipulated rate of interest on its face value. The face value of a bond is paid on its maturity date, but interest is paid to bondholders over the life of the bond. For example, an 8 percent, 10-year, $1,000 bond with interest payable on June 30 and December 31 will pay 4 percent or $40 ($1,000 × .08 = $80 × $^{6}/_{12}$) every interest payment period for the 10-year life of the bond. Total interest of $800 ($40 × 2 = $80 per year × 10 years) will be paid to bondholders over the life of the bond, and the face value of the bond will be paid to bondholders on the maturity date.

TYPES OF BONDS

Two types of bonds are issued, secured or unsecured (unsecured bonds are called debenture bonds). A *secured bond* guarantees the bondholder payment on its maturity date, because a trustee is usually given title to property of equal value as security for the bondholders until the maturity date of the bond. If the issuing company defaults on the payment date of a secured bond, the trustee may sell the property and pay the bondholders the maturity value of the bond plus any unpaid interest. *Debenture bonds* or unsecured bonds do not have any property pledged for the protection of bondholders, and the bondholders have no assurance that the bonds will be paid on their maturity date. However, there is usually little risk involved because debenture bonds are normally issued by large, well-established, reputable companies with a high credit rating. Secured and debenture bonds may be issued with one or more of the following conditions.

Registered Bond. A *registered bond* requires the name and address of bondholders to be on file at all times with the issuing company. When a registered bond is sold by a bondholder before its maturity date, a change of ownership form must be filed with the issuing company giving the name and address of the new bondholder. Interest payments are mailed to the registered bondholders on each interest payment period. Most of the corporate bonds issued today are registered.

Coupon Bond. A *coupon bond* has coupons attached to the bond—one for each interest payment period. A 10-year coupon bond with two interest periods per year would have 20 coupons. The issuing corporation normally establishes a special account with a bank and deposits funds each interest payment period. When bondholders present their coupons to the bank, payments are made from the special fund.

Serial Bond. A *serial bond* specifies that a portion of its face value will be paid to bondholders on different dates. For example, $250 of a $1,000, 10-year bond may mature at the end of Year 7, Year 8, and Year 9, until the final $250 payment is paid to the bondholders on the maturity date in Year 10.

Convertible Bond. A *convertible bond* gives a bondholder the option of exchanging bonds on or before their maturity date for cash or for a specified number of shares of the company's common stock.

Callable Bond. A *callable bond* permits the issuing company to "call" in bonds before the maturity date, retire the bonds, and pay bondholders a specific amount which is usually more than face value.

QUOTATION OF BONDS

Bonds, like stocks, are sold and traded on the open market. The selling price of bonds is quoted the same as the quotation for stock; however, the quotation has a different meaning for bonds. A quotation of 97 for stock means that stock is selling for $97 per share. A quotation of 97 for bonds means that bonds are selling for $970 ($97 × 10) for each $1,000 bond, or 97 percent of the cost of a $1,000 bond. If the face value (value of bond on maturity date) of a bond was $500, selling price would be $485 (97% × $500).

Bonds may be sold at face value, or they may be sold above or below face value. If bonds are sold above face value, they are sold at a premium; if bonds are sold below face value, they are sold at a discount. For example, if two, 8 percent, $1,000 bonds were sold at face value, the selling price would amount to $2,000 ($100 × 10 = $1,000 × 2). A quotation of 101 for the two bonds would result in a selling price of $2,020 ($101 × 10 = $1,010 × 2), a premium amounting to $20 ($2,020 − $2,000 face value). A quotation of 99 for the two bonds would result in a selling price of $1,980 ($99 × 10 = $990 × 2), a discount amounting to $20 ($2,000 face value − $1,980). When bonds are sold, a long-term liability account entitled **Bonds Payable** is credited for the face value multiplied by the number of bonds sold.

Bond interest expense, the cost of borrowing money through the issuance of bonds, is usually paid twice a year. The interest is paid on the face value not on the selling price of the bonds. When interest is paid, the Bond Interest Expense account is debited and the Cash account is credited. For example, interest incurred for 6 months on a $1,000, 8 percent bond would amount to $40 ($1,000 × .08 = $80 × $^{6}/_{12}$). Bond Interest Expense is classified as Other Expense on an income statement.

SELLING PRICE OF BONDS

Bonds are issued at face value, but they may be sold on the open market at different prices. The price is determined by market demand; the price a purchaser is willing to pay for an investment will depend on the type of bond, its special features, maturity date, and the rate of interest. For example, most investors want to earn a rate of return that is approximately equal to the current interest rate on the market on similar types of bonds with the same maturity date. They will purchase bonds at a price that is either:

1. Less than the face value of the bond if the bond interest rate is lower than the current market rate (discount)
2. More than the face value of the bond if the bond interest rate is higher than the current market rate (premium)

Assume that Smooth Tip Pen Company issued 100, 10-year, $1,000, 6 percent bonds when the interest rate on the market on similar types of bonds was $6^{1}/_{2}$ percent. The bonds will probably be sold at a discount to enable investors to earn a rate comparable to the market rate of $6^{1}/_{2}$ percent as shown below.

	Bonds Sold at 95 with Interest at 6%		Bonds Sold at 100 with Interest at 6½%	
Amount paid on maturity date		$100,000		$100,000
Add: Interest paid during 10-year life of bonds ($100,000 × .06 = $6,000 × 10 years); ($100,000 × .065 = $65,000 × 10 years)	60,000	$160,000	65,000	$165,000
Less: Selling price of bonds		95,000		100,000
Total amount paid to bondholders		$ 65,000		$ 65,000

Note that if the bonds sell at 95, the issuing company will pay interest over the 10-year life of the bond plus the face value on the maturity date that is equal to $6^{1}/_{2}$ percent bonds selling at 100 (face value).

Assume that Smooth Tip Pen Company issued 100, 10-year, $1,000, 6 percent bonds when the interest rate on the market on similar types of bonds was $5^{1}/_{2}$ percent. The bonds will probably be sold at a premium because investors will receive interest that is $^{1}/_{2}$ percent higher than the current market rate as shown below.

	Bonds Sold at 105 with Interest at 6%		Bonds Sold at 100 with Interest at 5½%	
Amount paid on maturity date		$100,000		$100,000
Add: Interest paid during 10-year life of bonds ($100,000 × .06 = $6,000 × 10 years); ($100,000 × .055 = $55,000 × 10 years)	60,000	$160,000	55,000	$155,000
Less: Selling price of bonds		105,000		100,000
Total amount paid to bondholders		$ 55,000		$ 55,000

Note that if the bonds sell at 105, the company will pay interest over the 10-year life of the bond plus the face value on the maturity date that is equal to $5^{1}/_{2}$ percent bonds selling at 100 (face value).

ACCOUNTING FOR BONDS

Accounting for the issuance of bonds requires a credit to a long-term liability account entitled **Bonds Payable.** When bonds are sold for more or less than their face value, the difference is credited or debited to a premium or discount account.

Bonds sold above face value are sold at a premium and the difference between the selling price and face value of the bond is credited to a long-term liability account entitled **Premium on Bonds.** Premium on Bonds will always have a credit or zero balance. Bonds sold below face value are sold at a discount and the difference between the face value and selling price is debited to a contra long-term liability account entitled **Discount on Bonds.** Discount on Bonds will always have a debit or zero balance. When bonds are sold above or below face value, the premium is revenue and the discount is an expense, and any premium or discount realized on the issuance of bonds is usually amortized (reduced or written off) over the life of the bond whenever bond interest expense is recorded. Amortizing a premium requires the premium account to be debited for a portion of the original amount of the premium resulting in a decrease to the Bond Interest Expense account for the period. Amortizing a discount requires a credit to the discount account resulting in an increase to the Bond Interest Expense account for the period. On the maturity date of the bond, the premium or discount account should have a zero balance if amortization has been recorded properly.

For example, assume Smooth Tip Pen Company issued 100, 8 percent, $1,000, 10-year bonds on July 1, 1983. The bonds pay interest on June 30 and December 31 and mature on July 1, 1993. Three examples are given below.

EXAMPLE 1 BONDS SOLD AT FACE VALUE

Assume that Smooth Tip Pen Company sold the 100 bonds at 100[1] or $100,000 ($100 × 10 = $1,000 × 100). The Cash account is debited and the Bonds Payable account is credited for the $100,000 selling price, the face value of the bonds, as shown in the following journal entry:

Journal entry for sale of bonds at face value

1983				
July	1	Cash	100,000	
		8% Bonds Payable		100,000
		To record issuance of 100, 8%,		
		$1,000, 10-year bonds at face value.		

On December 31, 1983, the first semiannual interest payment is paid to bondholders. The Bond Interest Expense account is debited and the Cash account is credited for the first semiannual interest payment of $4,000

---

[1] Quotation × 10 × number of bonds = selling price.

($100,000 × .08 = $8,000 × 6/12), as shown in the following journal entry:

Journal entry for semiannual payment for bond interest

1983				
Dec.	31	Bond Interest Expense	4,000	
		Cash		4,000
		To record interest payment for 100, $1,000 bonds.		

EXAMPLE 2 BONDS SOLD ABOVE FACE VALUE

Assume that Smooth Tip Pen Company sold the 100 bonds at 102 or $102,000 ($102 × 10 = $1,020 × 100). The Cash account is debited for cash received, $102,000; the Bonds Payable account is credited for $100,000, the face value of the bonds; and the Premium on Bonds account is credited for $2,000 ($102,000 − $100,000), the difference between selling price and face value of the bonds, as shown in the following journal entry:

Journal entry for bonds sold at a premium

1983				
July	1	Cash	102,000	
		8% Bonds Payable		100,000
		Premium on Bonds		2,000
		To record the issuance of 100, 8%, $1,000, 10-year bonds at $102,000, a premium of $2,000.		

On December 31, 1983, the first semiannual interest payment is paid to bondholders and the premium is amortized. There are 20 semiannual interest periods over 10-year life of bonds; therefore, the premium is amortized for $100, 1/20 of the $2,000 ($2,000/20). The Bond Interest Expense account is debited for $3,900 ($4,000 interest − $100 premium amortization), the Premium on Bonds account is debited for the $100 amortization, and the Cash account is credited for the semiannual interest payment of $4,000 ($100,000 × .08 = $8,000 × 6/12), as shown in the following journal entry:

Journal entry for amortization of premium on bonds

1983				
Dec.	31	Bond Interest Expense	3,900	
		Premium on Bonds	100	
		Cash		4,000
		Record interest payment for 100, $1,000 bonds and amortization of 1/20 of the $2,000 premium.		

The above entry is recorded each interest payment period for the life of bond.

**EXAMPLE 3
BONDS SOLD
BELOW FACE
VALUE**

Assume that Smooth Tip Pen Company sold the 100 bonds at 99 or $99,000 ($99 × 10 = $990 × 100). The Cash account is debited for the cash received, $99,000; the Discount on Bonds account is debited for the $1,000 ($100,000 − $99,000), the difference between selling price and face value of the bonds; and the Bonds Payable account is credited for $100,000, the face value of the bonds, as shown in the following journal entry:

Journal entry for sale of bonds at a discount

1983			
July 1	Cash	99,000	
	Discount on Bonds	1,000	
	8% Bonds Payable		100,000
	To record issuance of 100, 8%, $1,000, 10-year bonds at $99,000, a discount of $1,000.		

On December 31, 1983, the first semiannual interest payment is paid to bondholders and the discount is amortized. There are 20 semiannual interest periods over 10-year life of bonds; therefore, the discount is amortized for $50, 1/20 of the $1,000 discount ($1,000/20). The Bond Interest Expense account is debited for $4,050 ($4,000 interest + $50 amortization), the Discount on Bonds account is credited for the $50 amortization, and the Cash account is credited for the semiannual interest payment of $4,000 ($100,000 × .08 = $8,000 × 6/12), as shown in the following journal entry:

Journal entry for amortization of bond discount

1983			
Dec. 31	Bond Interest Expense	4,050	
	Discount on Bonds		50
	Cash		4,000
	Record interest payment for 100, $1,000 bonds and amortization of 1/20 of the $1,000 discount.		

Notice that the $4,000 paid for the 6 months interest on the bonds remains the same in all three examples.

YEAR-END ADJUSTMENTS FOR ACCRUED INTEREST ON BONDS

When the books are closed, any interest accrued on bonds is recorded with an adjusting entry debiting the Bond Interest Expense account and crediting a Bond Interest Payable account. For example, assume that the 100, 8 percent, $1,000 bonds issued by Smooth Tip Pen Company were dated September 30, 1983, and interest was payable on May 1 and October 1. If the bonds were sold at 100 on October 1, 1983, the following entry would be recorded:

Journal entry for sale of bonds at face value

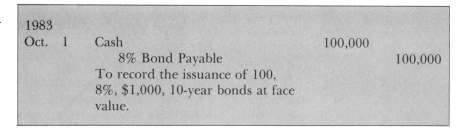

```
1983
Oct.   1     Cash                                        100,000
                   8% Bond Payable                                 100,000
                   To record the issuance of 100,
                   8%, $1,000, 10-year bonds at face
                   value.
```

On December 31, 1983, the books are closed. An adjusting entry is required to record the interest accrued on the bonds for October, November, and December. The Bond Interest Expense account is debited and the Bond Interest Payable account is credited for $2,000 ($100,000 × .08 = $8,000 × ¼), as shown in the following journal entry:

Adjusting entry for accrued interest on bonds

```
                              Adjusting Entry
1983
Dec.   31     Bond Interest Expense                      2,000
                   Bond Interest Payable                          2,000
                   Record interest payment for
                   3 months on 100, $1,000 bonds.
```

On April 1, 1984, the first semiannual interest payment is paid to the 100 bondholders. The Bond Interest Expense account is debited for the January, February, and March interest of $2,000 ($100,000 × .08 = $8,000 × ¼); the Bond Interest Payable account is debited for $2,000 to eliminate the liability account; and the Cash account is credited for the first semiannual interest payment of $4,000, as shown in the following journal entry:

Journal entry for payment of bond interest

```
1984
Apr.   1     Bond Interest Expense                       2,000
                 Bond Interest Payable                     2,000
                    Cash                                            4,000
                 Record interest payment for 1984
                 on 100, $1,000 bonds and remove
                 interest liability for 1983.
```

RETIREMENT OF BONDS

On the maturity date of bonds, the Bonds Payable account is debited and the Cash account is credited for the face value of bonds as shown below.

Journal entry for retirement of bonds on maturity date

1993			
July 1	8% Bonds Payable	100,000	
	Cash		100,000
	To record payment to 100,		
	bondholders on maturity date of		
	bonds.		

If bonds are retired prior to their maturity date, any balance remaining in the discount or premium account must be removed. Any remaining discount is credited to the Discount on Bonds account, and any remaining premium is debited to the Premium on Bonds account. The difference between the carrying value (see page 527) of bonds (Bonds Payable − discount or Bonds Payable + premium) and the cost of retiring the bonds is debited to an expense account entitled ***Loss on Retirement of Bonds*** for a loss and credited to a revenue account entitled ***Gain on Retirement of Bonds*** for a gain. A loss realized on the retirement of bonds is usually classified as Other Expense and a gain realized on the retirement of bonds is usually classified as Other Revenue on the income statement. If the loss or gain is material in amount, it is classified as an extraordinary item on an income statement to comply with the standards established by the Financial Accounting Standards Board (FASB), Statement No. 4.

For example, assume Smooth Tip Pen Company retired 100 bonds (Example 2, page 523) on January 1, 1988, 4½ years after the issuance date. The company purchased the bonds on the open market at a total cost of $100,500, and the loss or gain on retirement of bonds was determined by the following computation:

Computation of gain realized on retirement of bonds

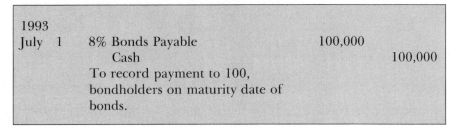

1. Carrying value of bonds:			
Balance in Bonds Payable		$100,000	
Plus: Balance in Premium on Bonds			
($2,000 − $900 amortized @			
$200 a year for 4½ years)		1,100	$101,100
2. Less: Cost of purchasing 100 bonds			100,500
3. Realized gain or loss on retirement			$ 600 gain*

* A gain is realized because the cost of retiring the bonds is less than their ***carrying value.***

The following journal entry would be recorded on the retirement date:

Journal entry for retirement of bonds prior to maturity date

1988			
Jan. 1	8% Bonds Payable	100,000	
	Premium on Bonds	1,100	
	Cash		100,500
	Gain on Retirement of Bonds		600
	To record retirement of 100, $1,000 bonds at a gain of $600 and to remove the liability accounts.		

Assume Smooth Tip Pen Company retired the 100 bonds (Example 2, page 523) on January 1, 1988, $4\frac{1}{2}$ years after the issuance date, by purchasing the bonds on the open market at a total cost of $102,000. The loss or gain on retirement of bonds was determined by the following computations:

Computation of loss realized on retirement of bonds

1. Carrying value of bonds:			
Balance in Bonds Payable		$100,000	
Plus: Balance in Premium on Bonds ($2,000 − $900 amortized @ $200 a year for $4\frac{1}{2}$ years)		1,100	$101,100
2. Less: Cost of purchasing 100 bonds			102,000
3. Realized gain or loss on retirement			$ 900 loss*

* A loss is realized because the cost of retiring the bonds is more than their carrying value.

The following journal entry would be recorded on the retirement date:

Journal entry for loss on retirement of bonds

1988			
Jan. 1	8% Bonds payable	100,000	
	Premium on Bonds	1,100	
	Loss on Retirement of Bonds	900	
	Cash		102,000
	To record retirement of 100, $1,000 bonds at a loss of $900 and to remove the liability accounts.		

CLASSIFICATION OF BONDS AND RELATED ACCOUNTS

Bonds Payable, Premium on Bonds, and Discount on Bonds are all classified as long-term liability accounts. The balance in the Premium on Bonds account is added to the face value of Bonds Payable and the balance in the Discount on Bonds account is deducted from Bonds Payable to arrive at the carrying value of bonds on the balance sheet date. For example, the balance sheet presentation for Bonds Payable (Example 2, page 523) as of December 31, 1983, follows.

Balance sheet presentation of long-term liabilities

Long-term Liabilities:		
8% Bonds Payable, due July 1, 1993	$ 100,000	
Add: Premium on Bonds	1,900*	
Total Long-term Liabilities		$101,900

* Premium of $2,000 less $100 amortization for 1983.

The balance sheet presentation for Bonds Payable (Example 3, page 524) as of December 31, 1983, is shown below.

Discount on bonds shown under long-term liabilities

Long-term Liabilities:		
8% Bonds Payable, due July 1, 1993	$100,000	
Less: Discount on Bonds	950*	
Total Long-term Liabilities		$ 99,050

* Discount of $1,000 less $50 amortization for 1983.

Bond Interest Payable is classified as a current liability on a balance sheet, because interest will be paid within the current operating cycle. The balance sheet presentation for Bond Interest Payable (example on page 525) as of December 31, 1983, is shown below.

Current Liabilities:
Bond Interest Payable $2,000

The interest on bonds payable is classified as Other Expense on an income statement. The Bond Interest Expense for the year ended December 31, 1983, (Example 2, page 523) is shown below.

Income statement presentation for Bond Interest Expense

Other Expense:
Bond Interest Expense $3,900

Assuming the gain on retirement of bonds is considered to be a material amount, it is classified as an extraordinary item on an income statement. Gain on Retirement of Bonds for the year ended December 31, 1983, is shown below.

Gains and losses classified as extraordinary items

Extraordinary Gain:
Gain on Retirement of Bonds $600

Assuming the loss on retirement of bonds is considered to be a material amount, it is classified as an extraordinary item on an income statement. Loss on Retirement of Bonds for the year ended December 31, 1983, is shown as follows:

Extraordinary Loss:
Loss on Retirement of Bonds $900

SUMMARY

Most long-term liabilities consist of notes, mortgages, or bonds that extend over a period of several years and involve the payment of interest. When a business needs a large amount of money for operations or for the purchase or construction of plant assets, it may obtain funds by issuing bonds. Bonds are a written promise to pay the amount designated on the bond certificate (face value) on the maturity date plus a promise to pay interest at a stipulated rate on face value over the life of bond.

Secured and debenture bonds are the two types of bonds issued, and they may or may not be registered and issued as a serial, convertible, callable, or coupon bond. Registered bonds require the name and address of bondholders to be on file at all times with the issuing company. Serial bonds pay a portion of the face value of a bond over several different periods. A convertible bond gives a bondholder the option of exchanging bonds on or before their maturity date for cash or for a specified number of shares of the company's common stock. Callable bonds permit the issuing company to "call" in bonds before the maturity date and pay bondholders a specific amount which is usually more than face value. Coupon bonds have coupons attached to them—one for each interest period. Bondholders receive interest payments by presenting coupons to a bank on the interest payment date.

Bonds are issued at face value, but they are sold on the open market at the price a purchaser is willing to pay. When bonds are sold, a liability account called Bonds Payable is credited for their face value. If the selling price of bonds is higher than their face value, the difference is credited to a Premium on Bonds account; if the selling price of bonds is lower than their face value, the difference is debited to a Discount on Bonds account. Bond premium or discount is amortized whenever bond interest is recorded. Amortizing a premium decreases bond interest expense; amortizing a discount increases bond interest expense.

When bonds mature, the bondholders are paid and the Bonds Payable account is debited and the Cash account is credited for the payment. When bonds are retired before their maturity date, any material gain or loss realized on the retirement is classified as an extraordinary item on an income statement to comply with the standards established by the Financial Accounting Standards Board, Statement No. 4.

The Bonds Payable, Premium on Bonds, and Discount on Bonds accounts are classified as a long-term liability on a balance sheet. Premium is added to the face value of Bonds Payable and a discount is deducted from the face value of Bonds Payable on a balance sheet to show book value or carrying value of bonds on the balance sheet date. Bond Interest Expense is classified as Other Expense on an income statement, and Bond Interest Payable is classified as a Current Liability on a balance sheet.

GLOSSARY

Bond Interest Expense: The cost of borrowing money through the issuance of bonds; usually paid twice a year. Bond Interest Expense is classified as Other Expense on an income statement.

Bond Interest Payable: A current liability account used to record interest owed to bondholders that will be paid within the current operating cycle.

Bonds: A written promise to pay the amount designated on bond certificate on maturity date plus a promise to pay a stipulated rate of interest on its face value over the life of bond.

Bonds Payable: A long-term liability account credited for the face value of the bonds multiplied by the number of bonds sold.

Callable Bonds: A bond that permits the issuing company to "call" in the bond before its maturity date, cancel the bond, and pay the bondholders a specified amount which is usually more than the face value of bonds.

Carrying Value: The face value of bonds plus the balance in the Premium on Bonds account or less the balance in the Discount on Bonds account equals the carrying value of bonds.

Convertible Bonds: A bond giving bondholders the option of exchanging their bonds on or before their maturity date for cash or for a specified number of shares of the company's common stock.

Coupon Bond: A bond that has coupons attached to the bond; one for each interest payment period. Interest is paid to bondholders when they present their coupons to a bank on the interest payment date.

Debenture Bond: Bonds that do not have any property pledged for the protection of bondholders, and the bondholders have no assurance that bonds will be paid on their maturity date. Most debenture bonds are issued by large, well-established, reputable companies with a good credit rating; therefore, very little risk is involved for bondholders.

Discount on Bonds: When bonds are sold below face value, they are sold at a discount. The difference between the face value and selling price is debited to a contra long-term liability account entitled Discount on Bonds. Discount on Bonds will always have a debit or zero balance.

Face Value: The amount designated on the bond certificate which is payable on its maturity date.

Gain on Retirement of Bonds: The title of a revenue account that is credited when bonds are retired for less than their carrying value. The gain realized is usually classified as Other Revenue on an income statement; however, if the realized gain is material in amount, it is classified as an extraordinary item.

Long-term Liabilities: Debts of a business that will not be paid without the current operating cycle.

Loss on Retirement of Bonds: The title of an expense account that is debited when bonds are retired for more than their carrying value. A loss realized is usually classified as Other Expense on an income statement; however, if the realized loss is material in amount, it is classified as an extraordinary item.

Maturity Date: The end of a bond period or the day a bond comes due for payment. Bondholders are paid the face value of the bonds on the maturity date plus any unpaid interest.

Premium on Bonds: When bonds are sold above face value, they are sold at a premium. The difference between the selling price and the face value is credited to a long-term liability account entitled Premium on Bonds. Premium on Bonds will always have a credit or zero balance.

Registered Bonds: A bond requiring the name and address of the bondholder to be on file at all times with the issuing company. Interest payments are mailed to the registered bondholders each interest payment period.

Secured Bonds: Bonds that have property pledged for payment of the bond on its maturity date. Title to the property is given to a trustee as security for the bondholders until the maturity date of the bond. If the issuing company defaults on the payment date of bonds, the trustee may sell property and pay off the bondholders.

Serial Bonds: A bond that pays a portion of its face value to bondholders on different dates throughout the life of bond.

QUESTIONS

1. List two advantages for issuing bonds instead of stocks.
2. State the difference between a secured and a debenture bond.
3. Give a brief explanation of a convertible and a callable bond.
4. What is the selling price of a $1,000 bond quoted at (*a*) 109 and (*b*) 94?
5. Give the balance sheet presentation for the sale of 100, 8 percent, 10-year, $1,000 bonds at 104. The bonds mature in 1990.
6. What is the carrying value on December 31, 19_B, of a 6 percent, $1,000, 10-year bond that was sold at 98 on January 1, 19_A?
7. What is the total amount of bond interest expense for the year 19_A for ten, 9 percent, 10-year, $1,000 bonds sold for 102 on February 1, 19_A?
8. The bonds in Question 7 were purchased on the open market at 101 and retired on January 1, 19_F. Compute the amount of realized gain or loss on the retirement of the ten bonds.
9. How is a realized loss of $2,500 on the retirement of bonds classified on an income statement if (*a*) the loss is considered to be a material amount, and (*b*) the $2,500 loss is insignificant?
10. Fill in the blanks for the following statements:
    (*a*) Some bonds are issued with _____ attached to the bond for each interest payment period.
    (*b*) Bonds with an interest rate that is higher than the current market rate will usually sell for _____ (more/less) than face value.

EXERCISES

Matching Items with Their Definition

1. Match the statements below with the items in column A.

Column A

(a) —————— property pledged for the payment of a bond
(b) —————— face value of bond is paid in install-ments
(c) —————— bond sold above face value
(d) —————— bonds retired for less than carrying value
(e) —————— bonds sold at 99

a Discount on bonds
b Serial bonds
c Premium on bonds
d Secured bonds
e Convertible bonds
f Realized gain
g Callable bonds

Journal Entries for Sale of Bonds

2. On July 1, 19__, the Toy Company sold 30, 9 percent, $1,000, 10-year bonds at face value. The bonds were dated June 30, 19__, and pay interest on July 1 and January 1 each year.

Required

Journalize the transactions for year one.

3. On January 1, 19__, Carpet Outlet sold 20, 8 percent, $1,000, 10-year bonds. The bonds were dated January 1, 19__, and pay interest on June 30 and December 31.

Required

Journalize the transactions for year one assuming the bonds were sold:
(a) At face value
(b) At 104

4. On July 1, 19__, Missouri Shoe Company sold 10, 6 percent, $1,000 10-year bonds. The bonds were dated June 30, 19__, and pay interest on June 30 and December 31.

Required

Journalize the transactions for year one assuming the bonds were sold:
(a) At face value
(b) At 94

Journal Entries for Sale of Bonds Plus Balance Sheet Presentation

5. On April 1, 19__, Cookie Company sold 40, 8 percent, $1,000, 10-year bonds at face value. The bonds were issued on March 31, 19__, and pay interest on March 31 and September 30.

Required

(*a*) Journalize the transactions for year one; the books are closed on December 31 each year.

(*b*) Give the balance sheet presentation for the bonds on December 31, year one.

6. On March 31, 19__, Joslin Manufacturing sold 20, 8 percent, $1,000, 10-year bonds at 102. The bonds were sold on the issuance date and pay interest on March 31 and September 30.

Required

(*a*) Journalize the transactions for year one; the books are closed on December 31 each year.

(*b*) Give the balance sheet presentation for the bonds on December 31, year one.

Journal Entries for Retirement of Bonds

7. On July 1, 19_F, Diamond Manufacturing purchased 20 of their own 9 percent, $1,000, 10-year bonds on the open market at 101 and retired them. The bonds were originally sold on January 1, 19_A, at face value, and interest was paid every June 30 and December 31 since the date the bonds were issued.

Required

Journalize the transactions for 19_F; the books are closed on December 31 each year.

Journal Entry for Retirement of Bonds and Income Statement Presentation

8. On July 1, 19_E, Home Fabrics purchased 40 of their own 8 percent, $1,000, 10-year bonds on the open market at 101 and retired them. The bonds were issued on July 1, 19_A, at a premium, and on July 1, 19_F, there was a balance in the premium account of $720.

Required

(*a*) Journalize the entry for the retirement of the bonds on July 1, 19_E.

(*b*) Give the income statement presentation for the gain realized on the retirement of the bonds assuming the gain is considered an ordinary item.

PROBLEMS

Journal Entries for Sale, Interest, and Retirement of Bonds on Maturity Date

19-1. On January 2, 1983, the Grade-A Beef Company received authorization to issue 60, 7 percent, $1,000, 10-year bonds. The bonds were sold on January 2, 1983, at face value. Interest is payable on June 30 and December 31 each year.

Required

(a) Journalize the transactions for 1983 and 1984 including the closing entries on December 31.

(b) Journalize the entry required on January 1, 1993, the maturity date of the bonds.

19-2. On July 1, 1983, Marion Industries received authorization to issue 40, 9 percent, $1,000, 10-year bonds. The bonds pay interest on June 30 and December 31 each year. All the bonds were sold on July 3, 1983, at face value.

Required

(a) Journalize the transactions for 1983 and 1984 including the closing entries.

(b) Journalize the transactions for 1993 including the retirement of the bonds on the maturity date.

19-3. On January 1, 1983, Swint's Music Company received authorization to issue 50, 6 percent, $1,000, 10-year bonds. The bonds pay interest on June 30 and December 31. All the bonds were sold on the issuance date at 96.

Required

(a) Journalize the transactions for 1983 including the closing entry.

(b) Journalize the transaction for the retirement of the bonds on January 1, 1993, the maturity date.

Journal Entries for Sale of Bonds at a Premium, Retirement of Bonds, Plus Balance Sheet Presentation

19-4. On September 1, 1983, the Family Company received authorization to issue 60, 8 percent, $1,000, 10-year bonds. The bonds pay interest on March 1 and September 1. All the bonds were issued on September 1, 1983, for 104.

Required

(a) Journalize the transactions for 1983 and 1984 including the adjusting and closing entries on December 31.

(*b*) Give the balance sheet presentation for the bonds on December 31, 1984.

(*c*) Journalize the transactions for 1993 including the retirement of the bonds on the maturity date.

19-5. Cellar Enterprises received authorization on June 1, 1983, to issue 80, 9 percent, $1,000, 10-year bonds. The bonds pay interest on May 31 and November 30. All the bonds were sold on the issuance date at 103. On June 1, 1988, 40 of the bonds were purchased by the company on the open market at 102 and retired. The balance of the bonds were retired on the maturity date of May 31, 1993.

Required

(*a*) Journalize the transactions for 1983, 1984, and 1988 including the adjusting and closing entries required on December 31.

(*b*) Journalize the entry required on May 31, 1993, the maturity date of the bonds.

Computation of Selling Price, Amortization, Interest, Cash Received, and Carrying Value of Bonds

19-6. The following $1,000, 10-year bonds were sold by three corporations:

Corporation	Number of Bonds Issued	Rate of Interest	Interest Payment Dates	Issuance Date	Sales Date	Selling Price
1	20	8%	6/30 & 12/31	7/1/83	7/1/83	104
2	30	7%	7/1 & 1/1	6/30/83	7/1/83	98
3	60	9%	4/1 & 10/1	4/1/83	4/1/83	106

Required

Complete the following table. (Round to nearest dollar.)

Corporation	Selling Price	Bond Amortization for 1983	Bond Interest Expense for 1983	Cash Received on Issuance Date	Carrying Value 12/31/83
1	___	___	___	___	___
2	___	___	___	___	___
3	___	___	___	___	___
Totals	___	___	___	___	___

Journal Entries for Sale and Retirement of Bonds Plus Balance Sheet Presentation

19-7. Spicy Foods received authorization on July 1, 1983, to issue 70, 7 percent, $1,000, 10-year bonds. Interest is payable on June 30 and December 31. Fifty bonds were sold on the issuance date at 98, and the balance of the bonds were sold at par on December 31, 1983.

Required

(*a*) Journalize the entries for 1983 and 1984 including the closing entries.

(*b*) Give the balance sheet presentation on December 31, 1983.

(*c*) Journalize the entries for 1993 including the retirement of the bonds on the maturity date.

19-8.   Three corporations sold 30, $1,000, 10-year bonds on July 1, 1984. Information relating to the sale of the 30 bonds for each corporation is shown below.

Corporation	Issuance Date	Interest Rate	Interest Payment Period	Sales Price	Maturity Date
1	6/30/84	8%	6/30 & 12/31	100	6/30/94
2	6/30/84	7%	6/30 & 12/31	99	6/30/94
3	6/30/84	9%	7/1 & 1/1	103	6/30/94

Required

(*a*) Journalize the entries for 1984 and 1985 including the adjusting and closing entries on December 31.

(*b*) Give the balance sheet presentation for the bonds as of December 31, 1985 for each corporation.

(*c*) Assume that corporation 3 retired the bonds on June 30, 1989, by purchasing the 30 bonds on the open market at 102. The balance in the premium account amounted to $450 on the retirement date. Journalize the entry for the retirement of the bonds.

(*d*) Journalize the entry required on the maturity date for corporations 1 and 2.

Investments in Stocks and Bonds

After reading this chapter, you should be able to:

1. **Journalize the entries for the purchase of stocks and bonds**

2. **Record the receipt of dividends on stock investments and interest earned on bond investments**

3. **Amortize the discount and premium for long-term investments in bonds**

4. **Give the balance sheet presentation for long-term and temporary investments**

5. **Classify the accounts for dividends earned on stock investments, interest earned on bond investments, and gains and losses realized on the sale of investments**

A business may invest any excess cash not needed for operations in securities consisting of stocks or bonds of another company. Investments purchased with the intention of holding them for a long period of time are usually recorded in an account entitled Investment in Stocks or Bonds that are classified as a long-term investment[1] on a balance sheet. They are classified as a *long-term investment,* because the investment will not be used in the operations of the business and they are purchased with the intention of holding them for more than a year. Long-term investments are shown as the second classification of assets on a balance sheet, listed directly below the current assets.

Investments purchased with the intention of holding them for a short period of time are called *temporary investments,* and they are usually recorded in an account entitled Marketable Securities. *Marketable securities* are classified as a current asset on a balance sheet because the company plans to sell the securities and convert them into cash within a relatively short period of time (a year or less). Temporary investments are listed after the cash accounts in the Current Asset section of a balance sheet.

When stocks or bonds are purchased, they are recorded by the cost method[2] (Chapter 1), the same method used for recording the purchase of other types of assets. The cost of these securities include the cash paid or market value of an asset given in exchange plus brokers' fees, commissions, or other expenses incurred in obtaining them.

LONG-TERM INVESTMENTS

Generally a company invests in long-term securities for two reasons:

1. To earn additional revenue

---

[1] Large corporations usually classify all their investments as a current asset on a balance sheet because these assets may be readily converted into cash.

[2] The *cost method* requires assets to be recorded at the cost or actual dollars paid.

2. To gain control over a competitor, customer, or a supplier of material needed in manufacturing the company product

To gain control of a competitor, customer, or supplier, a company will usually purchase common stock, because the common stockholders of a corporation receive one vote for each share of stock they own. Purchasing a sufficient number of voting stock will give the company the power to influence and control its operations as explained in the appendix to this chapter.

Long-term Investment in Stock

Stocks purchased with the intention of holding them for more than a year are classified as a long-term investment on a balance sheet. Long-term *investments in stocks* are recorded as a debit to the asset account Investment in Stocks for their cost plus all other expenses incurred in obtaining the stock. For example, assume that on December 19, 19_A, Smooth Tip Pen Company purchased 1,000 shares of the common stock of Ink Company at $12 per share plus a broker's fee of $100. The asset account, Investment in Stocks, would be debited and the Cash account would be credited for $12,100 (1,000 × $12 = $12,000 + $100 broker's fee) as shown in the following journal entry.

Journal entry for long-term investment in stocks

19_A				
Dec.	19	Investment in Stocks	12,100	
		Cash		12,100
		Purchased 1,000 shares of the common stock of Ink Company at $12 per share plus a brokerage fee of $100.		

The balance sheet presentation of the stock investment is shown below.

Balance sheet presentation of long-term investments in stocks

Assets	
Total Current Assets	$58,000
Long-term Investments:	
Investment in Stocks	12,100

Stock investments that give investors control of a company are discussed in the parent and subsidiary corporations section of the appendix at the end of this chapter.

Receipt of Dividends on Stock Investments

When dividends are received on an investment in stocks, the asset account Cash is debited and the revenue account **Dividends Earned** is credited. For example, assume that on June 1, 19_B, the Ink Company paid a dividend of $0.50 per share to their common stockholders. Smooth Tip Pen Company received $500 (1,000 shares × $0.50) in dividends from the Ink Company and recorded the following entry:

Journal entry for receipt of cash dividends

19_B			
June 1	Cash	500	
	Dividends Earned		500
	To record dividend of $0.50 per share on 1,000 shares of Ink Company common stock.		

For the year ended December 31, 19_B, the net operating income for the Smooth Tip Pen Company amounted to $18,000 before reporting any other type of revenue earned during the period. Dividends earned on the stock investment is classified as Other Revenue on the income statement because the dividends do not represent revenue earned from operations. The Other Revenue section of the income statement is shown after the net operating income as shown below for Smooth Tip Pen Company.

Income statement presentation for dividends earned

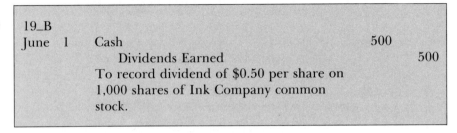

Net Operating Income	$18,000	
Other Revenue:		
Dividends Earned	500	
Net Income		$18,500

Sale of Long-term Investment in Stock

Accounting for the sale of a long-term investment in stock is no different than accounting for the sale of a plant asset. The asset account is credited for its cost, and any difference between the cost and selling price of the investment is debited to an expense account for a loss or credited to a revenue account for any gain realized on the sale. When stock is sold above its cost, the difference between the selling price of the investment and its cost is credited to a revenue account entitled *Gain on Sale of Investments.* When stock is sold below its cost, the difference between its cost and the selling price is debited to an expense account entitled *Loss on Sale of Investments.* Any gain realized on the sale of an investment is recorded in the Other Revenue section of an income statement. Any loss realized on the sale of an investment is recorded in the Other Expense section of an income statement. Any gain or loss realized on the sale of an investment is classified as Other Revenue or Other Expense because the amount does not represent revenue earned or expenses incurred from operations.

For example, assume that on April 10, 19_E, Smooth Tip Pen Company sold the investment consisting of 1,000 shares of common stock of Ink Company for $14 per share and the broker deducted a fee of $120. Smooth Tip Pen Company received $13,880 (1,000 shares × $14 =

$14,000 − $120 broker's fee) from the sale and realized a gain of $1,780 ($13,880 − $12,100 cost). The entry for the sale would be recorded as follows:

Journal entry for gain realized on sale of investment

19_E			
Apr.	10	Cash	13,880	
		Investment in Stock		12,100
		Gain on Sale of Investment		1,780

To record sale of 1,000 common shares of Ink Company at $14 per share less a $120 brokerage fee. A gain of $1,780 was realized over its cost of $12,100.

Gains realized from the sale of an investment are classified as Other Revenue on an income statement because they do not represent revenue earned from operations. To illustrate, the gain realized by Smooth Tip Pen Company on the sale of their investment in the common stock of Ink Company is shown in the partial income statement presentation below. The net operating income for the year ended December 31, 19_E, amounted to $29,000 before recording any other types of revenue earned during the period.

Income statement presentation for a gain realized on sale of an investment

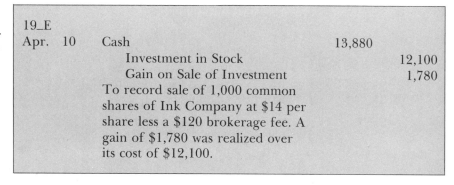

Net Operating Income	$29,000	
Other Revenue:		
Gain on Sale of Investment	1,780	
Net Income		$30,780

Assume that Smooth Tip Pen Company sold the 1,000 shares of common stock of Ink Company at $11.50 per share less a brokerage fee of $120. Smooth Tip Pen Company would receive $11,380 (1,000 shares × $11.50 = $11,500 − $120 brokerage fee) from the sale and incur a loss of $720 ($12,100 cost − $11,380). The entry for the sale would be recorded as follows:

Journal entry for loss incurred on sale of investment

19_E			
Apr.	10	Cash	11,380	
		Loss on Sale of Investment	720	
		Investment in Stock		12,100

To record sale of 1,000 shares of common stock of Ink Company at $11.50 per share less a brokerage fee of $120. A loss of $720 was realized over its cost of $12,100.

A loss realized from the sale of an investment is classified as Other Expense on an income statement because the loss does not represent an expense incurred from operations. To illustrate, the loss realized by Smooth Tip Pen Company on the sale of their investment in the common stock of Ink Company is shown in the partial income statement presentation below.

Income statement presentation for a loss realized on sale of an investment

Net Operating Income	$29,000
Other Expenses:	
Loss on Sale of Investment	720
Net Income	$28,280

Long-term Investment in Bonds

Bonds may be purchased at their *face value* (value of bond on its maturity date), or they may be purchased above or below its face value. If bonds are purchased above their face value, they are purchased at a *premium;* if bonds are purchased below their face value, they are purchased at a *discount.* When bonds are acquired with the intention of holding them for a period longer than a year, an asset account entitled *Investment in Bonds* is debited and the asset account Cash is credited for their purchase price. Inasmuch as the investment account is an asset, the account will always have a debit or zero balance. To illustrate the purchase of an investment in bonds, assume that Sales Corporation purchased two, 8 percent, $1,000, 10-year bonds with the intention of keeping them for 5 years or more. If the two bonds were purchased for their face value, the investment account would be debited and the cash account would be credited for $2,000 ($1,000 × 2). If the two bonds were purchased at $200 above their face value, the investment account would be debited and the cash account would be credited for $2,200, a premium of $200 ($2,200 − $2,000 face value). If the two bonds were purchased at $300 below face value, the investment account would be debited and the cash account would be credited for $1,700, a discount of $300 ($2,000 face value − $1,700).

Interest on an investment in bonds is usually paid twice a year, and the interest is paid on the face value of the bonds and not on their purchase price. When interest is received, the asset account Cash is debited and a revenue account entitled *Bond Interest Earned* is credited. For example, interest earned for 6 months on the two $1,000 bonds purchased by the Sales Corporation would amount to $80 ($2,000 × .08 = $160 × $6/12$). Remember that interest is paid on the face value of the bonds not on their purchase price. Bond Interest Earned is classified as Other Revenue on an income statement because the interest received on the bond investment does not represent revenue earned from operations.

Accounting for the Purchase of Bonds

The purchase of a long-term investment in bonds above or below their face value requires the amount of the premium or discount to be amortized[3] whenever the interest earned on the bonds is recorded. When amortizing a premium, the revenue account Bond Interest Earned is decreased with a debit, and the asset account Investment in Bonds is decreased with a credit. When amortizing a discount, the asset account Investment in Bonds is increased with a debit, and the revenue account Bond Interest Earned is increased with a credit. Bonds purchased at their face value do not require any adjustments to the investment or revenue account, because there were no premiums or discounts involved when the bonds were purchased.

To illustrate, assume that on June 30, 19_A, Sales Corporation purchased two, 8 percent, $1,000, 10-year Wolverine Products bonds with the intention of holding them for 5 years or more. The bonds pay interest on June 30 and December 31 and mature on June 30, 19_K. Three examples for recording the purchase and interest earned on the bonds are shown below:

**EXAMPLE 1
BONDS
PURCHASED AT
FACE VALUE**

Assume that Sales Corporation purchased the two Wolverine Product bonds at their face value and paid cash in the amount of $2,000 ($1,000 × 2). The journal entry for the purchase is shown below.

Journal entry for a purchase of bonds at face value

19_A				
June 30	Investment in 8% Bonds	2,000	
	Cash		2,000
	To record purchase of two, 8 percent, $1,000, 10-year Wolverine Product bonds at their face value.		

The long-term investment section of the balance sheet for Sales Corporation as of December 31, 19_A, is illustrated next.

Long-term investment section of a balance sheet

Assets
Long-term Investments:
Investment in 8%, 10-year Bonds $2,000

On December 31, 19_A, Sales Corporation received the first semiannual interest payment of $80 ($2,000 × .08 = $160 × 6/12) on the bonds. The receipt of $80 for interest is debited to the asset account Cash and credited to the revenue account Bond Interest Earned. The journal entry is recorded every interest payment period during the 10-year life of the bonds as illustrated on the following page:

[3] Spreading the amount of a premium or discount over the life of a bond.

Journal entry for receipt of interest earned on an investment in bonds

```
19_A
Dec.  31     Cash                                              80
                  Bond Interest Earned                             80
                  To record receipt of the first semiannual
                  interest payment on two, 8 percent, $1,000
                  Wolverine Product bonds.
```

The Bond Interest Earned account is classified as *Other Revenue* on an income statement because the interest does not represent revenue earned from operations. Assuming that the net operating income earned by Sales Corporation for 19_A amounted to $32,000, the Other Revenue section of the income statement is illustrated below.

Other Revenue section of income statement

```
Net Operating Income          $32,000
Other Revenue:
    Bond Interest Earned            80
            Net Income                     $32,080
```

EXAMPLE 2 BONDS PURCHASED ABOVE FACE VALUE

Assume that Sales Corporation purchased the two Wolverine Product bonds at $200 above their face value and paid cash in the amount of $2,200. The journal entry for the purchase is shown below.

Journal entry for a purchase of bonds above their face value

```
19_A
June  30     Investment in 8% Bonds                        2,200
                  Cash                                           2,200
                  To record purchase of two, 8
                  percent, $1,000, 10-year Wolverine
                  Product bonds at $200 above their
                  face value.
```

When the first semiannual interest payment of $80 ($2,000 × .08 = $160 × 6/12) on the bonds is received on December 31, 19_A, the premium of $200 ($2,200 − $2,000 face value) is amortized. The straight-line method of amortizing a bond premium and a bond discount is a simple, acceptable method, and it is used throughout this chapter.[4] The premium on the Wolverine Product bonds is divided by 20 (10 years × 2), the number of semiannual interest periods over the 10-year life of bonds. In every interest payment period during the 10-year life of bonds, two entries are required. In the first entry, the Cash account is debited and the Bond Interest Earned account is credited for the $80 ($2,000 × .08 = $160 × 6/12) of interest received from the bond investment. In the second entry, the Bond Interest Earned account

---

[4] The AICPA, Accounting Principles Board, stated in Opinion No. 21 that the effective-interest method is preferred. However, the straight-line method may be used if the interest does not differ greatly from the interest calculated by the effective-interest method. Effective interest is discussed in advanced accounting texts.

is debited and the Investment in Bonds account is credited for the amortization of the premium amounting to $10 ($200 premium /20 interest payment periods).

The two journal entries required on the first semiannual interest payment period for the two Wolverine Product bonds are illustrated below.

<table>
<tr><td rowspan="9">*Journal entries for interest earned and amortization of premium on bonds*</td><td colspan="4">19_A</td></tr>
<tr><td>Dec. 31</td><td>Cash</td><td>80</td><td></td></tr>
<tr><td></td><td>   Bond Interest Earned</td><td></td><td>80</td></tr>
<tr><td></td><td>To record receipt of the first semiannual interest payment on two, 8 percent, $1,000 Wolverine Product bonds.</td><td></td><td></td></tr>
<tr><td>31</td><td>Bond Interest Earned</td><td>10</td><td></td></tr>
<tr><td></td><td>   Investment in Bonds</td><td></td><td>10</td></tr>
<tr><td></td><td>To record amortization for 6 months on two, $1,000, 10-year Wolverine Product bonds purchased for $200 above face value.</td><td></td><td></td></tr>
</table>

The ledger accounts in T account form for the Investment in Bonds and Bond Interest Earned accounts after the entries are posted for June 30 and December 31, 19_A, are shown below.

Investment in Bonds				Bond Interest Earned			
19_A		19_A		19_A		19_A	
June 30	2,200	Dec. 31	10	Dec. 31	10	Dec. 31	80

The long-term investment section of the balance sheet for Sales Corporation as of December 31, 19_A, is illustrated next.

Long-term investment section of a balance sheet

Assets

Long-term Investments:
    Investment in 8%, 10-year Bonds $2,190*

* Purchase price of $2,200 less amortization of premium amounting to $10 = $2,190, the carrying value (book value) of the bonds.

Notice that the Investment in Bonds account and the Bond Interest Earned account are decreased when a premium is amortized.

The Other Revenue section of the income statement for Sales Products is illustrated below.

Other Revenue section of an income statement

Net Operating Revenue	$32,000
Other Revenue:	
Bond Interest Earned	70*
Net Income	$32,070

* $80 interest received less the amortization of premium amounting to $10 = $70.

EXAMPLE 3
BONDS
PURCHASED
BELOW FACE
VALUE

Journal entry for a purchase of bonds below their face value

Assume that Sales Corporation purchased the two Wolverine Product bonds at $300 below their face value and paid cash in the amount of $1,700. The journal entry for the purchase is shown below.

19_A			
June 30	Investment in 8% Bonds	1,700	
	Cash		1,700
	To record purchase of two, 8 percent, $1,000, 10-year Wolverine Product bonds at $300 below their face value.		

When the first semiannual interest payment of $80 ($2,000 × .08 = $160 × ⁶/₁₂) on the bonds is received on December 31, 19_A, the discount of $300 ($2,000 face value − $1,700) is amortized. The discount on the Wolverine Product bonds is divided by 20 (10 years × 2), the number of semiannual interest periods over the 10-year life of bonds. Every interest payment period during the 10-year life of the bonds, the discount is amortized for $15 ($300 discount/20). The two entries required to record the receipt of the interest and the amortization of the discount for the two bonds on December 31, 19_A, the first semiannual interest payment date, is shown below.

Journal entries for interest earned and amortization of discount on bonds

19_A			
Dec. 31	Cash	80	
	Bond Interest Earned		80
	To record receipt of the first semiannual interest payment on two, 8 percent, $1,000 Wolverine Product bonds.		
31	Investment in Bonds	15	
	Bond Interest Earned		15
	To record amortization for 6 months on two, $1,000, 10-year Wolverine Product bonds purchased for $300 below face value.		

The ledger accounts in T account form for the Investment in Bonds and Bond Interest Earned accounts after the entries are posted for June 30 and December 31, 19_A, are shown below.

Investment in Bonds			Bond Interest Earned	
19_A			19_A	
June 30	1,700		Dec. 31	80
Dec. 31	15		31	15

The long-term investment section of the balance sheet for Sales Corporation as of December 31, 19_A, is illustrated as follows:

Long-term investment section of a balance sheet

Assets	
Long-term Investments:	
Investment in 8%, 10-year Bonds	$1,715*

* Purchase price of $1,700 plus the first amortization of
the discount amounting to $15 = $1,715,
the carrying value (book value) of bonds.

The Investment in Bonds and Bond Interest Earned accounts are increased when a discount is amortized. On the maturity date of the bonds, the investment account should have a balance of $2,000 representing the face value of the bonds.

The Other Revenue section of the income statement for Sales Products is illustrated below.

Other Revenue section of an income statement

Net Operating Income	$32,000	
Other Revenue:		
Bond Interest Earned	95*	
Net Income		$32,095

* $80 of interest received plus the amortization of the discount
amounting to $15 = $95.

On June 30, 19_K, the maturity date of bonds, the $2,000 face value of the two bonds would be received from Wolverine Products and the following journal entry would be recorded.

Entry for the payment of the bonds on the maturity date

19_K			
June 30	Cash	2,000	
	Investment in Bonds		2,000
	To record receipt of payment on maturity date for investment in two, 10-year Wolverine Product bonds.		

After the entry is posted into the ledger account, the Investment in Bonds account would have a zero balance. To illustrate, the ledger account with all the journal entries posted for the amortization of the $300 discount over the 10-year life of the bonds and the payment on their maturity date is shown in Figure 20-1.

Sale of Long-term Investment in Bonds

When bonds are sold before their maturity date, the asset account Investment in Bonds is credited for its carrying value. Any difference between the selling price and carrying value of the investment is debited to an expense account for a loss or credited to a revenue account for any gain realized on the sale. When bonds are sold above their carrying value, the difference between the selling price of the investment and its carrying value is

FIGURE 20-1

Ledger account for Investment in Bonds over its 10-year life

Title: Investment in Bonds **Account No.: 120**

Date		Explanation	Ref.	Debit	Credit	Balance
19_A June	30	Purchase Price		1,700		1,700
Dec.	31	Amortization		15		1,715
19_B June	30			15		1,730
Dec.	31			15		1,745
19_C June	30			15		1,760
Dec.	31			15		1,775
19_D June	30			15		1,790
Dec.	31			15		1,805
19_E June	30			15		1,820
Dec.	31			15		1,835
19_F June	30			15		1,850
Dec.	31			15		1,865
19_G June	30			15		1,880
Dec.	31			15		1,895
19_H June	30			15		1,910
Dec.	31			15		1,925
19_I June	30			15		1,940
Dec.	31			15		1,955
19_J June	30			15		1,970
Dec.	31			15		1,985
19_K June	30			15		2,000
	30				2,000	-0-

credited to a revenue account entitled Gain on Sale of Investment. When bonds are sold below their carrying value, the difference between its carrying value and the selling price is debited to an expense account entitled Loss on Sale of Investment.

To illustrate the computation of a realized gain, assume that the Wolverine Product bonds with a carrying value of $2,100 were sold on July 1, 19_F, for $2,300. The gain realized on the sale is computed as follows:

Selling Price of Bonds	$2,300
Less: Carrying Value of Bonds	2,100
Equals: Amount of Gain Realized	$ 200

When the selling price is greater than the carrying value of bonds, a gain is realized on the sale. The journal entry required on July 1, 19_F to record the sale of the bonds is shown below.

Journal entry for bonds sold for more than their carrying value

19_F				
July 1	Cash		2,300	
	Investment in 8% Bonds			2,100
	Gain on Sale of Investment			200
	To record sale of two, 8 percent Wolverine Product bonds at $2,300, a realized gain of $200 over its carrying value of $2,100.			

The gain of $200 realized on the sale of the bonds is classified as Other Revenue on the income statement because the gain does not represent revenue earned from operations.

To illustrate the computation of a realized loss, assume that the Wolverine Product bonds with a carrying value of $1,850 were sold on July 1, 19_F, for $1,750. The loss realized on the sale is computed as follows:

Carrying Value of Bonds	$1,850
Less: Selling Price of Bonds	1,750
Equals: Amount of Loss Realized	$ 100

When the carrying value is greater than the selling price of bonds, a loss is realized on the sale. The journal entry required on July 1, 19_F, to record the sale of the bonds is shown on the following page:

*Journal entry for bonds
sold at less than their
carrying value*

19_F			
July 1	Cash	1,750	
	Loss on Sale of Investment	100	
	Investment in 8% Bonds		1,850
	To record sale of two, 8 percent		
	Wolverine Product bonds at $1,750,		
	a realized loss of $100 less than their		
	carrying value of $1,850.		

The loss of $100 realized on the sale of the bonds is classified as Other Expense on the income statement because the loss incurred does not represent an expense from operations.

TEMPORARY INVESTMENTS IN STOCKS AND BONDS

Generally a corporation will invest in short-term securities consisting of stocks or bonds to earn additional revenue on any excess cash that is not needed for current operations. Short-term investments or temporary investments are classified as a current asset on the balance sheet because they are purchased with the intention of selling them within a year or less and they can be readily converted into cash. Temporary investments are usually debited to a current asset account entitled Marketable Securities, or they may be debited to an investment account. Marketable securities are listed after the cash accounts in the current asset section of the balance sheet.

Temporary Investments in Stock

Stocks purchased as a short-term investment are recorded at cost, the purchase price plus all other costs incurred in securing the stock to comply with the Cost Principle of accounting (Chapter 1). To illustrate, assume that on March 12, 19_A, Sales Corporation purchased 500 shares of Fort Company common stock at $30 per share plus a brokerage fee of $150 with the intention of holding them for a period of 9 months or less. The current asset account Marketable Securities is debited and the Cash account is credited for the cost of $15,150 (500 shares × $30 = $15,000 + $150 brokerage fee) as shown in the following journal entry.

*Journal entry for purchase
of a temporary investment
in stock*

19_A			
Mar. 12	Marketable Securities	15,150	
	Cash		15,150
	To record purchase of 500 shares		
	of Fort Company common stock at		
	$30 per share plus a $150		
	brokerage fee as a short-term		
	investment.		

The AICPA, *Financial Accounting Standards Board (FASB)*,[5] requires marketable securities to be reported at the lower of cost or market price on the balance sheet date. If the current market price of marketable securities owned by a company is less than their cost on the balance sheet date, the securities should be reported at the current market price. The cost price of the securities should be disclosed in the Current Asset section or as a footnote on the balance sheet. For example, assume that the 500 shares of Fort Company common stock had a market value of $14,500 when a balance sheet was prepared. The $14,500 market value of the stock is less than its cost of $15,150; therefore, the securities would be recorded at its market price on the balance sheet as illustrated below.

Balance sheet presentation of marketable securities

Assets	
Current Assets:	
Marketable Securities at Market, Cost, $15,150	$14,500

If the current market price of marketable securities owned by a company is more than their cost on the balance sheet date, the securities are reported at their cost. For example, assume that the 500 shares of Fort Company common stock had a market value of $16,000 when the balance sheet was prepared. The $16,000 market value of the stock is more than its cost of $15,150; therefore, the securities would be reported at their cost price on the balance sheet as illustrated below.

Assets	
Current Assets:	
Marketable Securities at Cost, Market, $16,000	$15,150

Receipt of Cash Dividends

On November 4, 19_A, a cash dividend of $0.50 per share was received from Fort Company for the 500 shares of common stock. The asset account Cash is debited and the revenue account Dividends Earned is credited for $250 (500 shares × $0.50) as shown in the following journal entry.

Journal entry for receipt of cash dividends

19_A				
Nov. 4	Cash		250	
	Dividends Earned			250
	To record dividends of $0.50 per share on 500 shares of Fort Company common stock.			

---

[5] An independent committee responsible for establishing the standards for recording accounting information and preparing financial statements. The FASB replaced the Accounting Principles Board in 1973.

Dividends received from a stock investment are shown in the Other Revenue section of an income statement because the dividends do not represent revenue earned from operations.

Temporary Investment in Bonds

Bonds purchased as a temporary investment are recorded at their purchase price plus all the other expenses incurred in acquiring the bonds to comply with the Cost Principle of Accounting (Chapter 1). The current asset account Marketable Securities is usually debited for the purchase of a temporary investment in bonds. For example, assume that on June 4, 19_A, Sales Corporation purchased five, 6 percent, $1,000, 10-year Raye Corporation bonds for $4,950 plus a commission of $80. Interest on the bonds is payable every June 1 and December 1. The entry to record the purchase of the bonds requires a debit to the Marketable Securities account and a credit to the Cash account for $5,030 ($4,950 + $80 commission) as shown in the following entry.

Journal entry for temporary investment in bonds

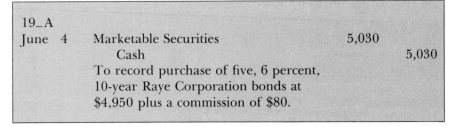

19_A			
June 4	Marketable Securities	5,030	
	Cash		5,030
	To record purchase of five, 6 percent, 10-year Raye Corporation bonds at $4,950 plus a commission of $80.		

Receipt of Interest on Bond Investment

On December 1, 19_A, the first interest payment of $150 ($5,000 × .06 = $300 × $^6/_{12}$) was received. Remember that interest is based on the face value of bonds and not on the purchase price. Amortization of a premium or a discount is not required on marketable securities, because they were purchased with the intention of keeping them for less than a year. Therefore, when the bond interest is received, the asset account Cash is debited and the revenue account Bond Interest Earned is credited for $150 as shown in the following entry.

Journal entry for receipt of interest on a temporary investment in bonds

19_A			
Dec. 1	Cash	150	
	Bond Interest Earned		150
	To record receipt of semiannual interest on five, 6 percent Raye Corporation bonds.		

Bond Interest Earned is classified as Other Revenue on an income statement because the interest does not represent revenue earned from operations.

Sale of Short-term Investments in Securities

Accounting for the sale of short-term investments in securities is no different than accounting for the sale of other types of assets. Any difference between the carrying value (purchase price) and selling price of the securities is debited to an expense account for a loss or credited to a revenue account for any gain realized on the sale. When securities are sold for more than their carrying value, the difference between the carrying value and the selling price is credited to the revenue account Gain on Sale of Investment. When securities are sold for less than their carrying value, the difference is debited to the expense account Loss on Sale of Investment. To illustrate, assume that on December 4, 19_A, the five Raye Corporation bonds purchased for $5,030 by the Sales Corporation were sold for $4,900 less a $75 commission, a total of $4,825. A loss of $205 ($5,030–$4,825 selling price) was realized on the sale as illustrated in the following entry.

19_A			
Dec. 4	Cash	4,825	
	Loss on Sale of Securities	205	
	Marketable Securities		5,030
	To record the sale of five, 6 percent, Raye Corporation bonds at $4,900 less a commission of $75, a difference of $205 less than their purchase price of $5,030.		

Journal entry for sale of marketable securities for less than their purchase price

The loss on the sale of the bonds is classified as an Other Expense on the income statement because the loss does not represent an expense incurred from operations.

SUMMARY

A business may invest excess cash not needed for current operations in securities consisting of stocks or bonds of another company. Investments purchased with the intention of holding them for more than a year are classified as long-term investments on a balance sheet. Investments purchased with the intention of holding them for less than a year are classified as a current asset on a balance sheet. Large corporations may classify all their investments as a current asset because they may readily be converted into cash.

Securities are recorded at their cost plus all the other expenses incurred in obtaining them. Any dividends received on a stock investment or interest received on a bond investment are classified as Other Revenue on an income statement because they do not represent revenue earned from operations.

The purchase of a long-term investment in securities is debited to an asset account entitled Investment in Stocks or Investment in Bonds. The purchase of short-term securities is usually debited to a current asset account entitled Marketable Securities. The Financial Accounting Standards Board (FASB) requires marketable securities to be shown at the lower of cost or market price on the balance sheet date. If the market price is lower, the securities should be reported at their market price with the cost disclosed in the current asset section or as a footnote on the balance sheet.

When bonds are purchased as a long-term investment, any premium or discount is amortized whenever bond interest earned is recorded. Amortization of a premium requires a credit to the investment account and amortization of a discount requires a debit to the investment account; therefore, on the maturity date of bonds, the investment account will have a balance that is equal to the face value of the bonds.

Accounting for the sale of a short- or long-term investment in securities is no different than accounting for the sale of other types of assets. The asset account is credited for the carrying value of the securities, and any difference between the carrying value and the selling price is debited to an expense account for a loss and a revenue account for any gain realized on the sale. Gains and losses realized on the sale of securities are classified as Other Revenue and Other Expense on the income statement.

GLOSSARY

Bond Interest Earned: Account title used to record interest earned on an investment in bonds. The account is classified as Other Revenue on an income statement because the interest does not represent revenue earned from operations.

Cost Method: A method requiring assets to be recorded at the purchase price plus commissions, brokerage fees, or other expenses incurred in obtaining them.

Discount: Bonds purchased below face value. The amount of a discount on a long-term investment in bonds is amortized over the life of the bond whenever bond interest is recorded. Discount on short-term investments in bonds are not amortized.

Dividends Earned: Account title used when recording dividends received from a stock investment. Dividends earned are classified as Other Revenue on an income statement because dividends do not represent revenue earned from operations.

Face Value: Value of a bond on its maturity date.

Financial Accounting Standards Board (FASB): An independent committee responsible for establishing the standards for recording accounting information and preparing financial statements. The FASB replaced the Accounting Principles Board in 1973.

Gain on Sale of Investments: Account title used to record the difference between the cost and the selling price of an investment when the investment is sold above its cost. The account is classified as Other Revenue on an income statement because the gain does not represent revenue earned from operations.

Investment in Bonds: Account title used to record an investment in bonds purchased with the intention of holding them for a period longer than a year.

Investment in Stocks: Account title used to record an investment in stocks purchased with the intention of holding them for a period longer than a year.

Long-term Investments: Classification on a balance sheet for securities purchased with the intention of holding them for more than a year. Long-term investments are shown as the second classification of assets on a balance sheet directly below the Current Asset section.

Loss on Sale of Investments: Account title used to record the difference between the cost and selling price of an investment when the investment is sold below its cost. The account is classified as Other Expense in an income statement because the loss does not represent an expense incurred in operations.

Marketable Securities: Account title used to record temporary or short-term investments in securities. They are classified as a current asset on the balance sheet because the securities are purchased with the intention of selling them within a year. Marketable Securities are listed after the Cash account in the Current Asset section.

Premium: Bonds purchased above their face value. The amount of a premium on a long-term investment in bonds is amoritzed over the life of a bond whenever bond interest is recorded. Premium on short-term investments is not amortized.

Temporary Investments: Securities purchased with the intention of holding them for less than a year. They are usually recorded in the asset account entitled Marketable Securities, and they are classified as a current asset on the balance sheet.

QUESTIONS

1. Name and briefly explain the methods used for recording investments in stocks and bonds.
2. Give the balance sheet presentation for (a) stock purchased for $12,000 as a temporary investment, market price is $12,100 on the balance sheet date, and (b) 20, 8 percent, 10-year bonds purchased as a long-term investment with a carrying value of $20,200.
3. What amount would be debited to the Marketable Securities account for the purchase of 1,000 shares of common stock at $35 per share. The broker charged a fee of $125.

4. Give the income statement classification for (*a*) dividends received from an investment in stocks, and (*b*) the sale of a $1,000 bond at $200 less than the carrying value.

5. What is the difference between purchasing a bond at a discount and purchasing a bond at a premium?

6. Marketable securities are classified as a current asset on the balance sheet. Where are they listed in the Current Asset section, and what are the Financial Accounting Standards Board (FASB) requirements concerning the reporting of marketable securities?

7. Determine the amount to be paid for the following investments: (*a*) 1,000 shares of common stock at $48 per share plus a commission of $175, and (*b*) four, 6 percent, $1,000 bonds at $4,160 plus a commission of $250.

8. What amount would be credited to the Bond Interest Earned account on the semiannual interest payment date for a long-term investment in two, 8 percent, 10-year, $1,000 bonds purchased at (*a*) $1,020, and (*b*) $990 each.

9. Give the explanation for the following journal entry:

19_A			
Mar. 2	Investment in 6%, 10-year Bonds	19,800	
	Cash		19,800

10. Fill in the following blanks:
    (*a*) Amortizing a premium on an investment in bonds _____ (increases/decreases) the investment account.
    (*b*) Amortizing a discount on an investment in bonds _____ (increases/decreases) the investment account.

EXERCISES

Classification of Investments

1. Classify the following: (*a*) Dividends Earned, (*b*) Marketable Securities, (*c*) Bond Interest Earned, (*d*) Gain on Sale of Securities, and (*e*) Loss on Sale of Investments.

Journal Entries for Long-term Investments

2. On January 2, 19_A, four, 6%, 10-year, $1,000 bonds were purchased as a long-term investment for $4,160. The bonds were issued January 1, 19_A, and interest is payable on June 30 and December 31. Give the journal entries required for 19_A including the closing entry.

3. On June 30, 19_A, 20, 7%, 10-year, $1,000 bonds were purchased as a long-term investment at $19,800. The bonds were issued on June 30, 19_A, and interest is payable June 30 and December 31. Give the journal entries required for 19_A and 19_B including the closing entry.

Journal Entries for Short-term Investments

4. Assume that the bonds in Exercises 2 and 3 were purchased as a short-term investment. Give the journal entries required for 19_A for each exercise including the closing entries.

5. On July 4, 19_A, 200 shares of common stock were purchased as a short-term investment at $18 per share plus a brokerage fee of $100. On October 1, 19_A, a dividend of $0.40 per share was received. On March 4, 19_B, the stock was sold for $16 per share and the broker deducted a fee of $100. Journalize the entries necessary for 19_A and 19_B including the closing entry.

6. On July 2, 19_A, four, 9%, 10-year, $1,000 bonds were purchased as a temporary investment at $4,040 plus a brokerage fee of $120. Interest is payable on June 30 and December 31. On January 2, 19_C, the bonds were sold at $4,080 less a fee of $120. Give the journal entries for 19_A and 19_C, including the closing entry.

Financial Statement Presentation of Investments

7. Give the balance sheet and income statement presentation for:
   (a) Marketable securities; cost, $18,000; market value, $16,500
   (b) Investment in 8%, 10-year bonds, $20,400
   (c) Dividends earned, $1,200
   (d) Loss on sale of securities, $600

8. Assume that the investment in Exercise 2 was purchased as a short-term investment and the investment in Exercise 6 was purchased as a long-term investment by Soapy Car Wash. The market value for the temporary investment had increased since the purchase date; therefore, it should be reported at cost price. Give the balance sheet and income statement presentation for 19_A, using the information in both exercises.

PROBLEMS

Journal Entries for Long- and Short-term Investments and Their Financial Statement Presentation

20-1. On January 1, 19_A, Sof Sole Shoes had marketable securities consisting of 30, 8%, 10-year, $1,000 Family Shoe Company bonds acquired at a cost of $30,200. During 19_A, the following selected transactions occurred:

19_A

Jan. 2 Purchased 20, 6%, 20-year, $1,000 Tread Easy Shoe Company bonds at $19,600 as a long-term investment. The bonds were dated January 2, 19_A, and pay interest on June 30 and December 31.

June 30 Received semiannual interest on Family Shoe Company bonds.

         30 Received semiannual interest on Tread Easy Shoe Company bonds.

Dec. 31 Received semiannual interest on Family Shoe Company bonds.

         31 Sold all the Family Shoe Company bonds at $30,300 less a commission of $200.

         31 Received the semiannual interest on Tread Easy Shoe Company bonds.

         31 Closed the necessary expense and revenue accounts.

Required

(*a*) Journalize the transactions for 19_A.

(*b*) Give the balance sheet presentation for Tread Easy Shoe Company bonds on December 31, 19_A.

(*c*) Give the income statement presentation for interest received and any gains or losses on sale of securities in 19_A.

20-2. The Wing Pasta Company had an excess amount of cash on hand not needed for current operations and purchased the following securities during 19_A and 19_B:

19_A

Jan. 3 Purchased 20, 8%, 20-year, $1,000 Curry Corporation bonds at $20,400 as a long-term investment plus a commission of $120. The bonds were dated January 1, 19_A, and pay interest on June 30 and December 31.

June 30 Received semiannual interest on Curry Corporation bonds.

July 1 Purchased five, 6%, 10-year, $1,000 Spicy Food Corporation bonds at $4,800 plus a commission of $30 as a temporary investment. The bonds were dated June 30, 19_A, and pay interest June 30 and December 31.

Dec. 31 Received semiannual interest on Curry Corporation bonds.

         31 Received semiannual interest on Spicy Food Corporation bonds.

         31 Closed the interest account.

19_B

June 30 Received semiannual interest on Curry Corporation bonds.

         30 Received semiannual interest on Spicy Food Corporation bonds.

July   1   Sold Spicy Food Corporation bonds at $4,900 less a commission of $125.

Dec.   31   Received semiannual interest on Curry Corporation bonds.

   31   Closed the necessary accounts.

Required

(*a*) Journalize the transactions for 19_A and 19_B.

(*b*) Give the balance sheet presentation for the investments as of December 31, 19_A: (Market value of securities, $4,750.)

(*c*) Give the balance sheet presentation for the investments as of December 31, 19_B.

20-3. On January 1 of the current year, Large Bottling Company had a temporary investment of 1,000 shares of B & B Bottling Company common stock at a cost of $22,250. The following selected transactions occurred:

Jan.   20   Received the regular quarterly dividend of $0.38 per share on B & B common stock.

Apr.   20   Received the regular quarterly dividend of $0.38 per share on B & B common stock.

   21   Sold 1,000 shares of B & B common stock for $22.25 per share less a brokerage fee of $110.

July   2   Purchased 2,000 shares of M & N Bottling Company common stock at $28 per share.

Aug.   10   Received a quarterly dividend of $0.42 per share on M & N common stock.

Nov.   10   Received a quarterly dividend of $0.42 per share on M & N common stock.

Dec.   31   Closed the necessary accounts.

Required

(*a*) Journalize the transactions for the year.

(*b*) Give the balance sheet presentation for the M & N stock as of December 31; the market value of the stock was $30 per share.

(*c*) Give the income statement presentation for dividends received and any gains or losses realized on the sale of the securities.

20-4. Small Corporation invested in the following securities during 19_A and 19_B:

19_A

Apr.   19   Purchased 2,000 shares of Willow Corporation common stock for $12 per share plus a brokerage fee of $130. Small Corporation plans to sell the stock in 19_B.

June   28   Purchased 1,000 shares of Warren Industries common stock for $54 per share plus a brokerage fee of $210 as a temporary investment.

Aug. 2 Received a dividend of $0.30 per share on Willow Corporation common stock.

Oct. 20 Received a dividend of $0.62 per share on Warren Industries common stock.

Nov. 2 Received a dividend of $0.30 per share on Willow Corporation common stock.

Dec. 31 Closed the necessary accounts.

19_B

Jan. 20 Received the quarterly dividend of $0.62 per share on Warren Industries common stock.

Feb. 2 Received a dividend of $0.30 per share on Willow Corporation common stock.

4 Sold 1,000 shares of Willow Corporation common stock at $12.50 per share less a brokerage fee of $75.

Apr. 20 Received a dividend of $0.62 per share on Warren Industries common stock.

21 Sold 500 shares of Warren Industries common stock at $55 per share less a commission of $125.

May 2 Received a dividend on $0.30 per share on Willow Corporation common stock.

July 20 Received a dividend of $0.62 per share on Warren Industries common stock.

Aug. 2 Received a dividend of $0.30 per share on Willow Corporation common stock.

22 Sold 1,000 shares of Willow Corporation common stock at $12 per share less a brokerage fee of $75.

Oct. 20 Received a dividend of $0.62 per share on Warren Industries common stock.

Dec. 31 Closed the necessary accounts.

Required

(a) Journalize the transactions for 19_A and 19_B.
(b) Give the balance sheet presentation for investment in Warren Industries common stock as of December 31, 19_B. The market value of the stock on December 31, 19_B, was $53.75 per share.
(c) Give the income statement presentation for dividends received and any gains or losses realized on sale of securities in 19_B.

Journal Entries for Short- and Long-term Investments

20-5. On January 1, 19_A, Easy Rider Trailer purchased 20, 8%, 10-year, $1,000 Wheels, Incorporated bonds at $18,800 plus a commission of $100. The bonds were dated January 1, 19_A, and pay interest on June 30 and December 31; bonds mature on January 1, 19_K.

Required

(a) Journalize the transactions for 19_A and 19_F, assuming the bonds were purchased as a long-term investment and were sold at $19,200 on July 1, 19_F. (Remember the closing entries.)

(b) Journalize the transactions for 19_A and 19_E, assuming the bonds were purchased as a short-term investment and were sold on July 1, 19_E, at $19,200.

(c) Journalize the entry required on maturity date, assuming the bonds were purchased as a long-term investment and were held to the maturity date.

20-6. On July 1, 19_A, Spinner Records purchased 10, 9%, 10-year, $1,000 Tape Deck Corporation bonds at $10,400. The bonds were issued July 1, 19_A, and pay interest on June 30 and December 31.

Required

(a) Journalize the transactions for 19_A and 19_B, assuming the bonds were purchased as a short-term investment and sold at $10,500 on January 1, 19_B. (Remember the closing entries.)

(b) Journalize the transactions for 19_A and 19_E, assuming the bonds were purchased as a long-term investment and sold at $10,100 on January 1, 19_E.

(c) Journalize entry on maturity date assuming the bonds were purchased as a long-term investment and bonds were held to the maturity date.

Review Problem for Investments

20-7. As of January 1, 19_D, the Service Enterprises owned the following investments:

1. Twenty, 8%, 20-year, $1,000 Ward Sales bonds were acquired on January 1, 19_A as a long-term investment, for $20,400. The bonds were dated January 1, 19_A, and pay interest on June 30 and December 31.

2. Two-thousand shares of Granary Corporation common stock acquired on January 20, 19_A, at a cost of $19,400 as a long-term investment. Quarterly dividends of $0.32 per share have been paid consistently each year on March 10, June 10, September 10, and December 10.

3. Five-hundred shares of Peterson Corporation common stock acquired on November 20, 19_A, at a cost of $15,240 as a short-term investment. Quarterly dividends of $0.58 per share have been received on January 10, April 10, July 10, and October 10 of each year since the stock was acquired. Stock was sold on December 31, 19_D, for $32 per share less a commission of $90.

4. Ten, 6%, 10-year, $1,000 Scooter Sales bonds acquired on July 1, 19_C, as a short-term investment at $10,100 plus a commission of $60. Bonds were dated July 1, 19_A, and pay interest on June 30 and December 31. Bonds were sold on December 31, 19_D, at $10,000 less a commission of $50.

Required

(a) Journalize all the entries required for 19_A, 19_B, and 19_C. (Remember closing entries.)

(b) Give the balance sheet presentation for the investments as of December 31, 19_C. The market value of the marketable securities on December 31 amounted to $24,600.

(c) Journalize the entries required for the sale of investments during 19_D.

(d) Give the income statement presentation for Other Revenue and Other Expense for the year ended December 31, 19_D. (Don't forget to include the bond interest and dividends earned.)

Chapter 20 Appendix:

Parent and Subsidiary Corporations and Consolidated Balance Sheets

Accounting for a parent and its subsidiary corporations and consolidated statements is a subject which is usually discussed in detail in an advanced accounting text. However, this appendix will give you a brief description of a parent and subsidiary relationship and consolidated statements. The discussion will also include the basic journal entries required when a company purchases a sufficient number of voting stock of another company to obtain control over their operations.

PARENT AND SUBSIDIARY CORPORATIONS

When one company purchases a sufficient number of voting stock of another company (usually 51 percent or more) to give them the power to influence and control its operations, the purchase is referred to as a *parent and subsidiary relationship.* Whenever a parent and subsidiary relationship exists, it is classified as a long-term investment on a balance sheet of the parent company.

Journalizing the investment in a subsidiary company on the parent company books requires a debit to an asset account entitled Investment in Subsidiary for the cost of the investment. After the subsidiary is purchased, any income earned or loss incurred, plus any dividends received by the parent company from its subsidiary, must be accounted for by a method called the *equity method* according to the Accounting Principles Board (APB)[1] Statement No. 15. The equity method assumes that income earned by a subsidiary increases the investment of the parent company. Any loss incurred by a subsidiary decreases the investment of the parent company. Dividends paid to a parent company by its subsidiary are considered to be a partial return of the investment. Therefore, the asset account Investment in Subsidiary on the books of the parent company is:

1. *Increased* (debited) for a parent company's shares of any net income earned by the subsidiary
2. *Decreased* (credited) for a parent company's share of any net loss incurred by the subsidiary
3. *Decreased* (credited) for any dividends a parent company received from the subsidiary

[1] A committee organized by the AICPA in 1959 that established accounting standards and concepts. In 1973, the APB was discontinued and responsibility for accounting standards was given to a committee known as the Financial Accounting Standards Board (FASB).

For example, assume that on December 31, 19_A, Putnam Company purchased 80 percent of the 10,000 authorized and outstanding shares of $10 par value common stock of Sentenial Corporation for $90,000. On December 31, 19_B, Sentenial Corporation reported net income of $20,000 and declared and paid an $18,000 dividend to their stockholders. The entries required by Putnam Company (parent) for 19_A and 19_B are shown in the following examples.

ENTRY 1   *Record Investment in Subsidiary*

19_A		
Dec. 31	Investment in Subsidiary/Sentenial Corporation	90,000
	Cash		90,000
	To record purchase of 80 percent of the 10,000 shares of authorized and outstanding $10 par value stock of Sentenial Corporation.		

ENTRY 2   *Recognize as Revenue the Income Earned by the Subsidiary*

19_B		
Dec. 31	Investment in Subsidiary/Sentenial Corporation	16,000
	Income Earned by Subsidiary		16,000
	To record 80 percent of the $20,000 of income earned by subsidiary.		

ENTRY 3   *Decrease Investment Account for Dividends Received from Subsidiary*

19_B		
Dec. 31	Cash	14,400
	Investment in Subsidiary/Sentenial Corporation		14,400
	To record 80 percent of the dividends amounting to $18,000 declared and paid by the subsidiary.		

On December 31, 19_C, Sentenial Corporation reported a net loss of $10,000; therefore, no dividends were declared or paid. The journal entry recorded by Putnam Company (parent) recognizing as an expense the loss incurred by the subsidiary is shown in Entry 4.

ENTRY 4 *Decrease Investment Account for Loss Incurred by Subsidiary*

19_C			
Dec. 31	Loss Incurred by Subsidiary	8,000	
	Investment in		
	Subsidiary/Sentenial		
	Corporation		8,000
	To record 80 percent of the		
	$10,000 loss incurred by the		
	subsidiary.		

INVESTMENT IN SUBSIDIARY

When one company purchases a sufficient number of voting stock of another company and obtains control, they purchase the stock at book value or for more or less than book value. If the amount paid for the investment is more or less than its book value of the total stockholders' equity of the subsidiary, the difference is debited or credited to an account entitled Excess of Cost Over Book Value. Excess of Cost Over Book Value is classified as an intangible asset on a balance sheet in an account entitled Goodwill. To illustrate, assume that Putnam Company (parent) paid $90,000 for 80 percent interest in Sentenial Corporation (subsidiary). Total stockholders' equity of Sentenial Company amounted to $106,000 at the time of purchase. The excess amount paid for the investment over the book value is computed as follows:

Amount paid for investment		$90,000
Book value of stockholders' equity of Sentenial		
Corporation	$106,000	
Multiplied by percentage of interest purchased by		
Putnam Company	× .80	84,800
Excess of cost over book value		$ 5,200

CONSOLIDATED STATEMENTS

The financial statements of a parent company and its subsidiaries may be combined or consolidated to present the results of operations and the fi-

FIGURE 20A-1

*Consolidated
Working Papers*

**PUTNAM COMPANY AND SENTENIAL CORPORATION
CONSOLIDATED WORKING PAPERS
For Year Ended December 31, 19_A**

	Balance Sheet		Elimination Entries		Consolidated Balance Sheet
	Putnam Company	Sentenial Corporation	Debit	Credit	
Assets					
Cash	8,000	6,000			14,000
Accounts Receivables	20,000	40,000		(a) 5,000	55,000
Other Current Assets	11,000	7,000			18,000
Investment in Sentenial Corp.	90,000			(b) 90,000	
Plant Assets	40,000	73,000			113,000
Excess of Cost Over Book Value			(b) 5,200		5,200
Total	169,000	126,000			205,200
Liabilities					
Accounts Payable	15,000	10,000	(a) 5,000		20,000
Other Payables	20,000	5,000			25,000
Bonds Payable	20,000	5,000			25,000
Stockholders' Equity					
Capital Stock	100,000	100,000	(b) 100,000		100,000
Premium on Capital Stock	9,000				9,000
Retained Earnings	5,000	6,000	(b) 6,000		5,000
Minority Interest				(b) 21,200	21,200
Totals	169,000	126,000	116,200	116,200	205,200

(a) Sentenial purchased merchandise on account from Putnam Company amounting to $5,000 representing an intercompany accounts receivable for the parent company and intercompany accounts payable for the subsidiary company.

(b) Putnam Company purchased 80 percent of the stockholders' equity of Sentenial Corporation for $90,000; $5,200 above book value ($106,000 × .80 = $84,800 book value; $90,000 − $84,800 = $5,200). The remaining stockholders (minority interest) own 20 percent of the book value amounting to $21,200 ($106,000 × .20 = $21,200).

nancial position for several companies under the same control. When preparing consolidated statements, all transactions that occurred between the parent company and its subsidiaries are eliminated so that the financial statements will show the effect of the activities for the parent company and its subsidiaries with their customers, creditors, or minority stockholders. Journal entries for these eliminations are not recorded in the accounting records of either the parent or the subsidiaries. However, these entries are recorded as elimination entries on working papers prepared for the purpose of combining all the financial information before preparing the consolidated statements. There are several different types of elimination entries. Two of the most common types that usually appear on consolidated working papers are as follows:

1. Eliminate intercompany receivables and payables
2. Eliminate the stockholder equity accounts of subsidiary, record minority interest in subsidiary, and record in the Excess of Cost Over Book Value account any difference between the amount paid by parent company for the investment and the book value of the total stockholders' equity of subsidiary

    To illustrate, working papers for Putnam Company (parent) and Sentenial Corporation (subsidiary) as of December 31, 19_A (date subsidiary was acquired) have been prepared in Figure 20A-1.

    A formal consolidated balance sheet prepared from the working papers for the Putnam Company is shown below.

Consolidated balance sheet

PUTNAM COMPANY AND SENTENIAL CORPORATION
CONSOLIDATED BALANCE SHEET
December 31, 19_A

Assets

Current Assets:			
Cash	$ 14,000		
Accounts Receivables	55,000		
Other Current Assets	18,000		
Total Current Assets		$ 87,000	
Plant Assets		113,000	
Goodwill (Consolidation)*		5,200	
Total Assets			$205,200

Liabilities

Current Liabilities:			
Accounts Payable	$ 20,000		
Other Payables	25,000		
Total Current Liabilities		$ 45,000	
Long-term Liabilities:			
Bonds Payable		25,000	
Total Liabilities			$ 70,000

Stockholders' Equity

Paid-in Capital:			
Capital Stock	$100,000		
Premium on Capital Stock	9,000		
Total Paid-in Capital		$109,000	
Retained Earnings		5,000	
Minority Interest		21,200	
Total Stockholders' Equity			135,200
Total Liabilities & Stockholders' Equity			$205,200

* Excess of Cost Over Book Value is shown as Goodwill on the formal balance sheet.

SUMMARY

When one company purchases a sufficient number of voting stock of another company (usually 51 percent or more) giving them the power to influence and control its operations, the purchase is referred to as a parent and subsidiary relationship. Whenever a parent and subsidiary relationship exists, it is classified as a long-term investment on the balance sheet of the parent company.

An investment in a subsidiary company on the parent company books is accounted for by the equity method. The equity method recognizes income earned and losses incurred by the subsidiary. When a subsidiary realizes income for an accounting period, the investment account is increased; when a subsidiary incurs a loss or when dividends are paid by the subsidiary, the investment account is decreased.

The financial statements of a parent and its subsidiaries may be combined or consolidated to present the results of operations and the financial position for several companies under the same control.

Budgets

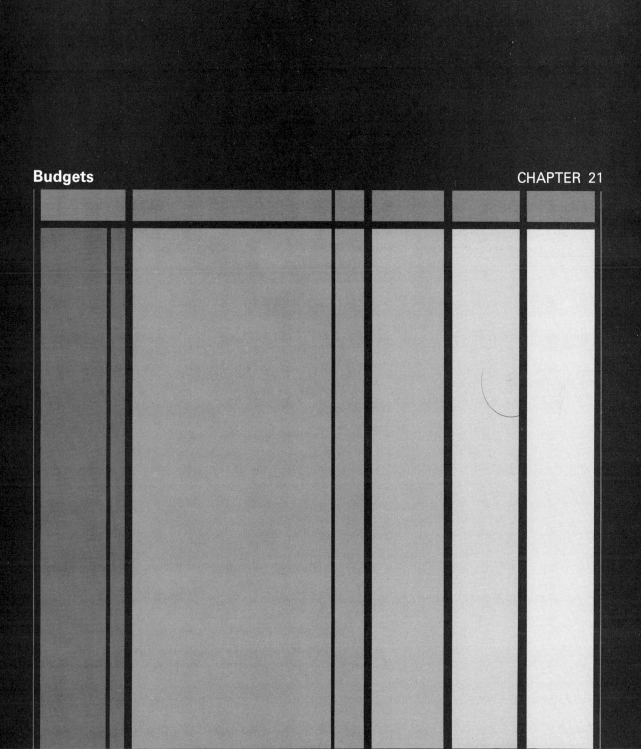

After completing this chapter, you should be able to:

1. **Define budgets and state the purpose of a sales, purchase, expense, and cash budget**

2. **Prepare a sales, purchase, expense, and cash budget**

3. **Complete a subsidiary schedule of expenses for the expense budget and a schedule of cash receipts and cash disbursements to accompany the cash budget**

4. **Know the difference between a fixed, semivariable, and variable expense**

5. **Give the meaning and purpose of a flexible budget**

6. **Prepare a flexible budget for various levels of sales and production**

Successful companies usually establish a set of objectives for their business to attain the same as individuals may establish a set of objectives for achieving their goals in life. To achieve the objectives, a plan is developed and short- and long-term goals are established to provide some direction and guidelines. For example, the objective of a dental lab may be to expand its business operations and open three additional labs within a 200-mile radius. To achieve this objective, a goal is established of opening one additional lab whenever sales for a 1-year period exceed $250,000 and a profit of 30 percent on sales is realized.

After plans for achieving the objectives are developed and the goals are established, a budget must be prepared. A budget is needed to provide a basis for comparing, evaluating, and controlling the objectives so that the desired results may be realized. The *budget* provides management with an estimate of revenues and expenses for each budget period to use as a tool or guide for measuring performance against the business objectives. A budget, therefore, is an effective tool that enables a business to check, control, compare, and evaluate sales and expenses to be realized during the budget period.

Previous chapters discussed the recording and reporting of the results of business operations; this chapter will discuss the budget, which is a method used to achieve business objectives. Objectives provide the means for recording and reporting accounting data for a budget period.

ADVANTAGES OF A BUDGET

A budget is a report which usually spells out in dollars and cents the goals established for each department or person responsible for the budget. The budget contains guidelines and provides direction for reaching the desired goals. A budget is necessary because it serves as a basis for measuring the performance of the department/s or individual/s responsible for the budget. In other words, a budget provides management with the means for comparing, evaluating, and controlling the results of business activities with the desired objectives.

PREPARING A BUDGET

Budgets are usually prepared at the beginning of an accounting cycle for a period of 1 year, although budgets may be prepared for shorter or longer periods. A *master budget* containing the overall objectives and goals for the budget period is prepared after all individual budgets are completed. Individual budgets for sales, purchases, expenses, and cash are prepared first, and the totals of these budgets are combined into the master budget. The master budget is normally prepared by a budget committee that works under the direction of the president of a business. A budget committee provides the person/s responsible for reaching the budget goals with the projections established for the budget period. A budget has a greater chance of success if the person/s responsible for achieving the budget goals are:

1. Allowed to participate in its preparation
2. Given realistic goals
3. Receive credit whenever they meet the budget requirements

Budgets are relatively easy to prepare, but their goals are difficult to obtain unless you have the cooperation of everyone responsible for its success. For a budget to be successful, individual/s must be assigned the responsibility of achieving the budget goals. Comparisons should be made periodically of the actual results and the budget estimates to evaluate and control the performance of the individual/s responsible for the budget. When the budget is used as a tool to evaluate the performance of individual/s, it serves as a means of encouraging them to achieve the budget goals.

SALES FORECAST

Before a budget can be prepared, management must forecast the number of products that will be sold and the amount of revenue that will be realized during the budget period. Sales estimates are usually based on the company's objectives and must be determined before the budget can be developed. The sales, purchases, expense, and cash budgets are prepared after the sales forecast because they are all dependent on the number of products to be sold and the amount of revenue to be realized.

A sales forecast may be established by obtaining estimates from the sales staff responsible for meeting the sales quotas. Experience has found that the sales staff is one of the best sources for obtaining future sales projections. These persons are usually in a better position to estimate the amount of future sales for their area because of their knowledge of the territory and the competition. Management may forecast future sales by studying sales of previous periods and by studying sales trends. This method tends to obtain a sales estimate based on a person's guess or intuition rather than on a knowledge of the problems involved in marketing the product. However, whatever method is used, the sales manager must be perceptive and aware of market fluctuations and changes to evaluate the sales staff projections and results of studies to determine if the forecast is realistic and not an underestimate or overestimate of sales.

SALES BUDGET

After the sales have been forecasted for the budget period, the sales budget is the first budget to be prepared. The purchases, expense, and cash budgets are all dependent upon the amount of revenue to be realized from sales; and these budgets are prepared after the sales budget is completed. Sales budgets are usually prepared for each type of product sold and for each department of the business. The *sales budget* contains the number of products to be sold by each department and the amount of revenue to be realized. For example, assume that the Crown Dental Lab made porcelain and gold crowns for dentists located in the southeastern part of Michigan. The Lab established an objective of monthly sales amounting to $7,700 for porcelain crowns and $14,000 for gold crowns for a yearly total of $92,400 ($7,700 × 12 months) for porcelain crowns and $168,000 ($14,000 × 12 months) for gold crowns for total yearly sales of $260,400. Each porcelain crown is to be sold for $55 and each gold crown for $50. A sales budget was prepared for each quarter to allow management to compare and evaluate the results for a 3-month period to determine if adjustments or revisions are necessary. The sales budget for the first 3 months of 19_A is shown in Figure 21-1.

PURCHASES BUDGET

The purchases budget is prepared after the sales budget is completed and the number of products that will be sold has been determined for the budget period. A sufficient amount of materials must be purchased to produce the orders as they are received during the period and to provide an ample supply of materials on hand to take care of any fluctuations in sales. This

FIGURE 21-1

Quarterly sales budget

CROWN DENTAL LAB
SALES BUDGET
For January, February, and March 19_A

Crowns	January		February		March		Totals	
	Units	Dollars	Units	Dollars	Units	Dollars	Units	Dollars
Porcelain—@ $55 each	60	$3,300	66	$ 3,630	70	$ 3,850	196	$10,780
Gold—@ $50 each	120	6,000	130	6,500	140	7,000	390	19,500
Totals	180	$9,300	196	$10,130	210	$10,850	586	$30,280

requires management to establish a policy to determine the amount of inventory to be on hand at the end of each monthly period. When purchasing merchandise, consideration must be given to prices based on the quantity purchased, shipping charges, and storage problems and costs. The **purchases budget** should be prepared for each type of product sold or for each type of material required to produce the product that is sold. To illustrate, assume that the Crown Dental Lab prepared a purchases budget for the materials needed in making the porcelain and gold crowns for the first 3 months of 19_A. The material required for making the crowns are porcelain, gold, solder, pins, plaster, stones, alloy, wax, investment material (utility wax, asbestos, and ring), and packaging material. A policy was established requiring an ending inventory of material sufficient to produce 50 percent of the porcelain and gold crowns to be sold in the following month. The material requirements for producing one porcelain and one gold crown is shown below.

Material requirements for production

Material for Crowns		Porcelain	Gold
Porcelain		$10.00	
Gold			$20.00
Solder	$2.00		
Pins	.25		
Plaster	.55		
Stones	1.10		
Alloy	.28		
Wax	.15		
Investment material	.20		
Packaging material	.12		
Totals	$4.65		
40% and 60% of $4.65		1.86	2.79
Cost of materials		$11.86	$22.79

FIGURE 21-2

Quarterly purchases budget

CROWN DENTAL LAB
PURCHASES BUDGET (IN UNITS)
For January, February, and March 19_A

	January		February		March		Totals	
	Porce-lain	Gold	Porce-lain	Gold	Porce-lain	Gold	Porce-lain	Gold
Budgeted Sales	60	120	66	130	70	140	196	390
Less: Beginning Inventory	30[1]	60[1]	33	65	35	70	98	195
Units Required for Sales	30	60	33	65	35	70	98	195
Units Required for Ending Inventory	33	65	35	70	35[2]	70[2]	103	205
Units to Be Purchased	63	125	68	135	70	140	201	400
Cost per Unit	× 12	× 23	× 12	× 23	× 12	× 23	× 12	× 23
Cost of Purchases	$756	$2,875	$816	$3,105	$840	$3,220	$2,412	$9,200

[1] Beginning inventory amounts to 50 percent of the sales budget for January (60 × .50 = 30 units for porcelain and 120 × .50 = 60 units for gold).
[2] Estimated sales for April are the same as the estimate for March.

Forty percent of the cost of material (except porcelain and gold) is for producing porcelain crowns, and 60 percent of the cost of materials is for producing gold crowns.

The purchases budget based on the material requirements for the first 3 months of 19_A is shown in Figure 21-2. (All amounts have been rounded to the nearest dollar.)

EXPENSE BUDGET

The *expense budget* consists of the general and administrative expenses. The general expense portion of the budget is usually prepared by the office manager, and the administrative expense portion of the budget is usually prepared by a person who works directly under the president of the company. Some of the amounts for general and administrative expenses will be fixed for the budget period. *Fixed expenses* do not vary with sales or production; they remain relatively the same for the budget period. For example, rent for an office building is usually fixed during the budget period. Some of the expenses will vary with sales and production, and they are known as the *variable expenses.* Variable expenses usually increase when sales and production increase and decrease when sales and production decrease. For example, the office supplies expense for Crown Dental Lab increases as sales increase, because additional statements and invoices are

FIGURE 21-3
*Subsidiary schedule
of expenses*

CROWN DENTAL LAB
SUBSIDIARY SCHEDULE OF EXPENSES*
For January, February, and March 19_A

	Fixed Expenses	Semivariable Expenses			Variable Expenses		
	January to March	January	February	March	January	February	March
Depreciation: Office Furniture & Equipment Lab Equipment	$ 50 200						
Insurance	70						
Office & Administrative Salaries	1,460						
Rent	250						
Lab Salaries, $2,600 + ⅓ of 1% of Sales		$2,600 31	$2,600 34	$2,600 36			
Telephone, $300 + 2% of Sales		300 186	300 203	300 217			
Mailing Costs: ½ of 1% of Sales					$ 47	$ 51	$ 54
Miscellaneous: 1% of Sales					93	101	109
Office Supplies: ½ of 1% of Sales					47	51	54
Postage: ½ of 1% of Sales					47	51	54
Travel: 4% of Sales					372	405	434
Utilities: ¾ of 1% of Sales					70	76	81
Total Expenses	$2,030	$3,117	$3,137	$3,153	$676	$735	$786

* Amounts rounded to nearest dollar.
Note: Sales amount to $9,300 in January, $10,130 in February, and $10,850 in March.

used for billing customers. The variable expenses are determined by the sales projections for the budget period. Some of the expenses will be **semivariable;** a portion of the expense will be fixed and a portion will vary with sales. For example, the telephone expense for Crown Dental Lab has a $300 fixed portion; and the balance varies with the number and length of calls made outside the service area.

To illustrate, assume that Crown Dental Lab had monthly fixed expenses of:

Depreciation/Office Furniture & Equipment	$ 50
Depreciation/Lab Equipment	200
Insurance	70
Office & Administrative Salaries	1,460
Rent	250

semivariable expenses of:

Lab Salaries	$2,600 plus $\frac{1}{3}$ of 1% of Sales
Telephone	$300 plus 2% of Sales

variable expenses of:

Mailing Costs	$\frac{1}{2}$ of 1% of Sales
Miscellaneous	1% of Sales
Office Supplies	$\frac{1}{2}$ of 1% of Sales
Postage	$\frac{1}{2}$ of 1% of Sales
Travel	4% of Sales
Utilities	$\frac{3}{4}$ of 1% of Sales

A subsidiary schedule (Figure 21-3) for the fixed, semivariable, and variable expenses for the budgeted sales for the first 3 months of 19_A support the figures in the expense budget shown in Figure 21-4.

FIGURE 21-4

Quarterly expense budget

CROWN DENTAL LAB
EXPENSE BUDGET*
For January, February, March 19_A

Expenses	January	February	March	Totals
Fixed	$2,030	$2,030	$2,030	$ 6,090
Semivariable	3,117	3,137	3,153	9,407
Variable	676	735	786	2,197
Total Expenses	$5,823	$5,902	$5,969	$17,694

* Amounts rounded to nearest dollar.

CASH BUDGET

The cash budget is prepared after the budget committee approves the sales, purchases, and expense budgets. *Cash budgets* are an important part of the budget process, because they provide a forecast of the cash receipts (sales, accounts receivable, and loans), cash disbursements, and the cash balance at the end of each month during the budget period. A forecast of cash receipts and disbursements will assist management in determining whether there will be sufficient cash on hand for operations and whether there will be sufficient cash on hand to meet the goals established for the period. If the budget indicates that a cash shortage will develop during the budget period, arrangements can be made to obtain funds in advance, thereby allowing management to shop around and secure a loan at the lowest interest rate possible.

Cash budgets are prepared by the accounting department usually for a period of 1 year. Yearly projections are divided into monthly figures for each quarter. At the end of each quarter, the cash budget is compared with actual results to determine if any adjustments are necessary for the next period. If significant differences arise, management has an opportunity to determine if they can be corrected or if an adjustment is necessary. Cash budgets usually have subsidiary schedules to support the cash receipts and cash disbursement figures as shown in Figure 21-5 for Crown Dental Lab.

After the cash budget is approved, copies are given to the person/s responsible so that they may know what goals they are expected to obtain for the budget period. Depreciation, depletion, and amortization are not shown in a cash budget, because they do not require a cash expenditure during the budget period. To illustrate, the cash budget for Crown Dental Lab for the first 3 months of 19_A is shown in Figure 21-6. Sales on account

FIGURE 21-5

Schedule of cash receipts

CROWN DENTAL LAB
SCHEDULE OF CASH RECEIPTS
For January, February, and March 19_A

Cash Receipts	January	February	March	Totals
Cash Sales: .10 of $ 9,300	$ 930			
.10 of $10,130		$1,013		
.10 of $10,850			$ 1,085	$ 3,028
Collections on Accounts Rec.:				
December: .50 of $ 8,500	$4,250			
January: .40 of $ 9,300	3,720			$ 7,970
.50 of $ 9,300		$4,650		
February: .40 of $10,130		4,052		8,702
.50 of $10,130			$ 5,065	
March: .40 of $10,850			4,340	9,405
Total Collections on Account	$7,970	$8,702	$ 9,405	$26,077
Total Cash Receipts	$8,900	$9,715	$10,490	$29,105

FIGURE 21-5 (*Continued*)
Schedule of cash disbursements

CROWN DENTAL LAB
SCHEDULE OF CASH DISBURSEMENTS
For January, February, and March 19_A

Cash Disbursements	January	February	March	Totals
Payments on Accounts Payable:				
December Balance	$ 842			
January: .70 of $3,631	2,542			$ 3,384
.30 of $3,631		$ 1,089		
February: .70 of $3,921		2,745		3,834
.30 of $3,921			$ 1,176	
March: .70 of $4,060			2,842	4,018
Total Payments on Accounts Payable	$3,384	$ 3,834	$ 4,018	$11,236
General & Adm. Expenses	5,573	5,652	5,719	16,944
Loan Payment	603	603	603	1,809
Gold Purchase			2,000	2,000
Total Cash Disbursements	$9,560	$10,089	$12,340	$31,989

for December amounted to $8,500; cash sales are budgeted at 10 percent of sales; collections of receivables (based on previous periods) amount to 40 percent during month of sale and 50 percent in the month following the sale. Seventy percent of the materials purchased on account is paid during the month of purchase, and the balance of 30 percent is paid in the month following the purchase. The balance of accounts payable for December amounted to $842.

FIGURE 21-6
Quarterly cash budget

CROWN DENTAL LAB
CASH BUDGET
For January, February, and March 19_A

	January	February	March	Totals
Beginning Cash on Hand	$ 1,950	$ 1,290	$ 916	$ 4,156
Cash Receipts:				
Cash Sales	930	1,013	1,085	3,028
Collections on Accounts Receivable	7,970	8,702	9,405	26,077
Total Cash Receipts	$10,850	$11,005	$11,406	$33,261
Cash Disbursements:				
Material Purchases	$ 3,384	$ 3,834	$ 4,018	$11,236
General & Administrative Expenses	5,573	5,652	5,719	16,944
Loan Payment	603	603	603	1,809
Gold Purchase*			2,000	2,000
Total Cash Disbursements	$ 9,560	$10,089	$12,340	$31,989
Ending Cash Balance	$ 1,290	$ 916	($ 934)	$ 1,272

* Gold is purchased in quantities required by supplier; an 8-ounce purchase was purchased on March 30 at a cost of $250 an ounce for a total of $2,000.

FLEXIBLE BUDGET

A *flexible budget* provides an estimate of revenues and expenses for various levels of business activities. When fluctuations for revenues and expenses are anticipated for a budget period, a flexible budget may be prepared to show the increases and decreases in revenues and expenses relating to sales or production. All the variable expenses are shown at the different levels of capacity, and the fixed expenses are shown at the same amount for all levels of capacity because these expenses are relatively stable.

To illustrate, assume that the Crown Dental Lab has the capacity of

FIGURE 21-7

Flexible budget

CROWN DENTAL LAB
FLEXIBLE BUDGET[1]
For the Month Ended March 31, 19_A

	Percentage of Capacity			
	50%	60%	70%	100%
Sales: (units)				
Porcelain Crowns	70	84	98	140
Gold Crowns	140	168	196	280
Total Sales (units)	210	252	294	420
Sales: (dollars)				
Porcelain Crowns	$ 3,850	$ 4,620	$ 5,390	$ 7,700
Gold Crowns	7,000	8,400	9,800	14,000
Total Sales (dollars)	$10,850	$13,020	$15,190	$21,700
Variable Expenses:				
Raw Material:				
Porcelain	$ 700	$ 840	$ 980	$ 1,400
Gold	2,800	3,360	3,920	5,600
Miscellaneous Material:				
Porcelain	130	156	182	260
Gold	391	469	547	781
Lab Salaries	36	43	50	72
Mailing Costs	54	65	76	109
Miscellaneous	109	130	152	217
Office Supplies	54	65	76	109
Postage	54	65	76	109
Telephone	217	260	304	434
Travel	434	521	608	868
Utilities	81	98	114	163
Total Variable Expenses	$ 5,060	$ 6,072	$ 7,085	$10,122
Contribution Margin[2]	$ 5,790	$ 6,948	$ 8,105	$11,578
Fixed Expenses[3]	4,930	4,930	4,930	4,930
Net Income	$ 860	$ 2,018	$ 3,175	$ 6,648

[1] Amounts rounded to nearest dollar.
[2] Term used for the difference between sales revenue and variable expenses.
[3] Depreciation, $250 + insurance, $70 + rent, $250 + telephone, $300 + lab salaries, $2,600 + office & administrative salaries, $1,460 = $4,930.

producing 140 porcelain crowns and 280 gold crowns per month. The budgeted sales for the month of March 19_A, was based on producing and selling approximately 50 percent of capacity. A flexible budget was prepared for 50 percent, 60 percent, 70 percent, and 100 percent of capacity to provide the lab with data for comparing and evaluating the results of operations in the event that budgeted sales reach a higher level than anticipated. The flexible budget for Crown Dental Lab is shown in Figure 21-7.

SUMMARY

Most businesses will set up a plan and establish short- and long-term goals for their company to provide some direction and guidelines. After the plans and objectives are established, a budget is needed to provide a basis for comparing, evaluating, and controlling the objectives so that the desired results will be reached. A budget provides management with an estimate of revenues and expenses for each budget period to use as a tool or guide for measuring performance.

Budgets are usually prepared at the beginning of an accounting cycle for a period of 1 year, although budgets may be prepared for shorter or longer periods. Individual budgets are prepared for sales, purchases, expenses, and cash, and they are all combined into a master budget.

Individual/s must be assigned responsibility for achieving the budget goals. Comparisons should be made periodically of the actual results and the budget estimates to evaluate and control the performance of the individual/s responsible for the budget.

Before a budget can be prepared, a forecast must be made of the number of products that will be sold and the amount of revenue that will be realized during the budget period. The sales, purchases, expense, and cash budgets are prepared after sales have been projected. After sales have been forecasted, the sales budget is the first budget to be prepared. The sales budget contains the number of products to be sold and the amount of revenue to be realized.

After the sales, purchases, and expense budgets have been approved, the cash budget is prepared. Cash budgets are an important part of the budget process because they provide a forecast of the cash receipts, cash disbursements, and the cash balance at the end of each month during the budget period. A cash budget will assist management in determining whether there will be sufficient cash on hand for operations and whether there will be sufficient cash on hand to meet the goals established for the period. Cash budgets are usually prepared by the accounting department for a period of 1 year. Yearly projections are divided into monthly figures for each quarter. Subsidiary schedules are usually prepared for the cash receipts and cash disbursements to support the figures on the cash budget. After the cash budget is prepared, copies are given to the person/s responsible so that they may know what is expected of them during the budget period.

A flexible budget provides an estimate of revenues and expenses for various levels of business activities. A flexible budget will show the increases and decreases in revenues and expenses relating to sales or production levels. All the variable expenses are shown at the different levels of capacity, and the fixed expenses are shown at the same amount for all levels of capacity because these expenses are relatively stable.

GLOSSARY

Budget: A plan containing an estimate of revenues and expenses for a period to use as a tool or guide for measuring performance against the objectives of a business. A budget is an effective tool enabling a business to check, control, compare, and evaluate performance during the budget period.

Cash Budget: A report containing a forecast of the cash receipts, cash disbursements, and the cash balance at the end of each month during the budget period.

Contribution Margin: Term used for the difference between sales and variable expenses.

Expense Budget: A report containing the general and administrative expenses for a budget period. The general expense portion of the budget is usually prepared by the office manager, and the administrative portion of the budget is usually prepared by a person who works directly under the president of the company.

Fixed Expenses: Expenses that do not vary with sales or production; they remain relatively the same for the budget period. Rent is an example of a fixed expense because the amount of rent is usually set at a fixed amount for a certain period.

Flexible Budget: A report that provides an estimate of revenues and expenses for various levels of business activities.

Master Budget: A report that contains the overall objectives and goals for a budget period. The master budget contains the totals for the individual sales, purchases, expense, and cash budgets.

Purchases Budget: A report that contains an estimate of the amount of products or materials that are to be purchased during a budget period. A purchases budget should be prepared for each type of product sold and for each type of material required to produce the products that are sold.

Sales Budget: A report showing the estimated number of products to be sold by each department and the estimated amount of revenue to be realized during a budget period.

Sales Forecast: A report showing an estimate of the number of products that will be sold during a budget period.

Semivariable Expenses: Expenses with a portion that is fixed and a portion that varies with sales or production. For example, Telephone Expense with a minimum charge plus an extra charge for the number and length of calls made outside the service area is a semivariable expense.

Variable Expenses: Expenses that vary with sales or production. Variable expenses increase when sales and production increase and decrease when sales and production decrease. If there are not any sales during a period or if the company is not in production, the variable expenses would be zero.

QUESTIONS

1. Why would a company establish a budget for the accounting period?
2. What is a master budget and who normally prepares the master budget for a company?
3. How may management achieve the budget goals? (List two ways.)
4. What is the first step in the budget process?
5. Name the two departments usually involved in the preparation of the expense budget.
6. Briefly define the three types of expenses shown on an expense budget.
7. Why is a cash budget prepared by a company?
8. What types of expenses are eliminated from the cash budget and why are they eliminated?
9. What is a flexible budget?

EXERCISES[1]

Estimating Sales Revenue

1. A furniture company established a sales budget for a 1-year period. The sales forecast estimated sales of 55 lounge chairs per month or a total of 720 lounge chairs to be sold during the 12-month period. Three types of lounge chairs are sold by the company. Type A sells for $195, type B for $250, and type C for $325 each. The sales forecast estimated sales each month of 30 type A, 15 type B, and 10 type C lounge chairs.

Required

Determine the estimated revenue to be realized each month from the sales of the three types of lounge chairs.

2. The sales forecast amounted to $38,000 for each of the first 6 months of 19_B, and a 2 percent increase for each of the last 6 months is predicted for 19_B. Ten percent of the sales are usually sold for cash, and the remaining 90 percent are sold on account. Collections on accounts receivable are estimated at 40 percent to be collected during the month of sale and the balance of 60 percent to be collected during the month following the sale. Sales for December 19_A, amounted to $36,700.

[1] Round all amounts to the nearest dollar.

Required

Compute the amount collected from sales during 19_B.

Determining Cost of Sales

3. The furniture company in Exercise 1 purchased type A lounge chairs for 65 percent of the selling price, and type B and type C lounge chairs for 75 percent of the selling price.

Required

Determine the total cost per month for the three types of lounge chairs sold by the furniture company.

Determining Fixed, Variable, and Semivariable Expenses

4. The estimated fixed, variable, and semivariable expenses for Office Furniture Company for a 1-month period are fixed, $2,400; variable, 3 percent of sales; semivariable fixed portion, $3,000 and variable portion, 4 percent of sales.

Required

Determine the amount to be shown on the expense budget for fixed, variable, and semivariable expenses for January based on estimated sales of $20,000.

Computation of Sales and Expenses

5. The Office Furniture Company estimated that business will improve in June and that sales of desks amounting to $20,000 will increase by 10 percent. Fixed expenses of $2,400 will increase 10 percent, variable expenses of $600 will increase to 5 percent of sales, and semivariable expenses will remain the same for the $3,000 fixed portion but the variable portion will increase to 6 percent of sales.

Required

Compute the amount of sales and expenses for June.

6. Office salaries and administrative salaries for Boswell Hose Company amounted to $5,600 and $32,500 respectively per month. The budget for 19_A estimates an increase of 8 percent for office salaries and 7 percent for administrative salaries.

Required

Compute the estimated salaries expense for 19_A.

7. A flexible budget prepared for various expenses of White Linen Company is shown as follows:

Expense	Capacity		
	70%	80%	100%
Depreciation	$1,000	$1,000	$1,000
Supplies	300	400	600
Wages	4,000	5,000	7,000
Telephone	400	450	550

Required

Determine the expense budget for 90 percent of capacity.

Estimating Net Income

8. Wrinkle-Free Drapes has a sales budget of $250,000, a purchases budget of $180,000, and an expense budget of $40,000.

Required

Determine the estimated amount of net income to be realized in 19_A if the sales are expected to increase 12 percent, the purchases to increase 12 percent, and the fixed expenses of $22,000 in the expense budget to remain the same but the variable portion to increase in proportion to sales.

PROBLEMS[2]

Preparation of Sales Budget

21-1. A sales forecast for the first 3 months of 19__ for product A and product B of Zippy Products amounted to 10,800 and 14,900 units respectively. Product A is sold for $14 each and product B is sold for $12 each. Estimated sales for each month are: January, 40 percent of product A and 45 percent of product B; February, 35 percent of product A and 30 percent of product B; and March, 25 percent of product A and 25 percent of product B.

Required

Prepare a sales budget for the first 3 months of 19_.

21-2. Canned Food Company sells canned fruits to food distributors. Estimated sales for the first 3 months of 19_A is given below.

Product	Units	Sales Price (24 per Case)
Applesauce	60,000	$6
Mandarin oranges	42,000	6
Pineapple	45,000	8

[2] Round all amounts to the nearest dollar.

Estimated sales per month are: January, 25 percent; February, 35 percent; and March, 40 percent.

Required

Prepare a sales budget for the first 3 months of 19_A.

Preparation of Purchases Budget

21-3. Zippy Products required an ending inventory each month for product A and product B equal to 30 percent of the estimated sales for the following month. The cost of purchasing both products amounted to 75 percent of the sales price of $14 each for product A and $12 each for product B.

Required

Prepare a purchases budget for the first 3 months of 19_A assuming budgeted sales for product A amounted to 4,320 units for January, 3,780 units for February, 2,700 units for March, and 4,200 units for April. Budgeted sales for product B amounted to 6,705 units for January, 4,470 units for February, 3,725 units for March, and 5,100 units for April.

21-4. Canned Food Company required an ending inventory each month for applesauce, mandarin oranges, and pineapple equal to 25 percent of the estimated sales for the following month. The cost of purchasing each product amounted to 70 percent of the sales price of $6 each for the applesauce and mandarin oranges and $8 each for the pineapple.

Required

Prepare a purchases budget for the first 3 months of 19_A assuming that budgeted sales for applesauce amounted to 15,000 units for January, 21,000 units for February, 24,000 units for March, and 26,400 units for April. Budgeted sales for mandarin oranges amounted to 10,500 units for January, 14,700 units for February, 16,800 units for March, and 18,480 units for April. Budgeted sales for pineapple amounted to 11,250 units for January, 15,750 units for February, 18,000 units for March, and 19,800 units for April.

Preparation of Expense Budgets

21-5. The sales forecast for Bart Sales for 19_A is estimated at $500,000. Estimated selling and general and administrative expenses relating to these sales are shown on page 586.

Required

Prepare the following budgets for 19_A:
(*a*) Subsidiary expense budget
(*b*) Expense budget

	Expenses	
	Fixed	**Variable**
Sales Salaries		5% of sales
Office Wages & Salaries	$10,000	+2¹/₂% of sales
Administrative Salaries	35,000	
Office Supplies		1% of sales
Depreciation:		
Office Furniture & Equipment	4,000	
Building	8,000	
Advertising		¹/₂ of 1% of sales
Miscellaneous:		
Selling	2,000	+1% of sales
General	1,500	+¹/₄ of 1% of sales
Administrative	1,200	

21-6. Estimated monthly general and administrative expenses for Paper Products Company for 19_A are given below.

	Expenses	
	Fixed	**Variable**
Office Wages & Salaries	$ 7,500	+3% of sales
Administrative Salaries	28,000	
Supplies		2% of purchases
Depreciation	800	
Miscellaneous:		
General	400	+2% of sales
Administrative	200	+1% of sales

Estimated sales for the first 3 months of 19_A are: January, $100,000; February, $90,000; and March, $120,000. Purchases per month average 70 percent of sales.

Required

For the first 3 months of 19_A, prepare:
(a) A subsidiary schedule of expenses
(b) An expense budget

Schedule of Cash Receipts and Cash Disbursement Plus a Cash Budget

21-7. The following information appeared in the sales, purchases, and expense budgets for the first 3 months of 19_A for R & S Sales.

	January	February	March	Totals
Sales (cash sales 12%)	$40,000	$35,000	$50,000	$125,000
Purchases	24,000	21,000	30,000	75,000
General & Administrative Expenses:				
Fixed	4,000	4,000	4,000	12,000
Variable	10,400	9,100	13,000	32,500

The balances for selected accounts on January 1, 19_A, are: Cash, $9,200; Accounts Receivable, $18,000; and Accounts Payable, $8,100. Sixty percent of the sales on account are collected during the month of the sale and the balance is collected the following month. All merchandise is purchased on account and 70 percent is paid in the month of purchase and the balance is paid the following month. Expenses are paid in the month they are incurred; however, 25 percent of the fixed expenses are for depreciation. A loan for $20,000 is due on March 31.

Required

Prepare the following for the first 3 months of 19_A:
(a) Schedule of cash receipts
(b) Schedule of cash disbursements
(c) Cash budget

21-8. The following information appeared in the sales, purchases, and general and administrative expense budgets for Dobson Company for the first 3 months of 19_A.

	January	February	March	Totals
Sales	$8,000	$8,400	$8,200	$24,600
Purchases	5,600	5,880	5,740	17,220
General & Administrative Expenses:				
Fixed	700	700	700	2,100
Variable	1,200	1,260	1,230	3,690

The balance for selected accounts on January 1, 19_A, are: Cash, $2,300; Accounts Receivable, $2,800; and Accounts Payable, $1,400. Cash sales amount to 10 percent of sales, and the balance of the sales are sold on account. Sixty-five percent of the sales on account are collected during the month of the sale and the balance is collected the following month. All merchandise is purchased on account and 70 percent is paid in the month of purchase and the balance is paid in the following month. Expenses are paid in the month they are incurred; however, 20 percent of the fixed expenses are for depreciation. A loan payment is due the last day of each month for $750.

Required

Prepare the following for the first 3 months of 19_A:
(*a*) Schedule of cash receipts
(*b*) Schedule of cash disbursements
(*c*) Cash budget

Flexible Budget

21-9. The R & S Sales operated at 80 percent capacity in March 19_A, with sales of $50,000, purchases of $30,000, and general and administrative expenses for fixed, $4,000 and variable, $13,000. Sales at 90 percent capacity amounted to $56,250 and $62,500 for 100 percent capacity.

Required

Prepare a flexible budget for 80 percent, 90 percent, and 100 percent capacity.

Determining Sales, Purchases, Expenses, Contribution Margin, Cash Receipts, Cash Disbursements, and Ending Cash Balance

21-10. The sales forecast for Perez Company for the first 3 months of 19__ amounted to 1,500 units per month. Sixty percent of the units sold are for product M and 40 percent are for product O. Product M sells for $36 each and product O sells for $52 each. Estimates for other costs and expenses are:

1. Purchases average 55 percent of sales.
2. Yearly fixed expenses: office salaries, $64,000; administrative salaries, $72,000; sales salaries, $24,200; depreciation of office furniture and equipment, $9,800; and depreciation of sales furniture and equipment, $10,000.
3. Variable expenses: office wages, 10 percent of purchases; sales commissions, 5 percent of sales; travel, $1/2$ of 1 percent of sales; advertising, $1/4$ of 1 percent of sales; selling expenses, 2 percent of sales; office and administrative expenses, 1 percent of sales; and supplies, 1 percent of purchases.
4. Cash sales amount to 20 percent of sales and the balance is sold on account. Forty percent of sales on account are collected in the month of sale and the balance is collected the following month.
5. All merchandise is purchased on account with payment of 60 percent in month of purchase and 40 percent the following month.
6. All expenses (except depreciation) are paid in the month they are incurred.

The March 1 balance for selected accounts is: Cash, $3,127; Accounts Receivable, $36,000; and Accounts Payable, $14,400.

Required

Determine the following for March 19__:
(*a*) Sales in units and in dollars for product M and product O
(*b*) Cost of purchases for product M and product O
(*c*) Total amount of fixed and variable expenses
(*d*) Contribution margin
(*e*) Cash receipts
(*f*) Cash disbursements
(*g*) Ending cash balance

After completing this chapter, you should be able to:

1. **Give the definition of the term funds as used in accounting**
2. **Define the term working capital**
3. **List the four sources and four uses of working capital**
4. **Prepare a statement of changes in working capital accounts**
5. **Complete working papers for analyzing the changes in noncurrent accounts**
6. **Prepare a statement of changes in financial position**

A *statement of changes in financial position* or funds statement is a financial statement that is prepared in addition to the income statement and balance sheet. This statement shows the sources and amount of funds that came into a business during an accounting period, and it shows how these funds were applied and used in the business operations. *Funds* in accounting is the difference between the amount of current assets and the amount of current liabilities; this difference is also called *working capital.* Remember that *current assets* are assets that will be converted into cash or used up by the business within a year or less. Examples are cash, marketable securities, receivables, inventory, and prepaid expenses. *Current liabilities* are the debts of a business that should be paid within a year or less. Examples are accounts payable, short-term notes payable, wages payable, taxes payable, etc.

PURPOSE OF PREPARING THE STATEMENT OF CHANGES IN FINANCIAL POSITION

There are two basic purposes for preparing a statement of changes in financial position. First, the statement shows the sources and amount of funds (working capital) that came into the business during the period and how these funds were used in the business during the same period. Second, the statement shows the amount of funds or working capital that are available at the end of the period. The amount of working capital available at the end of an accounting period shown on a statement of changes in financial position is useful to management, stockholders, creditors, and the employees because it indicates if a company is in a financial position to:

1. Purchase supplies, merchandise, and other assets
2. Declare dividends to their stockholders
3. Make payments to their creditors
4. Have sufficient cash on hand to pay the salaries and wages of their employees

Therefore, the amount of the sources and uses of working capital and the amount of working capital available at the end of an accounting period is useful in evaluating the ability of a company to meet their daily obligations.

Sources of Funds

Any business transaction that requires a debit to a ***current account*** (current asset or current liability) and a credit to a ***noncurrent account*** (long-term investments, plant assets, intangible assets, long-term liability, or stockholders' equity) results in a ***source of funds*** or increase in working capital. Any transaction that results in a debit and credit to a current account or a debit and credit to a noncurrent account would have no effect on working capital, because these transactions do not create a source or use of funds. There are basically four types of transactions that result in a source of funds (working capital). These four sources are listed below in the order that they usually appear on the statement of changes in financial position.

1. *Funds from Operations:* **Funds** provided *from operations* is the net income (the difference between the revenues earned during a period and the expenses incurred in earning the revenues) as shown on the year-end income statement adjusted for any expenses that did not require the use of funds during the period covered on the income statement. For example, depreciation of a plant asset and amortization of an intangible asset are expenses that have been deducted before arriving at the amount of net income. However, these expenses did not require the use of any funds during the period and they must be added back to net income to obtain the correct amount of funds provided from operations. Adjustments must also be made for any gains or losses realized from the sale of a noncurrent asset. Gains are deducted and losses are added back to net income because the total amount received from the sale of a noncurrent asset will be shown separately on the funds statement. To illustrate, assume that the net income of a company amounted to $22,000 which included a deduction for depreciation of a plant asset amounting to $1,200. The depreciation of $1,200 must be added back to net income to arrive at the correct amount of funds provided from operations as shown in the following illustration.

Net Income	$22,000	
Add Back Expenses Not Requiring the Use of Funds:		
Depreciation of Plant Asset	1,200	**Source**
Funds Provided from Operations	$23,200 ⟵	**of Funds**

2. *Sale of Noncurrent Assets:* Whenever a noncurrent asset is sold for cash or on account, the transaction results in a source of funds because a

current asset account is debited and a noncurrent asset account is credited for the sale. For example, assume that equipment purchased for $10,000 and depreciated for $6,000 was sold for $3,000. Inasmuch as the equipment was sold for $1,000 less than its book value ($10,000 cost − $6,000 depreciation = $4,000 book value − $3,000 selling price), a loss was realized on the sale. When recording the transaction, a current asset account was debited for $3,000, two noncurrent accounts were debited for $6,000 and $1,000, and a noncurrent asset account was credited for $10,000. The transaction resulted in a source of funds because a current asset account was debited and a noncurrent account was credited as illustrated in the following journal entry.

Cash	3,000 ←	**Source of Funds**
Accumulated Depreciation/Equipment	6,000	
Loss on Sale of Equipment	1,000	
Equipment		10,000

3. *Sale of Long-term Bonds or Issuing Long-term Note:* Whenever cash is received from the sale of long-term bonds or by obtaining a loan and signing a long-term note, the transaction results in a source of funds because a current asset account is debited and a noncurrent liability account is credited. For example, assume that $10,000 was borrowed by signing a note that is payable in 5 years. When recording the transaction, a current asset account is debited and a noncurrent liability account is credited for $10,000 resulting in a source of funds as shown in the following journal entry.

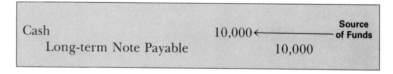

Cash	10,000 ←	**Source of Funds**
Long-term Note Payable		10,000

4. *Issuance of Capital Stock:* Whenever cash or a receivable is obtained from the issuance of capital stock or the receipt of a stock subscription, the transaction results in a source of funds because a current asset account is debited and a noncurrent equity account is credited. For example, assume that a company issued 400 shares of its $10 par value capital stock for $16 per share, receiving $6,400 (400 × $16) in cash. When recording the transaction, a current asset account is debited for $6,400 and two noncurrent equity accounts are credited for $4,000 and $2,400. The transaction resulted in a source of funds because a current asset account is debited and noncurrent equity accounts are credited as shown in the following journal entry.

		Source
		of Funds
Cash	64,000 ←	
Capital Stock		4,000
Premium on Capital Stock		2,400

Uses or Application of Funds

Any business transaction that requires a debit to a noncurrent asset or a noncurrent equity (liability or stockholders' equity) account and a credit to a current asset or a current liability account results in a *use* or application *of funds* or a decrease in working capital. There are basically four types of transactions that result in a use of funds (working capital). These four uses are listed below in the order that they usually appear on the statement of changes in financial position.

1. *Loss of Funds from Operations:* A loss of funds from operations is the net loss shown on the year-end income statement adjusted for any expenses that did not require the use of funds during the period covered on the income statement. For example, depreciation of a plant asset and amortization of an intangible asset are expenses that have been deducted before arriving at the amount of net loss. However, these expenses did not require the use of any funds during the period and they must be subtracted from the net loss to obtain the correct amount of funds lost from operations during the period. Adjustments must also be made for any gains or losses realized from the sale of a noncurrent asset. Gains are added and losses are subtracted from the net loss, because the total amount received from the sale of a noncurrent asset will be shown separately on the funds statement. To illustrate, assume that the net loss of a company amounted to $12,000 which included a deduction for the depreciation of a plant asset amounting to $800. The depreciation of $800 must be subtracted from the net loss to arrive at the correct amount of funds lost from operations as shown in the following illustration.

Net Loss	$12,000	
Deduct Expenses Not Requiring the Use of Funds:		
Depreciation of Plant Asset	800	Use
Funds Lost from Operations	$11,200 ←	of Funds

2. *Purchase of Noncurrent Assets:* Whenever a noncurrent asset is purchased for cash or on a short-term account payable, the transaction results in a use of funds because a noncurrent asset account is debited and a current asset or a current liability account is credited for the pur-

chase. For example, assume that equipment was purchased for $2,000 cash. When recording the transaction, a noncurrent asset account was debited and a current asset account was credited for $2,000 resulting in a use of funds as illustrated in the following journal entry.

Equipment	2,000	
Cash		2,000 ←— Use of Funds

3. *Payment on Long-term Liability:* Whenever a payment is made on a long-term bond or long-term note, the transaction results in a use of funds because a noncurrent liability account is debited and a current asset account is credited. For example, assume that on the maturity date of a 10-year bond, a company paid the maturity value of $5,000 to the bondholders and retired the bonds. When recording the transaction, a noncurrent liability account is debited and a current asset account is credited for $5,000 resulting in a use of funds as shown in the following journal entry.

Bonds Payable	5,000	
Cash		5,000 ←— Use of Funds

4. *Declaration of a Cash Dividend:* Whenever a cash dividend is declared to the stockholders of a company, the transaction results in a use of funds, because a noncurrent equity account is debited and a current liability account is credited. For example, assume that a company declared a cash dividend of $0.50 per share to its 10,000 stockholders. When recording the transaction, a noncurrent equity account is debited and a current liability account is credited for $5,000 (10,000 × $0.50), resulting in a use of funds as shown in the following journal entry.

Retained Earnings	5,000	
Dividends Payable		5,000 ←— Use of Funds

A summary of the sources and uses of funds or working capital are shown in Figure 22-1.

PREPARING THE STATEMENT OF CHANGES IN FINANCIAL POSITION

Before preparing the statement of changes in financial position, usually a statement analyzing the changes in working capital accounts (current assets

FIGURE 22-1

SUMMARY OF SOURCES AND USES OF FUNDS OR WORKING CAPITAL

Funds or Working Capital	
Sources	**Uses**

1. Net income from operations
    Add back: Depreciation, Depletion, Amortization, or Loss Realized from Sale of Noncurrent Asset
    Deduct: Gain Realized from Sale of Noncurrent Asset
	1. Net loss from operations
	    Add back: Gain Realized from Sale of Noncurrent Asset
	    Deduct: Depreciation, Depletion, Amortization, or Loss Realized from Sale of Noncurrent Asset

2. Sale of noncurrent asset
    (a) Long-term Investment
    (b) Plant Asset
    (c) Intangible Asset
	2. Purchase of noncurrent asset
	    (a) Long-term Investment
	    (b) Plant Asset
	    (c) Intangible Asset

3. Sale of long-term bonds or obtaining long-term note payable	3. Payment of long-term bonds and long-term note payable
4. Issuance of capital stock	4. Declaration of cash dividends or purchase of treasury stock

and current liabilities) and working papers analyzing the changes in non-current accounts are prepared. Information for the preparation of these statements and the working papers is obtained from comparative balance sheets (balance sheets for the current and previous year), the current income statement, and from analyzing the reason for changes to noncurrent accounts. To illustrate, the comparative balance sheets for the year ended December 31, 19_A, and December 31, 19_B, for Bailey Enterprises are shown in Figure 22-2.

Statement of Changes in Working Capital Accounts

Only the current asset and current liability accounts and their amounts appearing in the comparative balance sheets are used when preparing a *statement of changes in working capital* accounts. This statement has five columns consisting of an Account Title column, two amount columns for the current and previous year balances, and two amount columns to show the increases and decreases to working capital. The last two columns which show the increases and decreases to working capital is the difference beween the current asset and current liability account balances of the previous year and the current year. There are six steps in the preparation of a statement of changes in working capital accounts. These six steps prepared from the information in the comparative balance sheets of Bailey Enterprises (Figure 22-2) are listed below and illustrated in Figure 22-3 (p. 601).

Six steps for analyzing changes to working capital accounts

Step 1. Record the proper heading consisting of the name of the company, the title of the statement, and the period covered by the statement.

FIGURE 22-2

Comparative balance sheets for Bailey Enterprises

BAILEY ENTERPRISES
COMPARATIVE BALANCE SHEETS
For Year Ended December 31, 19_A and 19_B

	December 31,	
Assets	**19_A**	**19_B**
Current Assets:		
Cash	$18,000	$20,000
Accounts Receivable	8,900	7,800
Inventory	22,000	24,000
Prepaid Assets	1,400	1,200
Total Current Assets	$50,300	$53,000
Plant Assets (net)	34,000	36,000
Intangible Assets (net)	6,000	5,800
Total Assets	$90,300	$94,800
Liabilities		
Current Liabilities:		
Accounts Payable	$17,000	$18,700
Notes Payable	1,200	1,000
Miscellaneous Payables	6,900	5,800
Total Current Liabilities	$25,100	$25,500
Long-term Liabilities (net)	22,000	18,100
Total liabilities	$47,100	$43,600
Stockholders' Equity		
Paid-in Capital:		
Capital Stock	$32,000	$36,000
Premium on Capital Stock	8,000	10,400
Total Paid-in Capital	$40,000	$46,400
Retained Earnings	3,200	4,800
Total Stockholders' Equity	$43,200	$51,200
Total Liabilities & Stockholders' Equity	$90,300	$94,800

Set up one column for the account titles, two amount columns for the current asset and current liability balances for 19_A and 19_B, and two amount columns to show the increases and decreases to working capital during the period.

Step 2. Write the current asset and current liability account titles in the Account Title column.

Step 3. Record the 19_A and 19_B balances and totals of the current asset and current liability accounts in the first two amount columns.

Step 4. Record the changes to working capital in the last two amount columns showing the increases or decreases in their respective columns. When analyzing the changes in working capital accounts (current assets and current liabilities), the difference between the balance of the current year and previous year will result in an increase or a decrease to working capital. Whenever a working capital account is debited, there usually is an increase in working capital; whenever a working capital account is credited, there usually is a decrease in working capital. Keep in mind that if the amount of a current asset account at the end of the previous period has increased by the end of the current period, it results in an increase to working capital because assets are increased with a debit. When the amount of a current asset account at the end of the previous period has decreased by the end of the current period, it results in a decrease to working capital because assets are decreased with a credit. For example, the increases and decreases in the current asset accounts for Bailey Enterprises are listed in items *a* to *d*. The changes in the current asset accounts are recorded in the Increase and Decrease amount columns of the statement of changes in current accounts illustrated in Figure 22-3.

(a)   *Cash:* Cash increased from $18,000 in 19_A to $20,000 in 19_B. The $2,000 difference ($20,000 − $18,000) is recorded in the Increase column because an increase to a current asset account is debited resulting in an increase to working capital.

(b)   *Accounts Receivable:* Accounts receivable decreased from $8,900 in 19_A to $7,800 in 19_B. The $1,100 difference ($8,900 − $7,800) is recorded in the Decrease column because a decrease to a current asset account is credited resulting in a decrease to working capital.

(c)   *Inventory:* Inventory increased from $22,000 in 19_A to $24,000 in 19_B. The $2,000 difference ($24,000 − $22,000) is recorded in the Increase column because an increase to a current asset account is debited resulting in an increase to working capital.

(d)   *Prepaid Assets:* Prepaid assets decreased from $1,400 in 19_A to $1,200 in 19_B. The $200 difference ($1,400 − $1,200) is recorded in the Decrease column because a decrease to a current asset account is credited resulting in a decrease to working capital.

When analyzing the changes in current liabilities, keep in mind that if the amount of a current liability account at the end of the previous period increased by the end of the current period, it results in a decrease to working capital because liabilities are increased with a credit. When a current liability account decreases, it results in an increase to working capital because liabilities are decreased with a debit. For example, the increases and decreases in the current liability accounts for Bailey Enterprises is listed in items *e* to *g*. The changes in the current liability accounts are recorded in the Increase and Decrease amount columns of the statement of changes in current accounts illustrated in Figure 22-3.

(e)   *Accounts Payable:* Accounts payable increased from $17,000 in 19_A to $18,700 in 19_B. The $1,700 difference ($18,700 − $17,000) is recorded in the Decrease column because an increase to a current liability account is credited, resulting in a decrease to working capital.

(f) *Notes Payable:* Notes payable decreased from $1,200 in 19_A to $1,000 in 19_B. The $200 difference ($1,200 − $1,000) is recorded in the Increase column because a decrease to a current liability account is debited, resulting in an increase to working capital.

(g) *Miscellaneous Payables:* Miscellaneous payables decreased from $6,900 in 19_A to $5,800 in 19_B. The $1,100 difference ($6,900 − $5,800) is recorded in the Increase column because a decrease to a current liability account is debited, resulting in an increase to working capital.

Step 5. Record the difference between the total current assets and total current liabilities (the first two amount columns), and the total of the increase and decrease columns (the last two amount columns) on the next free line of their respective columns. Write the words "Working Capital" on the same line in the Account Title column. Double-underline the first two amount columns.

Step 6. The difference between the first two amount columns should be the same as the difference between the totals of the Increase and Decrease to Working Capital columns. The total of the Increase column for Bailey Enterprises is larger than the total of the Decrease column; therefore, there is an increase of $2,300 ($5,300 − $3,000) to working capital in 19_B. Record the $2,300 difference on the next line in the Decrease column for balancing purposes and write the words "Increase in Working Capital" in the Account Title column. Total the last two amount columns and double-underline the totals.

These six steps are illustrated in Figure 22-3.

Working Papers for Analyzing the Changes in Noncurrent Accounts

After the statement of changes in working capital accounts is prepared, the changes in noncurrent accounts are analyzed to show how funds were acquired and how funds were used during the period. All the changes to noncurrent accounts usually represent a source or use of working capital. Usually these changes to noncurrent accounts are shown on working papers before the statement of changes in financial position is prepared. The procedures for preparing working papers for analyzing noncurrent accounts are given (starting on page 601) for Bailey Enterprises for the year ended December 31, 19_B.

*Statement of changes in
working capital accounts*

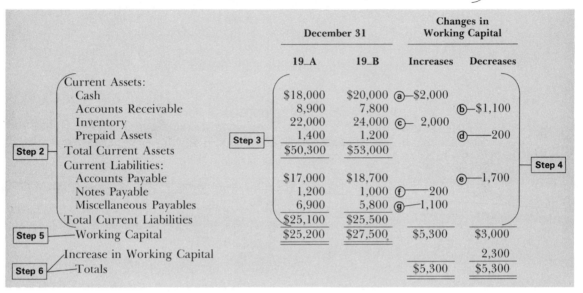

**BAILEY ENTERPRISES
STATEMENT OF CHANGES IN WORKING CAPITAL ACCOUNTS** Step 1
For the Year Ended December 31, 19_B

| | December 31 | | Changes in Working Capital | |
	19_A	19_B	Increases	Decreases
Current Assets:				
Cash	$18,000	$20,000	ⓐ—$2,000	
Accounts Receivable	8,900	7,800		ⓑ—$1,100
Inventory	22,000	24,000	ⓒ— 2,000	
Prepaid Assets	1,400	1,200		ⓓ——200
Total Current Assets	$50,300	$53,000		
Current Liabilities:				
Accounts Payable	$17,000	$18,700		ⓔ—1,700
Notes Payable	1,200	1,000	ⓕ——200	
Miscellaneous Payables	6,900	5,800	ⓖ—1,100	
Total Current Liabilities	$25,100	$25,500		
Working Capital	$25,200	$27,500	$5,300	$3,000
Increase in Working Capital				2,300
Totals			$5,300	$5,300

*Procedures for preparing
working papers analyzing
noncurrent accounts*

1. Record the proper heading on the working papers consisting of the name of the company, title of the statement, and the period covered by the statement. Set up an Account Title column and two amount columns for noncurrent asset and noncurrent equity (liabilities and stockholders' equity) account balances for 19_A and 19_B plus two amount columns for Sources and Uses of Working Capital.

**BAILEY ENTERPRISES
WORKING PAPERS FOR ANALYZING NONCURRENT ACCOUNTS
For Year Ended December 31, 19_B**

| | Balance, December 31 | | Working Capital | |
Account Title	19_A	19_B	Sources	Uses

2. Enter the words "Working Capital" in the Account Title column and record the amount of working capital for 19_A and 19_B from the statement of changes in working capital accounts in the first two amount columns. Enter the noncurrent asset accounts in the Account

Title column and record their respective balances as of December 31, 19_A, and December 31, 19_B, in the first two amount columns. Obtain a total for the first two amount columns, and write the words "Total Assets" on the next free line of the Account Title column. On the same line, record the totals in the amount columns, and double-underline the totals. Enter the noncurrent equity accounts in the Account Title column and record their respective balances as of December 31, 19_A, and December 31, 19_B, in the first two amount columns. Obtain a total for the first two amount columns for the noncurrent equity accounts, and write the words "Total Equities" on the next free line of the Account Title column. On the same line, record the totals in the amount columns and double-underline the totals.

BAILEY ENTERPRISES
WORKING PAPERS FOR ANALYZING NONCURRENT ACCOUNTS
For Year Ended December 31, 19_B

Account Title	Balance, December 31		Working Capital	
	19_A	19_B	Sources	Uses
Working Capital	25,200	27,500		
Plant Assets	34,000	36,000		
Intangible Assets	6,000	5,800		
Total Assets	65,200	69,300		
Long-term Liabilities	22,000	18,100		
Capital Stock	32,000	36,000		
Premium on Capital Stock	8,000	10,400		
Retained Earnings	3,200	4,800		
Total Equities	65,200	69,300		

3. Enter the changes to noncurrent accounts as either a source or use in the Working Capital columns and identify the changes at the bottom of the working papers. Whenever there is a decrease in a noncurrent asset account and an increase to a noncurrent equity account, it usually results in a source of working capital. Noncurrent assets are decreased with a credit and a noncurrent equity account is increased with a credit. These increases and decreases usually indicate that noncurrent assets and noncurrent equities have been sold or paid and a current asset or a current liability account (cash, receivable, or payable) have increased. Whenever there is an increase in a noncurrent asset account and a decrease to a noncurrent equity account, it usually results in a use of working capital. Noncurrent assets are increased with a debit and noncurrent equity accounts are decreased with a debit. These increases and decreases usually indicate that a noncurrent asset has been purchased and a noncurrent liability account has been paid or a noncurrent stockholders' equity account has been decreased because a cash dividend was declared, treasury stock was purchased, or preferred or common stock was retired and a current asset or current liability account (cash,

(a) receivable, or payable) has decreased. The changes to noncurrent accounts for Bailey Enterprises are listed in items *a* to *g*.

Plant assets for $3,000 were purchased for cash in 19_B resulting in a debit to a noncurrent plant asset account and a credit to a current account resulting in a use of working capital. The increase of $3,000 to the plant asset account is entered in the Use of Working Capital amount column, and the $3,000 is identified at the bottom of the working papers.

BAILEY ENTERPRISES
WORKING PAPERS FOR ANALYZING NONCURRENT ACCOUNTS
For Year Ended December 31, 19_B

Account Title	Balance, December 31		Working Capital	
	19_A	19_B	Sources	Uses
Working Capital	25,200	27,500		
Plant Assets	34,000	36,000		(a) 3,000
Intangible Assets	6,000	5,800		
Total Assets	65,200	69,300		
Long-term Liabilities	22,000	18,100		
Capital Stock	32,000	36,000		
Premium on Capital Stock	8,000	10,400		
Retained Earnings	3,200	4,800		
Total Equities	65,200	69,300		
Changes to Working Capital:				
(a) Purchase of plant assets.				

(b) Depreciation of plant assets amounted to $1,000 in 19_B. The entry required a debit to Depreciation Expense which decreased net in-

BAILEY ENTERPRISES
WORKING PAPERS FOR ANALYZING NONCURRENT ACCOUNTS
For Year Ended December 31, 19_B

Account Title	Balance, December 31		Working Capital	
	19_A	19_B	Sources	Uses
Working Capital	25,200	27,500		
Plant Assets	34,000	36,000	(b) 1,000	(a) 3,000
Intangible Assets	6,000	5,800		
Total Assets	65,200	69,300		
Long-term Liabilities	22,000	18,100		
Capital Stock	32,000	36,000		
Premium on Capital Stock	8,000	10,400		
Retained Earnings	3,200	4,800		
Total Equities	65,200	69,300		
Changes to Working Capital:				
(a) Purchase of plant assets.				
(b) Depreciation for plant assets.				

come and indirectly decreased the noncurrent Retained Earnings account; the entry also required a credit to the noncurrent plant asset account. No funds were used for depreciation during the period; therefore, the $1,000 for depreciation expense is added back to net income resulting in a source of working capital. The decrease of $1,000 to the plant asset account is entered in the Source of Working Capital amount column and the $1,000 is identified at the bottom of the working papers, as shown on page 603.

(c) Intangible assets were amortized for $200 in 19_B. The entry required a debit to Amortization Expense which decreased net income and indirectly decreased the noncurrent Retained Earnings account; the entry also required a credit to a noncurrent intangible asset account. No funds were used during the period for amortization; therefore, the $200 for amortization expense is added back to net income resulting in a source of working capital. The decrease of $200 to the intangible asset account is entered in the Source of Working Capital amount column, and the $200 is identified at the bottom of the working papers.

BAILEY ENTERPRISES
WORKING PAPERS FOR ANALYZING NONCURRENT ACCOUNTS
For Year Ended December 31, 19_B

Account Title	Balance, December 31		Working Capital	
	19_A	19_B	Sources	Uses
Working Capital	25,200	27,500		
Plant Assets	34,000	36,000	(b) 1,000	(a) 3,000
Intangible Assets	6,000	5,800	(c) 200	
Total Assets	65,200	69,300		
Long-term Liabilities	22,000	18,100		
Capital Stock	32,000	36,000		
Premium on Capital Stock	8,000	10,400		
Retained Earnings	3,200	4,800		
Total Equities	65,200	69,300		
Changes to Working Capital:				
(a) Purchase of plant assets.				
(b) Depreciation for plant assets.				
(c) Amortization of intangible assets.				

(d) Payments of $3,900 on long-term liabilities were made during 19_B. The entry required a debit to a noncurrent liability account and a credit to a current asset account resulting in a use of working capital. The $3,900 decrease in the long-term liability account is entered in the Use of Working Capital amount column, and the $3,900 is identified at the bottom of the working papers.

BAILEY ENTERPRISES
WORKING PAPERS FOR ANALYZING NONCURRENT ACCOUNTS
For Year Ended December 31, 19_B

| Account Title | Balance, December 31 | | Working Capital | |
	19_A	19_B	Sources	Uses
Working Capital	25,200	27,500		
Plant Assets	34,000	36,000	(b) 1,000	(a) 3,000
Intangible Assets	6,000	5,800	(c) 200	
Total Assets	65,200	69,300		
Long-term Liabilities	22,000	18,100		(d) 3,900
Capital Stock	32,000	36,000		
Premium on Capital Stock	8,000	10,400		
Retained Earnings	3,200	4,800		
Total Equities	65,200	69,300		
Changes to Working Capital:				
(a) Purchase of plant assets.				
(b) Depreciation for plant assets.				
(c) Amortization of intangible assets				
(d) Payment on long-term liabilities.				

(e)   Capital stock was sold for $6,400, $2,400 above par value. The entry required a debit to a current asset account and a credit to two noncurrent stockholders' equity accounts resulting in a source of

BAILEY ENTERPRISES
WORKING PAPERS FOR ANALYZING NONCURRENT ACCOUNTS
For Year Ended December 31, 19_B

| Account Title | Balance, December 31 | | Working Capital | |
	19_A	19_B	Sources	Uses
Working Capital	25,200	27,500		
Plant Assets	34,000	36,000	(b) 1,000	(a) 3,000
Intangible Assets	6,000	5,800	(c) 200	
Total Assets	65,200	69,300		
Long-term Liabilities	22,000	18,100		(d) 3,900
Capital Stock	32,000	36,000	(e) 4,000	
Premium on Capital Stock	8,000	10,400	(e) 2,400	
Retained Earnings	3,200	4,800		
Total Equities	65,200	69,300		
Changes to working capital:				
(a) Purchase of plant assets.				
(b) Depreciation for plant assets.				
(c) Amortization of intangible assets.				
(d) Payment on long-term liabilities.				
(e) Sale of capital stock for $6,400; $2,400 over par value.				

working capital. The increase of $4,000 in the Capital Stock account and the increase of $2,400 in the Premium on Capital Stock account is entered in the Source of Working Capital amount column, and the $6,400 is identified at the bottom of the working papers, as shown on page 605.

(f) Dividends of $1,000 were declared during 19_B. The entry required a debit to a noncurrent stockholders' equity account and a credit to a current liability account resulting in a use of working capital. The decrease of $1,000 in the Retained Earnings account is entered in the Use of Working Capital column, and the $1,000 is identified at the bottom of the working papers.

BAILEY ENTERPRISES
WORKING PAPERS FOR ANALYZING NONCURRENT ACCOUNTS
For Year Ended December 31, 19_B

| Account Title | Balance, December 31 | | Working Capital | |
	19_A	19_B	Sources	Uses
Working Capital	25,200	27,500		
Plant Assets	34,000	36,000	(b) 1,000	(a) 3,000
Intangible Assets	6,000	5,800	(c) 200	
Total Assets	65,200	69,300		
Long-term Liabilities	22,000	18,100		(d) 3,900
Capital Stock	32,000	36,000	(e) 4,000	
Premium on Capital Stock	8,000	10,400	(e) 2,400	
Retained Earnings	3,200	4,800		(f) 1,000
Total Equities	65,200	69,300		
Changes to working capital:				
(a) Purchase of plant assets.				
(b) Depreciation for plant assets.				
(c) Amortization of intangible assets.				
(d) Payment on long-term liabilities.				
(e) Sale of capital stock for $6,400;				
$2,400 over par value.				
(f) Dividends declared for $1,000.				

(g) Net income of $2,600 was earned during 19_B. The entry required a debit to the Income Summary account which indirectly results in a debit to Cash or Accounts Receivable and a credit to Retained Earnings. A debit to a current account and a credit to a noncurrent account represents a source of working capital. The increase of $2,600 in Retained Earnings is entered in the Source of Working Capital amount column, and the $2,600 is identified at the bottom of the working papers.

BAILEY ENTERPRISES
WORKING PAPERS FOR ANALYZING NONCURRENT ACCOUNTS
For Year Ended December 31, 19_B

Account Title	Balance, December 31 19_A	Balance, December 31 19_B	Working Capital Sources	Working Capital Uses
Working Capital	25,200	27,500		
Plant Assets	34,000	36,000	(b) 1,000	(a) 3,000
Intangible Assets	6,000	5,800	(c) 200	
Total Assets	65,200	69,300		
Long-term Liabilities	22,000	18,100		(d) 3,900
Capital Stock	32,000	36,000	(e) 4,000	
Premium on Capital Stock	8,000	10,400	(e) 2,400	
Retained Earnings	3,200	4,800	(g) 2,600	(f) 1,000
Total Equities	65,200	69,300		

Changes to working capital:
(a) Purchase of plant assets.
(b) Depreciation for plant assets.
(c) Amortization of intangible assets.
(d) Payment on long-term liabilities.
(e) Sale of capital stock for $6,400;
    $2,400 over par value.
(f) Dividends declared for $1,000.
(g) Net income of $2,600 earned.

4. Total the amount columns for sources and uses of working capital. The difference between the amount of the sources and the amount of the uses of working capital represent the amount of increase or decrease to working capital. Inasmuch as the total of $10,200 for the sources of working capital for Bailey Enterprises is larger than the total of the uses amounting to $7,900, there is an increase to working capital of $2,300 ($10,200 − $7,900) for 19_B. Record the increase to working capital in the Use of Working Capital amount column for balancing purposes, and write the words "Increase in Working Capital" on the same line in the Account Title column. Total the two columns and double-underline the totals, as shown in Figure 22-4. If the amount of the uses of working capital is larger than the amount of the sources of working capital, it would result in a decrease in working capital. The decrease would be recorded in the Source of Working Capital amount column for balancing purposes, and the words "Decrease in Working Capital" would be written on the same line in the Account Title column.

Statement of Changes in Financial Position

The statement of changes in financial position is prepared from the information in the working papers analyzing the changes in noncurrent accounts. This statement consists of two sections, one section listing the

FIGURE 22-4

Completed working papers
for analyzing
noncurrent accounts

BAILEY ENTERPRISES
WORKING PAPERS FOR ANALYZING NONCURRENT ACCOUNTS
For Year Ended December 31, 19_B

Account Title	Balance, December 31		Working Capital	
	19_A	19_B	Sources	Uses
Working Capital	25,200	27,500		
Plant Assets	34,000	36,000	(b) 1,000	(a) 3,000
Intangible Assets	6,000	5,800	(c) 200	
Total Assets	65,200	69,300		
Long-term Liabilities	22,000	18,100		(d) 3,900
Capital Stock	32,000	36,000	(e) 4,000	
Premium on Capital Stock	8,000	10,400	(e) 2,400	
Retained Earnings	3,200	4,800	(g) 2,600	(f) 1,000
Total Equities	65,200	69,300		
Total Sources & Uses			10,200	7,900
Increase to working capital				2,300
Totals			10,200	10,200

Changes to working capital:
(a) Purchases of plant assets.
(b) Depreciation for plant assets.
(c) Amortization of intangible assets.
(d) Payment on long-term liabilities.
(e) Sale of capital stock for $6,400;
      $2,400 over par value.
(f) Dividends declared for $1,000.
(g) Net income of $2,600 earned.

sources of working capital and the other section listing the uses of working capital. Sources of working capital and the amounts (how funds were acquired during the period) are usually listed in the first section of the statement. Uses of working capital and the amounts (how funds were applied) are usually listed in the last section of the statement. If the amount of funds applied during the period are larger than the amount of funds acquired during the same period, the uses of funds may be listed in the first section and the sources of funds may be listed in the last section.

The proper heading consists of the name of the company, the name of the statement, and the period of time covered by the statement. In the first section of the statement, the title Sources of Working Capital is entered on the first line. The first item listed in this section is the net income with its amount and the adjustments (depreciation, amortization, gains, or losses) that are added back or subtracted are listed next to arrive at the correct amount of funds provided from operations. Other sources of working cap-

FIGURE 22-5

Increase to working capital shown on statement of changes in financial position

BAILEY ENTERPRISES
STATEMENT OF CHANGES IN FINANCIAL POSITION
For Year Ended December 31, 19_B

Sources of Working Capital:		
Net Income	$2,600	
Add back: Depreciation/Plant Assets	1,000	
Amortization/Intangible Assets	200	
Funds Provided from Operations		$ 3,800
Sale of Capital Stock above Par Value		6,400
Total Sources of Working Capital		$10,200
Uses of Working Capital:		
Purchase of Plant Assets	$3,000	
Payment on Long-term Liabilities	3,900	
Declaration of Cash Dividends	1,000	
Total Uses of Working Capital		7,900
Increase in Working Capital		$ 2,300

ital are listed next with their amounts, and a total is obtained for the sources of working capital.

In the last section of the statement, the title Uses of Working Capital is written on the next free line. The uses of working capital are listed with their amounts, and a total is obtained for the uses of working capital. The difference between the total of the sources and uses of working capital representing the increase to working capital during the period is the last item recorded on the statement. This amount should agree with the amount of increase shown on the statement of changes in current accounts and the working papers analyzing the changes to noncurrent accounts. Double-underline the total amount of increase to working capital to complete the statement. To illustrate a statement of changes in financial position, a statement for Bailey Enterprises for the year ended December 31, 19_B, was prepared from the information in the working papers (Figure 22-4), and is shown in Figure 22-5.

SUMMARY

The statement of changes in financial position shows the sources and amount of funds that came into a business during an accounting period, and it shows how these funds were applied and used in the business operations. Funds in accounting is the difference between the current assets and the current liabilities; this difference is also called working capital. Before preparing a statement of changes in financial position, usually a statement is prepared showing the changes to working capital accounts and working papers are prepared analyzing the changes to noncurrent accounts. Information for these two statements and the working papers is obtained from comparative balance sheets (balance sheets for the current and previous year), from the current income statement, and from analyzing the reason for changes to noncurrent accounts.

The statement of changes in financial position consists of two sections, one listing the sources of working capital and one listing the uses of working capital. If there is an increase to working capital for the period, the sources are usually listed first followed by the uses. If there is a decrease to working capital for the period, the uses are usually listed first followed by the sources.

GLOSSARY

Current Account: Any current asset or current liability account. Current assets are assets that will be converted into cash or used up by the business within a year or less. Current liabilities are the debts of a business that should be paid within a year or less.

Funds: The difference between the amount of current assets and the amount of current liabilities is called funds in accounting; this difference is also called working capital.

Funds from Operations: Funds from operations is the net income shown on the year-end income statement plus any depreciation or amortization expense that did not require the use of funds during the period. Adjustments must also be made for any gains or losses realized from the sale of a noncurrent asset. Gains are deducted and losses are added back to net income because the total amount received from the sale of a noncurrent asset will be shown separately on a funds statement.

Noncurrent Account: Noncurrent accounts are any long-term investment, plant assets, intangible assets, long-term liabilities, and owner equity or stockholders' equity accounts.

Source of Funds: Any business transaction that requires a debit to a current asset or a current liability account and a credit to a noncurrent asset or a noncurrent equity (liability or stockholders' equity) account results in a source of funds or increase in working capital. Sources of funds (working capital) are obtained from the sale of a noncurrent asset, long-term bond, capital stock, obtaining a loan by borrowing on a long-term note, and funds provided from operations.

Statement of Changes in Financial Position: A statement showing the sources and amount of funds that came into a business during a period and how these funds were used by the business during the same period.

Statement of Changes in Working Capital Accounts: A statement showing the balances of the current asset and current liability accounts for the previous period and the current period and the amount of the increase or decrease to these accounts to arrive at the increase or decrease to working capital for the period covered on the statement.

Uses of Funds: Any business transaction that requires a debit to a noncurrent asset or a noncurrent equity (liability or stockholders' equity) account and a credit to a current asset or a current liability account results in a use or application of funds or a decrease in working capital. Funds are usually used to cover the loss from operations, the purchase of a noncurrent asset, the payment on a long-term liability, or the declaration of a cash dividend to the stockholders.

Working Capital: The difference between the amount of current assets and the amount of current liabilities for a period; this difference is also called funds in accounting.

QUESTIONS

1. What is the purpose for preparing a statement of changes in financial position?
2. Different types of transactions result in a source of working capital. Give an example of two types of transactions that would cause working capital to increase.
3. Would a sale of capital stock above par value increase or decrease working capital? Explain.
4. List four types of transactions that would result in a decrease to working capital.
5. If the difference between the amount of current assets for the current year and the previous year amounted to a decrease of $1,800, what does this difference represent?
6. What effect would an increase in the amount of Accounts Payable have on working capital?
7. If the net income for the current year amounted to $14,600 after deducting depreciation of $1,200 and amortization of $400, what would be the amount of funds provided from operations?
8. What effect does the declaration of a cash dividend have on working capital?

EXERCISES

Determining Sources and Uses of Funds

1. For each of the following items, determine if the transaction would result in (*a*) a source of funds, (*b*) a use of funds, or (*c*) is neither a source or use of funds. Use the identifying letter (*a, b,* or *c*) for your answer.
   (*a*) Sale of long-term bonds
   (*b*) Purchase of a building for cash
   (*c*) Purchase of equipment on a long-term note
   (*d*) Loss from operations
   (*e*) Declaration of a cash dividend

2. The balance sheets for the years ended December 31, 19_A, and December

31, 19_B, for Percy Manufacturing contained the following selected account balances.

	Balance on December 31	
	19_A	19_B
Bonds Payable	$10,000	$ 8,000
Capital Stock	20,000	24,000
Retained Earnings	7,100	8,200

Note: Cash dividends amounting to $600 were declared during 19_B.

Required

(*a*) Indicate the amount of sources and uses of working capital for 19_B.
(*b*) Determine the amount of the increase or decrease to working capital in 19_B.

Determining Effect of Transactions on Working Capital

3. For each of the following items, determine if the transaction resulted in an increase or decrease to working capital. Use an I for increase and a D for decrease.
(*a*) Increase in cash
(*b*) Decrease in accounts payable
(*c*) Increase in short-term notes payable
(*d*) Decrease in accounts receivable
(*e*) Decrease in inventory

Journal Entries for Working Capital

4. Give the journal entries required for the following transactions and indicate the effect of each transaction on working capital.
(*a*) Sale of 10, $1,000 long-term bonds for cash of $12,000
(*b*) Declaration of a cash dividend amounting to $1,200
(*c*) Purchase of equipment for $5,000 cash

Statement of Changes in Working Capital Accounts

5. The balance sheets for Curtis Industries for the years ended December 31, 19_A, and December 31, 19_B, contained the following selected account balances.

	Balance on December 31	
	19_A	19_B
Cash	$7,200	$6,000
Accounts Receivable	5,800	7,000
Prepaid Assets	3,100	3,000

Required

Prepare a partial statement of changes in working capital accounts.

Determining the Amount of Funds Provided from Operations

6. The work sheet for analyzing noncurrent accounts for Taylor Products showed a balance in the Retained Earnings account of $12,100 on December 31, 19_A, and $19,600 on December 31, 19_B. During 19_B, cash dividends amounting to $1,500 were declared.

Required

Determine the amount of funds provided from operations.

Determining Capital from Changes in Plant Assets

7. The balance of the plant assets on December 31, 19_A, amounted to $21,800 and $19,700 on December 31, 19_B. During 19_B, plant assets were sold for their book value of $4,100 and additional plant assets were purchased.

Required

Determine the following:
(a) Amount of plant assets purchased during 19_B
(b) Amount of sources or uses of working capital resulting from the changes in plant assets during 19_B

PROBLEMS

Statement of Changes in Current Accounts

22-1. The balances of the current accounts shown in the comparative balance sheets for the years ended December 31, 19_A, and December 31, 19_B, for Orr Corporation are shown below.

	December 31	
	19_A	19_B
Cash	$11,000	$10,100
Marketable Securities	5,400	5,200
Accounts Receivable	8,400	10,100
Inventory	2,600	3,700
Supplies	900	700
Accounts Payable	8,100	8,300
Short-term Notes Payable	5,300	3,300
Interest Payable	150	100
Taxes Payable	1,050	900

Required

Prepare a statement analyzing the changes in current accounts.

22-2. The balances of the current accounts shown in the comparative balance sheets for the years ended December 31, 19_A, and December 31, 19_B, for Bouton Candy Company are shown below.

	December 31	
	19_A	19_B
Cash	$19,000	$22,000
Accounts Receivable	9,200	8,700
Inventory	6,300	6,000
Office Supplies	1,400	1,800
Accounts Payable	14,400	13,900
Accrued Payables	2,300	3,550
Taxes Payable	1,200	900
Interest Payable	400	250

Required

Prepare a statement analyzing the changes in current accounts.

Work Sheet Analyzing Noncurrent Accounts

22-3. The balances shown in the comparative balance sheets for the years ended December 31, 19_A, and December 31, 19_B, for Excellence Manufacturing are shown below.

	December 31	
	19_A	19_B
Current Assets	$40,000	$48,000
Building	80,000	80,000
Accumulated Depreciation/Building	12,000	14,000
Land	20,000	24,500
Furniture & Equipment	32,000	32,000
Accumulated Depreciation/Furniture & Equipment	9,600	12,800
Current Liabilities	22,000	22,700
Mortgage Payable	30,000	27,000
Capital Stock	61,000	67,000
Premium on Capital Stock	28,000	29,500
Retained Earnings	9,400	11,500

Additional Data

(*a*) Cash dividends declared amounted to $3,000.
(*b*) Net income amounted to $5,100.

(c) Additional land was purchased for cash of $4,500.

(d) Additional shares of capital stock were issued for $1,500 above par value.

(e) Payment on mortgage amounted to $3,000.

(f) Depreciation on the building amounted to $2,000 and depreciation on the furniture and equipment amounted to $3,200.

Required

Prepare a work sheet analyzing the noncurrent accounts for the year ended December 31, 19_B.

22-4. The balances shown in the comparative balance sheets for the years ended December 31, 19_A, and December 31, 19_B, for Lexington Corporation are shown below.

	December 31	
	19_A	19_B
Current Assets	$46,900	$56,250
Land	10,000	8,000
Equipment	18,000	18,000
Accumulated Depreciation/Equipment	5,400	6,400
Patents	4,800	3,850
Current Liabilities	20,000	21,000
Long-term Notes Payable	6,000	4,800
Capital Stock	30,400	34,400
Premium on Capital Stock	9,000	9,800
Retained Earnings	8,900	9,700

Additional Data

(a) Net income amounted to $2,200.

(b) Land that was purchased for $2,000 was sold for its purchase price.

(c) Depreciation on equipment amounted to $1,000 and amortization of the patent amounted to $950.

(d) Capital stock was sold for $4,800, $800 above par value.

(e) Cash dividends declared amounted to $1,400.

(f) Payment on long-term note amounted to $1,200.

Required

Prepare a work sheet analyzing the noncurrent accounts for the year ended December 31, 19_B.

Statement of Changes in Financial Position

22-5. The amounts for the current and noncurrent accounts that increased and decreased from December 31, 19_A, to December 31, 19_B, for Shapley Sales are listed on the following page.

	Increase	Decrease
Current Assets	$8,000	
Accumulated Depreciation/Building	2,000	
Land	4,500	
Accumulated Depreciation/Furniture	3,200	
Current Liabilities	700	
Mortgage Payable		$3,000
Capital Stock	6,000	
Premium on Capital Stock	1,500	
Retained Earnings	2,100	

Additional Data
(a) Cash dividends declared amounted to $3,000.
(b) Net income amounted to $5,100.
(c) Additional land was purchased for cash.
(d) Six hundred shares of $10 par value capital stock was issued for $12.50 per share.

Required

Prepare a statement of changes in financial position for the year ended December 31, 19_B.

22-6. The amounts for the current and noncurrent accounts that increased and decreased from December 31, 19_A, to December 31, 19_B, for One-Way Products are listed below.

	Increase	Decrease
Current Assets	$9,350	
Land		$2,000
Accumulated Depreciation/Equipment	1,000	
Patents		950
Current Liabilities	1,000	
Long-term Notes Payable		1,200
Capital Stock	4,000	
Premium on Capital Stock	800	
Retained Earnings	800	

Additional Data
(a) Net income amounted to $2,200.
(b) Land was sold for its purchase price.
(c) Three hundred shares of $10 par value capital stock was issued for $16 per share.
(d) Cash dividends were declared in the amount of $1,400.

Required

Prepare a statement of changes in financial position for the year ended December 31, 19_B.

Statement of Changes in Current Accounts, Work Sheet Analyzing Noncurrent Accounts, and Statement of Changes in Financial Position

22-7. The balances shown in the comparative balance sheets for the years ended December 31, 19_A, and December 31, 19_B, for Cindy Sales are shown below.

	December 31	
	19_A	**19_B**
Cash	$ 9,200	$10,300
Marketable Securities	1,800	1,200
Accounts Receivable	16,000	14,000
Inventory	8,200	7,900
Supplies	2,100	1,900
Investment in Long-term Bonds	5,600	6,900
Land	10,000	10,000
Building	55,000	55,000
Accumulated Depreciation/Building	4,400	5,500
Furniture	18,000	26,500
Accumulated Depreciation/Furniture	7,200	8,400
Accounts Payable	18,000	15,000
Taxes Payable	3,100	2,800
Interest Payable	500	400
Mortgage Payable	30,000	27,000
Capital Stock	42,000	52,000
Premium on Capital Stock	13,100	14,400
Retained Earnings	7,600	8,200

Additional Data
(a) Purchased bonds as a long-term investment for $1,300.
(b) Purchased additional furniture for cash.
(c) Paid $3,000 on the mortgage.
(d) Sold 1,000 shares of $10 par value capital stock for $11.30 per share.
(e) Net income amounted to $2,680.
(f) Cash dividends amounting to $2,080 were declared during the period.

Required

Prepare the following for 19_B.
(a) Statement of changes in current accounts.
(b) Work sheet analyzing the changes in noncurrent accounts.
(c) Statement of changes in financial position.

Chapter 22 Appendix:

Cash Flow

After this appendix to Chapter 22, you should be able to:

1. **State the purpose for preparing a cash flow statement**

2. **List the three steps for converting an income statement to a cash basis**

3. **Give the format for preparing a cash flow statement**

4. **List the four sources and four uses of cash**

Chapter 22 discussed the importance of preparing a funds flow statement, a report showing the sources and uses of working capital for a period of time. In this appendix the importance of preparing a cash flow statement will be discussed. A cash flow statement is a report showing the sources and amounts of cash that came into a business during an accounting period and how the cash was used by the business during the same period. Cash in accounting, as explained in Chapter 10, refers to the coins, paper money, bank drafts, checks, money orders, certified checks, cashiers checks on hand, and the amount of cash on deposit in checking and other types of bank accounts.

PURPOSE FOR PREPARING A CASH FLOW STATEMENT

An important objective of a successful business is having enough cash on hand for operations and having enough cash on hand to meet their obligations as they become due. Therefore, a cash flow statement is prepared to show the amount of cash that is readily available to enable management to control the cash disbursements for the following period.

In this appendix a brief discussion of cash flow is given; a complete discussion of cash flow is given in advanced accounting texts.

CONVERSION OF INCOME STATEMENT TO A CASH BASIS

An income statement is a report of revenues earned and expenses incurred for a period of time, but it does not show the amount of actual cash received or the actual amount of cash paid for merchandise and expenses during the period. To determine the amount of cash received from operations, the income statement is usually converted to a cash basis before a cash flow statement is prepared.

Cash Received from Customers

Revenue earned from selling a product or a service is the first item that is converted to a cash basis. To determine the amount of cash received from sales, the amount of the cash sales during the current period is added to the amount of cash received from customers for payment on accounts receivable. These payments may represent credit sales for the current period, credit sales of a prior period, or advance payments for credit sales of a future period. The Accounts Receivable account appearing on a comparative balance sheet is analyzed to determine the amount of increase or decrease during the period. Cash received as payment on account is determined by

1. *Subtracting* the amount of *increase* in accounts receivable
2. *Adding* the amount of *decrease* in accounts receivable to the amount of revenue earned from selling a product or a service

For example, whenever a product or service is sold on account, the Accounts Receivable account is debited and the Sales account is credited. Whenever cash is received from customers as payment on account, Cash is debited and Accounts Receivable is credited. Therefore, a decrease in accounts receivable results in an increase to cash as shown in the following journal entry.

A decrease in accounts receivable increases cash	Cash	1,000
	Accounts Receivable	1,000
	To record the receipt of $1,000 from customers in payment on account.	

To illustrate a decrease in accounts receivable on the conversion statement, assume that sales for Windy Products amounted to $10,000 during January of the current year and the amount of accounts receivable decreased $2,000. Cash received from sales during January is computed as follows:

Decrease in accounts receivable is added to sales	Sales	$10,000
	Add: Decrease in Accounts Receivable	2,000
	= Cash Received from Sales	$12,000

If the amount of accounts receivable had increased, it would result in a decrease to the amount of sales shown on the conversion statement. The amount of an increase to accounts receivable is subtracted from the sales amount shown on the income statement to show the actual amount of cash received from customers during the period. For example, assume that sales for Windy Products amounted to $10,000 during January of the current period and the amount of accounts receivable increased $2,000. Cash received from sales is computed as follows:

Increase in accounts receivable is subtracted from sales

Sales	$10,000
Less: Increase in Accounts Receivable	2,000
= Cash Received from Sales	$ 8,000

Cash Paid for Merchandise Sold

The cost of goods sold is the second item on an income statement converted to a cash basis. To determine the amount of cash paid for the sale of merchandise, the amount of merchandise purchased for cash is added to the amount of cash paid to creditors for payment on accounts payable. These payments may represent purchases of merchandise on credit during the current period, credit purchases of a previous period, or credit purchases for a future period. The Accounts Payable account appearing on a comparative balance sheet is analyzed to determine the amount of increase or decrease during the period. Cash paid on account is determined by:

1. *Adding* any *decrease* in the amount of accounts payable
2. *Subtracting* any *increase* in the amount of accounts payable to the cost of goods sold

For example, whenever merchandise is purchased on account, the Merchandise Inventory account (perpetual inventory system) is debited and the Accounts Payable account is credited. Whenever cash is paid to creditors on accounts, Accounts Payable is debited and Cash is credited. Therefore, a decrease in accounts payable results in a decrease to cash as shown in the following journal entry:

Decrease in accounts payable decreases cash

Accounts Payable	1,000	
Cash		1,000
To record payment of $1,000 to creditors on account.		

To illustrate a decrease in accounts payable on the conversion statement, assume that during January of the current year, Windy Products received cash of $12,000 from sales, cost of goods sold amounted to $6,000, and accounts payable decreased $1,000. Gross profit realized on a cash basis for Windy Products during January is computed as follows:

Decrease in accounts payable increases cost of goods sold

Cash Received from Sales		$12,000
Cost of Goods Sold	$6,000	
Add: Decrease in Accounts Payable	1,000	
= Cash Paid for Merchandise Sold		7,000
= Gross Profit (Cash Basis)		$ 5,000

If the amount of accounts payable had increased, it would result in a decrease to the cost of goods sold shown on the conversion statement. The amount of an increase to Accounts Payable is subtracted from the cost of goods sold shown on the income statement to show the actual amount of cash paid for merchandise sold during the period. For example, assume that during January of the current year, Windy Products received cash of $12,000 from sales, cost of goods sold amounted to $6,000, and accounts payable increased $1,000. Gross profit realized on a cash basis for Windy Products during January is computed as follows:

Increase in accounts payable decreases cost of goods sold

Cash Received from Sales		$12,000
Cost of Goods Sold	$6,000	
Less: Increase in Accounts Payable	1,000	
= Cash Paid for Merchandise Sold		5,000
= Gross Profit (Cash Basis)		$ 7,000

Cash Paid for Operating Expenses

The last items to be converted to a cash basis on an income statement are the expenses. To determine the amount of cash paid for the expenses, it requires the addition or subtraction to the expense account shown on the income statement for the increases and decreases to the related prepaid asset and liability accounts. The cash paid for expenses may represent expenses incurred during the current period, expenses of a previous period, or expenses for a future period. The related prepaid asset and liability accounts appearing on a comparative balance sheet must be analyzed to determine the amount of increase and decrease to these accounts during the period. Cash paid for expenses involving a prepaid asset account is determined by

1. *Adding* any *increase* in the related prepaid asset account
2. *Subtracting* any *decrease* in the related prepaid asset account to the expense
3. *Adding* any *decrease* in the related liability account
4. *Subtracting* any *increase* in the related liability account to the expense

For example, whenever expenses are paid in advance, a Prepaid Asset account is usually debited and the Cash account is credited. Whenever the prepaid asset has expired or has been used, the related expense account is debited and the prepaid asset account is credited. Therefore, an increase to a prepaid asset results in a decrease to cash; a decrease to a prepaid asset results in a decrease to the expense shown on the conversion statement.

Whenever expenses are incurred, an expense account is debited and a liability account is credited. When the related liability account for the expense is paid, a liability account is debited and cash is credited. Therefore, a decrease in the liability results in a decrease to cash; an increase in the liability results in a decrease to the expense shown on the conversion statement.

To illustrate an increase in prepaid assets and an increase in a liability, assume that during January of the current year miscellaneous expenses amounted to $1,000 for Windy Products. Prepaid miscellaneous expenses increased $200 and miscellaneous liabilities increased $100 during January. Cash paid for miscellaneous expenses during January for Windy Products amounted to $1,100 as shown below.

Increase in prepaid assets is added and an increase in a liability is subtracted from an expense

Miscellaneous Expense	$1,000	
Add: Increase in Prepaid Asset	200	$1,200
Less: Increase in Miscellaneous Liability		100
= Cash Paid for Miscellaneous Expenses		$1,100

If the prepaid asset and liability had decreased for Windy Products during January, it would result in a decrease of $200 and an increase of $100 to the $1,100 amount of miscellaneous expenses shown on the conversion statement. The amount of the decrease to prepaid assets is subtracted and the amount of the decrease in the liability is added to the $1,100 to obtain the actual amount of cash paid for miscellaneous expenses during the period as shown below.

Decrease in prepaid assets is subtracted and a decrease in a liability is added to an expense

Miscellaneous Expense	$1,000	
Less: Decrease in Prepaid Asset	200	$800
Add: Decrease in Miscellaneous Liability		100
= Cash Paid for Miscellaneous Expenses		$900

Any depreciation, depletion, or amortization shown on an income statement is eliminated on a conversion statement, because they represent noncash items.

Preparing the Conversion of Income Statement to a Cash Basis

After all the items appearing on an income statement are analyzed to determine the amount of cash received and the amount of cash paid for operations, the conversion statement is prepared. The conversion of an income statement to a cash basis will show the revenues and expenses for a period on an accrual and cash basis to arrive at the net income.

To illustrate, assume that during January of the current year, Windy Products received cash amounting to $12,000 from sales, paid cash of $7,000 for merchandise sold and miscellaneous expenses of $1,100, and they reported depreciation expense of $400. The income statement converted to a cash basis for Windy Products for January of the current year is shown in Figure A22-1.

FIGURE A22-1.
*Income statement
converted to a cash basis*

WINDY PRODUCTS
CONVERSION OF INCOME STATEMENT TO CASH BASIS
For Month Ended January 31, 19___

	Accrual Basis	Adjustments	Cash Basis
Operating Revenue:			
Sales	$10,000		
Add: Decrease in Accounts Receivable		$2,000	$12,000
Cost of Goods Sold	6,000		
Add: Decrease in Accounts Payable		1,000	7,000
Gross Profit	$ 4,000		$ 5,000
Operating Expenses:			
Miscellaneous Expenses	$ 1,000		
Add: Increase in Prepaid Asset		200	
Less: Increase in Miscellaneous Liability		(100)	$ 1,100
Depreciation Expense	400		
Less: Noncash Item		(400)	–0–
Total Operating Expenses	$ 1,400		$ 1,100
Net Income	$ 2,600		$ 3,900

CASH FLOW STATEMENT

The cash flow statement is prepared after the income statement has been converted to a cash basis. A cash flow statement consists of two sections: one to show the cash receipts and one to show the cash disbursements for the period. The sources and amounts of cash received are listed in the first section of the statement; the amount of cash disbursements and how the cash was used during the period are listed in the second section.

Preparing the Cash Flow Statement

The proper heading consisting of the name of the business, name of statement, and the period of time covered on the statement is recorded first. Cash realized from operations (obtained from the income statement converted to a cash basis) is the main source of cash for a business; therefore, it is listed as the first item in the Cash Receipts section. If a cash loss was realized from operations, it would be listed as the first item in the Cash Disbursements section. Other sources of cash with their amounts are listed next, and the cash receipts are totaled.

How the various amounts of cash received were used during the period are listed in the Cash Disbursements section. The difference between

FIGURE A22-2
Cash flow statement

WINDY PRODUCTS
CASH FLOW STATEMENT
For Month Ended January 31, 19___

Cash Receipts:		
Cash from Operations (Figure 22-1)	$3,900	
Sale of Stock above Par Value	1,200	
Loan from Bank	500	
Total Cash Receipts		$5,600
Cash Disbursements:		
Purchase of Equipment	$1,000	
Payment of Cash Dividends	600	
Total Cash Disbursements		1,600
Increase in Cash		$4,000

the amount of cash receipts and the amount of cash disbursements equals the amount of increase or decrease to cash. This amount should be the same as the difference between the amount of cash shown on the current balance sheet and the amount of cash shown on the previous balance sheet. A work sheet may be prepared for analyzing the changes in balance sheet accounts to determine the amounts and sources of cash and the amount and uses of cash. A cash flow work sheet will not be discussed in this appendix.

Sources of Cash. There are basically four ways that a business may obtain cash. They are:

Four sources of cash

1. Cash from operations
2. Sale of assets
3. Sale of stocks or bonds
4. Borrowing cash and signing a note payable

Uses of Cash. There are basically four ways that a business may use the cash they have on hand. They are:

Four uses of cash

1. Purchase of assets
2. Payment of debts
3. Purchase of treasury stock
4. Payment of cash dividends to their stockholders

To illustrate, a cash flow statement is prepared for Windy Products for the month of January of the current year. Assume that the beginning cash balance on January 1 amounted to $5,000 for Windy Products. On January 31, cash on hand amounted to $9,000 representing a $4,000 increase ($9,000 − $5,000) during the month. This increase of $4,000 resulted from cash receipts amounting to $5,600 ($3,900 from operations, $1,200 from the sale of stock above par value, and $500 obtained as a loan from the local bank by signing a 60-day note), and cash disbursements amounting to $1,600 ($1,000 paid for equipment and $600 for the payment of cash dividends to the stockholders). The cash receipts and cash disbursements are shown on the cash flow statement in Figure A22-2.

SUMMARY

A cash flow statement is a report that shows the sources and amount of cash that came into a business during an accounting period and how the cash received was used by the business during the same period. The purpose of a cash flow statement is to show the amount of cash that is readily available to enable management to control the cash disbursements for the following period.

Before the cash flow statement is prepared, the income statement is usually converted to a cash basis to determine the amount of cash received from operations. Various asset and liability accounts appearing on a comparative balance sheet must be analyzed to determine the increase or decrease to these accounts.

Manufacturing Accounting

After completing this chapter, you should be able to:

1. **Give the definition of raw materials, direct labor, and factory overhead, the three elements of production**

2. **Give a brief description of Raw Materials, Goods in Process, and Finished Goods Inventory, the three types of inventories for a manufacturing concern**

3. **Journalize the five basic closing entries for a manufacturing concern**

4. **Prepare a manufacturing work sheet**

5. **Prepare a cost of goods manufactured statement, the cost of goods sold section of an income statement, and give the balance sheet classification for the three types of inventories**

A merchandising concern purchases a product for the purpose of re-selling the product for more than its purchase price. A *manufacturing concern* purchases materials for the purpose of using the materials in manufacturing a product that they will be able to sell for more than the cost of the materials, labor, and other manufacturing costs that will be incurred in the production process. Accounting for a manufacturing concern requires the use of several new accounts and the preparation of one additional financial statement called cost of goods manufactured. However, the journals, work sheet, and financial statements for a manufacturing concern are basically the same as those used for a merchandising business.

MANUFACTURING COSTS[1]

When a manufacturing concern purchases materials for the purpose of using them to make a finished product, two other types of costs will be incurred before the product is completed. These *manufacturing costs* are the materials used in the product called raw materials, the labor of the employees involved in making the finished product called direct labor, and the various other costs of operating the factory called factory overhead. These costs, raw materials, direct labor, and factory overhead, are called the three elements of production.

A manufacturing concern usually purchases and requisitions materials for the manufacturing process throughout the accounting period. At the end of the accounting period, any material that has not been requisitioned for the manufacturing process represents the ending raw materials inven-

---

[1] The AICPA has recommended that all costs for raw materials, direct labor, and factory overhead be described as a cost and not as an expense; expenditures made for operating, other, and extraordinary items should be described as an expense.

tory. Any partially finished products in the manufacturing process at the end of a period represent the ending goods in process inventory. Products finished and transferred out of the manufacturing process but not sold at the end of a period represent the ending finished goods inventory.

MANUFACTURING ACCOUNTS

Raw Materials

Raw materials are materials used in the manufacturing process that become or remain part of the finished product. For example, the raw materials used by a manufacturing concern that makes and sells office desks are the different types of wood, screws, nails, varnish, hardware, etc. These materials remain part of the finished desk, and they are referred to as the raw materials or direct materials.

Indirect Materials

Indirect materials are supplies that are used in the manufacturing process, but they do not remain part of the finished product. For example, indirect materials are the supplies used in making the desks, such as polishing rags, machine oil, sandpaper, etc., but these supplies do not remain a part of the finished product. When indirect materials are purchased, they are usually recorded in a current asset account entitled Factory Supplies. Factory supplies or indirect materials used during an accounting period are classified as a factory overhead cost.

Direct Labor

Direct labor consists of the wages or salaries paid to employees who are directly involved in making a product. Usually the employee/s operate a machine or use a tool in the manufacturing process.

Indirect Labor

Indirect labor consists of the wages or salaries paid to employee/s that are involved in the manufacturing operations but they are not directly involved in making the finished product. For example, indirect labor costs are the wages and salaries of factory supervisors, payroll clerks, maintenance persons, etc. Indirect labor is classified as a factory overhead cost.

Factory Overhead

The indirect costs of operating a factory and manufacturing a product are called *factory overhead*. For example, factory overhead costs are the factory rent, heat, electricity, telephone, insurance, depreciation, taxes, repairs, indirect materials, indirect labor, etc. A cost must be incurred in the factory or manufacturing process to be classified as a factory overhead item. Any expenses incurred in the selling or general and administrative departments would be classified as operating expenses.

MANUFACTURING INVENTORIES

A manufacturing concern has three different types of inventories that are classified as a current asset. These three types of inventories are called raw materials, goods or work in process, and finished goods inventories.

Raw Materials Inventory

Raw materials inventory consists of the material on hand at the end of an accounting period that was not used or put into the manufacturing process. Whenever material is purchased, the Raw Material Purchases account is debited and the Cash or Accounts Payable accounts are credited. At the end of an accounting period, a physical count would be taken of the raw materials on hand to determine the cost of the ending raw materials inventory. To record the cost of the ending raw materials inventory, a current asset account, Raw Materials Inventory, is debited and a temporary closing account entitled Manufacturing Summary is credited. The cost of the beginning Raw Materials Inventory account is removed from the records by debiting the Manufacturing Summary account and crediting the Raw Materials Inventory account.

Goods in Process Inventory

The *Goods in Process Inventory* account consists of the partially finished products in the manufacturing process. The cost of the goods in process at the end of an accounting period depends upon the cost of raw materials, direct labor, and factory overhead incurred for the unfinished products remaining in the manufacturing process. When the cost is determined, an entry is recorded debiting a current asset account, Goods in Process Inventory, and crediting a temporary closing account, Manufacturing Summary. The cost of the beginning Goods in Process Inventory is removed from the records by debiting the Manufacturing Summary account and crediting the Goods in Process Inventory account.

Finished Goods Inventory

The *Finished Goods Inventory* account consists of the products that are finished and ready to sell. At the end of an accounting period, a physical count would be taken of the finished goods on hand to determine the cost of the ending finished goods inventory. To record the cost of the ending finished goods inventory, a current asset account, Finished Goods Inventory, is debited and a temporary closing account entitled Income Summary is credited. The cost of the beginning Finished Goods Inventory account is removed from the records by debiting the temporary closing account entitled Income Summary and crediting the Finished Goods Inventory account.

The cost of the beginning and ending raw materials and goods in process inventories are shown on a financial statement entitled cost of goods manufactured or manufacturing statement. The cost of the beginning and ending finished goods inventory is shown in the Cost of Goods Sold section of an income statement.

COST OF GOODS MANUFACTURED STATEMENT

The first financial statement usually prepared by a manufacturing concern at the end of an accounting period is a statement entitled *cost of goods manufactured* or *manufacturing statement.* This information could be included in the Cost of Goods Sold section of an income statement, but because of its length, it is prepared separately and serves as a supporting schedule for the amount shown for the cost of manufacturing on the income statement. The first item on the cost of goods manufactured statement is the cost of the beginning goods in process inventory followed by the addition of the three elements of production (raw materials, direct labor, and factory overhead costs) to arrive at the cost of goods in process during the period. The last item on the statement is the deduction of the cost of the ending goods in process inventory to arrive at the cost of goods manufactured. The formula for preparing a cost of goods manufactured statement is shown below.

Formula for determining cost of goods manufactured

Beginning Goods in Process Inventory
Add: Cost of Raw Materials Used (beginning raw materials inventory + raw material purchases + transportation − returns and discounts − ending inventory of raw materials)
  Direct Labor
  Factory Overhead Costs
= Cost of Goods in Process during Period
Less: Ending Goods in Process Inventory
= Cost of Goods Manufactured

To illustrate, assume that the following balances appeared in the records of Forms Corporation as of December 31, 19__.

Raw Material Purchases	$91,000	Miscellaneous Factory Costs	$12,000
Direct Labor	82,000	Inventories:	
Indirect Labor	50,000	Raw Materials, 1/1/__	18,000
Depreciation on Machinery	2,000	12/31/__	28,000
Factory Insurance	500	Goods in Process, 1/1/__	25,000
Factory Supplies	11,000	12/31/__	30,000

This information from the records of the Forms Corporation was used to prepare the following cost of goods manufactured statement for the year ended December 31, 19__.

Year-end cost of goods manufactured statement

FORMS CORPORATION
COST OF GOODS MANUFACTURED STATEMENT
For Year Ended December 31, 19_A

Goods in Process Inventory, 1/1/__		$ 25,000
Raw Materials Used:		
Raw Materials Inventory, 1/1/__	$ 18,000	
Add: Raw Material Purchases	91,000	
Cost of Raw Materials Available	$109,000	
Less: Raw Materials Inventory, 12/31/__	28,000	
Cost of Raw Materials Used		81,000
Direct Labor		82,000
Factory Overhead:		
Indirect Labor	$ 50,000	
Factory Supplies	11,000	
Depreciation/Machinery	2,000	
Insurance	500	
Miscellaneous	12,000	
Total Factory Overhead Costs		75,500
Cost of Goods in Process during Year		$263,500
Less: Goods in Process Inventory, 12/31/__ ...		30,000
Cost of Goods Manufactured		$233,500

COST OF GOODS SOLD SECTION OF INCOME STATEMENT

An income statement for a manufacturing concern is prepared after completing the cost of goods manufactured statement. The statement is basically the same as an income statement prepared for a merchandising concern except the Cost of Goods Sold section consists of only three items as shown in the following formula:

Formula for Cost of Goods Sold section of income statement

Beginning Finished Goods Inventory
Add: Cost of Goods Manufactured
= Cost of Goods Available for Sale
Less: Ending Finished Goods Inventory
= Cost of Goods Sold

To illustrate, assume that the cost of goods manufactured amounted to $233,500 for 19_, and the finished goods inventory amounted to $30,000 on January 1 and $32,000 on December 31, 19__, for Forms Corporation. This information for the Forms Corporation was used to prepare the following Cost of Goods Sold section of the income statement for the year ended December 31, 19__.

Cost of Goods Sold section of income statement

Cost of Goods Sold:		
Finished Goods Inventory, 1/1/__	$ 30,000	
Add: Cost of Goods Manufactured	233,500	
Cost of Goods Available for Sale		$263,500
Less: Finished Goods Inventory, 12/31/__		32,000
Cost of Goods Sold		$231,500

MANUFACTURING WORK SHEET

The work sheet for a manufacturing concern usually has 14 columns, two columns more than the work sheet prepared for a corporation (Chapter 17). The two extra columns contain the information for preparing the cost of goods manufactured statement. To illustrate the work sheet for Forms Corporation, Figure 23-1 has been prepared for the year ended December 31, 19_B.

The work sheet begins with the Adjusted Trial Balance columns, and, for simplicity, some of the amounts for the assets, various costs, and expenses have been combined. Forms Corporation, a manufacturing company, uses a periodic system[2] for maintaining their inventories. Therefore, the three inventories are adjusted and closed in basically the same way as a merchandising concern using a periodic inventory system adjusts and closes their Merchandise Inventory account. Six steps for completing a manufacturing work sheet beginning with the adjusted trial balance are discussed below:

Step 1. The beginning inventory for raw materials and goods in process are entered as a debit in the Cost of Manufacturing columns. Beginning inventory for finished goods is entered as a debit in the Income Statement columns as shown in the partial work sheet.

FORMS CORPORATION
PARTIAL WORK SHEET
For Year Ended December 31, 19_B

Account Titles	Adjusted Trial Balance		Cost of Manufacturing		Income Statement	
	Debit	Credit	Debit	Credit	Debit	Credit
Raw Materials Inventory, 1/1	28,000		28,000			
Goods in Process Inventory, 1/1	30,000		30,000			
Finished Goods Inventory, 1/1	32,000				32,000	

Step 2. The words Raw Materials Inventory, 12/31/__, Goods in Process Inventory, 12/31/__, and Finished Goods Inventory, 12/31/__, are written on the next three free lines of the Account Title column. Enter the amount of $29,000 for ending raw materials inventory and $36,000 for ending goods in process inventory on their respective lines in the Cost of Manufacturing credit column. Enter the amount of $33,000 for the ending finished goods inventory on its respective line in the Income Statement credit column. Carry over all three ending inventory amounts to the Balance Sheet debit column as shown in the partial work sheet.

[2] Periodic inventory system is explained in Chapter 12.

FORMS CORPORATION
PARTIAL WORK SHEET
For Year Ended December 31, 19_B

Account Titles	Cost of Manufacturing		Income Statement		Balance Sheet	
	Debit	Credit	Debit	Credit	Debit	Credit
Raw Materials Inventory, 12/31		29,000			29,000	
Goods in Process Inventory, 12/31		36,000			36,000	
Finished Goods Inventory, 12/31				33,000	33,000	

Step 3. Carry over the manufacturing costs from the Adjusted Trial Balance columns to the Cost of Manufacturing debit column. Total the amounts appearing in the debit and credit Cost of Manufacturing columns. The difference between the amounts in the debit and credit column totals represents the cost of goods manufactured during 19__. Enter this difference in the credit column for balancing purposes, and write the words Cost of Goods Manufactured on the same line in the Account Title column. Total the amounts appearing in the same two columns and double-underline these final column totals. Final totals should be equal as shown in the partial work sheet.

FORMS CORPORATION
PARTIAL WORK SHEET
For Year Ended December 31, 19_B

Account Titles	Adjusted Trial Balance		Cost of Manufacturing	
	Debit	Credit	Debit	Credit
Raw Materials Inventory, 1/1	28,000		28,000	
Goods in Process Inventory, 1/1	30,000		30,000	
Raw Material Purchases (Net)	38,000		38,000	
Direct Labor	29,000		29,000	
Factory Overhead Control	55,000		55,000	
Raw Materials Inventory, 12/31				29,000
Goods in Process Inventory, 12/31				36,000
Totals			180,000	65,000
Cost of Goods Manufactured				115,000
Totals			180,000	180,000

Step 4. Carry over the amount of Cost of Goods Manufactured appearing in the credit column of the Cost of Manufacturing to the debit column of the Income Statement column. Carry over the revenue and expense amounts from the Adjusted Trial Balance columns to their respective Income Statement debit and credit columns, and subtotal the two columns. The total of the credit column is larger than the total of the debit column; therefore, net income was earned for 19__. Enter this difference in the debit column for balancing purposes and write the words Net Income on the same line in the Account Title column. Total the amounts appearing in the debit and credit columns and double-underline these final totals. Final totals should be equal as shown in the partial work sheet.

FORMS CORPORATION
PARTIAL WORK SHEET
For Year Ended December 31, 19_B

Account Titles	Adjusted Trial Balance		Cost of Manufacturing		Income Statement	
	Debit	Credit	Debit	Credit	Debit	Credit
Finished Goods Inventory, 1/1	32,000				32,000	
Sales		250,000				250,000
Operating Expenses Control	40,800				40,800	
Bond Interest Earned		4,000				4,000
Dividends Earned		600				600
Bond Interest Expense	3,600				3,600	
Income Tax Expense	38,000				38,000	
Finished Goods Inventory, 12/31						33,000
Cost of Goods Manufactured				115,000	115,000	
Totals			180,000	180,000	229,400	287,600
Net Income					58,200	
Totals					287,600	287,600

Step 5. Carry over the amount of net income from the Income Statement debit column to the Retained Earnings credit column. Carry over the amount of retained earnings on January 1, 19__, from the Adjusted Trial Balance credit column to the Retained Earnings credit column, and subtotal the debit and credit amount columns. The amount of the difference between the debit and credit columns represents retained earnings as of December 31, 19__. Enter the amount of ending retained earnings in the debit column for balancing purposes and write the words Retained Earnings, 12/31/_ on the same

FIGURE 23-1

FORMS CORPORATION
WORK SHEET
For Year Ended, December 31, 19_B

Accounts	Adjusted Trial Balance Debit	Credit	Cost of Manufacturing Debit	Credit	Income Statement Debit	Credit	Retained Earnings Debit	Credit	Balance Sheet Debit	Credit
Cash	18,000								18,000	
Marketable Securities	14,000								14,000	
Accounts Receivable (net)	12,000								12,000	
Raw Materials Inv. 1/1	28,000		28,000							
Goods in Process Inv. 1/1	30,000		30,000							
Finished Goods Inv. 1/1	32,000				32,000					
Prepaid Expenses	1,200								1,200	
Investment in 8% Bonds	50,000								50,000	
Furniture & Equipment	122,000								122,000	
Acc. Depreciation/ Furniture & Equipment		10,000								10,000
Accounts Payable		30,000								30,000
Accrued Liabilities		40,600								40,600
9% Bonds Payable, Due Year J		40,000								40,000
Common Stock, $10 Par Value		100,000								100,000
Premium on Common		23,400								23,400
Retained Earnings 1/1		13,000						13,000		
Sales (net)		250,000				250,000				
Raw Material Purchases (net)	38,000		38,000							
Direct Labor	29,000		29,000							
Factory Overhead Control	55,000		55,000							
Operating Expense Control	40,800				40,800					
Bond Interest Earned		4,000				4,000				
Dividends Earned		600				600				
Bond Interest Expense	3,600				3,600					
Income Tax Expense	38,000				38,000					
Totals	511,600	511,600								
Raw Materials Inv. 12/31				29,000					29,000	
Goods in Process Inventory 12/31				36,000					36,000	
Finished Goods Inv. 12/31						33,000			33,000	
Totals			180,000	65,000						
Cost of Goods Manufactured				115,000	115,000					
Totals			180,000	180,000	229,400	287,600				
Net Income					58,200			58,200		
Totals					287,600	287,600	-0-	71,200		
Retained Earnings 12/31							71,200			71,200
Totals							71,200	71,200	315,200	315,200

line in the Account Title column. Total the amounts appearing in the debit and credit columns and double-underline these final totals. Final column totals should be equal as shown in the partial work sheet.

FORMS CORPORATION
PARTIAL WORK SHEET
For Year Ended December 31, 19_B

Account Titles	Adjusted Trial Balance		Income Statement		Retained Earnings Statement	
	Debit	Credit	Debit	Credit	Debit	Credit
Retained Earnings, 1/1		13,000				13,000
Totals			229,400	287,600		
Net Income			58,200			58,200
Totals			287,600	287,600	-0-	71,200
Retained Earnings, 12/31					71,200	
Totals					71,200	71,200

Step 6. Carry over the amounts for asset, liability, and stockholders' equity accounts from the Adjusted Trial Balance columns to their respective debit and credit columns of the Balance Sheet, and subtotal the debit and credit amount columns. Carry over the amount of ending retained earnings from the Retained Earnings debit column to the Balance Sheet credit column. Total the amounts appearing in the debit and credit columns, and double-underline these final totals. Final column totals should be equal as shown on the completed work sheet, Figure 23-1.

FINANCIAL STATEMENTS FOR A MANUFACTURING CONCERN

Financial statements are prepared from the information appearing in a manufacturing work sheet. The cost of goods manufactured statement is prepared first followed by the income statement, retained earnings statement, and balance sheet. To illustrate, these statements are prepared from the work sheet in Figure 23-1 for Forms Corporation as shown in the cost of goods manufactured statement in Figure 23-2, income statement in Figure 23-3, retained earnings statement in Figure 23-4, and balance sheet in Figure 23-5.

FIGURE 23-2

Cost of goods manufactured statement

FORMS CORPORATION
COST OF GOODS MANUFACTURED STATEMENT
For Year Ended December 31, 19_B

Goods in Process Inventory, 1/1/__		$ 30,000
Raw Materials Used:		
Raw Materials Inventory, 1/1/__	$28,000	
Add: Raw Material Purchases	38,000	
Cost of Raw Materials Available	$66,000	
Less: Raw Materials Inventory, 12/31/__	29,000	
Cost of Raw Materials Used		37,000
Direct Labor		29,000
Factory Overhead		55,000
Cost of Goods in Process during 19_B		$151,000
Less: Goods in Process Inventory, 12/31/__		36,000
Cost of Goods Manufactured		$115,000

FIGURE 23-3

Income statement for manufacturing concern

FORMS CORPORATION
INCOME STATEMENT
For Year Ended December 31, 19_B

Operating Revenue:		
Sales		$250,000
Cost of Goods Sold:		
Finished Goods Inventory, 1/1/__	$ 32,000	
Add: Cost of Goods Manufactured	115,000	
Cost of Goods Available	$147,000	
Less: Finished Goods Inventory, 12/31/__	33,000	
Cost of Goods Sold		114,000
Gross Profit		$136,000
Operating Expense Control		40,800
Net Income before Other Revenue and Expense		$ 95,200
Other Revenue:		
Bond Interest Earned	$ 4,000	
Dividends Earned	600	
Total Other Revenue	$ 4,600	
Other Expenses:		
Bond Interest Expense	3,600	1,000
Net Income before Taxes		$ 96,200
Income Tax Expense		38,000
Net Income after Taxes		$ 58,200

FIGURE 23-4

Retained earnings statement for manufacturing concern

FORMS CORPORATION
RETAINED EARNINGS STATEMENT
For Year Ended December 31, 19_B

Retained Earnings, 1/1/__	$13,000	
Add: Net Income	58,200	
Retained Earnings, 12/31/__		$71,200

FIGURE 23-5

Balance sheet for manufacturing concern

FORMS CORPORATION
BALANCE SHEET
December 31, 19_B

Assets

Current Assets:		
Cash		$ 18,000
Marketable Securities		14,000
Accounts Receivable (Net)		12,000
Inventories:		
Raw Materials	$ 29,000	
Goods in Process	36,000	
Finished Goods	33,000	98,000
Prepaid Expenses		1,200
Total Current Assets		$143,200
Long-term Investments:		
Investment in 8% Bonds		50,000
Plant Assets:		
Furniture & Equipment	$122,000	
Less: Accumulated Depreciation	10,000	
Total Plant Assets		112,000
Total Assets		$305,200

Liabilities

Current Liabilities:		
Accounts Payable	$ 30,000	
Accrued Liabilities	40,600	
Total Current Liabilities		$ 70,600
Long-term Liabilities:		
9% Bonds Payable, Due 19_J		40,000
Total Liabilities		$110,600

Stockholders' Equity

Paid-in Capital:		
Common stock,[1] $10 Par Value, 10,000 shares authorized, issued, and out-standing	$100,000	
Premium on Common	23,400	
Total Paid-in Capital		$123,400
Retained Earnings		71,200
Total Stockholders' Equity		194,600
Total Liabilities & Stockholders' Equity		$305,200

[1] 10,000 shares of common stock was authorized, issued, and outstanding.

CLOSING ENTRIES PREPARED FROM MANUFACTURING WORK SHEET

Closing entries are prepared from the information in the Cost of Manufacturing and Income Statement columns of a manufacturing work sheet.

There are two closing entries prepared from the Cost of Manufacturing columns, and three closing entries prepared from the Income Statement columns, for a total of five closing entries. Entries for closing the beginning and recording the ending inventory for raw materials, goods in process, and finished goods are recorded through the closing process. All accounts appearing in the Cost of Manufacturing columns are closed into a temporary closing account entitled Manufacturing Summary. To illustrate, the first two closing entries are prepared from the Cost of Manufacturing columns of the work sheet for Forms Corporation in Figure 23-1.

In the first closing entry, ending raw materials and goods in process inventories with their amounts appearing in the Cost of Manufacturing credit columns are debited and the amount of the subtotal of the credit column is credited to the Manufacturing Summary account.

In the second closing entry, the Manufacturing Summary account is debited for the amount of the subtotal of the Cost of Manufacturing debit column, and the accounts with their amounts appearing in the debit column (beginning raw materials and goods in process inventories, raw material purchases, direct labor, and factory overhead costs) are credited.

	Closing Entries		
Closing entry 1			
19_B			
Dec. 31	Raw Materials Inventory	29,000	
	Goods in Process Inventory	36,000	
	Manufacturing Summary		65,000
	To record ending inventory for raw materials and goods in process.		
Closing entry 2			
31	Manufacturing Summary	180,000	
	Raw Materials Inventory		28,000
	Goods in Process Inventory		30,000
	Raw Material Purchases		38,000
	Direct Labor		29,000
	Factory Overhead Control		55,000
	To remove beginning raw materials and goods in process inventories, raw material purchases, direct labor, and factory overhead costs.		

Information for the next two closing entries (closing entries 3 and 4) is obtained from the Income Statement columns of a manufacturing work sheet. To illustrate, closing entries 3 and 4 are prepared from the work sheet of Forms Corporation in Figure 23-1.

In closing entry 3, the ending finished goods inventory, sales, and other revenue accounts with their amounts appearing in the credit column of the Income Statement columns are debited, and the temporary closing account entitled Income Summary is credited for the amount of the subtotal appearing in the credit column.

In closing entry 4, the temporary closing account entitled Income Summary is debited for the amount of the subtotal of the Income Statement debit column and the beginning finished goods inventory, operating expenses, other expenses, income tax expense, and Manufacturing Summary account with their amounts appearing in the Income Statement debit columns are credited.

Closing entry 3	19_B			
	Dec. 31	Finished Goods Inventory	33,000	
		Sales	250,000	
		Bond Interest Earned	4,000	
		Dividends Earned	600	
		Income Summary		287,600
		To record the ending finished goods inventory and to close the revenue accounts.		
Closing entry 4	31	Income Summary	229,400	
		Finished Goods Inventory		32,000
		Operating Expense Control		40,800
		Bond Interest Expense		3,600
		Income Tax Expense		38,000
		Manufacturing Summary		115,000
		To remove the beginning finished goods inventory and to close the expense accounts and Manufacturing Summary account.		

After the first four closing entries are journalized and posted, the difference between the subtotals of the Income Statement debit and credit columns representing the net income or loss for the period is closed into the Retained Earnings account. If the Income Statement subtotal of the credit column is smaller than the subtotal of the debit column, a loss has been realized. The Income Summary account is debited and the Retained Earnings account is credited for a profit, and the Retained Earnings account is debited and the Income Summary account is credited for a loss. To illustrate, the fifth and last closing entry is prepared from the Retained Earnings columns of the work sheet prepared for Forms Corporation in Figure 23-1. Inasmuch as the credit subtotal is larger than the debit subtotal of the Income Statement columns, the Income Summary account is debited and

Title: Manufacturing Summary   **Account No. 710**

Date		Explanation	Ref.	Debit	Credit	Balance
19_B Dec.	31				65,000	65,000
	31			180,000		115,000
	31				115,000	-0-

Title: Income Summary   **Account No. 720**

Date		Explanation	Ref.	Debit	Credit	Balance
19_B Dec.	31				287,600	287,600
	31			229,400		58,200
	31			58,200		-0-

the Retained Earnings account is credited for the net income realized for the period ending December 31, 19_B, as shown in the following journal entry.

Closing entry 5

19_B				
Dec.	31	Income Summary	58,200	
		Retained Earnings		58,200
		To close the Income Summary account and record the net income earned for 19_B into the Retained Earnings account.		

After the last two closing entries are posted, the two temporary closing accounts, Manufacturing Summary and Income Summary, should have a zero balance. To illustrate, the five closing entries prepared for Forms Corporation were posted to the Manufacturing Summary and Income Summary accounts and shown in Figure 23-6. Notice that these two accounts have a zero balance.

SUMMARY

A manufacturing concern purchases materials for the purpose of producing a product that they will be able to sell for more than the cost of the materials, labor, and other manufacturing costs that will be incurred in the production process. Accounting for a manufacturing concern requires the use of several new accounts incurred in the manufacturing process and factory operations.

Raw materials, direct labor, and factory overhead costs are called the three elements of production. Raw or direct materials are materials used in the manufacturing process that become or remain a part of the finished product. Indirect materials are supplies used in the manufacturing process and factory operations, but they do not remain part of the finished product. Direct labor consists of the wages or salaries paid to employees who are directly involved in making the product. Usually these employees operate a machine or use a tool in the manufacturing process. Indirect labor consists of the wages and salaries paid employees involved in the manufacturing operations, but they are not directly involved in the manufacturing of the finished product. All the indirect costs of manufacturing a product and operating a factory are classified as a factory overhead cost.

Three types of inventories of a manufacturing concern are called raw materials, goods in process, and finished goods inventories.

An additional financial statement is prepared by a manufacturing concern entitled cost of goods manufactured statement. This statement serves as a supporting schedule for the cost of manufacturing that is included in the Cost of Goods Sold section of an income statement.

A work sheet prepared for a manufacturing concern usually consists of 14 columns, two extra columns for the computation of the cost of manufacturing during the period covered on the work sheet. The manufacturing costs listed in these two columns are closed to a temporary closing account entitled Manufacturing Summary. Manufacturing Summary is also used to adjust the Raw Materials and Goods in Process Inventory accounts appearing in the Cost of Manufacturing columns. Revenues, expenses, and the Manufacturing Summary account appearing in the income statement columns are closed to the Income Summary account. Income Summary is also used to adjust the Finished Goods Inventory account appearing in the Income Statement columns. Income Summary is closed to the Retained Earnings account.

GLOSSARY

Cost of Goods Manufactured Statement: A statement prepared at the end of an accounting period to show the costs of manufacturing. The items listed on the statement begin with the cost of the beginning goods in process inventory followed by the addition of the costs for raw materials, direct labor, and factory overhead and ending with the deduction of the cost of the ending goods in process inventory to arrive at the cost of manufacturing.

Direct Labor: Wages and salaries paid to employees who are directly involved in making a product; usually the employees operate a machine or use a tool in the manufacturing process.

Factory Overhead: Indirect costs of operating a factory and manufacturing a product. For example, factory rent, heat, electricity, telephone, insurance, depreciation, taxes, repairs, indirect materials, indirect labor, etc.

Finished Goods Inventory: The products finished and transferred out of the manufacturing process but not sold at the end of an accounting period.

Goods in Process Inventory: Partially finished products in the manufacturing process at the end of an accounting period.

Indirect Labor: Wages or salaries paid to employees that are involved in the manufacturing operations but they are not directly involved in making the finished product. For example, indirect labor consists of the wages and salaries of factory supervisors, payroll clerks, maintenance persons, etc. Indirect labor costs are classified as a factory overhead cost.

Indirect Materials: Supplies that are used in the manufacturing process or factory operations, but they are supplies that do not remain a part of the finished product. For example, polishing rags, machine oils, sandpaper, etc. Indirect materials are classified as a factory overhead cost.

Manufacturing Concern: A company that purchases materials for the purpose of producing a product that they will be able to sell for more than the cost of the materials, labor, and other factory overhead costs that will be incurred in the production process.

Manufacturing Costs: Expenditures incurred for raw materials, direct labor, and factory overhead during an accounting period. The AICPA recommends that expenditures for manufacturing be referred to as costs, and expenditures for operating, other, and extraordinary items be designated as expenses.

Raw Materials: Material used in the manufacturing process that become or remain a part of the finished product; these materials are also called direct materials.

Raw Materials Inventory: Material on hand at the end of an accounting period that was not used or put into the manufacturing process.

QUESTIONS

1. Name and describe the three elements of production.
2. What two types of inventories are shown in a cost of goods manufactured statement?
3. State the difference between direct labor and indirect labor costs.
4. What is the difference between a cost and an expense as recommended by the AICPA?
5. Give the formula for preparing the cost of goods manufactured statement.
6. Give the explanation for the following journal entry:

Raw Materials Inventory
Goods in Process Inventory
Manufacturing Summary

7. How is the beginning and ending finished goods inventory shown on a manufacturing work sheet?

8. What accounts are debited and credited to close or remove the amount of the beginning raw materials and goods in process inventories from the accounting records.

9. What temporary accounts are used to close the (*a*) manufacturing accounts and (*b*) income statement accounts?

10. The subtotal of the cost of manufacturing debit column on a manufacturing work sheet is larger than the subtotal of the credit column. What does this difference represent?

EXERCISES

Determining Amount of Raw Materials Used

1. On January 1 of the current year, Brewster Manufacturing Company had $18,000 of direct materials on hand. During the year, raw materials amounting to $22,000 were purchased on account. On December 31, there were $14,000 of raw materials on hand.

Required

Determine the amount of raw materials used.

2. Wheel Corporation purchased $21,000 of raw materials during the current year and paid transportation costs of $2,600. The raw materials inventory on January 1 amounted to $6,600, and the inventory on December 31 amounted to $3,200.

Required

Determine the amount of raw materials used.

Determining the Amount of Cost of Goods Manufactured, Cost of Goods Sold, and Gross Profit

3. On June 30 of the current year, the following account balances appeared in the records of Paper Products Corporation: Raw Materials Inventory, January 1, $1,600, December 31, $2,300; Goods in Process Inventory, January 1, $3,800, December 31, $5,200; Finished Goods Inventory, January 1, $2,000, December 31, $7,500; Raw Material Purchases, $30,100; Direct Labor, $7,400; and Factory Overhead, $11,100.

Required

Determine:
(*a*) The cost of goods manufactured
(*b*) The cost of goods sold

4. The following account balances appeared on the records of Cosmetic Company on December 31 of the current year: Raw Materials Inventory, Jan-

uary 1, $32,000, December 31, $8,000; Goods in Process Inventory, January 1, $7,200, December 31, $8,100; Finished Goods Inventory, January 1, $1,400, December 31, $11,500; Raw Material Purchases, $68,000; Direct Labor, $48,000; Factory Overhead, $72,000; and Sales, $340,000.

Required

Determine:
(a) The cost of goods manufactured
(b) The cost of goods sold
(c) The gross profit

Closing Entries

5. Prepare the closing entries required on December 31 of the current year for Kay Corporation using the following information. Inventories: Raw Materials, January 1, $31,000, December 31, $9,000; Goods in Process, January 1, $7,000, December 31, $8,000; Finished Goods, January 1, $1,500, and December 31, $11,000; Raw Material Purchases, $69,000; Direct Labor, $49,000; Factory Overhead Costs, $71,000; and net income amounted to $34,000.

6. Prepare the closing entries required on December 31 of the current year for Wexler Corporation using the following information. Inventories: Raw Materials, January 1, $1,700, December 31, $2,400; Goods in Process, January 1, $4,800, December 31, $6,200; Finished Goods, January 1, $3,000, December 31, $8,500; Raw Material Purchases, $31,000; Direct Labor, $8,400; Factory Overhead Costs, $12,100; and net income amounted to $38,000.

Completion of a Partial Work Sheet

7. Complete the following partial work sheet for Swanson Brick Company:

Account Titles	Adjusted Trial Balance		Cost of Manufacturing		Income Statement	
	Debit	Credit	Debit	Credit	Debit	Credit
Raw Materials Inventory, 1/1	18,000					
Goods in Process Inventory, 1/1	9,000					
Finished Goods Inventory, 1/1	12,000					
Raw Material Purchases	50,000					
Operating Expenses	40,000					

8. Complete the following partial work sheet for Earthy Products:

	Adjusted Trial Balance		Cost of Manufacturing		Income Statement	
Account Titles	Debit	Credit	Debit	Credit	Debit	Credit
Raw Materials Inventory, 1/1	9,000					
Goods in Process Inventory, 1/1	7,100					
Finished Goods Inventory, 1/1	1,200					
Direct Labor	9,900					
Sales	90,000					

PROBLEMS

Matching Manufacturing Terms with Their Definition

23-1. Match items 1 to 8 with the following:

(a) Raw Materials Inventory   (e) Direct Labor
(b) Goods in Process Inventory   (f) Indirect Labor
(c) Finished Goods Inventory   (g) Indirect Materials
(d) Raw Material Purchases   (h) Factory Overhead Costs

1. Completed products on hand at end of a period
2. Direct material purchases
3. Factory superintendent's salary
4. Wages of factory machine operator
5. Supplies used by factory maintenance person
6. Partially finished products on hand at end of a period
7. Direct materials on hand at the end of a period
8. Factory costs for depreciation of factory machinery

23-2. Match items 1 to 10 with the following:

(a) Raw Materials   (f) Goods in Process Inventory
(b) Indirect Materials   (g) Raw Materials Inventory
(c) Indirect Labor   (h) Finished Goods Inventory
(d) Factory Overhead   (i) Cost of Goods Sold
(e) Operating Expenses   (j) Cost of Goods Manufactured

1. Nails used in production of product
2. Wages for factory maintenance person
3. Direct materials on hand at end of a period
4. Completed products on hand at the end of a period that are not sold
5. Cost of goods manufactured plus difference between beginning and ending finished goods inventory
6. Three cost elements of production plus the difference between beginning and ending goods in process inventory

7. Salaries of the salespeople
8. Cost of oil for factory machines
9. Factory insurance cost of factory building
10. Partially finished products on hand at the beginning of a period

Computation of Raw Materials Used, Ending Goods in Process Inventory, and Cost of Goods Sold

23-3. From the following data, compute the (*a*) raw materials used, (*b*) ending goods in process inventory, and (*c*) cost of goods sold. Raw Materials Inventory: 1/1, $5,000; 12/31, $10,700; Goods in Process Inventory: 1/1, $16,000; Finished Goods Inventory: 1/1, $9,800; 12/31, $18,300; Raw Material Purchases, $67,700; Direct Labor, $41,000; Factory Overhead, $61,500; and cost of goods manufactured during period, $162,500.

Computation of Ending Inventories

23-4. From the following data, compute the ending inventories for (*a*) raw materials, (*b*) goods in process, and (*c*) finished goods. Raw Material Purchases, $84,000; Raw Materials Inventory, 1/1, $5,600; Raw Materials Used, $71,000; Direct Labor, $40,000; Factory Overhead Costs, $60,000; Finished Goods Inventory, 1/1, $14,000; Goods in Process Inventory, 1/1, $20,000; Cost of Goods Sold, $137,000; and Cost of Goods Manufactured during period, $130,000.

Preparation of Cost of Goods Manufactured Statement and Cost of Goods Sold Section of an Income Statement

23-5. The following alphabetical list of accounts appeared in the records of Penrod Manufacturing Company as of December 31 of the current year: Direct Labor, $19,000; Factory Overhead, $38,000; Finished Goods Inventory, 1/1, $7,000; Goods in Process Inventory, 1/1, $11,000; Raw Materials Inventory, 1/1, $21,000; and Raw Material Purchases, $76,200. The inventory on December 31 amounted to: raw materials, $17,200; goods in process, $12,000; and finished goods, $18,000.

Required

Prepare the following:
(*a*) Cost of Goods Manufactured statement
(*b*) Cost of Goods Sold section of an income statement

23-6. The Home Ice Cream Company uses a periodic inventory system and closes their books on December 31 every year. The following data appeared in the accounting records on December 31 of the current year: Raw Materials Inventory: 1/1, $7,700; 12/31, $15,200; Goods in Process Inventory: 1/1, $9,600; 12/31, $17,050; Finished Goods Inventory: 1/1, $2,100; 12/31, $14,800; Direct Labor, $12,500; Raw Material Purchases, $16,200; Factory Overhead Costs, $6,900.

Required

Prepare the following:

(a) Cost of Goods Manufactured statement

(b) Cost of Goods Sold section of an income statement

Preparation of Closing Entries

23-7. The following data was obtained from the records of Hardy Cement Company at the end of January, the first month of operations: Raw Material Purchases, $39,000; Direct Labor, $32,000; Factory Overhead Costs, $37,400; Sales, $70,000; and Operating Expenses, $8,000. The ending inventories amounted to: Raw Materials, $10,000; Goods in Process, $400; and Finished Goods, $39,400.

Required

Journalize the closing entries required for the month ended January 31 of the current year.

Work Sheet, Financial Statements, and Closing Entries

23-8. The following list of accounts appeared in the records of Washington Paper Products on December 31 of the current year: Miscellaneous Current Assets, $62,000; Raw Materials Inventory: 1/1, $9,200; 12/31, $12,200; Goods in Process Inventory: 1/1, $4,000; 12/31, $7,800; Finished Goods Inventory: 1/1, $6,800; 12/31, $4,000; Plant Assets (net), $198,000; Current Liabilities, $31,000; Long-term Liabilities, $10,000; Capital Stock, $110,800; Retained Earnings, $6,000; Sales, $380,000; Raw Material Purchases, $76,200; Transportation on Raw Material Purchases, $4,800; Direct Labor, $10,000; Indirect Labor, $24,000; Factory Maintenance, $16,000; Depreciation/Factory Machinery, $4,800; Miscellaneous Factory Overhead, $17,000; Selling Expenses, $49,000; and General and Administrative Expenses, $56,000.

Required

Prepare the following:

(a) Work sheet beginning with the Adjusted Trial Balance columns

(b) Cost of goods manufactured statement

(c) Income statement

(d) Journalize the closing entries

23-9. Preston Wood Products has a periodic inventory system, and the following data appeared in their accounting records on December 31 of the current year: Cash, $35,000; Accounts Receivable, $6,000; Raw Materials Inventory: 1/1, $8,000; 12/31, $10,400; Goods in Process Inventory: 1/1, $2,800; 12/31, $7,200; Finished Goods Inventory: 1/1, $16,200; 12/31, $17,000; Factory Supplies, $6,200; Miscellaneous Current Assets, $5,000; Plant

Assets, $110,000; Accounts Payable, $10,000; Miscellaneous Current Liabilities, $6,000; Long-term Liabilities, $10,000; Capital Stock, $161,800; Retained Earnings, $4,000; Sales, $170,000; Raw Material Purchases, $28,400; Direct Labor, $29,000; Factory Overhead Costs, $80,200; Selling Expenses, $20,000; and General & Administrative Expense, $15,000.

Required

(a) Prepare a work sheet for the year ended December 31 of the current year beginning with the adjusted trial balance.
(b) Prepare a cost of goods manufactured statement.
(c) Prepare a partial income statement to gross profit on sales.
(d) Journalize the closing entries.

Job Order Cost System

After completing this chapter, you should be able to:

1. **Give a brief description of cost accounting and a job order cost system**

2. **Give the definition of a materials ledger card, a material requisition, and a labor time ticket**

3. **Prepare a job order cost sheet**

4. **Journalize the entries required for direct materials, direct labor, and factory overhead applied to production**

5. **Record the cost of jobs completed and sold in Finished Goods Inventory and Cost of Goods Sold**

6. **Summarize the six steps of a job order cost procedure**

Cost accounting is an accounting system designed to control and determine the unit costs of goods manufactured and the cost of goods sold. A cost accounting system maintains a record of the costs incurred in manufacturing a product/s to provide management with the information needed to:

1. Determine the cost of producing one unit of a product
2. Establish a selling price for the product
3. Determine the purchasing and production policies for future periods

MANUFACTURING COSTS

All the manufacturing costs incurred in production are classified as direct materials, direct labor, and factory overhead as discussed in Chapter 23. When a cost system is used, the unit cost for each of these three elements of production is determined to obtain the total unit cost for producing one unit of a product. It is necessary to obtain the unit cost of a product, because the unit cost is used to determine the amount of the ending goods in process inventory and to determine the cost of products completed and transferred to finished goods inventory.

COST ACCOUNTING SYSTEMS

There are two types of cost accounting systems used for determining the unit cost of a product. One is a job order cost system and the other is a process cost system. A job order cost system is discussed in this chapter and a process cost system is discussed in Chapter 25. Both systems need a perpetual inventory system[1] for maintaining inventories and for determining unit costs of direct materials, direct labor, and factory overhead.

JOB ORDER COST ACCOUNTING SYSTEM

A *job order cost accounting system* may be used by companies that manufacture a product according to the specifications of an order received from customers. However, a company may use a job order cost system when they produce different products for their inventory in anticipation of receiving future orders from customers. When a job order cost system is used, the cost of producing a product is based on a particular job or an order received from a customer. Therefore, it is possible to identify a particular job or order as it goes through the production process. A job order cost system may be used by a furniture company, cabinet maker, or an automobile manufacturer that makes furniture, cabinets, or automobiles according to the specifications received from a customer.

JOB ORDER COST SHEET

A job order cost system requires the preparation of a special ledger card called a *job order cost sheet* for each job or order received. These cost sheets are similar to the accounts receivable and accounts payable subsidiary ledgers maintained for each customer and creditor. Companies may use the job order cost sheets as a subsidiary ledger for the Goods in Process Inventory account and as a subsidiary ledger for the Cost of Goods Sold account in the general ledger.

All direct materials, direct labor, and factory overhead costs incurred in producing each job or order are accumulated and recorded on a job order cost sheet.

There are no standardized forms for a job order cost sheet; each company devises a form to accommodate its particular needs. Job order cost sheets usually are numbered and will have a space for the customer's name, type of product ordered, product number, date of order, due date, completion date, three sections for direct materials, direct labor, and factory overhead costs, plus a cost summary section. To illustrate, a job order cost sheet used by Custom Furniture Mart is shown in Figure 24-1.

Materials Ledger Card

A subsidiary ledger containing a separate record for each type of material used in producing a product is maintained on a *materials ledger card.*

[1] Perpetual inventory system is discussed in Chapter 11.

FIGURE 24-1

*Job order
cost sheet*

CUSTOM FURNITURE MART

JOB ORDER COST SHEET

Product: _____ Job Order No.: _____

Product No.: _____ Quantity Ordered: _____

Customer Name: _____ Date Shipped: _____

Date Ordered: _____ Date Promised: _____

Date Started: _____ Date Completed: _____

	Materials		Labor		Overhead Applied		
Date	Req. No.	Amount	Time Ticket No.	Amount	Date	Rate	Amount
						COST SUMMARY	
						Materials: _____	
						Labor: _____	
						Overhead: _____	
	Total					Total Cost: _____	
						Cost Per Unit: _____	

Whenever material is purchased or requisitioned for the production of a specific order or job, it is recorded on the related materials ledger card. The amount of material on hand, unit cost, and total cost is known at all times, because each requisition for production is subtracted and each pur-

FIGURE 24-2

*Materials ledger
card*

MATERIALS LEDGER CARD

No.: 10   Description: Material A—Antique Velvet

Supplier: Velour Fabric Company   Reorder Amount: 200 yards

		Purchases			Requisitions			Balance on Hand		
Date	Ref.	Units	Unit Price	Total	Units	Unit Price	Total	Units	Unit Price	Total
19— Nov. 1								400	$10	$4,000
1	R3447				42	$10	$420	358	10	3,580
15	R3448				9	10	90	349	10	3,490
15	R3450				58	10	580	291	10	2,910
23	R3452				15	10	150	276	10	2,760

chase is added to the beginning balance in the Balance on Hand column of the materials ledger card. To illustrate, a materials ledger card used by the Custom Furniture Mart for material A is shown in Figure 24-2.

Material Requisition

A *material requisition* is issued whenever material is needed for use in the factory operations. These requisitions show the type of material needed, quantity, and job order number. To illustrate, a material requisition for Custom Furniture Mart for Job Order 102 is shown in Figure 24-3.

Material requisitions are used as the basis for recording the cost of materials used on each job or order on the respective job order cost sheet and the materials ledger card. To illustrate, material requisitions No. 3447 and

FIGURE 24-3
Material requisitions

MATERIAL REQUISITION   3447

TO					DATE		
Materials Storeroom					November 1, 19—		
DELIVER TO					**CHARGE TO JOB**		
Department C					102		

	QUANTITY		STOREKEEPER: PLEASE SUPPLY	PRICE	AMOUNT	
1	42	yds.	Material No. A	10.00	420	00
2	20	yds.	Material No. C	2.50	50	00
3	350	ft.	Lumber No. 12	0.50	175	00
4	10	boxes	No. 620 Nails	1.50	15	00
5			Total		660	00
6						
7						
8						
9						

SIGNED

J. Booker

MATERIAL REQUISITION   3448

TO					DATE		
Materials Storeroom					November 15, 19—		
DELIVER TO					**CHARGE TO JOB**		
Department C					102		

	QUANTITY		STOREKEEPER: PLEASE SUPPLY	PRICE	AMOUNT	
1	9	yds.	Material No. A	10.00	90	00
2	32	yds.	Material No. D	3.00	96	00
3	2	boxes	Tape No. 32	7.00	14	00
4			Total		200	00
5						
6						
7						
8						
9						

SIGNED

J. Booker

FIGURE 24-4

*First step
in job order
cost system*

No. 3448 shown in Figure 24-3 for Custom Furniture Mart were used to record the cost of materials on the job order cost sheet for Job Order 102 as shown in Figure 24-4.

At the end of a cost period, the amounts shown on the material requisitions are totaled and used as the basis for debiting Goods in Process Inventory for the materials used in production and to credit Materials Inventory to show the decrease in the amount of materials on hand. For example, the total of material requisition Nos. 3447 to 3451 for Job Orders 102 to 105 amounted to $1,940 for the period ending November 15 for Custom Fur-

*Applying material
requisitions to production*

Nov.	15	Goods in Process Inventory	1,940	
		Materials Inventory		1,940
		To record material requisition Nos. 3447 to 3451 to production for Jobs 102 to 105.		

niture Mart. The Goods in Process Inventory account was debited and the Materials Inventory account was credited for $1,940 as shown in the journal entry at the bottom of page 656.

After posting the journal entry, the Goods in Process Inventory account will have a debit balance of $1,940 for materials requisitioned for Job Orders 102 to 105.

Goods in Process
Inventory account

Goods in Process Inventory   **No. 112**

| Nov. | 15 | Materials used | J1 | 1,940 | | 1,940 |

The amount debited to the Goods in Process Inventory account for materials used should agree with the amounts posted in the Materials column on all the job order cost sheets during the period.

Direct Labor Time Tickets

Recording the cost of direct labor on a job order cost sheet for each job or order is obtained from **direct labor time tickets** prepared by employees working on each job, the supervisor, or other authorized individuals. A separate time ticket is usually prepared on a daily basis for every employee working on a particular job showing the hours worked, hourly rate, and the amount. For example, if one or more employees work on Job Order 102 on November 1, a separate time ticket would be prepared for each employee.

The amounts shown on the time tickets for each job order are summarized and totaled periodically (usually weekly) and are entered on the job order cost sheet. To illustrate, the total amount for time ticket Nos. B12 to B16 from November 1 to November 5 for Job Order 102 were entered on the job order cost sheet for Custom Furniture Mart and shown in Figure 24-5.

At the end of each payroll period, the amounts on the time tickets are summarized and totaled to obtain the cost of direct labor. The total cost for direct labor is debited to Goods in Process Inventory and credited to Factory Payroll Payable. For example, the total cost of direct labor for Jobs 102 to 105 covering time ticket Nos. B12 to B30 dated November 1 to November 15 for Custom Furniture Mart amounted to $864. The Goods in Process Inventory account was debited and the Factory Payroll Payable account was credited for the $864 as shown in the following journal entry.

Direct labor applied
to production

Nov.	15	Goods in Process Inventory	864	
		Factory Payroll Payable		864
		To charge the amount of direct labor		
		for time ticket Nos. B12 to B30 dated		
		November 1 to November 15 for Jobs		
		102 to 105 to production.		

DAILY TIME

TICKET NO.: B12

Employee Name: _Swain Swanson_

DAILY TIME

TICKET NO.: B13

Employee Name: _Richard Horn_

No.: C

DAILY TIME

TICKET NO.: B14

Employee Name: _Sue Brownell_

No.: C

Amount

40.50

DAILY TIME

TICKET NO.: B15

Employee Name: _Bob Whitehall_

No.: C

Amount

64 —

DAILY TIME

TICKET NO.: B16

Employee Name: _Walter Zeda_

Employee No.: _217_   Date: _11-5_

Job Description: _upholstery_

Job Order No.: _102_   Department No.: _C_

No.: C

Amount

48 —

TIME				
Start	Stop	Total Hours	Hourly Rate	Amount
7	12	8 1/2	9 —	76.50
12:30	4			

Amount

35 —

Walter Zeda
Employee

J. Booker
Foreman

FIGURE 24-5

Time tickets used for recording direct labor on job order cost sheet

CUSTOM FURNITURE MART
JOB ORDER COST SHEET

Product: _Lawson Sofa_   Job Order No.: _102_

Product No.: _2840_   Quantity Ordered: _5_

Customer Name: _City Furniture Co._   Date Shipped: _____

Date Ordered: _10/15—_   Date Promised: _11/30/—_

Date Started: _11/1/—_   Date Completed: _____

	Materials		Labor		Overhead Applied		
Date	Req. No.	Amount	Time Ticket No.	Amount	Date	Rate	Amount
11/1	3447	$ 660					
11/5			B12–B16	$ 264			
11/12			B24–B30	450			
11/15	3448	200					
11/19			B40–B51	340			
11/26			B74–B78	250			
Total		$ 860		$1,304			

COST SUMMARY

Materials: _$ 860_

Labor: _1,304_

Overhead: _____

Total Cost: _____

Cost Per Unit: _____

After posting the journal entry, Goods in Process Inventory will have a debit balance of $2,804 ($1,940 for materials and $864 for direct labor) representing materials and direct labor applied to production for Jobs 102 to 105 as of November 15.

Goods in Process Inventory account

Goods in Process Inventory   **No. 112**

| Nov. | 15 | Materials used | J1 | 1,940 | | 1,940 |
| | 15 | Labor incurred | J1 | 864 | | 2,804 |

The amounts debited to Goods in Process Inventory for direct labor should agree with the amounts posted in the Labor column on all the job order cost sheets during the period.

Factory Overhead Costs

Factory overhead costs are difficult to determine at the time a job is completed or at the time a job is in the production process. All the overhead costs are not known at that time, because the bills for electricity, heat, taxes, etc., have not been received or determined. Also, overhead costs incurred for the period apply to all jobs in production and it may be difficult to determine the amount of overhead costs that apply to one particular job. Therefore, factory overhead costs for each job or order are usually recorded by using one of the following methods.

Methods for estimating overhead costs

1. Record factory overhead costs at the end of an accounting period when the actual costs are known. The total of actual overhead costs for a period would be allocated to the jobs in production or completed during the period and then recorded on each job order cost sheet. However, if this method is used, overhead costs could not be applied to each job until all costs are known and all bills have been received for utilities, taxes, etc.
2. Estimate the factory overhead costs based on previous periods and apply this estimate to the jobs in production during a cost period. If this method is used, overhead costs could be applied to each job as it is completed. A common method used for estimating overhead is to obtain a percentage of direct labor costs in relation to factory overhead costs. At the beginning of the production process, direct labor and factory overhead costs are estimated for the period. Estimated overhead costs are divided by estimated direct labor costs to obtain an estimated percentage of overhead costs for goods produced during the period. This estimated percentage is applied to the orders in production during the current cost period.

For example, assume that the estimated costs for factory overhead amounted to $50,000 and direct labor costs amounted to $100,000 for Custom Furniture Mart. The estimated percentage of factory overhead costs would amount to 50 percent of direct labor as shown on page 660.

$$\frac{\$50{,}000 \text{ estimated factory overhead costs}}{\$100{,}000 \text{ estimated direct labor costs}} = 50\%$$

COMPLETING THE JOB ORDER COST SHEET

When each job order is finished, the job order cost sheet is completed as follows:

Steps in completing job order cost sheet

1. Estimated factory overhead costs are recorded in the Overhead Applied section.
2. Materials and labor columns are totaled.
3. Column totals for materials, labor, and overhead applied are entered in the Cost Summary section.
4. The three cost elements in the Cost Summary section are added together to obtain the total cost of the completed job.
5. Cost per unit is determined by dividing the total cost by the number of units completed. The cost per unit is recorded as the last item in the Cost Summary section.

For example, Job Order 102 for Custom Furniture Mart was completed on November 30. The estimated factory overhead costs amounted to $652 ($1,304 × .50); 50 percent of the direct labor cost amounting to $1,304. Estimated factory overhead costs amounting to $652 was entered in the Overhead Applied section of the job order cost sheet. The columns were totaled, and the total amount of materials, labor, and overhead applied were entered in the Cost Summary section. The total cost and cost per unit for Job 102 was recorded in the Cost Summary section to complete the job order cost sheet as shown in Figure 24-6.

At the end of a cost period, a journal entry is recorded debiting Goods in Process Inventory and crediting Factory Overhead for 50 percent of the direct labor costs on all jobs, the estimated overhead applied to all jobs in process during the period. For example, the total amount of direct labor of Job Orders 102 to 105 for Custom Furniture Mart amounted to $2,734 for November. The Goods in Process Inventory account was debited and the Factory Overhead account was credited for $1,367 ($2,734 × .50); 50 percent of direct labor costs as shown in the following journal entry.

Overhead applied to production

Nov.	30	Goods in Process Inventory	1,367	
		Factory Overhead		1,367
		To apply overhead to Job Orders 102 to 105 based on 50 percent of direct labor costs amounting to $2,734.		

FIGURE 24-6

*Completed job order
cost sheet*

CUSTOM FURNITURE MART

JOB ORDER COST SHEET

Product: ___Lawson Sofa_____ Job Order No.: ___102_____

Product No.: ___2840_____ Quantity Ordered: ___5____

Customer Name: ___City Furniture Co._____ Date Shipped: ___11/30/—___

Date Ordered: ___10/15—_____ Date Promised: ___11/30/—___

Date Started: ___11/1/—_____ Date Completed: ___11/30/—___

	Materials		Labor		Overhead Applied		
Date	Req. No.	Amount	Time Ticket No.	Amount	Date	Rate	Amount
11/1	3447	$ 660			11/30	50% of	
11/5			B12–B16	$ 264		labor	$ 652
11/12			B24–B30	450			
11/15	3448	200					①
11/19			B40–B51	340			
11/26			B74–B78	250			
					COST SUMMARY		
					Materials:	$ 860	
					Labor:	1,304	③
					Overhead:	652	
Total		$ 860 ②		$1,304	Total Cost:	$2,816	④
					Cost Per Unit:	$ 563.20	⑤

After posting the journal entry, Goods in Process Inventory will have a debit balance of $6,411 ($1,940 + $370 = $2,310 for materials; $864 + $1,870 = $2,734 for direct labor, and $1,367 for factory overhead) for Job Orders 102 to 105 as shown below.

*Manufacturing costs
recorded in Goods in
Process Inventory*

Goods in Process Inventory   **No. 112**

Nov.	15	Materials used	J1	1,940	1,940
	15	Labor incurred	J1	864	2,804
	30	Materials used	J1	370	3,174
	30	Labor incurred	J1	1,870	5,044
	30	Overhead applied	J1	1,367	6,411

DISTRIBUTION OF COSTS ON JOB ORDER COST SHEET

After each job is completed, the costs accumulated on the job order cost sheet are totaled. The cost of producing one unit is determined and recorded on the job order cost sheet as shown in Figure 24-6 for Job Order 102.

The job order cost sheets may be used to determine:

1. Units completed and transferred to finished goods inventory
2. Goods in process inventory
3. Cost of goods sold and ending finished goods inventory

1. Cost of Units Completed and Transferred to Finished Goods Inventory. At the end of a cost period, the total amount of each job completed appears on the job order cost sheet. These completed job order cost sheets are used as the basis for debiting Finished Goods Inventory and crediting Goods in Process Inventory for the jobs completed and transferred out of the production process. For example, Jobs 102 and 103 were completed during November for Custom Furniture Mart at a total cost of $4,141 ($2,816 for Job 102 and $1,325 for Job 103). The entry for these two completed orders is shown in the following illustration.

Cost of jobs completed are debited to Finished Goods Inventory

Nov.	30	Finished Goods Inventory	4,141	
		Goods in Process Inventory		4,141
		To charge November costs of $2,816 for Job 102 and $1,325 for Job 103 to finished goods inventory.		

After posting the debit entry, Finished Goods Inventory will have a debit balance of $4,141 representing the cost of Jobs 102 and 103 as illustrated below.

Finished Goods Inventory as of November 30

Finished Goods Inventory No. 113

| Nov. | 30 | Jobs 102 & 103 | | J1 | 4,141 | | 4,141 |

After posting the credit entry, Goods in Process Inventory will have a debit balance of $2,270 on November 30 representing the costs incurred during November for Jobs 104 and 105. These two jobs are still in the production process because they are only partially completed as of November 30. The Goods in Process Inventory account is illustrated as follows:

Goods in Process Inventory
as of November 30

Goods in Process Inventory   No. 112

Nov.	15	Materials used	J1	1,940		1,940
	15	Labor incurred	J1	864		2,804
	30	Materials used	J1	370		3,174
	30	Labor incurred	J1	1,870		5,044
	30	Factory overhead	J1	1,367		6,411
	30	Jobs completed	J1		4,141	2,270

At the end of a cost period, the total amount of each job completed appearing on the job order cost sheets should agree with the cost of goods transferred to Finished Goods Inventory during the period. To illustrate, job order cost sheets for Jobs 102 and 103 and the ledger account for Goods in Process Inventory and Finished Goods Inventory are illustrated in Figure 24-7.

2. Goods in Process Inventory.   At the end of a cost period, the amounts appearing on the job order cost sheets for orders that have not been completed should agree with the balance in Goods in Process Inventory. For example, Job Orders 104 and 105 for Custom Furniture Mart were partially completed as of November 30, the end of the cost period. The amounts recorded for materials, direct labor, and factory overhead applied on these two partially completed job order cost sheets should agree with the balance shown in Goods in Process Inventory as shown in Figure 24-8.

3. Cost of Goods Sold and Ending Finished Goods Inventory.   Cost of goods sold may be obtained by totaling the amounts appearing on all the completed job order cost sheets for orders that have been delivered to customers. For example, Custom Furniture Mart completed Job Order 102 and delivered the five Lawson sofas ordered by City Furniture Company. The job order cost sheet for Job Order 102 shown in Figure 24-7 was used to record the cost of the sofas that were completed, sold, and delivered and to decrease the amount of the finished goods inventory. Cost of Goods Sold was debited and Finished Goods Inventory was credited for $2,816 (the cost of producing Job 102) as shown in the journal entry below.

Cost of completed job
debited to Cost of
Goods Sold

Nov.	30	Cost of Goods Sold	2,816	
		Finished Goods Inventory		2,816
		To charge cost of producing Job Order 102 to Cost of Goods Sold. The five Lawson sofas on Job Order 102 ordered by City Furniture Company were delivered today.		

FIGURE 24-7

CUSTOM FURNITURE MART
JOB ORDER COST SHEET

Product: Lawson Sofa   Job Order No.: 102
Product No.: 2840   Quantity Ordered: 5
Customer Name: City Furniture Co.   Date Shipped: 11/30/—
Date Ordered: 10/15—   Date Promised: 11/30/—
Date Started: 11/1/—   Date Completed: 11/30/—

| | Materials | | Labor | | Overhead Applied | | |
Date	Req. No.	Amount	Time Ticket No.	Amount	Date	Rate	Amount
11/1	3447	$ 660			11/30	50% of labor	$ 652
11/5			B12–B16	$ 264			
11/12			B24–B30	450			
11/15	3448	200					
11/19			B40–B51	340			
11/26			B74–B78	250			

COST SUMMARY
Materials: $ 860
Labor: 1,304
Overhead: 652

| | Total | $ 860 | | $1,304 | Total Cost: | $2,816 | |

Cost Per Unit: $ 563.20

CUSTOM FURNITURE MART
JOB ORDER COST SHEET

Product: Lounge Chairs   Job Order No.: 103
Product No.: 1201   Quantity Ordered: 10
Customer Name: Chairs, Inc.   Date Shipped:
Date Ordered: 10/29/—   Date Promised: 12/2/—
Date Started: 11/10/—   Date Completed: 11/25/—

| | Materials | | Labor | | Overhead Applied | | |
Date	Req. No.	Amount	Time Ticket No.	Amount	Date	Rate	Amount
11/10	3449	$ 320			11/30	50% of labor	$ 275
11/11			B17–B23	$ 150			
11/15	3450	180					
11/18			B31–B39	190			
11/25			B61–B73	210			

COST SUMMARY
Materials: $ 500
Labor: 550
Overhead: 275

| | Total | $ 500 | | $ 550 | Total Cost: | $1,325 | |

Cost Per Unit: $ 132.50

$2,816 + $1,325 = $4,141

Goods in Process Inventory			No. 112		
19–					
Nov.	15	Materials used	J1	1,940	1,940
	15	Labor incurred	J1	864	2,804
	30	Materials used	J1	370	3,174
	30	Labor incurred	J1	1,870	5,044
	30	Factory Overhead	J1	1,367	6,411
	30	Jobs completed	J1		4,141	2,270

Finished Goods Inventory			No. 113		
19–					
Nov.	30	Jobs 102 & 103	J1	4,141	4,141

After posting the journal entry, Finished Goods Inventory will show the balance as of November 30. Finished Goods Inventory for Custom Furniture Mart has an ending debit balance of $1,325. This balance represents the cost incurred for producing Job Order 103; a job that was started and completed in November but has not been delivered to the customer.

Finished Goods Inventory is credited when jobs are sold and delivered

Finished Goods Inventory					No. 113	
Nov.	30	Jobs 102 & 103	J1	4,141		4,141
	30	Sold Job 102	J1		2,816	1,325

FIGURE 24-8

CUSTOM FURNITURE MART
JOB ORDER COST SHEET

Product:	Sofabed	Job Order No.:	104
Product No.:	3840	Quantity Ordered:	10
Customer Name:	Sofa-Bed Company	Date Shipped:	
Date Ordered:	11/21/–	Date Promised:	12/15/–
Date Started:	11/15/–	Date Completed:	

| | Materials | | | Labor | | Overhead Applied | | |
Date	Req. No.	Amount	Time Ticket No.	Amount	Date	Rate	Amount
11/15	3451	$ 580			11/30	50% of	
11/22			B52–B60	$ 420		labor	$ 315
11/23	3452	120					
11/29			B79–B84	210			
Total							

COST SUMMARY
Materials:
Labor:
Overhead:
Total Cost:
Cost Per Unit:

CUSTOM FURNITURE MART
JOB ORDER COST SHEET

Product:	Bar Stools	Job Order No.:	105
Product No.:	81–	Quantity Ordered:	12
Customer Name:	Stools & Accessories	Date Shipped:	
Date Ordered:	11/24/–	Date Promised:	12/22/–
Date Started:	11/29/–	Date Completed:	

| | Materials | | | Labor | | Overhead Applied | | |
Date	Req. No.	Amount	Time Ticket No.	Amount	Date	Rate	Amount
11/29	3453	$ 150			11/30	50% of	
11/30			B85–B90	$ 250		labor	$ 125
11/30	3454	100					
Total							

COST SUMMARY
Materials:
Labor:
Overhead:
Total Cost:
Cost Per Unit:

($700 + $630 + $315)

$1,645

+

($250 + $250 + $125)

$625 = $2,270

Goods in Process Inventory No. 112						
19–						
Nov.	15	Materials used	J1	1,940		1,940
	15	Labor incurred	J1	864		2,804
	30	Materials used	J1	370		3,174
	30	Labor incurred	J1	1,870		5,044
	30	Factory Overhead	J1	1,367		6,411
	30	Jobs completed	J1		4,141	2,270

SUMMARY OF JOB ORDER COST PROCEDURE

Six steps in job order cost procedure

Six steps in the job order cost procedure are summarized below.

1. Record cost of materials for each job order from material requisitions to the job order cost sheets.

FIGURE 24-9

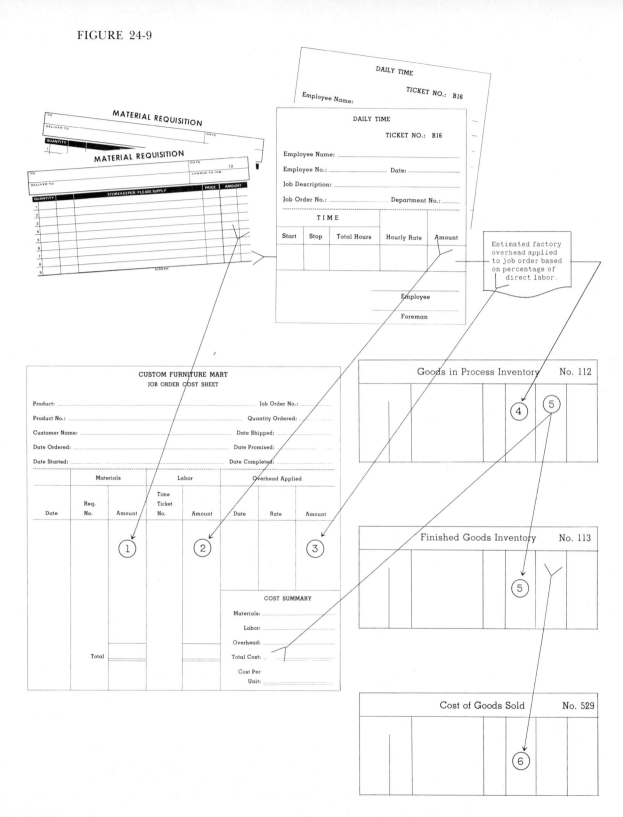

2. Record cost of direct labor charged to each job order from time tickets to the job order cost sheets.
3. Apply factory overhead to each job order based on a predetermined percentage of direct labor costs to the job order cost sheets.
4. Charge direct materials, direct labor, and factory overhead costs from material requisitions, time tickets, and job order cost sheets to Goods in Process Inventory.
5. Record cost of all jobs completed during period to Finished Goods Inventory and decrease Goods in Process Inventory.
6. Decrease Finished Goods Inventory for all orders sold and delivered during period and charge the costs of producing orders to Cost of Goods Sold.

These six steps are illustrated in Figure 24-9.

SUMMARY

Cost accounting is an accounting system designed to control and determine the unit costs of goods manufactured and the cost of goods sold. There are two types of cost accounting systems; one is called a job order cost system, and the other is called a process cost system. Both systems require the use of a perpetual inventory system for maintaining inventories and for determining unit costs of direct materials, direct labor, and factory overhead.

A job order cost accounting system may be used by companies that manufacture a product according to the specifications of an order received from customers. However, a company may use a job order cost system when they produce different products for their inventory in anticipation of receiving future orders from customers. Costs of producing a product is based on a particular job or an order received from a customer. A job order cost system may be used by a furniture company, cabinet maker, or an automobile manufacturer that makes furniture, cabinets, or automobiles according to the specifications received from a customer.

A job order cost sheet is prepared for each job or order received from a customer. These job order cost sheets serve as a subsidiary ledger for goods in process inventory and cost of goods sold.

Material requisitions are prepared for each type of direct material used in the production process and time tickets are prepared for the employees that work on producing the product. These material requisitions and direct labor time tickets are used as the basis for recording the cost of direct materials and direct labor on the job order cost sheets and for debiting the materials and direct labor costs to the Goods in Process Inventory account. Factory overhead costs are usually estimated and applied at the end of a cost period or when a job is completed. The estimate for factory overhead costs is recorded on the job order cost sheet. When a job is completed, the job order cost sheet is used as the basis for debiting Finished Goods Inventory and crediting Goods in Process Inventory for the goods transferred out of the production process. Job order cost sheets may be used to determine the cost of goods that have been sold and delivered to customers.

GLOSSARY

Cost Accounting: An accounting system designed to control and determine the unit costs of goods manufactured and the cost of goods sold.

Direct Labor Time Tickets: A form used to record the hours worked, hourly rate, and the amount of labor incurred by employees working on each job order. A separate time ticket is usually prepared daily for each employee. The amounts shown on the time tickets for each job order are summarized and totaled periodically (usually weekly) and are entered on the job order cost sheet. They are also used as the basis for debiting Goods in Process for the direct labor incurred during a cost period.

Job Order Cost Sheet: A special ledger card prepared for each job or order received. All direct materials, direct labor, and factory overhead costs incurred in producing each job or order are accumulated and recorded on a job order cost sheet. A job order cost sheet has a Cost Summary section which shows the total cost and unit cost of producing an order.

Job Order Cost System: A cost system used by companies that manufacture a product according to the specifications of an order received from customers. The cost of producing a product is based on a particular job or an order received from a customer. A job order cost system may be used by a furniture company, cabinet maker, or an automobile manufacturer that makes furniture, cabinets, or automobiles according to the specifications received from a customer.

Material Requisition: A form that is issued whenever material is needed for use in the factory operations. These requisitions show the type of material needed, quantity, and job order number. They are also used as the basis for recording the cost of materials used on each job or order on the respective job order cost sheet. They are also used as the basis for debiting Goods in Process Inventory for the materials used in production and to credit Materials Inventory to show the decrease in the amount of materials on hand.

Materials Ledger Card: A subsidiary ledger containing a separate record for each type of material used in producing a product. All the material purchased, requisitioned for production, and the balance on hand is recorded on a materials ledger card.

QUESTIONS

1. What is the purpose for installing a cost accounting system and what are the names of the two types of cost accounting systems?

2. What is the name of the report that is used to accumulate the direct materials, direct labor, and factory overhead costs for a job order cost system?
3. There are two specific forms used as the basis for charging the goods in process inventory for the direct materials and direct labor incurred for jobs or orders received from customers. What are the names of the forms used for (a) materials and (b) direct labor?
4. What accounts are debited and credited when a job or order is completed in the production process?
5. What is the name of the subsidiary ledger that contains a separate record for each type of material used in producing a product?
6. Give a brief definition of (a) a job order cost accounting system, (b) a materials ledger card, (c) a material requisition, and (d) a labor time ticket.
7. List the six steps in a job order cost procedure.

EXERCISES

Determining Ending Balance of Direct Materials

1. A materials ledger card for material P had a beginning balance of 100 units with a unit price of $4. Purchases for October amounted to 50 units at $4.10 each and 60 units at $4.15 each. Material requisitioned for production amounted to 110 units.

Required

Determine the quantity, unit price, and value of the ending inventory for material P using the FIFO method of inventory valuation.

Determining Cost of Materials Requisitioned for Production

2. Material ordered on material requisition No. 128 for the Planning Department of Brutte Products is given below:

18 feet	2 × 5 pine	@$1.10 per foot
20 rolls	Product C	@$4.80 per roll
16 boxes	Halfpenny nails	@$0.90 per box
48 yards	Cheesecloth	@$0.20 per yard

Required

Determine the total cost of material ordered on requisition No. 128.

Determining Unit Cost and Total Cost of Production

3. Frontier Furniture Company manufactured kitchen furniture according to the specifications of the customer. An order was received for six 5-piece

kitchen sets. Material requisitions amounted to $360, direct labor time tickets amounted to $800, and factory overhead was applied at the rate of 65 percent of direct labor costs.

Required

(*a*) Determine the total cost of producing the six kitchen sets

(*b*) Determine the unit cost of producing one kitchen set

Journal Entries for Cost and Sale of Merchandise to Customer

4. A furniture company sold six kitchen sets for $2,100 on account. The cost of manufacturing the kitchen sets amounted to $360 for materials, $800 for direct labor, and $520 for factory overhead.

Required

Journalize the entries required for the cost and sale of the six kitchen sets. Use February for the month and date the entries consecutively.

Completion of Materials Ledger Card and Material Requisition

5. Complete the following forms: (*a*) materials ledger card using the FIFO method and (*b*) the materials requisition by filling in the missing figures for items a to e.

MATERIALS LEDGER CARD

No.: 28   Description: Material X102 Plastic

Supplier: Plastic Products   Reorder Amount: 100, 50 ft. rolls

Date	Ref.	Purchases Units	Unit Price	Total	Requisitions Units	Unit Price	Total	Balance on Hand Units	Unit Price	Total
19–										
Jan. 1								90	$ 95	a) $ ___
3		30	$100	$3,000				90	b) ___	8,550
								30		100	c) ___
4					20	d) $___	e) $___	70	f) ___	g) ___
								30	h) ___	i) ___

MATERIAL REQUISITION

TO				DATE		
Materials Storeroom				February 2, 19—		
DELIVER TO				CHARGE TO JOB		
Department A				260		

QUANTITY			STOREKEEPER: PLEASE SUPPLY	PRICE	AMOUNT	
1	42	rolls	Material No. 24	$8.00	a) $	
2	16	yds.	Material Y46	b)	24	00
3	6	bxs.	Bolts, No. 28	1.30	c)	
4	100	ft.	2 x 6 Pine	d)	120	00
5						
6			TOTAL		e) $	
7						
8						
9			SIGNED			

Computation of Jobs Completed and Goods in Process Inventory

6. Century Desk Company had four jobs in production during the current month. Three jobs were 100 percent completed and one job was 75 percent completed at the end of the month. Data concerning the four jobs is shown below:

Job No.	Material Cost	Direct Labor Cost	Factory Overhead Cost
68	$120	$360	80% of direct labor
69	60	120	80% of direct labor
70	90	270	80% of direct labor
71	220	660	80% of direct labor

Jobs 68, 69, and 71 were completed during the month.

Required

(a) Compute the cost of jobs completed and transferred to the finished goods inventory.

(b) Compute the cost of goods in process at the end of the month.

Matching Cost Accounting Terms with Definitions

7. Match the items in column A with the items in column B shown on page 672.

Column A	Column B
_____ (a) Report showing cost of producing a job order	1. Goods in process inventory
_____ (b) Account debited for overhead costs applied to production	2. Job order cost sheet
_____ (c) Last item on job order cost sheet	3. Material requisition
_____ (d) Form used as basis for recording direct labor incurred	4. Materials ledger card
_____ (e) Form used to order material for production	5. Time tickets
_____ (f) Subsidiary ledger containing a separate record for each type of material used in production	6. Cost per unit

PROBLEMS

Materials Ledger Card and Journal Entry Requisitioning Material for Production

24-1. Requisitions for material X100 and material L802 are given below.

Material X100 with a Unit Price of $0.70 Each

Date	Requisition Number	Quantity
3/1	R101	20
3/5	R106	12
3/9	R102	18
3/14	R128	31
3/22	R121	6
3/31	R142	22

Material L802 with a Unit Price of $0.10 Each

Date	Requisition Number	Quantity
5/2	P28	30
5/8	P41	10
5/15	P62	45
5/22	P64	120
5/28	P81	210

Required

(a) Prepare a materials ledger card for March for material X100 that had 220 units on hand on March 1 and the supplier is the Hood Corporation.

(b) Prepare a materials ledger card for May for material L802 that had 590 units on hand on May 1 and the supplier is the Macy Company.

(c) Journalize the entry to transfer material X100 and material L802 to production.

Material Requisition

24-2. The supervisor, Amos Wheaton, in the assembly department of Woodcraft Sales requisitioned the following materials for production:

Material Requisition No. 3442 Dated April 4 of the Current Year for Job No. 26

Quantity	Material	Unit Price
12 yards	MC 40	$1.50 yard
10 boxes	No. 12 Screws	2.10 box
150 feet	2 × 4 Lumber	0.80 foot

Material Requisition No. 3443 Dated April 5 of the Current Year for Job No. 28

Quantity	Material	Unit Price
220 feet	1 × 6 Lumber	$1.10 foot
12 cases	A 64	8.20 case
31 boxes	No. 24 Screws	6.50 box
15 quarts	CM 8	4.50 quart

Required

Prepare a material requisition for No. 3442 and No. 3443.

Job Order Cost Sheet and Journal Entries

24-3. Montcalm Tool Company installed a job order cost accounting system for maintaining the cost of orders received from customers. During January, six orders were received and put into production. Job 5 for 900 claw hammers No. 690L ordered by M & L Company was received on January 6, started on January 7, promised for delivery on February 2, and completed on January 31. The following costs were incurred during January for job 5: January 7, material requisition Nos. A12 to A16, $126; January 31, direct labor time ticket Nos. 20 to 32, $360; and factory overhead applied on January 31 amounted to 120 percent of direct labor costs.

Required

(a) Prepare a job order cost sheet (Figure 24-1) for Job 5.

(b) Prepare journal entries required during January for Job 5.

(c) Prepare journal entry required on February 1 to record the cost for sale of Job 5.

24-4. Curly Hair Company maintained a job order cost system for all orders received for special wigs and hair pieces. Information relating to Job Order No. 56 received from Bentler Sales on May 1 of the current year for 100 Montclair Wigs, No. 26N is given below.

Materials Requisitioned for Production	Direct Labor Time Tickets
5/3 Req. No. 120-128, $160	5/3 B12-14, $320
5/10 Req. No. 162-169, $340	5/10 B20-23, $100
	5/17 B36-43, $400
	5/24 B61-69, $280

Factory Overhead Applied
5/25 150 percent of direct labor costs

Additional Data

Job Order No. 56 was promised for delivery on May 28; order was completed on May 25 and shipped on May 27.

Required

(*a*) Prepare a job order cost sheet.
(*b*) Prepare the journal entries required for May.

Determining Manufacturing Costs and Ending Goods in Process and Finished Goods Inventory

24-5. Custom Auto Company produced cars with special equipment and accessories according to the customer's specifications. On June 1 of the current year, Job No. 160 was in the finished goods inventory at a cost of $26,500. During June, four orders were received from car dealers, and two orders were completed by June 29. Costs for June pertaining to these four orders are shown below.

Job Order No.	Material	Direct Labor
161	$ 8,400	$16,600
162	9,100	12,900
163	6,600	10,400
164	10,800	22,200

Additional Data

Factory overhead was applied on the basis of 75 percent of direct labor costs; Jobs 161 and 163 were completed on June 29; Job 160 was shipped on June 10; and Job 161 was shipped on June 30 to the customer.

Required

(a) Determine the total cost of materials, direct labor, and factory overhead applied during June for Jobs 161 to 164.

(b) Determine the total cost of orders transferred to the finished goods inventory on June 29.

(c) Compute the cost of goods in process inventory on June 30.

(d) Compute the cost of finished goods inventory on June 30.

24-6. Baby Furniture Company manufactured custom baby furniture and used a job order cost accounting system. On July 1 of the current year, Job 49 was in process partially completed at a material cost of $200 and direct labor cost of $140, and Job 46 in the beginning finished goods inventory cost $640. During July, Jobs 50, 51, and 52 were received and Jobs 49 and 51 were completed. Costs for July are shown below.

Job Order No.	Material	Direct Labor
49	$210	$300
50	290	160
51	490	660
52	320	280

Additional Data

Factory overhead was applied on the basis of 125 percent of direct labor costs; Job 46 was shipped to the customer on July 3; and Jobs 49 and 51 were to be shipped to customers in August.

Required

Determine the following:

(a) Total cost of Job 51

(b) Total cost of Job 49

(c) Cost of goods in process inventory on July 31

(d) Cost of finished goods inventory on July 31

Review of Journal Entries, Job Order Cost Sheet, and Ending Finished Goods Inventory

24-7. Rawley Company manufactured booths for restaurants according to the specifications of orders received from customers. A job order cost system for the special orders was installed. Information pertaining to the job order cost system is given below.

During February, Job Order No. 129 was started but it was not completed by February 28. The total cost of Job Order No. 129 for February amounted to $2,090 (materials, $1,100; direct labor, $550; and overhead, $440). On March 1 there was a beginning balance of $6,200 in finished goods inventory for Job Order No. 128.

During March, the following selected transactions occurred:

Mar. 1 Materials were requisitioned as follows: Job 129, Req. No. 92, $400; Job 130, Req. No. 93, $940; and Job 131, Req. No. 94, $820.

6 Applied direct labor costs of $1,500 to production for the following job orders: No. 129, time ticket Nos. C84 to C86, $700; No. 130, time ticket No. C87, $500; and No. 131, time ticket No. C88, $300.

13 Applied direct labor costs of $600 to production for the following job orders: No. 129, time ticket Nos. C89 to C91, $200; No. 130, time ticket Nos. C92 and C93, $300; and No. 131, time ticket No. C94, $100.

16 Materials were requisitioned for production as follows: Job 131, Req. No. 97, $900.

20 Applied overhead to production based on 80 percent of direct labor costs.

20 Completed Job Order Nos. 129 and 130.

25 Shipped Job Order Nos. 128 and 129 to customers. (Journalize entry for cost of job order Nos. 128 and 129; assume journal entry for the sale has already been recorded.)

Required

(a) Journalize the entries for March.

(b) Prepare a job order cost sheet for Job Order No. 131, Product No. B200 for 40 booths. Job Order No. 131 was ordered by Taylor's Restaurant on February 28 and delivery was promised on April 10.

(c) Determine the cost of the finished goods inventory on March 31.

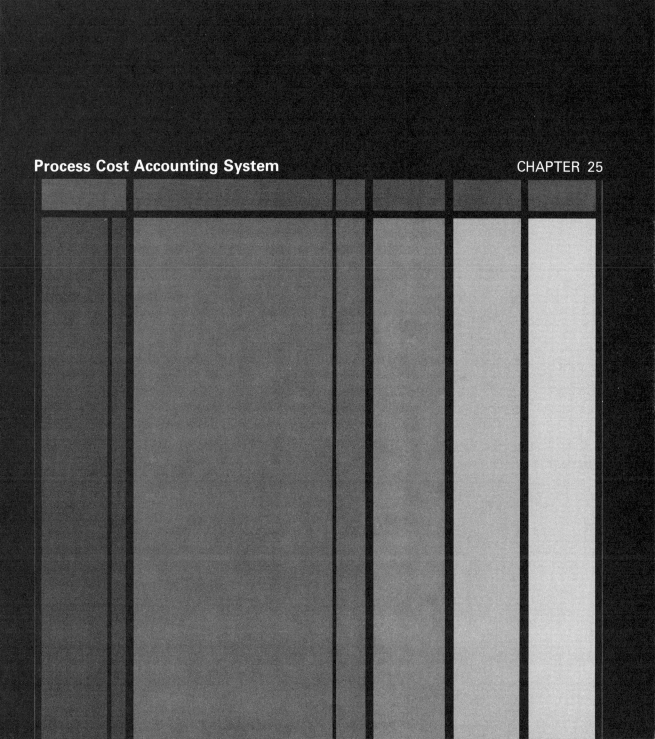

Process Cost Accounting System

After completing this chapter, you should be able to:

1. **Give a brief description of a process cost accounting system**

2. **Compute the equivalent units of production**

3. **Determine the unit costs for direct materials, direct labor, and factory overhead**

4. **Compute the cost of units completed and transferred to the finished goods inventory, cost of goods sold, and cost of the ending goods in process inventory**

5. **Prepare the basic journal entries for a process cost accounting system**

A *process cost system* is an accounting system that a company may use when it produces a single type of product or similar types of products for its inventory in anticipation of receiving future orders. In a process cost system, (1) the production process is continuous, (2) orders received from customers are filled from the finished goods inventory, and (3) the costs of production are based on the total costs incurred in each department of the production process. Whereas, in a job order cost system, (1) the production process is not started until an order is received from a customer, (2) orders are shipped to customers when the job is completed, and (3) the production costs are based on the costs incurred in producing each order received from a customer.

If a product goes through several departments in the production process, the costs of direct materials, direct labor, and factory overhead are recorded in a goods in process inventory account that is maintained for each department. For example, if a sewing manufacturing company produced shower curtains that required the material to be cut, sewn, sorted, and assembled, it would maintain three separate goods in process inventory accounts, one for each department. There would be a goods in process inventory account to record the costs of direct materials, direct labor, and factory overhead for the cutting department, sewing department, and assembly department. When the material is cut, the costs of the cutting department are transferred to the sewing department; when the sewing is completed on the curtains, the costs are transferred to the assembly department. When the curtains are sorted and boxed in the assembly department, the costs are transferred to the Finished Goods Inventory account until they are sold. When the curtains are sold, the costs are transferred from the Finished Goods Inventory account to the Cost of Goods Sold account as shown in the diagram in Figure 25-1.

Unit costs for each product produced during a period are determined by totaling the costs of direct materials, direct labor, and factory overhead for each department in the production process and dividing the total of these three elements of production by the number of units produced. A

FIGURE 25-1

*Flow of costs diagram for
process cost system*

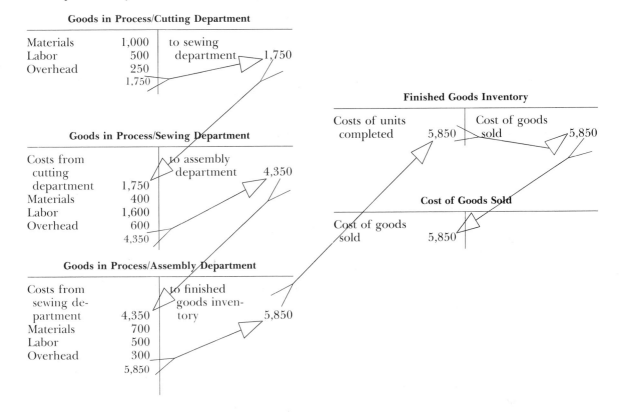

process cost system may be used by a company producing flour, sugar, steel, cement, rubber, paper, etc.

EQUIVALENT UNITS OF PRODUCTION

When the production process of a manufacturing company is continuous, there usually will be some products in production at the end of an accounting period that are partially completed. These partially finished products in process at the end of an accounting period plus the number of products that were started and completed are added together to determine the number of units produced. To obtain the number of units produced, it is necessary to determine the equivalent units of production. ***Equivalent units of production*** is an estimate of the number of units that would have been finished if all the units that were started during a period were completed by the end of the period. For example, if 100 units were put into the production process during the period and by the end of the period they were 40 percent completed, these 100 partially finished units would be equivalent to 40 (100 × .40) completed units; 40 units that could have been started and completed during the period. If these 100 units were 75 percent completed, they would be equivalent to 75 (100 × .75) completed units, etc.

When computing equivalent units of production, the equivalent units for the beginning and ending goods in process are added to the number of units that were started and completed during the period to obtain the total equivalent units as shown in the following three steps.

Three steps for computing equivalent units of production

1. Start with the number of units in the beginning goods in process inventory that must be completed in the current period (number of units in beginning goods in process inventory multiplied by the percentage that must be completed during the current period).
2. ADD: Number of units started and completed during the current period (number of units completed less number of units in the beginning goods in process inventory).
3. ADD: Number of equivalent units in the ending goods in process inventory (number of units in ending goods in process inventory multiplied by the percentage completed by end of current period).
EQUALS Equivalent units of production

To illustrate, assume that Michigan Company had 1,000 units in the beginning goods in process inventory that were 30 percent completed; 10,000 units that were completed during the current period; and 500 units that were in the ending goods in process inventory 60 percent completed. The equivalent units of production amounted to 10,000 units as computed below.

Computation of equivalent units of production

1. 1,000 units in beginning goods in process × 70 percent (100 percent − 30 percent completed in prior period) = 700
2. 10,000 units completed − 1,000 units in beginning goods in process inventory = 9,000
3. 500 units in ending goods in process inventory × 60 percent (percentage completed during current period) = 300
EQUALS Equivalent units of production = 10,000

In the previous example, it was assumed that materials, direct labor, and factory overhead costs for the beginning and ending goods in process inventory were applied evenly throughout the production process, and the products were all at the same level (percentage) of completion at the end of the period. For example, each time material was added to production, it was assumed that an equal amount of direct labor and factory overhead costs were added. Usually, however, the three elements of production are not applied in equal amounts during the production process. As the product is being processed, material may be added evenly throughout the production process, all the material may be added at the beginning of the production process, or various amounts of material may be added at different intervals (30 percent at the beginning, 30 percent when the product is 25 percent completed, etc.) and labor may be applied evenly throughout the production process. It is assumed that whenever direct labor costs are applied to production an equal amount of factory overhead costs are applied. Therefore, if materials, direct labor, and factory overhead are not applied evenly throughout the production process, the three elements of production will not be the same as they will be at different levels (percentages) of completion. For example, assume that the Michigan Company had:

1. 1,000 partially finished units on hand at the beginning of a period that were 60 percent complete as to materials and 30 percent complete as to direct labor and factory overhead
2. 10,000 units complete at the end of the period
3. 500 units in the ending goods in process inventory that were 90 percent complete as to materials and 60 percent complete as to direct labor and factory overhead

The equivalent units of production for materials would amount to 9,850 units and 10,000 units for direct labor and factory overhead computed as follows:

Equivalent units for materials, labor, and overhead

	Materials	Labor and Overhead
1. Beginning Goods in Process Inventory:		
1,000 units × 40 percent (100 percent − 60 percent completed in prior period) completed as to materials =	400	
1,000 units × 70 percent (100 percent − 30 percent completed in prior period) completed as to labor and overhead =		700
2. Units Started and Completed in Current Period:		
10,000 units − 1,000 units (beginning goods in process inventory) that were 100 percent completed as to materials, labor, and overhead	9,000	9,000
3. Ending Goods in Process Inventory:		
500 units × 90 percent complete as to materials =	450	
500 units × 60 percent complete as to labor and overhead =		300
Equivalent units of production =	9,850	10,000

UNIT COSTS

To calculate the cost of the ending goods in process and finished goods inventory plus the cost of the goods that were sold, the unit costs for materials, direct labor, and factory overhead are determined first. Determining the unit costs for materials, direct labor, and factory overhead for each department of the production process, the total costs of a period for each element of production is divided by its corresponding equivalent units of production. For example, assume that Michigan Company incurred costs of $19,700 for materials, $32,500 for direct labor, and $17,500 for factory overhead. The unit costs for each of the three elements of production is computed as follows:

Unit costs for materials, labor, and overhead

1. Raw material unit cost: $\dfrac{\$19,700}{9,850 \text{ equivalent units}}$ = $2.00

2. Direct labor unit cost: $\dfrac{\$32,500}{10,000 \text{ equivalent units}}$ = 3.25

3. Factory overhead unit cost: $\dfrac{\$17,500}{10,000 \text{ equivalent units}}$ = 1.75

Unit cost of producing one equivalent unit of product $7.00

COST OF ENDING GOODS IN PROCESS INVENTORY

After computing the equivalent units of production and the unit cost of a product, it is easy to calculate the cost of the ending goods in process inventory. The number of equivalent units for materials, direct labor, and factory overhead in the ending goods in process inventory is multiplied by its unit cost. The total of these three elements of production multiplied by the number of equivalent units in the ending goods in process inventory equals the cost of the ending goods in process inventory as illustrated for Michigan Company.

Computation of ending goods in process inventory

Element of Production	Number of Equivalent Units in Ending Goods in Process Inventory	× Unit Cost =	Total Unit Cost
Material (500 × 90 percent)	450	× $2.00 =	$ 900
Direct Labor (500 × 60 percent)	300	× 3.25 =	975
Factory Overhead (500 × 60 percent)	300	× 1.75 =	525
Cost of 500 Units in Ending Goods in Process Inventory			$2,400

COST OF GOODS TRANSFERRED TO FINISHED GOODS INVENTORY

There are two steps for computing the cost of the goods that are completed in the production process during a period. First, the cost of the units that are partially finished in the beginning goods in process inventory are added to the cost of completing these units during the current period. Second, the cost of the goods that were started and completed during the current period is determined. These two costs are added together to obtain the cost of the goods that were transferred to the finished goods inventory. For example, assume that costs of $2,600 were incurred by Michigan Company during the previous period for 1,000 units that were partially finished. The costs of completing these 1,000 partially finished units that were on hand at the beginning of the current period plus 9,000 additional units that were started and completed is computed as follows:

Cost of completing the beginning goods in process inventory

1. Costs incurred in previous period for the 1,000 partially finished units on hand at the beginning of period .... $ 2,600
2. ADD: Cost of completing the 1,000 partially finished units:
   Materials: 400 (1,000 × 40 percent) × $2.00 unit cost .... = $ 800
   Labor & Overhead: 700 (1,000 × 70 percent) × $5.00 ($3.25 + $1.75) unit cost .... = 3,500 ... 4,300
3. Cost to produce the 1,000 units .... $ 6,900
4. ADD: Cost to produce the 9,000 units (10,000 finished − 1,000 in beginning goods in process) started and completed during current period, 9,000 × $7.00 unit cost 63,000
   Cost to produce 10,000 units $69,900
5. Unit cost of one completed unit: $\dfrac{\$69,900}{10,000 \text{ units}}$ .... $ 6.99

COST OF GOODS SOLD AND COST OF ENDING FINISHED GOODS INVENTORY

When determining the cost of goods sold and cost of the ending finished goods inventory, consideration must be given to the cost of goods available for sale. To obtain the cost of goods available for sale, the cost of the beginning inventory and units completed during the period are added together. For example, assume that Michigan Company had 2,000 units in their beginning inventory that cost $6.50 for each unit produced, a total cost of $13,000 (2,000 × $6.50). During the current period, 10,000 units were completed and transferred to finished goods at a unit cost of $6.99 each, a total cost of $69,900 (10,000 × $6.99). The beginning inventory of 2,000 units plus the 10,000 units completed amounted to 12,000 units available at a total cost of $82,900 ($13,000 + $69,900).

To determine the cost of the ending finished goods inventory, cost of goods sold is subtracted from the cost of goods available for sale. For example, assume that Michigan Company sold 9,000 units and used the first in, first out (FIFO) method[1] of inventory valuation. The cost of goods sold and cost of the ending finished goods inventory amounted to $61,930 and $20,790 respectively as illustrated below.

Computation of cost of goods sold and finished goods inventory

	Units	Unit Cost	Total Cost
Beginning finished goods inventory	2,000	$6.50	$13,000
Units completed during period	10,000	6.99	69,900
Units available for sale	12,000		$82,900
Less sale of 9,000 units using FIFO method:			
Units from beginning inventory	2,000	6.50	$13,000
Units from completed units during period	7,000	6.99	48,930
Cost of Goods Sold	9,000		$61,930
Ending Finished Goods Inventory	3,000	6.99	$20,970

PRODUCTION COST REPORT

All the cost information obtained during a period for a company using a process cost system may be shown on a *production cost report.* This report contains the equivalent units of production, unit costs for direct materials, direct labor, and factory overhead, and the cost of the ending goods in process and finished goods inventories. To illustrate, the production cost report for Michigan Company for the month ended January 31, 19__ is illustrated in Figure 25-2. Note that in the first section of the report, it shows the total units and the total costs of these units to be accounted for during the month. The next section contains the unit costs, costs incurred during the period, and how these costs were charged to the goods in process and finished goods inventory. This illustration assumes that the product is started and completed in one department; however, if the production process required more than one department, a production cost report is usually prepared for each department.

JOURNAL ENTRIES FOR FLOW OF COSTS

A process cost system requires a perpetual inventory system for maintaining the materials, goods in process, and finished goods inventories. If the production process requires the product to be processed through several departments before it is completed, a separate Goods in Process Inventory account is maintained for each department. A subsidiary ledger, similar to the Accounts Receivable and Accounts Payable customer and creditor ledger, is usually maintained for the different materials used in the manufacturing process and for the various manufacturing overhead accounts.

Whenever direct materials, direct labor, and factory overhead is applied to the units in production, the Goods in Process Inventory account is

[1] A method that assumes that the first units produced are the first units sold.

FIGURE 25-2

Production cost report

MICHIGAN COMPANY
PRODUCTION COST REPORT
For Month Ended January 31, 19__

Units in Process:

Goods in Process 1/1	1,000
Units Started during Period	9,500
Total Units in Process	10,500

Units Accounted for:

Completed units	10,000
Goods in Process 1/31	500
Total Units Accounted for	10,500

Equivalent Units of Production:

	Materials	Labor & Overhead
Goods in Process 1/1:		
1,000 × 40%	400	
1,000 × 70%		700
Units Started and Completed	9,000	9,000
Goods in Process 1/31:		
500 × 90%	450	
500 × 60%		300
Equivalent Units	9,850	10,000

Costs to Be Accounted for:

	Materials	Labor & Overhead
Goods in Process 1/1		$ 2,600
Costs during period:		
Materials	$19,700	
Direct Labor	32,500	
Factory Overhead	17,500	69,700
Total Costs to Be Accounted for		$72,300

Unit Cost of Product:

Materials: $19,700/9,850	$2.00
Labor: $32,500/10,000	3.25
Overhead: $17,500/10,000	1.75
Total Unit Cost	$7.00

Costs Charged to Finished Units:

	Materials	Labor & Overhead
Cost to complete 1,000 units in process 1/1:		
Beginning Costs:	$ 2,600	
Materials: 400 × $2	800	
Labor & Overhead: 700 × $5	3,500	$ 6,900
Cost of units started and completed:		
9,000 × $7		63,000
Cost of 10,000 units finished		$69,900
Unit cost of 10,000 units (69,900/10,000)	$6.99	

Costs Charged to 500 units in Goods in Process 1/31:

	Materials	Labor & Overhead
Materials: 450 × $2.00	$ 900	
Labor: 300 × 3.25	975	
Overhead: 300 × 1.75	525	2,400
Total Costs Accounted for		$72,300

Journal entries to show flow of production costs

1. Materials used in the production process are purchased on account.

Materials Inventory	30,000	
Accounts Payable		30,000

Materials purchased for the production process.

2. Direct and indirect materials are requisitioned for production.

Goods in Process Inventory	19,700	
Factory Overhead	3,000	
Materials Inventory		22,700

Materials requisitioned for production.

3. Direct labor and indirect labor was incurred.

Goods in Process Inventory	32,500	
Factory Overhead	10,000	
Factory Payroll Payable		42,500

To record factory payroll costs incurred for direct and indirect labor.

4. Actual factory overhead costs were incurred.

Factory Overhead	4,500	
Various Accounts		4,500

To record actual factory overhead costs incurred during period.

5. Applied factory overhead costs to production.

Goods in Process Inventory	17,500	
Factory Overhead		17,500

To apply overhead costs to 10,000 units in production based on a cost of $1.75 for each unit.

6. Completed 10,000 units and transferred them to the finished goods warehouse.

Finished Goods Inventory	69,900	
Goods in Process Inventory		69,900

Transferred 10,000 units with a unit cost of $6.99 to finished goods warehouse.

7. Sold 9,000 units on account.

Accounts Receivable	80,000
Cost of Goods Sold	61,930
Sales	80,000
Finished Goods Inventory	61,930

To record sale of 9,000 units for $80,000
that cost $6.50 each for 2,000 units and
$6.99 each for 7,000 units.

debited and the Materials Inventory, Direct Labor, and Factory Overhead accounts are credited. When the units in the manufacturing process are completed, the Finished Goods Inventory account is debited and the Goods in Process Inventory account is credited. Whenever the product is sold, the Cost of Goods Sold account is debited and the Finished Goods Inventory account is credited. Therefore, the amount of the ending inventory for Materials, Goods in Process, and Finished Goods Inventory would be the balance remaining in these accounts.

Journal entries to show the flow of costs through the perpetual inventory accounts are shown below. For simplification, the journal entries for the period are recorded in one entry for each cost element although they are usually journalized whenever material is purchased or requisitioned for production and at the end of each payroll period.

After posting these entries to the three inventory accounts in the general ledger, the accounts will have the following balances. (*Note:* The entry numbers are placed in the date column.)

Title: Materials Inventory **Account No. 111**

Date		Explanation	Ref.	Debit	Credit	Balance
19__ Entry	1		J1	30,000		30,000
	2		J1		22,700	7,300

Title: Goods in Process Inventory **Account No. 112**

Date		Explanation	Ref.	Debit	Credit	Balance
19__ Jan.	1	Balance	✓			2,600
Entry	2		J1	19,700		22,300
	3		J1	32,500		54,800
	5		J1	17,500		72,300
	6		J1		69,900	2,400

Title: Finished Goods Inventory   **Account No. 113**

Date		Explanation	Ref.	Debit	Credit	Balance
19__ Jan.	1	Balance	✓			13,000
Entry	6		J1	69,900		82,900
	7		J1		61,930	20,970

SUMMARY

A process cost system may be used by a company that produces one type of product or similar types of products for inventory in anticipation of receiving future orders. The production process is continuous and orders received from customers are filled from the finished goods inventory. Therefore, the cost of production is based on the total costs of each department in the production process. Whereas, in a job order cost system, the costs of production are based on the costs incurred in producing each order received from a customer. A process cost system may be used by companies producing flour, steel, rubber, paper, etc. The unit cost of a product is determined by dividing the total cost of direct materials, direct labor, and factory overhead for the period by the number of equivalent units produced. Equivalent units of production is the estimated number of units that would have been finished if all the units that were started during a period were completed by the end of the period. Unit costs of a product are used to determine the costs for ending goods in process inventory and cost of goods completed and transferred to finished goods inventory.

All cost information obtained during a period for a company using a process cost system may be shown on a production cost report. This report shows the number of units in production, number of units produced, unit costs, and costs for the ending goods in process and finished goods inventory.

Whenever the costs for direct materials, direct labor, and factory overhead are applied to production, the Goods in Process Inventory account is debited. When the goods in the manufacturing process are completed, the Finished Goods Inventory account is debited and the Goods in Process Inventory account is credited. The Cost of Goods Sold account is debited and the Finished Goods Inventory account is credited whenever the product is sold. At the end of the period, the balance remaining in the Materials, Goods in Process, and Finished Goods Inventory accounts represents the ending balance for these accounts.

GLOSSARY

Equivalent Units of Production: An estimate of the number of units that would have been finished if all the units that were started during a period were completed by the end of the period. To obtain the equivalent units of production, the equivalent units in the beginning and ending goods in process inventory are added to the units started and completed during the period.

Process Cost System: A cost system that may be used by a company that produces a single type of product or similar types of products for their inventory in anticipation of receiving future orders. The production process is continuous, orders received from customers are filled from the finished goods inventory, and the costs of production are based on the total costs incurred in each department of the production process.

Production Cost Report: A report that contains all the cost information obtained during a period for a company using a process cost system. This report contains the equivalent units of production, unit costs for direct materials, direct labor, and factory overhead, and the cost of the ending goods in process and finished goods inventories.

QUESTIONS

1. What is the basic difference between a job order and process cost system?
2. Name the report that is used to accumulate the direct materials, direct labor, and factory overhead costs for a company that uses a process cost accounting system.
3. If the total costs of producing seven chairs for a customer amounted to $679, what is the unit cost of each chair?
4. What accounts would be debited and credited when the product is sold for a company that uses a process cost and perpetual inventory system?
5. What is the meaning of the term "equivalent units of production?"
6. Give the three steps for computing equivalent units of production.
7. How do you determine the cost of the goods completed and transferred to the finished goods inventory?

EXERCISES

Equivalent Units of Production

1. Thurmund Industries had 600 units in the beginning goods in process inventory that were 60 percent completed. During the current period, 1,200 additional units were started and 1,400 units were completed and transferred to the finished goods warehouse. The 400 units in the ending goods in process inventory were 40 percent completed.

Required

Determine the equivalent units of production.

2. Willow Corporation had 200 units in beginning goods in process that were 40 percent completed as to labor and overhead. During the current period, 700 additional units were started and 800 units were completed and transferred to the finished goods warehouse. The ending goods in process were 30 percent completed as to labor and overhead. All materials are added at the beginning of the production process.

Required

Determine the equivalent units of production for:
(*a*) Materials
(*b*) Labor and overhead

Equivalent Units of Production and Unit Costs

3. Becker Paper Company had direct materials costs of $1,896 for March, and the cost of materials in the beginning goods in process inventory amounted to $828. There were 800 units 90 percent completed as to materials in beginning goods in process, 600 units 50 percent completed as to materials in ending goods in process, and 2,000 units were completed during March.

Required

Compute the following:
(*a*) Equivalent units for materials
(*b*) Unit cost of materials

4. Jackson Company had direct labor costs of $3,984 and factory overhead costs of $5,976 for March of the current year. There were 800 units in beginning goods in process that were 50 percent completed at a cost of $1,860. During the period, 2,000 units were completed and 600 units were in the ending goods in process that were 10 percent completed.

Required

Compute the following:
(*a*) Equivalent units for labor and overhead
(*b*) Unit costs for labor and overhead

Determining Cost of Inventories

5. The following data applies to the Redwood Company for April of the current year:

  2,000 units in the beginning goods in process 40 percent completed at a cost of $6,040
  6,000 units completed during April

1,000 units in ending goods in process 60 percent completed
Costs for April amounted to $19,720 for materials, $16,240 for direct labor, and $12,180 for factory overhead

Required

Compute the following:
(a) Cost of the 6,000 units completed during period
(b) Cost of ending goods in process inventory
(c) Cost of ending finished goods inventory assuming 4,000 units were sold

6. Towel Fabric Company had 1,000 units in finished goods inventory on April 1 of the current year that cost $12 each to produce. During April, 6,000 units were completed at a total cost of $84,000. On April 30, 5,000 units were sold.

Required

Assuming a FIFO method of inventory valuation, determine:
(a) Cost of goods sold on April 30
(b) Cost of finished goods inventory on April 30

PROBLEMS

Equivalent Units of Production and Unit Costs

25-1. Wonder Fabrics produced several different types of drapery fabrics. The production of silk sheen fabric went through the dye, cutting, and finishing departments. On June 1, there were 5,000 yards in the dye department that were 80 percent completed as to materials and 60 percent completed as to labor and overhead at a cost of $21,000. During June, an additional 6,000 yards were started in the dye process and 9,000 yards were transferred to the cutting department. On June 30, the 2,000 yards in process were 70 percent completed as to materials and 50 percent completed as to labor and overhead. Materials for June cost $9,600, labor $24,500, and overhead amounted to 50 percent of the labor costs.

Required

Determine the following:
(a) Equivalent units of production for materials, labor, and overhead
(b) Unit costs for materials, labor, and overhead

25-2. Sift-Free Flour Company produced several different types of flour. The production of white flour went through the milling, blending, and packaging departments. On March 1, there were 1,000 pounds of white flour in the packaging department that were 75 percent completed as to materials and 40 percent completed as to labor and overhead at a total cost of $250. During March, 3,500 additional pounds of flour were transferred to the packaging department, and 4,000 pounds were transferred to the finished goods warehouse. On March 31, there were 500 pounds of white flour 75 percent completed as to materials and 30 percent completed as to labor and overhead in the packaging department. Production costs for March amounted to $725 for direct materials, $937.50 for direct labor, and $562.50 for factory overhead.

Required

Compute the following for the packaging department:
(a) Equivalent units for materials, labor, and overhead
(b) Unit costs for March

Equivalent Units, Unit Costs, and Ending Inventories

25-3. Executive Desk Company manufactures office desks, and the desks were processed through the planing, assembly, and finishing departments. On June 1, there were 400 desks in the assembly department that were 70 percent completed as to materials and 10 percent completed as to labor and overhead, a total cost of $6,600. During June, 1,200 desks were transferred from the planing department to the assembly department at a unit cost of $15 each, a total cost of $18,000. On June 30, the 400 desks in beginning goods in process and 1,000 of the desks transferred from the planing department for a total of 1,400 desks were completed and transferred to the finishing department. The 200 partially finished desks remaining in the assembly department were 90 percent completed as to materials and 70 percent completed as to labor and overhead. Costs in the assembly department for June amounted to $26,000 for direct materials, $45,000 for direct labor, and $54,000 for factory overhead.

Required

Compute the following for the assembly department:
(a) Equivalent units for direct materials, direct labor, and factory overhead
(b) Unit costs for June
(c) Cost of the 1,400 desks completed and transferred to the finishing department
(d) Cost of the goods in process inventory on June 30 (*Hint:* Don't forget to add the beginning unit cost of $15.)

25-4. Waxy Paper Company manufactured household wax paper and sold their products to distributors in the United States. Accounting records for the manufacturing process in April revealed the following:
Goods in Process Inventory, 4/1: 600 units 80 percent completed as to materials and 50 percent completed as to labor and overhead for a total cost of $210.

Products completed during April amounted to 20,000 units.

Goods in Process Inventory, 4/30: 800 units 60 percent completed as to materials and 30 percent completed as to labor and overhead.

Finished Goods Inventory, 4/1: 10,000 units at a unit cost of $0.50 each for a total cost of $5,000.

Finished Goods Inventory, 4/30: 5,000 units.

Costs for April: Direct Materials, $5,000; Direct Labor, $3,988; and Factory Overhead, $1,994.

Required

Compute the following for April:

(a) Equivalent units for direct materials, direct labor, and factory overhead
(b) Unit costs
(c) Cost of the 20,000 units completed and transferred to the finished goods warehouse
(d) Cost of the goods in process inventory on April 30

Production Cost Report and Journal Entries

25-5. During November, Acme Furnace Company completed 600 furnaces and transferred them to the finished goods warehouse. On November 1, there were 100 furnaces in production 50 percent completed as to materials and 20 percent completed as to labor and overhead at a total cost of $20,000. There were 200 furnaces in production on November 30 that were 60 percent completed as to materials and 30 percent completed as to labor and overhead. Costs of materials for November amounted to $268,000; labor, $320,000; and overhead, $160,000. Fifty furnaces were in the finished goods warehouse on November 1 with a unit cost of $1,100; 550 furnaces were sold on account during November at a selling price of $825,000.

Required

(a) Prepare a production cost report for November.
(b) Journal entries for materials, labor, and overhead applied to production in November.
(c) Journal entry for goods transferred to finished goods warehouse during November.
(d) Journal entry for cost of goods sold during November. (Use FIFO method of inventory valuation.)

Note: Use November 30 as the date for all journal entries.

Review Problem

25-6. Rawley Manufacturing manufactured a standard type of booth for restaurants. A process cost accounting system was established for the continuous production of the standard booth. Information pertaining to the production process for March is given below:

Finished Goods Inventory, 3/1: 100 booths at a unit cost of $180.

Goods in Process Inventory, 1/1: 500 booths 100 percent completed as to materials, 60 percent completed as to labor and overhead at a total cost of $65,000.

Goods completed during March: 1,000 booths.

Production costs for March: Materials, $40,250; Direct Labor, $63,000; and overhead, $44,100.

Goods in Process Inventory, 3/31: 200 booths 100 percent completed as to materials, 70 percent completed as to labor and overhead.

Finished Goods Inventory, 3/31: 200 booths.

Required

(*a*) Equivalent production for materials, labor, and overhead.

(*b*) Unit costs for materials, labor, and overhead.

(*c*) Total cost and unit cost of the 1,000 booths completed and transferred to finished goods warehouse.

(*d*) Cost of goods in process inventory on March 31.

(*e*) Cost of 200 booths on hand in finished goods warehouse on March 31.

(*f*) Journalize the entries for direct materials, direct labor, and factory overhead applied to production in March; booths completed and transferred to finished goods warehouse; and the cost of the goods sold assuming a FIFO method of inventory valuation.

Individual Income Tax

After completing this chapter, you should be able to:

1. **State the types of income excluded from taxes**

2. **Define gross income, adjusted gross income, zero bracket amount, and taxable income**

3. **Give the amount and number of exemptions allowed a taxpayer**

4. **Prepare Form 1040, and Form 1040 Schedules A, B, E, and Form 2106**

5. **Give the reasons for filing Form 1040, Schedules C, G, and SE**

6. **Compute the allowable sales tax deduction using the sales tax tables, and compute an individual's income tax using the tax tables or Schedules X, Y, or Z**

Although federal income taxes were proposed as early as 1815, it wasn't until July 12, 1909 when the Sixteenth Amendment was passed that Congress was given the power to lay and collect taxes on income. The amendment wasn't ratified until February 25, 1913, and income was taxed beginning March 1, 1913. Our current pay-as-you-go system was adopted in 1943 as a result of the Current Tax Payment Act. Many revisions have been made to this act which have simplified the procedures for collecting taxes while endeavoring to ease the burden of the taxpayer.

The discussion of taxes is an interesting and rewarding subject because taxes affect everyone. Generally, every person who is self-employed or receives income from an employer, an investment, a contest, or as a gift is required to file a tax return that may result in the payment of taxes. Even selling your personal residence or investment may result in filing additional forms and paying additional taxes.

Preparing an average income tax return is a relatively easy task, and every college student should be able to prepare his/her personal tax return. Chapter 26 will explain and help to simplify the procedures for filing an individual tax return to enable you to file your personal tax return with ease and self-confidence.

REQUIREMENTS FOR FILING AN INCOME TAX RETURN

Who must file an income tax return?

The Internal Revenue Service (I.R.S.) requirements for filing an income tax return are based on the amount of income received, marital status, and age. The 1981 requirements for filing an income tax return based on yearly income, marital status, and age are given below.

Requirements for filing tax return

$3,300 for a person who is single

$4,300 for a person who is single and 65 years of age or over

$4,400 for a surviving spouse

$5,400 for a surviving spouse who is 65 years of age or over

$5,400 for a married couple who files a joint tax return

$6,400 for a married couple who files a joint tax return and one of them is 65 years of age or over

$7,400 for a married couple who files a joint tax return and both of them are 65 years of age or over

However, there are two exceptions to the above requirements:

1. A self-employed person with yearly earnings of $400 or more from their own business or profession must file a tax return even if their earnings are not subject to any tax.
2. All persons with a yearly income of $1,000 or more are required to file an income tax return if:
   (*a*) They are married but are not living with each other at the end of the year.
   (*b*) They are married but each spouse files a separate tax return.
   (*c*) They are a dependent of another taxpayer.

INCOME EXCLUDED FROM TAXES

There are several types of income that have been excluded from taxes under the constitution of the United States, and this income does not have to be listed on an individual tax return. A list of income exclusions is given below:

Income excluded from taxes

1. Life insurance proceeds received by a taxpayer as the result of the death of an insured. For example, if a person is named the beneficiary of a life insurance policy and the insured person dies, the proceeds received by the beneficiary are not taxable.
2. Interest received on investments in state and municipal bonds are generally not taxable.
3. Payments received under workmen's compensation for a personal injury or sickness.
4. Payments received by a fireman or policeman for a permanent disability.
5. Payments received from an accident or health insurance policy purchased or paid for by a taxpayer.
6. Gifts or inheritances are excluded, but any income received from property received as a gift or inheritance is taxable.
7. Payments received for a personal injury as the result of a legal judgment or claim.

8. Payments from social security, unemployment benefits, and public assistance.
9. The first $200 of interest and dividends received from investments in domestic corporations. (Applicable in 1981.)

GROSS INCOME, ADJUSTED GROSS INCOME, AND TAXABLE INCOME

The income requirements for filing an income tax return are based on gross income. *Gross income* consists of all salaries, wages, commissions, fees, royalties, and bonuses earned by an individual plus interest and dividends (less $200 exclusion or $400 exclusion on a joint return), rent, or profits received from a trade or business and investments subject to taxes. The fair market value of any prize won by a person entering a contest or as a contestant on a quiz program is generally considered to be taxable income. The initials GI are often used when referring to gross income.

Adjusted gross income is the difference between gross income and allowable business expenses incurred in carrying on a trade, business, or profession owned by a taxpayer. This includes the business expenses of an outside salesperson and periodic alimony payments (excluding amounts paid for child support) that are required under a divorce or separate maintenance decree and written separation agreement. The initials AGI are often used when referring to adjusted gross income.

Taxable income is the amount used to compute an individual's income tax using tax tables or tax rate schedules provided by the I.R.S. Two ways of determining taxable income are given below:

Computation of taxable income

1. Adjusted gross income less personal exemption allowance equals taxable income for taxpayers who do not itemize their personal expense deductions and use the tax tables.
2. Adjusted gross income less difference between personal expense deductions (called itemized deductions) and zero bracket amount[1] less amount allowed for personal exemptions equals taxable income for taxpayers who itemize their personal expense deductions and use the tax tables or tax rate Schedules X, Y, or Z because they are not eligible to use tax tables.

Three formulas for figuring the amount of an individual's income tax are:

Three formulas for computing amount of tax

1. GI (gross income)
   − Adjustments to income

---

[1] Zero bracket amount is built into tax tables and tax rate schedules. Therefore, after itemizing and obtaining a total of personal expense deductions, $3,400 is deducted from the total if taxpayer is married and filing a joint return or is a qualifying widow, $2,300 if single or head of a household, and $1,700 if married and filing separate returns.

      = AGI (adjusted gross income)
      − Amount allowed for personal exemptions
      = TI (taxable income)
      = Tax using TI and locating tax on tax table

2. GI (gross income)
      − Adjustments to income
      = AGI (adjusted gross income)
      − personal expense (itemized) deductions
      − zero bracket amount
      − amount allowed for personal exemptions
      = TI (taxable income)
      = Tax using TI and locating tax on tax table

3. GI (gross income)
      − Adjustments to income
      = AGI (adjusted gross income)
      − personal expense (itemized) deductions
      − zero bracket amount
      − amount allowed for personal exemptions
      = TI (taxable income)
      = Tax using TI times tax rate on Schedule X, Y, or Z

DEDUCTIONS FOR EXEMPTIONS

Individual Taxpayer. A taxpayer is entitled to a $1,000 deduction for each *exemption* listed below:

1 exemption for taxpayer

2 exemptions if blind *or* 65 years of age or over

3 exemptions if blind *and* 65 years of age or over

Married Taxpayer. Married taxpayers filing a joint tax return with their spouse are entitled to:

1 additional exemption if spouse is under 65 years of age

2 additional exemptions if spouse is blind *or* 65 years of age or over

3 additional exemptions if spouse is blind *and* 65 years of age or over

    Taxpayers who are divorced or legally separated at the end of a tax year are *not* allowed an exemption for their spouse. When a taxpayer is in the process of a divorce and the final decree has not been received by the end of a tax year, an additional exemption may be taken for the spouse providing a joint tax return is filed.

*One additional exemption
for each qualified
dependent*

Dependent of a Taxpayer. A taxpayer is allowed one additional $1,000 exemption for each dependent child under the age of 19 who lived with the taxpayer during the year plus one additional $1,000 exemption for other persons who qualify as a dependent of the taxpayer. To qualify as a dependent,

1. A taxpayer must provide over one-half of the dependent's support.
2. Dependent must earn less than $1,000 of taxable income (unless dependent is a child under the age of 19 or a child over the age of 19 that attended school for at least 5 months during tax year).
3. Dependent must be a U.S. citizen.
4. Dependent must be a qualified relative of taxpayer or spouse (if a joint tax return is filed) or a member of the taxpayer's household.
5. If dependent is married, the dependent cannot file a joint tax return with his/her spouse.

A divorced parent with custody of the children for more than half of the tax year is usually entitled to the $1,000 exemption for each child. However, a parent who does not have custody of the children may be entitled to the exemption/s if the parent contributes at least $600 for each child's support and the divorce decree states he/she is entitled to the exemption/s. Also, a divorced parent who does not have custody of the children may be entitled to the exemption if the parent contributes at least $1,200 for each child's support and the parent with custody cannot prove he/she provided more than half the cost of the support of the children.

The I.R.S. Code defines support, citizenship, and relative or member of household as follows.

Support. Support of a dependent refers to food, lodging, clothing, medical and dental care, educational expenses, and church contributions.

Citizenship. Citizenship refers to a dependent who is a citizen or resident of the U.S. or a resident of Canada or Mexico at some time during the tax year. A child who is not a U.S. citizen but was adopted by a U.S. citizen and lived with the adopted parents during tax year satisfies the citizenship requirement.

Relative or Member of Household. A relative is a child, stepchild, mother, father, grandparents, brother, sister, grandchild, stepbrother, stepsister, mother-in-law, father-in-law, sister-in-law, daughter-in-law, son-in-law, uncle, aunt, nephew, or niece of a taxpayer or spouse. If a dependent is not a relative, he/she must be a member of the taxpayer's household for the entire tax year; but if it is illegal for the dependent to be living with a taxpayer, he/she does not qualify as a dependent.

FIGURE 26-1 *Page 1 of short form 1040A*

Form **1040A**

Department of the Treasury—Internal Revenue Service
U.S. Individual Income Tax Return 19 (0) OMB No. 1545-0085

Use IRS label. Other-wise, please print or type.	Your first name and initial (if joint return, also give spouse's name and initial)	Last name	Your social security number
	Present home address (Number and street, including apartment number, or rural route)		Spouse's social security no.
	City, town or post office, State and ZIP code	Your occupation ▶	
		Spouse's occupation ▶	

Presidential Election Campaign
▶ Do you want $1 to go to this fund? . . . . Yes No
If joint return, does your spouse want $1 to go to this fund? . . . Yes No

Note: *Checking "Yes" will not increase your tax or reduce your refund.*

For Privacy Act and Paperwork Reduction Act Notice, see page 23 of Instructions

Filing Status
Check Only One Box.

1 ___ Single
2 ___ Married filing joint return (even if only one had income)
3 ___ Married filing separate return. Enter spouse's social security no. above and full name here ▶--------
4 ___ Head of household (with qualifying person). (See page 8 of Instructions.) If he or she is your unmarried child, enter child's name ▶--------

Exemptions
Always check the box labeled Your-self. Check other boxes if they apply.

5a ___ Yourself ___ 65 or over ___ Blind
 b ___ Spouse ___ 65 or over ___ Blind
 c First names of your dependent children who lived with you ▶--------

Enter number of boxes checked on 5a and b ▶ ___

Enter number of children listed on 5c ▶ ___

| d Other dependents: (1) Name | (2) Relationship | (3) Number of months lived in your home. | (4) Did dependent have income of $1,000 or more? | (5) Did you provide more than one-half of dependent's support? |
| | | | | |

Enter number of other dependents ▶ ___

Add numbers entered in boxes above ▶ ___

6 Total number of exemptions claimed . . . .

Please Attach Copy B of Forms W-2 Here

7	Wages, salaries, tips, etc. (Attach Forms W-2. See page 10 of Instructions)	7	
8a	Interest income . . (Complete page 2 if over $400) (or you have any All-Savers interest)	8a	
b	Dividends . . . . . (Complete page 2 if over $400)	8b	
c	Total (add lines 8a and 8b)	8c	
d	Exclusion (See page 11 of Instructions)	8d	
e	Subtract line 8d from line 8c (but not less than zero)		8e	
9a	Unemployment compensation (insurance). Total received from Form(s) 1099-UC_____		
b	Taxable amount, if any, from worksheet on page 12 of Instructions . . .		9b	
10	Adjusted gross income (add lines 7, 8e, and 9b). If under $10,000, see page 13 of Instructions on "Earned Income Credit"	10	
11	Multiply $1,000 by the total number of exemptions claimed on line 6	11	
12	Taxable income (subtract line 11 from line 10)	12	
13a	Credit for contributions to candidates for public office. (See page 13 of Instructions).	13a	

IF YOU WANT IRS TO FIGURE YOUR TAX, PLEASE STOP HERE AND SIGN BELOW.

b	Total Federal income tax withheld (If line 7 is more than $29,700, see page 13 of Instructions)	13b	
c	Earned income credit (from page 14 of Instructions)	13c	
14	Total (add lines 13a, b, and c)		14	
15a	Tax on the amount on line 12. (See page 15 of Instructions; then find your tax in the Tax Table on pages 17-22)	15a	
b	Advance earned income credit (EIC) (from Form W-2). . .	15b	
16	Total (add lines 15a and 15b)		16	
17	If line 14 is larger than line 16, enter amount to be **REFUNDED TO YOU** . . . . . ▶	17	
18	If line 16 is larger than line 14, enter **BALANCE DUE**. Attach check or money order for full amount payable to "Internal Revenue Service." Write your social security number and "1981 Form 1040A" on it. ▶	18	

Attach Payment Here

Please Sign Here

Under penalties of perjury, I declare that I have examined this return, including accompanying schedules and statements, and to the best of my knowledge and belief, it is true, correct, and complete. Declaration of preparer (other than taxpayer) is based on all information of which preparer has any knowledge.

| Your signature | Date | Spouse's signature (if filing jointly, BOTH must sign even if only one had income) |

Paid Preparer's Use Only

Preparer's signature ▶	Date	Check if self-em-ployed ▶ ☐	Preparer's social security no.
Firm's name (or yours, if self-employed) and address ▶		E.I. No. ▶	
		ZIP code ▶	

Form **1040A** (1981)

FIGURE 26-1 (Continued)

Page 2 of short form
1040A

Form 1040A (1981)   Page **2**

CAUTION: You may **NOT** file Form 1040A (you must file Form 1040 instead) if any of the following apply to you:
- You could be claimed as a dependent on your parents' return AND had interest, dividends, or other unearned income of $1,000 or more.
- You had a foreign financial account or were a grantor of, or transferor to, a foreign trust.
- You received interest or dividends as a nominee (in your name) for someone else.
- You received or paid accrued interest on securities transferred between interest payment dates.
- You received any capital gain distributions.

Note: You may also be required to file Form 1040 for other reasons. See pages 4 and 5 of Instructions.

Part I Interest Income		Part II Dividend Income	
If you received more than **$400** in interest or you received any interest from All-Savers Certificates, you must complete Part I and list the names of the payers and the amounts of the interest on the lines below. See page 10 of the Instructions for what interest to report.		If you received more than **$400** in ordinary dividends and nontaxable distributions, list the names of the payers and the amounts of the dividends on the lines below. Be sure to include any nontaxable distributions on these lines. They will be deducted on line 5 below. See page 10 of the Instructions for a definition of ordinary dividends and nontaxable distributions.	
Name of payer	Amount	Name of payer	Amount
1a Interest income (other than qualifying interest from All-Savers Certificates).		3	
1b Total. Add above amounts			
1c Qualifying interest from All-Savers Certificates. (List payers and amounts even if $400 or less.) See page 11 of Instructions.			
1d Total			
1e Exclusion (See page 11 of Instructions) . .			
1f Subtract line 1e from line 1d. **Caution:** *No part of the amount on line 1f may be excluded on Form 1040A, line 8d*		4 Total. Add above amounts	
		5 Nontaxable distributions (See Instructions for adjustment to basis)	
2 **Total interest income** (add lines 1b and 1f). Enter here and on Form 1040A, line 8a		6 **Total dividend income** (subtract line 5 from line 4). Enter here and on Form 1040A, line 8b	

FORM 1040A AND FORM 1040

Every taxpayer is required to file an individual tax return on a short form, *Form 1040A*, or a long form, *Form 1040*. Taxpayers may use the short form 1040A shown in Figure 26-1 if they received all their income from wages or tips, did not receive over $400 in dividends or interest, and did not itemize personal expense deductions.

Taxpayers who do not qualify for the requirements of Form 1040A must file their individual tax returns on Form 1040. When filing a Form 1040A or Form 1040, a taxpayer must fill out the first section with personal data. Lines 1 to 6 on the form include the filing status and exemptions of the taxpayer.

To illustrate, Form 1040 is prepared for Suzanne Walters, who lives at 48124 Wixley Avenue, Plymouth, Michigan 48107. Suzanne is single, under the age of 65, teaches accounting at Plymouth College, and her social security number is 082-01-3619. The personal data section, filing status, and exemptions for Suzanne Walters are illustrated on Form 1040, Figure 26-2.

FIGURE 26-2

Personal data section and lines 1 to 6 on page 1 of Form 1040 completed for Suzanne Walters

Income received by Suzanne Walters during 1981 is given below:

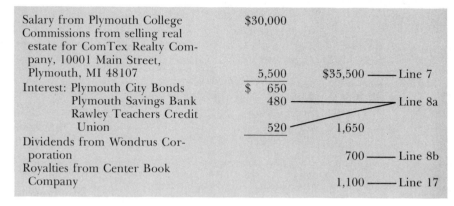

Income received by
Suzanne Walters

Salary from Plymouth College	$30,000		
Commissions from selling real estate for ComTex Realty Company, 10001 Main Street, Plymouth, MI 48107	5,500	$35,500	—— Line 7
Interest: Plymouth City Bonds	$ 650		
Plymouth Savings Bank	480		—— Line 8a
Rawley Teachers Credit Union	520	1,650	
Dividends from Wondrus Corporation		700	—— Line 8b
Royalties from Center Book Company		1,100	—— Line 17

Income received by a taxpayer is reported on Form 1040, lines 7 to 21, as illustrated for Suzanne Walters in Figure 26-3. Note that the interest and dividends are decreased $200 for the allowable exclusion in 1981, and note that the interest of $650 received from Suzanne's investment in Plymouth City Bonds is excluded. Remember that interest received from investments in municipal bonds is an exclusion allowed by the I.R.S.

Interest and Dividend Income

If a taxpayer received interest and/or dividends of more than $400, *Schedule B* must be completed and filed along with Form 1040 to show the source and amount of dividends and/or interest as shown in Figure 26-4 for Suzanne Walters. Note that the taxpayer's name and social security number appear at the top of all subsidiary schedules and forms.

Other Income

When a taxpayer receives taxable income from pensions, annuities, rents, royalties, or a partnership, the amount of income received is reported on Form 1040, line 18, page 1. The income must also be reported on Form 1040, *Schedule E.* Suzanne Walters received royalties of $1,100 from Center Book Company of New York for her share of the 1981 royalties as a coauthor of an accounting manual. Form 1040, Schedule E completed for Suzanne Walters is shown in Figure 26-5 *a* and *b*, pages 707–708.

Self-Employment Income

All taxpayers who are self-employed must file Form 1040, *Schedule SE* (Computation of Social Security Self-Employment Tax) unless they received wages of $29,700 or more in the year of 1981 that were subject to social security taxes and were reported on Form W-2, Wage and Tax Statement. Therefore, Suzanne Walters is not required to file Form 1040, Schedule SE to report the $8,500 she received in commissions from selling

FIGURE 26-3

Form 1040, lines 1 to 21
for Suzanne Walters

Form **1040**	Department of the Treasury—Internal Revenue Service **U.S. Individual Income Tax Return**	**1981**	(3)

For the year January 1–December 31, 1981, or other tax year beginning , 1981, ending , 19 — OMB No. 1545–0074

Use IRS label. Other-wise, please print or type.	Your first name and initial (if joint return, also give spouse's name and initial) Suzanne	Last name Walters	Your social security number 082 : 01 : 3619
	Present home address (Number and street, including apartment number, or rural route) 48124 Wixley Avenue		Spouse's social security no.
	City, town or post office, State and ZIP code Plymouth, MI 48107	Your occupation ▶ Prof. of Acct'g. Spouse's occupation ▶	

Presidential Election Campaign ▶ Do you want $1 to go to this fund? . . . . [X] Yes [ ] No
If joint return, does your spouse want $1 to go to this fund? . . . [ ] Yes [ ] No
Note: Checking "Yes" will not increase your tax or re-duce your refund.

For Privacy Act and Paperwork Reduction Act Notice, see Instructions.

Filing Status
Check only one box.

1 [X] Single
2 [ ] Married filing joint return (even if only one had income)
3 [ ] Married filing separate return. Enter spouse's social security no. above and full name here ▶ _____
4 [ ] Head of household (with qualifying person). (See page 6 of Instructions.) If he or she is your unmarried child, enter child's name ▶ _____
5 [ ] Qualifying widow(er) with dependent child (Year spouse died ▶ 19). (See page 6 of Instructions.)

Exemptions

Always check the box labeled Yourself. Check other boxes if they apply.

6a [X] Yourself [ ] 65 or over [ ] Blind
b [ ] Spouse [ ] 65 or over [ ] Blind

Enter number of boxes checked on 6a and b ▶ [1]

c First names of your dependent children who lived with you ▶ _____

Enter number of children listed on 6c ▶

d Other dependents: (1) Name	(2) Relationship	(3) Number of months lived in your home	(4) Did dependent have income of $1,000 or more?	(5) Did you provide more than one-half of dependent's support?

Enter number of other dependents ▶

e Total number of exemptions claimed . . . .

Add numbers entered in boxes above ▶ [1]

Income

Please attach Copy B of your Forms W-2 here.

If you do not have a W–2, see page 5 of Instructions.

Please attach check or money order here.

7	Wages, salaries, tips, etc.	**7**	35,500	00
8a	Interest income (attach Schedule B if over $400 or you have any All-Savers interest)	8a	1,000	00
b	Dividends (attach Schedule B if over $400)	8b	700	00
c	Total. Add lines 8a and 8b	8c	1,700	00
d	Exclusion (See page 9 of Instructions)	8d	200	00
e	Subtract line 8d from line 8c (but not less than zero)	**8e**	1,500	00
9	Refunds of State and local income taxes (do not enter an amount unless you de-ducted those taxes in an earlier year—see page 9 of Instructions)	**9**		
10	Alimony received	**10**		
11	Business income or (loss) (attach Schedule C) . . . . ▶	**11**		
12	Capital gain or (loss) (attach Schedule D)	**12**		
13	40% of capital gain distributions not reported on line 12 (See page 9 of Instructions) .	**13**		
14	Supplemental gains or (losses) (attach Form 4797)	**14**		
15	Fully taxable pensions and annuities not reported on line 16	**15**		
16a	Other pensions and annuities. Total received 16a			
b	Taxable amount, if any, from worksheet on page 10 of Instructions	**16b**		
17	Rents, royalties, partnerships, estates, trusts, etc. (attach Schedule E)	**17**	1,100	00
18	Farm income or (loss) (attach Schedule F) . . . . ▶	**18**		
19a	Unemployment compensation (insurance). Total received 19a			
b	Taxable amount, if any, from worksheet on page 10 of Instructions	**19b**		
20	Other income (state nature and source—see page 11 of Instructions) ▶ _____	**20**		
21	Total Income. Add amounts in column for lines 7 through 20 . . . . ▶	**21**	38,100	00

FIGURE 26-4 *Form 1040, Schedule B for Suzanne Walters*

Name(s) as shown on Form 1040 (Do not enter name and social security number if shown on other side)

Suzanne Walters

Your social security number

082 | 01 | 3619

Part I   Interest Income

If you received more than $400 in interest or you received any interest from an All-Savers Certificate, you must complete Part I and list ALL interest received. Also complete Part III if you received more than $400 in interest. See page 8 of the Instructions to find out what interest to report. Then answer the questions in Part III, below. If you received interest as a nominee for another, or you received or paid accrued interest on securities transferred between interest payment dates, please see page 20 of the Instructions.

Name of payer	Amount	
1a Interest income (other than qualifying interest from All-Savers Certificates).		
Plymouth Savings Bank	480	00
Rawley Teachers Credit Union	520	00
1b Total. Add above amounts	1,000	00
1c Qualifying interest from All-Savers Certificates. (List payers and amounts even if $400 or less.) See page 20 of Instructions.		
1d Total.		
1e Exclusion (See page 20 of Instructions) .		
f Subtract line 1e from line 1d.		
Caution: No part of the amount on line 1f may be excluded on Form 1040, line 8d. Total interest income (add lines 1b and 1f). Enter here and on Form 1040, line 8a	1,000	00

Part II   Dividend Income

If you received more than $400 in gross dividends (including capital gain distributions) and other distributions on stock, complete Part II and Part III. Please see page 9 of the Instructions. Then answer the questions in Part III, below. If you received dividends as a nominee for another, please see page 21 of the Instructions.

Name of payer	Amount	
3 Wondrus Corporation	700	00
4 Total. Add above amounts	700	00
5 Capital gain distributions. Enter here and on line 13, Schedule D. See Note below . . .		
6 Nontaxable distributions (See Instructions for adjustment to basis)		
7 Total (add lines 5 and 6)		
8 Total dividend income (subtract line 7 from line 4). Enter here and on Form 1040, line 8b	700	00

B

Note: If you received capital gain distributions for the year and you do not need Schedule D to report any other gains or losses or to compute the alternative tax, do not file that schedule. Instead, enter 40% of your capital gain distributions on Form 1040, line 13.

Part III   Foreign Accounts and Foreign Trusts

If you received more than $400 of interest or dividends, OR if you had a foreign account or were a grantor of, or a transferor to, a foreign trust, you must answer both questions in Part III. Please see page 21 of the Instructions.

	Yes	No
9 At any time during the tax year, did you have an interest in or a signature or other authority over a bank account, securities account, or other financial account in a foreign country?		X
0 Were you the grantor of, or transferor to, a foreign trust which existed during the current tax year, whether or not you have any beneficial interest in it?		X

If "Yes," you may have to file Forms 3520, 3520-A, or 926.

For Paperwork Reduction Act Notice, see Form 1040 Instructions.

FIGURE 26-5a *Form 1040, Schedule E for Suzanne Walters*

SCHEDULE E
(Form 1040)
Department of the Treasury
Internal Revenue Service (3)

Supplemental Income Schedule
(From rents and royalties, partnerships, estates and trusts, etc.)
▶ Attach to Form 1040. ▶ See Instructions for Schedule E (Form 1040).

OMB No. 1545-0074

1981

15

Name(s) as shown on Form 1040	Your social security number
Suzanne Walters	082 :01 : 3619

Part I Rent and Royalty Income or Loss.

1 Are any of the expenses listed below for a vacation home or similar dwelling rented to others (see Instructions)? . ☐ Yes ☒ No

2 If you checked "Yes" to question 1, did you or a member of your family occupy the vacation home or similar dwelling for more than 14 days during the tax year? . . . . ☐ Yes ☒ No

Rental and Royalty Income (describe property in Part V)		Properties			Totals	
		A	B	C		
3 a Rents received		1,100 00			3	1,100 00
b Royalties received						
Rental and Royalty Expenses						
4 Advertising	4					
5 Auto and travel	5					
6 Cleaning and maintenance	6					
7 Commissions	7					
8 Insurance	8					
9 Interest	9					
10 Legal and other professional fees . .	10					
11 Repairs	11					
12 Supplies	12					
13 Taxes (do NOT include Windfall Profit Tax, see Part III, line 35)	13					
14 Utilities	14					
15 Wages and salaries	15					
16 Other (list) ▶						
....						
17 Total deductions (add lines 4 through 16)	17				17	
18 Depreciation expense (see Instructions), or Depletion (attach computation)	18				18	
19 Total (add lines 17 and 18)	19					
20 Income or (loss) from rental or royalty properties (subtract line 19 from line 3a (rents) or 3b (royalties))	20	1,100 00				

21 Add properties with profits on line 20, and enter total profits here . . . . | 21 | 1,100 00

22 Add properties with losses on line 20, and enter total (losses) here . . . . | 22 | ( )

23 Combine amounts on lines 21 and 22, and enter net profit or (loss) here . . . . | 23 | 1,100 00

24 Net farm rental profit or (loss) from Form 4835, line 50 . . . . | 24 |

25 Total rental or royalty income or (loss). Combine amounts on lines 23 and 24. Enter here and include in line 37 on page 2 . . . . | 25 | 1,100 00

E

For Paperwork Reduction Act Notice, see Form 1040 Instructions.

FIGURE 26-5b

Part II   Income or Losses from Partnerships, Estates or Trusts, or Small Business Corporations

If you report a loss below, do you have amounts invested in that activity for which you are not "at risk" (see Instructions)? ☐ Yes ☐ No

If "Yes," and your loss exceeded your amount "at risk," did you limit your loss to your amount "at risk"? . . . . . ☐ Yes ☐ No

	(a) Name	(b) Employer identification number	(c) Net loss (see instructions for "at risk" limitations)	(d) Net Income
Partnerships				

26 Add amounts in columns (c) and (d) and enter here . . . . | **26** |(   )|

27 Combine amounts in columns (c) and (d), line 26, and enter net income or (loss) . . . . | **27** |

28 Additional first-year depreciation from 1980/1981 fiscal-year partnerships. Enter amount from Form 1065, Schedule K–1, line 2, but not more than $2,000 ($4,000 if a joint return) . . . | **28** |(   )|

29 Total partnership income or (loss). Combine lines 27 and 28. Enter here and include in line 37 . | **29** |

Estates or Trusts				

30 Add amounts in columns (c) and (d) and enter here . . . . | **30** |(   )|

31 Total estate or trust income or (loss). Combine amounts in columns (c) and (d), line 30. Enter here and include in line 37 . . . . | **31** |

Small Business Corporations				

32 Add amounts in columns (c) and (d) and enter here . . . . | **32** |(   )|

33 Total small business corporation income or (loss). Combine amounts in columns (c) and (d), line 32. Enter here and include in line 37 . . . . | **33** |

Part III   Windfall Profit Tax Summary

34 Windfall Profit Tax Credit or Refund received in 1981 (see Instructions) . . . . . . | **34** |

35 Windfall Profit Tax withheld in 1981 (see Instructions) . . . . | **35** |(   )|

36 Combine amounts on lines 34 and 35. Enter here and include in line 37 . . . . | **36** |

Part IV   Summary

37 TOTAL income or (loss). Combine lines 25, 29, 31, 33, and 36. Enter here and on Form 1040, line 17 . ▶ | **37** | 1,100 | 00 |

38 Farmers and fishermen: Enter your share of gross farming and fishing income applicable to Parts I and II . . . . | **38** |

Part V   Depreciation Claimed in Part I.—Complete only if property was placed in service before January 1, 1981. For more space, use Form 4562. If you placed any property in service after December 31, 1980, use Form 4562 for all property; do NOT complete Part V.

	(a) Description and location of property	(b) Date acquired	(c) Cost or other basis	(d) Depreciation allowed or allowable in prior years	(e) Depreciation method	(f) Life or rate	(g) Depreciation for this year
Property A							
	Totals (Property A)						
Property B							
	Totals (Property B)						
Property C							
	Totals (Property C)						

real estate; social security taxes for the maximum amount were deducted from the wages she received from Plymouth College. A Form 1040, Schedule SE is shown in Figure 26-6.

Allowable Business Deductions

All expenses incurred by a taxpayer in operating a trade, business, or profession are deductible from gross income to arrive at adjusted gross income. The expense must be directly related to the production of revenue for a trade, business, or profession of the taxpayer; and the expense must be reasonable in amount. A taxpayer who operates a trade, business, or professional practice is required to report their business income and allowable business deductions on Form 1040, *Schedule C* as illustrated in Figure 26-7.

Costs of maintaining property owned by a taxpayer for rental purposes are deductible as a nonbusiness expense, and the costs of earning commissions by a salesperson who is not paid by an employer are deductible as a business expense to arrive at gross income. A list of trade, business, and professional expenses are given below.

Allowable business expenses

Repairs to business property

Rental expense

Depreciation of business building, equipment, and furniture

Salaries, commissions, and fees paid to employees

Payroll tax expense

Travel and entertainment for business purposes

Telephone and utilities expense

Taxes and insurance

Contributions

Advertising and subscriptions to trade or professional publications

Dues of trade or professional organizations

Postage and supplies

Bank service charges and interest on notes

Accounting and legal fees

Business automobiles or pickup and panel trucks [taxpayers have two options: they may use the (*a*) regular method of reporting the actual costs of gasoline, oil, maintenance, depreciation, parking fees, etc.; or they may use (*b*) an optional method and deduct $0.20 per mile for the first 15,000 miles of business use and $0.11 per mile for each additional mile used for business plus cost of parking fees]

FIGURE 26-6 *Form 1040, Schedule SE*

SCHEDULE SE
(Form 1040)

Department of the Treasury
Internal Revenue Service (3)

Computation of Social Security Self-Employment Tax

▶ See Instructions for Schedule SE (Form 1040).
▶ Attach to Form 1040.

OMB No. 1545-0074

1981
22

Name of self-employed person (as shown on social security card)	Social security number of self-employed person ▶		

Part I Computation of Net Earnings from FARM Self-Employment

Regular Method

1 Net profit or (loss) from:

  a Schedule F (Form 1040) **1a**

  b Farm partnerships **1b**

2 Net earnings from farm self-employment (add lines 1a and 1b) **2**

Farm Optional Method

3 If gross profits from farming are:

  a Not more than $2,400, enter two-thirds of the gross profits . . . . } . . . **3**

  b More than $2,400 and the net farm profit is less than $1,600, enter $1,600 . . . . }

4 Enter here and on line 12a, the amount on line 2, or line 3 if you elect the farm optional method . **4**

Part II Computation of Net Earnings from NONFARM Self-Employment

SE

Regular Method

5 Net profit or (loss) from:

  a Schedule C (Form 1040) **5a**

  b Partnerships, joint ventures, etc. (other than farming) **5b**

  c Service as a minister, member of a religious order, or a Christian Science practitioner. (Include rental value of parsonage or rental allowance furnished.) If you filed Form 4361 and have not revoked that exemption, check here ▶ ☐ and enter zero on this line **5c**

  d Service with a foreign government or international organization **5d**

  e Other (specify) ▶_____ **5e**

6 Total (add lines 5a through 5e) **6**

7 Enter adjustments if any (attach statement, see instructions) **7**

8 Adjusted net earnings or (loss) from nonfarm self-employment (line 6, as adjusted by line 7). Enter here and on line 12b. (Note: If the amount on line 8 is less than $1,600, you may wish to use the nonfarm optional method instead. See instructions.) **8**

Nonfarm Optional Method (Use only if your earnings from nonfarm self-employment are less than $1,600 and less than two-thirds of your gross nonfarm profits.)

9 **a** Maximum amount reportable under both optional methods combined (farm and nonfarm) . . **9a** | $1,600 | 00

  b Enter amount from line 3. (If you have no amount on line 3, enter zero.) **9b**

  c Balance (subtract line 9b from line 9a) **9c**

10 Enter two-thirds of gross nonfarm profits or $1,600, whichever is smaller **10**

11 Enter here and on line 12b, the amount on line 9c or line 10, whichever is smaller **11**

Part III Computation of Social Security Self-Employment Tax

12 Net earnings or (loss):

  a From farming (from line 4) **12a**

  b From nonfarm (from line 8, or line 11 if you elect to use the Nonfarm Optional Method) . . . **12b**

13 Total net earnings or (loss) from self-employment reported on lines 12a and 12b. (If line 13 is less than $400, you are not subject to self-employment tax. Do not fill in rest of schedule) **13**

14 The largest amount of combined wages and self-employment earnings subject to social security or railroad retirement taxes for 1981 is . . . . **14** | $29,700 | 00

15 **a** Total FICA wages (from Forms W-2) and RRTA compensation **15a**

  b Unreported tips subject to FICA tax from Form 4137, line 9 or to RRTA **15b**

  c Add lines 15a and 15b **15c**

16 Balance (subtract line 15c from line 14) **16**

17 Self-employment income—line 13 or line 16, whichever is smaller **17**

18 Self-employment tax. (If line 17 is $29,700, enter $2,762.10; if less, multiply the amount on line 17 by .093.) Enter here and on Form 1040, line 48 . . . . **18**

For Paperwork Reduction Act Notice, see Form 1040 Instructions.

FIGURE 26-7 *Form 1040, Schedule C*

SCHEDULE C (Form 1040)	Profit or (Loss) From Business or Profession	OMB. No. 1545-0074

SCHEDULE C (Form 1040)
Department of the Treasury
Internal Revenue Service (3)

Profit or (Loss) From Business or Profession
(Sole Proprietorship)
Partnerships, Joint Ventures, etc., Must File Form 1065.
▶ Attach to Form 1040 or Form 1041. ▶ See Instructions for Schedule C (Form 1040).

OMB. No. 1545-0074

19 08

C

Name of proprietor

Social security number of proprietor

A Main business activity (see Instructions) ▶ _____ ; product ▶ _____

B Business name ▶ _____

C Employer identification number

D Business address (number and street) ▶ _____
City, State and ZIP Code ▶

E Accounting method: (1) ☐ Cash (2) ☐ Accrual (3) ☐ Other (specify) ▶ _____

F Method(s) used to value closing inventory:
(1) ☐ Cost (2) ☐ Lower of cost or market (3) ☐ Other (if other, attach explanation)

	Yes	No

G Was there any major change in determining quantities, costs, or valuations between opening and closing inventory? . . .
If "Yes," attach explanation.

H Did you deduct expenses for an office in your home? . . . .

Part I Income

1 a Gross receipts or sales	1a	
b Returns and allowances	1b	
c Balance (subtract line 1b from line 1a)	1c	
2 Cost of goods sold and/or operations (Schedule C–1, line 8)	2	
3 Gross profit (subtract line 2 from line 1c)	3	
4 a Windfall Profit Tax Credit or Refund received in 1981 (see Instructions) . . .	4a	
b Other income (attach schedule)	4b	
5 Total income (add lines 3, 4a, and 4b) . . . . ▶	5	

Part II Deductions

6 Advertising		29 a Wages . .		
7 Amortization		b Jobs credit		
8 Bad debts from sales or services .		c WIN credit		
9 Bank service charges		d Total credits		
10 Car and truck expenses . . .		e Subtract line 29d from 29a .		
11 Commissions		30 Windfall Profit Tax withheld in		
12 Depletion		1981 . . .		
13 Depreciation (see Instructions) .		31 Other expenses (specify):		
14 Dues and publications		a		
15 Employee benefit programs . .		b		
16 Freight (not included on Schedule C–1) .		c		
17 Insurance		d		
18 Interest on business indebtedness		e		
19 Laundry and cleaning . . .		f		
20 Legal and professional services .		g		
21 Office supplies and postage . . .		h		
22 Pension and profit-sharing plans .		i		
23 Rent on business property . .		j		
24 Repairs		k		
25 Supplies (not included on Schedule C–1) .		l		
26 Taxes (do not include Windfall Profit Tax, see line 30)		m		
27 Travel and entertainment . . .		n		
28 Utilities and telephone . . .		o		
		p		

32 Total deductions (add amounts in columns for lines 6 through 31p) . . . . ▶	32	
33 Net profit or (loss) (subtract line 32 from line 5). If a profit, enter on Form 1040, line 11, and on Schedule SE, Part II, line 5a (or Form 1041, line 6). If a loss, go on to line 34	33	

34 If you have a loss, do you have amounts for which you are not "at risk" in this business (see Instructions)? . . . ☐ **Yes** ☐ **No**
If you checked "No," enter the loss on Form 1040, line 11, and on Schedule SE, Part II, line 5a (or Form 1041, line 6).

For Paperwork Reduction Act Notice, see Form 1040 Instructions.

A taxpayer who is employed by a business as an outside salesperson and incurs expenses necessary in performing his/her duties that are not paid by the employer may claim these expenses as adjustments to gross income by filing *Form 2106* along with Form 1040.

To illustrate, assume that Suzanne Walters incurred the following business expenses when selling real estate as a part-time salesperson during 1981. These expenses were not paid by her employer, ComTex Realty Company.

Business expenses incurred by Suzanne Walters

Telephone	$ 170	
Travel and entertainment	750	
Advertising	141	
Real estate sales license	15	
6,845 business miles @ $0.20 per mile	1,369	
Total business expenses		$2,445

Form 2106 reporting the allowable business expenses for Suzanne Walters is shown in Figure 26-8*a* and *b*.

Allowable Nonbusiness Personal Deductions (Itemized Deductions)

Nonbusiness personal expenses paid by a taxpayer for medical and dental costs, taxes, interest, charitable contributions, casualty losses, and other miscellaneous expenses are the personal deductions allowed to an individual. The I.R.S. Code defines these personal deductions as listed below.

Allowable personal deductions

Medical Expenses. One-half of medical insurance payments (not to exceed $150) plus drug and medicine costs that exceed 1 percent of adjusted gross income are deductible. Also, payments for medical and dental expenses of a taxpayer, spouse, and dependents are deductible if they exceed 3 percent of adjusted gross income. The balance of the medical insurance payments are included with the medical and dental costs.

Taxes. A tax is deductible if it is imposed on the taxpayer and the taxpayer paid the tax during the current tax year. For example, real property taxes, city and state income taxes, city and state personal property taxes, and city and state sales taxes.

Interest. Interest pertains to the moneys paid for the use of borrowed money. For example, interest on a mortgage, note, debt, charge account, and installment purchase.

Charitable Contributions. A deduction not to exceed 50 percent of adjusted gross income is allowed for contributions to a charitable or educational organization. The organization must be a qualified institution, such as a church, educational institution, hospital, Red Cross, United Foundation, Salvation Army, and veteran organization.

FIGURE 26-8a *Form 2106, page 1 for Suzanne Walters*

Form **2106**

Department of the Treasury
Internal Revenue Service (O)

Employee Business Expenses

(Please use Form 3903 to figure moving expense deduction.)

▶ Attach to Form 1040.

OMB No. 1545-0139

1981

Your name	Social security number	Occupation in which expenses were incurred
Suzanne Walters	082 : 01 : 3619	Real estate salesperson

Employer's name	Employer's address
Com Tex Realty Company	10001 Main Street, Plymouth, MI 48107

Paperwork Reduction Act Notice.—The Paperwork Reduction Act of 1980 says we must tell you why we are collecting this information, how we will use it, and whether you have to give it to us. We ask for the information to carry out the Internal Revenue laws of the United States. We need it to ensure that you are complying with these laws and to allow us to figure and collect the right amount of tax. You are required to give us this information.

Instructions

Use this form to show your business expenses as an employee during 1981. Include amounts:

● You paid as an employee;
● You charged to your employer (such as by credit card);
● You received as an advance, allowance, or repayment.

Several publications available from IRS give more information about business expenses:

Publication 463, *Travel, Entertainment, and Gift Expenses.*
Publication 529, *Miscellaneous Deductions.*
Publication 587, *Business Use of Your Home.*
Publication 508, *Educational Expenses.*

Part I.—You can deduct some business expenses even if you do not itemize your deductions on Schedule A (Form 1040). Examples are expenses for travel (except commuting to and from work), meals, or lodging. List these expenses in Part I and use them in figuring your adjusted gross income on Form 1040, line 31.

Line 2.—You can deduct meals and lodging costs if you were on a business trip away from your main place of work. Do not deduct the cost of meals you ate on one-day trips when you did not need sleep or rest.

Line 3.—If you use a car you own in your work, you can deduct the cost of the business use. Enter the cost here after figuring it in Part IV. You can take either the cost of your actual

expenses (such as gas, oil, repairs, depreciation, etc.) or you can use the standard mileage rate.

The mileage rate is 20 cents a mile up to 15,000 miles. After that, or for all business mileage on a fully depreciated car, the rate is 11 cents a mile. If you use the standard mileage rate to figure the cost of business use, the car is considered to have a useful life of 60,000 miles of business use at the maximum standard mileage rate. After 60,000 miles of business use at the maximum rate, the car is considered to be fully depreciated. (For details, see **Publication 463.**)

Caution: You cannot use the mileage rate for a leased vehicle.

Figure your mileage rate amount and add it to the business part of what you spent on the car for parking fees, tolls, interest, and State and local taxes (except gasoline tax).

Line 4.—If you were an outside salesperson with other business expenses, list them on line 4. Examples are selling expenses or expenses for stationery and stamps. An outside salesperson does all selling outside the employer's place of business. A driver-salesperson whose main duties are service and delivery, such as delivering bread or milk, is not an outside salesperson. (For details, see **Publication 463.**)

Line 5.—Show other business expenses on line 5 if your employer repaid you for them. If you were repaid for part of them, show here the amount you were repaid. Show the rest in Part II.

Part II.—You can deduct other business expenses only if (a) your employer did not repay you, and (b) you itemize your deductions on Schedule A (Form 1040). Report these expenses here and under Miscellaneous Deductions on Schedule A. (For details, see **Publication 529.**)

You can deduct expenses for business use of the part of your home that you exclusively and consistently use for your work. If you are not self-employed, your working at home must be for your employer's convenience. (For business use of home, see **Publication 587.**)

If you show education expenses in Part I or Part II, you must fill out Part III.

Part III.—You can deduct the cost of education that helps you keep or improve your skills for the job you have now. This includes education that your employer, the law, or regulations require you to get in order to keep your job or your salary. Do not deduct the cost of study that helps you meet the basic requirements for your job or helps you get a new job. (For education expenses, see **Publication 508.**)

Part IV, line 8—Depreciation

Cars placed in service *before 1/1/81*:

You must continue to use either the standard mileage rate or the method of depreciation you used in earlier years. You cannot change to either of the new methods available in 1981.

Cars placed in service *12/31/80*:

If you placed a car in service in 1981 and you do not use the standard mileage rate, you must use the new Accelerated Cost Recovery System (ACRS). One method lets you deduct the following percentages of your cost basis regardless of what month you placed the car in service:

1981—25%
1982—38%
1983—37%

Example: You bought a new car, without a trade-in, for $10,000 in September 1981, and used it 60% for business. Your basis for depreciation is $6,000 ($10,000 × 60%). For 1981 your depreciation deduction is $1,500 ($6,000 × 25%). If your percentage of business use changes in 1982, you must refigure your basis for depreciation.

There is also an alternate ACRS method under which you may use a straight-line method over a recovery period of 3, 5, or 12 years.

Note: *If you use the mileage rate, you are considered to have made an election to exclude this vehicle from ACRS.*

You do not have to consider salvage value in either of these methods. Please see **Publication 463** for details on how to figure the deduction under either method.

PART I.—Employee Business Expenses Deductible in Figuring Adjusted Gross Income on Form 1040, Line 31

1	Fares for airplane, boat, bus, taxicab, train, etc.	
2	Meals and lodging	1369
3	Car expenses (from Part IV, line 21)	170
4	Outside salesperson's expenses (see Part I instructions above) ▶ _____ Telephone	750
	Travel and entertainment	
	Advertising	141
	Real estate license	15
5	Other (see Part I instructions above) ▶	
6	Add lines 1 through 5	2,445
7	Employer's payments for these expenses if not included on Form W-2	
8	Deductible business expenses (subtract line 7 from line 6). Enter here and include on Form 1040, line 23 .	2,445
9	Income from excess business expense payments (subtract line 6 from line 7). Enter here and include on Form 1040, line 20	

PART II.—Employee Business Expenses that are Deductible Only if You Itemize Deductions on Schedule A (Form 1040)

1	Business expenses not included above (list expense and amount) ▶ _____	
2	Total. Deduct under Miscellaneous Deductions, Schedule A (Form 1040)	

Form **2106** (1981)

FIGURE 26-8b

Form 2106, page 2 for
Suzanne Walters

Form 2106 (1981)

PART III.—Information About Education Expenses Shown in Part I or Part II

1 Name of educational institution or activity ▶ ....

2 Address ▶ ....

3 Did you need this education to meet the basic requirements for your job? . . . . ☐ Yes ☐ No

4 Will this study program qualify you for a new job? . . . . ☐ Yes ☐ No

5 If your answer to question 3 or 4 is Yes, you cannot deduct these expenses. If No, explain (1) why you are getting the education, and (2) what the relationship was between the courses you took and your job. (If you need more space, attach a statement.) ▶ ....

....

6 List your main subjects, or describe your educational activity ▶ ....

....

PART IV.—Car Expenses (Use either your actual expenses or the mileage rate.)

	Car 1	Car 2	Car 3
A. Number of months you used car for business during 1981 . .	12 months	_____ months	_____ months
B. Total mileage for months in line A	23,000 miles	_____ miles	_____ miles
C. Business part of line B mileage	6,845 miles	_____ miles	_____ miles

Actual Expenses (Include expenses on lines 1–5 for only the months shown in line A, above.)

1 Gasoline, oil, lubrication, etc.			
2 Repairs			
3 Tires, supplies, etc.			
4 Other: (a) Insurance			
(b) Taxes			
(c) Tags and licenses			
(d) Interest			
(e) Miscellaneous			
5 Total (add lines 1 through 4(e))			
6 Business percentage of car use (divide line C by line B, above)	%	%	%
7 Business part of car expense (multiply line 5 by line 6) . . .			
8 Depreciation (see instructions on front) . . . . . . **Caution:** *If you use ACRS, skip line 9 and enter the amount from line 8 on line 10.*			
9 Divide line 8 by 12 months			
10 Multiply line 9 by line A, above			
11 Total (add line 7 and line 10; then skip to line 19)			

Mileage Rate

12 Enter the smaller of (a) 15,000 miles or (b) the combined mileages from line C, above	6,845	miles
13 Multiply line 12 by 20¢ (11¢ if car is fully depreciated) and enter here	1,369	
14 Enter any combined mileage from line C that is over 15,000 miles	_____ miles	/////////
15 Multiply line 14 by 11¢ and enter here		
16 Total mileage expense (add lines 13 and 15)	1,369	
17 Business part of car interest and State and local taxes (except gasoline tax)		
18 Total (add lines 16 and 17)	1,369	

Summary

19 Enter amount from line 11 or line 18, whichever you used	1,369	
20 Parking fees and tolls		
21 Total (add lines 19 and 20). Enter here and in Part I, line 3	1,369	

Casualty Losses. A casualty loss is any unexpected damage or loss to personal property resulting from theft, fire, storm, accident, or shipwreck. The loss is deductible for the lower of the cost of the property or the decrease in the fair market value of property due to loss that exceeds $100 in any tax year. For example, if a taxpayer incurred a casualty loss of personal property for $800, only $700 would be deductible ($800–$100 exclusion). Form 4684 must be attached to Form 1040, *Schedule A* if the casualty loss or theft amounts to $1,000 or more or if the taxpayer had more than one casualty or theft loss during the tax year.

Miscellaneous Personal Expenses. If taxpayers are required to wear special clothing or shoes to perform their trade or profession, the cost of the clothing and shoes is deductible. If taxpayers are required to take special courses at an educational institution to maintain or improve their skills in a trade or profession, the costs are deductible. This includes the cost of any special trade or professional publications, subscriptions, and membership fees. Union dues, the cost of having your tax returns prepared, and the cost of renting a safety deposit box used for storing investments are also deductible for tax purposes. To illustrate, the personal expenses for Suzanne Walters for year 1981, listed on pages 716–717, are entered on Schedule A (Figure 26-10, page 718).

A schedule for the casualty loss of $600 is shown below for Suzanne Walters. This schedule is attached to Form 1040, Schedule A.

Schedule to report casualty loss

SCHEDULE FOR CASUALTY LOSS ON FORM 1040, SCHEDULE A

Name: Suzanne Walters		Social Security No.: 082-01-3619
1. Value of awnings before casualty		$600
2. Value after casualty (severe wind storm)		-0-
3. Difference		$600
4. Cost of awnings		750
5. Lesser of 3 or 4	Line 25, Schedule A	$600
6. Less: Insurance reimbursement	Line 26, Schedule A	-0-
7. Difference between 5 and 6	Line 27, Schedule A	$600
8. Less $100 reduction	Line 28, Schedule A	100
9. Casualty loss	Line 29, Schedule A	$500

Completing Form 1040

When a taxpayer completes all the subsidiary schedules and additional forms required to submit with Form 1040, the Adjustments to Income and Gross Income section of page 1 is completed. The $2,445 appearing on line 8, page 1 of Form 2106 is recorded on lines 23 and 30 of Form 1040 and subtracted from the total income of $38,100 appearing on line 21. The difference of $35,655 ($38,100 – $2,445) equals the adjusted gross income which is entered on line 31 of Form 1040 as shown in Figure 26-11.

Personal expenses for
Suzanne Walters

Section	Line		Amount
①		Medical and Dental Expenses (not covered by insurance): Medical insurance $ 210 Medical & dental 1,750 Medicines & drugs 413 These expenses are recorded on lines 1 to 10 as shown on page 718.	
	1	One-half of medical insurance $210 × ½	$ 105
	2	Medicines and drugs	$ 413
	3	1% of AGI: $35,655 (page 720) × .01	357
	4	Line 2 less line 3	$ 56
	5	Balance of medical insurance: $210 − $105	105
	6	Medical and dental expenses	1,750
	7	Total of lines 4 to 6	$ 1,911
	8	3% of AGI: $35,655 × .03	1,070
	9	Line 7 less line 8	$ 841
	10	Line 1 plus line 9	$ 946
②		**Taxes**	
	11	State income taxes	$ 1,495
	12	Property taxes on home	1,950
	13	State sales tax (see sales tax tables, Figure 26-9)	270
	15	Property taxes on land investment	126
	16	Total of lines 11 to 15	$ 3,841
③		**Interest**	
	17	Interest on home mortgage	$ 3,154
	18	Interest on charge accounts	140
	20	Total of lines 18 and 19	$ 3,294
④		**Contributions**	
		St. Marks Presbyterian Church	$ 468
		Salvation Army	100
		National Leukemia Foundation	25
		Disabled American Veterans	25
		United Foundation	100
		Plymouth College Scholarship Fund	100
	21	Total contributions	$ 818
	24	Total from line 21	$ 818
⑤		**Casualty Losses**	
		Loss from wind damage to awning on residence (not covered by insurance); Cost,	
	25	$750, value after storm	$ 600
	27	Total from line 25	$ 600
	28	Less: $100 exclusion	100
	29	Amount of deductible loss	$ 500

Section	Line		Amount
⑥		**Miscellaneous**	
	30	Michigan Education Association, union dues	$ 286
	31	Safe deposit box	23
	31	National accounting convention	275
	31	American Association of Accountants, dues	50
	32	Total of lines 30 and 31	$ 634
⑦		**Summary of Itemized Deductions**	
	33	Total of line 10, medical expenses	$ 946
	34	Total of line 17, taxes	3,841
	35	Total of line 20, interest	3,294
	36	Total of line 24, contributions	818
	37	Total of line 29, casualty loss	500
	38	Total of line 32, miscellaneous	634
	39	Total of lines 33 to 38, total deductions	$10,033
	40	Amount to be deducted by an unmarried tax-payer[1]	2,300
	41	Line 39 less line 40	$ 7,733

[1] Before 1977, taxpayers had the option of itemizing their personal expense deductions or taking a standard deduction based on marital status established by the I.R.S. However, this method was changed in the year 1977, and the standard deduction as build into the tax tables and tax rate schedules based on filing status and called the zero bracket amount. Therefore, when a taxpayer itemizes personal deductions on Schedule A, as shown for Suzanne Walters in Figure 26-10, $3,400 must be entered on line 40 if the taxpayer is married and filing a joint return or is a qualifying widow with one dependent, and $2,300 if the taxpayer is single or unmarried and head of a household, or $1,700 if the taxpayer is married and filing a separate return.

After completing page 1 of Form 1040, the $35,655 appearing on line 31 is entered on line 32a of page 2 (Figure 26-12). The $7,733 appearing on line 41 of Schedule A (Figure 26-10) is recorded on line 32b of Form 1040 and the $27,922 ($35,655 − $7,733) difference between line 32a and

FIGURE 26-9

1981 optional state sales tax tables for Michigan

Income [1]	Michigan Family size 1&2	3&4	5	Over 5
$1–$8,000	88	102	108	113
$8,001–$10,000	103	121	127	133
$10,001–$12,000	118	138	145	151
$12,001–$14,000	131	154	161	168
$14,001–$16,000	144	169	177	184
$16,001–$18,000	156	184	192	199
$18,001–$20,000	168	198	207	214
$20,001–$22,000	180	211	221	228
$22,001–$24,000	191	224	234	241
$24,001–$26,000	202	237	247	254
$26,001–$28,000	212	249	260	267
$28,001–$30,000	222	261	272	280
$30,001–$32,000	232	273	284	292
$32,001–$34,000	242	284	296	304
$34,001–$36,000	252	295	308	316
$36,001–$38,000	261	306	319	327
$38,001–$40,000	270	317	330	338
$40,001–$100,000 (See Step 3B)				

FIGURE 26-10

Schedule A—Itemized Deductions

Schedules A&B (Form 1040)
Department of the Treasury
Internal Revenue Service (3)

(Schedule B is on back)

▶ Attach to Form 1040. ▶ See Instructions for Schedules A and B (Form 1040).

OMB No. 1545-0074

1981
07

Name(s) as shown on Form 1040

Suzanne Walters

Your social security number
082 : 01 : 3619

Medical and Dental Expenses (Do not include expenses reimbursed or paid by others.) (See page 17 of Instructions.)

① 1 One-half (but not more than $150) of insurance premiums you paid for medical care. (Be sure to include in line 10 below.) ▶ **105 00**

2 Medicine and drugs . 413 00

3 Enter 1% of Form 1040, line 31 . 357 00

4 Subtract line 3 from line 2. If line 3 is more than line 2, enter zero . . . **56 00**

5 Balance of insurance premiums for medical care not entered on line 1 . . **105 00**

6 Other medical and dental expenses:

a Doctors, dentists, nurses, etc. . . **1,750 00**

b Hospitals . . . . . .

c Transportation . . . . . .

d Other (itemize—include hearing aids, dentures, eyeglasses, etc.) ▶ ....

7 Total (add lines 4 through 6d) **1,911 00**

8 Enter 3% of Form 1040, line 31 . . . **1,070 00**

9 Subtract line 8 from line 7. If line 8 is more than line 7, enter zero **841 00**

10 Total medical and dental expenses (add lines 1 and 9). Enter here and on line 33 ▶ **946 00**

Taxes (See page 18 of Instructions.)

② 11 State and local income **1,495 00**

12 Real estate (residence) **1,950 00**

13 a General sales (see sales tax tables) . **270 00**

b General sales on motor vehicles . .

14 Personal property . . . . . .

15 Other (itemize) ▶ .Real.estate. ...taxes.on.land.investments. **126 00**

16 Total taxes (add lines 11 through 15). Enter here and on line 34 . . . . ▶ **3,841 00**

Interest Expense (See page 18 of Instructions.)

③ 17 Home mortgage **3,154 00**

18 Credit and charge cards **140 00**

19 Other (itemize) ▶ ....

20 Total interest expense (add lines 17 through 19). Enter here and on line 35 ▶ **3,294 00**

Contributions (See page 19 of Instructions.)

21 a Cash contributions (If you gave $3,000 or more to any one organization, report those contributions on line 21b) . **818 00** ④

b Cash contributions totaling $3,000 or more to any one organization (show to whom you gave and how much you gave) ▶ ....

22 Other than cash (see page 19 of Instructions for required statement) . . . .

23 Carryover from prior years . . . .

24 Total contributions (add lines 21a through 23). Enter here and on line 36 ▶ **818 00**

Casualty or Theft Loss(es) (You must attach Form 4684 if line 29 is $1,000 or more, OR if certain other situations apply.) (See page 19 of Instructions.)

25 Loss before reimbursement **600 00**

26 Insurance or other reimbursement you received or expect to receive **0 00**

27 Subtract line 26 from line 25. If line 26 is more than line 25, enter zero . . . **600 00** ⑤

28 Enter $100 or amount from line 27, whichever is smaller. **100 00**

29 Total casualty or theft loss(es) (subtract line 28 from line 27). Enter here and on line 37 ▶ **500 00**

Miscellaneous Deductions (See page 19 of Instructions.)

30 a Union dues. **286 00**

b Tax return preparation fee . . . .

31 Other (itemize) ▶ Am.Acctg. Assoc. **50 00** ⑥
National Acctg. Convention **275 00**
Safe Deposit Rental **23 00**

32 Total miscellaneous deductions (add lines 30a through 31). Enter here and on line 38 . . . . ▶ **634 00**

Summary of Itemized Deductions (See page 20 of Instructions.) **A**

33 Total medical and dental—from line 10 . **946 00**

34 Total taxes—from line 16 . . . . **3,841 00**

35 Total interest—from line 20 . . . . **3,294 00** ⑦

36 Total contributions—from line 24 . . . **818 00**

37 Total casualty or theft loss(es)—from line 29 . **500 00**

38 Total miscellaneous—from line 32 . . . **634 00**

39 Add lines 33 through 38 . . . . . **10,033 00**

40 If you checked Form 1040, Filing Status box:
2 or 5, enter $3,400 . . . .
1 or 4, enter $2,300 . . . .
3, enter $1,700 . . . . **2,300 00**

41 Subtract line 40 from line 39. Enter here and on Form 1040, line 32b. (if line 40 is more than line 39, see the Instructions for line 41 on page 20.) . . . . ▶ **7,733 00**

For Paperwork Reduction Act Notice, see Form 1040 Instructions.

FIGURE 26-11 *Form 1040, page 1 for Suzanne Walters*

Form **1040**	Department of the Treasury—Internal Revenue Service **U.S. Individual Income Tax Return**	**1981**	(3)

For the year January 1–December 31, 1981, or other tax year beginning _____ , 1981, ending _____ , 19___ | OMB No. 1545-0074

Use IRS label. Other-wise, please print or type.	Your first name and initial (if joint return, also give spouse's name and initial) Suzanne	Last name Walters	Your social security number 082 01 3619
	Present home address (Number and street, including apartment number, or rural route) 48124 Wixley Avenue		Spouse's social security no.
	City, town or post office, State and ZIP code Plymouth, MI 48107	Your occupation ▶ Prof. of Acctg. Spouse's occupation ▶	

Presidential Election Campaign
Do you want $1 to go to this fund? . . . . X Yes / No
If joint return, does your spouse want $1 to go to this fund? . . . Yes / No
Note: Checking "Yes" will not increase your tax or reduce your refund.

Filing Status
Check only one box.

1 X Single
2 Married filing joint return (even if only one had income)
3 Married filing separate return. Enter spouse's social security no. above and full name here ▶ ....
4 Head of household (with qualifying person). (See page 6 of Instructions.) If he or she is your unmarried child, enter child's name ▶ ....
5 Qualifying widow(er) with dependent child (Year spouse died ▶ 19___). (See page 6 of Instructions.)

For Privacy Act and Paperwork Reduction Act Notice, see Instructions.

Exemptions
Always check the box labeled Yourself.
Check other boxes if they apply.

6a X Yourself   65 or over   Blind
  b   Spouse   65 or over   Blind

Enter number of boxes checked on 6a and b ▶ **1**

c First names of your dependent children who lived with you ▶ ....
Enter number of children listed on 6c ▶

d Other dependents: (1) Name	(2) Relationship	(3) Number of months lived in your home	(4) Did dependent have income of $1,000 or more?	(5) Did you provide more than one-half of dependent's support?

Enter number of other dependents ▶

e Total number of exemptions claimed . . . .
Add numbers entered in boxes above ▶ **1**

Income
Please attach Copy B of your Forms W-2 here.
If you do not have a W-2, see page 5 of Instructions.

7	Wages, salaries, tips, etc.			7	35,500 00
8a	Interest income (attach Schedule B if over $400 or you have any All-Savers interest)	8a	1,000 00		
b	Dividends (attach Schedule B if over $400)	8b	700 00		
c	Total. Add lines 8a and 8b	8c	1,700 00		
d	Exclusion (See page 9 of Instructions)	8d	200 00		
e	Subtract line 8d from line 8c (but not less than zero)			8e	1,500 00
9	Refunds of State and local income taxes (do not enter an amount unless you deducted those taxes in an earlier year—see page 9 of Instructions)			9	
10	Alimony received			10	
11	Business income or (loss) (attach Schedule C) . . . . ▶			11	
12	Capital gain or (loss) (attach Schedule D)			12	
13	40% of capital gain distributions not reported on line 12 (See page 9 of Instructions) .			13	
14	Supplemental gains or (losses) (attach Form 4797)			14	
15	Fully taxable pensions and annuities not reported on line 16			15	
16a	Other pensions and annuities. Total received	16a			
b	Taxable amount, if any, from worksheet on page 10 of Instructions			16b	
17	Rents, royalties, partnerships, estates, trusts, etc. (attach Schedule E)			17	1,100 00
18	Farm income or (loss) (attach Schedule F) . . . . ▶			18	
19a	Unemployment compensation (insurance). Total received	19a			
b	Taxable amount, if any, from worksheet on page 10 of Instructions			19b	
20	Other income (state nature and source—see page 11 of Instructions) ▶			20	
21	Total income. Add amounts in column for lines 7 through 20 . . . . ▶			21	38,100 00

Adjustments to Income
(See Instructions on page 11)

22	Moving expense (attach Form 3903 or 3903F)	22			
23	Employee business expenses (attach Form 2106) . . .	23	2,445 00		
24	Payments to an IRA (enter code from page 11 ....) .	24			
25	Payments to a Keogh (H.R. 10) retirement plan	25			
26	Interest penalty on early withdrawal of savings	26			
27	Alimony paid	27			
28	Disability income exclusion (attach Form 2440)	28			
29	Other adjustments—see page 12 ▶	29			
30	Total adjustments. Add lines 22 through 29 . . . . ▶			30	2,445 00

Adjusted Gross Income

31 Adjusted gross income. Subtract line 30 from line 21. If this line is less than $10,000, see "Earned Income Credit" (line 57) on page 15 of Instructions. If you want IRS to figure your tax, see page 3 of Instructions . . . . ▶ | 31 | 35,655 00

FIGURE 26-12 *Form 1040 page 2 for Suzanne Walters*

Form 1040 (1981)

Page **2**

Tax Computation (See Instructions on page 12)	32a Amount from line 31 *(adjusted gross income)*	32a	35,655	00
	32b If you do not itemize deductions, enter zero . . . . }	32b	7,733	00
	If you itemize, complete Schedule A (Form 1040) and enter the amount from Schedule A, line 41 . . . }			
	Caution: If you have unearned income and can be claimed as a dependent on your parent's return, check here ▶ ☐ and see page 12 of the Instructions. Also see page 12 of the Instructions if:			
	● You are married filing a separate return and your spouse itemizes deductions, OR			
	● You file Form 4563, OR			
	● You are a dual-status alien.			
	32c Subtract line 32b from line 32a	32c	27,922	00
	33 Multiply $1,000 by the total number of exemptions claimed on Form 1040, line 6e . .	33	1,000	00
	34 Taxable Income. Subtract line 33 from line 32c	34	26,922	00
	35 Tax. Enter tax here and check if from ☒ Tax Table, ☐ Tax Rate Schedule X, Y, or Z, ☐ Schedule D, ☐ Schedule G, or ☐ Form 4726	35	6,619	00
	36 Additional Taxes. (See page 13 of Instructions.) Enter here and check if from ☐ Form 4970, ☐ Form 4972, ☐ Form 5544, or ☐ Section 72(m)(5) penalty tax . . . . }	36		
	37 **Total.** Add lines 35 and 36 . . . . ▶	37	6,619	00

Credits (See Instructions on page 13)	38 Credit for contributions to candidates for public office . . .	38			
	39 Credit for the elderly (attach Schedules R&RP)	39			
	40 Credit for child and dependent care expenses (attach Form 2441) .	40			
	41 Investment credit (attach Form 3468)	41			
	42 Foreign tax credit (attach Form 1116)	42			
	43 Work incentive (WIN) credit (attach Form 4874)	43			
	44 Jobs credit (attach Form 5884)	44			
	45 Residential energy credit (attach Form 5695)	45			
	46 Total credits. Add lines 38 through 45	46			
	47 **Balance.** Subtract line 46 from line 37 and enter difference (but not less than zero) . ▶	47	6,619	00

Other Taxes (Including Advance EIC Payments)	48 Self-employment tax (attach Schedule SE)	48		
	49a Minimum tax. Attach Form 4625 and check here ▶ ☐	49a		
	49b Alternative minimum tax. Attach Form 6251 and check here ▶ ☐ . .	49b		
	50 Tax from recomputing prior-year investment credit (attach Form 4255) . . .	50		
	51a Social security (FICA) tax on tip income not reported to employer (attach Form 4137) . .	51a		
	51b Uncollected employee FICA and RRTA tax on tips (from Form W–2)	51b		
	52 Tax on an IRA (attach Form 5329)	52		
06	53 Advance earned income credit (EIC) payments received (from Form W–2)	53		
	54 **Total tax.** Add lines 47 through 53 . . . . ▶	54	6,619	00

Payments Attach Forms W–2, W–2G, and W–2P to front.	55 Total Federal income tax withheld	55	5,690	00	
	56 1981 estimated tax payments and amount applied from 1980 return .	56	850	00	
	57 Earned income credit. If line 32a is under $10,000, see page 15 of Instructions	57			
	58 Amount paid with Form 4868	58			
	59 Excess FICA and RRTA tax withheld (two or more employers)	59			
	60 Credit for Federal tax on special fuels and oils (attach Form 4136 or 4136–T)	60			
	61 Regulated Investment Company credit (attach Form 2439)	61			
	62 **Total.** Add lines 55 through 61 . . . . ▶	62	6,540	00

Refund or Balance Due	63 If line 62 is larger than line 54, enter amount **OVERPAID** . . . . ▶	63		
	64 Amount of line 63 to be **REFUNDED TO YOU** . . . . ▶	64		
	65 Amount of line 63 to be applied to your 1982 estimated tax . . . ▶	65		
	66 If line 54 is larger than line 62, enter **BALANCE DUE.** Attach check or money order for full amount payable to "Internal Revenue Service." Write your social security number and "1981 Form 1040" on it. ▶ (Check ▶ ☐ if Form 2210 (2210F) is attached. See page 16 of Instructions.) ▶ $	66	79	00

Please Sign Here

Under penalties of perjury, I declare that I have examined this return, including accompanying schedules and statements, and to the best of my knowledge and belief, it is true, correct, and complete. Declaration of preparer (other than taxpayer) is based on all information of which preparer has any knowledge.

▶ *Suzanne Walters* 4/15/82
Your signature   Date

Spouse's signature (if filing jointly, BOTH must sign even if only one had income)

Paid Preparer's Use Only	Preparer's signature ▶	Date	Check if self-employed ▶ ☐	Preparer's social security no.
	Firm's name (or yours, if self-employed) and address ▶		E.I. No. ▶	
			ZIP code ▶	

line 32b is entered on line 32c as shown in Figure 26-12. Suzanne is allowed to deduct $1,000 for her personal exemption allowance and this amount is recorded on line 33. The difference between $27,922 entered on line 32c and the $1,000 entered on line 33 represents the taxable income of Suzanne Walters amounting to $26,922 ($27,922 − $1,000), and this amount is entered on line 34.

Taxes are determined on the taxable income of $26,922 entered on line 34 of Form 1040 using the tax tables because the amount is below $50,000.

Tax rates will vary for different types of taxpayers. The I.R.S. requires some taxpayers to use the *tax tables* (Figure 26-13) and they require other taxpayers to use the *tax rate Schedules* X, Y, or Z (Figure 26-14). Most taxpayers will use the tax tables if their taxable income is $50,000 or less. Taxpayers who are not eligible to use the tax tables must use the tax rate Schedules X, Y, or Z if their taxable income exceeds $50,000 and they are using income averaging. If taxpayers are required to use the tax rate schedules, they must deduct the $1,000 personal exemption allowances from their taxable income before computing the amount of their tax.

By using the tax tables shown in Figure 26-13 and finding Suzanne's taxable income of $26,922, we see that her tax amounts to $6,619 for 1981. This amount is entered on lines 35, 37, 47, and 54 of Form 1040. During 1981, Plymouth College deducted $5,690 for federal income tax from Suzanne's wages, and she also paid estimated tax payments of $850, for a total tax payment amounting to $6,540 ($5,690 + $850).

The $5,690 of federal income tax withheld by her employer is entered on line 55 and the $850 paid in estimated tax payments is entered on line 56 of Form 1040. On line 62, the total amount of $6,540 is entered, and this amount is deducted from the amount of $6,619 appearing on line 54. The $79 difference ($6,619 − $6,540) is entered on line 66. This amount represents the amount of tax due by Suzanne Walters when she filed her 1981 tax return.

Before Form 1040 is mailed to the I.R.S. with a check for any tax due, the form must be signed and dated by the taxpayer. The completed tax return for Suzanne Walters is shown in Figure 26-12.

Itemizing Personal Deductions

When must a taxpayer itemize personal deductions?

The marital status of a taxpayer and the amount of his/her allowable personal deductions determine whether a taxpayer may have the option of itemizing or not itemizing personal expenses or if he/she is required to itemize.

Taxpayers *may have the option* of itemizing their personal expenses if they are:

1. Married and file a joint tax return with spouse or the taxpayer is a qualified widow/er with a dependent child and has allowable personal deductions of $3,400 or more

FIGURE 26-13   *Partial 1981 tax tables*

1981 Tax Table
Based on Taxable Income
For persons with taxable incomes of less than $50,000.

Example: Mr. and Mrs. Brown are filing a joint return. Their taxable income on line 34 is $23,270. First, they find the $23,250-23,300 income line. Next, they find the column for married filing jointly and read down the column. The amount shown where the income line and filing status column meet is $4,082. This is the tax amount they must write on line 35 of their return.

At least	But less than	Single	Married filing jointly *	Married filing separately	Head of a household
			Your tax is—		
23,200	23,250	5,208	4,069	6,438	4,805
23,250	23,300	5,224	(4,082)	6,462	4,820
23,300	23,350	5,241	4,096	6,486	4,836

If line 34 (taxable income) is—		And you are—				If line 34 (taxable income) is—		And you are—				If line 34 (taxable income) is—		And you are—			
At least	But less than	Single	Married filing jointly *	Married filing separately	Head of a household	At least	But less than	Single	Married filing jointly *	Married filing separately	Head of a household	At least	But less than	Single	Married filing jointly *	Married filing separately	Head of a household
			Your tax is—						Your tax is—						Your tax is—		
0	1,700	0	0	0	0	**3,000**						5,500	5,550	510	294	618	468
1,700	1,725	0	0	a2	0							5,550	5,600	519	302	627	476
1,725	1,750	0	0	5	0	3,000	3,050	100	0	189	100	5,600	5,650	528	310	635	484
						3,050	3,100	107	0	197	107	5,650	5,700	537	318	644	492
1,750	1,775	0	0	9	0	3,100	3,150	114	0	204	114	5,700	5,750	546	326	653	500
1,775	1,800	0	0	12	0	3,150	3,200	121	0	212	121						
1,800	1,825	0	0	16	0	3,200	3,250	128	0	220	128	5,750	5,800	554	334	662	508
1,825	1,850	0	0	19	0							5,800	5,850	563	342	671	515
1,850	1,875	0	0	22	0	3,250	3,300	135	0	228	135	5,850	5,900	572	350	680	5~~
						3,300	3,350	14?	0	236	1~	~ 900			2~~		
~ 25,5~~						~,250		,,139	5,610	24?	6,587	~1,000					
25,550	25,600	6,099	4,757	7,575	5,627	28,300	28,350	7,158	5,626	6,906	6,604	31,000	31,050	8,308	6,535	10,263	7,696
25,600	25,650	6,118	4,773	7,599	5,645	28,350	28,400	7,177	5,642	8,930	6,622	31,050	31,100	8,330	6,553	10,289	7,717
25,650	25,700	6,138	4,788	7,623	5,662	28,400	28,450	7,197	5,657	8,954	6,640	31,100	31,150	8,351	6,571	10,316	7,738
25,700	25,750	6,157	4,804	7,647	5,680	28,450	28,500	7,216	5,673	8,978	6,658	31,150	31,200	8,373	6,589	10,343	7,758
												31,200	31,250	8,395	6,608	10,369	7,779
25,750	25,800	6,176	4,820	7,672	5,698	28,500	28,550	7,235	5,689	9,002	6,676						
25,800	25,850	6,195	4,836	7,696	5,716	28,550	28,600	7,254	5,705	9,026	6,693	31,250	31,300	8,416	6,626	10,396	7,800
25,850	25,900	6,215	4,852	7,720	5,733	28,600	28,650	7,274	5,721	9,051	6,711	31,300	31,350	8,438	6,644	10,423	7,821
25,900	25,950	6,234	4,867	7,744	5,751	28,650	28,700	7,293	5,736	9,075	6,729	31,350	31,400	8,460	6,662	10,449	7,841
25,950	26,000	6,253	4,883	7,768	5,769	28,700	28,750	7,312	5,752	9,099	6,747	31,400	31,450	8,482	6,681	10,476	7,862
26,000												31,450	31,500	8,503	6,699	10,503	7,883
26,000	26,050	6,272	4,899	7,793	5,787	28,750	28,800	7,331	5,768	9,123	6,764						
26,050	26,100	6,292	4,915	7,817	5,805	28,800	28,850	7,352	5,784	9,147	6,784	31,500	31,550	8,525	6,717	10,529	7,903
26,100	26,150	6,311	4,931	7,841	5,822	28,850	28,900	7,374	5,800	9,172	6,804	31,550	31,600	8,547	6,735	10,556	7,924
26,150	26,200	6,330	4,946	7,865	5,840	28,900	28,950	7,395	5,815	9,196	6,825	31,600	31,650	8,569	6,754	10,583	7,945
26,200	26,250	6,349	4,962	7,889	5,858	28,950	29,000	7,417	5,831	9,220	6,846	31,650	31,700	8,590	6,772	10,609	7,966
						29,000						31,700	31,750	8,612	6,790	10,636	7,986
26,250	26,300	6,369	4,978	7,914	5,876	29,000	29,050	7,439	5,847	9,244	6,867						
26,300	26,350	6,388	4,994	7,938	5,893	29,050	29,100	7,461	5,863	9,268	6,887	31,750	31,800	8,634	6,809	10,663	8,007
26,350	26,400	6,407	5,010	7,962	5,911	29,100	29,150	7,482	5,879	9,293	6,908	31,800	31,850	8,655	6,827	10,689	8,028
26,400	26,450	6,426	5,025	7,986	5,929	29,150	29,200	7,504	5,894	9,317	6,929	31,850	31,900	8,677	6,845	10,716	8,049
26,450	26,500	6,446	5,041	8,010	5,947	29,200	29,250	7,526	5,910	9,341	6,950	31,900	31,950	8,699	6,863	10,743	8,069
												31,950	32,000	8,721	6,882	10,769	8,090
26,500	26,550	6,465	5,057	8,035	5,965	29,250	29,300	7,547	5,926	9,365	6,970	**32,000**					
26,550	26,600	6,484	5,073	8,059	5,982	29,300	29,350	7,569	5,942	9,389	6,991	32,000	32,050	8,742	6,900	10,796	8,111
26,600	26,650	6,503	5,089	8,083	6,000	29,350	29,400	7,591	5,958	9,414	7,012	32,050	32,100	8,764	6,918	10,823	8,132
26,650	26,700	6,523	5,104	8,107	6,018	29,400	29,450	7,613	5,973	9,438	7,032	32,100	32,150	8,786	6,936	10,849	8,152
26,700	26,750	6,542	5,120	8,131	6,036	29,450	29,500	7,634	5,989	9,462	7,053	32,150	32,200	8,808	6,955	10,876	8,173
												32,200	32,250	8,829	6,973	10,902	8,194
26,750	26,800	6,561	5,136	8,156	6,053	29,500	29,550	7,656	6,005	9,486	7,074						
26,800	26,850	6,580	5,152	8,180	6,071	29,550	29,600	7,678	6,021	9,510	7,095	32,250	32,300	8,851	6,991	10,929	8,215
26,850	26,900	6,600	5,168	8,204	6,089	29,600	29,650	7,700	6,037	9,535	7,115	32,300	32,350	8,873	7,010	10,956	8,235
26,900	26,950	6,619	5,183	8,228	6,107	29,650	29,700	7,721	6,052	9,559	7,136	32,350	32,400	8,894	7,028	10,982	8,256
26,950	27,000	6,638	5,199	8,252	6,124	29,700	29,750	7,743	6,068	9,583	7,157	32,400	32,450	8,916	7,046	11,009	8,277
27,000												32,450	32,500	8,938	7,064	11,036	8,297
27,000	27,050	6,657	5,215	8,276	6,142	29,750	29,800	7,765	6,084	9,607	7,178	32,500	32,550	8,960	7,083	11,062	8,318
27,050	27,100	6,677	5,231	8,301	6,160	29,800	29,850	7,786	6,100	9,631	7,198	32,550	32,600	8,981	7,101	11,089	8,339
27,100	27,150	6,696	5,247	8,325	6,178	29,850	29,900	7,808	6,116	9,656	7,219	32,600	32,650	9,003	7,119	11,116	8,360
27,150	27,200	6,715	5,262	8,349	6,196	29,900	29,950	7,830	6,133	9,680	7,240	32,650	32,700	9,025	7,137	11,142	8,380
27,200	27,250	6,735	5,278	8,373	6,213	29,950	30,000	7,852	6,151	9,704	7,261	32,700	32,750	9,046	7,156	11,169	8,401

*This column must also be used by a qualifying widow(er).

Continued on next page

FIGURE 26-14 *1981 tax rate Schedules X, Y, and Z*

1981 Tax Rate Schedules

Your zero bracket amount has been built into these Tax Rate Schedules.

Schedule X
Single Taxpayers

Use this schedule if you checked **Filing Status Box 1** on Form 1040—

If the amount on Form 1040, line 34 is: Over—	But not Over—	Enter on line 2 of the worksheet on this page:	of the amount over—
$0	$2,300	—0—	
2,300	3,400	.... 14%	$2,300
3,400	4,400	$154+16%	3,400
4,400	6,500	314+18%	4,400
6,500	8,500	692+19%	6,500
8,500	10,800	1,072+21%	8,500
10,800	12,900	1,555+24%	10,800
12,900	15,000	2,059+26%	12,900
15,000	18,200	2,605+30%	15,000
18,200	23,500	3,565+34%	18,200
23,500	28,800	5,367+39%	23,500
28,800	34,100	7,434+44%	28,800
34,100	41,500	9,766+49%	34,100
41,500	55,300	13,392+55%	41,500
55,300	81,800	20,982+63%	55,300
81,800	108,300	37,677+68%	81,800
108,300	....	55,697+70%	108,300

Schedule Z
Unmarried Heads of Household

(including certain married persons who live apart (and abandoned spouses)—see page 6 of the Instructions)

Use this schedule if you checked **Filing Status Box 4** on Form 1040—

If the amount on Form 1040, line 34 is: Over—	But not over—	Enter on line 2 of the worksheet on this page:	of the amount over—
$0	$2,300	—0—	
2,300	4,400	.... 14%	$2,300
4,400	6,500	$294+16%	4,400
6,500	8,700	630+18%	6,500
8,700	11,800	1,026+22%	8,700
11,800	15,000	1,708+24%	11,800
15,000	18,200	2,476+26%	15,000
18,200	23,500	3,308+31%	18,200
23,500	28,800	4,951+36%	23,500
28,800	34,100	6,859+42%	28,800
34,100	44,700	9,085+46%	34,100
44,700	60,600	13,961+54%	44,700
60,600	81,800	22,547+59%	60,600
81,800	108,300	35,055+63%	81,800
108,300	161,300	51,750+68%	108,300
161,300	....	87,790+70%	161,300

Schedule Y
Married Taxpayers and Qualifying Widows and Widowers

Married Filing Joint Returns and Qualifying Widows and Widowers

Use this schedule if you checked **Filing Status Box 2 or 5** on Form 1040—

If the amount on Form 1040, line 34 is: Over—	But not over—	Enter on line 2 of the worksheet on this page:	of the amount over—
$0	$3,400	—0—	
3,400	5,500	.... 14%	$3,400
5,500	7,600	$294+16%	5,500
7,600	11,900	630+18%	7,600
11,900	16,000	1,404+21%	11,900
16,000	20,200	2,265+24%	16,000
20,200	24,600	3,273+28%	20,200
24,600	29,900	4,505+32%	24,600
29,900	35,200	6,201+37%	29,900
35,200	45,800	8,162+43%	35,200
45,800	60,000	12,720+49%	45,800
60,000	85,600	19,678+54%	60,000
85,600	109,400	33,502+59%	85,600
109,400	162,400	47,544+64%	109,400
162,400	215,400	81,464+68%	162,400
215,400	....	117,504+70%	215,400

Married Filing Separate Returns

Use this schedule if you checked **Filing Status Box 3** on Form 1040—

If the amount on Form 1040, line 34 is: Over—	But not over—	Enter on line 2 of the worksheet on this page:	of the amount over—
$0	$1,700	—0—	
1,700	2,750	.... 14%	$1,700
2,750	3,800	$147.00+16%	2,750
3,800	5,950	315.00+18%	3,800
5,950	8,000	702.00+21%	5,950
8,000	10,100	1,132.50+24%	8,000
10,100	12,300	1,636.50+28%	10,100
12,300	14,950	2,252.50+32%	12,300
14,950	17,600	3,100.50+37%	14,950
17,600	22,900	4,081.00+43%	17,600
22,900	30,000	6,360.00+49%	22,900
30,000	42,800	9,839.00+54%	30,000
42,800	54,700	16,751.00+59%	42,800
54,700	81,200	23,772.00+64%	54,700
81,200	107,700	40,732.00+68%	81,200
107,700	....	58,752.00+70%	107,700

Caution

You must use the Tax Table instead of these Tax Rate Schedules if your taxable income is less than $50,000 unless you use Form 4726 (maximum tax), Schedule D (alternative tax), or Schedule G (income averaging), to figure your tax. In those cases, even if your taxable income is less than $50,000, use the rate schedules on this page to figure your tax.

Instructions

If you cannot use the Tax Table, figure your tax on the amount on line 34 of Form 1040 by using the appropriate Tax Rate Schedule. Then, unless you use Schedule G or Form 4726, figure your 1981 Rate Reduction Credit (1.25%) on the worksheet below.

Tax Computation Worksheet

(Do not use if you figure your tax on Schedule G or Form 4726.)

1. Taxable income from Form 1040, line 34 . _____
2. Tax on the amount on line 1 from Tax Rate Schedule X, Y, or Z . _____
3. Rate Reduction Credit. Multiply the amount on line 2 by .0125 . . . . . _____
4. Subtract line 3 from line 2. Enter here and on Form 1040, line 35 . . . . . _____

Do not file—keep for your records.

Note: If you use the alternative tax computation on Schedule D (Form 1040), enter the amount from Schedule D, line 32, on line 1 of the worksheet. Complete the worksheet and enter the amount from line 4 of the worksheet on Schedule D, line 33.

FIGURE 26-15 *Form 1040, Schedule G income averaging*

SCHEDULE G
(Form 1040)
Department of the Treasury
Internal Revenue Service   (O)

Income Averaging

▶ See instructions on back.
▶ Attach to Form 1040.

OMB No. 1545–0074

19
20

Name(s) as shown on Form 1040

Your social security number

Base Period Income and Adjustments

	(a) 1980	(b) 1979	(c) 1978	(d) 1977
1 Enter amount from: Form 1040—line 34 Form 1040A (1977 and 1978)—line 10 Form 1040A (1979 and 1980)—line 11 . .				
2 a Multiply $750 by your total number of exemptions each year, 1977 and 1978 .	/////	/////		
b Multiply $1,000 by your total number of exemptions each year, 1979 and 1980 .			/////	/////
3 Taxable income (subtract line 2a or 2b from line 1. If less than zero, enter zero . . .				
4 Income earned outside of the United States or within U.S. possessions and excluded under sections 911 and 931				
5 Base period income (add lines 3 and 4) . .				

Computation of Averageable Income

6 Taxable income for 1981 from Form 1040, line 34	6	
7 Certain amounts received by owner-employees subject to a penalty under section 72(m)(5)	7	
8 Subtract line 7 from line 6	8	
9 Excess community income	9	
10 Adjusted taxable income (subtract line 9 from line 8). If less than zero, enter zero	10	
11 Add columns (a) through (d), line 5, and enter here	11	
12 Enter 30% of line 11	12	
13 Averageable income (subtract line 12 from line 10)	13	

If line 13 is $3,000 or less, do not complete the rest of this form. You do not qualify for income averaging.

G

Computation of Tax

14 Amount from line 12	14	
15 20% of line 13	15	
16 Total (add lines 14 and 15)	16	
17 Excess community income from line 9	17	
18 Total (add lines 16 and 17)	18	
19 Tax on amount on line 18 (see caution below)	19	
20 Tax on amount on line 16 (see caution below)	20	
21 Tax on amount on line 14 (see caution below)	21	
22 Subtract line 21 from line 20	22	
23 Multiply the amount on line 22 by 4	23	

Note: *If no entry was made on line 7 above, skip lines 24 through 26 and go to line 27.*

24 Tax on amount on line 6 (see caution below)	24	
25 Tax on amount on line 8 (see caution below)	25	
26 Subtract line 25 from line 24	26	
27 Add lines 19, 23, and 26	27	
28 Multiply line 27 by .0125	28	
29 Tax (subtract line 28 from line 27). Enter here and on Form 1040, line 35 and check Schedule G box . .	29	

Caution: Use Tax Rate Schedule X, Y, or Z from the Form 1040 instructions, but do not use the Tax Computation Worksheet on that page. Do not use the Tax Table.

For Paperwork Reduction Act Notice, see Form 1040 instructions.

2. Married and filing a separate tax return and the allowable personal deductions amount to $1,700 or more
3. Single or an unmarried person qualified as head of household[2] with allowable personal deductions amounting to $2,300 or more

Taxpayers *may be required* to itemize personal expenses if they:

1. Are married and file a separate tax return and spouse itemizes personal expenses
2. Can be claimed as a dependent on parent's return and received interest, dividends, or other unearned income of $1,000 or more
3. Filed Form 4563 which allows a U.S. citizen to exclude any income received from sources outside the U.S. To qualify for the income exclusion, 80 percent of a taxpayer's gross income must be from sources within a U.S. possession for a 3-year period immediately preceding the tax year
4. Were a nonresident alien for part of the tax year and a resident alien or U.S. citizen for the other half of the tax year

Income Averaging

If the taxable income of taxpayers increases substantially for a tax year, they may file Form 1040, *Schedule G* (Income Averaging) providing the taxpayer qualifies. To qualify for income averaging, taxpayers must be U.S. citizens or residents for a 5-year period ending on December 31, 1981, and they must have furnished at least 50 percent or more of their support for the 5-year period. Form 1040, Schedule G is illustrated in Figure 26-15.

SUMMARY

An individual is required to file an income tax return based on the amount of income received during a tax year, marital status, and age. However, there are two exceptions to the income and marital status requirements. Individuals must file a tax return even if they are not subject to any taxes if (1) they are self-employed with yearly earnings of $400 or (2) they have yearly earnings of $1,000 or more and are a dependent of another taxpayer, they are married and are not living with their spouse at the end of tax year, or a spouse has filed a separate return.

[2] To qualify as head of household, a taxpayer must be unmarried on December 31, 1981; married but not living with spouse; be an abandoned spouse; or married but legally separated and the taxpayer must have paid more than half the cost of maintaining the main home of his/her parent/s that he/she can claim as a dependent (taxpayer does not have to live with parent/s). Or, the taxpayer must have paid more than half the cost of maintaining a home that was lived in all year by an unmarried child, fosterchild, grandchild, or stepchild (person does not have to be dependent of taxpayer); and mother-in-law, father-in-law, brother-in-law, sister-in-law, son-in-law, uncle, aunt, nephew, or niece that taxpayer can claim as dependent.

The income requirements for filing a tax return are based on gross income. Gross income consists of all salaries, wages, commissions, fees, royalties, and bonuses earned by an individual plus dividends and interest (less $200 exclusion), rent, or profits received from a trade or business and from investments that are subject to taxes. Adjusted gross income is the difference between gross income and allowable business expense deductions. Taxable income is the difference between adjusted gross income, allowable personal expense deductions (itemized deductions), and the amount of exemption allowance.

All taxpayers in the year 1981 were allowed one $1,000 exemption, an additional $1,000 exemption for the spouse if they were married and filed a joint return, if they were 65 years of age or over, if spouse was 65 years of age or over, if the taxpayer was blind, if spouse was blind, plus one additional exemption for each qualified dependent of the taxpayer.

Taxpayers must file a tax return on a short form, Form 1040A, or a long form, Form 1040. The short form, Form 1040A, may be used if taxpayers received all income from wages or tips, did not receive over $400 of dividends or interest, and did not itemize personal expense deductions. If taxpayers do not qualify for the short form, they must file a tax return on the long form, Form 1040.

Interest or dividend income received by a taxpayer exceeding $400 during the tax year must be reported on Schedule B and filed along with Form 1040. Any taxable income received from pensions, annuities, rents, royalties, or from a partnership must be reported on Schedule E and included with Form 1040.

Business expenses and personal expense deductions that a taxpayer is allowed to deduct from gross income are established by the I.R.S. Some taxpayers are required to itemize their personal expense deductions, and other taxpayers have the option of itemizing or not itemizing.

If the taxable income of taxpayers increased substantially during a tax year, they may file Schedule G and average all income over a 5-year period.

All self-employed individuals are required to file Schedule SE (Computation of Social Security Self-Employment Tax) unless they received other wages of $29,700 or more during 1981 that was subject to deductions for social security taxes.

GLOSSARY

Adjusted Gross Income: The difference between gross income and allowable business expense deductions.

Exemption: A $1,000 allowance given to each taxpayer plus one additional $1,000 allowance for (1) a taxpayer over 65 years of age, (2) a taxpayer who is blind, (3) a spouse (if a joint return is filed), (4) a spouse over 65 years of age, (5) a spouse who is blind, and (6) each qualified dependent of taxpayer or spouse.

Form 1040: A form for reporting the filing status, exemptions, income, adjustments to income, adjusted gross income, tax computation, credits, other taxes, tax payments, and the amount of refund or tax due.

Form 1040A: A short-form tax return that may be filed by a taxpayer who receives all income from wages or tips, did not receive over $400 in dividends or interest, and did not itemize allowable personal expense deductions.

Form 2106: A form used by a taxpayer who is employed by a business as an outside salesperson and incurs expenses necessary in performing his/her duties that are not paid by the employer may claim these expenses by filing Form 2106 along with Form 1040. Some of these business expenses may only be deducted if the taxpayer itemizes his/her personal deductions on Form 1040.

Gross Income: All salaries, wages, commissions, fees, royalties, and bonuses earned by an individual plus dividends, interest, rent, or profits received from a trade or business and investments that are subject to taxes.

Schedule A: A form for reporting the allowable personal expense deductions of a taxpayer. The schedule is filed with Form 1040.

Schedule B: A form for reporting the amount and source of taxable interest and dividend income received by a taxpayer. Taxpayers must file Schedule B if they received $400 or more in interest and dividends during the tax year, and the schedule must be filed along with Form 1040.

Schedule C: A form for reporting all the expenses incurred by a taxpayer in operating a trade, business, or profession. These expenses are deductible from gross income to arrive at adjusted gross income. The expense must be directly related to the production of revenue for a trade, business, or profession of the taxpayer, and the expense must be reasonable in amount. A taxpayer who operates a trade, business, or professional practice is required to report his/her business income and allowable business deductions on Form 1040, Schedule C. This schedule is filed with Form 1040.

Schedule E: A form for reporting the amount and source of taxable income received by a taxpayer from pensions, annuities, rents, royalties, or a partnership. The schedule is filed with Form 1040.

Schedule G: A form used if a substantial increase in taxable income has occurred. The income of the taxpayer is averaged over a 5-year period ending with the current tax year. The schedule is filed with Form 1040.

Schedule SE (Computation of Social Security Self-Employment Tax): A form for reporting self-employment income subject to social security taxes. The schedule is filed with Form 1040.

Tax Rate Schedule: A method of computing the amount of tax liability for a taxpayer who is not eligible to use the tax tables. Taxpayers with taxable income of more than $50,000 or using income averaging must use the tax rate schedule for computing his/her tax liability.

Tax Tables: A short-cut method of computing the amount of tax liability for taxpayers with taxable income of $50,000 or less.

Taxable Income: The amount used to compute an individual's income tax using tax tables or tax rate schedules.

QUESTIONS

1. Give the 1981 requirements for filing a tax return based on yearly income, marital status, and age for the following individuals.
   (a) An unmarried taxpayer
   (b) Surviving spouse
   (c) Married couple filing a joint tax return; husband is 65 years of age
   (d) Self-employed taxpayer
2. Define the initials AGI and TI.
3. State the formula for computing amount of taxable income by a taxpayer who itemizes expenses and is eligible to use the tax tables.
4. How many exemptions are married taxpayers entitled to if they are 60 years of age, blind, and file a joint tax return with their spouse?
5. A taxpayer provided all the support for a friend who had financial difficulties. The friend did not live in the household of the taxpayer. Would the taxpayer be entitled to a $1,000 exemption for the friend? Explain.
6. An unmarried student worked part time and earned $3,200 in taxable wages. The student is 19 years of age, attended college as a full-time student for 9 months during the year, lived with his parents, and was supported by them during the entire tax year. Is the student required to file a tax return, and may the parents claim their son as a dependent on their joint tax return?
7. What three tests must be met to qualify a person as a dependent of a taxpayer?
8. Name the form that is used to report deductible expenses of an outside salesperson.

EXERCISES

Computation of Gross Income, Adjusted Gross Income, and Taxable Income

1. Shelley Andrews earned $18,000 in salaries during 1981, received dividends of $400 and interest of $100, and received rental income of $3,600 from a home she owns for rental purposes. The allowable business expenses on her rental property amounted to $1,100, and her allowable personal expense deductions amounted to $4,100.

   Required

   Determine the following:
   (a) Gross income
   (b) Adjusted gross income
   (c) Taxable income

Determining Number of Allowable Exemptions and Gross Income

2. Helen Regal is 68 years of age and maintains a home for her 16-year-old grandchild. During 1981, Helen received the following income:

Pension (paid by employer)	$8,258
Social security	6,700
Interest from savings account	1,200
Dividends from stock investments	692

Required

Determine the following:
(a) Number of allowable exemptions
(b) Gross income

Determining Allowable Business Expense Deductions

3. A salesperson traveled 21,000 miles during 1981 of which 15,000 miles were for business purposes. Other automobile expenses incurred amounted to $1,520 for gas and oil; $35, car license; $295, car insurance; $442, car repairs and maintenance; and $50, parking fees for business purposes.

Required

Determine the amount of allowable business expense deductions for 1981 using the:
(a) Regular method
(b) Optional method

Determining Allowable Personal Expense Deductions, Gross Income, and Adjusted Gross Income

4. A taxpayer earned wages of $20,500 and filed a joint return with his/her spouse who earned wages of $15,000. The couple is less than 65 years of age and have one dependent child. During 1981, the couple's medical expenses amounted to $180 for medical insurance; $400 for medicines and drugs; and $1,400 for doctor bills not covered by insurance.

Required

Determine the amount of medical expense deduction allowed on a 1981 tax return.

5. An unmarried taxpayer with gross income of $29,000 which included dividends of $300 had the following business and personal expenses during 1981.

Car expenses for 18,000 miles, 12,000 business miles	$2,220
Parking fees for business	40
Contributions	495
Medical expenses: Doctor	520
Medicine and drugs	180
Interest on home mortgage and charge accounts	3,498
Real estate taxes	1,440
State income and state sales taxes	1,700

Required

Determine the following:
(a) Gross income
(b) Adjusted gross income
(c) Total amount of allowable personal expense deductions

Determining Amount of Income Taxes

6. A married taxpayer filing a joint return had adjusted gross income of $22,900 and allowable personal expense deductions of $8,100 and qualified for three exemptions. Federal income taxes of $2,235 were deducted from wages during 1981.

Required

Determine the amount of income tax due or to be refunded for 1981 assuming the total tax liability (joint return) using the tax tables amounted to $2,076.

PROBLEMS

Determining Number of Exemptions and Items to Be Included in Gross Income

26-1. Check the block in Chart A (on page 731) to indicate the number of exemptions taxpayers are entitled to claim on their income tax return for 1981. The first item has been completed as an example.

Check the block in Chart B (on page 731) to indicate the items that must be included in gross income for 1981. The first item has been completed as an example.

Determining Income Requirements, Gross Income, and Adjusted Gross Income

26-2. Income requirements for filing a tax return are established by the I.R.S. Check the appropriate block in Chart A (on page 732) to indicate if a taxpayer is required to file an income tax return for 1981.

For use with problem 26-1

CHART A

Taxpayer	Exemptions				
	1	2	3	4	5
1. Unmarried person	√				
2. Married filing joint return, both over 65 years of age					
3. Blind and less than age 65					
4. Blind and over age of 65					
5. Married filing joint return and mother-in-law over 65 years of age is a dependent of taxpayer					
6. Unmarried person supporting a brother who is living in France and is not a U.S. citizen					
7. Unmarried person supporting friend who lived all year in taxpayer's household and has income of $500					

CHART B

Type of Income	Included in Income	Not Included in Income
1. Commissions received by taxpayer	√	
2. Gift certificate received by employee from employer		
3. Pension benefits paid by taxpayer		
4. Social security benefits		
5. Proceeds of a life insurance policy to beneficiary		
6. Prize received as contestant on quiz show		
7. Dependent's income of $1,000 on tax return of parent		
8. Interest received from savings account in credit union		
9. Interest received on municipal bonds		
10. Interest received on investments inherited from father		
11. Health insurance premiums paid by employer		

For use with problem 26-2

CHART A

Income Received by Taxpayer	Tax Return Is Required Yes	No
1. Unmarried taxpayer with earnings of $2,900		
2. Unmarried taxpayer over 65 years of age receiving social security benefits of $549 per month plus dividends of $700 per year		
3. Taxpayer makes and designs handbags and sells them at shopping malls and bazaars; earnings for 1981 amounted to $3,400; cost of materials, $1,150		
4. Full-time student with part-time earnings of $2,400; student is qualified dependent of parents		
5. Married, filing joint return with taxable pension benefits of $4,600 and social security benefits of $7,100		
6. Surviving spouse maintaining home for dependent son with social security benefits of $6,000; insurance proceeds as beneficiary, $10,000; and part-time wages of $3,600		
7. Qualified dependent parents of a taxpayer with taxable pension benefits of $1,500		
8. A dependent relative with dividend and interest income of $1,000		

CHART B

Item	Gross Income +	Gross Income −	Adjusted Gross Income +	Adjusted Gross Income −	Not Reported or Not Deductible
1. Royalties received by taxpayer	X				
2. Inheritance received from relative					
3. Home mortgage interest					
4. Cost of life insurance policy					
5. Bonus received from employer					
6. Real estate taxes on personal residence					
7. Self-employment income of $600					
8. Wages received by taxpayer who is a dependent of parent, $990					
9. Loss of automobile due to accident not covered by insurance					
10. Auto repairs of family automobile					
11. Automobile expense of outside salesperson not paid by employer					

For each item listed in Chart B (on page 732), check the appropriate block to indicate if the item is an addition to gross income, subtraction from gross income, subtraction from adjusted gross income, or income that is not reported or is not deductible. The first item has been completed as an example.

Determining Gross Income, Personal Expense Deductions, Taxable Income, and Exemption Allowance

26-3. Maria and Alex Perez with three dependent children work and live in Michigan. During 1981, they received the following income and incurred the expenses listed:

Maria's salary as a legal secretary		$13,500
Alex's wages as a production worker		19,200
Dividends from stock investments owned jointly by Maria and Alex		1,800
Interest:		
Savings accounts	$1,200	
Credit union savings	480	
City of Wales bonds	620	2,300
Rental income		4,800
Expenses of rental property:		
Interest on mortgage	$3,200	
Depreciation	1,000	
Repairs and maintenance	400	4,600
Real estate taxes on residence		1,840
Mortgage interest on residence		2,460
Contributions to St. Edithe Church		540
State sales tax (use Figure 26-9)		?
State and local gasoline taxes		135
State income taxes		1,660
Repairs to family automobile		380

Required

Determine the following assuming Maria and Alex file a joint tax return.
(*a*) Gross income
(*b*) Personal expense deductions
(*c*) Taxable income
(*d*) Number of exemptions allowed to claim

26-4. Joan and Jack Carsun lived in Plymouth, Michigan, and had two dependent children, Wayne and John. John was 20 years of age, earned $1,600 during the summer, and attended college as a full-time student during the year 1981. Jack Carsun was employed as an electrician for a local electrical company and received wages of $22,614. Joan was laid off from her job as an assembler for a local parts company and received unemployment benefits of $2,340. Joan and Jack Carsun received rental income of $2,400 ($3,600 rental income less $1,200 allowable expenses), and they incurred the nonbusiness expenses listed on page 734 during 1981.

Medical insurance payments	$3,000
Medical and dental expenses (not covered by insurance)	601
Drugs and medicines	142
Real estate taxes on residence	1,950
State of Michigan income taxes	1,250
Michigan sales tax (use Figure 26-9)	?
Mortgage interest on residence	1,300
Interest on charge accounts	80
Contributions: Reformed Church of Michigan	520
Salvation Army	180
United Foundation	100
Goodwill Industries	25

During the year 1981, Joan and Jack also received interest on savings accounts of $1,090 ($490, Electrical Workers Credit Union and $600, Lowell National Bank), and Jack received $800 in dividends from stock investments ($540, Electrical Corporation and $260, Wondrus Corporation).

Required

Determine the following assuming Joan and Jack Carsun filed a joint tax return for 1981.
(a) Gross income
(b) Personal expense deductions
(c) Taxable income
(d) Number of exemptions

Preparation of Form 1040 and Form 1040, Schedules A and B

26-5. Referring to Problem 26-4, assume that Jack Carsun had $2,634 deducted for federal income tax, and the tax on taxable income (on a joint return) using the tax tables amounted to $2,574.

Required

Prepare the following using the forms provided in the Study Guide Workbook (some of the personal data has been entered on the forms).
(a) Schedules A and B
(b) Form 1040

26-6. Robert Axley was employed for Thompson Interiors located in Livonia, Michigan, as a salesperson during 1981. Robert was not married, but he provided the full support of his parents who lived in Redford, Michigan. Robert lived at 484 Stratton Lane, Livonia, Michigan 48052. During 1981, Robert earned salaries and commissions amounting to $28,600, he received dividends of $2,800 from stock investments ($1,800 from Munro Products and $1,000 from Dixboro Sales), and he incurred nonbusiness expenses as follows:

Medical and dental costs for parents (not covered by insurance)	$1,400
Medicine and drugs for parents	420
Real estate taxes on residence	2,350
Michigan income taxes	1,400
Michigan sales taxes (use Figure 26-9)	?
Mortgage interest on residence	4,280
Interest on automobile loan	190
Contributions: Michigan Presbyterian Church (Check)	780
United Foundation (Check)	100
Salvation Army (Check)	50
Red Cross (Check)	50
Goodwill Industries (Cash)	30
Theft loss of camera (not covered by insurance); value after loss, $250; cost, $250	250
Safe deposit box rental for storing investments	30

Required

Determine:

(a) The adjusted gross income and prepare the following for Robert Axley for year 1981. The forms are provided for you in the Study Guide Workbook.

(b) Schedules A and B

(c) Schedule for casualty loss

(d) Form 1040 using the following additional information:
Social Security No.: 001-264-3822
Parents: Mary and Robert Axley, Sr.
Income of parents: $700 each, total, $1,400
Federal income tax withheld from earnings: $3,900
Tax on taxable income (head of household) using the tax tables amounted to $3,887.

INDEX

Accelerated Cost Recovery System (ACRS), 345, 347
Account(s):
  chart of, 30, 31, 52
  classifications of, 134–135
    balance sheet, 9, 132, 134, 135
    basic, 5, 6
    of bonds and, 527–528
    definition of, 134–135
    income statement, 11, 176–179
  control (see Control account)
  debit versus credit side of, 31, 32
  definition of, 8, 19
  depreciation, 335, 336
  drawing, 50–51
  increase and decrease in, 32
  ledger (see Ledger account)
  mixed, 64, 77
  nominal, 128, 138
  noncurrent, 593, 600–607, 610
  normal balance of, 33, 35, 52
  numbers assigned to, 30–31
  parts of, 32–33
  permanent, 128, 138
  real, 128, 138
  temporary, 128, 138
Account balance, 33–35, 52
  footings (totals) in, 34
Account forms, running balance and T, 32, 33
Accountants:
  areas of specialization of, 3
  certified public accountant (CPA), 3, 4
  definition of, 3, 19
Accounting:
  acrual, 8–9, 20
  areas of specialization in, 3–4
  background of, 2
  for bonds: amortization of premium, 523
    interest on, 523–525
    journal entries for, 522–524
    sale of: above face value, 523
      at face value, 522–523

Accounting (Cont.):
  versus bookkeeping, 4, 5
  cash versus accrual, 8–9
  for common stock: for cash, 414–416, 431, 432
    on subscription, 432–435
  definition of, 2, 5
  double-entry, 36
  double-entry system, 8, 20
  financial, 2–3
  five basic parts of, 5–7
  government, 3
  managerial, 3
  pegboard systems (see Pegboard accounting systems)
  for preferred stock, 438–440
  present methods of, 2
  private, 3
  as a profession, 3–4
  public, 3
  purpose of, 4
  for stock transactions (see Common stock)
  structure of, 5
Accounting classifications, 5–7
Accounting cycle, 49, 52, 98, 136, 137
  illustration of, 136
Accounting equation, 9
Accounting manual:
  definition of, 31, 52
  illustration of, 31
Accounting period, 8
Accounting principles (see Principles and Concepts)
Accounting Principles Board (APB), AICPA, 505, 563
Accounting process, 13
Accounting terms, 7–9
Accounts Payable:
  balance sheet presentation of, 15
  definition of, 5, 6, 206
  journal entry for, 154–156, 369, 372, 374
  ledger account for, 213

Accounts Payable (Cont.):
  opposite balance, 215
  schedule of, 209, 220
Accounts payable control account, 206, 220
Accounts payable subsidiary ledger:
  definition of, 206, 220
  illustrations of, 208, 213
Accounts Receivable:
  balance sheet presentation of, 15, 181
  contra account for, 235
  definition of, 42, 201
  entry for sale: of merchandise, 150
    of service, 42, 43
  journal entry for, 42, 43, 89, 90, 150
  ledger account for, 46, 203, 211, 240
  opposite balance, 215
  in pegboard system, 216–218, 220
  reinstatement of, 240–241
  sales returns, 151–153
  schedule of, 202, 220
  writing off, 239–240
Accounts receivable control account, 201, 220
Accounts receivable subsidiary ledger:
  definition of, 201, 220
  illustrations of, 203, 211
Accounts receivable systems, pegboard, 216–218, 220
Accrual accounting, 8–9, 20
Accrued expenses:
  adjusting entries for, 65, 66, 70–73, 88
  definition of, 70, 77
  for depreciation, 73–76
  for interest, 72, 73
  for salaries and wages, 70, 71
Accrued revenue:
  adjusting entries for, 89–92

Accrued revenue (*Cont.*):
definition of, 89, 98
for repair service, 89, 90
for royalties, 90, 91
Accumulated depreciation:
adjusting entry for, 73–76, 336, 487
balance sheet presentation for, 76, 491
classification of, 73, 75
definition of, 73, 77, 336
examples of, 336
Adjusted gross income, 698, 726
Adjusted trial balance, 118–119
definition of, 97, 99
illustration of, 97
on work sheet, 125, 175, 486, 636
Adjusting entries, 64–78, 88–99
for accrued expense, 70–73, 487
for accrued revenue, 89–92
for corporation, 487
definition of, 65, 77
for depreciation, 73–76, 335–336, 487
for expenses, 65–77, 336, 487
four points to remember, 97–98
for merchandising concern, 181–182
for prepaid expense, 66–69, 487
for prior period income, 502, 503
for revenue, 88–95
received in advance, 92–96
statements affected by, 65
types of, 66, 88
from work sheet, 126, 487
on work sheet, 114–118, 486
Adjustments:
for accrued expense, 65–66, 70–73
for accrued interest, 72, 73
on bonds: definition of, 524
entries for, 525
for accrued revenue, 89–92
definition of, 65–66
for depreciation, 73–76, 335–336
for expenses (*see* Expense adjustments)
for insurance, 66–67
for office supplies, 67–69
for prepaid expenses, 66–69
reason for, 64
for repair service revenue, 73–76, 93–94
for revenue (*see* Revenue adjustments)
for royalties earned, 90–91
for salaries and wages, 70, 71

Adjustments (*Cont.*):
types of, 66
when prepared, 64
Administrative expenses (*see* General and administrative expenses)
Allowable business deductions:
definition of, 709
on Form 2106, 713, 714
list of, 709, 712
Allowable nonbusiness personal deductions (itemized deductions):
examples of, 715–717
itemizing, 721, 725
list of, 712
Allowance for doubtful accounts:
balance sheet presentation, 237, 240
definition of, 235, 242
journal entry for, 235, 238, 241
ledger illustration of, 236, 240
writing off, 239–240
American Institute of Certified Public Accountants (AICPA), 3
Accounting Principles Board (APB), 505, 563
Financial Accounting Standards Board (*see* Financial Accounting Standards Board)
Amortization:
of bond discount, 524
of bond premium, 523
definition of, 354, 357
example of, 355
Annual federal unemployment tax return (*see* Employer's Annual Federal Unemployment Tax Return)
Application of funds:
definition of, 595
types of, 595–597
Appropriated retained earnings, 500–501, 509
Articles of Co-Partnership, 391
Assets:
current, 66, 77, 134, 135, 137
decreasing, 32
definition of, 5, 20, 50
increasing, 32
intangible (*see* Intangible assets)
long-term investments (*see* Long-term investments)
noncurrent (*see* Noncurrent assets)
plant (*see* Plant assets)
revenue versus capital expenditures, 357

Assets (*Cont.*):
types of, 134
wasting, 326, 344, 348
Auditing, 3, 20

Bad debts:
adjusting for, 235
balance sheet method for, 237–238, 242
definition of, 235, 242
direct write-off method for, 238–239
journal entry for, 235, 236, 238
ledger account, 237
methods for estimating: percentage of accounts receivable or balance sheet, 237–238
percentage of sales or income statement, 236–237
Bad Debts Expense, 235–239, 242
Balance, 33–35
(*See also* Account balance; Trial balance)
Balance sheet:
classified, 132
for corporation, 491
definition of, 9, 20
format of, 132
illustrations of, 10, 15, 133, 181, 376, 419, 420, 491, 639
for manufacturing concern, 639
for merchandising concern, 179–181
when prepared, 491
from work sheet, 491, 639
on work sheet, 486, 636
Balance sheet equation, 9
Balance sheet method for bad debts, 237–238, 242
Balance sheet presentation of stock, 440–441
Bank checking account, 290, 292
Bank errors, 292
Bank reconciliation, 290–301
bank checking account, 290, 292
definition of, 295, 302
preparing statement, 295–298
procedure for, 292, 295
Bank reconciliation procedure, 292, 295
Bank reconciliation statement:
definition of, 292, 295
illustration of, 299–300
journal entries from, 299, 301
preparing, 295–298
procedure for, 292, 295
reconciling bank balance, 295–297

Bank reconciliation statement
    (*Cont.*):
    reconciling book balance,
        297–298
Bank service charge, 292, 302
Bank statement:
    definition of, 290, 302
    illustration of, 294
Basic accounting equation:
    definition of, 9, 20
    illustration of, 10
Bearer (possessor of note), 312, 320
Board of directors, 412
Bond interest earned:
    classification of, 542
    definition of, 542, 554
    income statement presentation
        of, 544, 545, 547
    journal entries for, 544–546, 552
    ledger account for, 545, 546
Bond interest expense, 520, 530
Bond interest payable:
    balance sheet presentation of,
        528
    definition of, 528, 530
Bonds, 518–519, 522–524
    classification of, 527–528
    computation of interest on,
        518–519
    definition of, 518–519, 530
    face value of, 518
    interest earned on (see Bond in-
        terest earned)
    investment in (*see* Investments, in
        bonds: in stocks or bonds)
    maturity date of, 518
    premium on (*see* Premium, on
        bonds)
    purchased at face value, 543–547
    quotation of, 520
    retirement of, 526–527
    selling price of, 520–521
    types of, 519–520
Bonds payable:
    balance sheet presentation of,
        528
    classification of, 527–528
    definition of, 522, 530
    journal entries for, 522–527
Book of final entry (*see* General
        ledger)
Book of original entry (*see* General
        journal)
Book balance of cash, 290
Book errors, 292, 294
Book value (carrying value):
    definition of, 74, 77, 339, 347
    of plant assets, 333

Book value (carrying value) (*Cont.*):
    per share of stock: definition of,
        507, 509
        formula for, 507
Bookkeeping, 4, 20
Budgets, 570–582
    advantages of, 570–571
    cash, 577–578, 581
    definition of, 570, 581
    expense, 574–576, 581
    flexible, 579–581
    goals for, 571
    master, 571, 581
    preparing, 571
    purchases, 572–574, 581
    sales, 572, 573, 581

Callable bonds, 520, 530
Callable option for preferred stock,
        437
Callable preferred stock:
    definition of, 437, 448
    journal entry for, 437
Capital:
    contributed, 430–431, 448
    definition of, 6, 20
    legal, 445, 446, 448
    owner's (*see* Owner's capital)
    partners', statement of, 401–403
    sources of, 430
    working (*see* Working capital)
Capital expenditures, 337, 347
Capital stock, issuance of, 575, 594
Carrying value, 527, 530
Cash:
    control of, 284
    definition of, 284, 302
    journal entries to correct, 299
    over and short, 288–290, 302
    petty (*see* Petty cash)
Cash accounting, 8, 20
Cash budget:
    definition of, 577, 581
    illustration of, 578
    schedule of cash receipts, 577
Cash control, objectives of, 284
Cash discount:
    computation for: on purchases, 155
        on sales, 153
    definition of, 152, 164
Cash dividend preference to pre-
        ferred stockholders, 461–464
    computations for, 463–464
    definition of, 462–464
    examples for, 463–464
    features of, 461–462
    variations of: cumulative, 462
        noncumulative, 462

Cash dividend preference (*Cont.*):
    nonparticipating, 464
    participating, 462–463
Cash dividends:
    computation of, 463–464
    declaration of, 461
    definition of, 460, 470
    important dates for, 460–461
    journal entries for, 461, 551
    receipt of, 551–552
    on retained earnings statement,
        503
Cash payments journal:
    definition of, 211, 220
    illustration of, 213
        summary, 214
    posting from, 212–213
Cash receipts journal:
    definition of, 209, 220
    illustration of, 211
        summary, 210
    posting from, 210–211
Casualty losses:
    definition of, 716, 717
    schedule for reporting, 717
    on Schedule A, 718
Certified public accountant (CPA),
        3, 4
Chart of accounts:
    definition of, 30, 31, 52
    illustration of, 31
Charter, corporate, 412
Circular E, I.R.S.:
    definition of, 249, 273
    illustration from, 250
Closing entries:
    for corporations, 488, 489
    cost of goods sold, 370, 375
    definition of, 137
    on expense accounts, 129, 183
    four parts to remember, 135
    income summary, 129, 182–184
    on inventories, 181–184, 640–641
    for manufacturing concern,
        639–642
    for merchandising concern,
        181–184
    owner drawing, 130, 184
    for partners, 393–395, 402
    procedures for, 129–130,
        181–185, 418
    for purchases, purchase return
        and allowances, and pur-
        chase discounts, 155, 183
    reason for, 128
    retained earnings, 417
    on revenue accounts, 184, 370,
        373, 375

Closing entries (*Cont.*):
  for sales, sales returns and allow-
    ances, and sales discounts,
    153, 183
  from work sheet, 128–130,
    181–184, 488–489, 640–642
Collection of notes, 295, 317
Combined income and retained
    earnings statement:
  definition of, 504, 509
  illustration of, 504
Common stock, 413–416, 431–436
  balance sheet presentation, 434,
    467, 468
  definition of, 414
  discount on, 431
  journal entries for, 415–416,
    431–433, 435–436
    stock dividend, 467
    stock split, 469
  ledger account for, 465–467, 469
  paid-in capital in excess of stated
    value, 431
  par or stated value, 414
  premium on (*see* Premium, on
    common stock)
  sold for cash, 415, 416, 418, 431,
    432
  sold on subscription: definition
    of, 432, 433
    journal entries for, 433–435
  stock split, 468, 469
  subscribed (*see* Common stock
    subscribed)
  subscriptions, 415–416, 432–435
Common stock dividend
    distributable:
  balance sheet presentation of,
    467
  entry for, 466–467
  ledger account for, 466–467
Common stock subscribed:
  classification of, 432, 434
  journal entries for, 415–416,
    433–435
Comparative balance sheets, 598
Compound entries:
  definition of, 36
  illustration of, 43
Concepts (*see* Principles and
    Concepts)
Consistency of reporting inventory,
    375
Contra account, 73, 77
Contra owner equity account, 51,
    52
Contra purchases account, 155
Contra revenue account, 152, 153
Contributed capital, 430–431, 448

Contribution margin, 579, 581
Control account:
  accounts payable, 206
  accounts receivable, 201
  definition of, 201, 220
Convertible bond, 519, 530
Convertible option issued with pre-
    ferred stock, 438, 448
Copyright, 355, 357
Corporate estimated tax:
  definition of, 480
  work sheet for (Form 1120–W),
    480–484
Corporate income taxes, 480–484
  adjusting entry for, 484
  computation of, 483–484
  definition of, 480, 492
  deposit form for, 483
Corporate work sheet:
  adjusting entries from, 487
  closing entries from, 488–489
  definition of, 484, 492
  financial statement from,
    489–491
  illustration of, 486
  six steps for preparing, 485–487
Corporations, 412–422, 431–445
  accounting differences, 417–418
  advantages and disadvantages of,
    413
  balance sheet presentation,
    420–421, 435, 440–441, 446
  board of directors of, 412
  capital stock, 413, 414
  cash dividends (*see* Cash
    dividends)
  charter for, 412
  common stock (*see* Common
    stock)
  definition of, 412
  financial statements for, 419–420,
    489–491, 638, 639
  incorporators of, 412
  officers of, 142
  organization costs, 413
  par value stock, 414
  preferred stock (*see* Preferred
    stock)
  retained earnings (*see* Retained
    earnings)
  versus single proprietorship, 418
  stated value stock, 414
  stock dividends (*see* Stock
    dividends)
  stock subscriptions, 415–416,
    432–435
  stock transactions, 414–416,
    431–436
  treasury stock (*see* Treasury stock)

Corporations (*Cont.*):
  work sheet for, 484–487
Cost of ending goods in process
    inventory:
  computation for, 682
  journal entries for, 686
Cost of goods manufactured
    statement:
  definition of, 631, 643
  formula for, 631
  illustrations of, 632, 638
Cost of goods sold:
  computation for, 684
  definition of, 177, 186
  formula on income statement,
    177, 186, 371
  journal entries for, 663, 686
  ledger account, 666
  for merchandising concern, 177
Cost of goods sold formula, 177,
    186, 371
Cost of goods sold section of in-
    come statement:
  illustrations of, 632, 638
  for manufacturing concern, 632
Cost of goods transferred to fin-
    ished goods inventory:
  computation of, 682, 683
  example of, 683
  journal entries for, 686
Cost accounting:
  definition of, 652, 658
  job order, 653, 667
  process (*see* Process cost system)
  two types of systems, 652
Cost method, 538, 554
Cost Principle, 16, 20, 327
Coupon bond, 519, 530
CPA (certified public accountant),
    3, 4
Credit, definition of, 32, 52
Credit memorandum:
  definition of, 160, 164
  illustration of, 160
Credit rules, debit-, 50
Credit terms, 152
Creditor's subsidiary ledger, 206
  (*See also* Accounts payable sub-
    sidiary ledger)
Cumulative preferred stock, 462,
    470
Current assets:
  on balance sheet, 134
  definition of, 66, 77, 135, 137,
    592, 593, 610
  examples of, 592
Current liabilities:
  on balance sheet, 133
  definition of, 134, 137, 592

Current liabilities (*Cont.*):
  examples of, 592
Customer's subsidiary ledger, 201
  (*See also* Accounts receivable subsidiary ledger)

Date of declaration for stock dividend, 419, 420
Date of payment for stock dividend, 419, 420
Date of record for stock dividend, 419, 420
Debenture bonds, 519, 530
Debit, definition of, 32, 52
Debit-credit rules, 50
Debit memorandum:
  definition of, 161, 164, 292
  illustration of, 291
Declaration of cash dividend, 593
Declaration date for dividends, 460–461, 470
Deductions for exemptions:
  for dependents of taxpayer, 700
  for individual taxpayer, 699
  for married taxpayer, 699
Defaulted note, 316–317
Deferred expense, 66, 77
Deferred revenue, 92, 99
Dependent of a taxpayer:
  definition of, 700
  I.R.S. code definition of, 700
Depletion:
  balance sheet presentation of, 345
  definition of, 344, 347
  examples for, 344
Deposit in transit, 292, 302
Deposit slips:
  definition of, 292, 302
  illustration of, 293
Depreciation:
  Accelerated Cost Recovery System (ACRS), 345
  accumulated (*see* Accumulated depreciation)
  adjusting entries for, 73–76, 335–336
  balance sheet presentation of, 336–337
  computations for, 329–333
  definition of, 73, 77, 326, 347
  effect of trade-in method on, 343–344
  income statement classification, 75
  for partial year, 333–335
  of plant assets, 73–77, 326
    adjusting entries for, 335–336

Depreciation, of plant assets (*Cont.*):
  definition of, 326
  methods of: double-declining balance, 332–333
    straight-line, 330
    sum-of-years'-digits, 331–332
    units-of-production, 330–331
  useful life, 329
  on work sheet, 116–118, 120–122, 124, 125, 175
Direct labor:
  on closing entries, 640
  definition of, 629, 643
Direct labor time tickets:
  definition of, 657, 668
  illustration of, 658, 666
  journal entries from, 657
Direct write-off method, 238–239
Discarding a plant asset (selling), 338–341
Discount, 542, 554
  on bonds: amortization of, 524
    balance sheet presentation, 528
    classification of, 527–528
    definition of, 522, 530
    journal entries for, 524
  on common: on balance sheet, 434, 441
    definition of, 431, 448
    journal entry for, 432
  on preferred stock: on balance sheet, 440, 441
    definition of, 439, 448
    journal entry for, 440
Discounted notes, 318
Dishonored notes, 316, 317
Disposing of plant assets, 337–339
Dissolving a partnership (*see* Partnerships, dissolving)
Dividends, 419–420
  in arrears, 462, 470
  stock (*see* Stock dividends)
Dividends earned:
  definition of, 539, 554
  income statement presentation for, 540
  journal entry for, 540
Dividends payable, 461, 470
Division of earnings in partnership, 392–395
Dollar signs, 16
Donated treasury stock:
  definition of, 445
  journal entries for, 445
Double-declining method:
  calculations for, 333
  definition of, 332, 347
  example of, 333
Double-entry accounting, 36

Double-entry system, 8, 20
Drawing account, 50–51
Drawings:
  classification of, 51
  definition of, 6, 20
  normal balance of, 50

Earnings per share:
  definition of, 504, 509
  formula for, 505
  on income statement, 506
Economic Recovery Act of 1981, 345
Employee earnings:
  record of, 258, 260
  rules for, 249, 251
Employee payroll taxes, 249, 251, 253, 264, 265
Employee's Withholding Allowance Certificate (Form W–4):
  definition of, 249, 273
  illustration of, 249
Employer's Annual Federal Unemployment Tax Return (Form 940):
  definition of, 263, 273
  illustration of, 254
Employer's payroll tax expense, 253, 255, 266–267
Employer's Quarterly Federal Tax Return (Form 941):
  definition of, 260, 273
  illustration of, 261–262
Entity Principle, 17, 20
Equities, 5, 20
Equity account:
  contra owner, 51, 52
  noncurrent (*see* Noncurrent equity account)
Equivalent units of production:
  computation of, 680
  definition of, 679, 689
  example of, 681
Errors in inventory, effect of, 375–377
Estimated salvage value, 329
Estimated systems, 366
Estimated useful life, 329
Exemptions, deductions for, 699–700, 726
Expense adjustments, 65–77
  accrued, 65, 70–73
  asset expiration, 66–68
  definition of, 65–66
  depreciation of plant assets, 73–76
  journalized from work sheet, 126, 182

Expense adjustments (*Cont.*):
  need for, 64–65
  prepaid, 66–69
  types of, 66
  on work sheet, 114–118,
    120–122, 124, 125, 175
Expense budget:
  definition of, 574, 581
  illustration of, 576
  subsidiary schedule for, 575
Expenses:
  accrued (*see* Accrued expenses)
  classification of, 176–179
  definition of, 6, 20, 50
  depreciation, 73–76
  examples of, 7
  fixed (*see* Fixed expenses)
  general and administrative,
    177–178, 186
  on income statement, 180
  increases and decreases in, 32
  operating (*see* Operating
    expenses)
  other (*see* Other Expense)
  prepaid (*see* Prepaid expenses)
  selling, 177, 178, 186
  semivariable (*see* Semivariable
    expenses)
  shipping, 157–158
  variable (*see* Variable expenses)
  on work sheet, 120–122, 124,
    125, 175
Experience rating, 255, 273
Extraordinary gain, 528
Extraordinary items:
  APB rules for, 505
  classification of, 505
  definition of, 505, 509
  examples of, 505
Extraordinary loss, 528–529

Face value, 542, 554
  of bonds, 518, 530
Factory overhead:
  in closing entries, 640
  definition of, 629–630, 644
  journal entries for flow of costs,
    686
Factory overhead costs, methods
    for estimating, 659–660
Fair Labor Standards Act, 257, 273
Federal income taxes, 696–727
  deductions for exemptions,
    699–700
  forms for (*see specific form*)
  history of, 696
  income excluded from, 697–698
  requirements for filing, 696–697

Federal income taxes (*Cont.*):
  taxable income, 698–699
  withheld from employee earn-
    ings, 249, 251
Federal Insurance Contributions
    Act (FICA), 251, 253, 273
Federal Tax Deposit form:
  definition of, 480, 492
  illustration of, 483
  instructions and work sheet for,
    482
Federal Unemployment Tax Act
    (FUTA), 251, 253, 273
Federal Wage and Hour Law, 257,
    273
FICA (Federal Insurance Contribu-
    tions Act), 251, 253, 273
Financial accounting, 2, 3, 20
Financial Accounting Standards
    Board (FASB), AICPA, 563
  definition of, 551, 555
  rules for presentation of tempo-
    rary investments, 551
Financial statements:
  balance sheet (*see* Balance sheet)
  for corporations, 419–420,
    489–491, 638–639
  cost of goods manufactured, 638
  definition of, 9, 131, 137, 175
  illustrations of, 10, 15, 132, 133,
    180, 181, 489–491, 638, 639
  income statement (*see* Income
    statement)
  for manufacturing concern, 632,
    637–639
  for merchandising concern,
    176–181
  for partnerships, 401–403
  prepared from work sheet,
    131–133, 489–491
  retained earnings, 490–638
  on work sheet, 125, 175, 486,
    636
Finished goods inventory:
  closing entries in, 641
  computation for, 684
  definition of, 630–631, 644
  determining cost of ending in-
    ventory, 683–684
  journal entries for, 662, 663, 686
  ledger account for, 662, 664,
    666, 688
First-in, first-out (FIFO) method:
  computations for, 364
  definition of, 364, 379
Fiscal period, 8, 20
Fixed expenses:
  definition of, 574, 581

Fixed expenses (*Cont.*):
  examples of, 576
  on expense budget, 576
  on flexible budget, 571
  on subsidiary schedule of ex-
    penses, 575
Flexible budget, 579–580
  definition of, 579, 581
  illustration of, 579
Flow of costs for process cost
    system:
  diagram of, 679
  journal entries for, 684, 686
FOB (free on board) destination:
  classification of, 157
  definition of, 157, 164
  examples of, 157
  journal entry for, 157
FOB (free on board) shipping
    point:
  definition of, 157, 164
  journal entries for, 158
Footings (totals), 34, 52
Form 940 (*see* Employer's Annual
    Federal Unemployment Tax
    Return)
Form 941 (*see* Employer's Quarterly
    Federal Tax Return)
Form 1040 (Individual Income Tax
    Return, long form):
  completing, 717, 721
  definition of, 703, 727
  illustrations of, 703, 705, 719,
    720
  Schedule A (itemized
    deductions), 718, 727
  Schedule B (interest and divi-
    dend income): definition of,
    704, 727
    illustration of, 706
  Schedule C (profit or loss from
    business or profession): defi-
    nition of, 709, 712, 727
    illustration of, 711
  Schedule E (supplemental in-
    come): definition of, 704,
    727
    illustration of, 707
  Schedule G (income averaging):
    definition of, 725, 727
    illustration of, 724
  Schedule SE (computation of so-
    cial security self-employment
    tax): definition of, 704, 709,
    712
    illustration of, 710
Form 1040A (Individual Income
    Tax Return, short form):

Form 1040A (*Cont.*):
  definition of, 703, 727
  illustration of, 701–702
Form 1099 (Information Return),
    263, 273
Form 1120–W (Corporation Esti-
    mated Tax), 480–484
  definition of, 480, 492
  illustration of, 482
  instructions for, 481
  worksheet for, 482
Form 2106 (Employee Business
    Expenses):
  definition of, 712, 727
  illustration of, 713–714
Formulas:
  for computation of earnings per
    share of common stock, 505
  for cost of goods manufactured
    statement, 631
  for preparing retained earnings
    statement, 503
Franchise, 355, 357
Full Disclosure Principle, 17, 20
Funds:
  definition of, 592, 610
  loss of, 595
  from operations: definition of,
    593, 610
    illustrations of, 593
  sources of, 593–595
  summary of, 597
  uses of, 595–597
FUTA (Federal Unemployment
    Tax Act), 251, 253, 273

Gain on retirement of bonds:
  computation of, 526
  definition of, 526, 530
  on income statement, 528
  journal entry for, 527
Gain on sale:
  of assets, 340
  of investments: classification of,
    540, 547, 549
    computation of, 549
    definition of, 540, 555
    income statement presentation
      for, 541
    journal entry for, 541, 549
General and administrative ex-
    penses, 177–178
  definition of, 178, 186
  example of, 178
General journal:
  definition of, 36, 52
  entries for, 38–43, 214–215
    (*See also* Closing entries)

General journal (*Cont.*):
  illustrations of, 37, 43
  journal entry, basic parts in,
    36–38
  journalizing transactions in, 36
General ledger:
  definition of, 44, 52
  illustration of, 46–48
  posting in, 44
Generally accepted accounting
    principles (GAAP), 16
Going Concern Principle, 17, 20
Goods in process inventory:
  closing entries for, 640
  definition of, 630, 644
  journal entries for: factory over-
    head applied to production,
    659–660
    goods completed, 662
    labor applied to production,
      657
    materials used in production,
      656
    process cost system, 686
  ledger account for, 657, 659,
    661, 663–666, 686
Goodwill, 355, 357
Government accounting, 3, 20
Gross earning, 265, 273
Gross income, 698, 727
Gross profit, 177, 186
Gross profit method, 367–368, 379
Gross sales, 177, 186

Imprest fund, 285
Income excluded from taxes,
    697–698
Income statement:
  classifications on, 176
  combined with retained earnings,
    504
  for corporation, 489, 638
  definition of, 11, 20
  format for, 131, 139
    expanded, 179
  formula for, 11, 21
  illustrations of, 12, 15, 132, 180,
    367, 368, 373, 376, 377, 401,
    489, 506, 638
  for manufacturing concern, 638
  for merchandising concern,
    176–180
  reason for, 15
  from work sheet, 489, 638
  on work sheet, 124, 125, 175,
    486, 636
Income statement method for bad
    debts, 236–237, 242

Income summary:
  to close: for corporations, 417,
    418
    for merchandise business, 153,
      156, 158–159, 182–184
    for partnerships, 393–395, 402
    for service business, 129, 130
  journal entries for, 640–642
  ledger account illustrations, 131,
    154, 157, 642
  for retained earnings, 417, 418
Income tax method for trading in
    plant assets:
  definition of, 341, 347
  examples for, 341, 342
Income taxes (*see* Federal income
    taxes)
Incorporators, 412
Indirect labor, 629, 644
Indirect materials, 629, 644
Information Return (Form 1099),
    263, 273
Insurance expense:
  adjusting for, 66, 67, 182
  income statement classification
    for, 67
Intangible assets:
  balance sheet presentation for,
    354
  definition of, 134, 137, 354
  types of, 355–357
    copyright, 355
    franchise, 355
    goodwill, 355
    leasehold and leasehold im-
      provements, 355–356
    patents, 356–357
    trademarks and trade names,
      357
Interest:
  on bank loan, 317–319
  computation of, 312–313
  definition of, 311, 320
  rate of, 312–313
  simple, 313
  sixty-day, 6 percent method,
    313–314
Interest and dividend income:
  definition of, 704
  on Schedule B, 706
Interest-bearing note, 317–318, 320
Interest expense:
  adjustment for, 72, 73
  income statement classification
    for, 72
Interest payable:
  adjustment for, 72, 73
  balance sheet classification for, 72

Internal control, 284
Internal Revenue Service (I.R.S.),
    249, 273
Inventories, 362–379
    adjusting and closing, 367, 370,
        373, 375
    consistency of reporting, 375
    definition of, 362
    effect of errors on, 375–377
    estimated systems for, 366
    of merchandise (see Merchandise
        inventory)
    methods of maintaining, 368–371
    methods of valuation, 362–366
    valuation of, 362, 377
Inventory valuation, 362, 377
Investments:
    in bonds, 543–550
        amortization: of discount, 546
            of premium, 545–546
        balance sheet presentation,
            543, 545
        definition of, 542, 555
        interest earned on, 542–544
        journal entry for, 542–544
        ledger account for, 545, 546,
            548
        long-term (see Long-term in-
            vestments, in bonds)
        sale of, 547, 549
    in stocks: balance sheet presenta-
        tion for, 539
        classification of, 539
        definition of, 539, 555
        dividends from, 539–540
        journal entry for, 539
    in stocks or bonds: balance sheet
        presentation for, 539
        classification of, 538
        definition of, 538
        journal entries for, 539
        method of recording, 538, 539
        purpose of, 538–539
    temporary (see Temporary
        investments)
Issuance of capital stock:
    definition of, 594
    journal entry for, 575
Issuing long-term note:
    definition of, 594
    journal entry for, 594

Job order cost procedure:
    illustration of, 666
    six steps in, 665–667
Job order cost sheet:
    definition of, 653, 668
    illustration of, 654, 656, 661, 666

Job order cost system, 652–668
    cost sheet for, 653, 664, 665
    definition of, 653, 656, 658, 666
    direct labor time tickets for, 657
    illustration of, 666
    journal entries: for direct labor,
        657
        for estimated overhead, 660
        for goods completed, 662
        for materials, 656
    material ledger card for, 653,
        654
    material requisition for, 655
    six steps in, 665–667
Journal entries:
    to correct cash balance, 299, 301
    definition of, 36, 52
    for dividends: cash, 461–464
        stock, 464–468
    illustrations of, 37–43
    six basic parts in, 36
    (See also Closing entries)
Journalizing:
    definition of, 36, 52
    format for, 36, 38
Journals:
    general (see General journal)
    special, 198–215
        cash payments, 211–214, 220
        cash receipts, 209–211, 220
        definition of, 198–199, 220
        proof of ledger accuracy, 202,
            209
        purchases (see Purchases
            journal)
        reason for, 198–199
        sales (see Sales journal)
        summary of journalizing and
            posting to, 214
        summary transactions, 201, 202,
            210, 211, 214

Last-in, first-out (LIFO) method of
    valuing inventory:
    computations for, 365
    definition of, 364, 379
Leasehold and leasehold improve-
    ments, 355–357
Ledger account, 131, 154, 157
    definition of, 44, 52
    illustration of, 45
Legal capital, 445, 446, 448
Liabilities:
    current (see Current liabilities)
    definition of, 5, 6, 20, 50, 52
    increase and decrease of, 32
    long-term (see Long-term
        liabilities)

Liabilities (Cont.):
    types of, 134–135
Limited life of partnerships, 391
List-price method for trading in
    plant assets:
    definition of, 341, 347
    examples for, 341, 342
Long-term investments, 538–555
    balance sheet presentation, 539,
        543, 545
    in bonds: balance sheet presenta-
        tion, 543, 545
        definition of, 542
        face value of, 542, 543
        interest earned on, 542
        journal entry for, 542–544, 546
        payment on maturity date, 547
        sale of, 547–548
            at a discount, 542
            at a premium, 542
        definition of, 132, 134, 138, 538,
            555
    in stock: balance sheet presenta-
        tion for, 539
        classification of, 539
        definition of, 539
        journal entries for, 539
        receipt of dividends on,
            539–540
        sale of, 540–542
Long-term liabilities, 518–531
    on balance sheet, 133, 486, 528
    definition of, 135, 138, 518, 530
Loss(es):
    casualty, 716–718
    extraordinary, 528–529
    of funds from operations, 595
    on retirement of bonds: compu-
        tations for, 527
        definition of, 526, 530, 531
        on income statement, 529
        journal entry for, 527
    on sale: of assets, 340
        of bonds, 553
        of investments: classification of,
            540
            computations of, 549
            definition of, 540, 555
            income statement presenta-
                tion for, 542
            journal entry for, 541, 550
        of securities, 553

Maker of the note (borrower),
    311–312, 320
Managerial accounting, 3, 20
Manufacturing accounts:
    closing entries for, 659–642

Manufacturing accounts (*Cont.*):
    definition of, 629
    direct labor, 629
    factory overhead, 629–630
    indirect labor, 629
    indirect materials, 629
    inventories, 630–631
    raw materials, 629
Manufacturing concern:
    closing entries, 639–642
    definition of, 628, 644
    inventories of, 630, 631
    statements: cost of goods manu-
        factured, 631–632
        cost of goods sold, 632
        financial, 637–639
    work sheet for, 633–637
Manufacturing costs:
    closing entries for, 639–641
    definition of, 628, 644, 652
Manufacturing summary:
    journal entries for, 640, 641
    ledger account illustration, 642
Manufacturing work sheet:
    closing entries prepared from,
        639–642
    definition of, 633
    illustration of, 636
    steps for preparing, 633–637
Marketable securities:
    classification of, 538
    definition of, 134, 138, 538, 555
    journal entries for, 550, 552–553
    method of recording, 538
    sale of, 553–554
Master budget, 571, 581
Matching Concept, 64, 77
Materiality Principle, 18, 21
Materials inventory:
    journal entries for, 656, 686
    ledger account, 687
Materials ledger card:
    definition of, 653, 654, 668
    illustration of, 654
Materials requisition:
    definition of, 655, 668
    illustration of, 655, 656, 666
Maturity date, 314–315, 320
    of bonds, 518, 531
Maturity value, 315, 320
Merchandising concern, 150, 164
    closing entries for, 181–184
    financial statements for, 176–181
    work sheet for, 175
Merchandise inventory:
    balance sheet classification, 160
    balance sheet presentation, 160
    closing entries for, 159, 183, 184,
        373

Merchandise inventory (*Cont.*):
    consistency of reporting, I.R.S.
        rules for, 375
    definition of, 159, 164, 363
    effect of errors on, 375–377
    estimated systems for, 366–368
        gross profit method, 366–368
        retail method, 366–367
    income statement presentation,
        178, 180, 367, 368, 373, 376,
        377
    journal entries for, 181, 182, 269,
        270, 272
    ledger accounts for, 182–184,
        370
    methods of maintaining, 368–371
    methods of valuing, 362–366
    perpetual versus periodic system
        of maintaining, 368–375
        periodic, 371–375
        perpetual, 368–371
    on work sheet, 175
Merit rating, 255, 273
Michigan state sales tax, tables,
    717
Mixed account, 64, 77
Mutual agency in partnerships,
    390–391

Natural resources:
    balance sheet presentation for,
        345
    definition of, 326, 344, 347
    example of, 344
Net earnings, 265, 273
Net income; definition of, 11, 12,
    50, 52
Net income formula, 11, 21, 50
Net loss, 12, 50
Net sales, 177, 186
Net worth, 6
1981 tax rate schedules, 723
1981 tax table, partial, 722
Nominal accounts, 128, 138
Noncumulative preferred stock,
    462, 470
Noncurrent accounts:
    definition of, 593, 610
    working papers for analyzing
        changes, 600–607
Noncurrent assets:
    analyzing changes on working
        papers, 602–607
    decrease and increase of,
        602–607
    definition of, 593
    purchase of, 595–596
    sale of, 593–594

Noncurrent equity account:
    analyzing changes on working
        papers, 602–607
    decrease and increase in,
        602–607
    definition of, 593
    as a use of funds, 596
Non-interest-bearing note, 318, 320
Nonparticipating preferred stock,
    464, 470–471
Nonsufficient funds (NSF) checks,
    292, 295, 302
Normal balance of accounts, 33, 35,
    52
Note payments by bank, 295
Notes:
    accounting entries, 316–318
    bearer of, 312
    collection of, 295, 317
    definition of, 311
    discount on non-interest-bearing,
        318
    dishonored or defaulted,
        316–317
    interest-bearing, 317
    maker of, 311, 312
    maturity date of, 314–315
    payee of, 312
    payments on, 316, 318
    principal, 312
    proceeds from, 318
    promissory, 311–312, 320
    rate of interest on, 312
    time of loan, 313
NSF (nonsufficient funds) checks,
    292, 295, 302

Objectivity Principle, 18, 21
Office supplies:
    adjustment for, 67–68
    balance sheet classification for, 68
Office supplies expense:
    adjusting entry for, 68
    income statement classification
        for, 68
One-write system for payroll,
    269–273
Operating expenses:
    classifications of, 177
    definition of, 67, 77, 177, 186
    examples of, 178
    income statement presentation
        for, 178
    subclassifications of, 177
Operating revenue, 90–94, 153,
    177
    adjusting entry for, 90, 93
    definition of, 90, 99, 177, 186

Operating revenue (*Cont.*):
  income statement presentation
    of, 90, 93, 177, 180
Organization costs:
  classification of, 436
  for corporation, 413
  definition of, 413
  journal entry for, 436
Other Expense:
  definition of, 72, 77, 178–179,
    186
  examples of, 506
  illustrations of, 72, 179
  income statement presentation
    for, 528, 542
Other Revenue:
  definition of, 91, 99, 177–179,
    186
  example of, 179, 506
  illustrations of, 91, 94, 179
  on income statement, 506, 540,
    541, 544, 545, 547
  for merchandising concern, 177
Other taxable income:
  definition of, 704
  on Schedule E, 707
Outstanding checks, 292, 302
Outstanding stock, 414, 422
Owner's capital:
  balance sheet presentation of, 12,
    133
  definition of, 6, 21, 50, 138
  increase and decrease in, 6, 32

Paid-in capital:
  on balance sheet, 440–441, 446
  definition of, 430–431, 448
  and donated treasury stock: defi-
    nition of, 445, 449
    journal entry for, 445
  in excess of stated value: balance
    sheet illustration, 434
    definition of, 431, 449
    journal entries for, 434, 435
    and preferred stock, 439
  and stock dividends: balance
    sheet presentation for, 467,
    468
    definition of, 465
    entry for, 466
    ledger account for, 466, 467
  and treasury stock: definition of,
    442, 449
    journal entry for, 442, 444
    ledger account for, 443, 444
Par value of stock, 414, 422
Participating preferred stock,
    462–463, 471

Partners' capital, statement of,
    401–403
Partnerships, 390–404
  accounting differences, 391–392
  advantages versus disadvantages
    of forming, 390–391
  agreement in, 391
  balance sheet presentation of
    partners' equity, 402–403
  closing entries, 393–395, 402
  definition of, 390
  dissolving, 396–401
    definition of, 396
    examples for, 396–401
    journal entries for, 397–401
  division of earnings in, 392–395
  formation of, 391
  income statement presentation of
    profits and losses, 401–403
  limited life of, 391
  mutual agency in, 390–391
  statement presentations for,
    401–403
  structure of, 390
  unlimited liability in, 390, 404
Patents, 356–357
Payables, 5
Payee (lender), 312, 320
Payment date for dividends, 461,
    471
Payroll accounting, 248–274
  Circular E, I.R.S., 249, 273
  controls for, 257, 267, 268
  employee earnings: recording,
    264–267
    rules for, 249
  employee earnings record, 258,
    260
  employee payroll taxes, 249, 250
  employer, rules for taxes on, 253,
    255
  Fair Labor Standards Act, 257
  federal forms for (*see* Payroll
    forms)
  federal income tax withheld, 249,
    251
  government regulations for, 248
  pegboard accounting for, 269
  points to remember, 264
  social security taxes (FICA), 251
  unemployment compensation tax,
    253–257
Payroll checks, 268
Payroll forms:
  940 (Employer's Annual Federal
    Unemployment Tax Return),
    254, 263, 273
  941 (Employer's Quarterly Fed-

Payroll forms (*Cont.*):
    eral Tax Return), 260–262,
    273
  1099 (Information Return), 263,
    273
  W–2 (Wage and Tax Statement),
    263, 264, 274
  W–4 (Employee's Withholding
    Allowance Certificate), 249,
    273
Payroll register:
  definition of, 257, 274
  how to figure payroll, 257, 260
  illustration of, 256
Payroll reports (*see* Payroll forms)
Payroll system, 269–272
Pegboard accounting systems,
    215–218, 269–272
  accounts receivable, 216–218, 220
  definition of, 215–216
  illustrations of, 216, 270, 271
  payroll, 269, 272
Percentage of accounts receivable
    method:
  definition of, 237, 242
  illustration of, 238
  journal entry for, 238
Percentage of sale method for bad
    debts:
  definition of, 236–237, 242
  illustration of, 236
  journal entry for, 236
Periodic inventory system:
  closing entries for, 373
  cost of goods sold formula, 371
  definition of, 371, 379
  examples of, 372
  income statement presentation
    for, 373
  summary of entries, 374–375
Permanent accounts, 128, 138
Perpetual inventory system:
  closing entries for, 370
  definition of, 368, 379
  journal entries for, 369, 370
  summary of entries, 374–375
Petty cash, 284–290
  balance sheet presentation of,
    286
  changing amount for, 287–288
  definition of, 285, 302
  forms for, 285
  journal entries for, 286–290
  ledger account for, 286, 288
Petty cash fund, 285–290
  changing original amount in,
    287–288
  decreasing, 288

Petty cash fund (*Cont.*):
  increasing, 287
  overage and shortage in,
    288–290
  replenishing, 286–287
Petty cash receipt:
  definition of, 285, 302
  illustration of, 285
Petty cash voucher, 285, 302
Petty cashier, 285, 302
Plant assets, 326–348
  balance sheet presentation of, 77,
    133, 336
  book value, 74, 77, 339
  costing of, 327–328
  definition of, 73, 77, 134, 138,
    326, 347
  depreciation of (*see* Depreciation,
    of plant assets)
  discarding or selling, 338–341
  disposing of, 337–338
  journal entries for, 327, 328
  ledger illustration, 327–329
  natural resources as, 344, 347
  salvage or scrap value of, 329,
    347, 348
  trade-in of: illustrations of,
    341–343, 347
    income tax method, 341–343,
      347
    list-price method, 341, 343, 347
  useful life, 329, 348
Post-closing trial balance:
  definition of, 135, 138, 185, 490,
    491
  illustrations of, 135, 185
  for merchandising concern, 185
Posting:
  definition of, 44, 52
  procedure for, 44
Preemptive right, 414
Preference as to assets, 436–437,
  449
Preference as to dividends, 436, 449
Preferred stock, 438–441
  on balance sheet, 440–441
  definition of, 449
  discount on, 439
  journal entry for: conversion to
    common stock, 438
    issuance above par, 439
    issuance at par, 439
    issuance below par, 439, 440
    paid-in capital in excess of stated
      value, 439
  preferences: as to assets, 436–437
    callable option, 437
    convertible option, 438

Preferred stock (*Cont.*):
  as to dividends, 436
  premium on (*see* Premium, on
    preferred stock)
Premium, 542, 555
  on bonds: amortization of, 523
    balance sheet presentation, 528
    classification of, 527–528
    definition of, 522, 531
    journal entries for, 523, 527
  on common stock: balance sheet
    presentation, 434, 441, 467,
      468
    definition of, 415, 431, 449
    ledger account for, 465–467
  on preferred stock: on balance
    sheet, 440, 441
    definition of, 439, 449
    journal entry for, 439
Prepaid expenses:
  adjusting entries for, 66–69, 88
  alternate method for adjust-
    ments, 69
  balance sheet presentation for,
    67–68
  classification of, 66
  definition of, 66, 77
  illustrated on work sheet, 114,
    115, 120–122, 175
  from work sheet, 126, 182
Prepaid insurance:
  adjustment for, 66, 67, 182
  balance sheet classification of, 66
Principal, 312, 320
Principles and Concepts:
  Cost, 16, 20, 327
  Entity, 17, 20
  Full Disclosure, 17, 20
  Going Concern, 17, 20
  Matching, 64, 77
  Materiality, 18, 20
  Objectivity, 18, 20
Prior period adjustments:
  definition of, 501, 509
  entries for, 502
  examples for, 502–503
  on retained earnings statement,
    503
Private accounting, 3, 21
Proceeds, 318, 321
Process cost system, 678–689
  cost of inventories for, 682–684
  definition of, 678, 689
  equivalent units for, 679–681
  flow of costs, 679
  journal entries for, 684, 686
  production cost report, 684, 685
  unit costs for, 681–684

Production cost report:
  definition of, 684, 689
  examples of, 685
Promissory note, 311–312, 320
Proprietorship, 6
Public accounting, 3, 21
Purchase of merchandise:
  classification for, 154
  closing entry for, 156
  definition of, 154, 164
  journal entry for, 154
  purpose for, 154
Purchase of noncurrent assets:
  definition of, 595, 596
  journal entry for, 596
Purchase budget:
  definition of, 572–574, 581
  illustration of, 574
  material requirement for, 573
Purchase discount:
  closing entry for, 156
  computations of, 155
  definition of, 155, 164
  journal entry for, 156
Purchase invoice:
  definition of, 204, 220
  illustration of, 199
Purchase order:
  definition of, 204, 220
  illustration of, 204
Purchase returns and allowances:
  classification of, 155
  closing entry for, 156
  definition of, 154, 164
  journal entry for, 155
Purchases, definition of, 154, 164
Purchases journal, 204–209
  definition of, 204, 220
  illustration of, 208
    summary, 207
  posting from, 206–207
  proof of ledger accuracy, 209

Quotation of bonds, 520

Raw material inventory:
  closing entries in, 640
  definition of, 630, 644
Raw materials, 629, 644
Real accounts, 128, 138
Receiving report:
  definition of, 205
  illustration of, 205
Record date for dividends, 461,
  471
Registered bond, 519, 531
Reinstatement of Accounts Receivable, 240–241

Requirements for filing income tax return, 696–697
  exceptions to, 697
Retail method of estimating cost of inventory, 366–367, 369
Retained earnings, 500–509
  appropriated, 500–501, 509
  balance sheet presentation, 446, 447, 468, 491
  definition of, 417, 430–431, 449, 500, 509
  effect on, for dividends, 460–461
  journal entries for, 417
    declaration and payment of dividends, 461, 465–466
  ledger account for, 465–467
  unappropriated, 500, 501, 509
Retained earnings statement:
  combined with income statement, 504
  for corporation, 490, 503, 638
  definition of, 490, 492, 503, 509
  formula for preparing, 503
  illustration, 490, 503, 638
  for manufacturing concern, 638
  from work sheet, 490, 638
  on work sheet, 486, 636
Retirement of bonds:
  definition of, 526
  gain on, 526, 527
  journal entries for, 526–527
  loss on, 526, 527
Returns and allowances (see Purchase returns and allowances; Sales returns and allowances)
Revenue:
  accrued (see Accrued revenue)
  adjustments for (see Revenue adjustments)
  classification of, 176
  closing entry for, 129, 184
  deferred, 92, 99
  definition of, 6, 21, 50
  examples of, 6
  increasing and decreasing, 32
  operating (see Operating revenue)
  other (see Other Revenue)
  received in advance: adjusting entry for, 88, 92–96, 117
    alternate method for recording adjustments, 95–96
    balance sheet presentation for, 90, 91, 93–94
    definition of, 92, 99
    income statement presentation for, 90–91, 93
    from rent, 94–95

Revenue (Cont.):
  from repair service, 93
  from royalties, 90–92
  from sale of merchandise, 150–151, 200
  from service fees, 13, 42–43
  sources of, 6
  types of, 88–89
  unearned, 92–96, 99
  on work sheet, 120–122, 124, 125, 175
Revenue adjustments, 88–96, 126
  accrued, 89–90
  definition of, 88–89
  received in advance, 92–96
  recognition of, 88–89
  for rent, 90, 91, 94
  for royalties, 90–92
  types of, 88
  for unearned revenue, 92–93
Revenue expenditures, 337, 347

Salaries and wages payable:
  adjusting entry for, 70–71
  balance sheet classification for, 71
Sale(s):
  cash discounts, 152, 154, 164
  closing entry for, 153, 184
  definition of, 150, 164
  income statement presentation for, 152, 180
  journal entries for, 150–151, 200
  of long-term bonds, 594
  of long-term investment in bonds, 547
  of merchandise, 150
  of noncurrent assets, 593, 594
  returns of (see Sales returns and allowances)
  trade discounts, 161–162, 164
Sales budget:
  definition of, 572, 581
  illustration of, 573
Sales discount, 152–154
  classification for, 153
  closing entry for, 153
  computation of, 153
  definition of, 152, 164
  income statement presentation for, 153
  journal entries for, 153
  terms for, 152
Sales forecast, 571, 581
Sales invoice:
  definition of, 204, 220
  illustration of, 199
Sales journal, 198–204
  definition of, 199, 220

Sales journal (Cont.):
  illustration of, 200, 203
  summary, 201–202
  posting from, 201–202
  proof of ledger accuracy, 202–204
Sales returns and allowances, 151–154
  classification for, 152
  closing entry for, 153
  definition of, 151, 164
  illustration for, 151
  income statement presentation for, 152, 153
  journal entry for, 151, 160
Sales taxes:
  classification of, 163
  definition of, 162
  entry for, 162–163
Salvage value, 74, 77, 329, 347
Schedule of accounts payable:
  definition of, 209, 220
  illustration of, 209
  proof of ledger accuracy, 209
Schedule of accounts receivable:
  definition of, 202, 220
  illustration of, 202
  proof of ledger accuracy, 202
Schedule of cash disbursements:
  definition of, 577
  illustration of, 578
Schedule of cash receipts:
  definition of, 577
  illustration of, 577
Scrap value, 329, 347
Secured bonds, 519, 531
Self-employment income:
  definition of, 704
  on Schedule E, 707, 708
Selling expenses:
  definition of, 177, 178, 186
  example of, 178
Selling price of bonds, 520
Semivariable expenses:
  definition of, 576, 581
  examples of, 576
  on expense budget, 576
  illustration on subsidiary schedule of expenses, 575
  on subsidiary schedule of expenses, 575
Serial bond, 519, 531
Shipping charges on merchandise:
  definition of, 157, 158
  FOB destination, 157
  FOB shipping point, 157
  journal entries for, 157, 158

Signature card:
  definition of, 290, 302
  illustration of, 291
Single versus double lines on in-
    come statements, 16
Single proprietorship, 6
Social Security Act, 251, 253
Source of funds:
  definition of, 593, 610
  summary of, 597
  types of, 593–595
Special journals (see Journals,
    special)
Specific invoice method of valuing
    inventory:
  computations for, 364
  definition of, 363, 379
State and city income tax withheld,
    251
State Unemployment Tax Act
    (SUTA):
  computations for, 255, 257
  definition of, 255
  merit rating, 255
Stated value of stock, 414
Statements:
  balance sheet (see Balance sheet)
  of changes: in financial position:
    definition of, 592, 610
    illustration of, 609
    preparation of, 596, 597
    prepared from working pa-
      pers analyzing noncurrent
      accounts, 607–609
    purpose of, 592, 593
  in working capital accounts:
    definition of, 597, 610
    six steps in preparation of,
      597–600
  financial (see Financial statements)
  income (see Income statement)
  partners' capital, 401–403
  on work sheet, 125, 175
Stock(s), 413
  common (see Common stock)
  investment in (see Investments, in
    stocks: in stocks and bonds)
  outstanding, 414, 422
  preferred (see Preferred stock)
  treasury (see Treasury stock)
Stock certificate, 413–414
Stock dividend distributable:
  balance sheet presentation for,
    465, 467
  classification of, 465
  definition of, 465, 471
  journal entry for, 465–467
  ledger account for, 466–467

Stock dividends:
  declaration of, 465
  definition of, 460, 464–465, 471
  effect of, on assets, 465
  important dates for, 460–461
  journal entries for, 465–468
  on retained earnings statement,
    503
Stock split:
  definition of, 468, 471
  effect of: on assets, 468
    on retained earnings, 468
  journal entry for, 469
Stock subscriptions, 415–416,
    432–435
Stockholders' equity, 419, 420,
    422
  illustration of, 419, 420, 434,
    440, 441, 446, 467, 468
Straight-line depreciation method:
  definition of, 330, 348
  formula for, 330
Subscribed stock, 415–416
Subscriptions on common stock,
    414–415
Subscriptions receivable:
  classification of, 416, 432, 449
  journal entries for, 416, 433–435
Subsidiary accounts:
  accounts payable, 206
  accounts receivable, 201
  definition of, 201
  illustration of, 203, 208, 211
Subsidiary ledger, 201, 206, 221
Subsidiary schedule of expenses,
    575
Sum-of-years'-digits depreciation
    method:
  definition of, 331, 348
  examples for, 332
  formula for, 332

T account, 31–32, 545
Take-home pay, 265
Tax rate schedules:
  definition of, 721, 727
  illustration of, 723
Tax tables:
  definition of, 721, 727
  illustration of, 722
Taxable earnings, 265, 274, 483,
    492
Taxable income:
  computation of, 698
  definition of, 698, 727
  three formulas for computing,
    698–699
Temporary accounts, 128, 138

Temporary investments:
  balance sheet presentation for,
    551
  in bonds: definition of, 552
    journal entry for, 552
    receipt of interest, 552–553
    sale of, 553
  definition of, 538, 550, 555
  FASB standards for, 551
  methods of recording, 538
  sale of, 553–554
  in stock: balance sheet presenta-
    tion for, 551
    definition of, 550
    FASB standards for, 551
    journal entry for, 550
    receipt of dividends, 511
Trade discounts:
  computations for, 161
  definition of, 161, 164
  examples of, 161–162
Trademarks and trade names, 357
Trading in plant assets, 341–343
Transactions:
  analyzing and journalizing, 36–43
  definition of, 7, 21
  financial, 7
    examples of, 7
  illustrations of, 13, 14, 38–43
    summary, 13, 14, 43
  recording, 44–48
  stock (see Common stock)
Transportation In:
  closing entry for, 158
  definition of, 158, 165
  journal entries for, 158
Transportation Out:
  classification of, 157
  closing entry for, 158
  definition of, 157, 165
  journal entires for, 157
Transporation terms, 157–158
Treasury stock, 441–446
  on balance sheet, 446
  classification of, 441
  definition of, 441, 449
  donated, 445
  how acquired, 441
  journal entries for: purchases of,
    442
    sales of, 442–445
  ledger account for, 442–444
  legal restrictions on, 445–446
  paid-in capital and, 442–445
Trial balance:
  adjusted (see Adjusted trial
    balance)
  definition of, 48, 49, 52

Trial balance (*Cont.*):
illustrations of, 49, 135
locating errors in, 49
post-closing (*see* Post-closing trial balance)
steps in preparation of, 48
on work sheet, 121, 122, 125, 175, 486

Unappropriated retained earnings, 500, 501, 509
Unearned revenue:
adjusting for, 92–96
balance sheet presentation, 93, 94
definition of, 92, 99
Unemployment compensation taxes:
computations for, 255, 257
definition of, 253, 255, 257
federal and state (FUTA and SUTA), 253
Unit costs:
for beginning goods in process inventory, 683
definition of, 681
for ending goods in process inventory, 682
example of, 682
for materials, labor, and overhead, 682
Units of production depreciation method:
definition of, 330, 348
examples for, 331
formula for, 331

Unlimited liability in partnerships, 390, 404
Useful life, 329, 348
Uses (application) of funds:
definition of, 595, 610
summary of, 597
types of, 595–597

Variable expenses:
definition of, 574, 582
examples of, 576
on expense budget, 576
on flexible budget, 579
on subsidiary schedule of expenses, 575

Wage and Tax Statement (Form W–2):
definition of, 264, 274
illustration of, 263
Wages (*see* Salaries and wages payable)
Wasting assets, 326, 344, 348
Weighted average method of inventory valuation:
computations for, 365–366
definition of, 365, 379
Work sheet:
adjusting entries from, 126, 180, 181, 487
closing entries from, 128–130, 181–184
for corporation, 484–487
definition of, 112, 138

Work sheet (*Cont.*):
financial statements from, 131–133, 176–181, 489–491, 637–639
illustration of, 113, 120–122, 125, 175, 486, 636
for manufacturing concern, 633–637
for merchandise concern, 112, 126
preparation of: corporate, 484–487
manufacturing, 633–637
merchandising, 174–176
service business, 112–123
steps in, 114–123, 174–176, 485, 487
summary of, 123–124
reason for, 112
steps for, 112–126, 174–176, 633–637
Working capital:
definition of, 529, 611
examples of, 592
summary of, 597
Working papers for analyzing changes in noncurrent accounts:
definition of, 600
illustration of, 601–608
procedures for preparation of, 600–607
Writing off Accounts Receivable, 239–240

CHECKLIST OF KEY FIGURES   *(continued from inside front cover)*

CHAPTER 15

15-1c Paid-in Capital, $754,000
15-2c Paid-in Capital, $1,075,000
15-3c Paid-in Capital, $183,500
15-4c Paid-in Capital, $366,000
15-5c Paid-in Capital, $412,000
15-6 Paid-in Capital, $293,000
15-7b Paid-in Capital, $267,000
15-9c Paid-in Capital, $2,461,500

CHAPTER 16

16-6 Stockholder Equity, $312,000
16-7 Stockholder Equity, 19_G, $323,300
16-8c Stockholder Equity, $733,500

CHAPTER 17

17-1d Net Income, $79,650
17-2 Income Tax Expense, $1,365
17-3 Income Tax Expense, $435
17-4 Income Tax Expense, $1,110
17-5a Net Income, $35,700
17-6a Net Income, $12,010

CHAPTER 18

18-1b Retained Earnings, $51,850
18-2b Retained Earnings, $53,900
18-3b Retained Earnings, $27,100
18-4b Retained Earnings, $24,480
18-5 Net Income, $53,910
18-6a Net Income, $40,000
18-7d Net Income, $24,750

CHAPTER 19

19-4b Total Long-term Liabilities, $62,080
19-5a Loss on Retirement of Bonds, $200
19-6 Total Carrying Value of Bonds, $113,520
19-7b Total Long-term Liabilities, $69,050
19-8c Loss on Retirement of Bonds, $150

CHAPTER 20

20-1b Carrying Value of Bonds, $19,620
20-2b Carrying Value of Bonds, $20,494
20-3c Dividends Earned, $2,440
20-4c Dividends Earned, $3,690
20-5a Loss on Sale of Investments, $305
20-5b Gain on Sale of Securities, $300
20-6a Gain on Sale of Securities, $100
20-6b Loss on Sale of Investments, $160
20-7b Carrying Value of Long-term Investments, $39,740